Advanced Financial Accounting

Sixth Edition

Richard Lewis MSc, FCA

Associate Chancellor of the US Open University

David Pendrill BSc(Econ), MSc, FCA, ATII, LTCL

Esmée Fairbairn Professor of Accounting and Financial Management,
University of Buckingham

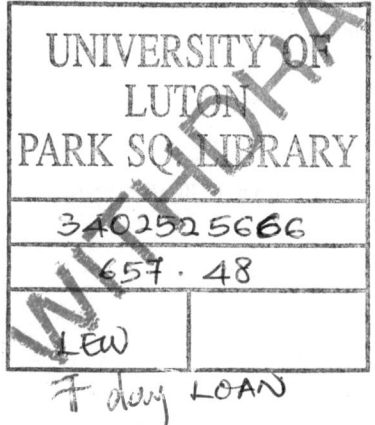

FINANCIAL TIMES

Prentice Hall

An imprint of **Pearson Education**

Harlow, England · London · New York · Reading, Massachusetts · San Francisco · Toronto · Don Mills, Ontario · Sydney
Tokyo · Singapore · Hong Kong · Seoul · Taipei · Cape Town · Madrid · Mexico City · Amsterdam · Munich · Paris · Milan

Pearson Education Limited

Edinburgh Gate
Harlow
Essex CM20 2JE
England

and Associated Companies around the world

Visit us on the World Wide Web at:
http://www.pearsoneduc.com

———————

First edition published in Great Britain under the Pitman imprint in 1981
Second edition published in 1985
Third edition published in 1991
Fourth edition published in 1994
Fifth edition published under the Financial Times Pitman Publishing imprint in 1996
Sixth edition published in 2000

ISBN 0 273 63833 5

British Library Cataloguing-in-Publication Data
A CIP catalogue record for this book can be obtained from the British Library.

Library of Congress Cataloging-in-Publication Data
A catalog record for this book can be obtained from the Library of Congress.

10 9 8 7 6 5 4 3 2 1
04 03 02 01 00

Typeset by 30 in Sabon 10/12pt.
Printed and bound in Great Britain by T.J. International Ltd., Padstow, Cornwall.

Contents

Preface   ix

Part 1 THE FRAMEWORK OF FINANCIAL REPORTING

1 The search for principles   3

Introduction · Accounting theory · The FASB conceptual framework project ·
The IASC framework · The Accounting Standards Board's Statement of
Principles · Summary · Recommended reading

2 Sources of authority   21

Introduction · Legislation · Stock Exchange rules · Accounting principles
and   conventions · Standardisation · International standardisation ·
Recommended reading

3 What is profit?   42

Introduction · Present-value approach · Measurement of wealth by reference to
the valuation of individual assets · Capital maintenance · The usefulness of
different profit measures · How do we choose? · The limitations of historical
cost accounting · Summary · Distributable profits · Realised profits ·
Recommended reading

Part 2 FINANCIAL REPORTING IN PRACTICE

4 Assets   73

Introduction · Value to the business · Tangible fixed assets · Depreciation ·
Intangible assets · Accounting for research and development · Impairment
reviews · Stocks and long-term contracts · Government grants ·
Recommended reading

5 Liabilities and related issues   115

Introduction · FRS 4 *Capital Instruments* · Derivatives and related financial
instruments · Provisions, contingent assets and liabilities · Provisions ·
Contingent assets and liabilities · Pension costs · Towards a new standard ·
Accounting for post balance sheet events · Recommended reading

6 Financial statements – form and content   153

Reporting financial performance · Off and on the balance sheet · SSAP 21
Accounting for Leases and Hire Purchase Contracts · Reflecting the substance
of transactions · Recommended reading

7 Taxation: current and deferred 199

Introduction · Current taxation · SSAP 8 · Accounting for deferred taxation · Recommended reading

8 Business combinations and goodwill 219

Business combinations · Goodwill · Recommended reading

9 Investments, groups, associates and joint ventures 252

Investments · Accounting for groups · Accounting for associates and joint ventures · The international accounting standards · Recommended reading

10 Overseas involvement 294

The problems identified · Accounting for foreign currency transactions · Translation of the financial statements of an overseas subsidiary · The international accounting standard · Recommended reading

11 Expansion of the annual report 333

Introduction · Cash flow statements · Value added statements · The operating and financial review · The historical summary · Reporting about and to employees · Summary financial statements · Interim reports and preliminary announcements · Recommended reading

12 Capital reorganisation, reduction and reconstruction 367

Introduction · Redemption and purchase of shares · Capital reduction · The legal background to other reorganisations · Capital reconstruction · Recommended reading

Part 3 INTERPRETATION AND VALUATION

13 Interpretation of financial statements 395

Introduction · Univariate analysis · Multivariate analysis · Segmental reporting and its problems · Related party disclosures · Recommended reading

14 The valuation of securities and businesses 416

Introduction · The valuation of securities · The valuation of a business · Appendix: FRS 14 'Earnings per share' · Recommended reading

Part 4 ACCOUNTING AND PRICE CHANGES

15 Accounting for inflation 451

Introduction · The progress of accounting reform · Current purchasing power (CPP) accounting · Recommended reading

16 Current cost accounting introduced 476

Introduction · Theoretical roots · The basic elements of current cost accounting · Recommended reading

17 Current cost accounting developed   499

Introduction · The Handbook: detailed treatment of assets · Operating capital
maintenance – two, three or four current cost adjustments? · Corresponding
amounts and trend information · Comprehensive example · Recommended
reading

18 Beyond current cost accounting   530

The utility of current cost accounts · Interim summary · CPP and CCA
combined · A real alternative – making corporate reports valuable · The
evolution of the ASB's thinking · Conclusion · Recommended reading

Appendix: Questions   555

Index   663

Preface

The rate of change of accounting regulation has not diminished since the publication of the previous, fifth edition of *Advanced Financial Accounting*. Attempts of the Accounting Standards Board to develop a conceptual framework, its Statement of Principles (*see* Chapter 1), have not slowed the more routine issue of Financial Reporting Standards, Financial Reporting Exposure Drafts and some voluminous Discussion Papers. This edition of *Advanced Financial Accounting* covers all extant Financial Reporting Standards as well as the latest thinking of the ASB and other bodies where proposals for change are under consideration.

With the globalisation of business and capital markets over the past decade, international developments in accounting have become much more important. In particular, the attempt of the International Accounting Standards Committee to develop a set of core standards acceptable to securities regulators around the world (*see* Chapter 2) has had a great impact on the thinking of the ASB as well as on that of standard setters in other countries. To reflect this we have introduced a section on the international position in each relevant chapter of Part 2, Financial reporting in practice.

There is no doubt that the ASB has achieved success in regulating areas where abuses have occurred in the past. Following its work with FRS 5 'Reporting the substance of transactions' (*see* Chapter 6), the ASB has tried to bring order to other areas of accounting with the issue of FRS 15 'Tangible fixed assets' (*see* Chapter 4), FRS 11 'Impairment of fixed assets and goodwill' (*see* Chapters 4 and 8) and FRS 12 'Provisions, contingent liabilities and contingent assets' (*see* Chapter 5). After much debate and controversy, it has also changed standard accounting practice significantly by the issue of FRS 10 'Goodwill and intangible assets' (*see* Chapter 8), although we have severe reservations about the usefulness of most of the figures which this standard requires us to calculate and disclose. Solutions are still awaited in the important areas of derivatives and financial instruments (*see* Chapter 5), deferred taxation (*see* Chapter 7) and pension costs (*see* Chapter 5).

The ASB has made it clear that, although it recognises the serious limitations of the present modified historical cost accounting system, it will continue to operate within that system. While it favours the greater use of current values in financial statements, especially in connection with financial instruments (*see* Chapter 5), its approach falls far short of the full-blooded alternative systems of accounting which we discuss in Part 4, Accounting and price changes. We are disappointed that the major debates and experiments of the 1970s and 1980s have achieved so little but recognise that more fundamental reform is politically unacceptable in an era of low inflation.

As academic accountants, we find it extremely difficult to assimilate and understand the vast volume of official pronouncements and, therefore, have considerable sympathy for accountants working at the coalface. We are now firmly of the view that there is too much detailed regulation and that there should be a pause to reflect on whether or not the extensive changes which have been made are actually bringing improvements in practice. In an era in which intangible assets are more valuable than tangible assets for many companies, any set of financial statements, based predominantly on those tangible assets, can only give a limited view of the results and position of an entity. Excessive regulation of the figures appearing in a balance sheet achieves only spurious accuracy when the most valuable assets do not appear in that balance sheet at all! In our view, a greater sense of perspective on the limitations of what we are doing would not go amiss.

As in previous editions, we have included an appendix containing a selection of questions from the professional examination papers of the ACCA, CIMA and ICAEW. We gratefully acknowledge the permission of these three bodies to reproduce their questions, although we are disappointed that the ACCA will not permit us to include questions set in the two years preceding the publication of this book. A separate *Solutions Manual* is available to assist lecturers using this book, and is available to them free of charge upon application to the publishers.

Our word processing skills have, at last, reached the stage where we do not have to thank our secretaries for all their hard work. However, we do wish to thank our long-suffering wives, Pamela and Louise, for all their help in reading and commenting on draft chapters, as well as for allowing our work on the sixth edition of *Advanced Financial Accounting* to encroach so much on our already limited leisure time.

RWL
DP

A Companion Web Site accompanies *Advanced Financial Accounting*

Visit the *Advanced Financial Accounting* Companion Web Site at www.booksites.net/lewispendrill to find valuable teaching and learning material including:

For students:
- Updates on all the latest developments in accounting
- Links to useful websites

For Lecturers, comprehensive resources including:
- A secure, password-protected site with teaching material
- A downloadable version of the full *Solutions Manual*
- A syllabus manager that will build and host your very own course web page

---

PART 1

The framework of financial reporting

1 The search for principles

Overview   In this chapter we introduce the subject matter of the book and explore some of the attempts which have been made to construct a conceptual framework for financial reporting.

We focus first on the US Conceptual Framework Project, which came to an end in the mid-1980s, and then more briefly on the IASC *Framework for the Preparation and Presentation of Financial Statements*, published in 1989. We then concentrate on the attempts of the ASB to develop its own Statement of Principles.

Introduction

One of the most difficult tasks facing authors is deciding how to start their books. An elegant epigram or an eye-catching sentence might well fix the attention of prospective readers or, more importantly, potential purchasers of the book, but such devices do not seem appropriate in this case. We feel that it would be best to start the book in a fashion which reflects its approach, i.e. we shall adopt a practical stance and start by discussing what we mean by the three words which constitute the title of the book – *Advanced Financial Accounting*. It will be convenient to start at the end of the title and then work back.

A number of definitions of accounting are available in the literature, and of these we will select the oft-quoted description provided by the Committee of the American Accounting Association (AAA), which was formed in order to prepare a statement of basic accounting theory. In its report, which was published in 1966, the Committee defined accounting as 'the process of identifying, measuring, and communicating economic information to permit informed judgements and decisions by users of the information'.[1]

We feel that the definition is a useful one in that it focuses not on the accounting process itself but on the reasons why information is required. It is all too easy for accountants to become obsessed with the techniques of their craft and to forget that the application of these techniques is not an end in itself but merely a means to an end. In this book we shall constantly reiterate such questions as 'Why is this information required?' or 'How will this data be used?' We believe that a proper study of accounting must start with an examination of the needs of decision makers.

The distinction between financial and management accounting is a convenient one to make, but it must not be regarded as one which divides the two areas of study into water-tight compartments. It would be better if the phrases 'financial' and 'management' accounting were replaced by 'external' and 'internal' accounting,

---

[1] *A statement of basic accounting theory*, AAA, New York, 1966, p. 1.

as management accounting has financial implications while managers have more than a passing interest in financial accounting. However one describes the differences, it is generally agreed that financial, or external, accounting is primarily concerned with the communication of information about an entity to those who do not share in its management, while management, or internal, accounting refers to the communication of information to the managers of the particular entity. Thus the American Financial Accounting Standards Board (FASB) has defined financial reporting as activities which are intended to serve 'the informational needs of external users who lack the authority to prescribe the financial information they want from an enterprise, and therefore must use the information that management communicates to them'.[2] This is a helpful definition which indicates that in this book we will be concerned with financial information that is given to users rather than information which is required by an individual or group of individuals who are in a position to enforce their request.

A more recent description of the objective served by financial statements has been provided by the British Accounting Standards Board (ASB), whose publications loom large in this book. In its Revised Exposure Draft for a *Statement of Principles for Financial Reporting*,[3] the Board states that:

> The objective of financial statements is to provide information about the reporting entity's financial performance and financial position that is useful to a wide range of users for assessing the stewardship of management and for making economic decisions.

The reference to the making of economic decisions links back to the AAA's description of accounting and reminds us of the essentially utilitarian nature of the activity. The concept of stewardship reminds us of accounting's historical roots which were based on the desire of owners of assets to receive reports from their stewards on the way in which the assets entrusted to their charge had been used.

A more modern interpretation of the concept of stewardship suggests that it has two aspects. The obligation to render accounts, or provide financial statements, might be expected to motivate stewards (managers) to act in ways which best serve the interests of owners, while the receipt of such information might help owners make economic decisions (e.g. sell shares or sack the managers), thus indicating that the two purposes of the provision of financial information identified by the ASB are closely interrelated.

Another way in which our attitude to stewardship has changed is that there is now the question of whether stewardship is owed to parties other than the economic owners of the assets. Do managers have an obligation to report to other groups such as employees? Although many would contend that economic ownership is all, and that reporting to other groups is simply a means to the end desired by the owners, there are others who would argue that in a modern business enterprise shareholders are not the only stakeholders entitled to receive reports. We shall return to this theme later in the book.

In this book we shall concentrate on the question of accounting for limited companies. We, of course, recognise that there are many other forms of entity which are of importance, including universities, charities, central and local government and their

---

[2] Statement of Financial Accounting Concepts (SFAC) 1, *Objectives of financial reporting by business enterprises*, FASB, Stamford, Conn., 1978, Para. 28.

[3] *Statement of Principles for Financial Reporting*, Revised Exposure Draft, ASB, London, March 1999.

associated agencies. Our reason for deciding to concentrate on the topic of limited companies is not because we think that the other forms of entity do not merit the concern of financial accountants, but because we recognise that, at least at present, most accounting courses are concerned with the private profit-seeking sector of the economy. Our readers will appreciate that many of the topics that will be discussed in the context of limited companies are of direct relevance to other forms of economic entity.

We should also provide some indication of the interpretation that should be placed on the adjective 'advanced' in the title of this book. It does not mean that the text will concentrate on detailed and complex manipulations of debits and credits, although we shall of course have to deal with such matters from time to time. In the context of this book, 'advanced' means that we shall concentrate on the identification, measurement and communication of economic information in the light of our acceptance of the view of the ASB that such information is required to help in decision making. Thus we shall concentrate on such questions as what information is relevant to decision makers, how the information is relevant to decision makers, how the information should be measured, and the manner in which it should be communicated. In so doing we shall describe and evaluate alternative approaches to the solution of accounting problems.

The definitions of accounting which we quoted above stop at the 'communication' of information. However, it must be emphasised that the interpretation of information is a vital part of an accountant's work, and it is clear that this aspect must be regarded as being an integral part of the process of communication. It should be noted that the definition of accounting does not extend to decision making. Of course, many accountants do become involved in decision making, but when they do so they are performing a managerial rather than an accounting role. We would not for one moment wish to argue that accountants should not become involved in management, but it is essential to distinguish between accounting and decision making. It is important that information provided by accountants should be as free as possible from personal bias but if accountants do not keep the distinction between accounting and decision making clear in their own minds, there is a great danger that they might, possibly quite unconsciously, bias the information provided towards the decision which they would wish to see made.

The above discussion might suggest that we see the work of an accountant as being of a purely technical nature in which he or she is allowed little latitude for professional judgement. This is not the case, because we believe that the accountant must strive to find out and attempt to satisfy the information needs of decision makers and, as we shall show, this is no easy task.

Accounting theory

Academic accountants tend to bemoan the lack of generally accepted accounting theory. This is understandable because theory is the stock in trade of academics. Some 'practical' accountants are probably rather pleased that there is no generally agreed theory of accounting because such practical people are suspicious of theory and theorising as they believe that it gets in the way of 'real work'. However, those who take this view are probably ignorant of the role that theory can play in practical matters and do not realise that an absence of theory does give rise to many real and practical difficulties.

The description of accounting theory provided by Hendriksen shows clearly the practical uses of theory. Hendriksen defines accounting theory as 'logical reasoning in the form of a set of broad principles that (i) provide a general frame of reference by which accounting practice can be evaluated and (ii) guide the development of new practices and procedures'.[4] Expressed in this way, it is obvious that the function of theory is to assist in the resolution of practical problems. The existence of a theory would mean that we could say and explain why, given a number of assumptions, method X (perhaps current cost accounting) is to be preferred to method Y (say historical cost accounting).

There have been numerous attempts to construct a theory of accounting.[5] In the early stages of development an *inductive* approach was employed. Thus the practices of accountants were analysed in order to see whether patterns of consistent behaviour could be derived from the observations. If a general principle could be observed, then procedures which deviated from it could be castigated as being unsound. These first attempts were mainly directed towards the establishment of explanatory theories, i.e. theories which explained why certain rules were followed.

This approach failed for two main reasons. One is the difficulty of distinguishing consistent patterns of behaviour from a mass of procedures which had developed with the growth of accountancy and the problem of establishing any general set of explanatory statements. The second, and possibly more important, reason was that the approach did not help to improve accounting practice in any significant way. The approach only allowed the theorist to say 'what is' and not 'what ought to be'.

In response to these problems a different method of theory construction emerged in the 1950s. This method was normative in nature, i.e. it was directed towards the improvement of accounting practice. The method also included elements of the deductive approach, which essentially consists of the derivation of rules on the basis of logical reasoning from a basic set of objectives. The theories generally consisted of a mixture of deductive and inductive approaches, the latter being used to identify the basic objectives. These approaches to theory construction were extremely valuable in that they generated a number of books and papers which have had a profound effect on the development of accounting thought, in particular in the area of current value accounting.[6]

Since that time, we have seen the development of numerous bodies throughout the world concerned with setting accounting standards. Perhaps not surprisingly, these standard setters have found it difficult to resolve particular accounting issues, so they have sought to construct a conceptual framework or set of principles which could be used to underpin accounting standards and to provide guidance to practitioners in areas where no accounting standard exists. Although the British Accounting Standards Steering Committee, a predecessor of the ASB, issued a discussion document *The Corporate Report*[7] as early as 1975, the most ambitious attempt to create such a framework has undoubtedly been that of the Financial Accounting Standards Board (FASB) in the USA in the late 1970s and the early 1980s. As we shall see, enormous expenditure on this project was not sufficient to prevent it running into difficulties such that work on the project ceased in the mid-1980s. In spite of these difficulties, the approach of the FASB

---

[4] E.S. Hendriksen, *Accounting Theory*, 4th edn, R.D. Irwin, Homewood, Ill., 1982, p. 1.

[5] Hendriksen, *op. cit.*, provides a detailed and authoritative description of these attempts.

[6] Some of the more important developments are summarised in Chapter 15.

[7] *The Corporate Report*, Accounting Standards Steering Committee, London, 1975. This important and wide ranging document did not receive the attention which it deserved because it was followed closely by the publication of the Report of the Inflation Accounting Committee, the Sandilands Report, which was considered to have much greater immediate relevance. We discuss the Sandilands Report in Chapters 15–17 of this book.

has had considerable influence on subsequent developments in other countries, including the following attempts to develop conceptual frameworks:[8]

Making Corporate Reports Valuable, Discussion Document by the Research Committee of the Institute of Chartered Accountants of Scotland, edited by Peter N. McMonnies, Kogan Page, London, 1988.

Framework for the Preparation and Presentation of Financial Statements, International Accounting Standards Committee (IASC), London, 1989.

Guidelines for Financial Reporting Standards, Report to the Research Board of the Institute of Chartered Accountants in England and Wales by Professor David Solomons, ICAEW, London, 1989.

The Future Shape of Financial Reports, Discussion paper by the ICAEW Research Committee and the ICAS Research Board, 1991.

Statement of Principles for Financial Reporting, Exposure Draft (November 1995) and Revised Exposure Draft (March 1999), ASB, London.

With the exception of the ICAS Discussion Document *Making Corporate Reports Valuable*,[9] which takes a much less blinkered approach, all of these documents work within the confines of a typical set of financial statements comprising position statement/balance sheet, performance statement or statements, cash or funds flow statement and supplementary notes. Their basic approach is summarised in Figure 1.1.

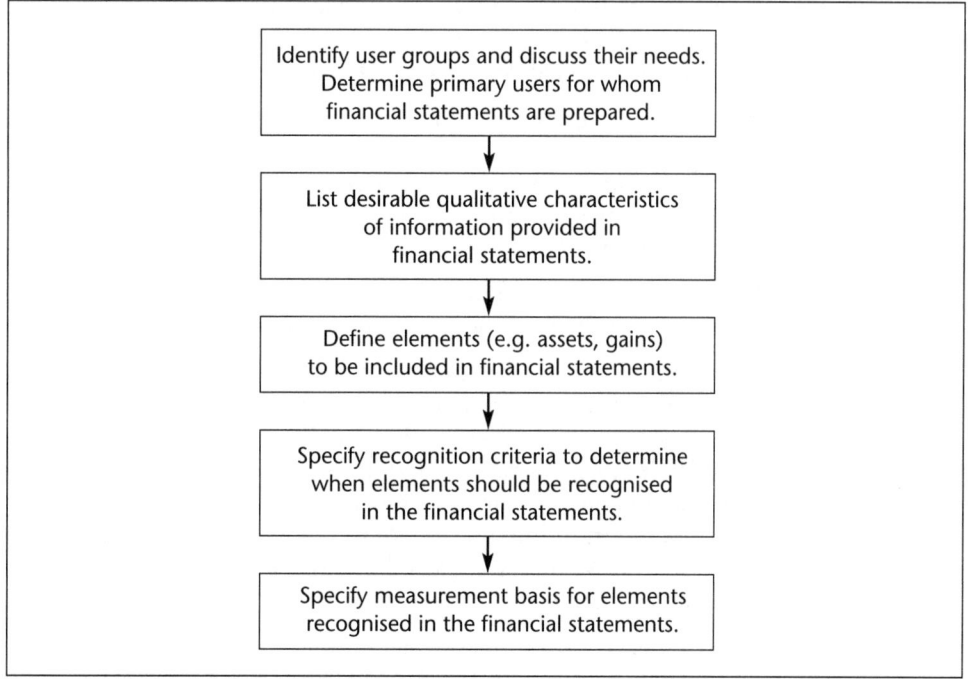

Fig. 1.1 Steps in the structure of a typical conceptual framework

---

[8] This is not intended as an exhaustive list. Many bodies in other countries have attempted to prepare conceptual frameworks and have drawn upon the work of the FASB. Examples include Australia, Canada and New Zealand.

[9] We shall examine some of the ideas of this report later in the book, particularly in Chapters 8 and 18.

As we shall see, problems arise at every stage of the process but, in particular, at the stages of recognition and measurement.

We shall look first at the US Conceptual Framework Project and then briefly at the IASC *Framework for the Preparation and Presentation of Financial Statements* before taking a more detailed look at the attempts of the ASB to prepare its Statement of Principles.

The FASB conceptual framework project

The US FASB was engaged, from the mid-1970s to the mid-1980s, in a major project to develop a 'conceptual framework' for accounting which it defined as:

> a constitution, a coherent system of interrelated objectives and fundamentals that can lead to consistent standards and that prescribes the nature, function and limits of financial accounting and financial statements.[10]

As the project developed, the FASB issued a number of documents entitled *Statements of Financial Accounting Concepts*, of which the following are relevant in the context of this book:[11]

1 *Objectives of Financial Reporting by Business Enterprises* (November 1978).
2 *Qualitative Characteristics of Accounting Information* (May 1980).
5 *Recognition and Measurement in Financial Statements of Business Enterprises* (December 1984).
6 *Elements of Financial Statements* (December 1985).

We shall briefly consider each in turn.

SFAC No. 1 *Objectives of Financial Reporting by Business Enterprises*
As we have seen earlier in the chapter, the FASB is firmly of the view financial reporting is intended to help users make decisions:

> Financial reporting is not an end in itself but is intended to provide information that is useful in making business and economic decisions . . . (Para. 9)

It follows that it is necessary to determine who the users are and to explore the sort of decision which they have to take. The FASB identifies a large number of user groups both with a direct interest and an indirect interest. The former include such groups as owners, lenders, suppliers, potential investors and creditors, customers, management, directors and taxing authorities while the latter include such groups as financial analysts and labour unions, who advise those with a direct interest. In spite of recognition of these user groups and discussion of their needs, the Statement comes to the conclusion that:

> . . . Thus, financial reporting should provide information to help investors, creditors and others assess the amounts, timing and uncertainty of prospective net cash inflows to the related enterprise. (Para. 37)

---

[10] *Scope and Implications of the Conceptual Framework Project*, FASB, Stamford, Conn., 1976, p. 2.
[11] SFAC No. 3 was superseded by SFAC No. 6 and SFAC No. 4 was concerned with Objectives of Financial Reporting by Nonbusiness Organizations', which is outside the scope of this textbook.

While some find it difficult to accept that this focus on investors and creditors follows logically from the identification of so many user groups and the discussion of their needs, the next step in the logic seems to be even more suspect.

> Financial reporting should provide information about the economic resources of an enterprise, the claims to those resources (obligations of the enterprise to transfer resources to other entities and owners' equity) and the effects of transactions, events and circumstances that change resources and claims to those resources. (Para. 40)

A cynical observer might comment that it is extremely convenient that the outcome of the user-oriented approach is the conclusion that users need the sort of reports that they have traditionally received in the past, namely a position statement or balance sheet together with an income statement!

SFAC No. 2 *Qualitative Characteristics of Accounting Information*
In SFAC No. 2, the FASB specifies a hierarchy of desirable characteristics for accounting information. Decision usefulness is paramount and to be useful information must be both relevant and reliable. While the statement provides numerous other desirable qualities in a hierarchy, it clearly recognises that there will often be a conflict between two or more of these characteristics. Thus at the highest level, relevant information may not be reliable while reliable information may not be relevant. We will examine a similar attempt to specify desirable characteristics later in the chapter within the context of the ASB Draft Statements of Principles.

SFAC No. 6 *Elements of Financial Statements (superseded SFAC No. 3)*
This Statement of Financial Concepts provides definitions of the ten elements of financial statements, namely:

- Assets
- Liabilities
- Equity
- Investments by owners
- Distributions to owners
- Comprehensive income
- Revenue
- Expenses
- Gains
- Losses

It follows that nothing should be included in the financial statements unless it satisfies one of the definitions provided. Even then, it should not be included in the financial statements unless it satisfies the recognition criteria laid down in SFAC No. 5.

SFAC No. 5 *Recognition and Measurement in Financial Statements of Business Enterprises*
Having set down the desirable characteristics of accounting information and the definitions of the elements of financial statements, the crucial step in the US Conceptual Framework Project came with Statement of Financial Accounting Concepts No. 5. This is the document which was intended to specify both when an element should be recognised (that is, included in the financial statements) and, once included, how it should be measured.

The Statement lays down four fundamental recognition criteria but accepts that trade-offs between them will have to be made in practice. It then discusses various different possible bases of measurement which could be used in a set of financial statements, including historical cost, current cost, current market value, net realisable value and present value of future cash flows. However, it does not come down clearly in favour of any one basis of measurement but, rather, leaves the choice of accounting measurement to standard setters and accountants.

This was the end for the Conceptual Framework Project for, instead of providing guidance of what should be included in financial statements and what basis of measurement should be used, it failed to do so. Three short quotations from the Statement will help readers appreciate why Professor David Solomons described SFAC No. 5 as a 'cop-out':[12]

> Items currently reported in financial statements are measured by different attributes, depending on the nature of the item and the relevance or reliability of the attribute measured. The Board expects the use of different attributes to continue. (Para. 66)

> The concept of earnings described in this statement is similar to net income in present practice . . . (Para. 33)

> The Board expects the concept of earnings to be subject to the process of gradual change or evolution which has characterized the development of net income . . . (Para. 35)

Here was a framework designed to help standard setters improve financial reporting providing little guidance but rather expecting things to continue much as they had done before! Such an outcome had been predicted by the British Professor Richard Macve in 1981 in a report commissioned by the Accounting Standards Committee, the predecessor of the ASB.[13] Professor Macve concluded that, while the quest for a conceptual framework or general theory is important in identifying questions that need to be answered, it would be idle to hope that such a framework could be developed that would give explicit guidance on practical problems.

In spite of Professor Macve's conclusion and the discontinuance of the US Conceptual Framework Project, other bodies have continued their search for this Holy Grail and we turn next to the attempt of the IASC.

The IASC framework

Given that national standard setters, like the FASB and ASB, were facing difficulties in resolving many accounting issues, it is perhaps not surprising that the IASC, with members drawn from some 100 countries, was facing even greater difficulties.[14] It too has attempted to construct a conceptual framework although on a much less grand scale than that which was originally envisaged by the FASB.

The IASC published its *Framework for the Preparation and Presentation of Financial Statements* in July 1989 and we may immediately obtain a feel for its contents by listing the major headings of the document:

---

[12] David Solomons, 'The FASB's Conceptual Framework: an evaluation', *Journal of Accountancy*, June 1986, pp. 114–24.

[13] Richard Macve, *A Conceptual Framework for Financial Reporting*, ICAEW, London, 1981.

[14] We discuss the IASC and its increasing role in international standard setting in Chapter 2, Sources of Authority.

- Introduction
- The Objective of Financial Statements
- Underlying Assumptions
- Qualitative Characteristics of Financial Statements
- The Elements of Financial Statements
- Recognition of the Elements of Financial Statements
- Measurement of the Elements of Financial Statements
- Concepts of Capital and Capital Maintenance

Most of these may be clearly related to the relevant Statements of Financial Concepts of the FASB, which we have outlined above. The additions are sections on 'Underlying Assumptions' and 'Concepts of Capital and Capital Maintenance'. The first of these describes the accruals basis and going concern concept while the second outlines the major capital maintenance concepts which can be used in the measurement of profit; namely financial capital maintenance (nominal or real) and physical capital maintenance, respectively, without chosing between them.[15]

Yet again, standard setters looking to this framework for help in resolving most accounting issues will be disappointed. Its failings are most evident at the measurement stage. Thus the section on measurement discusses four different measurement bases which are employed to different degrees and in varying combinations in financial statements; namely historical cost, current cost, realisable value and present value. However, no guidance is given on which should be selected for any given element recognised. When this is coupled with the lack of guidance on the capital maintenance concept to be employed in measuring profit for a period, the document seems unlikely to resolve many accounting issues. A quotation from the final paragraph (110) gives support to this conclusion:

> The selection of the measurement bases and concept of capital maintenance will determine the accounting model used in the preparation of financial statements. Different accounting models exhibit different degrees of relevance and reliability and, as in other areas, management must seek a balance between relevance and reliability. This Framework is applicable to a range of accounting models and provides guidance on preparing and presenting the financial statements constructed under the chosen model. At the present time, it is not the intention of the Board of IASC to prescribe a particular model other than in exceptional circumstances, such as for those enterprises reporting in the currency of a hyperinflationary economy. This intention will, however, be reviewed in the light of world developments.

Over a decade has now passed but this framework has not been tightened. With this background, let us now turn to the attempts of the ASB to develop its Statement of Principles.

The ASB's Statement of Principles

The ASB has been committed to the development of a Statement of Principles for Financial Reporting since its formation in 1990, as was made clear in paragraph 4 of the Foreword to accounting standards, issued in June 1993:

> FRSs (Financial Reporting Standards) are based upon the Statement of Principles for Financial Reporting currently in issue, which addresses the concepts underlying the information

---

[15] We will discuss these concepts in considerable depth later in the book, initially in Chapter 3 and subsequently in Part IV.

presented in financial statements. The objective of this Statement of Principles is to provide a framework for the consistent and logical formulation of individual accounting standards. The framework also provides a basis on which others can exercise judgement in resolving accounting issues.

Despite this brave statement, the Board has managed to issue some fifteen Financial Reporting Standards in the absence of such an agreed Statement of Principles.

The first attempt

Individual draft chapters of a Statement of Principles were issued by the ASB and, following amendment in response to comments, these were collected together in an Exposure Draft published in November 1995. The headings of the seven chapters in this exposure draft were as follows:

1 The objective of financial statements
2 The qualitative characteristics of financial information
3 The elements of financial statements
4 Recognition in financial statements
5 Measurement in financial statements
6 Presentation in financial statements
7 The reporting entity

The first five of these chapters covered material familiar from the FASB *Statements of Financial Accounting Concepts* and the IASC *Framework for the Preparation and Presentation of Financial Statements* which we have discussed above. Chapter 6 specified the contents of a set of financial statements and how information should be presented in those statements. Chapter 7 concerned itself with the treatment of different levels of investment, including subsidiaries, associates and joint ventures.

In the preparation of this draft, the ASB sensibly tried to start with a clean sheet by ignoring the constraints imposed by company law. Appendix 2 to the draft specifically drew attention to a number of important conflicts between the draft Statement and the law. However, where such conflicts exist, the principles could only be followed if use were to be made of the true and fair override or if the law were to be changed. The ASB undoubtedly hoped and still hopes that changes in the law would follow general acceptance of its Statement of Principles.

The draft Statement of Principles adopted a balance sheet focus. Thus, like its predecessors, it provided definitions of assets and liabilities and proposed that only items which satisfy those definitions may be recognised in the balance sheet and then only when certain recognition criteria are satisfied.

Given the greater relevance of current values to decision taking, it proposed a greater use of current values using a concept known as 'value to the business', to which we shall return many times in this book.

Ownership interest is defined as assets less liabilities and the total gains or losses for a period are to be calculated by deducting the opening ownership interest from the closing ownership interest and adjusting for any contributions from or distributions to owners. Such gains or losses were to appear in one of the two performance statements, either in the Profit and Loss Account or, as another gain or loss, in the Statement of Total Recognised Gains and Losses. The draft specified certain rules to guide this selection, in particular that gains and losses on fixed assets, whether realised or unrealised, should appear in the Statement of Total Recognised Gains and Losses rather than in the Profit and Loss Account.

Perhaps not surprisingly, the ASB received more comments on this document than any other document it has published. While many recognised the need for a Statement of Principles, criticism of this particular draft Statement was vociferous, with the firm of Ernst & Young playing a particularly important role.[16] This criticism was such that the ASB withdrew the draft Statement of Principles in July 1996 and issued a progress paper entitled 'Statement of Principles for Financial Reporting – the way ahead'. In that document, the ASB stated its intention to issue a revised exposure draft and this has been published, rather later than expected, in March 1999.

Although the ASB accused its critics of misunderstanding its proposals, much of the criticism seemed to have been well founded. The balance sheet focus adopted in the draft has a number of strengths but does not seem in accord with either current practice or with the principles on which the Board has based some of its published standards. The draft certainly failed to provide sufficient justification for such a fundamental departure from a position with which many accountants feel comfortable.

Although they may be accused of overlooking the fact that a large proportion of listed companies have revalued at least some of their fixed assets on a piecemeal basis, critics also attacked the proposals to move towards a greater use of current values. They pointed out that such values were less reliable and that, even if all assets and liabilities recognised in a balance sheet were to be shown at current values, the total ownership interest would not represent the wealth or value of the business as discussed in economists' models. Given this, any measure of gains and losses based upon comparing two such balance sheet totals is unlikely to provide a sensible measure of the increase in the wealth of owners.

The way in which gains and losses were to be recognised either in the Profit and Loss Account or Statement of Total Recognised Gains and Losses also came in for criticism. While the authors would applaud the attempts of the ASB to discard the confusing and rather unhelpful distinction between realised and unrealised profit, it is not surprising that practitioners, who have worked with such concepts for the whole of their working lives, are not willing to give them up without a fight.

With this brief look at the major criticisms made of the first draft Statement of Principles, let us now turn to the revised exposure draft issued in March 1999.

The revised exposure draft

The revised exposure draft was issued in March 1999, this time accompanied by both an introductory booklet and a technical supplement. The introductory booklet contains both a question and answer section and an overview of the draft statement. The technical supplement sets out the reasons for some of the Board's conclusions and why it has rejected possible alternatives. Having been taken by surprise by the negative reaction to the first exposure draft, the ASB was clearly concerned to defuse criticism of this second attempt at developing a Statement of Principles and has taken great pains to explain and sell its revised draft.

---

[16] *See*, for example: *The ASB's Framework: Time to Decide*, Ernst & Young, London, February 1996; *The ASB's Statement of Principles – Blueprint or Blind Alley?*, Ron Paterson (Ernst & Young), University of Wales (Aberystwyth), February 1998; Chapter 2 of *UKGAAP*, 5th edn, Mike Davies, Ron Paterson and Allister Wilson, Macmillan, London, 1997.

The revised exposure draft itself contains eight chapters, rather than the seven of its predecessor:

1 The objective of financial statements
2 The reporting entity
3 The qualitative characteristics of financial information
4 The elements of financial statements
5 Recognition in financial statements
6 Measurement in financial statements
7 Presentation of financial information
8 Accounting for interests in other entities

We shall provide a brief synopsis of each of these chapters before assessing the extent to which the revised draft overcomes the perceived defects of its predecessor and hence whether or not it is likely to prove acceptable in practice.

Chapter 1 The objective of financial statements

Perhaps not surprisingly the revised exposure draft provides us with the following objective:

> The objective of financial statements is to provide information about the reporting entity's financial performance and financial position that is useful to a wide range of users for assessing the stewardship of management and for making economic decisions. (p. 20)

It identifies a number of users of general purpose financial reports and discusses their needs for information. The user groups include investors, lenders, suppliers and other trade creditors, employees, customers, governments and their agencies and the public. Like the US Conceptual Framework Project, discussed above, the revised exposure draft comes to the conclusion that it is possible to meet the objective by focusing exclusively on the needs of investors, which it describes as the defining class of user.

It concludes that investors and others need information about the reporting entity's financial performance and financial position to help them to evaluate the entity's ability to generate cash (including the timing and certainty of its generation) and to assess its financial adaptability.

Chapter 2 The reporting entity

This chapter specifies the boundary of the reporting entity by reference to the scope of control. Thus an entity with direct control of its activities, assets and liabilities should prepare single entity financial statements while an entity which also has indirect control of the activities, assets and liabilities of a subsidiary should also prepare consolidated financial statements.

Control has two aspects: first, the ability to deploy the economic resources involved and, second, the ability to benefit (or to suffer) from this deployment. The exposure draft makes it clear that it is the relationship existing between entities in practice, rather than the theoretical level of influence, that is to be considered in determining whether or not control exists.

Chapter 3 The qualitative characteristics of financial information

The revised draft sets out the desirable characteristics of financial information in a hierarchy which we have reproduced as Figure 1.2. To be useful financial information must be (i) relevant to users, (ii) reliable, (iii) comparable, and (iv) understandable.

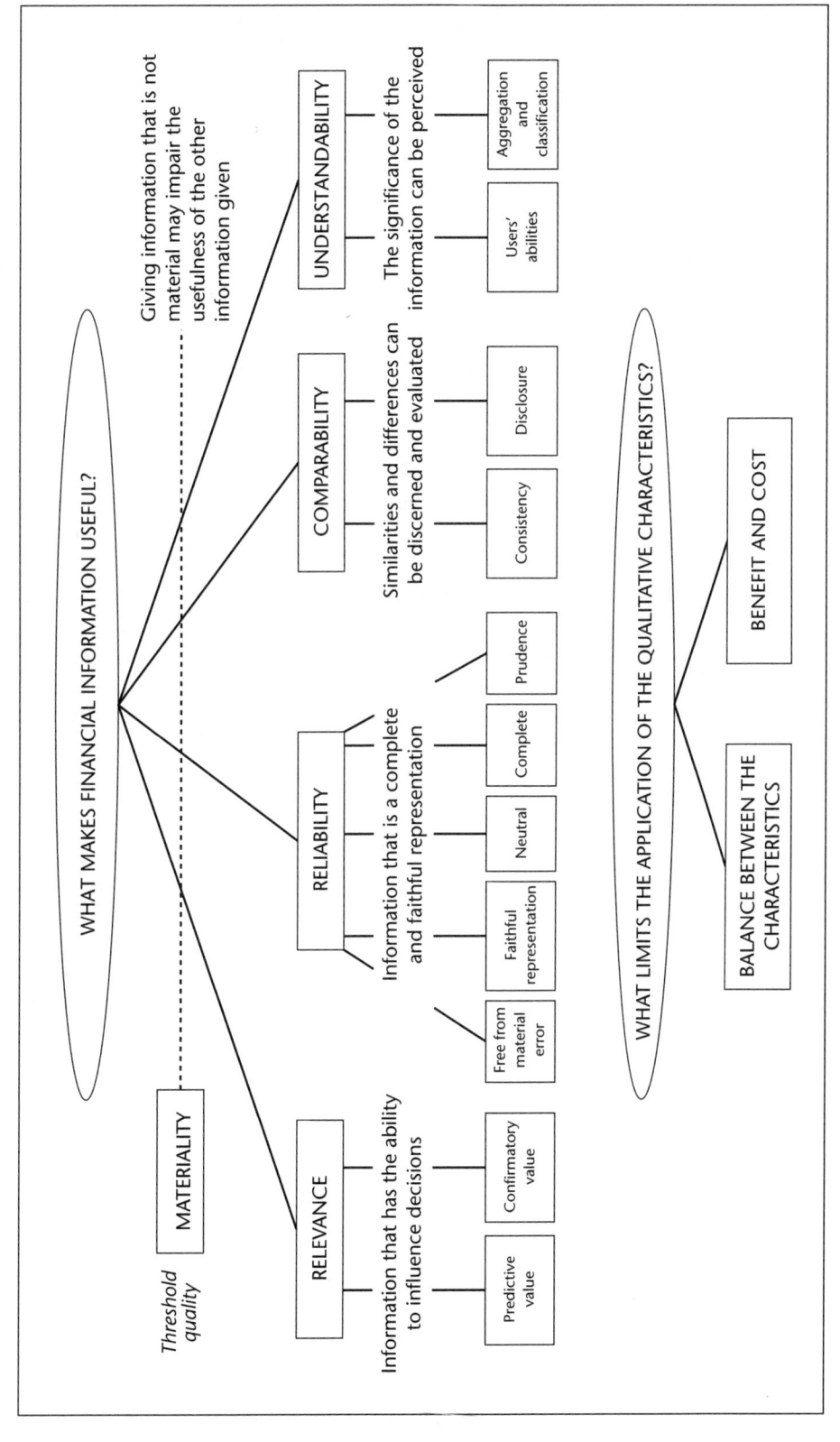

Fig. 1.2 The qualitative characteristics of financial information

Source: Statement of Principles for Financial Reporting, Revised Exposure Draft (March 1999), p.37. Accounting Standards Board. ©ASB Publications Limited 2000. Reproduced with permission.

Financial information is relevant if it would influence economic decisions and it would be able to do this if it has predictive value or confirmatory value. Information with predictive value would help users to assess what is likely to happen in future while information with confirmatory value would help them to confirm or correct previous predictions which they have made. In many, if not most, cases information will have both confirmatory and predictive value.

To be reliable, information must be free from material error and possess certain subsidiary characteristics:

- *Faithful representation.* It must faithfully represent what it purports to represent so that, for example, the substance of a transaction must be portrayed when this differs from its legal form.
- *Neutral.* The information should be neutral, in other words, it should not be subject to deliberate or systematic bias. We shall have more to say about this when we discuss prudence below.
- *Complete.* It should be complete to the extent possible.
- *Prudent.* In the revised exposure draft, prudence is defined as follows:

> Prudence is the inclusion of a degree of caution in the exercise of the judgements needed in making the estimates required under conditions of uncertainty, such that gains or assets are not overstated and losses and liabilities are not understated.

The ASB hopes that the application of such a concept will not cause the information presented to be biased and the exposure draft makes it clear that prudence should not involve the deliberate understatement of assets and gains or the overstatement of liabilities and losses. The making of excessive provisions and the creation of hidden reserves is unacceptable. Unfortunately the distinction between these different concepts of prudence is often difficult to make in practice and the disputes between directors and auditors about what is or is not prudent are unlikely to disappear as a result of this guidance.

Information should be comparable both for a reporting entity over time and across different reporting entities. This is a tall order but, in particular, requires disclosure of accounting policies as well as of details of changes and the effects of changes in accounting policies.

In order to specify understandability as a desirable characteristic, it is necessary to make some assumption about the ability of users. The ASB assumes that the targeted users 'have a reasonable knowledge of business and economic activities and accounting and a willingness to study with reasonable diligence the information provided'.

The exposure draft clearly recognises that there will be conflicts between these desirable characteristics such that trade-offs will be necessary. One example of such a conflict is between relevance and reliability: timely information may be highly relevant but not very reliable in an uncertain world but, if we wait for reliable information, it may no longer be timely and therefore no longer relevant. Another example is the conflict between neutrality and prudence, both subsidiary characteristics of reliability, to which we have drawn attention above.

Chapter 4 The elements of financial statements
This chapter defines seven elements of financial statements:

- assets
- liabilities

- ownership interest
- gains
- losses
- contributions from owners
- distributions to owners.

Ownership interest is defined as assets less liabilities while gains and losses, contributions from owners and distributions to owners are defined by reference to various changes in ownership interest. The crucial definitions are therefore those for assets and liabilities, which clearly demonstrates the determination of the ASB to retain a balance sheet focus in spite of the heavy criticism of that approach in its first exposure draft:

> Assets are rights or other access to future economic benefits controlled by an entity as a result of past transactions or events. (Para. 4.7)

> Liabilities are obligations of an entity to transfer economic benefits as a result of past transactions or events. (Para. 4.24)

We shall consider these terms later in the book, particularly in Chapters 4 and 5.

Chapter 5 Recognition in financial statements

There are two prongs to the recognition of transactions or events in a set of financial statements: first, there must be sufficient evidence that an asset or liability has been created or that there has been an addition to an asset or liability. Second, the new asset or liability, or addition thereto, must be capable of measurement at a monetary amount with sufficient accuracy.

So, to be included in a set of financial statements, the item must satisfy the definition of an element in Chapter 4 of the report and must be measured reliably. This would mean that certain expenditure previously treated as a deferred asset, such as deferred advertising expenditure, may not be recognised under the draft Statement of Principles. In this way the ASB hopes to limit the carrying forward of expenditure to match against perhaps dubious benefits in the future:

> The Statement imposes a degree of discipline on this process because only items that meet the definitions of, and relevant recognition criteria for, assets, liabilities or ownership interest are recognised in the balance sheet. (Para. 5.27)

Chapter 6 Measurement in financial statements

Having rejected, perhaps too easily, the notion that individual assets and liabilities should be reported on two or more bases of measurement, the ASB then has to choose whether assets and liabilities should be measured at historical cost or at some current value. The first exposure draft was explicit that the ASB favoured the use of current value as can be seen from the following quotation:

> The Board therefore believes that practice should develop by evolving in the direction of greater use of current values to the extent that this is consistent with the constraints of reliability and cost. (First exposure draft, Para. 5.38)

This was criticised as an attempt on the part of the ASB to move away from historical cost accounting towards a system of current cost accounting. This the ASB has denied and, certainly in the revised exposure draft, it is very careful not to expose this hostage to fortune.

The ASB now favours the use of the mixed measurement system, sometimes described as modified historical cost accounting. As envisaged by the revised exposure draft, some assets will be valued on a historical cost basis while others will be valued at current value. The draft statement would outlaw the practice by which some entities remeasure their tangible fixed to assets at a current value on one particular date but leave that revised value in the financial statements for many years to come.

The concept of current value which the ASB favours is Value to the Business, sometimes known as deprival value, which it defines as shown in Figure 1.3.

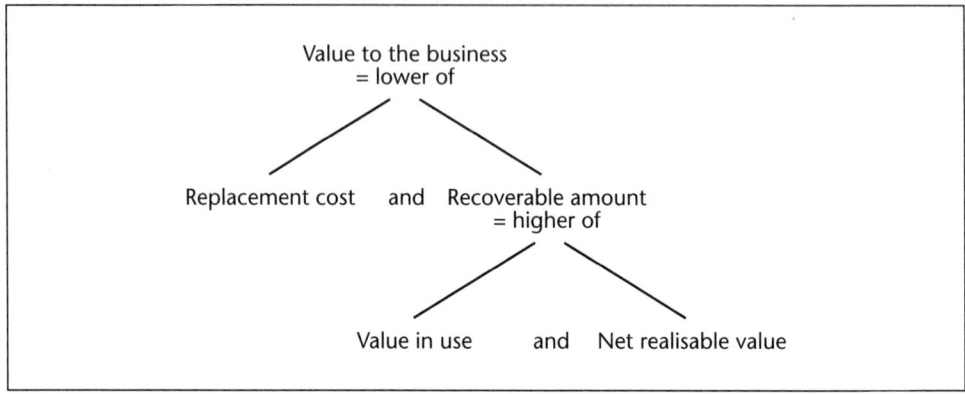

Fig. 1.3 The value to the business concept of current value

Source: Statement of Principles for Financial Reporting, Revised Exposure Draft (March 1999), p. 88. Accounting Standards Board. © ASB Publications Limited 2000. Reproduced with permission.

We shall return to this concept many times in this book, particularly in Chapters 3, 16, 17 and 18.

If some companies choose to measure assets and liabilities on an historical cost basis while others choose to use current value, it is difficult to see how their respective financial statements will satisfy the desirable quality of comparability.

Chapter 7 Presentation of financial information

According to this chapter, the primary financial statements comprise three documents:

- Statement of financial performance[17]
- Position statement or balance sheet
- Cash flow statement

It lays down general principles for presentation of the highly structured and aggregated information necessary in financial statements, the notes to these statements and in the accompanying information. The latter includes such documents as the Chairman's Report, the operating and financial review and five-year historical summaries.

---

[17] Present standard accounting practice requires the inclusion of two performance statements: a Profit and Loss Account and a Statement of Total Recognised Gains and Losses. It is suggested that the reference in the draft to 'Statement of performance' in the singular anticipates that the ASB proposal to combine these statements proves acceptable. This proposal is included in the Discussion Paper 'Reporting Financial Performance: Proposals for Change', published in June 1999. We shall discuss these proposals in Chapter 6.

Chapter 8 Accounting for interests in other entities

This final chapter deals with the treatment of investments in other entities in both the single-entity financial statements and in consolidated financial statements and is closely related to the material on the reporting entity discussed earlier in Chapter 2.

According to the exposure draft, the accounting treatment in financial statements should be determined by the degree of influence which the investor has over the investee. When there is significant influence but less than control, the investee is an associate or joint venture and the appropriate method of accounting to be used in the consolidated financial statements is the equity method of accounting. We shall discuss this thoroughly in Chapter 9.

An evaluation of the revised exposure draft

The revised exposure draft, together with the accompanying introductory booklet and technical supplement, clearly demonstrate the desire of the ASB to gain the acceptance of the various interested parties for its Statement of Principles. These documents explain the thinking of the ASB much more clearly than the first exposure draft and, in particular, respond to the criticisms of that earlier draft.

As we have seen, one of the major criticisms of the earlier exposure draft was that it adopted a balance sheet focus as opposed to the transactions focused and matching approach of present practice. The revised exposure draft reiterates this balance sheet focus and considers that it is necessary in order to prevent the attempts by some entities to delay the recognition of items of expenditure by carrying them forward to match against perhaps dubious future benefits.

A second major criticism of the first exposure draft was that the ASB was attempting to move away from a system of historical cost accounting to a system of current cost accounting. The ASB has always claimed that this was not its intention although it, quite sensibly, favours the greater use of current values where appropriate. In the revised exposure draft, it has undoubtedly stepped further back envisaging the use of a mixed measurement system using both historical costs and current values. However, if entities are permitted to choose whether to use historical cost based values or current values, the desirable quality of comparability across entities is lost completely.

A third criticism of the first exposure draft concerned the way in which gains and losses were divided between the Profit and Loss Account and the Statement of Total Recognised Gains and Losses. There is undoubtedly greater understanding and acceptance of the Statement of Total Recognised Gains and Losses now than when the first exposure draft was published.[18] Indeed, the Discussion Paper *Reporting Financial Performance: Proposals for change* (June 1999) advocates the combination of both documents into a single Statement of Performance. The major debate is therefore likely to focus on the more detailed proposals in that discussion paper.

In order to diffuse potential criticism, the ASB plays down the importance of the Statement of Principles by drawing attention to the many other factors which will have to be considered in setting accounting standards, namely:

(a) legal requirements,
(b) cost–benefit considerations,

---

[18] The first exposure draft was published in November 1995 just some three years after the issue of FRS 3 *Reporting Financial Performance* in October 1992. It was FRS 3 which introduced the requirement for entities to produce the new primary statement, a Statement of Total Recognised Gains and Losses, for accounting periods ending on or after 22 June 1993.

(c) industry-specific issues,

(d) the desirability of evolutionary change, and

(e) implementation issues.[19]

In particular, Part C of the technical supplement draws attention to the major conflicts between the exposure draft and existing company law. As in the past, the law will continue to constrain the activities of the ASB in the future.

All of this leaves the ASB considerable flexibility in future but does raise fundamental question about the role of any Statement of Principles if the principles which it lays down can be overridden on so many other grounds!

Summary

In this chapter we have stressed the need for 'theory' to guide and underpin practice and have examined some attempts to build such theories. After a brief examination of early attempts to develop theory, we have outlined the attempts of the US Financial Accounting Standards Board and International Accounting Standards Committee to develop frameworks for financial reporting. We have then focused, in more detail, on the attempts of the ASB to develop its more modestly titled Statement of Principles.

The revised exposure draft of this Statement of Principles for Financial Reporting goes to great pains to explain why the ASB has adopted its particular approach and, by so doing, hopes to head off the enormous criticism faced by its predecessor. Whether or not it proves effective in doing this remains to be seen.

There is no doubt that any Statement of Principles based on the revised exposure draft would leave the ASB with a considerable amount of flexibility. Inevitably choices will have to be made with trade-offs between different desirable characteristics and judgements on the necessary level of reliability for recognition of elements in the financial statements and the basis of their measurement. We would do well to remember that the setting of accounting standards is very much a political process which those with vested interests will wish to influence.

We have seen that, although the draft Statement of Principles is written without taking into account the constraints imposed by the law, these constraints cannot possibly be ignored in preparing accounting standards. The question of who does and who should set the rules by which the accounting game is played are important and complex issues and these form the subject matter of the next chapter.

Recommended reading

ASC, *The Corporate Report*, London, 1975.

E.S. Hendriksen and M.F. Van Breda, *Accounting Theory*, 5th edn, Irwin, Homewood, Ill, 1992.

Institute of Chartered Accountants of Scotland, *Making Corporate Reports Valuable*, Kogan Page, London, 1988.

R. Macve, *A Conceptual Framework for Financial Accounting and Reporting – Vision, Tool or Threat?*, Garland, New York/London, 1997.

K.V. Peasnell, 'The function of a conceptual framework for corporate financial reporting', *Accounting and Business Research*, Autumn 1982.

---

[19] *Ibid.*, Introduction, Para. 16.

2 Sources of authority

There is a large and increasing body of rules with which accountants need to be familiar when preparing or interpreting a set of financial statements. Such rules are laid down in the law, in the rules of the Stock Exchange and in accounting standards. In this chapter we look at these three rule makers and how they operate.

Here and throughout the book, we concentrate on 'big GAAP', the rules which apply to large companies and groups, rather than the special rules which apply to small and medium-sized companies.

Given the existence of the European Union and the globalisation of capital markets, international developments have assumed a much greater importance than they once enjoyed. We therefore examine the contribution which the International Accounting Standards Committee and the European Union have made and continue to make to the regulation of financial reporting.

Introduction

In Chapter 1 we have explained that there is no general theory of accounting in existence to guide us in the preparation of financial statements. We have explored the attempts of several bodies to build conceptual frameworks of accounting and have concentrated on the attempt of the ASB to develop its *Statement of Principles for Financial Reporting* and shown that the most recent revised exposure draft leaves many questions unanswered. In spite of the lack of theory, there are many rules which govern the preparation of financial statements and in this chapter we turn to the framework for the setting and enforcement of such rules in the United Kingdom.

Rule setters affecting the UK come in three main forms, each of which have different powers and sanctions available to them:

1 *Government at both the United Kingdom and European Union levels*: These operate through legislation.
2 *Securities markets*: In the UK the Stock Exchange imposes rules which must be complied with by companies which have their shares and other securities traded on the Exchange.
3 *Standard setting bodies in the private sector*: These may include professional accountancy bodies acting individually or collectively, perhaps in co-operation with non-accountants. In the UK, standard setting takes place nationally through the work of the Accounting Standards Board (ASB) and internationally through the work of the International Accounting Standards Committee (IASC).

In this chapter, we shall examine each of these sources of authority.

Legislation

Background

The advent of the limited liability company by registration under general Act of Parliament in the mid-nineteenth century made possible the separation of management from ownership, which is such a dominant feature of business organisation today. With this separation came the need for directors to render accounts to shareholders to show the performance and financial position of the company. It followed that it was necessary to determine what should be included in such accounts and how they should be prepared.

It would have been possible for the law to have left the specification of the form and content of such accounts to be determined by contract between the shareholders and directors, or even to have left the directors to decide what information should be made available in the particular circumstances. However, the law initially flirted with the regulation of accounting disclosure in the period 1844–56 and then became permanently involved with regulating the contents of company accounts early in this century. The Companies Act 1929 increased the information which companies had to disclose while extensive disclosure has been required since the Companies Act 1948.[1]

Before the Companies Act 1981, the accounting requirements of company law allowed companies considerable latitude. The directors were required to prepare accounts which showed a true and fair view and which contained the minimum information specified by the various Companies Acts. These accounts, together with the accompanying auditors' and directors' reports, had to be laid before the shareholders and filed with the Registrar of Companies within certain time limits. While the basic position is unchanged, substantial alterations were made by the Companies Act 1981.

The Companies Act 1981 was mainly concerned with the implementation of the EC Fourth Directive, a directive heavily influenced by the more prescriptive approach to accounting found in France and Germany. As a consequence, the Act was much more prescriptive than previous legislation in the UK. Although it still contained the overriding principle that accounts should give a true and fair view, it increased substantially the amount of information to be disclosed and reduced considerably the flexibility which companies previously enjoyed. Thus, whereas directors were previously able to choose the particular formats and valuation rules which seemed most appropriate in the circumstances, the Companies Act 1981 specified much more tightly the formats and valuation rules to be used.

The provisions of the Companies Act 1981 are now contained in the Companies Act 1985, which was a consolidating Act, but this in turn has been amended by the subsequent Companies Act 1989 and numerous Statutory Instruments.

The Companies Act 1989 implemented the EC Seventh Directive on consolidated accounts and the EC Eighth Directive on auditors, as well as dealing with many other matters.

Small and medium-sized companies have long enjoyed the opportunity of filing abbreviated accounts with the Registrar of Companies. However, as a consequence of

---

[1] Readers who wish to study this historical development of accounting further are referred to H.C. Edey, 'Company accounting in the nineteenth and twentieth centuries', in *The Evolution of Corporate Financial Reporting*, T.A. Lee and R.H. Parker (eds), Nelson, London, 1979, and J.R. Edwards, *A History of Financial Accounting*, Routledge, London, 1989: Chapters 9, 10 and 11 of the latter are particularly relevant.

the attempts of successive governments to reduce the burden of regulation on small companies, new rules were introduced in 1997 to reduce the volume of disclosure required of small companies and groups. The Companies Act 1985 (Accounts of Small and Medium-Sized Companies and Minor Accounting Amendments) Regulations 1997 established a revised Schedule 8 to the 1985 Companies Act, which now contains all the provisions of the law relating to the accounts which small companies must send to their members. This law, together with the accounting standard *Financial Reporting Standard for Smaller Entities* (FRSSE) now provides a less burdensome regulatory framework for small companies and groups.[2]

In this book we shall concentrate on what is sometimes called 'Big GAAP', that is Generally Accepted Accounting Practice for large companies and groups. While we will from time to time draw attention to some of the exemptions available to small and, to a lesser extent, medium-sized companies and groups, we will not deal with these systematically or in any detail.

Concentrating now on large companies, the law requires that full accounts, including group accounts where appropriate, are sent to all shareholders and debenture holders of the company, although permission is given for a listed public company to send a summary financial statement to its shareholders.[3] The latter provision was intended to reduce the cost of sending full accounts to large numbers of relatively unsophisticated shareholders, particularly following the large privatisation issues of the 1980s. Full accounts have to be laid before the company in general meeting except that a private company may elect not to do so.[4] Such provisions are designed to ensure that shareholders and debenture holders receive financial information about companies, while recognising that it may not be necessary formally to present the accounts of a private company at a general meeting.

In addition to the above, companies are required to make their accounts available to the public by filing them with the Registrar of Companies within certain time limits, namely ten months after the end of the accounting year for a private company and seven months after the end of an accounting year for a public company.

The current position

The Companies Act 1985, as amended by the Companies Act 1989, requires that the accounts of a large company give the information specified in Schedule 4 using one of the profit and loss account and balance sheet formats provided. However, compliance with this requirement is not sufficient to ensure compliance with the law for there is an overriding requirement that every balance sheet shall give a true and fair view of the state of affairs of the company and that every profit and loss account shall give a true and fair view of the profit or loss of the company for the financial year.[5]

Hence, having prepared the accounts containing the required disclosure, the accountant must then step back and decide whether or not the overall impression created is

---

[2] The first *Financial Reporting Standard for Smaller Entities* was issued in November 1997 and an updated version was issued in December 1998. It is intended that the Standard be updated periodically to incorporate relevant parts of new Financial Reporting Standards and Abstracts of the Urgent Issues Task Force (UITF).

[3] Companies Act 1985, Sec. 251 (as inserted by Companies Act 1989, Sec. 15). This section was implemented by The Companies (Summary Financial Statement) Regulations 1990, SI 1990/515. See Chapter 11, pages 362–3.

[4] Companies Act 1985, Sec. 252 (as inserted by Companies Act 1989, Sec. 16).

[5] Companies Act 1985, Sec. 226.

true and fair. If the accounts do not give such an impression, additional information must be provided. If the provision of additional information still does not result in a true and fair view, then the accounts must be changed, even if this means that they do not comply with the other statutory rules. Particulars of any departure, the reasons for it and its effect must be disclosed in the notes to the accounts.

The statutory requirements outlined above pose a number of problems for the accountant. Familiarity with the disclosure requirements of the Companies Acts is required, as is knowledge of the measurement or valuation rules to apply in arriving at the figures to be disclosed. Also the accountant must be aware of what is meant by the words 'true and fair'. We will look at each of these three aspects in turn.

The first problem involves detailed knowledge of the Companies Acts and the various guides thereto and considerable practice in applying those rules in various circumstances. We assume that readers have some knowledge of the requirements of the Companies Acts although, where relevant, we will reproduce the statutory rules in later chapters.

The second problem involves the selection of measurement or valuation rules to apply in arriving at the various figures which appear in the set of accounts. This requires a considerable knowledge of accounting, which this book will help to provide.

Until the Companies Act 1981 accountants would have looked to accounting principles, conventions, recommendations and standards to help them with this task. Although, as we shall see, such sources are extremely important, certain basic accounting principles have now been incorporated into the law. Thus, the law requires that accounts should be prepared in accordance with five accounting principles:

1 Going concern
2 Consistency
3 Prudence
4 Accruals
5 Separate determination of each asset and liability.

Statute law now requires that these principles must be applied unless there are special reasons for departing from them. Where such special reasons exist, a note to the accounts must state the details of the departure, the reason for it and its effect.[6] We shall discuss the first four of these principles later in this chapter and the fifth principle in Chapter 6.

The Act provides that companies may prepare their accounts using either historical cost accounting rules or alternative accounting rules.[7]

The alternative accounting rules are so framed to permit companies to use piecemeal revaluations in their historical cost accounts or to prepare current cost accounts as their main accounts, although in either case it is necessary to provide certain information to enable partial reconstruction of the historical cost accounts.

Some UK accountants are strongly opposed to the inclusion of such accounting principles and valuation rules in the law. They argue that it provides a straitjacket which may impede accounting development and two examples will illustrate their arguments.

First, as we have explained in Chapter 1, company law includes a provision that 'only profits realised at the balance sheet date shall be included in the profit and loss account.'

---

[6] Companies Act 1985, Schedule 4, Part II, Sec. A, Paras. 9–15.
[7] The historical cost accounting rules are contained in the Companies Act 1985, Schedule 4, Sec. B while the alternative accounting rules are contained in Schedule 4, Sec. C.

For reasons which we explain in Chapter 3, the ASB has taken the wise decision that a poorly defined concept of realisation is an inappropriate criterion for determining whether or not gains or losses should be recognised in the financial statements. However, while it has been possible for the ASB to ignore this legal constraint in drafting its Statement of Principles for Financial Reporting, it is not possible to ignore it when drafting accounting standards. As a consequence, the ASB is hampered in its attempts to reform accounting practice by a poorly thought out and somewhat dated legal provision.

Second, the alternative accounting rules permit the preparation of current cost accounts as a company's main accounts. As we explain in Part IV of the book, Current Cost Accounting was very much in vogue in the 1970s and early 1980s, when the Companies Act 1981 was enacted. However, it is now very much out of favour and, to the best of our knowledge, no British company prepares its financial statements using current cost accounting. The statutory reference to current cost now looks very dated and out of line with the current agenda of the ASB.

When accounts have been prepared, the accountant must decide whether they show a true and fair view and, if not, in what respects they need to be altered. These words 'true and fair' were first introduced together in the Companies Act 1948, following the recommendations of the Cohen Committee.[8] They have never been defined by statute but, rather, their meaning has become established by usage. A good definition has been provided by G.A. Lee:

> Today, 'the true and fair view' has become a term of art. It is generally understood to mean a presentation of accounts, drawn up according to accepted accounting principles, using accurate figures as far as possible, and reasonable estimates otherwise; and arranging them so as to show, within the limits of current accounting practice, as objective a picture as possible, free from wilful bias, distortion, manipulation or concealment of material facts.[9]

So, in order to decide whether or not a set of accounts presents a true and fair view, it is necessary for the accountant to have recourse to a body of accounting principles which have developed over many years, wedded mainly to the historical cost basis of valuation.[10]

Stock Exchange rules

Where companies have shares listed on the Stock Exchange or quoted on the Alternative Investment Market, they must comply with the additional disclosure requirements laid down by the Stock Exchange. These rules require the provision of both some more information and some more frequent information than that required by law.

Examples of greater disclosure are the requirements for more detailed analysis of certain creditors, namely bank loans, overdrafts and other borrowings, in the annual financial statements, as well as the requirement for directors to disclose whether or not they have complied with the provisions of the *Combined Code on Corporate Governance*.[11]

---

[8] *Report of the Committee on Company Law Amendment*, Cmnd 6659, HMSO, London, 1945.

[9] G.A. Lee, *Modern Financial Accounting*, 3rd edn, Nelson, London, 1981, p. 270.

[10] For a fuller discussion of the term 'true and fair' readers are referred to David Flint, *A True and Fair View in Company Accounts*, Gee and Co., London, 1982.

[11] *Combined Code on Corporate Governance*, The London Stock Exchange Limited, London, 1998. This Code has been developed from the earlier Cadbury and Greenbury Reports.

The best example of the requirement for more frequent information is the requirement for quoted companies to prepare and publish an interim report, containing certain minimum information. This provides investors and other users with more timely information on which to base their decisions.

Accounting principles and conventions

Accounting concepts

We have seen how statute law requires companies to disclose a considerable amount of information and lays down broad principles which must usually be applied in arriving at the figures disclosed. We have also seen how this information is extended for companies subject to the rules of the Stock Exchange.

In order to prepare accounts complying with the law and, where appropriate, the Stock Exchange rules, an accountant must turn to what are referred to as generally accepted accounting principles or generally accepted accounting conventions. These were first developed during the latter part of the nineteenth century but have been the subject of continuous development as new situations have arisen.

Many such principles or conventions could be listed, but a useful starting point would seem to be the fundamental accounting concepts of SSAP 2, 'Disclosure of accounting policies'. These are defined as 'the broad basic assumptions which underlie the periodic financial accounts of business enterprises'.[12]

Four concepts are listed and these are the same as the first four principles listed in the Companies Act 1985. Users of the accounts may assume that the concepts have been applied in the preparation of a set of accounts unless warning is given to the contrary.

The four concepts are as follows:

1 *Going concern*: Following the application of this concept, the accounts are drawn up on the basis that the enterprise will continue in operational existence for the foreseeable future. Thus, the accountant does not normally prepare the accounts to show what the various assets would realise on liquidation or on the assumption of a fundamental change in the nature of the business. It is assumed that the business will continue to do in the future the same sort of things that it has done in the past. If, of course, such continuation is not expected, then the going concern concept must not be applied. So if, for example, liquidation seems likely then the valuation of assets on the basis of sale values would be appropriate. The accountant must then give warning to the users that the usual going concern concept has not been applied.

2 *Accruals*: While this is an easy concept to describe and, indeed, to apply in situations which are commonly encountered, its implementation sometimes gives rise to problems. Revenues and costs are not calculated on the basis of cash received or paid. Revenues are recognised when they are earned, usually at the date of a transaction with a third party. Against such revenues are charged, not the expenditures of a particular period, but the costs of earning the revenue which has been recognised.

3 *Consistency*: The consistency concept requires like items to be treated in the same manner both within one set of accounts and from one period to another.

---

[12] SSAP 2, 'Disclosure of accounting policies', Para. 14.

Such a concept could easily prevent progress if applied too rigidly for, if a better accounting treatment than the existing method was discovered, it could never be applied because it would be inconsistent with the past! Obviously, it will be necessary to depart from this concept on occasions but then it is necessary to give warning that such departure has occurred and to show clearly what the effect has been.

4 *Prudence*: This concept has specified that accountants do not take credit for revenue until it has been realised but that they do provide for all known liabilities. This assymetrical approach was designed to introduce a bias which tended to understate profit and undervalue assets. Although such a concept might at first sight be thought to benefit users, it may instead damage their interests. Thus a shareholder may sell his or her shares at a low price because the financial statements show low profits and low asset values. As we have seen in Chapter 1, the ASB is attempting to refine the definition of the prudence concept along the following lines:[13]

> Prudence is the inclusion of a degree of caution in the exercise of the judgements needed in making the estimates required under conditions of uncertainty, such that gains or assets are not overstated and losses or liabilities are not understated. However, it is not appropriate to use this need for prudence as a reason for, for example, creating hidden reserves or excessive provisions, deliberately understating assets or gains, or deliberately overstating liabilities or losses, because that would mean that the financial statements are not neutral and, therefore, are not reliable.

It has to be recognised that the failure of accountants to come to grips with changing prices results in the overstatement of profits in inflationary periods. As we shall see in Chapter 15, adherence to historical cost accounting in these circumstances most certainly introduces a bias into accounting but one which is the opposite of that which the prudence concept would seem to require.

As we have seen in Chapter 1, it is also possible to have a conflict between two of the above concepts, and SSAP 2 explicitly deals with the situation where a conflict exists between the accruals concept and the prudence concept. In such a case, prudence is stated to prevail although, as we shall see, it has been difficult and indeed sometimes unreasonable for the standard setters to comply with this instruction in later Exposure Drafts and Standards.[14]

Even though an accountant follows the four fundamental accounting concepts, he or she still has considerable flexibility in the way in which assets are valued and profit determined. There are, for example, many methods of depreciating fixed assets or of valuing stocks and work-in-progress; there are many ways of accounting for deferred taxation and for translating the accounts of overseas subsidiaries. From the numerous accounting bases available, an accountant must choose the appropriate policy to apply in the circumstances of the particular company.

As we have seen in Chapter 1, there are many different users of financial accounts and their needs for information may conflict: in addition, as we have seen in this chapter, we have no precise idea of what is meant by the words 'true and fair'. Add to this the fact that the valuation of any asset or liability by its very nature, even under the historical cost system, involves taking a view of the future, and it is not surprising that different accountants will arrive at different views of the same business reality and hence report different figures.

---

[13] Para. 3.17, Revised exposure draft of *Statement of Principles for Financial Reporting*, ASB, London, March 1999.

[14] *See*, for example, the problem of accounting for foreign currency transactions discussed in Chapter 10.

Recommendations and freedom of choice

In order to help their members to choose the appropriate accounting policies, the various professional bodies have issued recommendations on accounting principles. For example, the Institute of Chartered Accountants in England and Wales (ICAEW) issued 29 such recommendations between 1942 and 1969, and these provided guidance on all manner of accounting matters. These recommendations were persuasive rather than mandatory and often permitted a choice from various methods of accounting for a particular set of transactions.

Most accountants appreciated the freedom which these recommendations provided and perhaps welcomed, as a bonus, the fact that the existence of flexibility made it difficult for anyone to prove that mistakes had been made. However, many thoughtful accountants took a more principled position and argued that the complexities of business were such that it was not desirable, nor even possible, to specify in advance a set of accounting rules to be applied rigidly in all circumstances. They argued that there would always be occasions when any preordained rules would be inappropriate and that the benefits resulting from the existence of flexibility, in terms of meaningful reporting on such occasions, more than outweighed the disadvantage that equally competent accountants might produce different results in the same circumstances.

A number of incidents in the late 1960s brought the existence of such flexibility to the attention of the general public and in 1968 Sir Frank Kearton, Chairman of Courtaulds and the Industrial Reorganisation Corporation, wrote to the President of the ICAEW to complain about 'the plethora of generally accepted accounting principles'. The problem was brought to a head in 1968 in connection with the GEC/AEI and Pergamon/Leasco affairs.[15]

In 1969 the late Professor Edward Stamp wrote a letter to *The Times* in which he was very critical of some aspects of the accountancy profession, in particular its lack of independence and its lack of a theoretical foundation for the preparation of accounts. His letter provoked an angry reaction from the accountancy profession in the person of Ronald Leach, President of the ICAEW. Suffice it to say that the criticism and ensuing debate led to the issue of a 'Statement of intent on accounting standards in the 1970s' by the ICAEW in 1969 and to the subsequent formation of the Accounting Standards Steering Committee.

Standardisation

From 1970 to 1990

The 'Statement of intent on accounting standards in the 1970s' issued by the Council of the ICAEW in 1969 set out a plan to advance accounting standards along the following lines:

(a) narrowing the areas of differences and variety in accounting practice;
(b) disclosure of accounting bases;
(c) disclosure of departures from established definitive accounting standards;

---

[15] These are dealt with in E. Stamp and C. Marley, *Accounting Principles and the City Code: the Case for Reform*, Butterworth, London, 1970.

(d) wider exposure for major new proposals on accounting standards;
(e) continuing programme for encouraging improved standards in legal and regulatory matters.

To this end, an Accounting Standards Steering Committee was set up by the Institute of Chartered Accountants in England and Wales, the Institute of Chartered Accountants of Scotland and the Institute of Chartered Accountants in Ireland. The Committee was later joined by representatives of the Association of Certified Accountants (now the Association of Chartered Certified Accountants) and the Institute of Cost and Management Accountants (now the Chartered Institute of Management Accountants) in 1971 and by representatives of the Chartered Institute of Public Finance and Accountancy in 1976. From 1 February 1976 its name was changed to the Accounting Standards Committee and it was reconstituted as a joint committee of the six member bodies acting through the Consultative Committee of Accountancy Bodies (CCAB).

Until 1982, the ASC consisted of more than 20 members, all of whom were qualified accountants. Membership of the committee was part-time and unpaid. The ASC had no power to issue standards in its own right but, once a standard had been set by the committee and approved and issued by the councils of the six CCAB members, individual members of the various professional accountancy bodies were required to comply with the standard. Thus, we had a body of professional accountants imposing rules above those required by the law of the land and attempting to enforce them through the constituent member bodies. Such a process was criticised on two counts.

First, the people who can be expected to benefit from standards are the users of accounts. If such is the case, then it may be argued that these users should have a larger say in the formulation of standards. Indeed, accounting standards may have considerable impact on economic behaviour which some would argue should, in a democratic state, be taken into consideration by duly elected Members of Parliament.[16] To give an example, a standard requiring companies to write off all research and development expenditure as it is incurred may cause firms to stop undertaking research and development due to its adverse effects on the profit figure. This may have severe consequences for the progress and competitive position of the nation.

Second, for standards to be effective, it is essential that they are enforced. However, the law places the onus for preparing accounts clearly on the shoulders of directors, and professional accountancy bodies have no authority over such directors unless the directors happen to be professional accountants. Even where professional accountants are involved, the ultimate penalty for non-compliance is disciplinary action against those members, and the professional bodies appear to have been loath to take such action.

The ASC was aware of these and other criticisms and a number of changes were made as a result of two papers: *Setting accounting standards: a consultative document*, known colloquially as the Watts Report after the then chairman of the ASC, Mr Tom Watts, published in 1978, and *Review of the standard setting process*, known as the McKinnon Report after its chairman, published in 1983.

As a consequence of these reports, membership of the ASC was opened up to include non-accountants representing user groups, and some new types of pronouncement were introduced. However, the Watts Report's recommendation that a panel be established to review non-compliance with accounting standards by listed companies was not acted upon at that time.

---

[16] For an account of the effect of standard setting on economic behaviour *see* S.A. Zeff, 'The rise of "economic consequences"', *Journal of Accountancy*, December 1978.

The 1983 Review introduced the publication of two new types of statement, the Statement of Intent (SOI) and the Statement of Recommended Accounting Practice (SORP). While the SOI, a short public statement explaining how the ASC proposed to deal with a particular accounting matter, was used very rarely, the SORP was a completely different type of statement issued on topics considered not to be of sufficient importance to warrant the issue of an accounting standard. These non-mandatory SORPs hark back to the earlier recommendations of the professional accountancy bodies. It was intended that such statements would be issued for matters which are of widespread application but not of fundamental importance, or for matters which are of limited application, in specific industries or particular areas of the public sector. In the case of statements of limited application, SORPs were prepared by the specific industry or areas of the public sector and then 'franked', that is approved, by the ASC.[17] In spite of the changes which were made, the ASC came under increasing criticism in the 1980s. Its lack of powers of enforcement became blatantly obvious in the context of SSAP 16 'Current Cost Accounting', when at one time only some 25 per cent of the companies to which it applied were actually complying with its provisions. In addition, the ASC faced enormous difficulties in developing standard practice for controversial areas such as accounting for business combinations and intangible assets.

A decline in the credibility of the ASC led to the establishment of the Dearing Committee, named after its chairman, now Lord Dearing, which produced its report *The Making of Accounting Standards* (the Dearing Report) in September 1988. This, in turn, has led to fundamental changes in the process of setting and enforcing accounting standards in the British Isles.

The current regime – structure

The Dearing Report took the view that standards should no longer be set by an inadequately financed ASC made up of part-time unpaid members, with only a small technical staff, and with no powers of ensuring compliance with its standards. It therefore recommended major changes.

In the view of the Dearing Report, effective standard setting required considerably more resources than had been available in the past. Given that a large constituency of users benefit from the existence of accounting standards, it was thought to be unreasonable for the process of standard setting to be financed wholly by the accountancy profession. Dearing therefore recommended a large increase in the finance available and a sharing out of the cost of standard setting.[18]

As a consequence of the Dearing Report, a Financial Reporting Council, drawn from a wide constituency of interests, was set up to guide the standard setting process and to ensure that it is properly financed. Standards are now set by the Accounting Standards Board, which has the power to issue standards in its own right. In addition, a Financial Reporting Review Panel was established to examine contentious departures from accounting standards by large companies.

---

[17] An example of the first type of SORP is SORP 2 'Accounting for Charities', issued in May 1988. Some examples of franked SORPs are those issued by the Oil Industry Accounting Committee and the Accounting Standards for Local Authority Group.

[18] The operating cost of the present regime, which amounted to some £2 600 000 in the year to 31 March 1998, comes from three main sources: the accountancy profession, government and city institutions, which include the London Stock Exchange. A substantial sum is also raised by the sale of ASB publications.

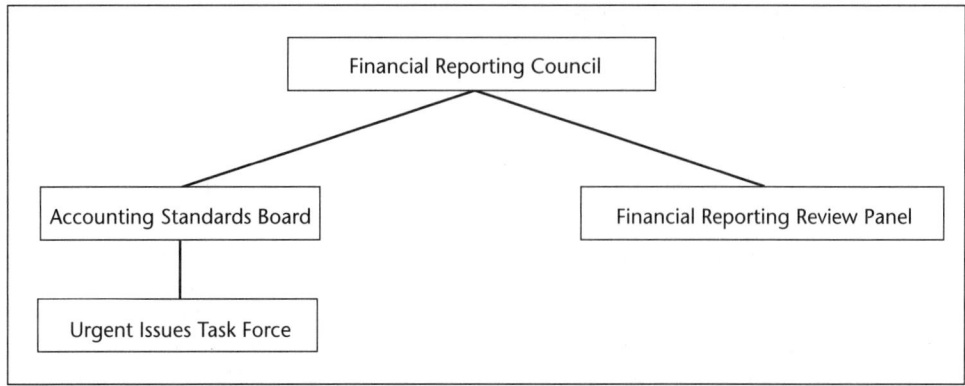

Fig. 2.1 Structure of the organisation for setting and enforcing accounting standards

An Urgent Issues Task Force has also been set up as a committee of the ASB to provide timely and authoritative interpretations on the application of standards. As a consequence, the present structure is as shown in Figure 2.1.[19]

The Accounting Standards Board is now a much smaller body than its predecessor. It consists of not more than nine members with a full-time Chairman and Technical Director, supported by a much larger technical and administrative staff to permit a higher level of research. As recommended by the Dearing Report, it has the power to issue standards in its own right and, for this, a two-thirds majority is required.

The introduction of a Financial Reporting Review Panel was more revolutionary, although the establishment of such a body had been proposed in the Watts Report in 1978. It is a panel of some twenty members chaired by a QC. The function of the Review Panel is to examine the accounts of large companies to ensure that they give a true and fair view and comply with the Companies Act 1985 and applicable accounting standards.

Although the government chose not to give statutory backing to accounting standards, it introduced provisions which facilitate the operations of the Review Panel. The first of these is a requirement for directors of all large (but not small or medium-sized) companies to state in the notes to the accounts whether or not those accounts have been prepared in accordance with applicable accounting standards, drawing attention to material departures and explaining the reasons for them.[20] The second is the introduction of procedures for the revision of accounts which are considered to be defective. These include a procedure whereby accounts can be revised voluntarily by the directors and a procedure whereby the Secretary of State for Trade and Industry or other authorised persons are able to apply to the court for an order requiring the revision of a company's accounts.[21] The Financial Reporting Review Panel is an 'authorised person' under these provisions and concentrates on the accounts of public and large private companies.

---

[19] There are other, more specialised, committees which support the work of the ASB. These include The Financial Sector and Other Special Industries Committee, The Public Sector and Not-for-Profit Committee and the Committee on Accounting for Smaller Entities (CASE).

[20] Companies Act 1985, Schedule 4, Part III, Para. 36A.

[21] These provisions are contained in Companies Act 1985, Sections 245–245C.

The current regime – progress

One of the many problems which confronted the ASB, and indeed the ASC before it, was the lack of a conceptual framework for accounting. As we have discussed in Chapter 1, the ASB immediately set to work to build such a framework and eventually published an exposure draft of its *Statement of Principles for Financial Reporting* in November 1995. Following a hostile reaction to that draft, it was withdrawn and a revised exposure draft was issued in March 1999.

While some people might argue that no standards should be set until the Statement of Principles has been finalised, it would have been quite impossible for the ASB to adopt such an approach. Indeed, it is becoming more widely recognised that the search for one conceptual framework is a search for the Holy Grail. Given the multiple users of accounts, there are probably many different conceptual frameworks, with a consequent implication for the adoption of multicolumn reporting.[22] If such is the case then we should not be under any illusion that the Statement of Principles will solve all the problems of accounting although, of course, it may enable us to remove some of the many inconsistencies which exist at present.

While work has been proceeding on the development of the Statement of Principles, the ASB has continued work on standard setting. In its first ten years of operation, it has produced an enormous volume of regulation in the form of Financial Reporting Standards, which we have listed in Table 2.1.

These standards have changed the face of financial reporting considerably. FRS 3 'Reporting Financial Performance', in particular, changed the presentation of the profit and loss account and introduced the new primary statement, the Statement of Total Recognised Gains and Losses. As we shall see in Chapter 6, the pace of change is now so fast that this standard is itself already under review.[23] Other standards, such as

Table 2.1 Financial reporting standards issued by ASB 1990–1999

1	Cash flow statements	1991, Revised 1996
2	Accounting for subsidiary undertakings	1992
3	Reporting financial performance	1992, Amended 1993
4	Capital instruments	1993
5	Reporting the substance of transactions	1994, Amended 1994
6	Acquisitions and mergers	1994
7	Fair values in acquisition accounting	1994
8	Related party disclosures	1995
9	Associates and joint ventures	1997
10	Goodwill and intangible assets	1997
11	Impairment of fixed assets and goodwill	1998
12	Provisions, contingent liabilities and contingent assets	1998
13	Derivatives and other financial instruments: Disclosures	1998
14	Earnings per share	1998
15	Tangible fixed assets	1999

---

[22] *See* Chapter 18.

[23] See Discussion Paper *Reporting Financial Performance: Proposals for Change*, ASB, London, June 1999.

FRS 4, FRS 5 and FRS 12 have addressed areas in which major abuses had occurred in the past. Yet other standards have tackled fundamental and difficult areas of accounting such as what to do with the large amounts paid for goodwill and intangible assets in an age when such assets may be far more important than tangible assets. Some of the more difficult topics still on the agenda of the ASB include the measurement of derivatives and other financial instruments and the treatment of both deferred taxation and pension costs. We shall, of course, deal with all of these topics later in this book.

While the ASB has been working on the above and many other issues, the Urgent Issues Task Force (UITF) has been providing timely guidance on contemporary accounting problems. Its guidance is provided in the form of Abstracts and, by the end of 1999, it had issued 22 such Abstracts.[24]

As explained above, the law now requires directors of large companies to state in the notes to accounts whether or not those accounts have been prepared in accordance with applicable standards, drawing attention to material departures and explaining reasons for them. This provision, introduced in 1989, is clearly set out, and so it came as something of a surprise and an indication of problems ahead when we learned that one of the first tasks undertaken by the Financial Reporting Review Panel in 1991 and 1992 was to write to the directors of some 240 companies who had failed to include the note required by law!

With regard to other apparent departures from the accounting requirements of the Companies Act and accounting standards, the Financial Reporting Review Panel does not systematically examine the accounts of all the companies within its ambit. Rather it acts only when something which appears to be wrong is drawn to its attention. Its references come from three broad sources: qualified audit reports or recorded non-compliance, cases referred by individuals or corporate bodies, and press comment.

Some of these references are not pursued beyond an initial examination but most have been pursued with the directors concerned. The Review Panel has not as yet considered it necessary to apply for a Court Order for rectification of accounts, although a fund of £2m is available to finance such action. In cases where companies have been found to be at fault, the Panel has been able to reach voluntary agreement with the directors concerned, usually requiring them to rectify errors in the next set of accounts or interim statement.

During 1998, the accounts of 32 companies were brought to the attention of the Panel.[25] This is the same as for the previous year but represents a significant decrease compared with references in earlier years. Whether this is due to more sophisticated cases of non-compliance slipping through the net or to greater compliance with the law and accounting standards will perhaps never be known.

Advantages and disadvantages of standardisation

Before we briefly examine international standardisation, it is perhaps helpful if we review both the advantages and the disadvantages of standardising accounting practice, for the process of standardisation is not without its critics.

---

[24] Some examples of the topics covered are:
UITF Abstract 6 'Accounting for post-retirement benefits other than pensions', November 1992,
UITF Abstract 9 'Accounting for operations in hyper-inflationary economies', June 1993,
UITF Abstract 14 'Disclosure of changes in accounting policy', November 1995, and
UITF Abstract 21 'Accounting issues arising from the proposed introduction of the euro', March 1998.
[25] 98 Annual Review, Financial Reporting Council: Report by Chairman of the Financial Reporting Review Panel, Page 61, Para. 17.

Accounting may be described as the language of business. As with any communication, it is important that the preparers of a document and the users adopt the same language. Standards may be regarded as the generally accepted language.

When directors prepare accounts for their companies, they are not likely to be indifferent to the position shown by those accounts for, after all, they will be judged on the basis of the results disclosed. Thus, given many generally accepted accounting bases, the choice of a particular policy may not be free from bias. The establishment of accounting standards, with the consequent need to justify departures from them, limits the possibility of exercising such bias and strengthens the hands of the auditor.

In addition it is clear that the issue of exposure drafts and standards has provoked considerable thought and discussion among members of the accounting profession, which has made accounting an exciting area of study.

One of the most pertinent criticisms of the process of standardisation was made by Professor W.T. Baxter writing about recommendations on accounting principles in 1953,[26] long before the Accounting Standards Steering Committee was formed. He argued that authoritative backing for one particular accounting treatment may have adverse effects. Although it may help practical men in their day-to-day work, in the longer run it may hinder experimentation and progress. An accountant or auditor may become loath to depart from a particular recommendation or standard and the educational process may become one of learning rules rather than searching for theories or truth. Indeed he argued that, if truth subsequently shows a recommendation or standard to have been wrong, then it may be hard for authoritative bodies to admit that they were wrong.

Both the ASC and the ASB have been well aware of these criticisms. Thus the 'Foreword to Accounting Standards', issued by the ASB in June 1993, makes it quite clear that the requirement to give a true and fair view may in exceptional circumstances require a departure from accounting standards and permits such a departure, although particulars of the departure, the reasons for it and its financial effects must then be disclosed in the financial statements (Paras. 18 and 19). It also recognises that the standards are not absolute but will require amendment as the business environment and accounting thought evolves (Para. 33). As we shall see later in the book, there have been many cases where standards have been revised and these have often involved substantial changes in required standard accounting practice.[27] The standard setters certainly do not hesitate to recognise that previous standards may have been, or have become, deficient.

International standardisation

Introduction

It seems reasonable to suggest that, if standards have merit within the boundaries of one country, there would be merit if they were applied more generally.

In a period in which investors based in one country choose between investments in many countries, a lack of comparability between accounts drawn up in different coun-

---

[26] W.T. Baxter, 'Recommendations on accounting theory', in *Studies in Accounting Theory*, 2nd edn, W.T. Baxter and S. Davidson (eds), Sweet & Maxwell, London, 1962, pp. 414–27.

[27] One example of such a change is the replacement of SSAP 22 'Accounting for goodwill' by FRS 10 'Goodwill and intangible assets'. As we shall see in Chapter 8, the latter takes a fundamentally different approach to that of SSAP 22.

tries may well lead to incorrect decision taking and thereby to an inefficient allocation of scarce resources. As individual countries have pursued a policy of standardisation, so too a number of bodies have become concerned with international standardisation. Both the United Nations and the Organisation for Economic Co-operation and Development have been concerned with the regulation of accounting. As might be expected, these bodies have been primarily concerned with the regulation of disclosure by multinational companies. In the more recent past, we have seen the formation of the 'G4+1' which is an international group of standard setters that consists of the standard setters from Australia, Canada, New Zealand, the UK and the USA. Representatives of the International Accounting Standards Committee (IASC) participate as observers. This grouping attempts to formulate a common, Anglo-Saxon approach to financial reporting issues and has begun to publish Position Papers intended to influence the work of the standard setters in their respective countries.[28]

For the remainder of this chapter, we shall concern ourselves with the two most important attempts at international standardisation relevant in Britain. We shall look first at the approach of the International Accounting Standards Committee (IASC) and then at the approach of the European Union (EU).

The International Accounting Standards Committee

Although the possibility of international standards has been debated since early this century, the most successful programme began with the formation of the IASC in 1973. The founder members were drawn from professional accountancy bodies in the following countries: Australia, Canada, France, Germany, Japan, Mexico, the Netherlands, the UK, the Republic of Ireland and the USA. One hundred and forty-three professional accountancy bodies, including nine associate and affiliate members, from 104 countries have now been admitted to membership and these represent countries at many different levels of economic development. Some examples are the Scandinavian countries, India, Nigeria, and Trinidad and Tobago.

The objectives of the IASC as stated in the original 1973 agreement were:

> to formulate and publish in the public interest basic standards to be observed in the presentation of audited accounts and financial statements and to promote their worldwide acceptance and observance.

Under a revised agreement entered into in 1982 the reference to basic standards was removed and the revised objectives became:

(a) to formulate and publish in the public interest accounting standards to be observed in the presentation of financial statements and to promote their worldwide acceptance and observance, and

(b) to work generally for the improvement and harmonisation of regulations, accounting standards and procedures relating to the presentation of financial statements.

In order to achieve these objectives, members joining the IASC enter into the following undertaking:

---

[28] *See*, for example, the G4+1 Position Papers 'Recommendations for achieving convergence on the methods of accounting for business combinations', subsequently published by the ASB as a Discussion Paper in December 1998, and 'Reporting Financial Performance: proposals for change', subsequently published by the ASB as a Discussion Paper in June 1999.

to support the work of IASC by publishing in their respective countries every International Accounting Standard approved for issue by the Board of IASC and by using their best endeavours:

(i)   to ensure that published financial statements comply with International Accounting Standards in all material respects and disclose the fact of such compliance;
(ii) to persuade governments and standard-setting bodies that published financial statements should comply with International Accounting Standards in all material respects;
(iii) to persuade authorities controlling securities markets and the industrial and business community that published financial statements should comply with International Accounting Standards in all material respects and disclose the fact of such compliance;
(iv) to ensure that the auditors satisfy themselves that the financial statements comply with International Accounting Standards in all material respects;
(v)   to foster acceptance and observance of International Accounting Standards internationally.

The undertaking emphasises the fact that the IASC has no direct power to implement or enforce its standards. Rather it must rely on its members to persuade the relevant institutions in their particular countries to adopt and enforce the standards.

Given the very different ways in which countries regulate accounting, in some countries this involves persuading the relevant standard-setting bodies to comply while, in other countries, it involves the much more difficult task of persuading the government that changes to the law are necessary.

Even before the IASC had been established, Irving Fantl identified three major barriers to international standardisation:[29]

(a) differences in background and traditions of countries;
(b) differences in the needs of various economic environments;
(c) the challenge to the sovereignty of states in making and enforcing standards.

These are enormous problems for the IASC, although it has taken steps to try and overcome the barriers. Thus, it tries to work closely with the major standard-setting bodies to ensure that it is involved before a country's position becomes entrenched. In addition, like the ASB, it consults widely and has formed a consultative committee drawn from a number of international bodies including the International Association of Financial Executives Institutes, the International Confederation of Free Trade Unions and the World Bank.

What then has been the progress of the IASC?

By 1990 the IASC had issued 31 International Accounting Standards and these provided a set of inexpensive ready-made standards which could be adopted by those countries which had not developed their own mechanism for standard setting. While many of the International Accounting Standards covered topics on which a standard had already been set in the British Isles, this was not always the case. For example, IAS 14 'Reporting Financial Information by Segments' (1981) was published many years before the issue of SSAP 25 'Segmental Reporting' (1990); and IAS 18 'Revenue Recognition' (1982) dealt with a subject on which neither the ASC nor the ASB has issued a standard.

As might have been expected, the activities of the IASC attracted considerable criticism and, during the 1980s, it was accused of Anglo-Saxon domination and of issuing standards which were too flexible. It took action on both counts.

---

[29] I.L. Fantl, 'The case against international uniformity', *Management Accounting*, May 1971.

The Committee has now had a number of non-Anglo-Saxon Chairmen, including Georges Barthès from France (1987–89), Eiichi Shiratori from Japan (1993–95) and Stig Enevoldsen from Denmark (1998–2000).

By the close of the 1980s, the IASC recognised that it had reached a new phase in its work and its emphasis changed from the production of new standards to the tightening of its existing standards. However, even now, more than ten years later, many international standards specify not just one *benchmark* treatment but also an, often very different, *allowed alternative* treatment.

The work of the IASC assumed a much higher profile from 1995, when it entered into an agreement with the International Organisation of Securities Commissions (IOSCO) to develop a set of 'core standards for cross-border capital raising and listing purposes'. If endorsed by IOSCO and accepted by the national securities regulators, this would permit quoted companies to produce their financial statements using International Accounting Standards rather than having to prepare a set of financial statements drawn up in accordance with the GAAP of the country in which the stock exchange is situated or to provide a reconciliation with the local rules of that country.

After a period of frenetic effort, the IASC concluded the development of this set of core standards with its approval of the last major standard IAS 39 'Financial Instruments: Recognition and Measurement' in December 1998.

Whether this set of standards will prove acceptable to IOSCO and the national stock exchange regulators is very much an open question and much hinges on the view taken by the powerful US Securities and Exchange Commission. If the IASC set of core standards is accepted, this would mean that foreign companies quoted in the USA would be able to prepare their financial statements in accordance with international standards rather than in accordance with the much more rigorous and voluminous rules of the SEC and FASB. Such an approach is unlikely to find favour with US corporations who are still subject to US GAAP, and might have serious implications for the subsequent development of that US GAAP. It is unlikely that national regulators will surrender their regulatory power to the IASC with great enthusiasm.

Harmonisation in the European Union

The use of Directives

When the European Economic Community was established by the Treaty of Rome on 25 March 1957 one of the objectives to be achieved by member states was 'the approximation of their respective national laws to the extent required for the common market to function in an orderly manner'.[30] To achieve this objective a number of programmes of law harmonisation have been undertaken. One of these is the company law harmonisation programme under the provisions of Article 54(3)(g) which calls for 'the co-ordination of the safeguards required from companies in the Member States, to protect the interests both of members and of third parties'.

When the EU Commission has obtained agreement on a set of proposals on a particular topic, it places a Draft Directive before the Council of Ministers. If the Directive is adopted, governments of member states then have a specified period to enact legislation and incorporate the provisions of the Directive into their national law.

---

[30] Treaty of Rome, Article 3(h).

In practice, many countries were unable to keep to the timetables imposed by the early Directives and, for the Seventh Directive, the time limits set were much longer than for previous Directives. This was, however, to a large extent necessary to accommodate fundamental changes which have been required in some member states.[31]

While a number of Directives have been adopted, the two of most concern to accountants are the Fourth Directive on company accounts and the Seventh Directive on consolidated accounts.[32]

The former was adopted on 25 July 1978 and implemented in the UK by the Companies Act 1981. The latter was adopted on 13 June 1983 and implemented by the Companies Act 1989.

In this section of the chapter we look briefly at these two Directives.

The Fourth Directive

The original draft of the Fourth Directive was published in November 1971, some time before the UK became a member of the European Economic Community. Not surprisingly the draft was heavily influenced by the current law and practice in France and Germany. When the UK joined the EEC in March 1973, it pressed for certain changes to the draft and, as a result, an amended draft was issued in February 1974. Although not all of the changes suggested by the UK were accepted, the requirement to give a 'true and fair view' was admitted as an overriding objective of accounts and the Directive was eventually adopted by the Council of Ministers on 27 July 1978.

As we have explained earlier in this chapter, the major changes prescribed by the Fourth Directive were as follows:

(a) limited companies have to adopt compulsory formats for both the balance sheet and the profit and loss account;
(b) defined methods of valuing assets, the so-called 'valuation rules', must be followed.

In addition, the Directive provided definitions of small and medium-sized companies and permitted member states to offer such companies exemptions from complying with certain requirements of the Directive.[33]

We have already seen how the provisions of the Fourth Directive have been implemented in the UK, but it is worth spending a little time looking at the impact of the Fourth Directive in what is now known as the EU as a whole.

Given the very different accounting systems which exist in member countries, it is perhaps not surprising that it took some ten years for the Fourth Directive to be adopted. Although this Directive undoubtedly moved the accounting requirements of the various countries closer together, there are two major factors which have limited its effectiveness in achieving harmonisation.

First, as we have seen, the Directive contains an overriding requirement that accounts must give a 'true and fair view'. Although it is difficult to define such a term, accountants in the UK have long experience of working with it and are thoroughly familiar with what it means. In many EU countries the term was unknown and, although it has been translated and included in their respective national legisla-

---

[31] *See below.*
[32] These directives may be found in the *Official Journal of the European Communities*. The text of the Fourth Directive is in Volume 21, L222, 14 August 1978, while the text of the Seventh Directive is in Volume L193/1, 18 July 1983.
[33] Fourth Directive, Articles 11, 27 and 47.

tion, it is certainly not interpreted or applied in the same way in all of those countries as it is in the UK.

Second, in order to be able to obtain agreement, it was necessary to include a large number of options in the Fourth Directive and there are over 60 points on which countries were able to exercise a choice.[34] Member states had to decide whether or not to incorporate the particular options in their national legislation and could, in fact, even permit individual companies a choice from alternative treatments under the national legislation.

One example is the possible exemptions for small and medium-sized companies. Some countries, such as the UK, gave most of these, while other countries did not. As a result, the information provided by small companies in different countries is not comparable.

A second example is that countries could adopt historical cost valuation rules or either permit or require the application of alternative accounting rules. In the UK the Companies Acts permit the use of such alternative accounting rules, while other countries do not do so. Given the requirement for information to reconstruct historical cost accounts when alternative accounting rules are used, this means that many international comparisons are possible only on the basis of the historical cost figures.

A third example is provided by the possible choice of formats. The Directive provided two balance-sheet formats and four profit-and-loss-account formats. Although part of the choice was merely between a horizontal and a vertical format, there are differences between the information disclosed in the two pairs of profit-and-loss-account formats.

Member states could either impose one balance-sheet format and one profit-and-loss-account format on all companies or they could specify all formats and permit companies to choose between them. The UK Companies Acts have given the widest possible choice with the result that, even in the UK, different companies disclose somewhat different information. Other countries have been more rigid and, hence, there is a lack of comparability.

Even if all countries were to adopt the same formats, the inability to define terms with precision means that there is a superficial comparability only. For example, the profit-and-loss-account format of Article 25 requires the disclosure of, *inter alia*, cost of sales, distribution costs and administrative expenses. Even if we ignore the flexibility of the underlying valuation rules, it is highly likely that different companies will analyse similar expenses between these three categories in different ways and, hence, although the same descriptions are used, the figures are not comparable.

The above examples are not given to belittle the efforts which have been made to try and achieve harmonisation in the EU but rather to ensure that readers do not overestimate their impact.

The Seventh Directive

Although a proposed Seventh Directive was first issued in May 1976 and an amended proposal was issued in December 1978, it was not until June 1983 that the Seventh Directive was actually adopted.[35] As with the Fourth Directive it has been a long and difficult task to reach agreement on when consolidated accounts should be prepared and what they should contain. This should not surprise us when it is realised that some

---

[34] T.R. Watts (ed.), *Handbook on the EEC Fourth Directive*, ICAEW, London, 1979, p. 1.
[35] *Official Journal of the European Communities*, Volume L193/1, 18 July 1983.

EU countries had no legal requirement for consolidated accounts at all.[36] One of the major difficulties was defining the circumstances in which consolidated accounts should be required and a large part of the Directive was devoted to this problem.[37]

In the UK the basic legal position was that group accounts were required when one company owned more than half of the equity share capital in another company or had the legal power of control over that other company, irrespective of whether the investing company actually exercised that power. The proposed Directive was initially concerned to ensure that information was provided about concentrations of economic power and, as a consequence, consolidated accounts were required when companies were managed in practice by a 'central and unified management'. Ownership was only important to the extent that it led to a presumption that such central management might exist.

A criterion based on the existence of an economic unit is much more difficult to apply than one based on the legal power of control, and accountants in the UK were relieved to find that the Directive came down in favour of a definition based on the existence of this legal power of control.[38]

Some other problems which had to be resolved in this connection were whether or not consolidated accounts should be required when an individual or partnership controls companies; whether consolidated accounts should be required for subgroup holding companies where the ultimate parent company is in another EU country or non-EU country; and whether horizontal consolidations should be required for companies in the EU where, for example, two French companies are both under the control of a US company.

The second part of the Directive is concerned with the preparation of consolidated accounts. As is the case for the accounts of individual companies, there is an overriding requirement that consolidated accounts give a 'true and fair view' as well as the requirement that they give the information specified by the Directive using the valuation rules and formats specified in the Fourth Directive as far as appropriate.

There is no doubt that the Seventh Directive has had a much greater impact on accounting in other EU countries than it has had in the British Isles, where many of its provisions were already established by existing law and accounting standards. However, this is not to say that it has had no impact at all in the British Isles. As in the case of the Fourth Directive, rules previously set by accounting standards are now a part of the law and the introduction of new definitions has widened the coverage of consolidated accounts to include certain off-balance-sheet finance schemes as well as certain partnerships and joint ventures. We deal with these topics in Chapters 6 and 9.

As in the case of the Fourth Directive, member states were given a large number of options in the Seventh Directive. The different ways in which they have exercised these options has inevitably limited the degree of harmonisation achieved.

No more Accounting Directives

It is now recognised that, in spite of all the efforts which led to their development, the Accounting Directives have achieved much less harmonisation in the European Union than was originally anticipated. Perhaps not surprisingly, they have been found to be

---

[36] Examples are Greece and Luxembourg.

[37] Seventh Directive, Sec. 1, 'Conditions for the preparation of consolidated accounts' (Articles 1–15).

[38] Seventh Directive, Sec. 1. As we shall see in Chapter 9 it is still possible for member states to require consolidated accounts where there is unified management but no legal power of control (Article 1, Para. 2).

an inflexible source of rules, difficult to change in a business world which is constantly changing.

The European Commission has explored the way forward on accounting harmonisation in the European Union.[39] It has rejected both the further use of Directives and the establishment of a European standard setting body. Instead it has opted to support the work of the IASC, accepting that there will be a consequent need to amend the existing Accounting Directives where necessary to enable companies to comply with International Accounting Standards.

As a consequence, it is likely that the standards of the IASC will grow in importance in countries of the European Union even if, for reasons we have explained above, they do not find favour on the other side of the Atlantic.

Recommended reading

W.T. Baxter, 'Accounting standards – boon or curse?' *Accounting and Business Research*, ICAEW, Winter 1981.

M. Bromwich and A.G. Hopwood (eds), *Accounting Standard Setting: An International Perspective*, Pitman Publishing, London, 1983.

R. Leach and E. Stamp (eds), *British Accounting Standards: The First Ten Years*, Woodhead-Faulkner, Cambridge, 1981.

The Making of Accounting Standards (*The Dearing Report*), ICAEW, London, 1988.

D.R. Myddelton, 'Accountants Without Standards? – Compulsion or Evolution in Company Accounting', IEA Hobart Paper 128, IEA, London, 1995.

C. Nobes and R. Parker, *Comparative International Accounting*, 6th edn, Financial Times Prentice Hall, Harlow, 2000.

---

[39] *See*, for example, 'Accounting Harmonisation: A new strategy *vis-à-vis* international harmonisation', Communication from the Commission, COM 95 (508), EN.

3 What is profit?

Overview   We start this chapter with a discussion of the economic concept of profit and consider a number of different ways in which profit may be defined and measured. This requires us to consider, first, the measurement of wealth at the beginning and end of a period and, second, the comparison of these opening and closing amounts when the value of the measuring rod, the pound, may be changing. We demonstrate that the traditional approach of historical cost accounting is just one of several approaches which could be adopted and that it has serious limitations for many of the purposes for which it is used. This section of the chapter also serves as an introduction to Part 4 of the book, where we discuss, in some depth, major alternatives to the traditional historical cost accounting approach.

The chapter also has a more immediate practical purpose in that the later sections explore the legal definition of profit, which is relevant when determining the maximum dividend that can be paid by a limited company, and the closely related question of when a profit is deemed to have been realised.

Introduction

The layman has no doubt about the way in which the question 'What is profit?' should be answered. Profit is the difference between the cost of providing goods or services and the revenue derived from their sale. If a greengrocer can sell for 10p an apple which cost him 6p, his profit must be 4p. Accountants also used to inhabit this seemingly comfortable world of simplicity, but they are now aware that such a world is not only uncomfortable but possibly dangerous. We can perhaps agree that profit is the difference between cost and revenue, but there is more than one way of measuring cost. Historical cost – the cost of acquisition – is only one alternative, which may indeed be one of the least helpful for many purposes. Furthermore, it is not even obvious that we should measure the difference between costs and revenue in monetary terms – actual pounds – for another unit of measurement has been suggested: the purchasing power of pounds.

In order to answer the question 'what is profit?' it is perhaps best to start by considering the most useful of hypothetical examples in accounting theory – the barrow boy who trades for cash and rents his barrow.

Consider such a barrow boy whose only asset at the start of a day's trading is cash of £2000. Let us suppose that he rents a barrow and a pitch for the day which together cost him £20. Let us further assume that he spends £150 in the wholesale market for a barrow-load of vegetables, all of which are sold for £240. The trader therefore ends the day with cash of £2070 and we can all agree that the profit for that day's trading is £70.[1] In other words we have taken the barrow boy's profit to be the increase in monetary wealth resulting from his trading activities.

Let us extend the illustration by supposing that the barrow boy has changed the style of his operation. He now owns his barrow and trades in household sundries of which he can maintain a stock. If we wish to continue to apply the same principle as before in calculating his profit, we would need to measure his assets at the beginning and the end of each day. Thus we would need to place a value on his stock and his barrow at these two points of time as well as counting his cash.

All this may appear to be very simple, but it is by no means trivial, for the above argument contains one important implication, that profit represents an increase in wealth or 'well-offness', and one vital consequence, that in order to measure the increase in wealth it is necessary to attach values to the assets owned by the trader at the beginning and end of the period.

Let us now consider the implied definition of profit in a little more detail. The argument is that a trader makes a profit for a period if either he is better off at the end of the period than he was at the beginning (in that he owns assets with a greater monetary value) or would have been better off had he not consumed the profits. This essentially simple view was elegantly expressed by the eminent economist Sir John Hicks, who wrote that income – the term which economists use to describe the equivalent, in personal terms, of the profit of a business enterprise – could be defined as 'the maximum value which [a man] can consume during a week and still expect to be as well off at the end of the week as he was at the beginning'.[2]

This definition cannot be applied exactly to a business enterprise since such an entity does not consume. The definition can, however, be modified to meet this point, as was done by the Sandilands Committee,[3] which defined a company's profit for a year by the following adaptation of Hicks's dictum: 'A company's profit for the year is the maximum value which the company can distribute during the year and still expect to be as well off at the end of the year as it was at the beginning'.[4]

The key questions that have to be answered in arriving at such a profit are 'How do we measure 'well-offness' at the beginning and end of a period?' and 'How do we measure the change in 'well-offness' from one date to another?'

This is not the end of the matter for we may wish to make a distinction between that part of the increase in 'well-offness' which is available for consumption and that which should not be so regarded. In traditional accounting practice a distinction has been made between realised and unrealised profits such that only the former is normally available for distribution. Subsequently company legislation[5] introduced into statute law the concept of distributable profits and the legal aspects of the assessment of this element of profit will be discussed in the final section of this chapter.

Turning to our two questions, we will first examine the question of how we may measure 'well-offness' or 'wealth' of a business at a point in time. There are two approaches. First, the wealth of a business can be measured by reference to the expectation of future benefits; in other words, the value of a business at a point of time is

---

[1] Actually this is not strictly true, for one might wish to impute a charge for the labour supplied by the barrow boy and would say that his profit is the excess of £70 over the imputed labour charge.
[2] J.R. Hicks, *Value and Capital*, 2nd edn, Oxford University Press, Oxford, 1948, p. 172.
[3] *Report of the Inflation Accounting Committee*, Cmnd 6225, HMSO, London, 1975.
[4] *Ibid.*, p. 29.
[5] Companies Act, 1980 and 1981.

the present value of the expected future net cash flow to the firm. The second approach is to measure the wealth of a business by reference to the values of the individual assets and liabilities of the business. Actually these two approaches can be linked by the recognition of an intangible asset, often called goodwill, which can be defined as the difference between the value of the business as a whole and the sum of the values of the individual assets less liabilities.

Present-value approach

We will assume that readers are familiar with the principles and mechanics of discounted cash flow techniques.

The present-value approach is based on the assumption that the owner of a business is only interested in the pecuniary benefits that will accrue from its ownership ('I am only in it for the money'). Well-offness at any balance sheet date is then measured by the present value of the expected future net cash flows at that date and profit for the period is the difference between the present values at the beginning and end of the period after adjustment for injections and withdrawals.[6]

This requires some formidable problems of estimation of both cash flows and appropriate discount rates, but such estimates are made either explicitly or implicitly (usually the latter) when businesses or individual assets are bought and sold. The present-value approach is an important and useful one when applied to the valuation of shares for an entire business to determine whether their sale or purchase would be worthwhile at a given price, and the methods used for such purposes will be discussed in Chapter 14.

It may well be thought, however, that the problems of estimation are such as to render the approach unsuitable for the measurement of an entity's periodic profit on a regular basis specifically given the qualitative characteristics of financial information discussed in Chapter 1. But there is a more fundamental objection to the use of this method for financial accounting in that it is agreed that the regular reporting of profits should not be based solely on future expectations. The present-value approach is, of course, based entirely on expectations of the future and depends on decisions involving the way in which assets will be employed. It is argued that one of the objectives of accounting is to aid decision making and it is hardly appropriate if the fundamental measure of profit is based on the assumption that all decisions have already been made. This point was made by Edwards and Bell, who wrote:

> A concept of profit which measures truly and realistically the extent to which past decisions have been right or wrong and thus aids in the formulation of new ones is required. And since rightness or wrongness must, eventually, be checked in the market place, it is changes in market values of one kind or another which should dominate accounting objectives.[7]

This quotation provides a neat introduction to the asset-by-asset approach.

---

[6] *See* T.A. Lee, *Income and Value Measurement*, 3rd edn, Van Nostrand Reinhold, Wokingham, 1985.
[7] E.O. Edwards and P.W. Bell, *The Theory and Measurement of Business Income*, University of California Press, Stanford, CA, 1961, p. 25.

Measurement of wealth by reference to the valuation of individual assets

In this section we shall discuss some of the different methods that may be used to value assets. We shall at this stage concentrate on the problems associated with the determination of an asset's value using the different bases and shall defer the question of the suitability of the different bases of asset valuation for profit measurement until later.

Historical cost

The historical cost of an asset can usually be determined with exactitude so long as the records showing the amount paid for the asset are still available. The matter, however, is not always that simple. The historical cost of a fixed asset purchased when new may well be known, but it will usually be impossible to say what proportion of the original total cost should be regarded as being applicable to that portion of the asset which remains unused at a point in time. For example, imagine that we are dealing with a two-year-old car which cost £20 000 and which we expect to have a total life of five years – do we say that the historical cost of the unused portion of the car is three-fifths of £20 000, i.e. £12 000? This is, of course, the class of question which is answered by the use of some more or less arbitrary method of depreciation. As we will show later, much the same sort of expedient is used in various forms of current-value accounting.

Readers will be aware of the difficulties involved in the determination of historical cost of trading stock – whether stock should be valued on the basis of 'average', FIFO, etc. The problem is even more acute when trading stock involves work in progress and finished goods, as the question of the extent to which overheads should be included in the stock figure must be considered. Similar problems arise when determining the cost of fixed assets which are constructed by a firm for its own use.

There is another class of assets for which it may be difficult to find the historical costs. These are assets which have been acquired through barter or exchange, a special case of which are assets which are purchased in exchange for shares in the purchasing company. In such instances it will usually be necessary to estimate the historical cost of the assets acquired. This is usually done by reference to the amount that would have been realised had the assets, which had been given in exchange, been sold for cash. In some cases it might prove to be extremely difficult to make the necessary estimates as there may not be a market in the assets concerned.

Yet further problems occur where a number of assets are purchased together; for example, where a company purchases the net assets of another company or unincorporated firm. For accounting purposes it is necessary to determine the cost of the individual assets and liabilities which have been acquired and this involves an allocation of the global price to the individual assets and liabilities which are separately identified in the accounting system. Any balancing figure represents the amount paid for all assets and liabilities not separately identified in the accounting system and is described as goodwill.[8] Such an allocation is made using 'fair values', which usually results in the individual assets being valued at their replacement costs and liabilities being valued at their face values.

The contents of this section may seem fairly obvious, but it is important to remember that the determination of an asset's historical cost is not always an easy task.

---

[8] Such an approach is also necessary when preparing consolidated financial statements and this is discussed in Chapter 9.

'Adjusted' historical cost

By 'adjusted' historical cost we mean the method whereby the historical cost of an asset is taken to be its original acquisition cost adjusted to account for changes in the value or purchasing power of money between the date of acquisition and the valuation date. This method of valuation forms the basis of the accounting system known as current purchasing power accounting (*see* Chapter 15).

The practical difficulties of this approach include all those which were discussed in the preceding section on historical cost but to these must be added the problems involved in reflecting the changes in the value of money. This is done by using a price index, which is an attempt to measure the average change in prices over a period.

Great care must be taken when interpreting the figures produced by the adjusted historical cost approach. It must be remembered that this method does not attempt to revalue (i.e. state at current value) the assets; it is money and not the asset which is revalued. The adjusted historical cost method can be contrasted with those approaches under which assets are stated at their current values which are the subjects of the following sections.

Replacement cost

Replacement cost (RC) is often referred to as an entry value because it is the cost to the business of acquiring an asset. In crude terms it may be defined as the estimated amount that would have to be paid in order to replace the asset at the date of valuation.

This is a useful working definition, but it is crude as it begs a large number of questions, some of which will be discussed below.

The definition includes the word 'estimated' because the exercise is a hypothetical one in that the method is based on the question 'How much would it cost to replace this asset today?' Since the asset is not being replaced, the answer has to be found from an examination of the circumstances prevailing in the market for the asset under review. If the asset is identical with those being traded in the market, the estimate may be reasonably objective. Thus, if the asset is a component which is still being manufactured and used by a business, its replacement cost may be found by reference to manufacturers' or suppliers' price lists. However, even in this apparently straightforward case, there may still be difficulties in that the replacement cost may depend on the size of the order. Typically a customer placing a large order will pay a lower price per unit than someone buying in small lots. In some types of business the difference between the two sets of prices may be significant, as is evidenced by the different prices paid for food by large supermarkets and small grocery shops. This observation leads to the conclusion that in certain instances it will be necessary to add to the above definition of replacement cost that the estimate should assume that the owner of the asset would replace it in 'the normal course of business', in other words that the replacement would be made as part of the normal purchasing pattern of the business.

The difficulties inherent in the estimation of replacement cost loom very much larger when we turn our attention to assets which are not identical to those which are currently being traded in the market, including those which have been made obsolete by technological progress. A special, and very important, class of non-identical assets are used assets because all used assets will differ in some respect or other from other used assets of a similar type.

A more detailed discussion of the ways in which the replacement cost of assets is found will be provided later in the book, but it will be helpful if we indicate some of the possible approaches at this stage:

1 *Gross/net replacement cost*: The most common approach, particularly if the asset has been the subject of little technological change, is to take the cost of a new asset (the gross replacement cost) and then deduct an estimate of depreciation; for example, if the asset is two years old and is expected to last for another three years then, using straight-line depreciation, the net replacement cost is $\frac{3}{5}$ths of the gross replacement cost.

2 *Market comparison*: In the case of some used assets, such as motor vehicles, the asset might be valued by reference to the value of similar used assets. It may prove necessary to adjust the value found by direct comparison to account for any special features pertaining to the particular asset. Thus, the approach includes a subjective judgement element which is combined with the reasonably objective comparison with the market.

3 *Replacement cost of inputs*: In certain cases – particularly fixed assets manufactured by owners for their own use and work in progress and finished goods – it might be possible to determine an asset's replacement cost by reference to the current replacement cost of the various inputs used in the construction of the asset. Thus the necessary labour input could be costed at the wage rates prevailing at the valuation date with similar procedures being applied to the other inputs – raw materials, bought-in components and overheads.

Whilst in practice the focus of valuation is often the physical asset itself, we need to recognise that this is a proxy for that which is actually being valued – the services provided by the asset.

Take, as an example, a machine which is expected to operate for another 2000 hours. A new machine might have a life of 4000 hours and have operating costs which are less than those of the machine whose replacement cost we are seeking to estimate. In this case, the replacement cost of the old machine would be half the cost of the new machine less the present value of the savings in the operating costs. If there is a 'good market' in second-hand machines the replacement cost of used machines will approximate for this value, but if this is not the case the replacement cost will be based on the cost of a new machine after adjusting for differences in capacity and operating costs.

Net realisable value

The net realisable value of an asset may be defined as the estimated amount that would be received from the sale of the asset less the anticipated costs that would be incurred in its disposal. It is sometimes called an exit value as it is the amount realisable when assets leave the firm.

One obvious problem with this definition is that the amount which would be realised on the disposal of an asset depends on the circumstances in which it is sold. It is likely that there would be a considerable difference between the proceeds that might be expected if the asset were disposed of in the normal way and the proceeds from a forced and hurried sale of the assets. Of course, it all depends on what is meant by the 'normal course of business' and, while the phrase may be useful enough for many practical purposes, it must be remembered that it is often not possible to think in terms of the two extreme cases of 'normal' and 'hurried' disposals. There may be all sorts of intermediate positions between these extremes. It can thus be seen that there may be a whole family of possible values based on selling prices which depend on the assumptions made about the conditions under which they are sold and that, particularly in the case of stock, great care must be taken when interpreting the phrase that the net realisable value of an asset is £x.

As is true for the replacement cost basis of valuation, the difficulties associated with the determination of an asset's net realisable value are less when the asset in question is identical, or very similar to, assets which are being traded in the market. In such circumstances the asset's net realisable value can be found by reference to the prevailing market price viewed from the point of view of a seller in the market. The replacement cost is, of course, related to the purchaser's viewpoint. If there is an active market, the difference between an asset's replacement cost and its net realisable value may not be very great and will depend on the expenses and profit margins of traders in the particular type of asset.

The relationship of the business to the market will determine whether, in the case of that business, an asset's replacement cost exceeds its net realisable value or vice versa. It is likely that the barrow boy to whom reference was made earlier would find that the replacement cost of his barrow could be greater than its net realisable value, while the reverse is likely to hold for his vegetables. It is generally, but not universally, true that a business will find that the replacement costs of its fixed assets will exceed their net realisable values, while in the case of trading stock the net realisable value will be the greater.

Generally the estimation of the net realisable value of a unique asset is even more difficult than the determination of such an asset's replacement cost. It may be possible to use a 'units of service' approach in that one could examine what the market is prepared to pay for the productive capacity of the asset being valued, but the process is likely to be more subjective. In the replacement cost case, the owner is the potential purchaser and will base his valuation on his own estimate of the productive capacity of the asset but, in the net realisable value case, the hypothetical purchaser will have to be convinced of the asset's productive capacity.

A further difficulty involved in the estimation of net realisable value is the last phrase in the definition – 'less the anticipated costs that would be incurred in its disposal'. This sting in the definition's tail can be extremely significant, especially in the case of work in progress, in relation to which the estimation of anticipated additional costs may be difficult and subjective.

Present value

It might be possible to apply the present-value approach to the valuation of individual assets. To do so would require the valuer to attach an estimated series of future cash flows to the individual asset and select an appropriate discount rate. This may be possible in the case of assets which are not used in combination with others, such as an office block which is rented out, but most assets are used in combination to generate revenue. Thus, a firm purchases raw materials which are processed by many machines in their building to produce the finished goods which are sold to earn revenue. In such circumstances as these it would seem impossible to say what proportion of the total net cash flow should be assigned to a particular machine.

Capital maintenance

Let us for a while ignore the practical problems associated with the valuation of assets at an instant in time and assume that one can generate a series of figures (depending on the basis of valuation selected) reflecting the value of the bundle of assets which constitutes a business and hence, after making appropriate deduction for creditors,[9] arrive at a series of figures showing the owners' equity in or net assets of the enterprise at different instants in time.

If this can be done, is the profit for a period found by simply deducting the value of the net assets at the start of the period from the corresponding value at the end of the period? In other words if, using the selected basis of valuation, the value of the assets at the time t_0 was £1000 and the value at the time t_1 £1500, is the profit for the period £500? The answer is, probably not.

We must remember that we have defined profit in terms of the amount that can be withdrawn or distributed while leaving the business as well-off at the end as it was at the beginning of the period. Now assume that in this simple example the valuation basis used is replacement cost and, for the sake of even more simplicity, that no capital has been introduced or withdrawn during the period and that the firm only holds one type of asset, the replacement cost of which has increased by 50 per cent. (Thus the company holds the same number of assets at the end as it did at the beginning of the period.) Let us also assume that prices in general have not increased over the period.

The question which has to be answered is, how much could be distributed by way of a dividend at the end of the period without reducing its 'well-offness' below that which prevailed at the start of the period? It could be argued that £500 could be paid, as that would leave the value of the assets constant. It could also be argued that nothing should be paid because in order to pay a dividend the company would have to reduce its holding of assets. If the latter view is accepted, it means that the whole of the increase in the value of the assets should be retained in the business in order to maintain its 'well-offness'. It will be seen that each of the approaches described in this simple example will be found in different accounting models, but at this stage we simply want to show that it is not sufficient to find the difference between values at two points in time. The profit figure will also depend on the amount which it is deemed necessary to retain in the business to maintain its 'well-offness', that is on the concept of *capital maintenance* which is selected. We shall describe the various approaches to capital maintenance in a little more detail below.

There are thus two choices to be made: the basis of asset valuation and the aspect of capital which is to be maintained. In theory each of the possible bases of valuation can be combined with any of the different concepts of capital maintenance with each combination yielding a different profit figure. In practice the two choices are not made independently of each other in that, as we will show, there are some combinations of asset value/capital maintenance which are mutually consistent and yield potentially helpful information, while others appear not to provide useful information, usually because the two choices are made on the basis of an inconsistent approach to the question of the objectives served by the preparation of financial accounts.

---

[9] The valuation of liabilities is an even less well developed subject than the valuation of assets, but things are changing and more attention is now being paid to this topic. However, in order to focus on the principles underlying the concept of capital maintenance and its relationship to the measurement of profit we will defer the subject of the valuation of liabilities to later chapters.

We can summarise the argument thus far by stating that the profit figure depends on (a) the basis of valuation selected, and (b) the concept of capital maintenance used, and is found in the following way:

1 Find the difference between the value of the assets less liabilities at the beginning and end of the period after adjusting for capital introduced or withdrawn.
2 Decide how much of the difference (if any) needs to be retained in the business to maintain capital.
3 The residual is then the profit for the period.

We will now turn to more detailed examination of the possible ways of viewing the capital of the company (or of its owners) which is to be maintained. It will be helpful to categorise the various approaches to capital maintenance in the following way:

- Financial capital maintenance
  - Not adjusted for inflation (Money financial capital maintenance)
  - Adjusted for inflation (Real financial capital maintenance)
- Operating capital maintenance[10]
  - From the standpoint of the entity
  - From the standpoint of the equity shareholders' interest.

We shall deal with the above in turn.

Money financial capital maintenance

With money financial capital maintenance the benchmark used to decide whether a profit has been earned is the book value of the shareholders' interest at the start of the period.

If money capital is to be maintained then in the absence of capital injections or withdrawals[11] the profit for the period is the difference between the values of assets less liabilities at the start and end of the period with no further adjustment. Money financial capital maintenance is used in traditional historical cost accounting which is not to say that, as we will show in Example 3.1, it cannot be combined with other bases of asset valuation.

Real financial capital maintenance

With real financial capital maintenance (which is often referred to simply as real capital maintenance) the benchmark used to determine whether a profit has been made is the *purchasing power* of the equity shareholders' interest in the company at the start of the period. Thus, if the equity shareholders' interest in the company is £1000 at the start and the general price level increases by 5 per cent in the period under review, a profit will only arise if, on the selected basis, the value of the assets less liabilities, and hence the equity shareholders' interest[12] at the time, amounts to at least £1050.

---

[10] There is as yet no consensus on the names of the various bases of capital maintenance. For example, the term 'nominal money' might be used instead of 'money capital', or 'physical capital' rather than 'operating capital'. We believe the terms used in this book both provide better descriptions and are more widely used in the literature than the alternatives.

[11] In order to save repeating this phrase readers should, for the remainder of this section, continue to assume the absence of capital injections and withdrawals.

[12] Preference shares being treated as liabilities for this purpose.

Both the money financial capital and real financial capital maintenance approaches concentrate on the equity shareholders' interest in the company and are hence sometimes referred to as measures of profit based on *proprietary capital maintenance*.

Operating capital maintenance

The operating capital maintenance concept is less clear-cut than the financial capital maintenance approach. Broadly, it is concerned with the physical assets of the enterprise and suggests that capital is maintained if at the end of the period the company has the same level of assets as it had at the start. A very simple example of the operating capital approach is provided by the following example.

Suppose a business starts the period with £100 in cash, 20 widgets and 30 flanges and ends the period with £130 in cash, 25 widgets and 32 flanges. Then the profit for the period, using the operating capital maintenance approach, could be regarded as being:

Profit = £30 in cash + 5 widgets + 2 flanges.

For certain purposes one could stop here, for the list of assets given above shows the increase in wealth achieved by that business over the period. To state profit in this way does provide a very clear picture of what has happened and shows in an extremely objective fashion the extent to which the business has grown in physical terms. Accountancy, however, is concerned with providing information stated in monetary terms.

In order to take this additional step it is necessary to select a basis of valuation, for this would then enable the accountant to place a single monetary value on the profit.

Let us assume that it is decided that replacement cost is the selected valuation basis and that the replacement costs at the end of the year are widgets £100 each and flanges £150 each. The profit for the period would then be stated as follows:

	£
Increase in cash	30
Increase in widgets, 5 × £100	500
Increase in flanges, 2 × £150	300
Profit	830

The above example is obviously simplistic in so far as companies hold a large number of different sorts of assets and, only in the most static of situations, will the assets held at the end of the year match those which are owned at the start of the period. However, the example does illustrate the sort of thinking which will be developed in later chapters.

The example was based on the variant of the operating capital maintenance measure which states that a company only makes a profit if it has replaced, or is in a position to replace, the assets which were held at the start of the period and which have been used up in the course of the period. A more sophisticated alternative would be to consider the output which is capable of being generated by the initial holding of assets and design an accounting model which would only disclose a figure for profit if the company is able to maintain the same level of output.

Most variants of the operating capital maintenance approach relate the determination of profit to the assets held by the business, i.e. look at the problem from the standpoint of the business. The operating capital approach is thus often referred to as an *entity measure of profit*. It is, however, possible to combine the operating capital maintenance concept with the proprietary approach. Thus, a profit based on an entity concept can be derived which can be adjusted to show the position from the point of view of the equity holders. If, for example, part of the assets are financed by long-term creditors, it might be assumed that part of the additional funds required, in a period of rising prices, to maintain the business's operating capital will also be contributed by the long-term creditors. Hence, the profit attributable to equity holders would be higher than the profit derived from the strict application of the entity concept. Assume that a company has the following opening balance sheet:

	£		£
Equity shareholders	60	Assets	
		10 items of stock at £10 each	100
Debentures	40		
	100		100

Stock is valued at its replacement cost and the proportion of debt finance in the capital structure (i.e. the gearing) is 40 per cent. For simplicity we will assume the debentures are interest free.

Assume that the company holds the stock for a period and then sells all 10 items for cash at £18 each so that the closing balance sheet includes just one asset, cash of £180. In the period the replacement cost of stock has risen from £10 to £15 per unit.

If the operating capital maintenance concept is followed, then, in order to maintain the operating capital of the entity, an amount of £150, that is 10 items at the new replacement cost of £15, would be needed. Thus, the entity profit would be:

	£
Closing capital in cash	180
less Amount necessary to replace 10 items at £15	150
Entity profit	30

However, in order to maintain the operating capital of the equity shareholders' interest in the entity, an amount of £90 rather than £150 would be needed. Shareholders were financing 60 per cent of the stock and 60 per cent of £150 is £90. Thus, the proprietary profit would be:

	£
Net assets at end of period:	
Cash	180
less Debentures	40
Equity interest	140
Amount necessary to maintain the equity interest in entity	90
Profit attributable to equity shareholders	50

The additional £20 of profit may be described as a gearing gain and represents the profit which accrued to the shareholders because the company borrowed money and invested it in stock which rose in value. It is therefore 40 per cent of the increase in the replacement cost of stock: $40\% \times (150 - 100)$.

If the gearing gain were distributed, the operating capital of the entity would fall, unless the debentures were increased to maintain the original gearing ratio of 40 per cent.

An extended illustration is provided in Example 3.1, in which the combinations of three different bases of valuation and three different concepts of capital maintenance are shown.

Example 3.1 Different profit concepts

In this example the three valuation bases used are historical cost (HC), replacement cost (RC) and net realisable value (NRV), and the three measures of capital maintenance are money financial capital, real financial capital and operating capital.

Suppose that a trader has an inventory consisting of 100 units at the start of the year (all of which were sold during the year) and 120 units at the end of the year, but has no other assets or liabilities.

Assume that the trader has neither withdrawn nor introduced capital during the period.

Suppose that the following prices prevailed:

Opening position (100 units)

Basis of valuation	Unit price £	Total capital £
Historical cost	10.00	1000
Replacement cost	11.00	1100
Net realisable value	11.50	1150

Closing position (120 units)

Basis of valuation	Unit price £	Total capital £
Historical cost	15.00	1800
Replacement cost	17.00	2040
Net realisable value	18.00	2160

In order to use the real financial capital approach it is necessary to know how a suitable general price index moved over the year. For illustrative purposes, we shall assume a high rate of inflation: We will assume that an index moved as follows:

	Index
Beginning of the year and date on which the opening inventory was purchased	100
Date on which the closing inventory was purchased	118
End of year	120

(a) Money financial capital

The opening money financial capital depends on the selected basis of asset valuation and profit is the difference between the value of the assets at the end of the period and the corresponding figure for opening money capital.

Basis of valuation	Closing value of assets £	Opening money capital £	Profit £
Historical cost	1800	1000	800
Replacement cost	2040	1100	940
Net realisable value	2160	1150	1010

(b) Real financial capital

(i) *Historical cost* The closing inventory of £1800 (as measured by its historical cost) was acquired when the general price index was 118. The index has risen to 120 by the year end and thus the historical cost of inventory expressed in terms of pounds of year-end purchasing power is £1800 × 120/118 = £1831.

Opening money capital based on historical cost was £1000. The index stood at 100 at the beginning of the year and rose to 120 by the year end. Thus the real financial capital which has to be maintained is £1000 × 120/100 = £1200.

The profit derived from the combination of historical cost valuation and real financial capital is hence £1831 – £1200 = £631 (expressed in 'year-end pounds').

(ii) *Replacement cost* As the replacement cost is a current value it is automatically expressed in year-end pounds and hence the closing value of inventory is £2040.

Opening money capital using replacement cost was £1100 which, expressed in year-end pounds, is equivalent to £1320 (£1100 × 120/100). The profit for this particular combination is thus £2040 – £1320 = £720.

(iii) *Net realisable value* The argument is similar to that which was used above and the profit derived from a net realisable value/real financial capital concept combination is calculated as follows:

	£
Closing inventory at net realisable value (automatically expressed in pounds of year-end purchasing power)	2160
Opening money capital (based on net realisable value) restated in year-end pounds, £1150 × 120/100	1380
Profit	780

(c) Operating capital

In this simple example it can be seen that the wealth of the business has increased by 20 units and the only question is how the 20 units should be valued:

Basis of valuation		Profit £
Historical cost (using first in, first out)	20 × £15.00	300
Replacement cost	20 × £17.00	340
Net realisable value	20 × £18.00	360

The various profit figures are summarised in the following table:

| | Capital maintenance concept | | |
| | Money financial £ | Real financial £ | Operating capital £ |
Basis of valuation			
Historical cost	800	631	300
Replacement cost	940	720	340
Net realisable value	1010	780	360

The usefulness of different profit measures

In Example 3.1 nine different profit figures emerged. It is impossible to say that one of these is the 'correct' figure. They are all 'correct' in their own terms, although it may be argued that some of them are generally more useful than others. The different measures reflect reality in different ways. We will meet some of these measures later in this book in the context of the various proposals that have been made for accounting reform.

It might be useful if at this stage we examined a number (but by no means all) of the different objectives which are served by the preparation of financial statements and consider which of the different profit measures would appear to be the more useful in each case.

We will first discuss the question of whether a business should be allowed to continue in existence. For simplicity we will assume that the business is a sole proprietorship. Consider the profit figure of £780 derived from the combination of the net realisable value asset valuation method and real financial capital maintenance. This figure shows the potential increase in purchasing power which accrued to the owner of the business by virtue of his decision not to liquidate the business at the beginning of the year. Had he taken that option, the owner would have received £1150, which expressed in terms of year-end pounds amounts to £1380, i.e. he could at the beginning of the year purchase an 'average' combination of goods and services amounting to £1150 but it would cost £1380 to purchase the same quantity of goods and services at the end of the year. By allowing the business to continue, the owner has increased his wealth by £780 in that, should he liquidate the business at the end of the year, he would release purchasing power amounting to £2160. Now this analysis does not enable the owner to tell whether he was right to allow the business to continue in operation, but the figures do allow him to compare his increase in wealth with that which he would have achieved had he liquidated the business at the beginning of the year and invested his funds elsewhere. In the words of Edwards and Bell (*see* p. 44) the owner has been able to check in the market place his decision not to wind up the business.

But, of course, the past is dead and it is current decisions which are important, the decision to be taken in this case being whether or not the business should be liquidated at the end of the year. It would be naive to assume that the figure of past profit can be expected to continue in the future. However, the decision maker has to start somewhere and most people find it easier to think in incremental terms. With this approach the decision maker might say: 'In the conditions which prevailed last year I made a profit of £x. I accept that next year there will be a number of changes in the circumstances facing the business and I estimate that the effect of these changes will be to change my profit by £y.' It is clear that if this approach is adopted a profit figure related to the decision maker's objectives (in this case assumed to be the maximisation of the potential consumption) is a valuable input to the decision-making process.

Let us now consider the subject of taxation. A government might well take the view that a company should be able to maintain its productive capacity and that taxation should only be levied on any increase in the company's wealth as measured against that particular yardstick. In that case, one of the set of profit figures derived from the application of physical capital maintenance might be thought to be most suitable on the grounds that, to use the figures given in our example, if the company started the year with 100 units, then in order to maintain the productive capacity it should hold 100 units at the end of the year. The government would, if it took this view, wish to base its taxation levy on the physical increase of wealth of 20 units. Arguments for and against the use of one of the three members of the physical capital maintenance set could be deployed, but these will not be pursued at this stage. There are obviously severe practical difficulties in the use of the physical units approach where the company owns more than one type of asset and, as will be discussed later, other more practical methods have been used which allowed governments to apply a taxation policy which approximated to that postulated above.

Later in this chapter we will point out the limitations of the historical cost approach and, in fairness, we should now consider whether the profit derived from the traditional accounting system (historical cost asset values and money capital maintenance) could be said to be particularly apposite for any purpose. It is sometimes suggested that the traditional profit figure is of use in questions concerned with distribution policy, for, to quote Professor W.T. Baxter:

> The ordinary accounting concept has obvious merits; it is familiar and (inflation apart) cautious, and most of its figures are based on objective data; its widespread use has therefore been sensible where the decisions are about cash payments (e.g. tax and dividends), since it reduces the scope for bickering and the danger of paying out cash before the revenue has been realized.[13]

How do we choose?

We have identified nine different methods of measuring profit and pointed out that many other different methods are available. One possible way forward would be to include in a company's annual financial statements a list of different profit figures. However, if this is not considered practical, the question becomes which basis or bases is/are the most suitable for inclusion in published accounts. The reference to the plural 'bases' holds upon the possibility that it might be found desirable to include more than one profit concept in the published accounts.

A sensible approach to this question would be a consideration of the purposes for which a knowledge of a company's profits are used, which is in effect the considera-

---

13 W.T. Baxter, *Accounting Values and Inflation*, McGraw-Hill, London, 1975, p. 23. It may be strange to quote the words of one of the foremost advocates of current value accounting in support of historical cost accounting. However, Professor Baxter, on whose work this section of the book is largely based, was seeking to show that different profit concepts may be useful for different purposes.

tion of the aims and objectives of published financial accounts. A very long list of such purposes can be provided, but it might be helpful if these were analysed under four different headings, i.e. control, consumption, taxation, valuation. It must, however, be recognised that the divisions between these headings are not watertight and that they share numerous common features.

The limitations of historical cost accounting

Later chapters of this book deal with the subject of current purchasing power and current value accounting and will, by implication, highlight some of the deficiencies of the traditional form of accounting, i.e. historical cost basis of valuation and money financial capital maintenance.[14] It might, however, be helpful if by way of introduction we tested the traditional system against the objectives enumerated above.

Control

It is a widely held view that the prime objective of the preparation and publication of regular financial reporting is – so far as public limited companies are concerned – to provide a vehicle whereby the directors can account to the owners of the company on their *stewardship* of the resources entrusted to their charge. This involves providing shareholders with information about the progress of the company as well as details of the amounts paid to directors by way of remuneration. In theory shareholders can, when supplied with this information, take certain steps to remedy the position if the information suggests that all is not well. One mechanism that is available to shareholders is to effect a change in directors, but in practice it is rare for shareholders directly to oust directors because of the publication of unfavourable results. This end might be achieved by the indirect process of a takeover, in that shareholders might accept an offer for their shares on the grounds that they believe that the new management will be more effective than existing management. An individual shareholder can, of course, achieve similar ends by selling his shares but in so doing he must compare what he considers to be the value of the shares with the existing management with the current market price (see the section on valuation below).

The above discussion is based on the view that the directors need only account for their stewardship to their shareholders, but it has been suggested that the concept of stewardship should be extended – at least so far as large companies are concerned – to cover the need to report to the community at large. This view, propounded for example in *The Corporate Report*,[15] is based on the view that large companies control the use of significant proportions of a country's scarce resources and that, consequently, large companies should report to the community at large on the way in which the resources have been used. It will be realised that such a view does not attract the support of all businesspeople and accountants, who might well be concerned with the nature of the control devices which might follow if this view were adopted. The pressure of public

---

[14] The weaknesses of the traditional accounting model are lucidly and concisely set out by the Accounting Standards Committee in *Accounting for the Effects of Changing Prices: a Handbook*, published in 1986, and by the Accounting Standards Board in its Discussion Paper 'The Role of Valuation in Financial Reporting', published in 1993. See Chapters 17 and 18.

[15] Scope and Aims Committee of the Accounting Standards Steering Committee, *The Corporate Report*, Accounting Standards Steering Committee, London, 1975.

opinion might be an acceptable control device, but many would be concerned that this might not be regarded as being sufficiently strong and that recourse might be made to government intervention or 'interference' or, ultimately, nationalisation.

If stewardship is narrowly defined to cover simply the reporting by directors to shareholders of how they have used shareholders' funds, then it is possible to argue that historical cost accounting is reasonably adequate. An historical cost balance sheet lists the assets of the company and the claims by outsiders (liabilities) on the company; however it will not identify *all* the assets, as it will usually omit many intangible assets such as the skill and knowledge of the employees, degree of monopoly power, etc. The main point, however, is whether stewardship should be narrowly defined in the manner suggested above. If shareholders, and others, are to apply effective control they should be helped to form judgments about how well the directors have used the resources entrusted to them.

As we indicated earlier in the chapter there are a number of different possible approaches to the question of how one can measure how successful a company – and by implication its managers – has been over a period. At this stage it is perhaps sufficient to point out that historical cost accounting will not – except in the simplest of cases where a high proportion of a company's assets is made up of cash – be of much assistance. Historical cost accounts, in general, simply show the acquisition cost or the depreciated historical cost of a company's assets and not their current values, let alone the value of the company as a whole.

It is sometimes argued that, even if historical cost accounts do not provide an absolute measure of success, they can at least allow comparisons to be made between the quality of performance achieved by different companies. This statement is sometimes justified by arguments such as, 'Inflation affects all companies to more or less the same extent and therefore a comparison of profitability measured on an historical cost basis, e.g. rate of return on capital employed, enables a rough comparison to be made of relative success'.

Two points need to be made. The first concerns inflation. As will be shown, the problem is not just inflation – a general increase in prices or fall in the value of money – but includes the treatment of changes in relative prices. For, even in an inflation-free economy, there will be changes in individual prices. The limitations of historical cost accounting in the context of changes in relative prices can be seen by considering the following simple example.

Suppose that two companies start operations as commodity dealers, in an inflation-free environment, with £1000 each. Company A spent its £1000 on commodity A while Company B invested its £1000 in commodity B. Assume that neither company bought or sold any units during the period and that over the period the market value[16] of commodity A increased by 2 per cent and commodity B increased by 20 per cent. Historical cost accounts will not show that Company B performed better in the sense that it chose to invest in a commodity which experienced a greater increase in value.

The second point which should be made about the argument advanced above is that it is not true that inflation affects all companies to more or less the same extent. This point will be developed later when we will show that price changes (both general and relative) affect different companies in very different ways and that it is in fact the case that historical cost accounts are most unhelpful when it comes to the comparison of performance.

---

[16] For simplicity we will ignore transaction costs and assume, in the case of both commodities, that there is no difference between the commodities' replacement costs and net realisable values.

Consumption

Probably one of the most important uses of the profit figure is in determining the amount of any increment of wealth which is available for distribution and how it should be shared between the various groups entitled to share in such a distribution, i.e. the different classes of shareholders, the directors and employees (either directly through profit-sharing schemes or indirectly through wage claims) and the community through taxation. There are what might be called 'legal' and 'economic' aspects to this question. Company law requires that dividends may only be paid out of profits, and tax law specifies the amount of taxation which has to be paid; however, subject to these constraints, plus any other legal limitations arising from such things as profit-sharing agreements, it is for the directors to make economic judgments about the level of dividends and, again subject to numerous institutional and possible legal constraints, the level of wages. Empirical evidence suggests that companies' dividends are related to the level of reported profit. It is also safe to suggest that sole traders and partners act in a similar fashion in that, when deciding on the level of their drawings, they will be influenced by the profits of their businesses.

The concept of capital maintenance based on historical cost accounting principles has, in periods of anything but modest price changes, proved to be a dangerous benchmark when used to assess the amount which a company can pay out by way of dividend or through taxation. For example, the maintenance of money financial capital is not, except in the simplest of cases, the same as the maintenance of the company's productive capacity. The point is an obvious one, for we could visualise a company which started business with £10 000 which it invested in 1000 units of stock. If the price of the stock increases and if the whole of the company's historical cost profit is taxed or consumed away, its money financial capital will be maintained, but it is clear that the company will have to reduce the physical quantity of stock.

It should be recognised that there is a great deal of difference between using the capital maintenance approach as a benchmark to measure profit and requiring companies to maintain their capital. Presumably distribution decisions should be made on the basis of consumption needs and perceived future investment opportunities inside and outside the company, and in many cases it would be sensible not to restrict distributions to profits. It is necessary that company law should attempt to provide a measure of protection to creditors, but this should not be done in an inflexible way.[17]

It will be argued in later chapters that there is a need to devise a measure of profit that will provide a signal that if more than the amount of profit is consumed or taxed away then the substance of the business – however that may be defined – will be eroded. However, this is not to say that the substance of the business should never be reduced by way of dividend: in other words, a partial liquidation of the business might in certain circumstances be beneficial to shareholders without being detrimental to the interests of creditors and employees.

Taxation

In Britain, as in many other countries, a company's tax charge is based on its accounting profit, although numerous adjustments might have to be made when computing the profit subject to taxation. The general rule is, however, clear: the higher the accounting profit, the higher, all other things being equal, the amount that will be paid in tax.

---

[17] Current legal practice regarding distributable profit is outlined in the final section of this chapter.

For reasons similar to those discussed in the above section on consumption, the traditional accounting system does not constitute a suitable basis for the computation of the taxation obligations of businesses. This view depends on the not unreasonable assumption that governments would wish companies to be at least able to maintain the substance of their businesses. As we have shown, it is possible for historical cost accounting to generate a profit figure even when there has been a decline in the productive capacity of the business or, in less extreme cases, the reported profit might far exceed the growth in the company's productive capacity. Thus the use of historical cost accounting as the basis for taxation means that in periods of rising prices the proportion of the increase in a company's wealth which is taken by taxation may be very much larger than that which is implied by the nominal rate of taxation. In extreme cases taxation might be payable even where there has been a decline in the productive capacity of the business.

The rapid and extreme inflation of the mid-1970s made governments and others very much aware of the inadequacy of historical cost accounting for the purposes of taxation. Special measures were enacted which allowed businesses some relief against taxation for the impact of increasing prices, namely stock appreciation relief and accelerated capital allowances. In contrast, financial accounting practice remained and remains essentially rooted in the traditional model of historical cost valuation combined with money financial capital maintenance, although, as described later in this book, the debate on possible reforms continues.

Valuation

The information contained in a company's accounts is a significant, but not the sole, input to decisions concerning the valuation of a business or of a share in a business. This subject will be discussed in detail in Chapter 14. At this stage it is perhaps sufficient to point out that the value of any asset, including a business or a share, depends on the economic benefits which are expected to flow to the asset's owner. It requires neither much space nor forceful argument to suggest that a knowledge of the historical cost of a company's assets will not be of much help in assessing the value of a company or of its shares. Indeed, it was never the view of accountants that historical cost accounts should be used in this way. However, this view has never fully been accepted by the users of accounts, who have, understandably from their point of view, believed that the information provided by a company's accounts should help them form judgments concerning valuation. In fact the case for accounting reform does not simply rest on the existence of inflation, which still appears to be a permanent feature of our economy, but on the recognition that the wish of users to be supplied with information which will help them assess the value of companies and shares therein is a legitimate demand and one which will be better served by accounts based on current value principles than by historical cost accounts.

Summary

So far in this chapter, we have considered the meaning of profit and have shown that there are very many ways of measuring this elusive concept. These depend essentially on the choice made regarding the basis of asset valuation and the aspect of capital which is to be maintained. We have also discussed the limitations of historical cost accounting when tested against the more important purposes which a 'reasonable person' might expect financial accounts to serve. In the later chapters we will consider in some detail a number of the more important accounting models which have been developed and used in practice. But before doing so, we will turn our attention briefly to the subject of distributable profits.

Distributable profits

Because the liability of its shareholders is limited to the amount which they have paid or agreed to pay in respect of their shares, creditors of a failed limited company will normally only have recourse to the assets of the company itself. The assets representing the share capital, and any other reserves which are treated as being similar to share capital, may be seen as a buffer or cushion which provides some protection to creditors in the event of a failure. If a company were permitted to use its assets to repay this 'permanent' capital, the buffer would be reduced or disappear entirely with the result that the creditors' position would be more risky.

Although the law cannot prevent companies from reducing their 'permanent' capital by making losses, it does attempt to restrict the reduction of capital in other circumstances and, where a reduction of capital is permitted, it is strictly regulated. One way in which the law achieves its aim is by restricting payments of dividends to the distributable profits of the company. Another way is by the regulation of any transactions involving the purchase or redemption of a company's own shares and of any capital reduction or reorganisation schemes. We look at the former here and the latter in Chapter 12.

It has long been the case that dividends can only be paid out of profits but, surprisingly, until the passage of the Companies Act 1980, statute law offered no guidance on what constituted profits available for distribution. There were a number of leading cases, some of which were distinguished by their age rather than their economic rationale, which combined to produce some rather odd and confusing results.[18]

The implementation of the Second and Fourth EU Directives necessitated the inclusion of provisions relating to distributable profits in UK statute law and, as a result, the Companies Act 1985 contains the following definition:

> . . . a company's profits available for distribution are its accumulated, realized profits, so far as not previously utilized by distribution or capitalization, less its accumulated, realized losses, so far as not previously written off in a reduction or reorganization of capital duly made.[19]

The above represents the only legal requirement placed on private companies, but additional rules apply to public companies and investment companies.

A public company may not pay a dividend which would reduce the amount of its net assets below the aggregate of its called-up share capital plus its undistributable reserves.[20] For this purpose the Act defines undistributable reserves as:

(a) the share premium account;
(b) the capital redemption reserve;
(c) excess of accumulated unrealised profits over accumulated unrealised losses (to the extent that these have not been previously capitalised or written off);
(d) any other reserve which the company may not distribute.

---

[18] Interested readers are referred to E.A. French, 'Evolution of the Dividend Law of England', in *Studies in Accounting*, W.T. Baxter and S. Davidson (eds), ICAEW, London, 1977.
[19] Companies Act 1985, Sec. 263(3).
[20] Companies Act 1985, Sec. 264(1).

Before turning to the special case of investment companies we will discuss the implications of the above for public and private companies. Note that no distinction is made between revenue and capital profits, both are distributable; the key element is whether the profits have been *realised*, a term which will be discussed in further detail below.

A private company may, legally, pay a dividend equal to the accumulated balance of realised profits less realised losses, irrespective of the existence of unrealised losses. In contrast, the effect of the 'net asset rule' or 'capital maintenance rule' imposed on public companies is to require such a company to cover any net unrealised losses.

Thus, suppose a company's balance sheet is as given below:

	£	£
Share capital		50
Share premium		25
Unrealised profits	20	
Unrealised losses	(35)	(15)
Realised profits less realised losses		40
Net assets		100

If the concern were a private company it could pay a dividend of £40, but if it were a public company the maximum possible dividend would, because of the net asset rule, be restricted as follows:

	£	£
Net assets		100
less Share capital and undistributable reserves		
Share capital	50	
Share premium	25	
Excess of unrealised profits over unrealised losses[21]	0	75
Maximum dividend payable by public company		25

The effect of the net asset rule is to reduce the possible dividend by the net unrealised losses:

	£
Realised profits less realised losses	40
less Excess of unrealised losses over unrealised profits	15
Maximum dividend	25

Given the general bias in accounting to treat all losses and provisions as being realised, it has to be recognised that unrealised losses are likely to be somewhat rare.

An investment company is a listed public company whose business consists of investing its funds in securities with the intention of spreading the risk and giving its shareholders the benefits of the results of its management of funds. Such a company can, if it satisfies a number of conditions,[22] including a prohibition on the distribution of capital profits, give notice to the Registrar of Companies of its intention to be regarded as an investment company.

---

[21] Note that the excess of realised profits over unrealised losses is zero rather than the 'mathematical' excess of minus 15.

[22] For a detailed list of conditions readers should refer to Companies Act 1985, Section 266.

Except for the fact that it may not distribute capital profits, an investment company may calculate its maximum dividend on the same basis as any other public company. However, it is afforded greater flexibility by Sec. 265 of the Companies Act 1985 which provides an alternative method of calculating the maximum dividend payable. An investment company can, subject to a number of conditions, pay a dividend equal to the amount of its accumulated realised revenue profits less its accumulated revenue losses (both realised and unrealised). Thus, it may ignore any capital losses subject to the restriction that, after the payment of the dividend, the company's assets must be equal to or greater than $1\frac{1}{2}$ times its liabilities. Thus, if an investment company wishes to take advantage of the provision in Sec. 265 of not restricting its dividend by virtue of the existence of capital losses, it must apply this 'asset ratio test'.

It should be noted that the asset ratio test will be affected by the way in which it is proposed to fund the dividend, in that the result will depend on whether the dividend, will reduce assets (if paid out of a positive cash balance) or increase liabilities (if paid from an overdraft). Suppose, for example, that an investment company has assets of £1200 and liabilities of £600. Then the maximum dividend on each basis will be:

(a) Dividend paid out of cash (i.e. liabilities held constant)

	Initial position £	After dividend £	Maximum dividend £
Assets	1200	900(3)	300
Liabilities	600	600(2)	

(b) Dividends paid out of an overdraft (assets held constant)

	Initial position £	After dividend £	Maximum dividend £
Assets	1200	1200(3)	
Liabilities	600	800(2)	200

The various provisions outlined above are summarised in Table 3.1 and illustrated in Example 3.2.

Table 3.1 Tests for maximum dividend

Type of company	Test
Private	The dividend must not exceed accumulated realised profits less accumulated realised losses.
Public (other than investment companies)	The dividend must not exceed accumulated realised profits less accumulated realised losses, less accumulated net unrealised losses.
Investment companies	The maximum dividend is the higher of: (a) the amount derived from the above rule applicable to all public companies with the modification that realised capital profits must be excluded; and (b) the amount of accumulated realised revenue profits less accumulated revenue losses, both realised and unrealised, provided that, after payment of the dividend, assets are equal to at least one and a half times the liabilities.

Example 3.2

The balance sheet of Company A is summarised below:

	£	£
Total assets		4000
less Total liabilities		1000
		3000
Share capital		200
Share premium account		800
Unrealised profits		
Revenue	100	
Capital	200	300
Unrealised losses		
Revenue	(200)	
Capital	(800)	(1000)
Realised profits less realised losses		
Revenue	2300	
Capital	400	2700
		3000

We will now work out the maximum dividend on the assumption that Company A is (a) a private limited company, (b) a public limited company, and (c) an investment company.

(a) Private company

For such a company, the maximum dividend is the accumulated net realised profits, that is £2700.

(b) Public company

The public company is subject to the capital maintenance rule that, after distribution, the net assets must equal the share capital plus undistributable reserves. In this case the undistributable reserves comprise only the share premium account, for the excess of unrealised profits over unrealised losses is zero. Hence, the maximum dividend is given by:

	£	£
Net assets		3000
less Share capital	200	
Share premium	800	1000
Maximum dividend		2000

In the case of the public company, the maximum dividend of the private company (£2700) has been reduced by the net unrealised losses of £700. (Unrealised losses £1000 less unrealised profits £300.)

(c) Investment company

By definition, an investment company must not distribute its capital profits. Hence our starting point must be realised revenue profits of £2300 subject, however, to the capital maintenance rule. Under this rule, the maximum dividend would be £2000 as for the public company in (b) above.

Using the alternative method allowed by Sec. 265, the maximum dividend is the excess of the realised revenue profits over net unrealised revenue losses, i.e. £2300 – (200 – 100) = £2200, subject to the application of the asset ratio test.

(i) If a dividend of £2200 were paid in cash, total assets would fall from £4000 to £1800, which is more than 1.5 times the liabilities of £1000.

(ii) If the dividend of £2200 was paid by overdraft, liabilities would increase to £3200, which would require asset cover of 1.5 × £3200 = £4800, i.e. more than the existing assets of £4000.

Hence the maximum dividend is £2200, but only if such a payment did not increase the liabilities. The lower limit of the maximum dividend is £2000 (as this can be justified on the alternative capital maintenance rule) while a dividend of between £2000 and £2200 would be possible if only a proportion of the dividend was paid out of an overdraft.

Realised profits[23]

It is clear from the above discussion that the most important task in determining a company's distributable profits is deciding what constitutes its realised profits less losses. Given the importance of the term, we might expect the Companies Acts to provide us with a comprehensive definition, but we would be extremely disappointed.

The Companies Acts provide both specific and general guidance; although the specific guidance is helpful, the general guidance is much less helpful. Let us look at the more detailed guidance first.

Section 275 of the Companies Act 1985 states that provisions are realised losses except for a provision made in respect of a fall in value of a fixed asset appearing on a revaluation of all the fixed assets of the company, whether including or excluding goodwill. It also provides that where a fixed asset is revalued and depreciation is subsequently based on the revalued amount, the excess of depreciation based on the revalued amount over depreciation based on historical cost is to be treated as a realised profit. Thus the unrealised profit on revaluation is gradually converted into realised profit over the remaining useful life of the asset. Put another way, whatever is done in the profit and loss account, it is necessary only to charge depreciation based on historical cost in arriving at the realised profits of a company.

To give an example of such depreciation, let us suppose that a company purchased a fixed asset for £50 000 when its expected useful life was ten years and its expected residual value was zero. Using the straight line method of depreciation, the annual charge would be £5000 and, after four years, the net book value would be £30 000. If, after these four years, the asset were revalued to £42 000, there would be an unrealised revaluation surplus of £12 000, that is £42 000 less £30 000. The future annual depreciation charge in accordance with FRS 15 'Tangible Fixed Assets' would normally be £42 000 ÷ 6 = £7000.

The excess of the revised depreciation charge of £7000 over historical cost depreciation of £5000 will then be treated as realised profits of the company year by year for the purpose of determining its distributable profits. Thus, by the end of the ensuing

---

[23] This section on realised profits draws heavily on the ICAEW research paper *The Reporting of Profits and the Concept of Realization*, B.V. Carsberg and C.W. Noke, ICAEW, 1989.

six years, the original unrealised revaluation surplus of £12 000 will have been regarded as realised and hence distributable.

Quite clearly the realised profits of a company may be a different figure from the balance on its profit and loss account!

Let us turn next to the more general guidance provided by the law. As a consequence of Companies Act 1989, the Companies Act 1985, Section 275, now contains the following definition:

> References . . . to 'realised profits' and 'realised losses', in relation to a company's accounts, are to such profits or losses of the company as fall to be treated as realised in accordance with principles generally accepted, at the time when the accounts are prepared, with respect to the determination for accounting purposes of realised profits or losses . . . .

This hardly provides an adequate definition of realised profits. Rather it leaves the definition of realised profits to accountants, subject, of course, to the need for judicial interpretation in the Courts if the accountants' methods are challenged. For reasons which we discuss below, accounting standard setters have found it extremely difficult to provide a satisfactory definition of realised profits.

A basic problem is that the definition includes reference, not to generally accepted accounting principles, but to 'principles generally accepted with respect to the determination for accounting purposes of realised profits'. There is some considerable doubt over whether such principles actually exist. Accounting principles have been primarily concerned with a different objective, namely providing a true and fair view of a company's position and results. In attempting to achieve such an objective, accountants have been more concerned with the recognition of profit than with whether it is realised or distributable.

Paragraph 12 of Schedule 4 to Companies Act 1985 further complicates matters by stating that:

> The amount of any item shall be determined on a prudent basis, and in particular:
> (a) only profits realized at the balance sheet date shall be included in the profit and loss account . . . .

Many accountants see this as providing an undesirable constraint on the development of more informative accounting.[24] Indeed the ASC invoked the true and fair override to avoid the requirement to comply with the above principle in cases where it was thought to be inappropriate. One example is the treatment of exchange gains on foreign currency loans outstanding on a balance sheet date, which we discuss in Chapter 10.

Given the above position, it is perhaps not surprising to find little guidance on how to determine realised profits. One source of guidance was the ICAEW Technical Release 481, issued in 1982, which came to the conclusion that:

> A profit which is required by SSAPs to be recognized in the profit and loss account should normally be treated as a realized profit, unless the SSAP specifically indicates that it should be treated as unrealized.

Although this might have seemed an attractive way forward, it does seem to be a rather suspect interpretation of the law. Indeed, it appears to be somewhat close to a tautology: a profit and loss account must only include realised profits but, by definition, whatever an accountant puts in the profit and loss account is realised!

---

[24] See, for example, 'The ASC in chains: whither self-regulation now?', Professor David P. Tweedie, *Accountancy*, March 1983, pp. 112–20. This article was written many years before David Tweedie became Chairman of the Accounting Standards Board in 1990.

Given the above difficulties, the ASC requested the Research Board of the ICAEW to commission a study, and the resulting paper 'The Reporting of Profits and the Concept of Realization', by B. V. Carsberg and C. W. Noke, was published in 1989. If the ASC was expecting guidance on what was and what was not a realised profit, it must have been extremely disappointed. Carsberg and Noke identified six different meanings of realisation which have been used.

We shall focus on just two of these possible concepts of realisation. The narrower of the two is that embodied in the definition of prudence contained in SSAP 2:

> revenue and profits are not anticipated, but are recognized by inclusion in the profit and loss account only when realized in the form either of cash or of other assets the ultimate cash realization of which can be assessed with reasonable certainty; provision is made for all known liabilities (expenses and losses) whether the amount of these is known with certainty or is a best estimate in the light of the information available. (Para. 14.)

This concept concentrates on the reasonable certainty of the ultimate receipt of cash. Clearly realisation has occurred if cash has been received but realisation is also deemed to occur if certain types of assets, such as debtors, are held which are reasonably certain to be turned into cash.

The wider concept regards profit as realised if it can be assessed with reasonable certainty. Thus, it considers the main purpose of the concept as being to ensure reliability of measurement.

Readers may find the distinction between these two concepts difficult to grasp so it is perhaps helpful to look at some examples.

Where a company makes a cash sale, there is no doubt that the profit is realised under either concept. Similarly, where a sale is made on credit, the profit is treated as realised subject to the possible need for a provision for doubtful debts. The creation of the debt payable in the short term provides evidence of the ultimate cash proceeds and also provides a reliable measure of the profits.

Let us think next of an investment in a listed security which increases in price during a period. Under the narrower concept of realisation, profit would not be considered realised because the ultimate cash proceeds at some unspecified time in the future cannot be assessed with reasonable certainty. However, under the wider concept, profit would be treated as realised because the listed price of the share on the balance sheet date provides reliable evidence that a profit has been made. Conventionally accountants would adopt the narrower concept and would treat the holding gain as unrealised.

When we turn to foreign exchange gains on unsettled short-term debtors and creditors, we find that SSAP 20 requires that such gains be taken to the profit and loss account as realised profits. Under the narrower concept of realisation, these would not be treated as realised profits in view of the fact that the exchange rate may reverse between the balance sheet date and the date of receipt or payment. However, under the wider concept, there is reliable evidence, in the form of a published exchange rate, for the fact that a profit has been made. It is true that this may be reversed in the subsequent period but that will be a matter for the subsequent period. Here the ASC appears to have adopted the wider concept of realisation, although, interestingly, the adoption of this wider concept is not applied to the treatment of exchange gains on unsettled long-term monetary items, for here the gains are specifically described as unrealised.

We hope that these examples provide an indication of the lack of consistency in defining realised profits in practice. In order to provide some consistency, Carsberg and Noke recommended that the standard setters should prepare a statement defining realisation and, in their view, the definition should be framed in terms of the reliability of measurement. Instead of attempting to define or redefine realisation, the ASB has taken a rather different approach in the development of its draft Statement of Principles. As we have seen in Chapter 1, it has developed recognition criteria which do not depend upon realisation; we shall return to this below.

Do the provisions make sense?

It is possible to question the philosophy on which the law of distributable profits is based and to press for changes to that law. Why, after all, should dividends be restricted to distributable profits defined in terms of realisation?[25]

Let us approach the question in two stages. First, why should dividends be restricted to profits and, second, if such a restriction is to apply, why should it relate to realised profits?

If a company's directors are acting in the interests of its shareholders then the decision on whether or not a distribution is made should depend on the rates of return available to shareholders outside the company, compared with the rates of return available within the company. If the company has inferior investment opportunities to those of the shareholders, then the restriction of a dividend to the distributable profits of the company would lead to an inefficient allocation of economic resources. The position of creditors needs to be considered and there is a case for protecting the 'buffer' available to creditors. In practice it is likely that the buffer will only be of relevance if the company goes into liquidation or substantially reduces its scale of operations. In such circumstances the real protection for creditors is the amount which will be realised from the sale of assets. In the case of some assets, especially current assets, realisable values may be well in excess of book values, but in the case of many fixed assets, particularly of a failed company, book value might exceed net realisable value. Hence, it might be argued that the test that should be applied is to specify that after distribution the realisable value of the company's assets exceed, possibly by a safety margin, the amounts due to creditors.

Even if we accept that dividends should be restricted to profits, why should the distribution be limited to realised profits?

It is sometimes argued that if a gain is realised, then the money is available to pay the dividend without the need to consider asset valuation. However, as Professor Egginton has pointed out, the argument has two weaknesses, one damaging and the other fatal! The damaging weakness is that conventional accounting often treats profits as realised well before cash is received. The fatal weakness is that even when profits have been received in cash, this cash will usually have been converted into other assets long before any dividends are paid. Hence, whether profits have been received or not, there is no guarantee that cash is available.

This is an area of the law which includes a number of poorly thought-out rules based on dubious reasoning, and accountants are forced to operate within an extremely unhelpful framework. It is of some consolation that in the vast majority of cases the

---

[25] The ideas which follow may be explored in E.A. French, 'Evolution of the dividend law of England', in *Studies in Accounting*, W.T. Baxter and S. Davidson (eds), ICAEW, London, 1977, and D.A. Egginton, 'Distributable profit and the pursuit of prudence', in *Accounting and Business Research*, Number 41, Winter 1980.

limiting factor in determining a dividend is not the availability of distributable profits but the availability of cash and the alternative uses to which it may be put!

The ASB approach

According to the law, only profits realised at a balance sheet date may be included in a profit and loss account. However, given the difficulties which we have discussed above, it is not surprising that the ASB has found the concept of realisation a poor test of whether or not a gain or loss should be recognised in financial statements. As we have explained in Chapter 1, the revised exposure draft of its Statement of Principles[26] is drawn up ignoring the realisation constraint as well as other constraints imposed by the law.

The revised exposure draft contains recognition criteria which are based upon the reasonable certainty that an asset or liability exists and whether it can be measured with sufficient reliability. This would achieve the purpose intended by the recommendation in the report by Carsberg and Noke, discussed above, but in a rather different way. In the view of the authors, this attempt to separate recognition from realisation makes good sense.

The ASB hopes that its approach will in due course lead to changes in company law. However, changes in the law usually involve a long gestation period and it has to be recognised that the approach taken by the ASB is likely to lead to all manner of difficulties and possible confusion in the foreseeable future. While it is possible to ignore the constraints imposed by law in drawing up a draft Statement of Principles, it is certainly not possible to do so in developing accounting standards. The ASB clearly recognises that it will inevitably be forced to produce accounting standards which are in conflict with its own Statement of Principles.

Recommended reading

R.H. Parker, G.C. Harcourt and G. Whittington (eds), *Readings in the Concept and Measurement of Income*, 2nd edn, Philip Allan, Oxford, 1986.

B.V. Carsberg and C.W. Noke, *The Reporting of Profits and the Concept of Realization*, ICAEW, London, 1989.

---

[26] *Statement of Principles for Financial Reporting*, Revised Exposure Draft, ASB, London, March 1999.

Financial reporting in practice

4 Assets

Overview
A key practical and theoretical issue in accounting is when should an asset be recognised and how it should be measured. In what circumstances does expenditure result in an asset and when in an expense? If an asset is to be recognised should it be recorded at cost, and how should that cost be measured, or at a current value that may be more or less than the asset's historical cost? Most assets do not last for ever and so we must decide how we should measure the consumption of the asset.

In this chapter we are concerned with both fixed and current assets as well as special topics such as investment properties and accounting for research and development expenditure while in the context of the measurement of the consumption of fixed assets the chapter deals with depreciation and impairment reviews. Finally the chapter also includes a description of the treatment of government grants.

The various statements and standards covered in the chapter are:

- FRS 15 *Tangible fixed assets* (February 1999)
- SSAP 19 *Accounting for investment properties* (amended July 1994)
- FRS 10 *Goodwill and intangible assets* (December 1997)
- SSAP 13 *Accounting for research and development* (revised January 1989)
- FRS 11 *Impairment of fixed assets and goodwill* (July 1998)
- SSAP 9 *Stocks and long-term contracts* (revised September 1988)
- SSAP 4 *Accounting for Government grants* (revised July 1990)

Introduction

In Chapter 3 we introduced the three bases for the valuation of assets – replacement cost, net realisable value and present value. We shall, in Part 4 of the book, explore these concepts in the context of what came to be called current cost accounting, but in this chapter we will deal with the way in which valuation issues have impacted on the development of reporting standards that relate to assets.

In this and the following chapters, we will discuss a number of problems of accounting measurement and disclosure in the context of current financial accounting practice, which might be described as a 'modified historical cost accounting' system. While efforts to replace historical cost accounting by current cost accounting as the main basis of accounting have failed, the debate has had a considerable impact on financial accounting practice. Of course, in the UK at least, historical cost accounting has always been 'modified' to the extent that assets could be revalued for the purposes of the accounts and in that company legislation required limited information to be provided about the market value of assets.

It was during the 1970s and 1980s, those inflationary decades, that both the accountancy profession and the government made moves that placed more emphasis on the use of current values in financial statements: the main elements of that particular saga are described in Chapter 15. In a period of relatively low inflation much of the heat has gone out of the debate, but there are some important legacies of the controversy including the 'alternative accounting rules' of the Companies Act 1985 and the fact that the subject of the revaluation is now an important aspect of any financial reporting standard dealing with assets.

The ASB deals with the general nature of assets in the revised version of its Revised Draft Statement of Principles issued in 1999, in which assets are defined thus:

> Assets are rights or other access to future economic benefits controlled by an entity as a result of past transactions or events. (Para. 4.7)

This definition is very close to that which was included in the ASB's earlier attempt to produce a draft statement of principles in 1995, the only difference being that in the earlier version the singular 'past transaction or event' was used rather than the plural. The more recent definition recognises that the asset might be the result of a series rather than a sole event.

Note that the key elements are *control* (not ownership), *future economic benefit* and the need to identify *past transactions or events* that gave rise to the asset. We shall show how these elements affect the treatment of assets in the course of the chapter.

Accountants are prone to make distinctions between tangible and intangible assets. Tangible assets are real, you can see them and touch them, and people are reasonably comfortable with them. Intangible assets, such as patents, trademarks and brands, are things without physical substance, and seem to be surrounded by greater risks and uncertainties than tangible assets. The distinction is actually very unhelpful because it deflects us away from understanding the basic principle that an asset is only an asset if it is a source of future economic benefit. Its tangibility or intangibility has nothing to do with it. A piece of plant and equipment is a potential heap of rust; the right to the 'Mars' brand is a very 'real' source of wealth.

In a world where the production and sale of knowledge is becoming increasingly important the major assets owned by more and more businesses are likely to be intangible and the weakness of the traditional accounting model in dealing with such assets is becoming an issue of great importance. There is a great danger that the setters of accounting standards will lead the profession towards the land of spurious accuracy in which there are increasingly sophisticated ways of measuring and reporting on some types of assets and liabilities but where others, which may be of greater significance to many entities, are ignored.

In its recent work the Board has tended to distinguish between tangible and intangible assets and has more closely linked the issues surrounding the special case of the intangible asset of goodwill arising from a business combination with intangible assets in general. One consequence is that there are now three key interlinking standards, FRS 10, 11 and 15, which are, however, based on consistent principles, as well as three surviving SSAPs, 19, 9 and 13, which deal with investment properties, stocks and work in process, and research and development. We shall, in this chapter, deal in some depth with the SSAPs and FRS 15 and 10. We shall also discuss some elements of FRS 11 but will return to this standard in Chapter 8 where we deal with business combinations.

The nature of the issues

Before proceeding to the detailed discussion it might be helpful to identify the main issues relating to accounting for assets that need to be considered:

1 What is the actual nature of the asset that is to be recorded? It may be necessary to distinguish between the economic benefits that accrue from the ownership of the asset, the right to acquire the asset (an option), or the right to receive some or all of the returns that will be generated by the asset.

2 Who controls the right to benefit from the use of the asset? This might not be the same entity as its legal owner.

3 What is the cost of acquiring an asset?

4 Does the asset have a finite useful economic life? If so, how should it be depreciated?

5 What is the current value of the asset? This is needed even in historical cost accounts to help decide whether the net book value of the asset should be reduced.

6 To what extent, and how, should current values be recognised in historical cost accounts?

7 The treatment of gains and losses from the revaluation and disposal of assets.

Value to the business

The ASB permits entities to record their assets either on the basis of historical cost or on the basis of their current values. In recent standards, the AASB has attempted to indicate what it means by current value. While it is, for reasons which we will discuss later, not always as clear as it might be, the basis of valuation underlying the treatment of assets in the more recent financial reporting standards is the *value to the business* model that we briefly introduced in Chapter 1 and to which we will return, in more detail, in Chapter 16. The selection of this approach as the most appropriate way of determining the current value of an asset is evidenced by its inclusion in the ASB's Revised Draft Statement of Principles.[1]

The key question in determining an asset's value to the business (the loss the entity would suffer if deprived of the asset) is whether an entity would, if deprived of the asset, replace it. If it would, the loss, and hence the value to the business, is the asset's replacement cost.[2] But in some instances the entity would not choose to replace the asset because the economic benefit that comes from ownership is less than the cost of replacement. In which case the value to the business, which would be less than the replacement cost, would depend on what a 'rational entity' is intending to do with the asset; the critical question is whether the asset is being held for sale or not. If the best thing the entity could do is sell the asset (but not replace it) then the value to the business is the asset's net realisable value; sales proceeds less the future costs of sale.

However, there may be some assets which are not worth replacing but which it would not be sensible to sell, because they are worth more to keep than would be realised through their sale. A good example of such an asset is an old specialised machine which would not be replaced but which is still producing cash flows with a net present value far in excess of its net realisable value. In such a case, the asset would be retained and used rather than sold.

---

[1] *See* Paras 6.27–6.30.

[2] Strictly, the loss includes any consequent costs due, for example, to delays in production. In practice these consequential losses are, unless they are substantial, ignored.

Assets that fall into this intermediate category are valued by reference to their value in use that is defined as:

> The present value of the future cash flows obtainable as a result of the asset's continued use, including those resulting from its ultimate disposal.[3]

The higher of the net realisable and value in use is the assets *recoverable amount*; we will discuss this subject in more detail later in the chapter when we introduce FRS 11.

So when a company exercises its option to show assets at current value, rather than on the basis of historical cost, the value to the business will usually be its replacement cost, or to be more precise in the case of a fixed asset, the replacement cost of that portion of the assets that has not been consumed. If the asset is not worth replacing, its value to the business is its recoverable amount.

All this is shown concisely and graphically in Figure 1.3 in Chapter 1, taken from the Revised Draft Statement of Principles. It can be summarised as follows:

Summary of value to the business concept

Value to the business	=	lower of:	Replacement cost
			Recoverable amount
Recoverable amount	=	higher of:	Value in use
			Net realisable value

The confusion that we mentioned earlier refers to the use of the phrase *fair value* in many of the standards and its unhelpful definition provided in FRS 7 *Fair Values in Acquisition Accounting*. In that standard fair value is defined, at paragraph 2, as:

> The amount at which an asset or liability could be exchanged in an arm's length transaction between informed and willing partners, other than in a forced or liquidation sale.

Thus it seems clear that fair value is a market-based value but one that ignores the different hypothetical situations of a potential buyer or seller. While it is true that one party's replacement cost is another party's net realisable value, life is not as simple as that. There is not only the question of the costs of realisation there is also the question of the entity's relation to the market. Take, as a simple example, the case of an apple. If the two willing parties are an individual consumer and the supermarket from whom he or she purchases the 'asset' the price may be, say, 20 pence but that will far exceed the amount at which those 'two informed and willing' parties, the supermarket and the grower, will exchange for the apple. Hence, in applying the definition attention needs to be given to the position in which the owner of the asset stands in relation to the market.

But the definitional problem does not end there. The problem is compounded by the ASB itself, elsewhere in FRS 7, where it moves away from the seemingly clear implication of paragraph 2 that *fair value* is a market derived value. Consider the following extract from the introductory summary to FRS 7.

> d Fair values should be based on the value at which an asset or liability could be exchanged in an arm's length transaction. The fair value of monetary items should take into account the amounts expected to be received or paid and their timing.

---

[3] FRS 11, Para. 2.

e Unless they can be measured at market value, the fair values of non-monetary assets will normally be based on replacement cost, but should not exceed their recoverable amount as at the date of acquisition. The recoverable amount reflects the condition of the assets on acquisition but not any impairments resulting from subsequent events. The FRS specifies the methods for determining fair values of individual categories of assets and liabilities.

In order to analyse this extract we will also need to examine the definition of *recoverable amount*. This is defined in paragraph 2 of FRS 7 as follows:

The greater of the net realisable value of an asset and, where appropriate, the value in use.

While *value in use* is defined in the same paragraph as:

The present value of the future cash flows obtainable as a result of an asset's continued use, including those resulting from the ultimate disposal of the asset.

This is the same as the present value model of valuation that we introduced in Chapter 3.

In paragraph e of the introduction the ASB seems to suggest, in fact, states explicitly, that replacement cost is not a market value, which seems more than a little odd given that assets are replaced in the market. But what they probably mean is that, if there is no market in that asset, then its fair value should be measured in terms of the current cost of its replacement, in other words the summation of the current costs, or market values, of the asset's components plus the current, or market, price of labour. Sometimes the phrase *depreciated replacement cost* is used which means that the normal depreciation calculations are applied to the current cost of replacement of a new asset to take account of the age and condition of the asset under review.

But there is more. Fair value should not exceed the asset's recoverable amount, which itself might be based on the asset's value in use, which is certainly not a market value as it depends on, for example, the way in which the asset in question can be used in combination with the other assets owned by the entity.

The above discussion may appear to be a little complicated, but we believe the main points are fairly clear. These are that the 'apparent' definition of fair value provided in FRS 7 is profoundly unhelpful (a polite way of saying that it is wrong) and that a close reading of the standard suggests that *fair value* really must mean the same thing as *value to the business*, a position that seems to be confirmed by the ASB in its Draft Statement of Accounting Principles.

Tangible fixed assets

For convenience we will consider the various issues surrounding the accounting treatment of tangible fixed assets in the same order as is found in FRS 15 *Tangible Fixed Assets* that was issued in 1999.[4] The main issues and related provisions of FRS 15 are summarised in Table 4.1.

---

[4] It is perhaps surprising that a standard on such an important topic did not emerge until 1999. The International Accounting Standards Committee (IASC) came much earlier to the field in that the original version of IAS 16 *Property, Plant and Equipment* was issued in 1982 and revised in 1993 and 1998.

Table 4.1 Summary of main issues and related provisions of FRS 15

Issues	Provisions
Initial measurement of tangible fixed assets (TFAs)	At cost
Capitalisation of finance costs	Optional
Write down of TFAs to their recoverable amounts	Required
Treatment of subsequent expenditure on TFAs	Write off to P&L, with three exceptions
Revaluation of TFAs	Optional
Depreciation of TFAs	Required, other than for land and investment properties, but may be immaterial
Treatment of gains and losses on disposal and revaluation of TFAs	Show in P&L if due to consumption of economic benefits otherwise in STRGL, but with exceptions
Disclosure requirements	Various

Tangible fixed assets are defined in FRS 15 as:

> Assets that have physical substance and are held for use in the production or supply of goods or services, for rental to others, or for administrative purposes on a continuing basis in the reporting entity's activities. (Para. 2)

This definition seems clear enough but it does beg at least one important question. To what extent should an item be regarded as a single asset or a collection of assets? A factory is clearly a collection of assets while a motor car would almost always be treated as a single asset. But the question is not always capable of a simple answer. Take, as an example, trailers that are towed by articulated trucks. The tyres of the trailers constitute a substantial portion of the total cost of the trailer but have a much shorter life than that of the bodies of the trailers. The owner of a large trailer fleet might well find it sensible to treat the tyres separately from the bodies and, for example, to apply a different depreciation pattern to the tyres as compared to the bodies.

This is an important topic that FRS 15 touches upon but does not completely resolve. It is recognised that when an asset is made up of two or more major components with substantially different useful economic lives, then each component should be accounted for separately for depreciation purposes (FRS 15, Para. 83). But this, perhaps, does little more than shift the debate to what is the nature of a component.

One way of approaching the question is to consider the acquisition of the asset and argue that an identifiable asset is one which was acquired as a result of a single event but, as described earlier, that possibility has been removed by the ASB's decision to replace singular by plural events in the definition of a tangible fixed assets. Thus, in Appendix IV to FRS 15, which deals with the development of the standard, the Board is reduced to relying on such phrases as that the decision will '*depend upon the individual circumstances*' and expressing the expectation that entities will use '*a common sense approach*' (FRS 15, p. 77). The use of such phrases by standard setters is usually a pretty fair indication that there are issues still to be resolved.

The initial cost of a tangible fixed asset

Whether acquired or self-constructed, the initial cost of a tangible fixed asset is made up of its purchase price and '*any costs directly attributable to bringing it into working condition for its intended use*' (Para 8). Thus general overheads should not be included, but the cost does include, as well as any directly attributable labour costs, *'the incremental costs to the entity that would have been avoided only if the tangible fixed asset had not been constructed or acquired'* (Para. 9(b)).

While it is clear that the Standard calls for the identification of truly marginal costs, it is likely that, in practice, the usual overhead recovery rates will be used as proxy to arrive at the incremental costs.

Of particular interest are the costs that the ASB say should not be included, paragraph 11 states:

> Abnormal costs (such as those relating to design errors, industrial disputes, idle capacity, wasted materials, labour or other resources and production delays) and costs such as operating losses that occur because a revenue earning activity has been suspended during the construction of a tangible fixed asset are not directly attributable to bringing the asset into working condition for its intended use.

This paragraph seems both impractical and inconsistent. Its impractablity stems from the assumption that such things as design errors are 'abnormal'. Anyone who has experience of any large-scale construction knows that designers and engineers do not get everything right the first time and that a reasonable amount of rectification and redesign is part of the normal cost of construction.

The inconsistency is to be found in the different treatments of acquired and self-constructed tangible fixed assets. In the case of an acquisition the cost is the cost, which may or may not be the 'best price' at which it might have been purchased in the market and, in the case of complex assets, is likely to include an element for cost recovery of the 'inefficiencies' listed in paragraph 11 of FRS 15. Hence, it is possible to capitalise the entity's purchasing inefficiency and the supplier's production inefficiency and excess profit, but not the entity's production inefficiency.

A more consistent and realistic approach would be to measure and record the cost actually incurred in constructing the asset, warts (inefficiencies) and all, and then apply the usual tests of impairment to determine whether the carrying value should be written down its recoverable value (*see* p. 99).

Another major problem that can arise in determining the initial cost of an asset occurs when the asset is not acquired in solitary isolation but as part of a package that might, in the extreme, involve the purchase of an entire business. As we will show in Chapter 8 it is necessary, in such circumstances, to attempt to arrive at the fair values, or to be more precise, values to the business, of the assets involved using the bases we described earlier.

The capitalisation of finance costs

Considerable uncertainty surrounds the question of whether finance costs should be capitalised when the asset, say a building, is paid for in advance, often by a series of progress payments, or when an asset takes a considerable time to bring into service. The debate about whether or not finance costs should be capitalised is often conducted with a fervour reminiscent of the more extreme medieval religious conflicts, but the basic point is, however, extremely simple.

The only point at issue is when the cost of finance should be charged to the profit and loss account. If the cost is not capitalised it will be charged over the life of the loan, whereas if it is capitalised the cost will be charged to the profit and loss account over the life of the asset as part of the depreciation expense. The rationale for the view that borrowing costs should be capitalised can best be demonstrated by the use of a simple example.

Assume that the client, A Limited, is offered the following choice by the builder, B Limited: 'The building will take two years to construct, you can either pay £1.0 million now or £1.2 million in two years' time.' If A Limited decides to select the first option, it may well have to borrow the money on which it will have to pay interest. If A Limited selects the second option, it will still have to pay interest, but in this case the interest will be included in the price paid to B Limited.

The above example is extreme, but it does highlight the principles involved. If we assume that both companies have to pay the same interest rate, then A Limited will be in exactly the same position at the end of two years whatever option is selected, and it does not seem sensible to suggest that the cost of the building is different because in one case the interest is paid directly by the client while in the second case the interest is paid via the builder.

The basic stance adopted in FRS 15 is that an entity can choose to capitalise or not to capitalise finance costs but having chosen it must be consistent.

The Board acknowledges that it would have been better if it climbed off the fence and either prohibited the capitalisation of finance costs or made it mandatory. It agrees that there are conceptual arguments for the capitalisation on the grounds of comparability as demonstrated in the above example. However, the ASB was influenced by the argument that, if capitalisation were made mandatory, then companies would demand that notional interest charges should also be capitalised. This would be relevant in cases where entities did not need to resort to borrowing to acquire the fixed asset but instead relied on its internal resources that have, not a direct cost, but an opportunity cost related to the benefit that the entity would have obtained had the resources not been used for this particular project. This is, the Board states 'a contentious issue' and, until an internationally acceptable approach is agreed, the Board will continue with the optional approach that it says is consistent with that taken by IAS 23 *Borrowing Costs* as revised in 1993.

The provisions of FRS 15 relating to the capitalisation of finance costs may be summarised as follows:

1 When an entity adopts a policy of capitalisation of finance costs that are directly attributable to the construction of tangible fixed assets, the finance cost should be included in the cost of the asset and the policy should be consistently applied (Paras 19 and 20).
2 When the entity borrows funds specifically to be used for the project the amount to be capitalised should be restricted to the actual costs incurred and should be capitalised on a gross basis, i.e. before the deduction of any tax relief (Paras 21 and 22).
3 If the funds used are part of the entity's general borrowings the amount to be capitalised should be based on the average cost of capital but in calculating the cost funds raised for specific purposes should be excluded (Paras 23 and 24).
4 Capitalisation should begin when:
  (a) finance costs are being incurred and
  (b) expenditure for the asset are being incurred and
  (c) activities to get the asset ready for use are in progress (Para. 25).
5 Capitalisation should stop when all the activities are substantially complete. If the asset is being completed in parts the relevant capitalisation should cease when the part is completed (Paras 29 and 30).

6 Where a policy of capitalisation is adopted that fact should be disclosed together with:
(a) the aggregate amount of finance costs included in the cost of tangible fixed assets;
(b) the amount of finance costs capitalised during the period;
(c) the amount of finance costs recognised in the profit and loss account during the period;
(d) the capitalisation rate used to determine the amount of finance costs capitalised during the period (Para. 31).

The writing down of new tangible fixed assets to their recoverable amounts

This is, as we shall see, a main theme of FRS 11 'The impairment of fixed assets and goodwill' and we deal with this later in the chapter. At this stage it is necessary to comment on paragraphs 32 and 33 that state that when a new tangible fixed asset is acquired, either through purchase or construction, that it should not be carried at an amount that exceeds its *recoverable amount*. This concept was discussed on p. 76.

Subsequent expenditure

'Subsequent expenditure' is a relatively new, useful term that covers all expenditure on the tangible fixed asset after it has come into use.

One of the more slippery areas of accounting is the distinction between repairs and enhancement with the temptations often pulling in opposite directions. The enterprise wishing to minimise its tax bill would tend to write off as much as possible to repairs, while an enterprise more concerned with showing a good profit would opt for capitalisation.

FRS 15 is clear that expenditure to ensure that a fixed asset maintains its previously assessed standard of performance should be written off to the profit and loss account as it is incurred (Para. 34). The circumstances under which subsequent expenditure can be capitalised are set out in paragraph 36, which we will reproduce in full.

Subsequent expenditure should be capitalised in three circumstances:
(a) where the subsequent expenditure provides an enhancement of the economic benefits of the tangible fixed asset in excess of the previously assessed standard of performance.
(b) where a component of the tangible fixed asset that has been treated separately for depreciation purposes and depreciated over its individual useful economic life is replaced or restored.
(c) where the subsequent expenditure relates to a major inspection or overhaul of a tangible fixed asset that restores the economic benefits of the asset that have been consumed by the entity and have already been reflected in depreciation.

The drafting of the paragraph is not all that clear but the concepts are pretty simple. Paragraph 36(a) states that capitalisation is appropriate when the asset has been improved in some way, such as extending its life or improving its efficiency. Paragraph 36(c) refers to situations, such as those found in the airline industry, where there is a mandatory inspection and overhaul of the asset every, say, three years. Then the cost of the inspection and the overhaul can be capitalised and written off over the period until the next inspection is due. Paragraph 36(b) takes us back to the question of when an asset is an individual asset or a bundle of assets. As mentioned earlier, an asset with two or more major components may have different depreciation patterns for each of the components and this clause is simply a consequence of this.

The revaluation of tangible fixed assets

The various attempts to introduce a system of financial reporting based primarily on current values are described elsewhere in this book. In this section we will be concerned with what has been termed 'modified historical cost accounting' where some items are carried in the balance sheet at their current values and some are not. While in the USA historical costs accounts have required the writing down of assets, by, for example, depreciation, revaluation in an upward direction has not been permitted,[5] the revaluing of certain assets has long been the practice in the UK, and has been given additional legislative force by the inclusion of the alternative accounting rules in the Companies Act 1985.

In previous pronouncements the ASB and its predecessor, the Accounting Standards Committee, set out the arguments for and against the greater use of current values, sometimes tending to favour such a practice[6] and sometimes not.[7] In FRS 15 the ASB's position seems to be one of studied neutrality as evidenced by the awe inspiring declaration in a paragraph printed in bold and hence part of the standard itself that

> Tangible fixed assets should be revalued where the entity adopts a policy of revaluation. (Para. 42)

So it should only be done when you want to do it!

Given that the entity has adopted a policy of revaluation the standard sets out the parameters within which the policy should be applied. These are summarised below

1 The policy should be applied consistently to all assets within an individual class of tangible fixed assets but need not be applied to all classes of such assets (Para. 42).
2 Assets subject to the policy of revaluation should be included in the balance sheet at their current values (Para. 43).

Classification of tangible fixed assets

In the UK the formats for financial reporting contain three groups for tangible fixed assets:

- Land and buildings
- Plant and machinery
- Fixtures, fittings, tools and equipment

However, in applying the provisions of this standard entities may adopt narrower classes, e.g. freehold properties. Little guidance is given as to what would be an appropriate class other than the not very forceful phrase that 'entities may, within reason, adopt . . . narrower classes' (Para. 62).

There is one exception to the rule that requires all assets within the same class to be revalued. These are assets that are held outside the UK or Republic of Ireland for which it is impossible to obtain a reliable valuation. Such assets can continue to be carried at historical cost but the fact that this override has been used must be stated.

---

[5] One of the authors used a machine with an American spell check which gave an error message every time he typed revalued.
[6] See *Accounting for the Effects of Changing Prices* published in 1986.
[7] See *ED51 Accounting for Fixed Assets and Revaluations* issued in 1990.

Frequency

Most quoted entities have made use of the alternative accounting rules but have generally done so on a spasmodic basis. An analysis of the *Company Reporting Database* disclosed that about 65 per cent of the companies making up the database had revalued certain of their assets, but in about half of these cases the companies concerned had not revalued any of their assets within the last five years.[8] Thus it seems that in addition to 'historical cost accounting' and 'current value accounting' there has been added a new system 'obsolete current values'. This third model is obviously unhelpful in that it tells the user nothing of value. Historical cost shows what the asset cost, current values say what they are now worth but out-of-date values are of no utility.

Hence, the standard requires that, if an entity opts for a policy of revaluation in respect of a particular class of tangible fixed assets, the balance sheet should reflect the current values of those assets. This does not mean, however, that revaluation need be an annual process (Para. 44). In general, the requirements of the standard would be satisfied if there were a full revaluation every five years with an interim valuation in year 3. In addition an interim valuation should be carried out in any year where it is 'likely that there has been a material change in value' (Para. 45).

Special considerations apply to entities that hold a portfolio of non-specialised properties.[9] In such cases it is suggested that a full valuation could be achieved on a rolling programme designed to cover all the properties over a five-year cycle, together with interim valuations where it is likely that there has been a material change in value.

We have in the preceeding paragraphs been free with the phrases *'full valuation'*, *'interim valuation'* and *'likely to be a material change in value'*. What do these phrases actually mean?

The differences between full and interim valuations are described in the case of properties but not for other types of tangible fixed assets. For properties a full valuation would include a detailed inspection of the property, enquiries of local planning authorities, solicitors etc. and research into market transactions of similar properties and the identification of market trends (Para. 47). The less detailed interim valuation would involve the last of these together with the confirmation that there have been no significant changes either to the physical fabric of the property and an inspection (but not a detailed inspection) if there are indications that such would be necessary (Para. 48).

No effective guidance is provided as to what is meant by a material change. In attempting this the standard does little more than restate its position by explaining that 'A material change in value is a change in value that would reasonably influence the decision of a user of the accounts' (Para. 52).

Who should make the valuations?

With only the exception referred to below revaluations should be made by qualified valuers. These may be internal, employed by the entity, but if they are, then the valuation process should be reviewed by a qualified external valuer.

The exception relates to those assets for which there exists an active second-hand market, as is the case for used cars, or where suitable indices exist that enable the

---

[8] FRS 15, p. 73.

[9] FRS 15 follows the definitions used by the Royal Institute of Chartered Surveyors (RICS) that are reproduced in Appendix 1 to the standard. In summary non-specialised buildings are those which can be used for a range of purposes.

entity's directors to establish the asset's value with reasonable certainty. In such instances the valuations can be made by the directors but if this option is selected the valuations should be done an annual basis.

Bases of valuation

Assets other than properties

This is a key provision but, for the reasons stated earlier, (*see* p. 76) the less than well-informed reader might understandably be confused. The key basic principle for the revaluation of all tangible assets, other than property, is set out in paragraph 59:

> Tangible fixed assets other than properties should be valued using market value, where possible. Where market value is not obtainable, assets should be valued on the basis of depreciated replacement cost.

As we explained earlier the 'practical interpretation' of this paragraph leads to the use of the value-to-the business model.

Properties

A distinction must be made between *specialised properties* and *non-specialised properties*. Drawing on the work of the RICS, the ASB states that specialised properties are 'those which, due to their specialised nature, are rarely, if ever, sold on the open market for single occupation for continuation of their existing use, except as part of a sale of the business in occupation' (page 57). Examples of specialised properties listed include oil refineries, power stations, hospitals, universities and museums. In addition a property may be regarded as specialised if, although otherwise normal, it is of such a substantial size given its location that there is no market for such properties.

Valuation of specialised properties

Because of the lack of a market for such assets they should be valued by reference to their depreciated replacement cost (Para. 53(c)).

Valuation of non-specialised properties

It will come as no surprise to be told that the value of non-specialised properties should be based on their market values. However, an important difference between properties and most other tangible assets is that the value of properties depends heavily on the use to which the property is put. Consider as an example a warehouse in the middle of an area which had once been industrial but which is now increasingly residential. The value of the property as a warehouse might be much less than it would if it is used as a shell for conversion into flats, but, even so, the entity needs a warehouse and would, if deprived of the asset, replace it. Thus following the principles underlying value to the business, the asset should be valued on the basis of its replacement cost. But we must be clear as to what is being replaced, in this case it is a warehouse not a potential housing site. Hence, FRS 15 specifies that non-specialised assets:

> should be valued on the basis of existing use value (EUV), with the addition of notional directly attributable acquisition costs where material. Where the open market value (OMV) is materially different from EUV, the OMV and the reasons for the difference should be disclosed in the notes to the accounts. (Para. 53(a))

If the asset is surplus to the entity's requirements the above argument does not hold and hence these should be valued on the basis of OMV less any expected material directly attributable selling costs (Para. 53(c)).

Detailed definitions of EUV and OMV are provided in the standard. Both models are based on an opinion of the best price at which the sale of an interest in the property would have been completed unconditionally for cash consideration at the date of valuation, on the assumption that there is a good market for the property and specifically excludes the possibility of a bid by a prospective purchaser with a special interest. The last of these factors means that the value would not be enhanced by the possibility that a specific potential purchaser, perhaps the owner of the adjacent property, might be prepared to pay more for the property than anyone else.

The essential difference between the two bases, EUV and OMV, is that the estimate of existing use value is based on the additional assumption 'that the property can be used for the foreseeable future only for the existing use' (page 60).

Reporting losses and gains on revaluation

There can be no question that losses on revaluation reduce owners' equity and gains on revaluation enhance it. The only issue that presently detains us is how the loss or gain should be reported; should it be through the profit and loss account or through the statement of total recognised gains and losses (STRGL)?

In FRS 15 a distinction is made between those losses that are caused by 'clear consumption of economic benefits' and other losses. A loss of the first type, which is regarded as being akin to depreciation, is usually due to a factor which is intrinsic to the asset, such as physical deterioration, while the second type of loss may be characterised by a general fall of value in the type of asset concerned.

The starting position is that 'All revaluation losses that are caused by a clear consumption of economic benefits should be recognised in the profit and loss account' (Para. 65).

Otherwise losses should be recognised in the STRGL.

Now for the complications. If the carrying amount falls below the depreciated historical cost then, in general, any further revaluation losses, whatever their cause, should be recognised in the profit and loss account. But there is an exception to this where it can be shown that the recoverable amount exceeds the revalued amount, in which case the loss should be recorded in the STRGL to the extent that the recoverable amount exceeds the revalued amount (Para. 65).

In order to help understand this it might be helpful to be reminded that a non-specialised property is valued by reference to its OMV. It may well be that the value of the property has fallen, because of a general fall in the market, but the directors of the entity can demonstrate that the recoverable amount (the present value of the cash flows that flow from the ownership of the asset) is greater than the OMV. The asset is still written down to its OMV, and owners' equity reduced, but as the loss is not regarded as resulting from a consumption of economic benefit it can be recorded in the STRGL.

Revaluation gains should in general be recognised in the STRGL other than to the extent that gain reverses revaluation losses on the same asset that were recognised in the profit and loss account (Para. 63).

There is one slight twist if any part of the gain is credited to the profit and loss account, that may be relevant when, as a result of the reduction in the carrying value, the depreciation charged to date is less than it would have been had the asset not been written down. In such a case the credit to the profit and loss must be reduced by the amount of the 'lost depreciation', thus restoring the position to what would have been had the reduction in value had not taken place (Para. 64).

Reporting losses and gains on disposal

The profit or loss on the disposal of a tangible fixed asset should be accounted for in the profit and loss account of the period in which the disposal occurs as the difference between the disposal proceeds and the carrying amount, whether carried at historical cost (less any provisions made) or at a valuation. (Para. 72)

This formulation that follows the relevant provision of FRS 3, Para. 21, does give rise to a serious inconsistency. If the entity had, at some stage in the past, revalued the asset the revaluation gain would not have passed through the profit and loss account but instead been recorded in the STRGL. But if the asset had not been revalued the whole of the gain goes through the profit and loss account. The ASB recognises that this is inconsistent and in FRED 17, the exposure draft for FRS 15, it proposed that the whole of the gain should appear in the STRGL.

For a number of reasons the responses made it clear that this proposal was not acceptable. It seems that the main reasons for this reaction was the view that it would be premature to make the change in advance of a more far reaching review of the Statement of Total Recognised Gains and Losses and that the proposed treatment was inconsistent with the treatment of gains and losses on the disposal of businesses, subsidiaries and investments. Thus it appears, as we discuss in Chapter 6, that further changes are on their way.

Disclosures relating to revaluation

Paragraph 74 specifies what has to be disclosed including details of the timing of valuations, the names and status of those who carried them out as well as the total amount of material notional directly attributable acquisition costs or expected selling costs that are included in the valuation.

Depreciation

Prior to the issue of FRS 15 depreciation merited its own standard. It was the subject of SSAP 12 that was issued in 1977, amended in 1981 and revised in 1987. The 1977 version was firmly rooted in the historical cost tradition while the 1987 revision was relevant to both historical cost and current value accounting.

To those well versed in the ethos of historical cost accounting and the mechanics of double entry bookkeeping depreciation is a pretty straightforward matter. The asset that the entity owns will be a source of economic benefit for a number of time periods and hence the recognition of the cost of the asset should be spread over the same period. To such folk, depreciation is all about spreading the cost or, to use a clumsier expression, expensing the asset.

To many other people, including many who run successful businesses, the idea is not so simple because they have difficulty in grasping the concept that the accountant wants to recognise the using up of an asset. The layman has difficulty in distinguishing this from a fall in the value of the asset and becomes completely confused when told that depreciation is necessary in a period in which the value of the asset is actually increasing.

Well brought-up accountants, on the other hand, know we must distinguish between two events; the consumption of a portion of the asset and the increase in value of that part of the asset that remains:

> The fundamental objective of depreciation is to reflect in operating profit the cost of the use of the tangible fixed assets (i.e. amount of economic benefits consumed) in the period. This requires a charge to operating profit even if the asset has risen in value or been revalued. (FRS 15, Para. 78)

Business people are generally not so understanding and their antipathy towards what people saw as a one-sided approach was even stronger under a system of historical cost accounting. Thus one element of the continuing saga of Accounting Standards for depreciation is the desire of standard setters to ensure that all assets other than land, the one asset which standard setters agree might not be consumed, are depreciated and pressure from the business community to identify other exceptions. Investment Properties provide an interesting example of an asset about which there has been a continuing debate. The requirement that Investment Properties be depreciated was included in the original 1977 version of SSAP 12 but was dropped, after pressure from property companies, from the 1981 version. In that year the ASC issued SSAP 19 'Accounting for Investment Properties' which, although threatened with review, is still in issue. We discuss SSAP 19 later in this chapter.

As we shall see, the ASB accepts that there are some assets either whose life is so long or whose likely residual value is so high that an annual depreciation charge would not be material. They do not, it must be noted, retreat from the position that all tangible assets (except land) depreciate, but they are prepared to concede that some do not depreciate very much. FRS 15 is therefore more flexible than its predecessors in accepting that depreciation need not be recognised in certain limited circumstances, but it extracts a price, the *Impairment Review*. If depreciation is not to be recognised on the grounds of immateriality the entity must undertake an impairment review. We will discuss this topic later in the chapter and at this point simply explain that an impairment review is a systematic process that tests whether an asset's carrying value exceeds its recoverable amount.

Depreciation is more easily applied to a single identifiable asset whose cost and condition can be relatively easily measured and whose economic contribution to the entity easily assessed, the latter point being relevant to decisions as to whether the carrying value of the asset should be reduced to its recoverable value. But life is not always as conveniently simple as this and assets are often used in combination. A particularly noteworthy feature of FRS 15 is the way in which it deals with the topic of combined and inter-related assets (*see* p. 89).

FRS 15 and depreciation

The topics covered in the depreciation section of FRS 15 can be summarised as follows:

- General principles
- Changes in the methods used to account for depreciation
- Changes in estimates of remaining useful life and residual value
- Combined assets
- Renewals accounting
- Disclosure

General principles

Depreciation is defined as:

> The measure of the cost or revalued amount of the economic benefits of the tangible fixed asset that have been consumed during the period.
>
> Consumption includes the wearing out, using up or other reductions in the useful economic life of a tangible fixed asset whether arising from use, effluxion of time or obsolescence through other changes in technology or demand for the goods and services produced by the asset. (Para. 2)

While the underlying principle is:

> The depreciable amount of a tangible fixed asset should be allocated on a systematic basis over its useful economic life. The depreciation method used should reflect as fairly as possible the pattern in which the asset's economic benefits are consumed by the entity. The depreciation charge for each period should be recognised as an expense in the profit and loss account unless it is permitted to be included in the carrying amount of another asset. (Para. 77)

Depreciable amount is defined as:

> The cost of a tangible fixed asset (or, where an asset is revalued, the revalued amount) less its residual value. (p. 10)

The final sentence in paragraph 77 is logically necessary if depreciation is to be included in the costs of stocks and work in process or the cost of a self-constructed fixed asset.

There are, of course, a number of methods of charging depreciation and two, straight line and reducing balance, are described in the text of the standard. In general, the method of depreciation employed should be consistent with the pattern of consumption of the benefit. If, proportionally, greater benefit were derived in the earlier years of ownership then reducing balance would likely be the more appropriate method. While, if the pattern of consumption is uncertain, the Board notes that the straight-line method is usually employed (Para. 81).

As we noted earlier one of the more interesting features of FRS 15 is its acceptance that the depreciation charge may not always be material. The drafting of the relevant part of the standard is a little strange in that it does not say that depreciation need not be recognised but instead says what must happen when it is not recognised.

> Tangible fixed assets, other than non-depreciable land, should be reviewed for impairment, in accordance with FRS 11, at the end of each reporting period when either:
> (a) no depreciation charge is made on the grounds that it would be immaterial(either because of the length of the estimated remaining useful life or because the estimated residual value of the tangible fixed asset is not materially different from the carrying value of the asset); or
> (b) the estimated remaining economic life of the tangible fixed asset exceeds 50 years.
> (Para. 89)

Of the two grounds for immateriality, high residual value is generally more problematic than long life, as assets with very long lives, such as paintings and sculptures, can usually be readily identified. This is much less true of the high residual value group and hence the standard sets out a number of factors which could be used to justify the case for immateriality, including whether the assets are regularly maintained and whether, in the past, similar assets have been sold for amounts close to their carrying values.

Changes in the method of depreciation

A change is only permitted on the grounds that the new method will give a fairer presentation of the results and financial position (Para. 82). The change is not to be regarded as a change in accounting policy and hence the carrying amount of the asset at the date of change is simply depreciated, using the new method, over its remaining useful life.

Changes in estimated useful remaining life and residual value

The useful remaining economic life of a tangible fixed asset should be reviewed at the end of each accounting period if 'expectations are significantly different from previous estimates' (Para. 93) while 'Where the residual value is material it should be reviewed at the end of each reporting period' (Para. 95).

The standard, in respect of remaining useful life, seems rather unhelpful and tautological in that it is not possible to know whether expectations have changed without carrying out a review, albeit a superficial one.

The residual value should be measured on the basis of the same prices as apply to the carrying value of the asset, either the prices at acquisition or subsequent valuation.

Note that one review, that for assets with long lives, only has to be carried out if there are significantly different expectations while the other, for assets with high residual values, has to be done annually. But this does depend on what is regarded as material in the case of the residual value. Of course if it is very material, depreciation may not be recognised in which case an annual impairment review would be required.

The accounting consequences in changes of estimates of both types are the same, in each case no change is made to past results and the current carrying value is written off over the revised period or on the basis of the new assumption of residual value.

Combined assets

When an asset is made up of two or more of what the standard describes as 'major components' that have substantially different economic lives then each component should be treated separately for the purposes of depreciation (Para. 83). This is, of course, an approach that has been adopted for many years in the case of land and buildings but there are many other circumstances where it might sensibly be applied.

Renewals accounting

Renewals accounting is a technique that has been developed to deal with what might be termed an *infrastructure system* or *network*. An example of such might be a subway or light railway system. The trains, stations and other major identifiable assets can be treated as separate items but the system also includes, and depends on, a myriad of wires, computer chips and other small components. Such a situation poses some interesting questions. Should the cost of the small components be written off in the year of acquisition or should they be treated as other tangible fixed assets (for tangible fixed assets they surely are) and written off over their useful economic lives?

Neither approach is satisfactory. The first is unsatisfactory because it might produce a very unrealistic charge to profit and loss that would not adequately reflect the economic benefit consumed. It also would allow for manipulation of the reported profit, cut back essential expenditure if you want to increase profit, spend heavily in advance if you want to reduce profit. The alternative approach is unrealistic in a practical sense, in that it would cost far too much to account individually for the millions of small components.

Renewals accounting can – in appropriate circumstances – be used to overcome the dilemma. The use of renewal accounting depends on knowing the level of expenditure required to maintain the operating capacity of the system. As an example it might be agreed that it requires £20 million per annum to be spent on the replacement of the smaller components in order to maintain the operating capacity of the system, which might be defined as the ability to operate the same number of trains travelling at the same average speed at the same level of reliability. Then, under renewals accounting, £20 million is the annual depreciation charge to be made to the profit and loss account and added to accumulated depreciation. The actual expenditure per year is capitalised and added to the cost of the asset. Hence, if the entity actually spends £20 million in a year, the carrying value would be maintained, if less, the carrying value, is reduced and if more it would be increased. Note the primacy that is given to the charge to the profit and loss account. Assuming that £20 million is indeed a good estimate of the average cost then £20 million is the annual expense irrespective of the pattern of spending.

The treatment is not without its theoretical problems, for it could be argued that any excess expenditure over the £20 million is in effect a prepayment because less will have to be incurred in future years, while the effect of spending less is to create something very akin to an accrued expense. In other words would it be better to reflect the differences between actual and planned expenditure in the working capital part of the balance sheet rather than in the cost of fixed assets?

In practice it is unlikely that the differences between planned and actual expenditure would be all that great in that one of the conditions that has to be satisfied, if renewals accounting is to be used, is that the system is mature, or in a steady state, and that the annual cost of maintenance is relatively constant (Para. 99). The other significant condition is that the required level of annual expenditure is derived from an asset management plan that has been certified by a suitably qualified and independent person (Para. 97).

Disclosure requirements relating to depreciation

The disclosure requirements are to be found in paragraph 100. In summary they require that, for each class of tangible fixed asset, the following be shown:

- the depreciation method used;
- the useful economic lives or the rates of depreciation used;
- the financial effects of any changes in estimates of either the remaining useful life or residual value, but only if material;
- the cost, or revalued amount, accumulated depreciation and net carrying amount at the beginning of the financial period and at the balance sheet date;
- a reconciliation of the movements.

In addition, paragraph 102 requires that if there has been a change in the method of depreciation, the effect, if material, and the reason for the change should be disclosed.

Compliance with International Accounting Standards

The IAS equivalent to FRS 15 is IAS 16 *Property, Plant and Equipment* (revised 1998) but IAS 23 *Borrowing Costs* (revised 1993) also contains some relevant material.

There are no differences in principle between the UK and International Standards. The most significant differences in approach are as below.

- IAS 16, like FRS 15, requires that if a policy of revaluation is adopted tangible fixed assets should be shown at current values. The difference is that the International Standard defines current values as *fair values* that are usually market values or otherwise depreciated replacement costs while FRS 15 relies on the better developed value-to-the-business approach where the current value is the lower of replacement cost and recoverable amount.
- FRS 15 specifies that revaluation losses that are due to the consumption of economic benefits be recognised in the profit and loss account. IAS 16 does not contain this provision.
- IAS 16 is more restrictive in its approach to losses that can be charged to the STRGL; only those that reverse revaluation losses can be so charged. FRS 15 requires that other losses should also be recognised in the STRGL to the extent that the asset's recoverable amount exceeds its revalued amount.
- Only FRS 15 requires that an impairment review (*see* p. 99) be undertaken at the end of each reporting period where depreciation is not charged on the grounds of immateriality or where the remaining useful life exceeds 50 years.
- IAS 16 includes a number of additional disclosure requirements.

Investment properties

One important group of tangible fixed asset, investment properties, needs to be considered separately because of the different accounting treatment that applies in their case. Investment properties have been a major feature of two interrelated debates; to depreciate or not depreciate and to revalue or not to revalue.

The original, 1977, version of the first standard on depreciation, SSAP 12, did not exclude investment properties from its scope and required all buildings, including those held for investment, to be depreciated. This was fiercely contested by property companies whose profits would, of course, be substantially reduced if they had to provide for depreciation on their buildings. It was argued that the profits of property companies would be distorted if depreciation were charged to the profit and loss account while the surpluses on revaluation had, under the provisions which were then in force of SSAP 6 ('Extraordinary Items and Prior Year Adjustments'), to be credited to reserves.

The ASC's response (which may, according to taste, be described as reflecting the committee's weakness or flexibility) was to allow companies owning investment properties exemption from this provision and this exemption was confirmed with the issue, in 1981, of SSAP 19 'Accounting for Investment Properties', which specified the conditions under which depreciation need not be charged on properties held as investments.

It was argued in SSAP 19 that, for the proper appreciation of the position of the enterprise, it is of prime importance for users of the accounts to be aware of the current value of the investment properties and the changes in their values. For this purpose investment properties are defined as an interest in land and/or buildings:

(a) in respect of which construction work and development have been completed; and
(b) that is held for its investment potential, any rental income being negotiated at arm's length.

The following are specifically excluded from the definition.

(a) A property that is owned and occupied by a company for its own purposes is not an investment property.
(b) A property let to and occupied by another group company is not an investment property for the purposes of its own accounts or the group accounts.

The standard was revised in July 1994, to take account of the introduction of the new performance statement, the statement of total recognised gains and losses, but otherwise the revised version is virtually identical to the original version and reflects more the attitudes of 1981 than those of 1994.

In outline, SSAP 19 specifies:

• 'Investment properties should not be subject to a depreciation charge as otherwise required by SSAP 12 (now FRS 15), except for properties held on a lease which should be depreciated on the basis set out in SSAP 12 at least over the period when the unexpired term is 20 years or less' (SSAP 19, Para. 10). In other words, leaseholds with more than 20 years to run can be depreciated while other leases must be depreciated.
• Investment properties should be included in the balance sheet at their 'open market value', which might be defined as the best price at which the asset might reasonably be expected to be sold. The bases of valuation should be disclosed in a note to the accounts.
• The names of the persons making the valuation, or particulars of their qualification, should be disclosed together with the bases of valuation used by them. If the person making the valuation is an employee or officer of the company or group that owns the property, this should be disclosed.
• The carrying value of the investment properties and the investment revaluation reserve should be displayed prominently.
• With one exception (see below), changes in the market value of investment properties should not be taken to the profit and loss account but should be treated as a movement on an investment revaluation reserve and, consequently, be included in the statement of total recognised gains and losses. The exception is when there is a deficit on an individual property that is expected to be permanent; in this case the deficit should be charged to the profit and loss account.[10]

The ASB notes that the application of the standard will usually represent a departure from the legal requirement to provide depreciation on any fixed asset which has a limited economic life, but justifies this on the grounds that this treatment will more closely adhere to the overriding requirement to provide a true and fair view. In such circumstances the financial statements must include a statement giving particulars of the departures from the specific requirements of the Act with the reasons for and effect of the departure.[11]

Not everyone would agree with the stance, originally taken by the ASC in 1981 and confirmed by the ASB in 1994, in that it does appear that a fuller, truer and fairer picture would be revealed if both the increase in value and the proportion of the total value that has been consumed by the passage of time were shown in the financial statements.

---

[10] There is an exception to the exception in the case of investment companies and unit trusts where deficits on individual investments properties may only be shown in the statement of total recognized gains and losses (SSAP 19, p.13, as amended 1994).
[11] Companies Act 1985, Sec. 222(5) as amended by Companies Act 1989, Sec. 4.

It does appear that the life of SSAP 19 is limited in that in FRS 15 the ASB makes the point that it was considering the treatment of investment properties, in tandem with the international project on this subject. The board believe that it is appropriate to maintain the status quo until this work is completed[12] and hence investment properties were excluded from the scope of FRS 15.

Intangible assets

Some intangible assets are very identifiable and separable; patents, the right to use a famous brand name, is an example. Intangible assets like these can be easily bought and sold. But this is not true for other types of intangible assets.

In this *Information Age* the skill and loyalty of its staff may be an entity's only significant asset. While this is an economically significant asset it is not, since the abolition of slavery, readily saleable. In practice the only way that the owner of such an entity can sell this asset is to dispose of the company that employs the skilled staff, in which case the sales proceeds will be very much greater than the sum of the carrying values of the assets and liabilities that have been recocognised and there will, in accounting terms, be a massive amount of goodwill resulting from the sale of the entity.

In many cases it is very difficult to disentangle intangible assets from other residual elements that make up goodwill. This is the reason why the ASB has chosen to deal with both goodwill and intangible assets in the same Standard, FRS 10 *Goodwill and Intangible Assets*.

In the Discussion Paper[13] that preceded FRS 10 the Board expressed the view that certain intangible assets such as brands and publishing titles could not be disposed of separately from the business and that there was, in any event, no generally agreed way of valuing such assets. Hence, the Board intimated that it was of a mind to specify that intangible assets that were part of a business acquisition should be subsumed within the value attributable to goodwill. This was met with strong opposition as corporate respondents said that such assets were critical to their business and that it was important to account for them separately (App. III, Para. 22).

The Board accepted that point and hence accepted that intangible assets can be separated from goodwill and shown as such, as long as they satisfy the legal and conceptual requirements for identifiability and can, at the time they are initially recognised, be measured with sufficient reliability. However, given what will in many cases be a pretty hazy distinction, the second principle underlying FRS 10 is that in order to avoid the results of the entity being shown in a more, or less, favourable light, merely by classifying expenditure as an intangible asset rather than goodwill, the accounting treatment of intangible assets and goodwill should be aligned (App. III, Para. 23).

We will return to FRS 10 in Chapter 8 when dealing with goodwill, and in this chapter we shall concentrate on the standard's treatment of intangible assets.

FRS 10 and its treatment of intangible assets

In this section of the chapter we will discuss the following topics:

- the nature of intangible assets and the conditions necessary for recognition as a separate asset

---

[12] FRS 15, p. 94.
[13] *Goodwill and Intangible Assets*, ASB, 1993.

- the determination of their carrying value at initial recognition
- the depreciation of intangible assets
- the revaluation of intangible assets
- disclosure requirements.

The nature of intangible assets

Intangible assets are defined as

> Non-financial fixed assets that do not have a physical substance but are identifiable and are controlled by the entity through custody or legal rights. (Para. 2)

Identifiable assets are, in line with company legislation, defined in FRS 10 as assets that are capable of being disposed of without disposing of a business of the entity.[14] So the test is, in simple terms, can the asset be sold without forcing the entity to get out of one or more of its businesses?

It is recognised that control can be exercised other than through the possession of legal rights, it can also be exercised through *custody*. An example of control through custody is technical or intellectual knowledge that is maintained secretly.

Initial carrying value

In determining the value at initial recognition we need to consider three cases – *intangible assets purchased separately from a business, internally developed intangible assets*, and *those that are purchased as part of the acquisition of a business*.

The first is straightforward, an intangible asset purchased separately **should** be capitalised at its cost (Para. 9).

An internally developed intangible fixed asset **may** be capitalised only if it has a readily ascertainable market value (Para. 14). Note that in this case the entity has the choice whether to capitalise the asset. In the case of purchased intangible assets capitalisation is mandatory as long as the specified conditions are satisfied. This means that it is very difficult to compare the results of companies in industries where, by the nature of the business, internally generated intangible assets are of significance.

The test of whether the internally generated asset can be recognised is whether it has a readily ascertainable market value which is a value that is established by reference to a market where:

(a) the asset belongs to a homogenous population of assets that are equivalent in all material respects; and

(b) an active market, evidenced by frequent transactions, exists for that population of assets. (Para. 2)

This is a stringent condition for recognition and would preclude assets such as brands and publishing titles that are one-offs that are not equivalent 'in all material respects' to a group of other assets.[15]

The third type of asset, an intangible fixed asset acquired as part of a purchase of a business:

> should be capitalised separately from goodwill if its value can be measured reliably on initial recognition, It should initially be recorded at its fair value, subject to the constraint that,

---

[14] This seems to be a case where the use of the word does not accord with its basic meaning, as there are many 'identifiable' assets, such as the human resource of a business that are readily identifiable but do not satisfy the accounting definition.

[15] As we will explain later in this chapter FRS 10 does not cover the potential intangible assets that might result from development expenditure.

unless the asset has a readily ascertainable market value, the fair value should be limited to an amount that does not create negative goodwill arising on acquisition. (Para. 10)

So there are two tests for recognition. Is the asset separable and, if so, can it be measured reliably?

The measurement test depends on whether it is possible to determine the asset's *fair value*. We discussed the problematic definition of fair value provided by FR 7 earlier in the chapter, and would repeat our conclusion here, that is that fair values may well be based on market values but can be arrived at in other ways. In the case of intangible fixed assets FRS 10 recognises that many intangible assets are unique and are not traded in the market and the ASB accepts that acceptable techniques for their valuation have been developed including multiples of turnover and, where these exist, they can be used to provide a fair value for intangible assets.

In order to avoid the creation of negative goodwill a restriction is placed on the fair value that can be assigned to intangible assets. The fair value is reduced until the negative value of goodwill disappears unless, that is, the carrying value of the intangible asset satisfies the more stringent test of being based on a readily ascertainable market value.

Depreciation of intangible fixed assets

We have already, in the context of FRS 15, discussed the arguments as to whether all fixed assets, other than land, should be depreciated. Intangible assets provide, of course, a very fruitful field for this debate.

FRS 10 takes a more relaxed line in the need to depreciate than FRS 15 where the line was 'all tangible fixed assets, other than land, depreciate but the amount may not be material'. It is recognised in FRS 10 that certain intangible assets, not possessing a physical form which must wither with time, can have an indefinite life. Thus:

> Where goodwill and intangible assets are regarded as having indefinite useful economic lives, they should not be amortised. (Para. 17; note the should.)

The estimation of the useful life of a fixed asset is usually fairly subjective but this is particularly true in the case of intangible assets. The standard does specifically warn against using the uncertainty of the estimate as grounds for selecting an unrealistically short life (Para. 22). In addition to the impairment reviews, the useful lives of intangible assets should be reviewed at the end of each reporting period and revised if necessary (Para. 33).

The standard draws a distinction between those assets whose estimated lives are less than 20 years and those which have either an estimated life of 20 or more years or an indefinite life. The choice of 20 years as the cut-off is 'based largely on judgement' (App. III, Para. 33).

Assets with life not exceeding 20 years

Because of the greater subjectivity, and because of the problems of separability when they are acquired as part of a purchase of a business, intangible assets are subject to more rigorous requirements than tangible assets. Intangible assets must be the subject of an impairment review.

(a) at the end of the first full financial year following the acquisition (the 'first year' review): and

(b) in other periods if events or changes in circumstances indicate that the carrying values may not be recoverable. (Para. 34)

Assets with a life of 20 years or more including those with an indefinite life

There is a rebuttable presumption that the useful life of purchased goodwill and intangible assets are limited to periods of 20 years or less. This presumption can be rebutted only if:

(a) the durability of the acquired business or intangible asset can be demonstrated and justifies estimating life to exceed 20 years: and

(b) the goodwill or intangible asset is capable of continued measurement (so that annual impairment reviews will be feasible). (Para. 19)

Thus a case has to be made to justify a life of 20 years or more and an annual impairment review is required.

Revaluation of intangible assets

Only an intangible asset that has a readily ascertainable market value (*see* p. 94) may be revalued to its market value. If such a policy is selected then, in line with the provisions of FRS 15 for tangible assets, if one asset is revalued all intangible assets of the same class must be revalued and the operation must be repeated sufficiently often to ensure that the carrying value does not differ materially from the market value (Para. 43).

The effect of paragraph 43 is that those intangible assets that were recognised as part of the purchase of the business on the grounds *inter alia* that they could be reliably measured, but for which a readily ascertainable market value does not exist, cannot be revalued. One of the members of the ASB argued, in a note of dissent, that it was inconsistent to accept that the reliability of measurement that was sufficient for initial recognition could not be the basis of subsequent valuation (App. IV, Para. 8).

Impairment losses can be reversed only in respect of those assets that have a readily ascertainable market value or, in what are regarded as rare circumstances, where both the original impairment loss and its subsequent reversal are attributable to external events. (Para. 44). It is argued that to allow reversal in other circumstances would, in effect, be allowing the capitalisation of internally generated intangible assets.

Disclosure requirements

In general the disclosure requirements, to be found in paragraphs 52 to 59, are similar to those set out in FRS 15 in respect of tangible fixed assets. The additional requirements include the need to state, if appropriate, the grounds for rebutting the 20 year presumption, which should be a reasoned explanation based on the specific factors contributing to the durability of the asset.

Compliance with International Accounting Standards

The corresponding international standard IAS 38, issued in 1998, does not differ from FRS 10 in substance but there are some differences in detail, including

- IAS 38 does not accept that intangible assets can have an indefinite life and hence requires amortisation of such assets in all circumstances
- Internally developed intangibles can, under the international standard, be capitalised as long as costs can be measured reliably, thus a readily ascertainable market value is not required. But since IAS 38 specifically states that the costs of generating brands, mastheads and similar assets cannot be measured reliably there are unlikely to be significant differences in practice between the two approaches.

Accounting for research and development

Many enterprises spend large sums of money on research and development in the hope that, by incurring such expenditure, future profits will be higher than they otherwise would be. In other words, they incur expenditure on research and development in the expectation of creating an intangible asset that will yield benefits in the future. By the very nature of the process, some research and development activities will be unsuccessful and hence no asset will be created. Any expenditure on such projects must certainly be written off against profits of the year in which it is incurred. Other research projects will be successful and will result in the creation of an asset. Under historical cost accounting, it would be reasonable to suggest that expenditure on unsuccessful projects should be written off against the profits of the year in which they were incurred, while expenditure on successful projects should be capitalised at an appropriate figure and written off against profits of the periods in which benefits are expected to arise.

The accounting treatment proposed above seems quite clear, but two major problems arise as soon as an attempt is made to apply it. First, even where a project appears to have been successful, the size and timing of future benefits are often very uncertain; if such is the case, the prudence convention would appear to require the expenditure to be written off. Second, the people who must make the decision on whether or not the research and development has been successful are not independent of the entity but are the directors who are interested in the outcome of the research and development. Because of their involvement, such directors may be susceptible to bias, either innocent or fraudulent, and, in view of the uncertainties involved, it may be extremely difficult for an auditor to challenge the views of the directors.

SSAP 13 *Accounting for Research and Development*

Accounting for research and development was the subject matter and title of SSAP 13, originally issued in 1977. A later version SSAP 13 (revised), which was issued in 1989, follows the same principles, although it increases the amount of disclosure required. We shall refer to SSAP 13 (revised) 'Accounting for Research and Development' (January 1989). This SSAP, like its predecessor, follows the definitions of research and development expenditure adopted by the Organisation for Economic Co-operation and Development, which divides such expenditure into three categories:

1 Pure (or basic) research: experimental or theoretical work undertaken primarily to acquire new scientific or technical knowledge for its own sake rather than directed towards any specific aim or application.
2 Applied research: original or critical investigation undertaken in order to gain new scientific or technical knowledge and directed towards a specific practical aim or objective.
3 Development: use of scientific or technical knowledge in order to produce new or substantially improved materials, devices, products or services, to install new processes or systems prior to the commencement of commercial production or commercial applications, or to improve substantially those already produced or installed.

Given the uncertainties surrounding the benefits from research and development expenditure and the requirement of SSAP 2 that, in case of conflict, prudence should prevail over the accruals concept, one approach, would be to write off all such expenditure to the profit and loss account as incurred.[16]

Although this approach may be simply applied and removes the need for judgement on the part of directors and auditors, many people would argue that it makes little economic sense. To take an example, we may think of two similar companies that have spent an identical amount on research and development. The efforts of one company have been successful while the efforts of the other company have not. If both companies are required to write off all research and development expenditure as it is incurred, then this essential difference between the two companies is not apparent from an examination of their financial statements. An important element of business reality does not feature in those statements.

SSAP 13 takes a less conservative approach. Although it requires companies to write off all expenditure on pure and applied research as it is incurred, it permits, but does not require, the capitalisation of certain development expenditure which must then be matched against the revenues to which it relates.

The adoption of this permissive approach introduces the possibility of bias on the part of directors, who must decide whether or not an asset exists on a balance sheet date. In order to reduce this bias to a minimum, the standard lists the following conditions that must be satisfied before development expenditure may be carried forward:[17]

(a) there is a clearly defined project; and
(b) the related expenditure is separately identifiable; and
(c) the outcome of such a project has been assessed with reasonable certainty as to:
   (i) its technical feasibility; and
   (ii) its ultimate commercial viability considered in the light of factors such as likely market conditions (including competing products), public opinion, consumer and environmental legislation; and
(d) the aggregate of the deferred development costs, any further development costs, and related production, selling and administration costs is reasonably expected to be exceeded by related future sales or other revenues; and
(e) adequate resources exist, or are reasonably expected to be available, to enable the project to be completed and to provide any consequential increases in working capital.

It will be seen that, unlike the position with the generality of internally generated intangible fixed assets, development expenditure can be recognised in the absence of readily ascertainable market value but, instead, expenditure can only be capitalised if the above, reasonably stringent conditions, are met.[18]

In order to facilitate interpretation, the standard requires that the notes to the accounts contain a clear explanation of the accounting policy followed, although this would, in any case, be required under the provisions of SSAP 2. It requires disclosure of the total amount of research and development expenditure charged in the profit and loss account, analysed between the current year's expenditure and the amortisation of deferred development expenditure. Finally, it requires disclosure of movements

---

[16] This was, in fact, the approach proposed in the original exposure draft on the subject, ED 14 *Accounting for Research and Development*, issued in 1975.

[17] SSAP 13(revised), Para. 25.

[18] The Companies Act 1985 requires that costs of research are charged to the profit and loss account (Schedule 4, Para. 3(2)(c)) but permits the carrying forward of development costs 'in special circumstances' (Schedule 4, Para. 20(1)). Satisfaction of the criteria for the carrying forward of development expenditure in SSAP 13 is generally accepted as providing the 'special circumstances' referred to in the Act.

on the deferred development expenditure account each year. The Companies Act 1985 specifically requires that the directors explain why expenditure has been capitalised and state the period over which the costs are being written off.[19]

Compliance with International Accounting Standards

Research and development expenditure is covered by IAS 38 *Intangible Assets* which, as we described earlier, does not require an intangible asset to have a readily ascertainable market value for it to be recognised. Hence, SSAP 13 is consistent with the general approach of IAS 38.

Impairment reviews

It is a long established principle that a fixed asset should be written down if its carrying value exceeds its economic worth to the entity but, prior to the publication of FRS 11 *Impairment of Fixed Assets and Goodwill*, there was little guidance on how to measure the economic worth of the asset and how any losses should be treated.

FRS 11 Impairment of Fixed Assets and Goodwill

This standard is the last of the trinity dealing with fixed assets. Its main purpose is to set the principles and methodology for accounting for the impairment of fixed assets and goodwill which necessities the reduction of their carrying values to their recoverable amounts. We have already introduced the term *recoverable amount*, which we defined as the higher of an asset's net realisable value and value in use.

The standard does not cover investments covered by the Board's projects on derivatives and other financial instruments.

An impairment review is an exercise involving the valuation of an individual asset, where it is possible to assign the generation of cash flows to an individual asset, or, otherwise, the smallest bundle of assets to which a series of cash flows can be related.

In discussing FRS 11 we will cover the following topics.

- When to perform an impairment review
- The calculation of recoverable amount
- The bundle of assets to be valued or the 'income generating unit'
- The estimation of cash flow
- The choice of discount rates
- The allocation of impairment losses
- Subsequent monitoring of cash flows
- Disclosure

When to perform an impairment review

We have already touched upon the special requirements for goodwill and intangible assets (*see* p. 93). For the generality of assets a review need only be carried out if 'events and changes in circumstances indicate that the carrying amount of the fixed asset or goodwill may not be recoverable' (Para. 8).

The events or circumstances can relate specifically to the asset, such as the emergence of a new, more efficient version, or to the business in which the asset is used,

---

[19] Companies Act 1985, Schedule 4, Para. 20(2).

perhaps the making of large losses over an extended period. It is, of course, not possible to define precisely what constitutes a significant event that should trigger a review. This must be a matter of judgement at the margin, although there will be events of such magnitude that the there will be no doubt as to the need for a review.

The calculation of recoverable amount

The recoverable amount depends on a comparison of the asset's carrying value with the higher of the asset's net realisable value and value in use. In making the comparison between value in use and net realisable value regard must be paid to deferred tax balances that would arise in each case (Para. 19). Otherwise the calculations are made on the basis of pre-tax flows.

While the standard sets out, in some considerable detail, how the calculations of value in use should be made, it also points out that in many cases a simple estimate will be enough to demonstrate that the value in use is either above the carrying value or below net realisable value thus obviating the need for a more detailed calculation.

Income-generating units

Ideally, the value in use of assets should be estimated on an individual basis but this is often not possible because of the impossibility of dividing the cash flows generated by the business between the individual assets. Thus, it is necessary to identify *income-generating units* that are found by dividing the total income stream of the entity into as many largely independent income streams as is reasonable possible. With the exception of any central assets which cannot meaningfully be apportioned across the units, all the identifiable assets and liabilities, excluding deferred tax balances, interest-bearing debt, dividends payable and other items relating wholly to finance should be attributed to, or apportioned between, the various income-generating units.

Thus the main business is divided into two or more, as independent as possible, 'mini-businesses', although the businesses may not be very mini. Given the highly integrated nature of many enterprises it may not be possible to break down some very large entities into more than two or three income-generating units. An illustration of this is one of the examples provided in the standard. This is of a transport company that operates a number of trunk routes each fed by a number of supporting routes. In this case the units are each of the trunk routes together with their supporting routes.

In some cases it is possible to apportion central assets, such as the head office, to the different units using some rule of thumb such as proportion of turnover. This is more likely to be possible when the units are fairly homogeneous in nature. When they are very different, involving say a large volume manufacturing plant and a small highly specialised research laboratory, this might not be possible. In such cases it may be necessary first to undertake a review at the level of the individual units ignoring the asset value and the income flows relating to the central asset and then to combine the units with the central assets and to again compare carrying value with recoverable amount. It might be that no impairment is identified at the individual unit level but is found at the aggregate level.

As we will explain in Chapter 8 a similar approach is used for goodwill.

The estimation of the cash flows

The standard is quite prescriptive in the way it requires the cash flows necessary to allow an asset's (or more likely an income-generating unit's) value in use to be estimated. The estimates must be based on two elements, first the most up-to-date budgets and plans that have been approved by management which, other than in exceptional circumstances, should be for a period not exceeding five years. Thereafter the cash flows should be based on the assumption of steady or declining (but not increasing) growth rates and that, again with a let-out in exceptional circumstances, the rate used should not exceed the long-term average of the country or countries in which the entity operates (Para. 36). Note that the rules are framed in terms of the growth rate not the rate itself, hence if the average rate of growth in the period covered by the budgets was, say, 3 per cent it would be permissible to extrapolate this rate of growth into the future so long as it was consistent with estimates of the growth rate in the appropriate country or countries.

In general the cash flow estimates should be based on the current condition of the assets and should include neither future expected cash savings from future reorganisations for which provision has not yet been made nor future capital expenditure that will enhance the asset in excess of its originally assessed standard of performance (Para. 38). There is one exception to this provision that applies in the case of a newly acquired income-generating unit such as a subsidiary. In instances such as these the purchase price might well reflect the synergies that will result from the acquisition but which will depend on additional expenditure. In this cases the cash flow estimates can, up till the end of the first full year following the acquisition, take the costs and benefits resulting from that expenditure into account (Para. 39).

Discount rate

> The present value of the income generating unit under review should be calculated by discounting the expected cash flows of the unit. The discount rate used should be an estimate of the rate the market would expect on an equally risky investment. It should exclude the effects of any risk for which the cash flow has been adjusted and should be calculated on a pre-tax basis. (Para. 41)

The standard goes on to suggest ways by which the rate can be estimated placing great emphasis on the need to ensure that the rates used for comparison are derived from cash flows from operations with the same risk profile or are adjusted for risk. The ASB is a trifle sanguine about the ease with which adjustments can be made for risk. As an example, it states (Para. 45) that it is likely that the use of a discount rate equal to the rate or return that the market would expect on an equally risky investment is likely to be the easiest way of dealing with risk, which begs the question of how one finds an equally risky investment, but that an equally acceptable alternative is to adjust the cash flows for risk and then to discount using a risk-free rate, e.g. government bond rate, which begs the question of how to adjust the cash flows for risk! (Para. 45).

The standard warns against the danger of double counting inflation, if cash flows are expressed in current prices they should be discounted using a real discount rate, if expressed in future prices a nominal discount rate should be employed (Para. 46).

The allocation of impairment losses

When the impairment review is conducted at the level of the income-generating unit it might not be possible to identify the asset whose carrying value should be reduced. If it is not obvious then the procedure specified in FRS 11 is to allocate the impairment loss first to those assets whose value is the most subjective. Hence the order is:

1 Goodwill
2 Any capitalised intangible asset
3 The tangible assets, on a pro rata or more appropriate bases (para. 48).

Subsequent monitoring of cash flows

In those cases where the recoverable amount is based on the, generally, more subjective of the possible two measures, the asset's *value in use*, the standard requires that, for the period of five years following the review, the cash flows actually achieved should be compared with those used in the review (Para. 54). Such a comparison can only have three outcomes: the actual cash flows may be broadly in line with those that had been estimated, in which case no further action is required, or the position may turn out to be better or worse than had been originally anticipated.

If the cash flows turn out to be better than had been forecast then it might be possible to recognise a complete or partial reversal of the impairment loss.

If the actual cash flows are worse than had been expected, then the additional loss that would have been shown, had the actual cash flows been used, must be recognised. However, it might be the case that the reason that the actual cash flows had been worse was because a major cash flow in had been delayed. Hence, the standard allows entities to calculate the current value in use that might indicate that the apparent additional loss had been, in whole or in part, reversed. In such a case and, so long as the general conditions for recognition of the reversal of the loan are satisfied, the additional loss need not be recognised but the potential additional loss and its reversal must be disclosed (Para. 71).

Disclosure requirements

These appear at paragraphs 67–73 and may be summarised as follows:

- impairment losses shown in the profit and loss account should, if appropriate, be shown as an exceptional item; those appearing in the statement of total recognised gains and losses should be disclosed separately;
- for assets shown other than at market value, the impairment losses should be included within cumulative depreciation;
- if the loss is measured by reference to value in use the discount rates used should be disclosed, if a risk-free rate is used an indication of the risk adjustments made to the cash flow should be provided;
- if an impairment loss is reversed information relating to the circumstances and assumptions used in the calculation of the recoverable amount must be provided;
- if, because of the use of actual cash flows, a greater loss is recognised which is then reversed, both the loss and the reversal should be disclosed;
- if, in the measurement of value in use, the period before the assumption of steady or declining growth extends to more than five years, the note should state both the length of the period and its justification; if the long-term growth rate exceeds the average, the rate used and its justification should also be provided.

It can be seen that superficially a great deal of information has to be provided especially in relation to value-in-use calculations, but in practice there must be some doubt as to the extent that will be useful to users of the accounts who will have difficulty in determine the reasonableness of the assumptions underpinning the calculations.

Compliance with International Accounting Standards

The equivalent international standard is IAS 36 *Impairment of Assets*, which was issued in 1998. The basic approach of the two standards is the same and, while the detailed requirements are very similar, among the more interesting differences are:

- the FRS treats intangible assets in much the same way as goodwill while the IAS aligns their treatment to that of tangible assets. As a consequence, for the allocation of impairment losses, the FRS sets them off first against intangible assets, while the IAS sets them off against all assets pro rata, and for the recognition of the reversal of impairment losses, the IAS does not restrict the reversal of losses in respect of intangible assets;
- if an acquired business is merged with an existing business the IAS does not require any subsequent impairment to be allocated between the existing and acquired goodwill;
- the FRS requires estimates of value in use to be monitored for five years, the IAS does not;
- the IAS has additional disclosure requirements.

Stocks and long-term contracts

It used to be said in jest that in drawing up the annual accounts of an enterprise the first figure to be set down was that of profit, then all the ascertainable figures, until finally the value of stock emerged as a balancing item. This sentiment is certainly echoed in the introductory remarks to the original version of SSAP 9, 'Stocks and Work in Progress', issued in May 1975:

> No area of accounting has produced wider differences in practice than the computation of the amount at which stocks and work in progress are stated in financial accounts. This statement of standard accounting practice seeks to define the practices, to narrow the differences and variation in those practices and to ensure adequate disclosure in the accounts.

Partly, but not wholly, due to changes in company law, the treatment of long-term contracts in the original version of the standard was found to be unsatisfactory and a revised version of the standard was issued in September 1988. From now on all references will be to the revised version.

SSAP 9 differs from most other statements in that a large proportion of the document is devoted to appendices that deal with practical problems. The ASC was of the view that the problems that arise in this area are of a practical rather than of a theoretical nature. Appendix 1 deals with the relevant practical considerations but, as was always the case with appendices, it did not form part of the statement of standard accounting practice. There are two other appendices; Appendix 2, which consists of a glossary of terms, and Appendix 3, which is concerned with the presentation of information relating to long-term contracts.

We will assume that readers are familiar with the basic principles of stock valuation and the different methods employed in the historical cost system and, hence, we will concentrate on the few, but important, principles underlying SSAP 9.

Stocks other than long-term contracts

> The amount at which stocks are stated in periodic financial statements should be the total of the lower of cost and net realizable value of the separate item of stock or of groups of similar items. (SSAP 9, Para. 26)

A simple enough statement. Stock should normally be shown at cost but might sometimes be written down. But to state that stock should normally be stated at cost does not take us very far, for, as readers will be aware, the determination of the cost of stock and work-in-progress is by no means a simple task and much of the statement, including the appendices, is devoted to that subject. The basic principle is that the cost of stock and work-in-progress should comprise:

> that expenditure which has been incurred in the normal course of business in bringing the product or service to its present location and condition. Such costs **will** [our emphasis] include all related production overheads, even though these may accrue on a time basis. (SSAP 9, Paras 17–19)

The cost of stock and work-in-progress is to include costs of production and conversion (as defined in the statement). The specification of the treatment of overheads reflects one way in which the standard fulfils its objective of narrowing variations in practice. There has been much debate on the extent to which production overheads should be included in the valuation of stock. At one extreme – the variable costing approach – is the view that overhead allocation is by its very nature arbitrary and that stock should be valued by reference to the costs (usually just direct material and labour) that can be directly related to the stock in question. A view that lies between this extreme and the ASC's position is that production overheads that relate to activity rather than time (e.g. cost of power) should be included in the cost of stock. These approaches are rejected by SSAP 9, which requires the inclusion of all production overheads, including those that accrue on a time basis. It appears that this alternative was adopted because the ASC felt that all production overheads, whether or not they arise on a time basis, are required to bring the stock to its 'present location and condition'.

Costs which include time-related production overheads will, all other things being equal, vary with the level of output; the lower the output the greater cost of, say, rent per unit. Thus, the statement refers to the need to base the allocation of overheads on the company's normal level of activity,[20] so ensuring that the cost of unused capacity is written off in the current year. Appendix 1 of SSAP 9 provides some guidance on the question of how the normal level of activity should be determined, but it is clear that judgement will have to play a part in the resolution of this matter.

The ASC specifically rejected the argument that the omission of production overheads can be defended on the grounds of prudence. This emerges in Appendix 1, Para. 10, which states:

> The adoption of a conservative approach to the valuation of stocks and long-term contracts has sometimes been used as one of the reasons for omitting selected production overheads. In so far as the circumstances of the business require an element of prudence in determining the amount at which stocks and long-term contracts are stated, this needs to be taken into account in the determination of net realizable value and not by the exclusion from cost of selected overheads.

The conventional methods of stock valuation (FIFO, LIFO, etc.) are described in the glossary of terms. The actual standard does not give any guidance about the methods that should be used; but the ASC's view of the principle that should be followed is given in Appendix 1, where it is stated that 'management must exercise judgment to ensure that the methods chosen provide the fairest practicable approximation to cost'.[21] It can be seen that the ASC placed emphasis on the need to show as accurately as possible the cost of stock and rejected those methods such as LIFO which are used, especially in the United States, to produce a profit figure which approximates to a current cost operating profit (see Chapter 16).

---

[20] SSAP 9, Appendix 1, Para. 8.
[21] SSAP 9, Appendix 1, Para. 12.

We will now turn to the methods that must be adopted when stock is to be written down. We will not, however, at this stage refer to the problems of establishing the net realisable value, which has been dealt with in Chapter 3.

SSAP 9 requires that stock should be written down to its net realisable value. Prior to the publication of the standard, some companies stated stock at replacement cost where this was lower than net realisable value and cost. The use of replacement cost is rejected in SSAP 9 on the grounds that it may result in the recognition of 'a loss that is greater than that which is expected to be incurred' (SSAP 9, Para. 6).

Our final comment on the provisions of SSAP 9, Para. 26, quoted at the beginning of this section, relates to the requirement that the comparison of cost and net realisable value should be on an item-by-item basis or by reference to groups of similar items. The reason for this is that this provision is given in Para. 2, where it is stated that 'to compare the total realisable value of stocks with the total cost could result in an unacceptable setting off of foreseeable losses against unrealised profits'. In other words, the practice contravenes the concept of prudence.

Long-term contracts

Long-term contracts merit separate consideration. Because of the time taken to complete such contracts, to defer recording turnover and the recognition of profit until completion might in the words of the standard 'result in the profit and loss account reflecting not so much a fair view of the activity of the company during the year but rather the results relating to contracts which have been completed by the year end' (SSAP 9, Para. 7).

Thus, SSAP 9 states that it is appropriate to (and by appropriate the ASC meant that companies should) take credit for ascertainable turnover and profit while contracts are in progress, subject to various conditions specified in the standard.

This may well be an eminently practical and sensible view, but it does seem to be in conflict with the attitude adopted in SSAP 2, 'Disclosure of Accounting Policies', where it is stated that 'where the accruals concept is inconsistent with the prudence concept, the latter prevails'. The provision of SSAP 9 relating to long-term contracts does appear to suggest that the accruals concept should prevail over prudence. We should, however, note that in the Draft Revised Statement of Principles the ASB is attempting to change the definition of prudence (see Chapter 1).

The provision that attributable profit should (not might) be recognised in the financial statements was perhaps the most controversial aspect of the original SSAP 9. A number of large companies had consistently eschewed the recognition of profit on uncompleted contracts and some continued this practice after the implementation of SSAP 9, accepting the consequential qualifications in their audit reports.

In addition, there would appear to be a conflict between this requirement of SSAP 9 and the legal requirement that only realised profits may be credited to the profit and loss account (see Chapter 3). Even if attributable profit on long-term contract work in progress is not realised, it may, nonetheless, be included in the profit and loss account if this is necessary to give a true and fair view. The use of this true and fair view override on a number of occasions in the UK has aroused considerable criticism from other members of the EU, who did not envisage that it would be used so often.

Definition of long-term contracts

A long-term contract can relate to the design or construction of a single substantial asset or the provision of a service (or a combination of assets or services which constitute a single project) where the activity falls into different accounting periods. If a contract is to fall within the definition, it will normally have to last for more than a year, but shorter contracts may also be included if they are sufficiently material so that the failure to record turnover and attributable profit would distort the financial statements.

Turnover, related costs and attributable profit

> Long-term contracts should be assessed on a contract by contract basis and reflected in the profit and loss account by recording turnover and related costs as contract activity progresses. (SSAP 9, Para. 28)

Also:

> Where it is considered that the outcome of a long-term contract can be assessed with reasonable certainty before its conclusion, the prudently calculated attributable profit should be recognized in the profit and loss account as the difference between the reported turnover and related costs for that contract. (SSAP 9, Para. 29)

So the accounting seems pretty straightforward and obvious:

$$\text{Reported turnover} - \text{Related costs} = \text{Attributable profit}$$

But how are the various elements determined? The actual standard does not help very much, although some guidance is given:

> Turnover is ascertained in a manner appropriate to the stage of completion of the contract, the business and the industry in which it operates. (SSAP 9, Para. 28)

Some assistance is also provided in Appendix 1 (Para. 23) where it is stated that turnover may be ascertained by reference to valuation of the work carried out to date. Alternatively there may be specific points where separately ascertainable sales values and costs can be identified because, for example, delivery or customer acceptance has taken place. The section goes on to state that the standard does not provide a definition of turnover because of the number of different possible approaches. It does, however, point out that the standard does require disclosure of the means by which turnover is ascertained.

Neither the standard nor any of the appendices refer to the calculation of related cost, so we will now turn to this and the estimation of attributable profit. We will start with two conceptually simple cases.

If the outcome of a long-term contract cannot be ascertained with reasonable certainty, no profit should be reflected in the profit and loss account. However, if, despite the uncertainty, the contract is not expected to make a loss, 'it may be appropriate to show as turnover a proportion of the total contract value using a zero estimate of profit' (SSAP 9, Para. 10). In the latter situation in order to satisfy the relationship between turnover, cost and profit, the related costs would be made equal to the reported turnover. If, on this basis, related costs appeared to be greater than the actual costs incurred to date, the turnover would be reduced and made equal to the actual costs.

The second 'simple' case is where the contract is expected to make a loss, then, in accordance with the prudence concept, the whole of the loss should be recorded as soon as it is foreseen. Turnover would be determined in the normal way and the related cost would be equal to the actual cost to date plus the provision for foreseeable future losses.

Now let us consider a case where it would be necessary to recognise some profit. Attributable profit is defined as:

> that part of the total profit currently estimated to arise over the duration of the contract, after allowing for estimated remedial and maintenance costs and increases in costs so far as not recoverable under the terms of the contract, that fairly reflect the profit attributable to that part of the work performed at the accounting date. (SSAP 9, Para. 23)

Thus, it is first necessary to estimate the total profit and then decide how it should be allocated. The principles involved are illustrated in Example 4.1.

Example 4.1

Suppose that Engineer Limited started a three-year contract at the beginning of year 1 with a total contract value of £18 000 and costs of £12 000 that it is anticipated will be incurred as follows:

Year 1	Year 2	Year 3	Total
£3000	£6000	£3000	£12 000

The expected profit is thus £6000.

Case 1

We will assume that both turnover and profit are to be recognised in proportion to the costs incurred. Hence, assuming all goes to plan, the contract would be reported in the profit and loss accounts as follows:

	Year 1 (25%) £	Year 2 (50%) £	Year 3 (25%) £
Reported turnover	4 500	9 000	4 500
Related costs	3 000	6 000	3 000
Attributable profit	£1 500	£3 000	£1 500

Case 2

Depending on the nature of the contract it might be deemed appropriate to record turnover on a different basis, perhaps on the values placed on the work completed to date by an independent consultant.

Assume that the value of the work certified is as follows:

	Value of work certified £	Value of work completed in year £	Fraction
End of year 1	3 000	3 000	$\frac{1}{6}$
End of year 2	9 000	6 000	$\frac{1}{3}$
End of year 3	18 000	9 000	$\frac{1}{2}$

Profit might be based on cost (Case 2a) or turnover (Case 2b) that would result in the reporting of the following figures.

Case 2a
Profit related to cost

	Year 1 £	Year 2 £	Year 3 £
Reported turnover	3 000	6 000	9 000
Related cost	1 500	3 000	7 500
Attributable profit	£1 500 (25%)	£3 000 (50%)	£1 500 (25%)

Case 2b
Profit related to turnover

	Year 1 £	Year 2 £	Year 3 £
Reported turnover	3 000	6 000	9 000
Related cost	2 000	4 000	6 000
Attributable profit	£1 000 ($\frac{1}{6}$)	£2 000 ($\frac{1}{3}$)	£3 000 ($\frac{1}{2}$)

Thus, we can see that under the provisions of SSAP 9, even in this simple case, three different patterns of turnover, cost and profit might be reported, and in practice more variations are possible.

Now let us assume that all does not go to plan and the actual cost in Year 2 was £8000 rather than the expected £6000, but that no further difficulties are expected and that the original estimate for the cost of Year 3 of £3000 still holds.

Consider the position as at the end of Year 2; there are two possibilities which will be illustrated by reference to Case 2a above. Either the additional unexpected expenditure can be written off in Year 2 reducing the profit for the year by £2000 to £1000, leaving the profit for Year 3 at £1500, or the revised profit less that already recognised in Year 1 could be spread over Years 2 and 3 on the basis of cost, i.e. in the ratio 8:3.

The revised profit is £4000 and the profit recognised in Year 1 was £1500, hence the profits for the remaining two years would be:

Year 1	£1 818	(8/11)
Year 3	£682	(3/11)
	£2 500	

Thus, we have the paradox that the profit for Year 3 is reduced because of difficulties experienced in Year 2. This does not appear to be sensible, but the approach would be permissible under the terms of SSAP 9.

Example 4.1 illustrates the point that the related cost is normally a balancing figure derived from the relationship between reported turnover and attributable profit. The statement does not deal with the situation where related costs exceed actual costs. Suppose that we have the following for the first year of a contract:

	£
Turnover	20 000
Related cost	16 000
Attributable profit	£4 000
Actual cost to date	£13 000

In practice it is likely that the turnover figure would be reduced to £17 000 to make the equation balance.

Long-term contracts and the balance sheet

Before moving to a discussion of the way in which long-term contract balances are shown in the balance sheet, we need to introduce another factor, payments on account, which is defined as 'all amounts received and receivable at the accounting date in respect of contracts in progress ' (SSAP 9, Para. 25).

The relevant section of the standard reproduced below is perhaps unnecessarily complex.

> Long-term contracts should be disclosed in the balance sheet as follows:
> (a) the amount by which recorded turnover is in excess of payments on account should be classified as 'amounts recoverable on contracts' and separately disclosed within debtors;
> (b) the balance of payments on account (in excess of amounts (i) matched with turnover; and (ii) offset against long-term contract balances) should be classified as payments on account and separately disclosed within creditors;
> (c) the amount of long-term contracts, at costs incurred, net of amounts transferred to cost of sales, after deducting foreseeable losses and payments on account not matched with turnover, should be classified as 'long-term contract balances' and separately disclosed within the balance sheet heading 'Stocks'. The balance sheet note should disclose separately the balances of:
>   (i) net cost less foreseeable losses; and
>   (ii) applicable payments on account;
> (d) the amount by which the provision or accrual for foreseeable losses exceeds the costs incurred (after transfers to cost of sales) should be included within either provisions for liabilities and charges or creditors as appropriate.
> (SSAP 9, Para. 30)

To unravel the above it is best to start by concentrating on the situation where there are no losses, either incurred or contemplated.

Let us start by looking at the costs.

If the actual costs incurred to date exceed the cumulative related costs (the total charged to cost of sales), there is an asset, long-term contract balances, which is separately disclosed within stocks.

As stated earlier the standard does not consider a situation where related costs exceed actual costs; in practice this will not arise because, in all probability, turnover would be adjusted.

Let us now consider the receipt of cash from the customer.

If the cumulative reported turnover exceeds cumulative payments on account there is an asset, amounts recoverable on contracts, which is separately disclosed within debtors.

If the reverse holds (more cash received on account than reported as turnover), the credit balance is set off against long-term contract balances. If the credit (payments less turnover) is greater than the debit (long-term contract balances), the resulting credit is described as payments on account, which is separately disclosed within creditors.

Thus in respect of each contract, which has to be considered separately, the possible combinations of assets and liabilities are:

(a) two assets: long-term contract balances and amounts recoverable on contract; or
(b) a liability: payments on account.

The above points are illustrated in Example 4.2.

Example 4.2

No losses

Assume that the position on three contracts at a year-end is as follows:

	(1) £	(2) £	(3) £
Cumulative turnover	520	520	520
Cumulative actual cost	510	510	510
Cumulative related cost	450	450	450
Cumulative payments on account	440	555	630

The cumulative attributable profit for each of the contracts is £70, i.e. £520 – £450.

The relevant balance sheet items are shown below. Note that each contract will be considered on an individual basis, balances arising on one contract are not set-off against balances on other contracts and hence the figures that will appear in the balance sheet are shown in the total column.

	Contract (1) £	Contract (2) £	Contract (3) £	Total £
Stock – long-term contract balances	60 [a]	25 [b]	NIL	85
Debtors – amount recoverable on contracts	80 [a]	NIL	NIL	80
Creditors – payments on account	NIL	NIL	50 [c]	50

Notes

(a) Actual costs less related costs; £510 – £450 = £60

(b) Long-term contract balance as (a), £60
less Excess of payments on account
over turnover, £555 – £520 £35
£25

(c) Long-term contract balance, as (a) £60
less Excess of payments on account
over turnover, £630 – £520 £110
(£50)

Foreseeable losses

All losses, as soon as they are foreseen, should be recognised in the financial statements. The estimate of future loss should be charged to the profit and loss as part of the related cost. The credit is first offset against the long-term contract balance (before any set-off for the excess of cumulative payments on account over cumulative reported turnover). If the long-term contract balance is insufficient to cover the expected loss, the balance is included within either provisions for liabilities and charges or creditors, as appropriate, i.e. depending on the degree of certainty with which the estimate is made.

Example 4.3

Consider the following two contracts:

	(1) £	(2) £
Cumulative turnover	200	110
Cumulative actual costs	250	200
Cumulative related costs	250	110
Cumulative payments on account	180	160
Losses to date (£250 – £200)	50	–
Expected future losses	40	70

If we assume that this is the first year of each contract, the profit and loss account will include the following:

	(1) £	(2) £	Total £
Turnover	200	110	310
Related costs (cost of sales)	290	180	470
Gross loss	90	70	60

If the projects were other than in their first year, the amounts included would depend on what had been charged or credited in the previous years.

The various balance sheet figures are:

	(1) £	(2) £	Total £
Stock – long-term contract balances	NIL	NIL	NIL
Debtors – amounts recoverable on contracts	20(a)	NIL	20
Creditors – payments on account	NIL	30(b)	30
Provision/accrual for foreseeable losses	40	NIL	40

Notes

(a) Cumulative turnover less cumulative payments on account, £200 – £180 = £20.

(b) For contract 2, actual costs exceed related costs so we start with a long-term contract balance of £90, i.e. £200 – £110.

Expected future losses of £70 are set off against that balance, reducing it to £20.

But, there are excess payments on account, £50 since payments on account, £160, exceed turnover, £110. This credit balance, £50, is set off against the debit, £20, representing the long-term contract balance.

The net credit of £30 will appear in the balance sheet as a provision or accrual as appropriate.

Government grants

It is appropriate to deal with the accounting treatment of government grants as a postscript to a chapter on assets because the topic is often closely related to the subject of fixed assets and depreciation. The topic is the subject matter of SSAP 4, 'The Accounting Treatment of Government Grants', which was originally issued in 1974.

The standard proved to be inadequate, not only because it was itself poorly conceived but also because of other developments. Grants themselves became more complex than was envisaged when SSAP 4 was published, while the provisions of the standard proved to be inconsistent with those of the Companies Act 1985 and of International Accounting Standard No 20 *Accounting for Government Grants and Disclosure of Government Assistance* which was issued in 1982. Hence a revised standard, SSAP 4 (revised), 'Accounting for Government Grants', was issued in July 1990.

The two accounting concepts on which SSAP 4 (revised) is based are accruals and prudence. The first implies that grants should be credited to the profit and loss account so as to match the expenditure towards which they are expected to contribute; the second that grants should not be recognised in the profit and loss account until the conditions for their receipt have been satisfied and that there is a reasonable assurance that the grants will be received.

Readers may feel that the reference to the accruals and prudence conventions is unnecessary because they are two of the four fundamental accounting concepts. However, by presenting the accruals concept in the way stated above, the ASC avoided a discussion of a fundamentally different alternative approach that all government grants should be regarded as a source of finance provided by government and hence retained in the balance sheet as a non-distributable reserve; including it as a reserve would imply that it is an element of owners' equity, but a part which has been provided by the government.

There are certain advantages of such an approach including clarity – it would describe clearly what has actually happened – and comparability in that it would assist comparisons between, for example, the two companies, one operating in an area where grants are available and the other not.

Revenue-related grants

Revenue-related grants, according to the original SSAP 4, did not produce any accounting problems 'as they clearly should be credited to revenue in the same period in which the revenue expenditure to which they relate is charged' (SSAP 4, Para. 2).

This may have been a reasonable description of the situation in 1974, but subsequently grants took many different forms and were derived from different sources than was the case in 1974. In the latter context it is noteworthy that, in the original SSAP 4, the ASC did not see a need to define government; by implication government was the UK Central Government. In contrast, the revised SSAP 4 defines government as including 'government and intergovernmental agencies and similar bodies whether local, national or international' (SSAP 4, Para. 21); it thus includes the European Union.

The matching of grants received to expenditure is straightforward when the grant is made towards specified items of expenditure. However, certain grants might not be related to specific items of expenditure; they might, for example, be paid to encourage job creation. In such circumstances the recognition of the grant in the profit and loss account should be matched with the identifiable net costs of achieving the objective. As is pointed out in the explanatory note to the revised standard, this may not be straightforward, as account needs to be taken of the associated income generated by the activity in arriving at the net cost. If, for example, the grant is given on condition that jobs are created and sustained for a period of, say, three years, the grant should be matched to the net cost of providing the jobs. Thus, if the revenue generated by the activity is higher in the third year, a higher proportion of the grant should be recognised in the earlier years.

In some cases the grant may be paid to support one activity – training, for instance – but will only become payable when the company incurs expenditure in another, usually related, area – perhaps the purchase of capital equipment. In other words, the grant will not be paid unless the company purchases the equipment, but the size of the grant depends on the company's training expenditure. SSAP 4 provides that where such a link is established the grant should be matched to the expenditure which it is intended to support, in this case training, but, as is the general rule under SSAP 4, nothing should be credited to the profit and loss account until the necessary conditions have been fulfilled – in this case until the equipment has been purchased.

The part of any revenue-related grant received but not yet recognised in the profit and loss account should be included in the balance sheet as deferred income.

Capital-related grants

Two methods of dealing with capital-related grants are identified in SSAP 4 (revised).

(a) Show the grant as deferred income that is credited to the profit and loss account over the life of the asset on a basis consistent with the depreciation policy adopted for the asset.
(b) Reduce the cost of the asset and hence reduce the annual depreciation charges.

The other possible option of not crediting the grant at any stage to the profit and loss account but retaining it in the balance sheet as a source of funds is not considered for the reasons given earlier.

In choosing between the two alternatives, the ASC came to the surprising, if not astonishing, conclusion that 'both treatments are acceptable and capable of giving a true and fair view' (SSAP 4 (revised), Para. 15). It is difficult to see how showing in the balance sheet the cost of an asset at 100 per cent of its purchase price or, say, depending on the size of the grant, 80 per cent of the price, can both show a 'true and fair' view. It does seem the ASC had, on this occasion, distorted that splendidly elastic phrase too far.

The ASC's position appears even stranger in that it records that it had received Counsel's opinion that the second alternative, the reduction in cost, is illegal in the light of Paragraphs 17 and 26 of Schedule 4 of the Companies Act 1985. However, the ASC stuck to its guns. Both alternatives are available to enterprises under the provisions of SSAP 4 (revised), but only the first can be used by enterprises whose financial statements are governed by the Companies Acts.

Disclosure requirements

The disclosure requirements of SSAP 4 (revised) require the following information to be revealed.

(a) The accounting policy adopted in respect of government grants (this in any case is required by SSAP 2 'Disclosure of Accounting Policies').
(b) The effects of government grants on the results of the period and the financial position of the enterprise.
(c) Information regarding any material effect on the results of the period from government assistance other than grants (for example, free consultancy or subsidised loans) including, if possible, quantitative estimates of the effect of the assistance.
(d) Any potential liability to repay grants should, if necessary, be disclosed in accordance with SSAP 18 'Accounting for Contingencies' which has now been replaced by FRS 12 'Provisions, Contingent Assets and Liabilities'.

Recommended reading

Excellent up-to-date and detailed reading on the subject matter of this chapter and on much of the contents of this book is provided by the most recent edition of:

UK GAAP, principal authors and editors M. Davies, R. Paterson and A. Wilson, Ernst & Young, Butterworths, London, 1999.

5 Liabilities and related issues

Overview Liabilities used to be the poor relation in the standard setting family but far more attention is now being paid to the subject.

In this chapter we will deal with the 'credit side' of the balance sheet. The chapter has three elements. One deals with the general issues. These are of two types, the first is concerned with the differences between the various elements of that section of the balance sheet. There is first the fundamental distinction between debt and ownership interest, then there are the divisions within each group. In the case of debt, what should be regarded as a provision and what a contingent liability and in the case of ownership interest the distinction between equity and non-equity. The second general issue is the recognition of the cost of liabilities and the way in which they are recognised in the financial statements.

This part of the chapter includes an introduction to the complex world of derivatives and related financial instruments. We focus on the sort of information that will help users of financial statements form a view as to the impact of financial instruments on an entity's risk profile and how these risks are being managed. It is perhaps the potentially devastating risks, which go alongside the prospect of very considerable rewards, associated with financial instruments that have brought the treatment of liabilities to the fore in recent years.

This section of the chapter also includes an interloper in the shape of contingent assets, as it is convenient to deal with them alongside contingent liabilities.

The second element of the chapter is devoted to a very special case, that of pensions, an obligation which can have a major impact on an entity, and will certainly be of considerable importance to its employees.

The final part of the chapter deals with post balance sheet events and so is not exclusively concerned with liabilities but, for all the usual reasons relating to prudence, it is more likely to affect the reporting of liabilities than of assets, which is why the subject is included in this chapter.

The various standards and other documents discussed in this chapter include

- FRS 4 *Capital Instruments* (December 1993)
- FRS 13 *Derivatives and other financial instruments: disclosures* (September 1998)
- FRS 12 *Provisions, Contingent Liabilities and Assets* (September 1998)
- SSAP 24 *Accounting for pension costs* (May 1988)
- ASB Discussion Paper *Aspects of accounting for pension costs* (July 1998)
- FRED 20 *Retirement Benefits* (October 1999)
- SORP 1 *Pension scheme accounts* (May 1986)
- SSAP 17 *Accounting for post balance sheet events* (August 1980)

Introduction

A company acquires capital funding through three sources:

- from owners – either through direct contribution of share capital or the retention of profits
- by borrowing
- through gifts.

The last named might seem an unusual source but in fact governments and other agencies do make significant contributions to some companies.

We discussed the subject of accounting for government grants in Chapter 4 where we pointed out that a logical case could be made for retaining on the balance sheet a section, separate from owners' equity and liabilities, representing the volume of funds that have been provided by government and similar agencies; however, as we pointed out, SSAP 4 'Accounting for Government Grants' does not take this line. Instead the standard requires that the government grant should be credited to the profit and loss account either immediately or over time. Hence, a transfer is made between the 'gift' source of finance and shareholders' funds; the grant is thus treated as a gift to the owners rather than to the business itself. A more unusual form of gift is sometimes found in small family-owned businesses where a very long-term loan is granted, possibly interest free, where, under foreseeable circumstances, there is no intention that the loan should be repaid. In such, admittedly rare, cases the source of finance would be treated as a liability.

Apart from gifts, we have two sources of capital funding which are often referred to as debt and equity.[1] There are two key issues associated with the subject of accounting for these sources of funds. The first relates to separating the sources of funds between liabilities and shareholders funds.[2] The second issue is how the interest on liabilities should be calculated and how it should be allocated over the life of the respective liability.

In order to deal with the first issue we should turn to the Revised Draft Statement of Principles which provides a succinct definition of liabilities:

> Liabilities are obligations of an entity to transfer economic benefits as a result of past transactions or events. (Para. 4.24)

The concepts involved are straightforward. Perhaps the key word in the definition is 'obligations'. A liability only exists when the entity cannot avoid the future transfer of economic benefit – which might take the form of cash or the provision of goods or services. The word obligation is not, in this context, always capable of objective interpretation. There can be no doubt about the nature of a legal or contractual obligation but there may be other circumstances where the entity has no realistic alternative other than to transfer economic benefit. An example could be a business which may, for commercial considerations, have no realistic alternative to refunding the price of goods that fail to meet the expectations of customers, even though it has no legal obligation to do so.

---

[1] The use of the word equity to describe the source of funds provided by owners can sometimes lead to confusion, because in the context of companies with share capital the distinction is made between equity shares and other forms of share capital, such as preference shares.

[2] While the twofold categorisation holds for the accounts of single companies, a third category, minority interest, will be found in consolidated financial statements.

The ASB places great stress on the need for there to have been a past transaction or event for a liability to be created, but it is doubtful whether that phrase takes us very much further than the need to assess the possibility of avoiding the obligation. As the Revised Draft Statement of Principles points out, the mere decision of a board of directors cannot bind a company because, what the directors decide, they can undecide. However, the event that creates an obligation may be the communication of the decision to another party if, in consequence of such an announcement, the entity cannot realistically avoid the future transfer of benefit, such obligations which are not legally binding are often termed *constructive obligations*.

Ownership interest or *equity* is what is left on the 'credit side' of the balance sheet after the liabilities have been removed, or to put in the words of the Revised Draft Statement of Principles

> Ownership interest is the residual amount found by deducting all the entity's liabilities from all of the entity's assets. (Para. 4.38)

Another source of authority on both the issue of the difference between debt and equity and the subject of the allocation of interest costs is FRS 4 *Capital Instruments*, issued in December 1993.

FRS 4 *Capital Instruments*

The objective of FRS 4 is:

> to ensure that financial statements provide a clear, coherent and consistent treatment of capital instruments, in particular as regards the classification of instruments as debt, non-equity shares or equity shares; that costs associated with capital instruments are dealt with in a manner consistent with their classification, and, for redeemable instruments, allocated to accounting periods on a fair basis over the period the instrument is in issue; and that financial statements provide relevant information concerning the nature and amount of the entity's sources of finance and the associated costs, commitments and potential commitments. (Para. 1)

We should start by defining the term *capital instruments*.

> All instruments that are issued by reporting entities which are a means of raising finance, including shares, debentures, loans and debt instruments, options and warrants that give the holder the right to subscribe for or obtain capital instruments. In the case of consolidated financial statements the term includes capital instruments issued by subsidiaries except those that are held by another member of the group included in the consolidation. (Para. 2)

Another important definition is that of *finance costs*, these are:

> The difference between the net proceeds of an instrument and the total amount of the payments (or other transfers of economic benefits) that the issuer may be required to make in respect of the instrument. (Para. 8)

With these two definitions in mind the main points of FRS 4 can be summarised.

Balance sheet presentation

Capital instruments must be categorised into four (single companies) or six (consolidated accounts) groups as shown in Table 5.1.

Table 5.1 Categorisation of capital instruments

	Analysed between	
Shareholders' funds	Equity interests	Non-equity interests
Liabilities	Convertible liabilities	Non-convertible liabilities
Minority interests in subsidiaries	Equity interests in subsidiaries	Non-equity interests in subsidiaries

The period prior to the issue of FRS 4 had seen the issue of various hybrid forms of capital instruments that seemed to combine elements of debt and equity. Examples of the hybrid securities are convertible bonds where holders are given the right to convert into equity shares at a favourable price at some future time. Often the terms are such that the conversion is virtually certain to occur and existing shareholders benefit from obtaining capital at a relatively low rate of interest until conversion, when their ownership interest in the company is diluted.[3]

Because of their complexity, and the lack of a clear accounting standard, there was inconsistency in treatment and opportunities, which were from time to time taken, to paint the balance sheet in a more favourable light than reality might otherwise have allowed. All other things being equal, the higher the level of debt relative to shareholders' funds the higher the degree of risk, because failure to pay interest could lead to the insolvency of the company, whereas the failure to pay dividends would not have such a devastating effect. Similarly, from the point of view of equity shareholders, a high level of non-equity shares means that equity holders are subject to greater uncertainty in terms of their returns because of the prior claims of the non-equity holders. Hence the opportunity of painting the balance sheet in a rosy hue if there are possibilities that instruments which are essentially debt can be presented as part of shareholders' funds, or if non-equity interests can be classified as part of equity shares. As will be seen, the provisions of FRS 4 are such as to ensure that if an instrument contains any element of debt it should be treated as debt or, if the instrument is properly part of shareholders' funds, then if the instrument contains any trace of non-equity, it should be recorded as non-equity.

Allocation of finance costs

Finance costs associated with liabilities and shares, other than equity shares, should be allocated to accounting periods at a constant rate on the carrying amount. This is the actuarial method that is illustrated in the examples that follow. Initially capital instruments should be recorded at the net amount of the issue proceeds and only the direct costs incurred in connection with the issue of the instruments should be deducted from the proceeds in arriving at this net amount. The finance cost for the period is added to the carrying amount and payments deducted from it. Thus, as will be seen, the carrying figure in the balance sheet may not be the same as the nominal

---

[3] For an introduction to these hybrid forms of financial instruments, readers are referred to D.J. Tonkin and L.C.L. Skerratt (eds), *Financial Reporting 1988–1989*, ICAEW, 1989: chapter entitled 'Complex Capital Issues', by B.L. Worth and R.A. Derwent; and L.C.L. Skerratt and D.J. Tonkin (eds), *Financial Reporting 1989–1990*, ICAEW, 1989: chapter entitled 'Complex Capital Issues'.

value of the liability, but in the case of redeemable instruments this would result in the carrying amount at the time of redemption being equal to the amount payable at that time. Gains and losses will only occur on purchase or early redemption and the standard specifies clearly how these should be treated.

> Gains and losses arising on the repurchase or early settlement of debt should be recognised in the profit and loss account in the period during which the repurchase or early settlement is made. (FRS 4, Para. 32)

Accrued finance costs, to the extent that they will be paid in the next period, may be included with accruals, but even if this option is exercised, the accrual must be included in the carrying value for the purpose of calculating the finance costs and any gains or losses on repurchase or early settlement (FRS 4, Para. 30).

In some cases the amount payable on the debt may be contingent on uncertain future events such as changes in a price index. Such events should not be anticipated and the finance costs and carrying amount should only be adjusted when the event occurs (FRS 4, Para. 31).

We shall illustrate both the actuarial method specified in FRS 4 and the conflict between the provisions of the standard and the more economically illiterate aspects of company legislation by considering the example of the issue of three hypothetical debentures under terms that look more different than they actually are.

Example 5.1

Let us consider three issues of debentures, each with a nominal value of £100 and each for a five-year period.

(a) Debenture A carries a coupon rate of 20 per cent per annum: it is to be issued and redeemed at par.

(b) Debenture B carries a coupon rate of 16 per cent per annum: it is to be issued at a discount of £12, at a price of £88, and is to be redeemed at par.

(c) Debenture C carries a coupon rate of 18 per cent per annum: it is to be issued at par but redeemed at a premium of £15 at £115.

We shall assume that the interest on each debenture is payable annually at the end of each year and shall ignore taxation and transaction costs.

The effective interest rate on Debenture A is 20 per cent and the terms of Debentures B and C have been chosen to produce identical effective interest rates of 20 per cent. In other words, if we discount the cash flows from and to the debenture holders, all these debentures produce a net present value (NPV) of zero at a 20 per cent discount rate (Table 5.2).

In all cases the effective rate of interest, that is the cost of the finance, is 20 per cent, but whereas for Debenture A this is all paid in interest, for Debentures B and C the cost is partly paid as a difference between the redemption price and the issue price.

Accounting for Debenture A poses no problems. The annual interest expense of £20 (20 per cent of £100) will be charged in the profit and loss account each year, while the liability will appear at the nominal value of the debentures, that is £100. Accounting for Debentures B and C does pose some problems and we will deal with each in turn.

Discount on debentures

Debenture B is issued at a discount. While the interest of £16 (16 per cent of £100) will undoubtedly be charged to the profit and loss account each year, it is also necessary to decide how to account for the discount on issue, the amount of £12.

Table 5.2 Net present values of debentures

Debenture	NPV at 20%
A	$+100 - 20a_5 - 100v^5$
$=$	$+100 - 20(2.9906) - 100(0.4019)$
$=$	$+100 - 59.8 - 40.2$
$=$	0
B	$+88 - 16a_5 - 100v^5$
$=$	$+88 - 16(2.9906) - 100(0.4019)$
$=$	$+88 - 47.8 - 40.2$
$=$	0
C	$+100 - 18a_5 - 115v^5$
$=$	$+100 - 18(2.9906) - 115(0.4019)$
$=$	$+100 - 53.8 - 46.2$
$=$	0

The liability would be recorded at the nominal value of £100 and company law gives us permission to treat the discount on debentures as an asset.[4] Once we have recorded the discount as an asset, the next question is how this should be dealt with. As the discount is effectively part of the cost of the finance, we might expect this cost to be reflected in the profit and loss account. However, company law specifically permits the writing off of discounts on debentures to a share premium account.[5]

Thus, where a company has a share premium account, we may either write off the discount to share premium account or we may write off the discount to profit and loss account. In the latter case it is possible to write off the discount immediately or to write it off over the five-year period. Let us look at each possibility in turn.

Use of share premium account

Although company law clearly permits the writing off of this discount to share premium account, this results in part of the cost of borrowing bypassing the profit and loss account and hence in an overstatement of profits. This odd quirk of company law has been around for some time, as have its critics.

As long ago as 1962, the Jenkins Committee, which was set up to advise the government on changes in company legislation, reported that it thought that the law should be amended:

> . . . to prohibit the application of the (share premium) account in writing off the expenses and commission paid and discounts allowed on any issue of debentures or in providing for any premiums payable on redemption of debentures, since these are part of the ordinary expenses of borrowing.[6]

Despite the numerous Companies Acts that have been enacted since 1962, this oddity remains and it is difficult to see how it can be justified. The charging of a discount to the share premium account means that the profit and loss account does not bear the full cost of the borrowing, but it also seems to be inconsistent with the rationale for creating a share premium account in the first place. The purpose of a share premium account is to ensure that, with certain exceptions, subscribed capital cannot be repaid to shareholders. If the

---

[4] Companies Act 1985, Schedule 4, Para. 24(1).
[5] Companies Act 1985, Sec. 130(2).
[6] Report of the Company Law Committee, Cmnd 1749, HMSO, London, 1962, Para. 163.

profit and loss account is relieved of part of the cost of the business, then, effectively, part of the subscribed capital is available for distribution.

Charge to profit and loss account

If it is to be charged to the profit and loss account the 1985 Act merely states 'it shall be written off by reasonable amounts each year and must be completely written off before repayment of the debt'.[7]

While FRS 4 requires that the 'finance cost of debt should be allocated to periods over the term of the debt at a constant rate on the carrying amount'.[8]

Using the actuarial method[9] the liability is recorded at the present value of the cash flows discounted at the market rate of interest, which we have assumed to be 20 per cent. The interest expense each year would be found by multiplying the present value of the cash flows at the start of the year by the effective interest rate. As can be seen from Table 5.3 this results in an increasing liability and an increasing interest expense throughout the term of the loan.

Table 5.3 Actuarial method for Debenture B

(i) Year	(ii) Opening balance	(iii) Interest 20% of (ii)	(iv) Total (ii) + (iii)	(v) Payment at year end	(vi) Closing balance (iv) − (v)
	£	£	£	£	£
1	88.0	17.6	105.6	16.0	89.6
2	89.6	17.9	107.5	16.0	91.5
3	91.5	18.3	109.8	16.0	93.8
4	93.8	18.8	112.6	16.0	96.6
5	96.6	19.4*	116.0	116.0†	–

* Includes rounding adjustment.   † Interest 16.0 + Redemption price 100.0.

In addition to satisfying the requirements of FRS 4 this is the approach that is required in the USA[10] and by SSAP 21 'Accounting for Leases and Hire Purchase Contracts' when accounting for the obligation under a finance lease (*see* Chapter 6).

Premium on redemption

Debenture C, which carries a coupon rate of interest of 18 per cent is issued at par but redeemed at a premium of £15. Under the existing legal framework it is not clear whether the liability should be recorded initially at the nominal value of £100 or at the amount payable, the redemption price of £115. If it is recorded initially at £100, then a premium must be provided by the end of the five-year period. If it is recorded initially at £115, then an asset 'premium on debentures' must also be established and we have a situation analogous to the issue of a debenture at a discount that has been discussed above. In either case it is necessary to decide how to deal with the premium.

---

[7] Companies Act 1985, Schedule 4, Para. 24(2)(a).
[8] FRS 4, Para. 28.
[9] Which is also called the effective rate method; the 'compound yield method' (Inland Revenue) or the 'interest method' (FASB).
[10] Readers are referred to Richard Macve, 'Accounting for long-term loans', in *External Financial Reporting*, Bryan Carsberg and Susan Dev (eds), Prentice-Hall, 1984. This essay in honour of Professor Harold Edey discusses the treatment of long-term loans in both the UK and USA.

Not surprisingly we find that the law permits the write-off of this premium to share premium account but, for the reasons explained above, the authors are of the view that it should be charged to the profit and loss account over the life of the debentures. Using the actuarial method the liabilities at the balance sheet dates and the annual expense figures can be calculated as shown in Table 5.4.

Table 5.4 Actuarial method for Debenture C

(i) Year	(ii) Opening balance	(iii) Interest 20% of (ii)	(iv) Total (ii) + (iii)	(v) Payment at year end	(vi) Closing balance (iv) – (v)
	£	£	£	£	£
1	100.0	20.0	120.0	18.0	102.0
2	102.0	20.4	122.4	18.0	104.4
3	104.4	20.9	125.3	18.0	107.3
4	107.3	21.5	128.8	18.0	110.8
5	110.8	22.2	133.0	133.0*	–

* Interest 18.0 + Redemption price 115.0.

Finance costs for non-equity shares

The treatment of finance costs relating to non-equity shares is based on the same principles as debt (FRS 4, Para. 42) with two additional specific rules. These are:

> Where the entitlement to dividends in respect of non-equity shares is calculated by reference to time, the dividends should be accounted for on an accruals basis except in those circumstances (for example where profits are insufficient to justify a dividend and dividend rights are noncumulative) where ultimate payment is remote. All dividends should be reported as appropriations of profit. (Para. 43)

> Where the finance costs for non-equity shares are not equal to the dividends, the difference should be accounted for in the profit and loss account as an appropriation of profits. (Para. 44)

An example of a situation where there may be a difference between the finance costs and the dividends are shares which may be redeemed at a premium.

We have already introduced the actuarial method earlier in this chapter. There we showed that the method was logical and allocated the cost of borrowing fairly over the period of the loan, as well as ensuring that the whole of the finance costs are charged to the profit and loss account. The use of the method would also achieve consistency across the wide range of different capital instruments in issue.

Issue costs

The calculation of the constant rate of interest and the initial carrying value in the balance sheet depends upon the 'net proceeds' of the issue of the capital instruments. The net proceeds are defined as

> The fair value of the consideration received on the issue of a capital instrument after deduction of issue costs. (Para. 11)

Issue costs are defined as:

> The costs that are incurred directly in connection with the issue of a capital instrument, that is, those costs that would not have been incurred had the specific instrument in question not been issued. (Para. 10)

The use of the phrase 'fair value' reminds us that the carrying value of the capital instrument will not always be found without some degree of estimation. An example of such a case would be the joint issue of a debt and warrant. The amount received for the issue of the joint instrument will need to be allocated to provide the fair value of the debt and warrant; the most likely source of evidence is market values.

The standard is restrictive as to what should be included in issue costs (Para. 96). Such costs should not include any which would have been incurred had the instrument not been issued, such as management remuneration or indeed the costs of researching and negotiating alternative sources of finance. Those costs that do not qualify as issue costs should be written off to the profit and loss account as incurred. The standard requires that issue costs be accounted for by reducing the proceeds of the issue of the instrument and should not be regarded as assets because they do not provide access to any future economic benefits. The consequence of setting the issue costs against the net proceeds is to increase the interest charge in the profit and loss account; in other words, it ensures that the issue costs are written off over the life of the capital instrument.

Use of the share premium account

It might be thought that the proposals would include the stipulation that entities subject to the Companies Act should no longer take advantage of the provision whereby they can charge issue costs and discounts against the share premium account. The proposals only go some way towards this desirable end. Issue costs, which would include discounts, have to be charged to the profit and loss account but the standard specifically draws attention to the fact that the issue costs may subsequently be charged to the share premium account by means of a transfer between reserves (Para. 97).

The distinction between shareholders' funds and liabilities

A capital instrument is a liability if it contains an obligation to transfer economic benefit, including contingent obligations, otherwise it is part of shareholders' funds. It is usually clear whether an instrument requires the company to make some sort of transfer to the owner of an instrument or whether any such transfer is made at the discretion of the company but there are two exceptions to the general rule. The first relates to an obligation that would only arise on the insolvency of the issuer. If there is no expectation of that event, and the entity can be accounted for on a going concern basis, that contingent liability can be ignored. Similarly, an obligation that would only crystallise if a covenant attached to a capital instrument were breached can also be disregarded unless, of course, there is evidence that such a breach will occur.

Warrants

Share warrants are instruments that state that the holder or bearer is entitled to be issued with a specified number of shares, possibly upon the payment of an additional fixed price. In the view of the ASB, the original amount paid for the warrant must be regarded as part of the subscription price of the shares which may, or may not, be issued at some time in the future, and it is for this reason that FRS 4 specifies that warrants be reported within shareholders' funds (Para. 37).

The Board does, however, recognise that the topic of warrants raises a number of issues that are outside the scope of FRS 4. It refers[11] in particular to the view that if the price paid on the exercise of the warrant is less than the fair value of the shares issued, this should be reflected in the financial statements by, presumably, increasing shareholders' funds and recognising as an expense the 'cost' incurred in issuing shares in this way. Another controversial issue is what should be done if the warrant lapses without being exercised. Should the amount initially subscribed to the warrant continue to be treated as part of share capital or be regarded as a gain by the company? The issue depends essentially on whether the warrant holders are regarded as sharing in the ownership of the company. If they are so regarded then the benefit from the lapse in the warrant is not a gain to the company but a transfer between owners, and hence the initial subscription should be treated as part of share capital. If, on the other hand, the warrant holders are not regarded as owners (the view taken by the ASB), the amount released by the lapse of the warrants should be reported as a gain within the statement of recognised gains and losses.

In summary, the provisions of FRS 4 relating to the taking up and lapsing of warrants are:

1 When a warrant is exercised, the amount previously recognised in respect of the warrant should be included in the net proceeds of the shares issued (Para. 46).
2 When a warrant elapses unexercised, the amount previously recognised in respect of the warrant should be reported in the statement of total recognised gains and losses (Para. 47).

The distinction between equity and non-equity

FRS 4 reinforces the requirements of company legislation by requiring that the balance sheet should show the total amount of shareholders' funds with an analysis between the amount attributable to equity interests and the amount attributable to non-equity interests (Para. 40).

The need therefore is to distinguish between equity and non-equity interests. Company law provides a succinct definition of equity share capital, which means:

> in relation to a company, its issued share capital excluding any part of that capital which, neither as respects dividends nor as respects capital, carries any right to participate beyond a specified amount in a distribution.[12]

The ASB believes that this definition does not give sufficient guidance in the more complex cases and hence it provides a far more detailed statement of the distinction that starts with a definition of non-equity shares. These are shares possessing any of the following characteristics:

(a) Any of the rights of the shares to receive payments (whether in respect of dividends, in respect of redemption or otherwise) are for a limited amount that is not calculated by reference to the company's assets or profits or the dividends on any class of equity share.

---

[11] *See* the section on the development of the standard, paragraphs 11–13.
[12] Companies Act 1985, Sec. 744.

(b) Any of their rights to participate in a surplus in a winding-up are limited to a specific amount that is not calculated by reference to the company's assets or profits, and such limitation has a commercial effect in practice at the time the shares were issued or, if later, at the time the limitation was introduced.

(c) The shares are redeemable according to their terms, or the holder, or any party other than the issuer, can require their redemption.

(Para. 12)

Following all the above, equity shares are defined simply as 'shares other than non-equity shares' (Para. 7).

The general drift of the ASB thinking is clear. Its definition attempts to ensure that only 'true' equity is treated as such. In so far as the existence of non-equity capital represents a risk that may be taken into account by equity shareholders when making investment decisions, this approach can be seen as being protective of the interest of existing and potential equity shareholders.

The distinction between convertible and non-convertible liabilities

A convertible debt is one that allows the holder of the security to exchange the debt for shares in the issuing company on the terms specified in the loan instrument.

Prior to the issue of FRS 4 existing practice was to report convertible debt as a liability, a practice that FRS 4 noted is uncontroversial where conversion is uncertain or unlikely. But there are those who would argue that if conversion were probable then convertible debt should be reported outside liabilities in order to give a fairer representation of the economic position of the company. In drafting FRS 4, the ASB, arguing that a balance sheet is a record of the financial position of a company at a point of time, not a forecast of future events, specified that all convertible debt should be included with liabilities. As we shall see, in the section of this chapter dealing with the disclosure requirements of the standard, adequate information must be provided regarding the terms and conditions relating to the various capital instruments in issue.

There is a more sophisticated line of argument that suggests that merely reporting convertible debt as part of liabilities ignores the equity rights which are inherent in the issue of convertible debt. The International Accounting Standard Committee, for example, in IAS 32, 'Financial Instruments: Disclosure and Presentation', requires split accounting for convertible debt. Under this approach the proceeds of issue of convertible debt are allocated between the two components, the equity rights and the liabilities. The consequence of this is that the finance charge relating to the debt is increased over that which would be recorded if the whole of the proceeds of the issue were treated as a liability. The reason for this is that the total amount payable to the convertible debt holders, assuming no conversion, consists of a string of interest payments and the redemption price remains the same irrespective of the method of accounting used. If the initial recorded value of the debt were smaller, as it would be if the proceeds of the issue were split, then the finance cost would be increased to cover the amount of the proceeds that were allocated to the equity interest.

Happily for lovers of simplicity, the ASB rejected this more complex presentation and the relevant standard practice for the presentation of convertible debt is straightforward:

> Conversion of debt should not be anticipated. Convertible debt should be reported within liabilities and the finance cost should be calculated on the assumption that the debt will never be converted. The amount attributable to convertible debt should be stated separately from that of other liabilities. (Para. 25)

When convertible debt is converted, the amount recognised in shareholders' funds in respect of the shares issued should be the amount at which the liability for the debt is stated as at the date of conversion. No gain or loss should be recognised on conversion. (Para. 26)

Debt maturity

As recognised in company legislation, users of accounts need to be given adequate information about the scheduling of the repayment of debt in order to help them assess the companies' short-term solvency and long-term liquidity position.

The requirements of FRS 4 are a little more extensive than those of the Companies Act in that they include an additional cut-off date of two years. The requirement is that:

An analysis of the maturity of debt should be presented showing amounts falling due:
(a) in one year or less, or on demand;
(b) in more than one but not more than two years;
(c) in more than two years but not more than five years; and in more than five years.
(Para. 33)[13]

The maturity of the debt should be determined by reference to the earliest date on which the lender can require repayment. (Para. 34)

Life is of course not without its complications and the ASB had to consider the case of a borrower who had already made arrangements to refinance the existing loan. The question here is whether the maturity of the loan should be measured by reference only to the capital instrument currently in issue, or whether account should be taken of the re-financing arrangements that have been established. It would clearly be misleading to ignore the significant fact that facilities have been established in order to extend the period of the loan and therefore the ASB states:

Where committed facilities are in existence at the balance sheet date that permit the refinancing of debt for a period beyond its maturity, the earliest date at which the lender can require repayment should be taken to be the maturity date of the longest refinancing permitted by a facility in respect of which all the following conditions are met:
(a) The debt and the facility are under a single agreement or course of dealing with the same lender or group of lenders.
(b) The finance costs for the new debt are on a basis that is not significantly higher than that of the existing debt.
(c) The obligations of the lender (or group of lenders) are firm: the lender is not able legally to refrain from providing funds except in circumstances the possibility of which can be demonstrated to be remote.
(d) The lender (or group of lenders) is expected to be able to fulfil its obligations under the facility.
(Para. 35)

This is clearly a stringent set of conditions.

In order that the users of the accounts are made aware of the use of the above provision it is also required that:

Where the maturity of debt is assessed by reference to that of refinancing permitted by facilities in accordance with paragraph 35, the amounts of the debt so treated, analysed by the earliest date on which the lender could demand repayment in the absence of the facilities, should be disclosed. (Para. 36)

---

[13] This is a correction of the original version that was effected in FRS 13. The original, incorrect version, referred to periods of less than 2 or 5 years and more than 2 or 5 years thus leaving in doubt the treatment of liabilities that had exactly two or five years to run.

FRS 4 and consolidated financial statements

There are a number of special issues relating to consolidated financial statements.

There may be circumstances when shares issued by a subsidiary and held outside the group should be included in liabilities rather than minority interest (Para. 49). This treatment is required when the group, taken as a whole, has an obligation to transfer economic benefit; for example, if another member of the group has guaranteed payments relating to the shares.

In addition:

(a) The amount of minority interests shown in the balance sheet should be analysed between the aggregate amount attributable to equity interests and amounts attributable to non-equity interests (Para. 50).
(b) The amounts attributed to non-equity minority interests and their associated finance costs should be calculated in the same manner as those for non-equity shares. The finance costs associated with such interests should be included in minority interests in the profit and loss account (Para. 51).

Some further explanation is required regarding the circumstances under which shares issued by subsidiaries would not be shown in minority interest. As already noted, one of the FRS 4 principles is that if any element of obligation to transfer economic resources attaches to a capital instrument, then it should be treated as a liability. Thus, if guarantees have been given in respect of dividends payable on the shares or on their redemption, there is a liability, albeit contingent, to transfer economic resources. In such circumstances the shares should be included under liabilities.

Disclosure requirements

FRS 4 is very much concerned with the provision of adequate, some might argue more than adequate, disclosure, and in the previous pages we have referred to a number of the proposals that bear on this matter. The remaining disclosure requirements may be summarised as follows:

(a) Disclosure relating to shares (Paras 55–59)
  (i) An analysis should be given of the total amount of non-equity interests in shareholders' funds relating to each class of non-equity shares and series of warrants for non-equity shares.
  (ii) A brief summary of the rights of each class of shares should be given, other than for equity shares with standard characteristics. Details should also be provided of classes of shares which are not currently in issue but which may be issued as a result of the conversion of debt or the exercise of warrants.
  (iii) Details of dividends for each class of shares and any other appropriation of profit in respect of non-equity shares should be disclosed.
(b) Disclosure relating to minority interests (Paras 60–61)
  (i) The minority interests charge in the profit and loss account should be analysed between equity and non-equity interests.
  (ii) If there are non-equity minority interests the rights of the holders against other group companies should be described.
(c) Disclosure relating to debt (Paras 62–64)
  (i) Details of convertible debt should be provided.
  (ii) Brief descriptions should be provided where the legal nature of the instrument differs from that associated with debt; for example, when the obligation to repay is conditional.

(iii) Gains and losses on the repurchase or early settlement of debt should be disclosed in the profit and loss account as separate items within or adjacent to 'interest payable and similar charges'.

(d) General disclosure requirements

(i) When the disclosure requirements relating to the amounts of convertible debt, non-equity interests in shareholders' funds and non-equity interests in minority interests are given in the notes, the relevant balance sheet caption should refer to the existence of the relevant capital instruments (Para. 54).

(ii) Where the brief summaries required in respect of a(ii), b(i), c(i) and c(iii) above cannot adequately provide the information necessary to understand the commercial effect of the relevant instruments, that fact should be stated together with particulars of where the relevant information may be obtained. In any event the principal features of the instruments should be stated (Para. 65).

Application notes

FRS 4 includes a section on Application Notes that describes how the principles of the reporting standard should be applied to capital instruments with certain features. The instruments covered in this section are:

Auction market preferred shares (AMPS)	Index-linked loans
Capital contributions	Limited recourse debt
Convertible capital bonds	Participating preference shares
Convertible debt with a premium put option	Perpetual debt
Convertible debt with enhanced interest	Repackaged perpetual debt
Debt issued with warrants	Stepped interest bonds
Deep discount bonds	Subordinated debt
Income bonds	

Space does not allow coverage of these notes and the interested reader should refer to the standard itself.

Derivatives and related financial instruments

The vast majority of derivatives are quite simple financial instruments, such as a call option which could involve Smith saying to Jones 'I will pay you 5 pence per share for the right to buy, in three months time, 5000 shares in Blank plc for 57 pence per share', or it could be a forward purchase of currency where, instead of buying US dollars at, say, 1.60 dollars to the pound for immediate delivery, the purchaser agrees to a rate of 1.62 dollars for delivery in three months. It has to be admitted that other derivatives are not as simple, ask the former directors of Barings, but even in very complex cases it is as well to remember that all such instruments are essentially about the balance between risk and expected return. Probably the majority of those involved in the various derivative markets are attempting to protect themselves against risk (or to hedge) but for the markets to exist there need to be others present whose purpose is to speculate in the hope of profit.

FRS 13 *Derivatives and other Financial Instruments: Disclosures*

This standard is unusual in a number of ways, not only is it the most complicated standard issued to date, containing many terms and concepts which do not impinge on the professional life of the vast majority of accountants, but it is also an admission that the present state of the art of financial accounting is not capable of dealing adequately with the reporting of the more complex forms of derivatives and other types of financial instruments. The ASB's concerns were expressed in a discussion paper *Derivatives and other Financial Instruments*, issued in July 1996, which focused on three main issues: the measurement of financial instruments, the use of hedge accounting and the disclosures relating to financial instruments. Among what FRS 13 describes (page 137) as the tentative conclusions of the discussion paper, was the view that it was not appropriate to measure financial instruments on a historical cost basis, but that they should be measured at fair value, a term that the Board now seems to prefer rather than current value, the term used in the discussion document. However, the Board is not yet able to advance on the measurement front, nor deal with the issue of hedge accounting, but felt it was necessary to promulgate a standard on disclosure.

Scope and objective

FRS 13 is concerned only with those entities that have one more of their financial instruments listed or publicly traded on a stock exchange or market as well as all banks and similar institutions. Its provisions do not apply, however, to insurance companies.

A financial instrument is defined as:

> any contract that gives rise to both a financial asset of one entity and a financial liability or equity instrument of another entity. (FRS 13, Para. 2)

Financial instruments include both primary financial instruments – such as bonds, debtors, creditors and shares – as well *derivative financial instruments*, which are themselves defined in the same section as FRS 13 as:

> a financial instrument that derives its value from the price or rate of some underlying item.

The underlying items can take a variety of forms including equities, commodities, interest rates, exchange rates and stock market and other indices.

However so complicated the nest of interrelations contained within the instrument may be, there must be a chain of events that leads to the transfer of either cash or an equity instrument from one party to another. Thus, just to give a few examples, debtors, shares, forward contracts and options are financial instruments while physical assets, prepayments and obligations, like many warranties that will be satisfied by the provision of services are not. Lest it be thought that any entity that has debtors will be covered by the standard, remember that to qualify the financial instruments must be publicly traded.

The objective of the standard is to ensure that entities within its scope disclose information to help users assess its objectives, policies and strategy for holding or issuing financial instruments. In particular, the information should help users assess:

(a) the risk profile of the entity for each of the main financial risks that arise in connection with financial instruments and commodity contracts with similar characteristics; and

(b) the significance of such instruments and contracts to the reported financial position, performance and cash flows, regardless of whether the instruments or contracts are on the balance sheet (recognized) or off the balance sheet (unrecognized).

(Para. 1)

Risks associated with financial instruments

The standard identifies the following four types of risk associated with financial instruments of which only the first two have, and even then to a limited extent, been reported upon in financial statements.

- *Credit risk* – the possibility that a party to the contract may fail to perform according to the terms of the contract.
- *Liquidity risk* – the chance that an entity will fail to raise the funds that would enable it to meet its commitments under the contract.
- *Cash flow risk* – the possibility that future cash flows will fluctuate in amount.
- *Market price risk* – the possibility that future changes in market prices will change the value, or burden, of a financial instrument. The main components of market price risk are:
  - *Interest rate risk*
  - *Currency risk*
  - *Other market risk*, this includes the risks associated from changes in commodity and share prices.

The structure of FRS 13

The standard requires both narrative and numerical disclosures; the same narrative disclosures are required of all entities while the requirement for numerical disclosure differs between:

- entities that are not financial institutions
- banks and similar institutions
- other types of financial institutions.

We are in this section dealing only with the first of the above.

One of the more helpful features of the standard is the three examples provided in Appendix III of hypothetical disclosures that might be provided by different entities. One relates to a bank, the others to non-financial entities; of these, one, that is said to be representative of the vast majority of entities, is fairly simple, the other is more complex. Interested readers should refer to this appendix.

Mode of presentation

It is envisaged, but it is not required, that the disclosures specified by the standard should be placed in context of a discussion of the entity's activities, structure and funding. This discussion should typically also consider the financial risk profile as a whole. This means that it will be helpful to provide the narrative requirements of the standard in a statement such as an operating and financial review. The way in which the information is presented is left to the entity, but it is required to ensure that the narrative information is cross-referenced to the Notes to the Financial Statements. The required numerical information should be included in the notes.

The standard covers a lot of ground and large entities with numerous complex schemes, involving many types of financial instruments, could nullify the objective of the standard by providing data in excessive detail. The Board is aware of this point and enjoins entities to be prepared to use a high degree of aggregation in fulfilling their obligations under the standard, which could mean that it might be impossible to relate the explanations directly to the balance sheet captions (another unusual feature of FRS 13), and entities are encouraged to provide additional information to allow the figures to be traced back to the balance sheet unless that would unduly complicate the position (Para. 25).

Main elements to be disclosed

The length of the standard makes it impossible for us to do anything more than provide a highly simplified and selective summary of the main points that have to be disclosed. In making our selection we have been influenced by those areas, such as the use of current values, that we have emphasised elsewhere in this book. The following are the main aspects for which disclosure is required:

- *Objectives, policies and strategies.*
- *Interest rate disclosures* indicating liabilities at fixed interest rates, variable interest rates and on which no interest is paid.
- *Currency rates disclosure* providing an analysis of the net amount of financial (or monetary) assets and liabilities in terms of the principal currencies involved.
- *Liquidity disclosure* including a breakdown of the dates at which financial liabilities fall due for payment.
- *Fair value disclosure* providing information about both the carrying values and fair values of financial assets and liabilities.
- Disclosures about *financial assets and financial liabilities used for trading.*
- Disclosures about *hedging.*
- Disclosures about *commodity contracts.*

Compliance with International Accounting Standards

The relevant International Standard is IAS 32 *Financial Instruments: Disclosure and Presentation*. This standard covers topics that, in the UK, are the subject of FRS 13, FRS 4, *Capital Instruments*, FRS 5, *Reporting the Substance of Transactions*, and company legislation. Compliance with these standards and company law ensures compliance with IAS 32 in all material respects other than the following:

- IAS 32 applies to all entities, which does seem a trifle excessive.
- There are some differences in what are regarded as being financial instruments.
- In general the disclosure requirements of the UK's standards are more extensive and specific than those of IAS 32, although there are some aspects where it calls for more detailed information.

The IASC is one jump ahead of the ASB in that it has issued a statement dealing with measurement and not just disclosure. IAS 39 *Financial Instruments: Recognition and Measurement*, issued in December 1998, establishes rules for the recognition and measurement of financial assets and liabilities, including hedging transactions. The International Standard draws heavily on the equivalent US standard and is regarded by the IASC as an interim standard pending further work. IAS 39, and any successor will undoubtedly increase the use of fair values in financial statements.

Some comments on FRS 13

The standard has many commendable features, one of the most significant being its general approach to reporting on risk and uncertainty. One of the weaknesses of traditional accounting, which was perpetuated in the initial phases of standard setting, is the mistaken view that complex realities can be expressed in a single figure. This is reflected in the reluctance to contemplate the production of financial statements where two or more valuation bases are given equal prominence and the insistence of always providing a single value, rather than a range of possible values, for items whose estimation is subject to a high degree of error.

The more 'grown up' approach of FRS 13 can be seen in its encouragement in the use of sensitivity analysis in reporting to users. Sensitivity analysis helps identify the factors that of most significance and can help users assess the numerical significance of changes in circumstances. For example, in determining the effect of interest rate risk users could be told that, say, if in the year under review, average interest rates had been 5 per cent higher the reported profit would have been reduced by 2 per cent. Such information is undoubtedly useful in forming a general impression of an entity's financial position and the hypothetical example provided for a 'simple' company does appear to provide information that could help the user. It may be more difficult, even on the part of a skilled analyst, to assimilate the data that will be provide in the more complex cases. Much will depend on the willingness of reporting entities to make their best efforts to help users and to avoid, particular when they have things to hide, the opportunities, which surely exist, for obfuscation.

Provisions, contingent assets and liabilities

Provisions and contingent items are bound up with doubt and uncertainty. There may be no doubt that a provision is a liability – something is owed or an obligation has to be discharged – but there may be doubt as to how much is owed or when it has to be paid. While in the case of a contingent asset or liability there may doubt as whether the thing exists at all. Doubt and uncertainty very easily give rise to uneven accounting treatment and, as we shall show, prior to the intervention of the ASB this was particularly true in the case of provisions and, to a lesser extent, contingent assets and liabilities. The ASB issued a Discussion Paper in November 1995 and an Exposure Draft, FRED 14, in June 1997 that was followed by FRS 12 in September 1998.

FRS 12 *Provisions, Contingent Liabilities and Assets*

We deal first with provisions and then go on to consider contingent liabilities and assets, the last named being included in a Standard which is largely devoted to liabilities because the treatment of contingent assets and contingent liabilities share many common features.

The need for a standard

It has long been recognised that there was considerable variation in the treatment of provisions. For example, provisions were almost always recognised when there is likely to be expenditure resulting from goods sold under warranty, whereas they were far less frequently recognised in the case of potential environmental liabilities. But there was more to the problem than inconsistent practice: the lack of clarity allowed accountants to manipulate the figures for profit.

If provisions can be related to intention ('we think we will do this') rather than obligation ('we must do this') it would be possible to smooth profits by creating provisions in years in which the profit is high and releasing them in years in which profits are low (using the defence that 'we changed our mind').

Another way of apparently creating a healthy growth in profits was to engage in 'big bath' accounting. This often occurred in a reorganisation of some kind – possibly following a change in management following disappointing financial results – when the profit and loss account was charged not only with committed expenditure but also with planned expenditure for several years. The failure of users of financial statements to understand the significance of excess provisions and its beneficial effect on the reported profits of the years following reorganisation helped to boost the careers of a number of so-called 'company doctors'.

FRS 12 is a standard which is concerned with measurement and hence addresses three main issues: When should a provision be recognised? How should it be measured? How should it be disclosed?

We will deal with these in turn.

Provisions

Recognition of provisions

The summary of FRS 12 (paragraph d) provides a succinct statement of the main issues:

> A provision should be recognised when an entity has a present obligation (legal or constructive) as a result of a past event, it is probable that a transfer of economic benefits will be required to settle the obligation, and a reliable estimate can be made of the amount of the obligation. Unless these conditions are met, no provision should be recognised.

A provision should only be made if a liability cannot be avoided and this particular condition will usually be easily dealt with if there is a legal contract involved, but the standard also refers to non-legal or constructive obligations. These are obligations that arise because the reporting entity has created a valid expectation on the part of other parties that it will discharge its responsibilities towards them either because of its past actions or because it has clearly stated that it will do so (Para. 2).

If a provision is to be made a liability it must have arisen from a *past event* or *obligating event*, in other words it must result from some past action of the entity such that it has 'no realistic alternative to settling the obligation created by the event' (Para. 17). The ASB strongly makes the point that financial statements deal with the entity's financial position at the end of its reporting period, and not its possible position in the future, and that no provision should be made for the costs of operating in the future or for providing against occurrences which the entity can avoid by changing its style of operations. An example of this is provided in the Standard (Para. 19) which is of an entity which might, because of commercial pressures or legal requirements, have good evidence that it will need to incur certain expenditures if it is to operate in a particular way in the future, the example quoted is the possible need to fit a smoke filter in a certain type of factory. It is argued that this should not give rise to a provision because the entity can avoid the expenditure by changing its operating methods and, hence, there is no present liability. Intuitively, there is something a bit odd about this for it implies that the financial statement should ignore what might potentially be a catastrophic event if, say, the likely costs of complying with new environmental requirements means that the existing business ceases to be economically viable. The answer is that, if the potential event is high in probability and large in magnitude, its impact on the business might be reflected through the write down of certain assets (see Impairment of Assets in Chapter 4) or by the removal of the assumption that the business is a going concern. These two actions are related to the future while a provision has to be firmly rooted in the past.

The decision as to whether a constructive liability exists may not be straightforward especially if we need to identify the past or obligating event. That event might simply be the announcement of a decision. Consider the situation of a company, which, possibly because it wants to construct a plant with an 'uncertain' environmental impact, needs to build up the goodwill of the local community and so decides to underwrite the costs of a local arts festival. Suppose that following the announcement of the possibility of the grant the local organisers take some action resulting from that announcement which increases their financial exposure. Should the company recognise a provision even if it had not yet signed a formal agreement and could legally change its mind? If, as seems likely given the facts stated, the company believes that it must stand by the announcement, then a provision should be recognised.

The measurement of provisions

The basic rule is that:

> The amount recognised as a provision should be the best estimate of the expenditure required to settle the present obligation at the balance sheet date. (Para. 36)

Of course, but how in a world of uncertainty do we measure it?

In some cases use can be made of elementary statistical techniques such as *expected values*. For example, a store might at its year-end have 100 000 items still under warranty and, on the basis of experience, estimate that 5 per cent will need to be repaired, and that the average cost of repair is £300.

Then the expected value of the cost of servicing the warranty that should be recognised as a provision is:

$$(0.95 \times 0 + 0.05 \times £300) \times 100\,000 = £1\,500\,000$$

In the case of a single event a distinction needs to be drawn between the *best estimate* and *most likely outcome*. Consider the example provided in the Standard. It is of an obligation to rectify a serious fault in a plant where the 'most likely' outcome is that the repairs can be completely rectified at the first attempt at a cost of £1m. But this is not certain, so the provision should be for a greater amount, or 'best estimate', to allow for the possibility of additional expenditure. This is a variant of the expected value approach in that the additional amount would depend on both the magnitude of the cost of the additional work but also on the probability that it will be necessary.

The need for prudence as conventionally defined – the asymmetric statement that profits and assets should not be overstated and expenses and liabilities not overstated – is introduced in paragraph 43 but the ASB goes on quickly to warn against going too far. To quote directly '. . . if the projected costs of a particularly adverse outcome are estimated on a prudent basis, that outcome is not then deliberately treated as more probable than is realistically the case' (Para. 43). This phrase, which must of one of the least elegant examples of ASB drafting, seems to mean be prudent but do not overdo it.

Present values

> Where the effect of the time value of money is material, the amount of the provision should be the present value of the expenditures expected to be required to settle the obligation. (Para. 45)

In the case of provisions it is recommended that the easiest way of dealing with risk is to use a discount rate that reflects the risks specific to the liability, but if this option is selected the cash flows to be discounted should not themselves be adjusted for risk, the 'best estimates' should be used. An acceptable alternative is to adjust the cash flows for risk and use a risk-free rate of discount.

Changes in provisions

> Provisions should be reviewed at each balance sheet date and adjusted to reflect the current best estimate. (Para. 62)

Disclosure requirements

The disclosure requirements are set out in paragraphs 89 and 90; the first paragraph deals primarily with numbers, the second mainly with words. The numerical statement should reflect the changes in provisions that have occurred during the accounting period: provisions created, used and reversed as well as increases in present values due to the passage of time and the consequences of changes in the discount rate. The words that should be supplied include, for each class of provision, the nature of the liability, some indication about the associated risk and a note of the extent of any expected reimbursements.

Contingent assets and liabilities

Company law has for a long time required the disclosure, by way of a note to the accounts, of information concerning contingent liabilities but there is no such requirement concerning contingent assets.

Accounting for Contingencies was the subject of SSAP 18, issued in 1980, and this called for both the recognition, within financial statements, of certain contingent liabilities, but only in extreme cases, and the provision of note information about contingent assets but only where there was a high probability that they would unwind in the entity's favour. FRS 12, which replaced SSAP 18, also forbids the recognition of contingent assets under any circumstances but adopts a different, less useful, definition of contingent liabilities.

Contingent assets

It will be helpful to start the discussion with the definition of a contingent asset.

> A possible asset that arises from past events and whose existence will be confirmed only by the occurrence of one or more uncertain events not wholly within the entity's control. (Para. 2)

A bet on a horse race would seem to satisfy the definition pretty well, so too, to take a more commercial example, would be a drug which is the subject of clinical trials. However, prudence will usually dictate that such possible assets are not accorded the status of contingent assets that will continue to be very rare beasts.

Contingent assets: disclosure requirements

'An entity should not recognise a contingent asset' (Para. 31), but what should be disclosed? This is covered in paragraph 94 which states that where 'an inflow of economic benefits is probable', the nature of the contingent assets should be disclosed with, if practicable, an estimate of their financial effect measured on the same principles as FRS 12 applies to provisions.

Contingent liabilities

The definition of a contingent liability has two elements; the first is the counterpart of the contingent asset while the second breaks new ground. A *contingent liability* is defined as:

(a) A possible obligation that arises from past events and whose existence will be confirmed only by the occurrence of one or more uncertain future events not wholly within the entity's control; or

(b) a present obligation that arises from past events but is not recognised because:

(i) it is not probable that a transfer of economic benefits will be required to settle the obligation: or

(ii) the amount of the obligation cannot be measured with sufficient reliability.

(Para. 2)

The second part of the definition (which was not included in the SSAP 18 definition) provides a convenient vehicle for picking up items which are actually provisions, insofar that they represent *present obligations*, but which do not fully satisfy the tests for recognition set out in paragraph 14 either because it is 'not probable' that the liability will have to be discharged or because it is not possible to make a 'reliable estimate' of the liability. Thus FRS 12 requires that such pseudo provisions should be treated in the same way as 'real' contingent liabilities. This may be convenient but it seems unfortunate that, as a result, the concept of contingency is muddied.

Figure 5.1, which is taken from FRS 12, shows a decision tree for distinguishing between provisions and contingent liabilities. The figure shows that, if it is unlikely that there is a present obligation, and that there is only a remote possibility that the liability, if it did exist, would have to be discharged, then the item can be ignored. But, if there is a reasonable chance that there is an obligation, but with very little chance that it will have to be discharged, then it should be disclosed by way of a note to the financial statements as part of contingent liabilities.

Contingent liabilities: disclosure requirements

As is the case with contingent assets, contingent liabilities should not be recognised but, as might be expected, the test for whether the item should be shown in the notes to the financial statements is not the same for the two items. In the case of contingent assets note disclosure is required when the inflow of benefits *is probable* while in the case of contingent liabilities disclosure can only be avoided if *the possibility of payment is remote* (Para. 91). For each class of contingent liability that passes the test information should be provided on their estimated financial effect, the uncertainties relating to the amount or timing of any outflow and an indication of the possibility of any reimbursement.

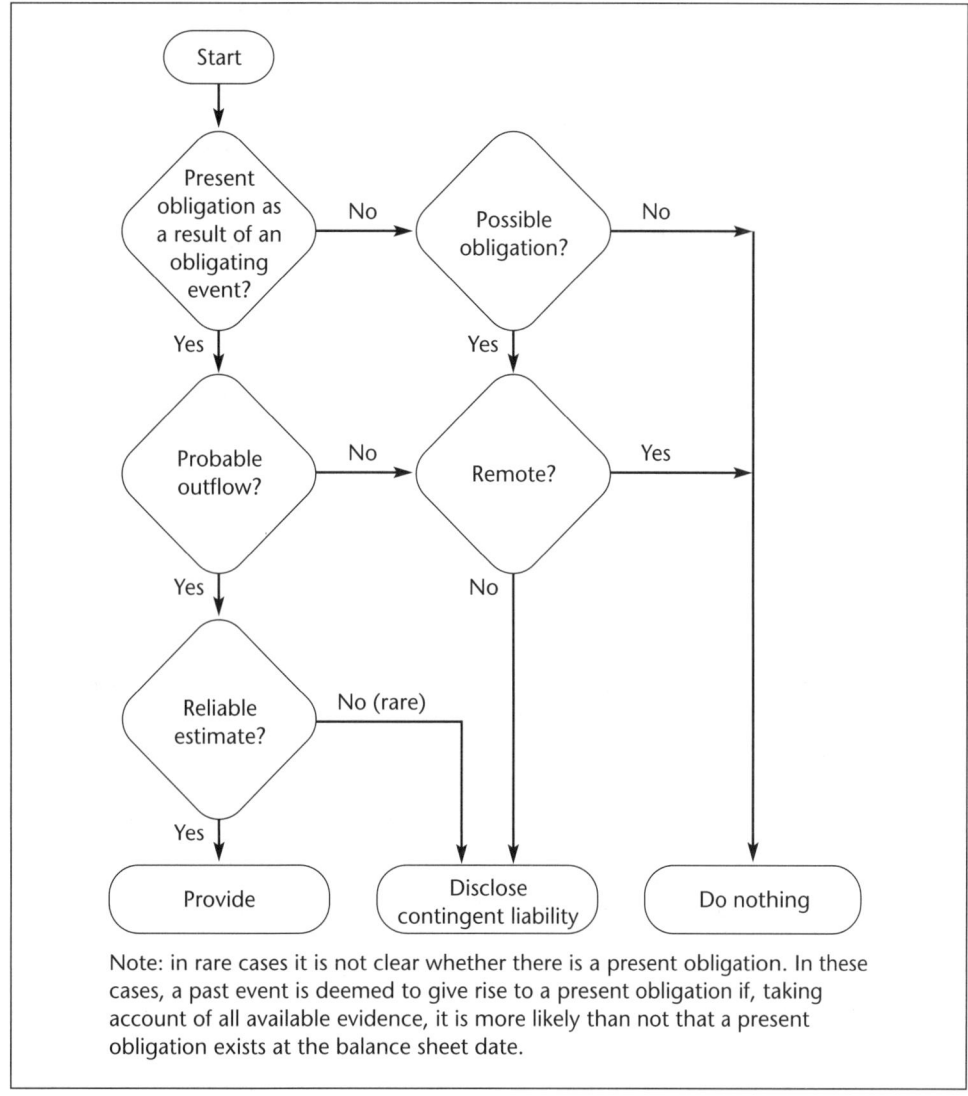

Fig. 5.1 Decision Tree

Source: ASB FRS 12, Provisions, Contingent Liabilities and Assets. © ASB Publications Limited 2000.

Pension costs

Introduction

The provision of occupational pension schemes for employees is now common practice in the UK. Some schemes are contributory, that is the cost is shared by both employees and employer, while others are non-contributory, that is the whole cost falls on the employer. In either case the cost to the employer may be both substantial and difficult to determine, but the legal disclosure requirements are minimal and, in the past, accounting practice was rudimentary. The publication of SSAP 24,

'Accounting for Pension Costs', in 1988, represented an important development in that it sought to fill a large hole in the accounts of many companies.

In order to understand accounting for pensions it is necessary to know something about pension schemes.

One distinction which may be made between pension schemes is whether they are funded or unfunded. In the case of the funded scheme, contributions are paid into a separate fund that is usually administered by trustees, who invest the contributions and meet the pension commitments. The contributions are invested in a portfolio of property and/or securities either directly or indirectly by the purchase of insurance policies. In unfunded schemes contributions are not placed in a separate fund but are reinvested in the employer's business and pensions are subsequently paid on a 'pay-as-you-go' basis. An unfunded pension scheme is obviously the more risky from the point of view of the employees and the vast majority of pension schemes in the UK are funded.

Another distinction that needs to be made is between defined contribution schemes and defined benefit schemes.

Under defined contribution schemes the contributions are determined and the employees receive pensions on the basis of whatever amounts are available from those contributions and the returns earned from their investment. Such a scheme poses few problems for the accountant. As the contributions are fixed, the amount to be charged as the cost of providing pensions is clearly determinable as the amount payable by the employer in respect of a particular year.

Under a defined benefit scheme the retirement benefits are determined, sometimes on the basis of average salary over the employee's period of service, but more often on the basis of salary in the final year or years before retirement. For such a scheme the cost of pensions in a particular year is much more difficult to determine. It depends not upon the contribution payable in respect of a year but upon the pensions that will be paid in the future. The pensions payable depend on such factors as the future rate of increase in wages and salaries, the number of staff leaving the scheme before retirement and the life expectancy of pensioners and, where relevant, their dependants. In addition, the cost in the year of providing future pensions depends upon the rate of return to be earned on contributions and reinvested receipts. It is the need to take a very long-term view in the face of great uncertainties that makes accounting for defined benefit schemes such a difficult problem for the accountant.

Fortunately for employees, but unfortunately for accountants, most UK pension schemes, certainly those of major employers, are of the defined benefit variety. We will first examine how the costs of these schemes are estimated.

Defined benefit schemes – actuarial considerations

Given the long-term nature of pension schemes, it is necessary to involve actuaries in the calculation of the costs of defined benefit schemes. Most schemes are subject to a formal actuarial review every three years. The task of the actuary is to assess the level of contribution required to fund the estimated pension payments.

There are a number of different methods that are used by actuaries that, in general, share a common aim of finding a level contribution rate, as a proportion of pensionable pay, which, if the actuary's assumptions are correct, would ensure that the pension fund would be sufficient to pay the pensions as they fall due. Suppose, for example, that we have a new pension scheme, which has one employee, aged 41, due to retire in 24 years' time at 65 and with a life expectancy thereafter of 15 years.

The actuarial calculations might proceed as follows:

Present salary	£20 000

Assume, that his or her salary will increase by 6% per year.
Hence, salary on retirement = £20 000 $(1.06)^{24} \approx$ £81 000.

If on retirement a pension of half final salary is payable, the fund will require to be sufficient to pay £40 500 per annum for 15 years. Assuming, for simplicity, that the pension contribution is paid at the end of each year and that the assets in the fund will earn 8 per cent per annum for that period, the capital value of the fund at retirement age will need to be £346 660.

Assume, that in the period until retirement, the annual return on investments is only 7 per cent. Then 13 per cent of the staff member's salary will need to be paid into the fund.[14]

Two approaches are mentioned in SSAP 24[15] – the accrued benefits and prospective benefits methods. In broad terms, accrued benefits methods are based on the assumption that the flow of new entrants to the scheme will be such as to preserve the existing average age of the workforce. In contrast, prospective benefit methods normally only consider the existing workforce and seek to find a stable contribution rate for that group until the last member retires or leaves. The size of the fund will, hence, tend to be larger in the case of a scheme using a prospective benefit approach because it takes the ageing of the existing workforce into account.

The accounting principles underlying SSAP 24

Prior to the adoption of SSAP 24 many companies simply showed their contribution to the pension scheme as the pension cost for the period. The contribution may have been affected by factors other than those relating solely to the needs of the fund. Employers might, for example, increase the contribution for a year or for a limited period, with a view to reducing contributions in the future. Conversely, employers have in periods of financial stringency reduced their contributions. Such actions may have been effective in achieving the desired ability to manipulate the levels of reported profit, but they did little to help users of accounts assess the total costs of employment for the period.

The accounting objective set by SSAP 24 is to require employing companies to recognise the cost of providing pensions on a systematic and rational basis over the period in which they benefit from the services of their employees. This cost may well not be equal to the contribution made to the pension scheme in any period. [16]

Thus, in a very simple world the actuary's task is to estimate what proportion of pensionable pay would be needed to be paid into the scheme each year to pay for the

---

[14] On the date of retirement the required balance on the fund x is given by:

$$x = £40\,500 \sum_{i=1}^{15}(1.08)^{-i} = £346\,660$$

Let y be the required fraction of the annual salary which needs to be paid into the fund, then

$$£346\,660 = y\, £20\,000 \sum_{i=1}^{24}(1.06)^{i}\,(1.07)^{24-i}$$

from which $y = 0.13$.

[15] Other methods will be found in a paper published jointly by the ICAEW and the Faculty of Actuaries in May 1986, Pension Fund Terminology: Specimen Descriptions of Commonly-used Valuation Methods.

[16] Since tax relief is based on the contributions paid to the scheme the difference has deferred tax implications. See Chapter 7.

pensions, and the whole of this (in the case of a non-contributory scheme) or a part of this (in a contributory scheme) would represent the cost to the employer. This cost can be regarded as the regular pension cost.

But we do not live in such a state of simplicity and both the world and employers change their minds. The world changes its mind through altered interest rates, changes in the level of earnings and by allowing people to die other than when predicted by the actuary. Employers can also change their minds (or have their minds changed for them) and vary the conditions under which pensions are paid.

Thus, there will be variations to the regular cost and a large part of SSAP 24 is devoted to discussing how to account for these variations. Variations from the regular cost may be due to the following:

(a) the results of the world not being as the actuary expected it to be when he or she last worked out the regular cost – *experience surpluses or deficiencies*;
(b) changes in actuarial assumptions and methods and retroactive changes in benefits or conditions of membership;
(c) discretionary pensions increases.

Experience surpluses or deficiencies

In deciding whether the fund is in balance, that is whether it has sufficient assets to pay the required pensions given all the necessary assumptions about salary increases, rates of return and the like, the pension fund's assets are compared with its liabilities. Part of any difference may be due to changes in policy and assumptions about the future; these will be dealt with in the reassessment of the regular costs but, as noted above, part of the difference will, in all likelihood, because some of the assumptions made at the last review proved to incorrect, for example the rate of wage and salary increases might have been under or over estimated. This part of the difference is known as experience surpluses or deficiencies, which are defined in SSAP 24 as follows:

> An experience surplus or deficiency is that part of the excess or deficiency of the actuarial value of the assets over the actuarial value of the liabilities, on the basis of the valuation method used, which arises because events have not coincided with the actuarial assumptions made for the last valuation. (Para. 63)

The definition refers, not to the market value of the assets, but to their 'actuarial value', which is a value based on assumptions about future cash flows and interest rates and which may well, from time to time, differ significantly from the current market value. As we will discuss later in the context of the review of the standard the use of actuarial rather than market values is a controversial issue.

But at this stage we will concentrate on the treatment of experience surpluses and deficiencies. Should they be credited (or charged) to the past, the current year or to the future?

SSAP 24 specifies that with certain exceptions, to which we will refer later, material experience deficiencies, and surpluses, should be dealt with by adjusting current and future costs and not by immediately expensing (or crediting) the amount. In accordance with the main accounting objective of SSAP 24, the normal period over which the effect of the deficiency or surplus should be spread is the expected remaining service life of the current employees in the scheme after making suitable allowances for future withdrawals, or the average remaining service lives of the current membership. There are three exceptions to the general rule:

(a) Where there is a significant reduction in the number of employees covered by the scheme (see below).

(b) Where prudence requires a material deficiency to be made up over a shorter period. This exception is strictly limited to cases where a significant additional payment has to be paid into the scheme arising from a major transaction or event outside the actuarial assumptions and normal running of the scheme; a possible example is the consequence of a major mismanagement of the assets of the pension scheme. The standard does not specify the period over which the additional charge should be spread; it merely allows a shorter period than would otherwise be required.

(c) Where a refund is made to employers subject to deduction of tax within the provisions of the Finance Act 1986, or similar legislation. In such cases the employer may (not must) depart from the normal spreading rule and recognise the refund in the period in which it occurs.

The exception arising from a significant reduction of employees merits further comment. There have been many instances in recent years where reorganisation schemes have resulted in significant redundancies. These have often led to large surpluses on the pension funds with a result that future contributions are reduced, eliminated for a period (a 'contribution holiday') or contributions refunded.

In such instances the benefit should not be spread over the lives of the remaining workforce but instead recognised in the periods in which the benefits are received. They should, in general, not be anticipated in the sense of taking credit immediately the facts are known, but recognised on a year-by-year basis. But to this rule there is an exception, where the redundancies are related to a sale or termination of an operation, for in such a case FRS 3 *Reporting Financial Performance* must be followed. (SSAP 24, which of course predates FRS 3, refers to SSAP 6 in this context.) It may not be appropriate to defer recognition of a pension cost or credit because FRS 3 requires that provisions relating to the sale or termination of an operation be made after taking into account future profits of the operation or on the disposal of the assets.

The following example serves as a summary of the above and illustrates the variations between the contributions made to the scheme and the costs of pensions charged to the profit and loss account.

Example 5.2

Slick Limited is a small company which established a non-contributory defined benefit funded scheme in 20X1. Its year end is 31 December.

For arithmetical simplicity we will assume that the annual pensionable salary bill was £1 000 000 before the reorganisation referred to in paragraph C below and £600 000 thereafter.

(A) On the inception of the fund in 20X1 the actuary estimated that a contribution rate of 20 per cent on pensionable salaries would be required.

20X1–20X3
The charge to the profit and loss account will equal the contribution paid to the fund in each year, that is 20 per cent of £1 000 000 = £200 000.

(B) At the first triennial actuarial valuation in 20X4 the regular cost was estimated to be 21 per cent. There was at that stage an experience deficit of £75 000 which was paid into the fund by the employer in 20X4. The average remaining service life of the employees at that date was 15 years.

The position for each of the years 20X4–20X6 will be as follows:

20X4	£	£
Charge to profit and loss account		
Regular cost: 21% of 1 000 000		210 000
Experience deficit spread over 15 years		
75 000 ÷ 15		5 000
Amount paid to fund		
21% of 1 000 000	210 000	
Experience deficit	75 000	
	285 000	215 000
Prepayment at 31 December 20X4		70 000
	285 000	285 000

20X5	£	£
Prepayment at 1 January 20X5	70 000	
Charge to profit and loss account –		
as above		215 000
Amount paid to fund – regular cost –		
21% of 1 000 000	210 000	
	280 000	215 000
Prepayment at 31 December 20X5		65 000
	280 000	280 000

20X6	£	£
Prepayment at 1 January 20X6	65 000	
Charge to profit and loss account –		
as above		215 000
Amount paid to fund – regular cost –		
as above	210 000	
	275 000	215 000
Prepayment at 31 December 20X6		60 000
	275 000	275 000

(C) The next valuation took place in 20X7, a year in which the company undertook a major reorganisation involving a substantial number of redundancies.

The surplus resulting from redundancies was estimated to be £200 000 which is to be recouped by a reduction of £50 000 in the contributions otherwise payable for each of the four years 20X7–20Y0. We shall assume that this event constitutes a 'sale or termination' of an operation as defined in FRS 3.

In addition there was an experience surplus of £56 000 arising from events other than the reorganisation. The remaining average service life of the employees was 14 years.

The regular cost is estimated to be 18 per cent of £600 000 and the experience surplus of £56 000 is to be deducted in arriving at the 20X8 (not 20X7) payment.

For each of the years 20X7–20X9 the accounting treatment will be as follows:

20X7	£	£	£
Prepayment at 1 January 20X7		60 000	
Charge to profit and loss account in respect of regular cost and experience deficit/surplus.			
Regular cost – 18% × 600 000	108 000		
add 20X4 experience deficit			
75 000 ÷ 15	5 000		
	113 000		
less 20X7 experience surplus			
56 000 ÷ 14	4 000		109 000
Credit to profit and loss account in respect of surplus on termination		200 000	
Amount paid to fund			
18% × 600 000	108 000		
Reduction in respect of surplus on termination	50 000	58 000	
		318 000	109 000
Prepayment at 31 December 20X7			209 000
		318 000	318 000

20X8	£	£	£
Prepayment at 1 January 20X8		209 000	
Charge to profit and loss account – as above			109 000
Amount paid to fund – as above	58 000		
less Experience surplus	56 000	2 000	
		211 000	109 000
Prepayment at 31 December 20X8			102 000
		211 000	211 000

20X9		£	£
Prepayment at 1 January 20X9		102 000	
Charge to profit and loss account – as above			109 000
Amount paid to fund – as 20X7		58 000	
		160 000	109 000
Prepayment at 31 December 20X9			51 000
		160 000	160 000

The above may be summarised as follows:

	Profit & loss account expense	Cash payment	Balance prepayment at year end
	£000	£000	£000
(A) 20X1–20X3			
20X1	200	200	–
20X2	200	200	–
20X3	200	200	–
(B) 20X4–20X6			
20X4	215	285	70
20X5	215	210	65
20X6	215	210	60
(C) 20X7–20X9			
20X7 Ordinary	109 ⎫	58	209
Extraordinary	(200) ⎬		
20X8	109 ⎭	2	102
20X9	109	58	51

The prepayment at 31 December 20X9 may be analysed as follows:

	£
20X4 Experience deficit $\frac{9}{15} \times £75\,000$	45 000
20X7 Experience surplus $\frac{11}{14} \times £56\,000$	(44 000)
	1 000
20X7 Surplus on reorganisation £200 000 – £(3 × 50 000)	50 000
	51 000

Note:
The deferred tax implications have been ignored.

Changes in actuarial assumptions and methods and retroactive changes to the scheme

The effect of changes in the assumptions and methods used by the actuary should be treated in the same way as experience deficits and surpluses – they should be spread over the period of the expected remaining service lives of the current employees.

The same rule should be applied if there are retroactive changes in benefits and membership. Such changes, often called past service costs, may give improved benefits, e.g. increasing the proportion of final salary which will be paid as pension, or give employees credit for periods of service before they joined the scheme.

In some cases a surplus on a pension fund may be used to improve benefits and if, as a result, a provision that the company had made in its own accounts is no longer necessary, that provision should be released over the estimated remaining service life of the current employees.

Discretionary pension increases

A pension scheme might allow for pension increases within its rules, in which case they will be taken into account in the actuarial calculations, as should any increases required by legislation.

Other increases are discretionary on the part of the employer, whether paid direct or through the pension scheme. If such increases are granted on a regular basis, SSAP 24 states that the preferred treatment is to allow for them in the actuarial calculations. If this is not done, the full capital value of the increase should be provided in the year in which it is granted, not in the years in which it is paid, to the extent to which the increase is not covered by the surplus on the fund.

The same procedure should be followed in the case of an ex gratia pension granted to an employee on retirement, such as a long-serving member of staff who for some reason has not been a member of the scheme. Thus, for example, if it is estimated that the amount which would need to be invested to produce the desired pension at the estimated rates of interest is £400 000 then that amount should be charged to the profit and loss account in the year of retirement.

A non-recurring increase, which is granted for one period only with no expectation of repetition, should be charged to the period in which it is paid to the extent that it is not covered by a surplus.

We have now completed our main discussion of the accounting principles underlying SSAP 24, but we will deal with a number of related issues before turning to disclosure.

Related issues

The effect of discounting

The statement points out that financial statements normally show items at their face value without discounting, but by their very nature actuarial assumptions do make allowances for interest so that future cash flows are discounted to their present values. The statement points out that the question of whether items should be discounted in financial statements is a general one and on this general issue SSAP 24 should not be regarded as establishing standard practice.

In the special case of unfunded schemes the question of discounting cannot be avoided. The annual charge for pensions in any unfunded scheme is made up of two elements: the charge for the year (which is equivalent to the contribution to a funded scheme) plus interest on the unfunded liability. In an unfunded scheme the assets to support the pension are retained within the business and the latter element represents the return on those investments.

Group schemes

It is common for a number of companies in a group to use a single group scheme in which it is accepted that a common contribution rate can be used, even if when calculated company by company different rates would emerge. The standard allows this practice to continue and for lesser disclosure in the case of subsidiary companies, although full details have to be provided in the accounts of the holding company.

Foreign schemes

In principle all pension costs should be accounted for in accordance with the standard and hence consolidation adjustments may be required in the case of overseas subsidiaries. However, where countries overseas have very different pension laws or where the cost of making the necessary actuarial calculations is excessive, the contributions to the relevant overseas scheme can be treated as the costs for the period.

Scope

The standard is not restricted to instances where employers have a legal or contractual commitment to pay pensions; it also covers cases where the employers implicitly, through their actions, provide or contribute to employees' pensions.

Disclosure requirements

The main accounting principle is fairly straightforward. Estimate the regular cost and, subject to certain exceptions, spread the cost or benefit from variations over the remaining service lives of the current employees.

Given the uncertain nature of the estimates that are involved and the length of the time period over which they have to be made, it is not surprising that the standard requires extensive disclosure of surpluses or deficiencies in respect of defined benefit schemes, just stopping short of asking for the colour of the actuary's eyes.

It would not be helpful to repeat the requirements here but they can be summarised as follows:

(a) nature of the scheme;
(b) accounting and funding policies;
(c) date of last actuarial review and status of the actuary; i.e. whether or not an officer of the company;
(d) the pension cost for the period, together with an explanation of significant changes compared with the previous period, and any provisions or prepayments included in the balance sheet;
(e) the amount of any deficiency and action, if any, being taken in consequence;
(f) details of the last formal valuation or review of the scheme including:
    (i) actuarial method used and main actuarial assumptions;
    (ii) market value of the assets;
    (iii) level of funding expressed in percentage terms of the benefits accrued by members and comments on any material surpluses or deficiency so revealed;
(g) details of any commitments to make additional payments and the effect of any material changes in the company's pension arrangements.

An appendix to the standard provides some useful hypothetical examples of what might be disclosed by different types of companies but, a little surprisingly, does not provide an example of an unfunded scheme.

Towards a new standard

The introduction of SSAP 24 in 1988 resulted in some reduction in the range of methods used for accounting for pension costs but, given the pioneering aspects of the standard, there was a need for a reasonably early review of the lessons learnt from its implementation. The review led initially to the publication of two discussion papers, *Pension Costs in the Employers Financial Statements* in 1995 and *Aspects of Accounting for Pension Costs* in 1998, which were followed by FRED 20 *Retirement benefits* issued in October 1999.

SSAP 24 had, even when it was issued, an old fashioned air about it. It was, in some ways, a radical document in that it attempted to bring some order to an important aspect of financial reporting that had previously been largely unregulated but it was backward looking in that it did not seek to ensure that an entity's assets and liabilities were properly recorded. Examples of this include the provision that pension funds assets should be valued at the actuarial rather than their market value and that actuarial surpluses and deficits should be recognised over time rather than immediately.

The IASC was meanwhile, taking the alternative approach in that it was focusing on the 'balance sheet' approach in which an entity's assets are recognised, preferably at their current values. The result of the ASB's review, as evidenced by FRED 20, is an acceptance of the IASC position even in those aspects where it appears that the ASB think that the IASC is in error.

There are five main areas of differences between the provisions of SSAP 24 and the recommendations of FRED 20, these are

- the measurement of pension fund assets and liabilities;
- the discount rate used in estimating the pension liability;
- the treatment of actuarial gains and losses (which are made up of experience surpluses and deficiencies and changes in actuarial assumptions);
- the treatment of past service costs;
- disclosure requirements.

Measurement of pension fund assets and liabilities

There are basically two ways of measuring pension fund assets: the *actuarial approach* (the basis underlying SSAP 24) and the *market approach* which is the one most commonly used in other countries and is now the method specified by the relevant International Standard IAS 19 *Employee Benefits* (revised 1998). The actuarial basis measures both the obligations of the fund and the assets of the fund by reference to the present values of the expected cash flows. In contrast, the market basis, as the name implies, values the assets by reference to their current market values while, in theory at least, the liabilities would be measured by the price that would have to be paid to purchase appropriate deferred annuities. These two methods are obviously not unconnected; for example, a change in the market's view as to long-term interest rates will affect the actuary's calculations of present values, the current value of investments and, in particular, the market value of deferred annuities. But in the short term, there may be considerable variations due to the short-term market fluctuations.

The 1995 discussion paper set out the two alternative methods but the response was overwhelmingly in favour of the actuarial method, the main reasons being the volatility of market values and the impossibility of estimating the market values of the pension liability. A majority of the Board members agreed with this consensus, but at the same time the Board recognised that there is no prospect of other countries adopting the actuarial approach and hence, as part of the move to international harmonisation, the 1998 paper proposed the acceptance of the market value approach.

This position is reaffirmed in FRED 20 that proposes the use of the market approach for the valuation of assets. It would, ideally, like to recommend the same approach to be used for liabilities but it recognises that it would be impracticable to do so because there is no active market for most defined benefit scheme liabilities. Instead, it proposes the use of the *accrued benefit* method (*see* p. 139) that, because it is based on the estimated present value of the obligations of the fund to current employees and pensioners, is closer to the fair value of the liability than that provided by the *prospective benefits* approach.

The ASB believes that the concerns about the volatility due to short-term fluctuations can be addressed by ensuring that these fluctuations appear in the Statement of Total Recognised Gains and Losses and not the profit and loss account. The Board believes that the variation reported in any one year is not significant, rather that it is the pattern that emerges over a number of years that is important and that 'users of accounts are sufficiently sophisticated to view them (annual gains and losses on pension fund assets and liabilities) in their proper context'[17] We shall see.

The discount rate for pension liabilities

This was another area of disagreement between UK and international standard setters. IAS 19 requires that pensions be discounted at the market rate on high-quality fixed-rate corporate or government bonds, in other words a reasonably risk-free rate. The ASB disagrees; it pointed out in the 1998 paper that this would lead to an excessive investment in the pension fund, because of the lower rate of return assumed on the assets, and instead argues for the use of a rate derived from what it describes as 'matching assets'. The basic notion is that the matching assets are those that are likely to move in the same direction and, more or less, at the same pace as the pension liability. Thus as salary rates are affected by the growth in the economy the best way to match the pension liability is to invest in a well-diversified equity portfolio.

It appears from Appendix 5, which describes the development of the FRED, that the ASB has not really changed its view but 'In the interests of objectivity and international harmonisation, the Board has therefore decided to propose a standard discount rate: the rate of return on an AA corporate bond' (FRED 20, p. 62).

Treatment of actuarial gains and losses

The basic question remains when should the changes be recognised, in the past, now or in the future?

SSAP 24 specifies, with the exceptions we described, that the changes should be recognised over the service lives of the employees. IAS 19 adopts a similar position, the only significant difference being that it permits relatively small variations, up to 10 per cent of the value of the fund, to be ignored.

However, the ASB is now of the, eminently sensible, view that actuarial gains and losses should be treated in a like manner to changes in the value of tangible assets that result from causes other than operations. That is they should be recognised immediately but reported in the Statement of Total Recognised Gains and Losses. It is expected that the IASC will also adopt this approach when it incorporates a performance statement similar to the Statement of Total Recognised Gains and Losses into the International Standards which, given the pace of the drive towards international harmonisation is unlikely to be long delayed.

Treatment of past service costs

These occur when there has been an increase in the benefits promised from the scheme, in other words they are granted in retrospect for services that the employees

---

[17] FRED 20, p. 5.

have already provided. Present practice under SSAP 24 is to recognise costs relating to former employees immediately in the profit and loss, other than those covered by a surplus in the scheme, but to spread the cost of current employees over their service lives. In contrast IAS 19 requires the immediate recognition of all past service costs and FRED 20 also favours this approach.

Disclosure requirements

It would not be sensible to attempt to summarise the FRED's proposed disclosure requirements at this stage but we would mention two points. First, the principle that service costs, both current and past, should appear in the profit and loss account, together with the expected return (as estimated at the beginning of the year) on the pension scheme assets and the interest cost on pension liabilities. The difference between the actual return and the expected return on pension scheme assets would be shown in the Statement of Total Recognised Gains and Losses as would experience gains and losses and the effect of the changes in assumptions relating to the scheme. The principle is that the profit and loss should, as far as is possible, show what might be thought of as the 'regular charge' with the consequences of changes in market values, expectations and estimates appearing in the Statement of Total Recognised Gains and Losses.

The second point worth making at this stage is that a consequence of recognising experience gains and losses immediately is that a surplus or deficit on the scheme may appear in the balance sheet. Under the provisions of SSAP 24 this would not happen as, in general, the recognition of, say, a deficit would have had no immediate impact on the financial statements, it would only have resulted in a change in the amounts to be contributed to the fund in the future.

Pension scheme accounts

In the previous sections, we have considered the measurement of pension costs and the disclosure of pension information in the accounts of an employer. A related, although somewhat different, problem is the form and content of the accounts of the pension scheme. The ASC first published a Standard of Recommended Practice (SORP) on the topic in 1986 but that was replaced when the ASB published a new version in 1996.[18] This is an example of the ASB franking the work of others, in this case the SORP was produced by the Pensions Research Accountants Group (PRAG).

This is too specialised a topic for a general textbook on advanced financial accounting but, for completeness, we have decided to include a very brief summary of the statement.

A pension fund's annual report will usually include the following:

- The report of the trustees that will include sections on the management of the scheme and investment policy and performance.
- Reports by professional advisors viz auditors and actuaries.
- The financial statements.

The financial statements are normally comprised of two elements; a fund statement, which reports on the resources acquired and expended by the fund in the period and

---

[18] Financial Reports of Pension Schemes, SORP. The ASB seems to have given up numbering SORPS.

which reconciles the assets at the beginning of the year with those at the end of the year, and a net assets statement in which investments should be shown at current values.

Accounting for post balance sheet events

One of the desirable characteristics of accounting reports discussed in Chapter 1 was 'timeliness', i.e. the need to publish accounts as quickly as possible. However, there will inevitably be some delay between the end of the accounting period and the date of publication (which is not to say that the duration of the delay could not often be reduced), and this leads one to the question of how the accountant should treat significant events which occur during this period.

The main principle underlying SSAP 17 *Accounting for Post Balance Sheet Events*, issued in 1980, is that users should be presented with information that is as up-to-date as possible and be informed of any significant events that have occurred since the end of the accounting period. The provisions are uncontroversial and straightforward and may therefore be briefly summarised.

A distinction is drawn between events that occur before and after the date on which the directors approved the financial statements, and the standard covers only those events which occurred prior to the date of approval. The point is made, however, that directors have a duty to ensure the publication of details of any events that occur after the date of approval if they have a material effect on the financial statements.

The date of approval is normally the date of the board meeting at which the financial statements are formally approved. In the case of group accounts the date is that on which the accounts are approved by the directors of the holding company.

Post balance sheet events are classified as either *adjusting* or *non-adjusting* events.

Adjusting events are those that provide additional evidence in respect of conditions existing at the balance sheet date and will therefore call for the revision of the amounts at which items are stated in the financial statements. A very obvious example of an adjusting event would be the receipt of cash from a debtor that could affect the provision against doubtful debts. Events such as the proposal of a dividend, a transfer to reserves and a change in the tax rate are also regarded as being adjusting events.

Non-adjusting events are those that do not relate to conditions existing at the balance sheet date and will not affect the figures included in the financial statements. Examples of non-adjusting events are the issue of shares, major changes in the composition of the company and the financial effect of the losses of fixed assets or stocks as a result of a disaster such as fire or flood. The last-mentioned instance is an example of a non-adjusting event because the fire or flood would not affect the condition of the asset concerned at the balance sheet date.

The standard also requires the disclosure, as a non-adjusting event, of the reversal after the balance sheet date of transactions undertaken before the year end with the prime intention of altering the appearance of the company's balance sheet. These alterations comprise those commonly referred to as 'window dressing'; for example, the borrowing of cash from an associated company to disguise an acute short-term liquidity problem.

It may be that some event occurs after the balance sheet date which, because of its effect on the company's operating results or financial position, puts into question the application of the going concern convention to the whole (or to a significant part) of the company's accounts. The standard (Para. 22) requires that the accounts should be amended as a consequence of any material post balance sheet event, which casts doubt on the application of the going concern convention, even though Para. 21 specifies that the financial statements should be prepared on the basis of conditions exisiting at the balance sheet date.

The actual standard may be summarised as follows:

1 Financial statements should be prepared on the basis of conditions existing at the balance sheet date.
2 A material post balance sheet event requires changes in the amounts to be included in financial statements where:
   (a) it is an adjusting event; or
   (b) it indicates that the application of the going concern concept to the whole or a material part of the company is not appropriate. (Note that this seems to conflict with requirement 1.)
3 A material post balance sheet event should be disclosed where:
   (a) its non-disclosure would hinder the users' ability to obtain a proper understanding of the financial position; or
   (b) it is the reversal or maturity after the year end of a transaction, the substance of which was primarily to alter the appearance of the company's balance sheet (window dressing).
4 In respect of any material post balance sheet event which has to be disclosed under the provisions of (3) above, the following should be stated in the notes to the accounts:
   (a) the nature of the event; and
   (b) an estimate of its financial effect or a statement that it is not practicable to make such an estimate. The financial effect should be shown without any adjustment for taxation but the taxation implications should be explained if such is necessary to enable a proper understanding of the financial position to be obtained.
5 The date on which the financial statements are approved by the Board of Directors should be disclosed.

It should be noted that the Companies Act 1985 requires that all liabilities and losses in respect of the financial year (or earlier years) shall be taken into account including those which only became apparent between the balance sheet date and the date of the approval of the accounts.

Recommended reading

Excellent up-to-date and detailed reading on the subject matter of this chapter is provided by the most recent edition of:

UK GAAP, principal authors and editors M. Davies, R. Paterson and A. Wilson, Ernst & Young, Butterworth Tolleys, London.

More specialised reading includes the following:

A.T. Cabourne-Smith, 'Accounting for post balance sheet events', *Accountants Digest* No. 101, ICAEW, London, 1981.

P.G.C. Carne and P.P.E. Ogwuazor, 'Accounting for pension costs', *Accountants Digest* No. 237, ICAEW, London, Winter 1989/90.

R. Macve, 'Accounting for Long-term Loans', in *External Financial Reporting*, Bryan Carsberg and Susan Dev (eds), Prentice Hall, London, 1984.

C.J. Napier, *Accounting for the Cost of Pensions*, ICAEW, London, 1983.

T. Sienkiewicz and D. Campbell, *Accounting for Pension Costs*, Tolleys, Croydon, 1990.

J.M. Young and N.J.C. Buchanan, *Accounting for Pensions*, Woodhead-Faulkner, Cambridge, 1981.

6 Financial statements – form and content

Overview This chapter is primarily concerned with two related issues, the way in which the financial statements are structured and what goes into them.

For many years the basic structure of all company accounts for a single company was a profit and loss account and balance sheet, as remains the position for small entities. The introduction of statements of source and application of funds and, subsequently, cash flow statements in 1991 did not represent a radical change, as they were additional statements that had no impact on the other elements. A more fundamental change was brought about in 1992 with the publication of FRS 3 *Reporting Financial Performance*, which introduced the Statement of Total Recognised Gains and Losses (STRGL) that did have an impact on the other statements, especially the profit and loss account. The ASB is in the process of reviewing FRS 3 and as part of this review published in 1999 a discussion paper *Reporting Financial Performance: Proposals for Change*. FRS 3 and the Discussion Paper are the main subjects of the first part of the chapter.

The second part of the chapter starts with a discussion of the treatment of leases and in particular the circumstances under which the leased asset, and the related liability, are recognised in the balance sheet, *finance leases*, and when they are not, *operating leases*. Leases are the subject of SSAP 21 *Accounting for Leases and Hire Purchase Contracts* and we discuss this standard in some depth. The accounting treatment of leases is yet another subject that is under review. As part the review the United States Financial Accounting Standards Board (FASB) published in 1996, on behalf of a consortium comprising the IASC and bodies from five countries, including the UK in the form of the ASB, a special report *Accounting for Leases: A New Approach*. We will also deal with this paper as part of our discussion.

Things are not always what they seem, even in accounting, and FRS 5 *Reporting the Substance of Transactions* published in April 1994 deals with a number of situations where to account on the basis a strict legalistic interpretation would give a misleading impression. The objective of FRS 5, the discussion of which concludes this chapter, is to ensure that substance triumphs over form.

The standards and discussion papers discussed in this chapter are:

- FRS 3 *Reporting Financial Performance* (1992)
- ASB Discussion Paper *Reporting Financial Performance: Proposals for Change* (1999)
- SSAP 21(1984) *Accounting for Leases and Hire Purchase Contracts*
- FASB special paper *Accounting for Leases: A New Approach* (1996)
- FRS 5 *Reporting the Substance of Transactions* (1994)

Reporting financial performance

Financial statements report on past performance but they are also used as an aid in the prediction of future performance. Prediction is usually heavily dependent on an extrapolation of the past. Suppose, to take a simplistic example, one wants to predict future profits in order to place a value on a business. The obvious starting point is the current level of profit and recent rates of growth (or decline). Suppose the current profit is £3.0 million and growth has been on average 3 per cent per year over the recent past, the predictor would start by thinking whether the growth rate is likely to continue into the future or whether a different rate should be used. But in performing this simple extrapolation the predictor will need to consider the extent to which the future will differ from the past; what proportion, for example, of the company's existing activities will be sustained in the future and what will be eliminated.

The desire to show separately what might be termed continuing and non-recurrent elements of the business resulted, in the past, in a loss of comparability in that different companies dealt with the issue in different ways. From time to time, abuses occurred because companies attempted to play down the effect of bad decisions by treating the resulting losses as a non-recurring item.

The ASC first dealt with this topic in April 1974 through the issue of SSAP 6 *Extraordinary Items and Prior Adjustments*, which was reissued in a revised form in August 1986. SSAP 6 was replaced in 1992 by the more wide ranging FRS 3 *Reporting Financial Performance*. The subject is now under review by the ASB and, as part of this work, the Board published a discussion paper *Reporting Financial Performance: Proposals for Change* in 1999.

SSAP 6 *Extraordinary Items and Prior Adjustments*

Since FRS 3 is in many respects a development of SSAP 6 it will be useful to briefly summarise SSAP 6 before dealing in more detail with the provisions of the FRS.

The problem that gave rise to the issue of SSAP 6 was the variety of practice concerning the treatment of income and expenditure that was regarded as being 'non-recurring'. Two extreme positions could be identified. At one extreme all items were passed through the profit and loss account, while at the other extreme any items which could be argued as not relating to the normal activities of the business (non-recurring items) were charged or credited direct to reserves or adjusted against the opening balance of retained profits. The latter method is known as 'reserve accounting'.[1] In practice, most companies adopted a position between the two extremes.

The argument in favour of reserve accounting was that a profit or loss based only on the 'normal activities' of the business gave a fairer indication of the business's maintainable profit. It was suggested that such a profit figure would provide the more useful basis for estimating future profits than the profit resulting from a profit and loss account that included all items irrespective of their nature.

The view of the ASC, as evidenced by the provisions of SSAP 6, was that all revenue items should pass through the profit and loss account. The reasons for this view were as follows:

(a) The inclusion and disclosure of the non-recurring items enables the profit and loss account for the year to give a better view of a company's profitability and progress.

---

[1] The two approaches are also often described, particularly in the USA, as '*all inclusive income*' and '*current income*', respectively.

(b) The exclusion of non-recurring items requires the exercise of subjective judgement and may lead to variation in the treatment of similar items and hence to a loss of comparability between the accounts of different companies.

(c) The exclusion of non-recurring items could result in them being overlooked in any review of results over a series of years. Thus, while the nature of the items will, by definition, change, many businesses, especially larger ones, will often have items that are 'non-recurrent' and continually to exclude them from the profit and loss account would result in a distorted view of profit being shown.

The wholly sensible view of the ASC was that the legitimate advantages of reserve accounting could be obtained, without the drawbacks listed above, if adequate disclosure is provided in accounts. In essence SSAP 6 required that all profits and losses recognised in the year should be shown in the profit and loss account. There were, however, two exceptions – prior year adjustments and certain items that, either by law or under the provisions of an accounting standard, were specifically permitted or required to be taken directly to reserves.

While the standard did in general reject the use of reserve accounting, it did accept the notion that it is possible, and helpful to users, to distinguish between the results of ordinary activities of the business and *extraordinary* (non-recurring) profits and losses. Thus the standard prescribed, if there were any extraordinary items, that the following elements should be included in the profit and loss account:

- post-tax profit before extraordinary items
- extraordinary items (less taxation attributable thereto)
- post-tax profit after extraordinary items.

In addition, items of an abnormal size and incidence but which may be regarded as deriving from the ordinary activities of the business, *exceptional items*, should be disclosed but included in the derivation of the profit before extraordinary items.

The above provisions of SSAP 6 were incorporated into statute law by the Companies Act 1985 but the Act does not attempt to define the various terms, a task left to the standard setters.

FRS 3 *Reporting Financial Performance*

FRS 3 is based on the same principles as SSAP 6 but includes three important changes.

(a) It provides more precise and more useful definitions of the key terms and in particular limits drastically the circumstances under which an item can be classed as extraordinary.

(b) It puts greater emphasis on reporting the effects of discontinued operations. This has led to a change in the format of the profit and loss accounts of enterprises that have discontinued operations during an accounting period.

(c) It requires the inclusion of three additional elements in the financial statements:
   (i) a statement of total recognised gains and losses, including the profit or loss for the period together with all other movements on reserves reflecting recognised gains and losses attributable to shareholders;
   (ii) a reconciliation of movements in shareholders' funds bringing together the performance of the period, as shown in the statement of recognised gains and losses, and all other changes in shareholders' funds in the period, including capital contributed by or repaid to shareholders;

(iii) a note, which would be of relevance to companies which had revalued assets at some stage in their history, reconciling the profit or loss disclosed in the accounts with that figure which would have been disclosed had the company not revalued assets, i.e. the profit based on the strict application of the unmodified historical cost convention.

We will deal with each of these later in the chapter.

Exceptional and extraordinary items

The key definitions relating to ordinary activities and exceptional and extraordinary items provided in FRS 3 are:

Ordinary activities

> Any activities which are undertaken by a reporting entity as part of its business and such related activities in which the reporting entity engages in furtherance of, incidental to, or arising from, these activities. Ordinary activities include the effects on the reporting entity of any event in the various environments in which it operates, including the political, regulatory, economic and geographical environments, irrespective of the frequency or unusual nature of the events. (Para. 2)

Exceptional items

> Material items which derive from events or transactions that fall within the ordinary activities of the reporting entity and which individually or, if of a similar type, in aggregate, need to be disclosed by virtue of their size or incidence if the financial statements are to give a true and fair view. (Para. 5)

Extraordinary items

> Material items possessing a high degree of abnormality which arise from events or transactions that fall outside the ordinary activities of the reporting entity and which are not expected to recur. They do not include exceptional items nor do they include prior period items merely because they relate to a prior period. (Para. 6)

The last sentence of the definition of 'Extraordinary items', which has to be read a few times to be understood, simply means that an item does not become extraordinary simply because it is recognised in the profit and loss account in a period following the one in which it occurred.

The definition of ordinary activities contained in FRS 3 is much wider than the corresponding definition in SSAP 6. As a consequence the definition of extraordinary items provided in FRS 3 is very much more restricted than the SSAP 6 version, with the result that, in the words of the ASB, extraordinary items are now likely to be '*extremely rare*' (FRS 3, Para. 48). Because of this, FRS 3, unlike SSAP 6, does not provide examples of extraordinary items. An illustration of the extent of the change is one of the examples provided in SSAP 6, the expropriation of assets, which is now regarded as part of the ordinary activities of the business because of the revised definition of that term. Another of the major examples of extraordinary items provided in SSAP 6 is the consequence of the discontinuity of a separate segment of the business that, as we will explain below, is now treated in an entirely different way.

The question of whether an item should be regarded as exceptional is essentially a matter of judgment related to whether knowledge of the item will provide the users of the financial statement with a clearer picture of the performance of the company. By definition, exceptional items must be material but thereafter the recognition of such items depends on size or incidence. The meaning of 'incidence' in this context is not clear, nor is it explained in FRS 3, but it presumably relates to items which lie somewhere between material and large but which will nonetheless have some significance in assessing the maintainable profits of the enterprise. Thus, for example, the profit or loss on the sale or termination of operations of a type which do not satisfy the rather tight conditions for recognition as discontinued operations (*see* p. 159) may not be large but may yet be significant in judging the future profitability of the business, perhaps because had the operation not been terminated large losses would have been sustained in the future.

Prior period adjustments

These are defined as:

> Material adjustments applicable to prior periods arising from changes in accounting policies or from the correction of fundamental errors. They do not include normal recurring adjustments or corrections of accounting estimates made in prior periods. (Para. 7)

In some ways it is unfortunate that the ASB did not use a different name for this type of adjustment because, as is pointed out in FRS 3 (Para. 60), the vast majority of items relating to prior periods arise from the corrections and adjustments which are the natural result of estimates inherent in periodic financial reporting and are therefore not covered by the definition of prior period adjustment; perhaps a title such as Fundamental Prior Period Adjustment would have been preferable.

The normal run of adjustments relating to prior periods are dealt with in the profit and loss account of the period in which they are identified. They are not exceptional or extraordinary merely because they relate to a prior period, but if their effect is material then they would be disclosed as an exceptional item or, in very rare cases, an extraordinary item.

The importance of consistency as a fundamental accounting concept is emphasised and it is stated that a change in accounting policy should therefore be made only when it can be justified that the new policy gives a fairer presentation of the financial position of the reporting company. An adaptation or modification of an accounting basis caused by transactions or event that are clearly different in substance from those which occurred in the past does not give rise to a change of accounting policy and hence does not result in a prior period adjustment (FRS 3, Para. 62).

The second element in the definition of prior period adjustments is the correction of fundamental errors. To be treated as prior period adjustments such errors would need to be of such significance that the financial statements that contained them could not show a true and fair view.

Prior period adjustments and disclosure requirements

> Prior period adjustments should be accounted for by adjusting the opening balance of reserves for the cumulative effect of the adjustments and by restating the comparative figures for the preceding period. In addition, the cumulative effect of the adjustment should be noted at the foot of the statement of total recognised gains and losses of the current period whilst the effect of the prior period adjustments on the results for the preceding period should be disclosed where practicable. (FRS 3, Para. 29)

Reflecting the results of discontinued operations

A company cannot maintain the profits of operations which it no longer carries out, and thus it seems reasonable to ensure that financial statements discriminate clearly between the results which have been achieved by that part of the enterprise which will continue, and the results achieved or losses sustained by those parts of the organisation which had been closed or sold during the course of the year.

In order to achieve this, FRS 3 calls for what is, in effect, two profit and loss accounts; one covering those operations that will continue in the future, which includes acquisitions made during the year, and one dealing with any part of the enterprise that was sold or terminated during the course of the year.

The way in which the information is disclosed, whether by way of note or on the face of the profit and loss account, is to a large measure left to the accountant, guided by two examples provided in the Appendix to FRS 3. The discretion is not unlimited, however, because as a minimum there should be shown on the face of the profit and loss account analyses of turnover and operating profit as between discontinued and continuing operations.

Adjustments are also required in the comparative figures because only the results of those operations which are regarded as continuing at the year end should be included in the preceding year's figures for continuing operations. This is an important measure that helps the users of the financial statements to gain a clearer picture of the progress of the company.

One of the two illustrations provided in the standard is reproduced below:

	Continuing operations		Discontinued operations	Total	Total
	1993	Acquisitions 1993	1993	1993	1992 as restated
	£ million	£ million	£ million	£ million	£ million
Turnover	550	50	175	775	690
Cost of sales	(415)	(40)	(165)	(620)	(555)
Gross profit	135	10	10	155	135
Net operating expenses	(85)	(4)	(25)	(114)	(83)
Less 1992 provision			10	10	
Operating profit	50	6	(5)	51	52
Profit on sale of properties	9			9	6
Provision for loss on operations to be discontinued					(30)
Loss on disposal of discontinued operations			(17)	(17)	
Less 1992 provision			20	20	
Profit on ordinary activities before interest	59	6	(2)	63	28
Interest payable				(18)	(15)
Profit on ordinary activities before taxation				45	13
Tax on profit on ordinary activities				(14)	(4)
Profit on ordinary activities after taxation				31	9
Minority interests				(2)	(2)
[Profit before extraordinary items]				29	7
[Extraordinary items] (included only to show positioning)				–	–
Profit for the financial year				29	7
Dividends				(8)	(1)
Retained profit for the financial year				21	6

	1993	1992
Earnings per share	39p	10p
Adjustments	*x*p	*x*p
[to be itemised and an adequate description to be given]		
Adjusted earnings per share	*y*p	*y*p

[Reason for calculating the adjusted earnings per share to be given]

Required Note:	1993			1992 (as restated)		
	Continuing	Dis-continued	Total	Continuing	Dis-continued	Total
	£ million	£ million	£ million	£ million	£ million	£ million
Turnover				500	190	690
Cost of sales				385	170	555
Net operating expenses						
Distribution costs	56	13	69	46	5	51
Administrative expenses	41	12	53	34	3	37
Other operating income	(8)	0	(8)	(5)	0	(5)
	89	25	114	75	8	83
Operating profit				40	12	52

The total figure of net operating expenses for continuing operations in 1993 includes £4 million in respect of acquisitions (namely distribution costs £3 million, administrative expenses £3 million and other operating income £2 million).

What constitutes discontinuity?

FRS 3 defines discontinued operations in the following way:

> Operations of the reporting entity that are sold or terminated and that satisfy all of the following conditions:
> (a) The sale or termination is completed either in the period or before the earlier of three months after the commencement of the subsequent period and the date on which the financial statements are approved.
> (b) If a termination, the former activities have ceased permanently.
> (c) The sale or termination has a material effect on the nature and focus of the reporting entity's operations and represents a material reduction in its operating facilities resulting either from its withdrawal from a particular market (whether class of business or geographical) or from a material reduction in turnover in the reporting entity's continuing markets.
> (d) The assets, liabilities, results of operations and activities are clearly distinguishable, physically, operationally and for financial reporting purposes.
> Operations not satisfying all these conditions are classified as continuing. (Para. 4)

The objective of FRS 3 is clearly laudable in attempting to help users extrapolate past results into the future but the drawing of a distinction between continuing and discontinued operations is clearly open to abuse. Most businesses continually modify their range of operations; some product lines or activities will be dropped in the course of the year and these will usually be those that are less successful. Hence, if there were no limits on what could be designated as discontinued operations a business could make the 'continuing operations' part of the profit and loss account look very healthy by shunting the results of all abandoned product lines or activities into the discontinued operations section.

In order to prevent, or rather minimise, the opportunity for whitewashing the profit and loss account in this way, the ASB has laid down a reasonably rigorous definition of what constitutes discontinuity. As can be seen above there are four tests all of which must be satisfied. The first two tests are fairly clear; the discontinuity must be completed either in the year or within three months of the balance sheet date, or even earlier if the date of approval of the financial statements is within that three-month period. Also, the termination must be permanent and not a temporary withdrawal from a particular market. Condition (d) is also reasonably straightforward. It requires that the 'operation' must have constituted a distinct chunk of the business in operational, physical and financial terms. Further elaboration of that point is provided in paragraph 44 of the standard. To satisfy the condition, the operation must have been a revenue and cost centre to which all material items of revenue and costs were specifically assigned or, to put it another way, one where only a very small reliance had to be placed on the allocation of joint costs and revenues.

Paragraph (c) of the definition requires that the sale or termination must have had a material effect on the nature and focus of the enterprise but this does seem to beg the question of what is meant by the focus of the reporting entity's operations. The ASB goes some way to answering the question in so far as it states 'including the aspects of both quality and location' (FRS 3, Para. 42). The nature and focus of the reporting entity's operations refers to the position of its products or services in their markets

An example is given of a hotel company that sells its existing chains of hotels that operate at the cheaper end of the market and then buys a chain of luxury hotels. This, it is stated, can be regarded as 'changing its focus' and hence the sale could be treated as a discontinued operation even though the company stays in the hotel business. Similarly, a sale of all its hotels in one country might also be regarded as a discontinuity, even if, as a result, hotels are purchased in another country.

Two points need to be made about this example. The first relates to the use of the term 'chain' which implies that the hotels were operated as an identifiable group that was sold in its entirety. The sale of only the cheap hotels in a chain which were operated under the same name as the remaining luxury hotels and which shared common services would probably not satisfy the 'separateness' tests specified in paragraph (d).

The second point is that paragraph (c) requires that for the sale to be treated as a discontinuity it must represent 'a material reduction in its operating facilities resulting either from its withdrawal from a particular market (whether class of business or geographical) or from a material reduction in turnover in the reporting entity's continuing markets' (FRS 3, Para. 4(c)).

There is, perhaps, an ambiguity here. Can the sale be treated as a discontinuity if the material reduction in operating facilities in one market is replaced by an equivalent increase in another market? The example provided in paragraph 42 suggests that it can but this is not clear from the wording of paragraph (c) of the definition that places stress on the 'material reduction in operating facilities'. In reviewing the standard, the ASB might consider revising its definition to make it clear that a change in the style of operation that does not materially affect the totality of operating facilities can still be treated as a discontinuity for the purposes of the standard.

Acquisitions

In estimating future results account needs to be taken of the effect of any acquisitions made during the year. Normally (the 'exception' being the use of the merger method of consolidation, see Chapter 8, Business Combinations and Goodwill) only post-acquisition results will be included in the profit and loss account but the user of the accounts will want to know the full year results of the company acquired. The Companies Act 1985 (Schedule 4A, Para. 13) requires that information relating to the profit or loss of any group or company acquired from the start of the financial year of the acquired undertaking to its date of acquisition should be shown in a note to the financial statement. The note must also state the date of the start of the financial year of the acquired undertaking and provide information relating to the previous accounting period.

The additional requirements of FRS 3 are that there should be shown:

(a) on the face of the profit and loss account: analyses between continuing operations, acquisitions (as a component of continuing operations) and discontinued operations of turnover and operating profit;

(b) on the face of the profit and loss account or in the notes: a similar threefold analysis of each of the statutory profit and loss format items between turnover and operating profit.

Acquisitions are shown as part of continuing operations except when an operation is both acquired and discontinued in the course of the year; then it should be treated as discontinued.

If it is not possible to determine the post-acquisition results of the new operation, then either an indication of the contribution of the acquired operation to turnover and operating profit should be disclosed or, if that is not possible, an explanation should be provided of the reasons for the company's inability to provide the information.

What should be included in the results of discontinued operations?

If an operation is sold or terminated in a year, two elements of profit or loss arise. One is the trading profit or loss to the date of termination, the other is the profit or loss on the disposal of the assets constituting the operation. FRS 3 provides that both should be included in the determination of the profit or loss on ordinary activities before taxation, albeit separately identified. This is in contrast to the provisions of SSAP 6, whereby profits or losses on the sale of a business segment were treated as extraordinary items and hence shown after the derivation of profit or loss on ordinary activities.

One of the members of the ASB, Robert Bradfield, did not vote for the adoption of the standard and one of his reasons for this, explained in his dissenting view (published alongside the standard), was the inclusion of profits or losses on the disposal of operations in the figure for pre-tax profit. Bradfield believed that the standard placed undue emphasis on the pre-tax profit figure which may be misleading if it includes the profits or losses on disposal, especially as the tax effects, as allowed by FRS 3, are only shown in the notes. The view of the majority of the members of the ASB, expressed in the section of the standard entitled 'A Development of the Standard', is that the FRS 3 approach does not place emphasis on a single number because the admittedly complex presentation is based on an 'information set' approach that highlights a range of important components of performance. However, if a single measure of performance is to be used – for example in calculating earnings per share – then it should be based on its 'all-inclusive' concept which avoids the inconsistencies which were experienced in the application of SSAP 6.

Provision for future losses

There is a great temptation to say that if the company has to take its medicine then it should drink deeply of it. Thus if the company decides that it should either eliminate entirely or reduce extensively its loss-making operations in, say, the United States, the announcement will have an adverse effect on share prices and there would be less confidence in the company's future; a confidence which the company will want to restore as quickly as possible. One way of helping to restore confidence quickly may be to lump as much of the loss into the 'bad news' year as possible and to relieve future years of the burdens of those losses.

To provide for everything in sight, and possibly just a wee bit more, may well be prudent but it is likely to be exceedingly misleading.

Consider the following two series of numbers:

Results (£ million)

Year:	1	2	3	4	5	Total
A	L10	L2	–	P2	P4	L6
B	L16	P1	P2	P3	P4	L6

(L = Loss, P = Profit)

To oversimplify, let us suppose that series A represents the 'truth' but B represents the results of the company if an excess provision of £6 million is made in the 'bad news' year, year 1. The 'prudent' approach under B suggests that the company is immediately restored to profit in year 2 and then makes steady growth, whereas in fact the 'true' position is that profit is not restored until year 4 but that the real rate of improvement is then higher than is shown by the prudent approach.

Now let us see how this matter is dealt with in FRS 3, remembering that in accordance with normal practice any permanent diminution in asset values should be recorded. The essential point of FRS 3 (Para. 18) is that provisions should be made for the direct cost of sale or termination and any operating losses of the operation up to the future date of sale or termination (after in each case taking account of related profits), if and only if there exists a binding sale agreement or the company is demonstrably committed to the sale or termination because, for example, the action is covered by detailed formal plans from which the company cannot realistically withdraw.

The provision would be included as part of discontinued operations only if the related event qualifies as a discontinuity. Note that the conditions for discontinuity and the condition precedent for making a provision are different and that provisions can be made for operations that are for the purposes of FRS 3 treated as continuing.

When in the subsequent period the operation is actually closed, its results for that period should not be lumped together but shown under the statutory format headings, but there also needs to be full disclosure on the face of the profit and loss account showing the way in which the provisions made in prior years have been utilised, indicating how much has been used to cover operating losses and how much to cover the loss on sale or termination of the discontinued operation.

The treatment of provisions for future losses specified in FRS 3 is consistent with the position adopted by the ASB in FRS 12 *Provisions, Contingent Liabilities and Assets*.

Taxation

In deciding how taxation should be disclosed, the ASB had before it two main options. One was to relate the tax charge on the face of the profit and loss account to its basic elements – for example, continuing and discontinuing operations, and extraordinary and exceptional items – and to show the total tax charge by way of a note.

The alternative was to show the total tax charge on the face of the accounts and provide the analysis in the notes. By and large, with the exception of extraordinary items, the ASB adopted the latter approach.

The disclosure provisions are of both a general and specific nature. The general elements of the standard (Para. 23) are:

(a) Any special circumstances that affect the overall tax charge or credit for the period, or that may affect those of the future periods, should be disclosed by way of a note to the profit and loss account and their individual effects quantified.
(b) The effects of a fundamental change in the basis of taxation should be included in the tax charge or credit for the period and separately disclosed on the face of the profit and loss account.

In addition there are specific disclosure provisions relating to:

(a) Profits or losses on the sale or termination of an operation.
(b) Costs of fundamental reorganisation or restructuring.
(c) Profits or losses on the disposal of fixed assets.

In each case relevant information should be provided in the notes showing their effect on the tax charge.

Taxation and extraordinary items

FRS 3 provides (Para. 22) that the tax on extraordinary items should be shown separately as a part of the extraordinary profit or loss either on the face of the profit and loss account or in a note. Any subsequent adjustments to the tax on extraordinary profit or loss should also be shown as extraordinary items.

A dissenting view

We have already referred to the dissenting view of Robert Bradfield. One of the major elements of Bradfield's opposition to the provision of FRS 3 was his belief that users of accounts would not fully appreciate the taxation effect on the trading results attributable to shareholders (he made a similar point relating to minority interest). As an example, Bradfield quotes the case of an international group of companies where the pre-tax trading profits in a low tax regime fell and those in a high tax regime increased by an identical amount. Such a change would leave the shareholder materially worse off but this would be masked in FRS 3.

The point is a good one and needs further consideration. This needs to be conducted in the light of a broader consideration relating to the reaction of shareholders and other users of accounts to the far more complex structure of financial statements that are appearing as a result of FRS 3. A particular issue is the balance between the information disclosed on the face of the accounts and in the notes to the accounts.

Minority interests

In the case of consolidated financial statements the information disclosure requirements for minority interests are very similar to those for taxation. The effect of three specific items referred to above (the termination of an operation, the fundamental reorganisation of operations and the profit or loss on disposal of fixed assets) on minority interests should be noted. If there are any extraordinary items that affect minority interests then the extent of the extraordinary profit and loss attributable to minority shareholders should be shown separately as a part of the extraordinary item, either on the face of the profit and loss account or in a note.

The statement of total recognised gains and losses

One of the confusing aspects, especially so for the layperson, of pre-FRS 3 traditional accounting was the ambiguity surrounding the treatment of gains and losses which were thought sufficiently significant to be allowed to have an impact on the balance sheet but yet were not reflected in the profit and loss account, and were instead dealt with by direct transfer to and from reserves. A good example of this type of transaction was the unrealised surplus on the revaluation of assets.

The traditional profit and loss account was based on a 'narrow concept' of realisation that treats as profits only those gains that have resulted in the receipt of cash or the acquisition of assets that are reasonably certain to be turned into cash. Unrealised gains were shunted into reserves (because of the prudence convention, anticipated losses were generally taken to the profit and loss account) and were reported as part of the movement of reserves, a statement the significance of which was not readily appreciated by many users of financial statements.

FRS 3 did not fundamentally challenge the narrow concept of realisation but, in drafting the standard, the ASB emphasises that gains and losses may be excluded from the profit and loss account only if they are specifically permitted or required to be taken to reserves by an accounting standard or, in the absence of a relevant accounting standard, by law (Para. 37). However, even with this stipulation the ASB believes that an incomplete impression of the company's financial performance would be obtained if attention were directed exclusively to the profit and loss account.

Accordingly FRS 3 requires that companies publish an additional primary statement, which should be presented with the same prominence as the other primary statements, the 'Statement of Total Recognised Gains and Losses', which shows the total of recognised gains and losses in so far as they are attributable to shareholders.

As we pointed out in Chapter 3 the ASB now takes a more relaxed attitude to realisation and in particular the extent to which unrealised gains and losses should be kept out of the profit and loss account. The important distinction, argues the ASB, is not between realised and unrealised gains and losses but between those which derive from operating activities and those which derive from changes in the value of those assets and liabilities that are held on a continuing basis for use in the entity's business and which provide its infrastructure. It is suggested that changes in value that do not directly affect current trading (including those resulting from the disposal of infrastructure assets) should be reported separately from the result of operating and financing.

Hence the ASB requires that 'gains and losses on those assets and liabilities that are held on a continuing basis primarily in order to enable the entity's operations to be carried out are reported in the statement of total recognised gains and losses, and not in the profit and loss account' (Para. 6.27), while 'all other gains and losses are reported in the profit and loss account' (Para. 6.28).

The Revised Draft Statement of Principles goes further in this direction by not referring to realisation at all. In the context of the entity's operating cycle gains should be recognised at the incidence of the *critical event*[2] that normally occurs when the reporting entity has completed all its obligations while, in the case of revaluation, the critical consideration is reliability of measurement.[3]

---

[2] Revised Draft Statement, Para. 5.32.
[3] Revised Draft, Para. 6.15.

The illustration in FRS 3 of the statement of total recognised gains is reproduced below.

Statement of total recognised gains and losses	1993	1992 as restated
	£ million	£ million
Profit for the financial year	29	7
Unrealised surplus on revaluation of properties	4	6
Unrealised (loss)/gain on trade investment	(3)	7
	30	20
Currency translation differences on foreign currency net investments	(2)	5
Total recognised gains and losses relating to the year	28	25
Prior year adjustment	(10)	
Total gains and losses recognised since last annual report	18	

It is, perhaps, worth making the obvious point that gains and losses should not be double counted. Hence, a gain that was previously recorded as unrealised should not be recognised again in the period in which it is realised. For example, the realisation of a profit previously recognised when a fixed asset was revalued would be reflected in the statement of the movement of reserves, where it would appear as a transfer from the revaluation reserve to the profit and loss account reserve.

The prominence given to the statement of total recognised gains and losses is an example of the 'information set' approach which the ASB hopes will divert the focus of attention from the single 'bottom line' figure of profit for the period.

Two additional notes

Reconciliation of movements in shareholders' funds
The profit or loss for the period together with any recognised gains or losses not reflected in the profit and loss account measures the performance of the company during the period but there are other changes in shareholders' funds that affect the company's financial position, notably the declaration of dividends and the injection and withdrawal of capital. FRS 3 hence requires the publication of an additional note reconciling the opening and closing balance of shareholders' funds.

Reconciliation of movements in shareholders' funds	1993	1992 as restated
	£ million	£ million
Profit for the financial year	29	7
Dividends	(8)	(1)
	21	6
Other recognised gains and losses relating to the year (net)	(1)	18
New share capital subscribed	20	1
Net addition to shareholders' funds	40	25
Opening shareholders' funds (originally £375 million before deducting prior year adjustment of £10 million)	365	340
Closing shareholders' funds	405	365

The note may be included as a primary statement but, if it is, it should be shown separately from the statement of total recognised gains and losses (Para. 59).

It is important to see how the profit and loss account, statement of total recognised gains and losses and the reconciliation of movements in shareholders' funds fit together. This can best be seen by studying the comprehensive note showing the movement of reserves required by company legislation. The example shown below is consistent with the previous illustrations.

Reserves	Share premium account £ million	Revaluation reserve £ million	Profit and loss account £ million	Total £ million
At beginning of year as previously stated	44	200	120	364
Prior year adjustment			(10)	(10)
At beginning of year as restated	44	200	110	354
Premium on issue of shares (nominal value £7 million)	13			13
Transfer from profit and loss account of the year			21	21
Transfer of realised profits		(14)	14	0
Decrease in value of trade investment		(3)		(3)
Currency translation differences on foreign currency net investments			(2)	(2)
Surplus on property revaluation		4		4
At end of year	57	187	143	387

Note: Nominal share capital at end of year £18 million (1992 £11 million).

Note of historical cost profits and losses

If there is a material difference between the results disclosed in the profit and loss account and that which would have been produced by an 'unmodified' (i.e. no asset revaluations) financial statement, a note of the historical cost profit or loss for the period should be presented. The note should include a reconciliation of the reported profit on ordinary activities before taxation to the equivalent historical cost figure and show the retained profit from the financial year as would have been reported on the historical cost basis.

The more common types of adjustments that will be found include:

(a) Gains recognised in prior periods in the statement of total recognised gains and losses but realised in the current period, as under the strict historical cost convention the whole of the gain would be reported in the current period.
(b) The difference between the depreciation charges based on historical cost and such charges based on the revalued amounts.

The standard allows two exceptions (Para. 55):

(a) adjustments made to cope with hyper-inflation in foreign operations; and
(b) the practice of market makers and other dealers in investments of marking to market value where this is an established industry practice.

Where full historical cost information is unavailable or cannot be obtained without unreasonable expense or delay, the earliest available values should be used.

The note should be presented immediately following the profit and loss account or the statement of total recognised gains and losses. The FRS 3 example of the note is presented below:

Note of historical cost profits and losses

	1993	1992 as restated
	£ million	£ million
Reported profit on ordinary activities before taxation	45	13
Realisation of property revaluation gains of previous years	9	10
Difference between an historical cost depreciation charge and the actual depreciation charge of the year calculated on the revalued amount	5	4
Historical cost profit on ordinary activities before taxation	59	27
Historical cost profit for the year retained after taxation, minority interests, extraordinary items and dividends	35	20

Two reasons are cited by the ASB to support the publication of this additional note:

- Currently undertakings are allowed to decide whether to revalue assets and, if so, when. The results of undertakings that have revalued assets at different times are thus not comparable but the strict historical cost profit figures can be compared.
- Some users of financial statements wish to assess the profit or loss on the sale of assets on the basis of their historical cost rather than, as required by the standard, on their revalued carrying amount.

Review of FRS 3

Accountants have struggled for a long time to find a way of separating out unusual items in order to help users make an informed judgment of the progress of the company and estimate its potential for the future. FRS 3 was an important milestone in that development.

Its provisions have resulted in the production of far more complex profit and loss accounts than had traditionally been produced, a development in tune with the view of the ASB that the desire for understandability should not mean that complex items should be excluded from financial statements if the information is relevant to decision making (ASB, Statement of Principles; Revised Exposure Draft, Para. 3.35).

A number of factors have led to the recognition that a review of the standard was appropriate, particularly the view that, although the ASB had made great strides with FRS, 3 there remained a number of areas, such as the treatment of gains and losses on assets, that would benefit from further work. Another point is that it does not appear that the user community has yet fully grasped the significance of the standard.

As part of the move towards international harmonisation of accounting standards the first stage of the review was carried out at an international level and this has produced a different form of paper that comes in two parts. The first part is the discussion paper itself issued by the ASB while the second part consists of a 'position paper' produced by the 'G4+1' of standard setters that consists of representatives of the standards bodies of Australia, Canada, New Zealand, UK and USA together with staff of the IASC as observers.

Reporting financial performance: proposals for change

In the first part of the paper the ASB sets out its thinking and poses questions that it would like answered in the consultative period; the detailed discussion is found in the second, international, part of the paper.

In its introduction the ASB reiterates its view that the performance of a complex enterprise cannot be summarised by a single number and reaffirms its belief in the 'information set' approach, as introduced in FRS 3, which attempts to highlight a number of components of performance. However, this is not yet a view widely held by users, many of whom still give undue prominence to the profit and loss account at the expense of the STRGL.

If the proposals in the discussion paper were adopted the main changes to FRS 3 would affect the following matters:

- The introduction of a single performance statement combining the profit and loss account and the STRGL
- Exceptional items
- Correction of errors
- Reporting of Dividends.

Single performance statement

In a sense the STRGL is a single performance statement in so far that it combines the operating profit or loss with other gains and losses but, as indicated earlier, it is believed that undue prominence is given to those items that appear in the profit and loss account.

The view of the G4+1 is that the best way forward would be to have a single operating statement comprising three parts

the results of operating (or trading) activities
the results of financing and other treasury activities
other gains and losses.

There can be no clear set of rules about the section of the statement in which a particular item should appear as it depends on the nature of the business of the entity. Thus, the gain from the sale of property would appear in the first section of the statement in the case of a property dealer but in the third section if the profit was made by, say, a manufacturer and is incidental to its main business; and what most businesses would put into the second section of the statement, financial institutions would probably include in the first.

The ASB in FRED 20 (p. 67) sets out a matrix which it is proposing to use to decide what items of financial performance should appear in the 'operating/trading' component of a single performance and which should be reported in 'other gains and losses'.

Characteristics more typical of operating items	Characteristics more typical of other gains and losses
Operating activities	Non-operating activities
Recurring	Non-recurring
Non-holding items	Holding items
Internal events (e.g. value adding activities)	External events (e.g. price changes)

The principle that the first section of the statement is to do with normal operations might help resolve some of the more tricky issues surrounding the treatment of gains and losses on fixed assets to which we referred in Chapter 4. The basic principle would be that if the loss or gain is to do with operations it should appear in the first section, otherwise it would appear in the third section, and in this context it should be noted that impairments might be thought of as an accelerated depreciation and so it would be recognised in the operating section.

The position paper does not seek to go into great detail and recognises that the final formulation will have to depend on the outcome of a number of other reviews that are presently being undertaken. Thus, in advance of the outcome of the review of financial instruments, little is said about the content of the financing and other treasury section. Given the rather tentative tone of the paper, we present an example of a single performance standard based on the one provided in the paper (Example 6.1).

Example 6.1   Statement of Financial Performance

Operating (trading) activities		
Revenues		775
Cost of sales		(620)
Other expenses		(104)
Operating Income		**51**
Financing and other treasury activities		
Interest on debt	(26)	
Gains and losses on financial instruments	8	
Financing Income		**(18)**
Operating and financing income before taxation		33
Taxation on Income		(12)
Operating and financing income after taxation		21
Other gains and losses		
Profit on disposal of discontinued operations	3	
Profit on sale of properties in continuing operations	6	
Revaluation of long-term assets	4	
Exchange translation differences on foreign currency net investments	(2)	
Other gains and losses before taxation	11	
Taxation on other gains and losses	(4)	
Other gains and losses after taxation		7
Total recognised gains and losses		**28**

Note the treatment of taxation in the example. The paper discusses various possibilities including showing a single tax charge or apportioning the charge across the different parts. While the arbitrariness of any apportionment is acknowledged, it is felt that it would be useful to help users assess the taxation implications of the different activities. On balance the preferred option is to break down the charge into two components, one relating to operating and financing income the other to other gains and losses

Most of the countries represented in the G4+1 group require, like UK in FRS 3, specific information about discontinued operations. The paper suggests that all three sections of the performance review could be broken down into three subcomponents covering continuing, discontinued and acquired activities.

Exceptional and extraordinary items

The paper recommends the final extinction of extraordinary items. It points out that, to be classed as such, the item cannot be part of the normal operating activities of the business and hence its special nature would be evidenced by inclusion in the third section of the statement. Its proposals, if implemented, would also do much to get rid of abnormal and exceptional items, at least as a special group of items. The paper recognises that there might well be, in any year, exceptional items information about which will help the user of the accounts, but what it firmly rejects is the notion of aggregating all the exceptional items and providing a total figure implying that the exceptional items have something in common.

Thus the paper proposes that exceptional items be shown on the face of the performance statement next to the item to which they relate. It also suggests that a price be extracted from an entity that emphasises a figure for profit before exceptional items. Such entities should be required to produce a summary of the results for, say, the last five years that show the results pre and post exceptional items. The purpose of such a statement is obviously to demonstrate the frequency with which 'exceptional items' occur, albeit from different causes.

Correction of errors

In general, the paper suggests, the correction of errors and estimates should be recognised in the current year without separate disclosure, unless the item falls to be treated as an exceptional item. The paper would make an exception in the case of those errors of such materiality that, had they been discovered in the course of preparation of the financial statements, the statements would have been amended before issue. The paper does not include anything that is equivalent to the FRS 3 requirement that for the change to be treated as a prior year adjustment it must be the consequence of a fundamental error.

Reporting of dividends

Unlike the other items discussed above the subject of dividends is raised only in the opening, ASB, section of the paper.

In the UK and the Republic of Ireland company law requires that dividends be shown on the face of the profit and loss account that might be inferred as suggesting that dividends are expenses rather than appropriations of profit. The ASB has taken advantage of the publication of this paper to float the suggestion that dividends should not be included in the statement of financial performance but should instead be shown as part of changes in equity.

Off and on the balance sheet

In order for the reader of accounts to judge properly the progress and standing of a company, it is necessary for the accounts to show all the assets which are used to generate its profit and to describe fully its liabilities. With the present state of its art, accountancy is not capable of listing and valuing all assets. Those which relate to people – their skill, contacts and knowledge – are often the most important assets of a business which are as yet not shown separately in balance sheets. Other intangible assets are also important but, particularly where they have been generated internally and not acquired for an identifiable cost, these too are often absent from the balance sheet. But accepting all this, it would not be unreasonable to expect the accounts to reflect all the tangible assets employed in a business and to show all its liabilities. A reasonable expectation, but one not always achieved.

A phenomenon, which has long been with us but which has grown in importance in recent years, is 'off balance sheet finance' schemes whereby what are, or have all the essential economic characteristics of, liabilities are excluded from the balance sheet. Since 'nothing is for nothing', the avoidance of recording the liability also means the exclusion of assets. While the phenomenon is as old as accounting, the term 'off balance sheet financing' is a relatively new one; many of the activities which are now so described would probably in the past have been described as 'window dressing', a much less respectable term.

There are a number of reasons for adopting off balance sheet financing. In some instances taxation is the spur, in other cases a desire not to show the true level of borrowing. Highly-geared companies are regarded with some caution and it might be extremely advantageous to eliminate both assets and liabilities from the balance sheet, if, by so doing, the gearing ratio is reduced. It might also be that a company's articles or agreements with existing creditors set a limit on its level of borrowings; off balance sheet financing might be used to circumvent such a restriction.[4]

The ASC first addressed the subject in 1984 when it issued SSAP 21 'Accounting for Leases and Hire Purchase Contracts' which as the title suggests dealt with only one, albeit important, aspect of the general problem. Hence, in March 1988 the ASC published ED 42 'Accounting for Special Purpose Transactions' which, following a period of consultation, was withdrawn and replaced in May 1990 by ED 49 'Reflecting the Substance of Transactions in Assets and Liabilities'. This was itself replaced in 1993 when the ASB issued FRED 4 'Reporting the Substance of Transactions' which, with only relatively minor modifications, was issued with the same title as FRS 5 in April 1994. We will deal in this section of the chapter with SSAP 21 and FRS 5.

Accounting for leases and hire purchase contracts

Under a hire purchase agreement the user has the option to acquire the legal title to the asset upon the fulfilment of the conditions laid down in the contract, usually that all the instalments are paid. By contrast, under a leasing agreement in the UK no legal title passes to the lessee at any time during the currency of the lease. The lessor rents the asset to the lessee for an agreed period and, although the lessee has the physical possession and use of the asset, the legal title remains with the lessor.

In some cases a lease will be for a relatively short period in the life of the particular asset and the lessor may lease the same asset for many short periods to different lessees and in such cases he/she will usually be responsible for the repairs and maintenance of the asset. This type of lease is described as an operating lease. In other

---

[4] A useful description of different forms of off balance sheet finance will be found in K.V. Peasnell and R.A. Yaansah, *Off Balance Sheet Financing*, Certified Accountant Publications, London, 1988.

instances the lease may be for virtually the whole life of the asset with the lessor taking the whole of his/her profit from one transaction; such a lease is known as a finance lease. Typically, the lessee of a finance lease will in practical terms treat the leased asset in very much the same way as it would an owned asset; the lessee, for example, will often be responsible for the asset's repair and maintenance.

The distinction between finance and operating leases is, however, not clear cut and we will return to the way in which they can be differentiated in our discussion of SSAP 21 'Accounting for Leases and Hire Purchase Contracts' later in this chapter.

For the accountant, operating leases pose few problems. Amounts are payable for the use of an asset. From the point of view of the lessee the amounts payable are the cost of using an asset for particular periods and hence are charged to the profit and loss account using the accruals concept. So far as the lessor is concerned the amounts receivable represent revenue from leasing the asset and are credited to the profit and loss account. The leased asset is treated as a fixed asset by the lessor and depreciated in accordance with normal policy.

It is the financing lease that poses problems for the accountant. Prior to the introduction of SSAP 21, financing leases were usually treated by both the lessee and lessor in the same way as operating leases. However, it was widely recognised that such treatment, while being justified on a strict legal interpretation of the agreement, failed to recognise the financial reality or substance of the transaction. The substance of the transaction was that the lessee acquired an asset for his exclusive use with finance provided by the lessor; which in economic terms has few (if any) differences from the case of an asset purchased on credit. If accounts are to be 'realistic' it is necessary to find a way of accounting for finance leases which accords with the reality of the transaction rather than its legal form. As we shall see, the general issue is the subject of FRS 5 'Reporting the Substance of Transactions' but, because of the growth of the leasing industry and the distorting effects of the then prevalent accounting treatment, the ASC issued SSAP 21 in advance of a comprehensive standard. Fortunately SSAP 21 is consistent with the provisions of FRS 5. The International Accounting Standards Committee also specifically requires that the substance and financial reality of a transaction, rather than its legal form, should determine the appropriate accounting treatment.[5]

The alternative treatment which accords with the substance of the transaction is, from the point of view of the lessee, to include in the lessee's balance sheet an asset representing the lease and a liability representing the obligation to make payments under the terms of the lease. At the inception of the lease the asset would be equal to the liability but this relationship does not hold thereafter. The asset would be written off over its life (or the length of the lease if shorter) while the liability would be eliminated by the payments. These payments are not, as in the case of an operating lease, charged entirely to the profit or loss account nor are they, in general, wholly set off against the liability. Instead the payments are split between that element which is regarded as representing the repayment of the liability and the remainder that is debited to the profit and loss account as the financing (or interest) charge. The alternative approach is referred to as the capitalisation of the lease.

The lack of reality consequent upon the failure of a lessee to capitalise financial leases is highlighted by the problems that would be experienced when comparing two companies, one of which leases most of its assets, with the other purchasing fixed assets using loans of one sort or another. The latter company's balance sheet would

---

[5] IAS 1, Paras 9b and 17.

show the assets which it used to generate its revenue thus allowing users of accounts to estimate the rate of return earned on those assets, whereas the former company's balance sheet would, if the leases were not capitalised, understate its assets. Similarly, the latter company's balance sheet would indicate the liabilities that would have to be discharged if it is to continue in business with its existing bundle of assets, whereas the former company's balance sheet would not.[6]

We have so far considered only how the lessee should treat a finance lease. Let us now consider the matter from the point of view of the lessor. The lessor's balance sheet would not include the physical asset but a debtor for the amounts receivable under the lease. Thenceforth the payments received under the terms of the lease should be split between that which goes to reducing the debt and the balance being credited to the profit and loss account. We shall see later in this section how the division can be made.

In order to understand part of the reason why leasing became popular, the reluctance on the part of most companies to capitalise leases, and the provisions of SSAP 21, it is necessary to understand the way in which leases are treated for the purposes of taxation. Unlike hire purchase contracts and credit sales agreements, where the user obtains grants and capital allowances, in the case of a lease it is the legal owner, the lessor, who receives grants and capital allowances on the asset. The lessee receives no allowances but obtains tax relief on the amounts payable under the lease. Capital allowances are only of value to a company that has sufficient taxable profit. Hence, to their mutual advantage, one company with large taxable profits is able to lease assets to another company that does not have sufficient taxable profits to take full advantage of capital allowances. Thus the company with insufficient taxable profits can acquire fixed assets at a lower effective cost than would have been the case with alternative methods of financing.

The effect of what might well be described as the distortion of the tax system described above was undoubtedly one of the major causes of the growth of leasing. Hence, there was a good deal of opposition to the proposal that lessees should capitalise finance leases, as it was feared that a change in accounting practice might precipitate changes in taxation law whereby finance leases would be treated in the same way as hire purchase contracts.

Other factors which hindered the development of a standard requiring the capitalisation of finance leases included concerns about the possible extension of the principle to other types of non-cancellable contracts, for example those for the regular supply of raw materials or labour, and fears about the potential complexity of any standard. However, the ASC did issue SSAP 21 'Accounting for Leases and Hire Purchase Contracts' in August 1984 and, amongst other things, this required lessees to capitalise finance leases, and lessors to include in their balance sheets not the fixed asset but the debtor for the net investment in the lease. It is perhaps somewhat ironic that, after studying the problem for some nine years, the ASC issued this standard just after the Finance Act 1984 had considerably reduced the tax advantages of leasing.

We will start by examining the treatment of finance leases in the books of the lessee. This will not only enable us to show the basic principles involved but also introduce some terms which will make it easier to understand SSAP 21.

Let us start with a simple example.

---

[6] It is for this reason that finance leases were described as providing an 'off balance sheet' source of finance.

Lonbok Limited, a company whose year end is 31 December, leases a machine from Salat Limited on 1 January 20X1. Under the terms of the lease Lonbok is to make four annual payments[7] of £35 000 payable at the start of each year. Lonbok Limited is responsible for all the maintenance and insurance costs, so these are not covered by the payments under the lease.

The first step is to decide the amount at which the leased asset should be capitalised, i.e. shown as an asset and a liability in the first instance. SSAP 21 requires that:

> At the inception of the lease the sum to be recorded both as an asset and as a liability should be the present value of the minimum lease payments, derived by discounting them at the interest rate implicit in the lease. (SSAP 21, Para. 32)

To do that we need to know what is meant by the minimum lease payments and the interest rate implicit in the lease. These terms are as defined in SSAP 21.

Minimum lease payments

The minimum lease payments are the minimum payments over the remaining part of the lease term (excluding charges for services and taxes to be paid by the lessor) and:

(a) in the case of the lessee, any residual amounts guaranteed by him or by a party related to him; or
(b) in the case of the lessor, any residual amounts guaranteed by the lessee or by an independent third party.
(SSAP 21, Para. 20)

In the Lonbok example we will assume that there are no residual amounts and thus the minimum lease payments at the inception of the lease are the four annual payments of £35 000.

Interest rate implicit in a lease

> The interest rate implicit in a lease is the discount rate that at the inception of a lease when applied to the amounts that the lessor expects to receive and retain produces an amount (the present value) equal to the fair value of the leased asset. The amounts which the lessor expects to receive and retain comprise (a) the minimum lease payments to the lessor (as defined above) plus (b) any unguaranteed residual value, less (c) any part of (a) and (b) for which the lessor will be accountable to the lessee. If the interest rate implicit in the lease is not determinable, it should be estimated by reference to the rate that a lessee would be expected to pay on a similar lease. (SSAP 21, Para. 24)

A key element in the above definition is fair value and hence we need to know how this is found.

Fair value

> Fair value is the price at which an asset could be exchanged in an arm's length transaction less, where applicable, any grants receivable towards the purchase or use of the asset.
>
> (SSAP 21, Para. 25)

---

[7] In practice lease payments are usually made at monthly, quarterly or six-monthly intervals, but, in order to illustrate more clearly the principles involved, in our example we will assume that the payments are made at annual intervals. More realistic examples of the type of calculations that have to be made in practice, including leases which do not, conveniently, start on the first day of the year can be found in the guidance notes to SSAP 21.

Note that while knowledge of the implied interest rate is required to determine the appropriate accounting treatment in the books of the lessee, it is found by reference to the cash flows of the lessor. In practice the lessee may not know or be able to estimate the various cash flows but we, at this stage, assume that the lessee can obtain all the necessary data.

If we let FV be the fair value, L_j the lease payment in year j (payable at the beginning of each year) and R_n the estimated residual values received at the end of year n, the last year of the lease, then using standard present value techniques the implied rate of interest r is found from the solution of the following equation:

$$FV = \sum_{j=0}^{n-1} \frac{L_j}{(1 + r)^j} + \frac{R_n}{(1 + r)^n}$$

If we assume in the case of the Lonbok/Salat lease that the fair value is £108 720 and that there is no residual value (i.e. $R_n = 0$) then substituting in the above equation we get:

$$£108\,720 = \sum_{j=0}^{3} \frac{£35\,000}{(1 + r)^j} \quad \text{or} \quad \sum_{j=0}^{3} \frac{1}{(1 + r)^j} = 3.1064$$

Inspection of tables showing the present value of an annuity shows that 3.1064 represents an interest rate of 20 per cent.[8]

Thus the interest rate implicit in the lease is 20 per cent and hence the present value PV of the minimum lease payments can be found as follows:

$$PV = £35\,000(3.1064)$$
$$= £108\,720$$

This is of course equal to the fair value as, in the simple case, the only cash flows that the lessor will receive are the minimum lease payments. Later we will describe the circumstances where the two series of cash flows (i.e. the lessee's and the lessor's) might be different and the effect of these differences on the calculations.

We can now show how the lease will be treated in the books of Lonbok (the lessee). The original entry recording the lease is:

Dr Leased asset	£108 720	
Cr Liability under lease		£108 720

From this time onwards the two accounts are dealt with separately. The leased machine will be depreciated over the shorter of the length of the lease or the asset's expected life, using the company's normal depreciation policy for assets of its type, while the liability will be gradually extinguished as payments are made during the primary period of the lease. The only problem that remains is how to spread the total interest charge over the primary period of the lease. This same problem is, of course, encountered in accounting for hire purchase transactions.

The total interest charge may be calculated as follows:

Payments under lease, 4 × £35 000	£140 000
less 'Cost' as above	108 720
Interest	£31 280

---

[8] This and other necessary present value calculations can be made by use of standard computer packages.

Theoretically the best approach is to use the actuarial or annuity method that produces a constant annual rate of interest (in this case 20 per cent) on the outstanding balance on the liability account. This is the method specified in SSAP 21, which does, however, allow the use of any alternative method that is a reasonable approximation to the annuity method.[9]

Assuming that all payments are made on the due dates, the liability account in the books of Lonbok for the term of the lease can be summarised as follows:

	20X1	20X2	20X3	20X4
	£	£	£	£
1 Jan opening balance (20X1 cost)	108 720	88 470	64 170	35 000
1 Jan Cash	35 000	35 000	35 000	35 000
	73 720	53 470	29 170	–
31 Dec Interest, 20% of above	14 750	10 700	5 830	–
31 Dec closing balance	£88 470	£64 170	£35 000	–

The account provides us with the interest charge to the profit and loss account for each year and the liability for inclusion in each balance sheet, although it is of course necessary to distinguish between the current portion of the liability (i.e. due within a year) and the rest for the purpose of balance sheet presentation. The amount of interest charged to the profit and loss account declines over the life of the lease because the outstanding balance is reduced by the annual payments.

One commonly used alternative to the annuity method is the 'sum of the year's digits' method or 'Rule of 78'.[10] If the sum of the digits method were used in the above illustration the results would be:

Total interest charge		£31 280
Sum of the year's digits, 1 + 2 + 3		6
Interest charged to profit and loss account		
20X1, $\frac{3}{6}$ of £31 280	15 640	
20X2, $\frac{2}{6}$ of £31 280	10 430	
20X3, $\frac{1}{6}$ of £31 280	5 210	
	£31 280	

Although the use of the annuity method is conceptually superior, a comparison of the annual interest charges under the two methods reveals similar patterns of interest charge and thus the 'sum of the year's digits' method is often used as a convenient approximation to the annuity method:

Year	Annuity method	Sum of the year's digits method
	(£)	(£)
20X1	14 750	15 640
20X2	10 700	10 430
20X3	5 830	5 210
	£31 280	£31 280

---

[9] The method is the only one permitted under the provisions of FRS 4 'Capital Investments'.

[10] It is called the Rule of 78 because if the method is based on the monthly intervals and if the digit 1 is assigned to January, 2 to February and so on, the sum of the digits for the year is 78.

The impact of residual values

Let us now complicate matters by assuming that the asset that is the subject of the lease has a residual value. We will assume that the manufacturer who originally supplied the asset to Salat has agreed to reacquire the asset at the end of the lease. The sum is dependent on the condition of the machine and the market factors at the end of the lease, but the manufacturer has guaranteed to pay £10 000 whatever the circumstances. Let us assume that at the inception of the lease it is anticipated that the manufacturer will actually pay £20 000. Let us also assume that Lonbok and Salat agree that they will divide any sums realised on the disposal of the asset in the ratio 35:65. Thus, at the inception of the lease it is estimated that Lonbok will receive £7000 (of which £3500 is guaranteed) and Salat £13 000 (£6500 guaranteed).

For the purposes of calculating the implicit interest rate, the distinction between the guaranteed and unguaranteed elements of the residual value can be ignored as both have to be taken into the calculation, but the distinction may be important when deciding whether the lease is a finance or operating lease (*see* p. 178).

If we return to the equation on p. 175 and substitute the estimated value on realisation receivable by Salat, the equation becomes:

$$£108\,720 = \sum_{j=0}^{3} \frac{35\,000}{(1 + r)^j} + \frac{13\,000}{(1 + r)^4}$$

Use of tables or a programmable calculation on a computer shows that the above equation will be satisfied when r is approximately 25 per cent. This is a higher rate of interest than the 20 per cent that was previously calculated as Salat obviously earns a higher return due to the introduction of the residual value as an additional cash flow.

So far as Lonbok is concerned the minimum lease payments are unchanged but they will now be discounted at the higher rate of 25 per cent that will produce an initial value of the leased asset of:

$$£35\,000(2.952) = £103\,320$$

The annual payments of £35 000 are the same as in the original example except that the liability that is to be paid off is lower (£103 320 not £108 720). Hence the finance charge in the profit and loss account will be higher in the second example. This reflects the fact that in the first example the lease payments can be regarded as acquiring the whole of the productive use of the asset, in that a zero residual value was assumed, whereas in the second case the same annual lease payments only acquired a proportion of the asset's productive capacity.

It will be noted that the estimated realisable value that Lonbok expects to receive had no effect on the calculation of the amount by which the lease should be capitalised or on the way in which the annual lease payments should be split. This is because these depend on the minimum lease payments. The recognition of the estimated realisable value does have an effect on the amount that has to be depreciated which is the present value of the minimum lease payments less the estimated realisable value. Thus, the depreciation charges that would emerge from our two sets of assumptions are as follows (assuming the straight-line method is used):

$$\text{Assumption 1} \qquad \frac{£108\,720}{4} = £27\,180$$

$$\text{Assumption 2} \qquad \frac{£(103\,320 - 7000)}{4} = £24\,080$$

In the above examples we assumed that the lessee knows (or is able to find out from the lessor) the fair value of the asset and the estimated realisable value that the lessor expects to receive. In practice this may well not be the case and certain estimates will have to be made. Often the fair value will be known [11] and the interest rate estimated from a knowledge of other leases of a similar type.

SSAP 21 *Accounting for Leases and Hire Purchase Contracts*

We are now in a position to discuss the specific requirements of SSAP 21. This is a detailed standard and we will not attempt to cover all its aspects but will instead concentrate on the important elements and those that might give rise to particular difficulties of understanding. The ASC published guidance notes on SSAP 21 and readers should refer to this booklet for a more detailed explanation of the provisions of the standard.

We will first deal with a number of general issues before concentrating on the impact of the standard on the accounts of lessees and hirers. A discussion of the more specialised topic of accounting for lessors will be deferred to the concluding part of this chapter.

Scope

The standard covers leases and hire purchases contracts and is applicable to accounts based on both the historical cost and current cost conventions. The standard does not apply to leases of the rights to exploit natural resources such as oil or gas, nor does it apply to licensing agreement for items such as motion pictures, videos, etc. Stress is also laid on the point that the standard does not apply to immaterial items. Thus a company that leases some of its office equipment may not need to capitalise the lease but continue to treat a finance lease in the same way as an operating lease.

Distinction between finance and operating leases

The basic distinction between the two different types of leases has already been explained (*see* p. 171). SSAP 21 states that:

> A finance lease is a lease that transfers substantially all the risks and rewards of ownership of an asset to the lessee. (Para. 15)

It is presumed that a lease is a finance lease if at the start of the lease the present value of the minimum lease payments amounts to substantially all (normally 90 per cent or more) of the fair value of the leased asset. The present value should be calculated by using the interest rate implicit in the lease. However, the standard recognises that in exceptional circumstances this initial presumption may be rebutted if the lease in question does not transfer substantially all the risks and rewards of ownership to the lessee. It may sometimes be the case that the lessor will receive part of his return by way of a guarantee from an independent third party, possibly the manufacturer of the asset, in which case the lease may be treated as a finance lease by the lessor but as an operating lease by the lessee.

---

[11] Unless the asset concerned is highly specific the prudent lessee will obviously wish to know how much it would cost to purchase the asset before signing a lease.

Hire purchase contracts

With the vast majority of hire purchases contracts the 'risks and rewards' pass to the hirer and hence may be regarded as being akin to finance leases. In such cases the standard specifies that they should be treated in a similar way to finance leases. However, in exceptional circumstances a hire purchase contract may be accounted for on the same principles as an operating lease.

Accounting by lessees

Finance leases

A finance lease should be capitalised; hence the lease should be recorded as an asset and an obligation to pay rentals. At the inception of the lease the asset will equal the liability (although this equality will not hold over the life of the lease) and will be the present value of the minimum lease payments, derived by discounting them at the interest rate implied in the lease.

The standard states:

> that the fair value of the asset will often be a sufficiently close approximation to the present value of the minimum lease payments and may in these circumstances be substituted for it. (Para. 33)

In most circumstances the fair value will be a sufficiently close approximation to be used, for, by definition, if the present value of the minimum lease payments does not equal 90 per cent or more of the fair value, then it is presumed that the lease is an operating and not a finance lease.

If the fair value cannot be determined, possibly because the asset concerned is unique, then the present value can be found by discounting the minimum lease payments by the interest rate implicit in the lease. If the latter cannot be determined the rate may be estimated from that which applied in similar leases.

Total payments less than fair value

In some circumstances the combined impact of any grants which may be available and taxation allowances received by the lessor may be such as to bring the total (i.e. not the present value) lease payments below the fair value. The standard specifies (Para. 34) that if this occurs the amount to be capitalised and depreciated should be reduced to the minimum lease payments. A negative finance charge should not be shown.

In other words if, say, the total of the payments to be made under the lease is £10 000 and the fair value of the asset is £12 000, the asset and liability on the inception of the lessee are both £10 000. The payments under the lease will all be applied to reducing the liability and no part of them will be charged to the profit and loss account as a finance charge. The only charge in the profit and loss account will be the annual depreciation charge.

Rentals

Rentals payable should be apportioned between the finance charge (if any) and a reduction of the outstanding obligation. The total finance charge should be allocated to accounting periods so as to produce a constant annual rate of charge (i.e. the annuity method), or a reasonable approximation thereto.

The guidance notes suggest that in most circumstances, especially where the lease is for seven years or less and interest rates are not high that the Rule of 78 (*see* p. 176)

179

will be an acceptable approximation to the actuarial method. In the case of small (relative to the size of the companies) leases it is suggested that the straight-line method, whereby the total finance charge is recognised on a time basis, may be acceptable.

Note that FRS 4 'Capital Instruments' does not give any latitude as to use of the method of allocating finance charges (or finance costs as they are called in FRS 4); only the actuarial (or annuity) method is allowed. However, the concept of materiality could be cited to justify the use of a simpler method such as the Rule of 78 if the figures produced by the two methods are fairly close or the totals are not material in the context of the entity's total operation.

Depreciation

A leased asset should be depreciated over the shorter of the length of the lease or the asset's useful life. However, in the case of hire purchase contracts, because of the presumption that the asset concerned will be acquired by the hirer, the asset should be depreciated over its useful life.

Operating leases

The accounting treatment by the lessee in respect of operating leases is fairly straightforward in that the whole of the payments are charged to the profit and loss account. The only slight complication is that the standard requires the rental to be charged on a straight-line basis over the lease term (unless another systematic and rational basis is more appropriate) even if the payments are not made on such a basis. Hence, if the term of the lease requires a heavy initial payment, a proportion of the payment can be treated as a prepaid expense.

More commonly, lessees are granted so-called 'rental holidays' in that they do not have to pay anything for an initial period. In such circumstances the standard requires a charge to be made to the profit and loss account for the period of the rental holiday that would be treated as an accrual in the balance sheet. Thereafter the charge to the profit and loss account would be less than the payments made in the year (as rental, like other holidays, has to be paid for), with the excess reducing the balance sheet accrual. Particularly significant examples of this type of arrangement are leases of buildings by government agencies to business in areas where the government wants to encourage the creation of jobs.

Disclosure requirements in the accounts of lessees and hirers

Finance leases

For disclosure purposes information relating to hire purchase contracts with characteristics similar to finance leases should be included with the equivalent information regarding leases.

1 *Fixed assets and depreciation.* The lessee may either:
   (a) show separately the gross amounts, accumulated depreciation and depreciation expense for each major class of leased asset; or
   (b) group the above information with the equivalent information for owned assets[12] but show by way of a note how much of the net amount (i.e. net book value) and the depreciation expense relates to assets held under finance leases.

---

[12] Since it is the right to use the asset rather than the asset itself which is capitalised there is some doubt as to whether it should be called a tangible asset and included with the owned tangible assets. The ASC ignored such niceties and for the purposes of balance sheet presentation the leases are regarded as tangible assets.

2 *Obligations.* The lessee must both:
(a) disclose the obligations related to finance leases separately from other obligations and liabilities; and
(b) analyse the net obligations under finance leases into three components (the figures may be combined with other obligations):
– amounts payable in next year
– amounts payable in second to fifth years
– amounts payable thereafter.
3 *Finance charges.* The lessee must disclose the aggregate finance charge allocated to the period.
4 *Commitments.* The lessee must show by way of a note the amount of any commitment existing at the balance sheet date in respect of finance leases which have been entered into but whose inception occurs after the year end.
5 *Accounting policies.* Accounting policies adopted for finance leases must be stated.

Operating leases

1 *Current rentals.* The lessee must disclose the total rentals charged as an expense, analysed between amounts payable in respect of the hire of plant and machinery and those charged in respect of other operating leases. (The Companies Act, of course, requires disclosure of the charge for the hire of plant and machinery.)
2 *Future rentals.* The lessee must show the payments which he or she is committed to make during the next year, analysed between those in which the commitment expires:
(a) within that year;
(b) in the second to fifth years inclusive; and
(c) over five years from the balance sheet date.
Commitments in respect of leases of land and buildings and other operating leases must be shown separately.
3 *Accounting policies.* The accounting policies adopted for operating leases must be stated.

Accounting for finance leases by lessors – general principles

The provisions of SSAP 21 regarding the accounting treatment of finance leases by lessors are relatively difficult for two main reasons. First, the basic method is itself not simple since – as will be shown – it depends on complex calculations of what constitutes the lessor's investment in a particular lease and, second, the standard permits the use of alternative methods and simplifying assumptions so that a host of different methods can be justified under the terms of the standard.

We will first describe the basic principles underlying the provisions of SSAP 21 relating to the treatment of finance leases by lessors.

Balance sheet presentation – the measurement of net investment

Lessors should not include in their balance sheets the assets subject to the leasing contracts but instead record as a debtor the *net investment* in the lease after making any necessary provisions for bad and doubtful debts. In order to explain this term and describe how profit is recognised, we will need to reproduce certain definitions included in SSAP 21.

Net investment

The net investment in a lease at a point in time comprises:

(a) the gross investment in a lease; less
(b) gross earnings allocated to future periods.
(SSAP 21, Para. 22)

Thus, we need to know what is meant by the gross investment and gross earnings.

Gross investment

The gross investment in a lease at a point in time is the total of the minimum lease payments [see p. 174] and any unguaranteed residual value accruing to the lessor. (SSAP 21, Para. 21)

Gross earnings

Gross earnings comprise the lessor's gross finance income over the lease term, representing the difference between his gross investment in the lease [see above] and the cost of the leased asset less any grants receivable towards the purchase or use of the asset.[13] (SSAP 21, Para. 28)

In order to illustrate the effect of the above definitions assume that the details relating to a particular lease are as follows:

Cost of asset	£12 000
Grant receivable by lessor	£2 000
Lease term	5 years
Annual rental	£3 000
Estimated residual value accruing to the lessor	£500

Let us see how one measures the net investment at the inception of the lease and at the end of the first year.

At inception:	£
Minimum lease payments, 5 × £3000	15 000
Estimated residual value	500
Gross investment	15 500
less Gross earnings (£15 500 – £10 000)	5 500
Net investment	£10 000

Hence, at inception the net investment is equal to the cost of the asset less grants receivable by the lessor.

Assume that the gross earnings recognised in the profit and loss account in the first year are £2500 (we shall describe in the following section how this figure is calculated). Then the net investment at the end of the first year is:

	£
Minimum lease payments, 4 × £3000	12 000
Estimated residual value	500
	12 500
less Gross earnings allocated to future periods	
£5500 – £2500	3 000
Net investment	£9 500

---

[13] The paragraph goes on to modify the definition to deal with the use of a possible option available in SSAP 21 relating to the treatment of tax-free grants.

The recognition of gross earnings

The total gross earnings on any lease are reasonably easy to calculate since the minimum lease payments will be known and, generally, the residual value, if any, can be estimated. The difficulty lies in allocating the gross earnings to the different accounting periods. The standard followed existing practice in the leasing industry by specifying that (other than in the case of hire purchase contracts) the interest should be allocated on the basis of the lessor's *net cash* investment in the lease and not on the basis of the net investment. Specifically, Para. 39 of SSAP 21 states:

> The total gross earnings under a finance lease should normally be allocated to accounting periods to give a constant periodic rate of return on the lessor's net cash investment in the lease in each period. In the case of a hire purchase contract which has characteristics similar to a finance lease, allocation of gross earnings so as to give a constant periodic rate of return on the finance company's net investment will in most cases be a suitable approximation to allocation based on the net cash investment. In arriving at the constant periodic rate of return, a reasonable approximation may be made.

To an extent the above is familiar in that it is the counterpart of the annuity method prescribed for use by lessees in that the annual finance charge should be such as to produce a constant rate based on the decreasing obligation. The difference is that although the reduction in the obligation is relatively easy to calculate, the determination of the net cash investment is somewhat more difficult.

The meaning of net cash investment

The meaning of the net cash investment can be more easily understood if one assumes that a separate company is established by the lessor for each lease and then measuring or estimating the cash flows in and out of that company. The net cash investment is then the balance of cash, which might be positive or negative, in the company at any point in time. The various cash flows may be summarised in Table 6.1.

If one thinks in terms of a single lease company and the cash flows associated with it, it can be seen that the company will start with an 'overdraft' – the cost of the asset and of setting up the lease – but that this will be reduced if a grant is received and as capital allowances for the purchase of the asset are received. The overdraft will be reduced as lease payments are received but will be increased by

Table 6.1 Summary of cash flows

Cash flows out	Cash flows in
1 Cost of the asset	(a) Grants recieved against purchase or use of asset
2 Cost of setting up the lease	(b) Rental income recieved
3 Tax payments on rental and interest recieved	(c) Tax reductions on capital allowances[14] and on interest paid
4 Interest payments on cash invested in the lease	(d) Interest earned when the net cash investment becomes a surplus
5 Profit withdrawn	(e) Residual value at the end of the lease

[14] Since in actuality the 'single-lease' company is not separate and distinct, the reductions in tax payments due to the receipt of capital allowance and the charging of expenses can be treated as cash receipts since they are covered by tax payment otherwise payable by the lessor (if this were not the case the lessor should not be in the leasing business in the first place!).

virtue of the interest payments made on the overdraft. Profit may also be withdrawn (and for this purpose profit may be regarded as including the contribution made by the 'single lease' company to the operating expenses of the enterprise of which it actually forms part) which will also increase the overdraft. At some stage the overdraft may be eliminated and replaced by a cash surplus on which interest may be deemed to be earned. The interest 'payments' and 'receipts' will also have taxation consequences that will respectively increase the cash surplus (or reduce the overdraft) or decrease the cash surplus. Finally, if the lessor receives a residual value this will increase the surplus.

It is on the basis of the above considerations that SSAP 21 defines net cash investment as follows:

> The *net cash investment* in a lease at a point in time is the amount of funds invested in a lease by a lessor, and comprises the cost of the asset plus or minus the following related payments and receipts:
> (a) government or other grants receivable towards the purchase or use of the asset;
> (b) rentals received;
> (c) taxation payments and receipts, including the effect of capital allowances;
> (d) residual values, if any, at the end of the lease term;
> (e) interest payments (where applicable);
> (f) interest received on cash surplus;
> (g) profit taken out of the lease.
> (SSAP 21, Para. 23)

The actuarial method after tax

The guidance notes to SSAP 21 describe a number of ways of allocating the gross revenue to accounting periods based on the net cash investment. Of these the most accurate is the 'actuarial method after tax'. This method produces a constant rate of return on the net cash investment over that period of the lease in which the lessor has a positive investment (i.e. before any cash surplus is generated). The phrase 'after tax' does not imply that it is after tax profit which is allocated but simply that the tax cash flows are included in the measurement of the net cash investment.

The actuarial method after tax is illustrated in Example 6.1.

Example 6.1

Gasp plc, the lessor, acquired an asset for £7735 that it leased out on the following terms:

Period   5 years
Rental   £2000 per year payable in advance on 1 January of each year
Residual value Zero

Gasp's year end is 31 December and tax in respect of any year is payable on 1 January of the next year but one. The tax rate is 50 per cent and capital allowances of 100 per cent are receivable in the first year. (These rates are unrealistic but they have been chosen to simplify the figures and hence clarify the example.)

The annual rate of return earned over the period when there is a net cash investment is 12 per cent while it is estimated that surplus cash can be invested at 5 per cent (both rates are before tax).

The interest paid by Gasp on the funds invested in the lease will be ignored.

The cash flows and the profit recognised on the lease are set out in Table 6.2.

Table 6.2 Hypothetical cash flows – figures in brackets represent cash flows out

Date	Cost £	Rent £	Tax £	Profit taken on lease £	Interest on cash surplus £	Net cash investment £
1 Jan X0	(7 735)	2 000				(5 735)
31 Dec X0				(688)		(6 423)
1 Jan X1		2 000				(4 423)
31 Dec X1				(531)		(4 954)
1 Jan X2		2 000	2 868			(86)
31 Dec X2				(11)		(97)
1 Jan X3		2 000	(1 000)			903
31 Dec X3					45	948
1 Jan X4		2 000	(1 000)			1 948
31 Dec X4					98	2 046
1 Jan X5			(1 023)			1 023
31 Dec X5					52	1 075
1 Jan X6			(1 049)			26
1 Jan X7			(26)			–

Notes:

(a) The profit taken on the lease has been calculated at 12 per cent of the net cash investment at the start of each year (e.g. £688 = 0.12 × £5735) while the interest on the cash surplus has been calculated at 5 per cent of the opening balance (e.g. £45 = 0.05 × £903). Interest on the cash surplus in 20X6 has been ignored (otherwise the calculation would never end).

(b) The tax computation for 20X0 (tax payable on 1 January 20X2) is as follows:

	£
Capital allowances (100%)	7 735
less Rental income received	2 000
Adjusted profit	5 735
Tax thereon, 50% of £5 735	£2 868

In subsequent years the tax payment is 50 per cent of the sum of the rental income and the interest earned on the cash surplus.

Although the lease will generate an annual rental of £2000 for each of the five years after tax, profit recognised in respect of the lease is £688 in year 1, £531 in year 2 and £11 in year 3.[15]

It may be thought that this is a very imprudent way of recognising profit in that most of the profit is taken in the first two years of the lease. However, it must be recognised that the profit reported is that which is generated by the lessor's financing activities and is calculated by reference to the amount that the lessor has invested in the lease. As Table 6.2 shows, the investment falls to zero, to be replaced by a cash surplus by 1 January 20X3.

---

[15] Observant readers will note that the sum of these is, at £1230, more than the 50 per cent of the difference between the minimum lease payments and the cost of the asset, i.e. 50 per cent of (£10 000 – £7735) = £1132. This is because the interest on the cash surplus is included in the total profit, i.e. £1230 = 50 per cent of £(10 000 – 7735 + 45 + 98 + 52).

Arithmetically all the figures in Table 6.2 can be found if you know the cash flows, which will be specified in the agreement, and either the profit on the lease (12 per cent) or the re-investment rate (5 per cent). Thus, if one of the two rates is known the other can be calculated, with the aid of a computer or a lot of patient trial and error. In practice, of course, the lessor will have made the calculations of these rates when agreeing the terms of the rental with the lessee. Thus the lessor would start by deciding, on the basis of market conditions and competitive forces, the return required on the lease (taking into account the return on any surplus cash invested[16] and hence work out the rent that would need to be charged.

The next step is to calculate the proportion of the annual receipts of £2000, which is deemed to represent the reduction in the amount due from the lessee. The calculation is based on the figures in Table 6.3. This table also shows the necessary transfers to and from the deferred taxation account if it is judged necessary to establish such an account.

Table 6.3 is constructed from the bottom up. The figures in line 9 are taken from Table 6.2. The net profit is then grossed up at the appropriate tax rate (50 per cent) to give line 5. Line 6, which shows the actual tax payments, is also taken from Table 6.2 which means that line 8 (deferred tax) can be derived. Line 4 is taken from Table 6.2 and hence the gross earnings (line 3) and capital repayments (line 2) can be deduced. If, taking into consideration the affairs of the company as a whole, it is decided that it is not necessary to account for deferred tax, one could start Table 6.3 at line 5 and work up from there.

Table 6.3 To calculate capital repayment and deferred taxation transfers

	20X0 £	20X1 £	20X2 £	20X3 £	20X4 £	20X5 £	Total £
1 Rental	2 000	2 000	2 000	2 000	2 000		10 000
2 Capital repayments	(624)	(938)	(1 978)	(2 045)	(2 098)	(52)	(7 735)
3 Gross earnings	1 376	1 062	22	(45)	(98)	(52)	2 265
4 Interest				45	98	52	195
5 Profit before tax	1 376	1 062	22	–	–	–	2 460
6 Taxation	2 868	(1 000)	(1 000)	(1 023)	(1 049)	(26)	(1 230)
7	4 244	62	(978)	(1 023)	(1 049)	(26)	(1 230)
8 Deferred tax	(3 556)	469	989	1 023	1 049	26	–
9 Net profit	£688	£531	£11	–	–	–	£1 230

It must be emphasised that Table 6.3 is used only to calculate the capital repayment and, if appropriate, the deferred taxation transfers. For the purposes of the balance sheet presentation SSAP 21 requires that the amount due from the lessee should be the net investment (not the net cash investment) in the lease. Thus in the instance of Gasp plc the asset would be recorded as follows:

---

[16] The surplus cash will probably be invested in another lease, thus the rate of return on the surplus cash will be the return from the new lease. The return on the new lease will inter alia depend on the return on any surplus cash it may generate which it may be presumed will be invested in yet another lease and so on ad infinitum. In practice, to avoid having to estimate returns on leases (or other investments) which will arise in the future, a prudent estimate of the return on surplus cash is used in the calculations.

Balance sheet date	Gross investment £	Gross earnings allocated to future periods £	Net investment £
31 Dec X0	8 000	889	7 111
31 Dec X1	6 000	(173)	6 173
31 Dec X2	4 000	(195)	4 195
31 Dec X3	2 000	(150)	2 150
31 Dec X4	–	(52)	52

The gross earnings allocated to future periods are found from line 3 of Table 6.3. Thus, for example, the figure at 31 December 20X0 is £(1062 + 22 – 45 – 98 – 52) = £889 and so on.

The method produces the apparently absurd result that the net investment at certain dates is greater than the remaining lease payments, the extreme case being that at 31 December 20X4 when a net investment of £52 is produced notwithstanding the fact that the lease has terminated. This odd result derives from the fact that a larger profit is taken in the early years of the lease in consequence of the anticipated return on the surplus cash invested; thus, for example, the net investment at 31 December 20X3 of £2150 can be regarded as representing the final lease payment of £2000 plus the anticipated interest receipts of £150 (£98 in 20X4 and £52 in 20X5).

The above example assumed the existence of 100 per cent first-year capital allowances and a high nominal rate of corporation tax as these assumptions make it easier to show the effect of tax on the net cash investment.

Alternative approaches to accounting for finance leases and hire purchase contracts

As stated on p. 183, Para. 39 of SSAP 21 specifies that in the case of hire purchase contracts gross earnings can be allocated on the basis of the company's net investment. The reason for this is that in the case of hire purchase, capital allowances are granted to the hirer and hence the tax cash flows will not have the same significance to the hire purchase company as they have for a leasing company.

The same paragraph allows the use of alternative methods for both hire purchase and leasing companies that give 'reasonable approximations' to that, which produces a constant rate of return of the net cash investment. A number of alternatives are described in the guidance notes to SSAP 21, which include the investment period method, which is similar to the actuarial method after tax. Other methods described are the 'Rule of 78' and the actuarial method before tax. These two methods are primarily intended for use with hire purchase contracts but they can be used for finance leases where the amounts concerned are not judged to be material.

Lessors may, if they choose, write off the initial direct costs in arranging a lease over the period on a 'systematic and rational basis' (SSAP 21, Para. 44). This provision applies to both finance and operating leases.

Accounting for operating leases by lessors – general principles

The basic principles are contained in Paras. 42–44 of SSAP 21. These are:

An asset held for use in operating leases by a lessor should be recorded as a fixed asset and depreciated over its useful life. (Para. 42)

Rental income from an operating lease, excluding charges for services such as insurance and maintenance, should be recognized on a straight-line basis over the period of the lease, even if the payments are not made on such a basis, unless another systematic and rational basis is more representative of the time pattern in which the benefit from the leased asset is receivable. (Para. 43)

Initial direct costs incurred by a lessor in arranging a lease may be apportioned over the period of the lease on a systematic and rational basis. (Para. 44)

The accounting treatment of operating leases by the lessor is thus straightforward, subject only to the problems of dealing with cases where payment is not received on a straight-line basis and deciding on the circumstances where an alternative systematic and rational basis would be appropriate. These issues are similar to those faced by the lessee (*see* p. 180).

Disclosure requirements for the lessor in respect of finance and operating leases and hire purchase contracts

The requirements, contained in Paras 58–60 of SSAP 21 are as follows:

1 The net investment in (i) finance leases and (ii) hire purchase contracts should be disclosed. Note that separate totals need to be given for leases and hire purchase contracts. In the case of the remaining disclosure requirements, information regarding leases and hire purchase contracts can be combined.
2 The gross amount of assets held for use in operating leases and the related accumulated depreciation charge should be disclosed.
3 Disclosure should be made of:
    (a) the policy adopted for accounting for operating leases and finance leases and, in detail, the policy for accounting for finance lease income;
    (b) the aggregate rentals receivable in respect of an accounting period in relation to (i) finance leases and (ii) operating leases; and
    (c) the cost of assets acquired, whether by purchase or finance lease, for the purpose of letting under finance leases.

Sale and leaseback transactions

The standard makes specific reference to sale and leaseback transactions that arise when the vendor/lessee sells an asset but continues to have the use of it on the basis of a lease granted by the purchaser/lessor. No problems arise with regard to the treatment of a sale and leaseback transaction in the accounts of the lessor who will record the asset purchased at cost and then, depending on the nature of the lease, follow the provisions of SSAP 21 in the usual way. The position regarding the vendor/lessee is different in so far as there are circumstances where the sales and leaseback transactions will have to be accorded special treatment. The nature of the circumstances depends on the type of lease.

Finance leases

The key characteristic of a finance lease is that the 'risk and reward' associated with the asset rests with the lessee. Hence when a vendor engages in a sale and finance leaseback transaction, the 'risk and reward' is retained. It is therefore argued that in such circumstances it would be wrong to recognise a profit or loss on the sale of the asset concerned in the year in which the sale and leaseback is effected.

Thus SSAP 21 states:

> In a sale and leaseback transaction which results in a finance lease, any apparent profit or loss (that is, the difference between the sale price and the previous carrying value) should be deferred and amortized in the financial statements of the seller/lessee over the shorter of the lease term and the useful life of the asset. (Para. 46)

If the asset was sold for its fair value, the provisions of Para. 46 could be avoided by revaluing the asset prior to sale and hence removing any difference between the sale price and the carrying value. However, to the extent that the vendor retains the 'risk and reward' any profit on the sale should not be regarded as being realised, but it would be reasonable to recognise gradually the realisation of any profit over the shorter of the lease term and the useful life of the asset.

If the asset were not sold for its fair value it is likely that the consequence would be that the lease rental payments would be higher (if the asset were sold for more than its fair value) or lower than those which would be charged if the asset had been sold for its fair value. Hence it is reasonable to set the apparent profit or loss against the rental charges.

Operating leases

In the case of an operating lease the 'risks and rewards' are transferred along with the legal title to the asset. Hence any profit or loss on the sale of the asset should be recognised immediately as long as the asset was sold at its fair value.

If the asset is sold for an amount in excess of its fair value, the excess should be written back to the profit and loss account over the shorter of the remainder of the lease term or the period to the next rent review (if any).

Tax-free grants

SSAP 21 was amended in 1997 to cover tax-free grants that may be available to the lessor against the purchase price of assets acquired for leasing. These should be spread over the period of the lease and dealt with by treating the grant as non-taxable income (Para. 41).

Postscript to SSAP 21

Since accounting for lessors is a specialised subject, we have concentrated on the main principles. Interested readers will need to study SSAP 21 and the associated guidance notes to gain a full understanding of the topic.

Accounting for Leases: A New Approach

This paper, *Accounting for Leases: A New Approach*, Financial Accounting Standards Board, 1996, whose principal author was Warren McGregor, is a report of a working party made up of representatives of the IASC and groups from five countries.[17] It reports that leasing continues to be a major source of financing and suggests that it may be even more important in the future.

The authors of the paper, drawing largely on research carried out in Australia and the USA, conclude that there are many examples of lease agreement for what are, in all material respects, finance leases that were drawn up in such a way to ensure that they qualified for treatment as operating leases and hence appear 'off the balance sheet'. It does seem that the authors were sceptical of the ability of standard setters to produce criteria that would overcome the problem. They also took an alternative approach and examined the issue from first principles largely relying on the definitions of assets and liabilities contained in the IASC's Framework. These are:

> An asset is a resource controlled by the enterprise as a result of past events and from which future economic benefits are expected to flow to the enterprise. (IASC Framework, Para. 49(a))

> A liability is a present obligation of the enterprise arising from past events, the settlement of which is expected to result in an outflow from the enterprise of resources embodying economic benefits. (IASC Framework, Para. 49(b))

The report argues that, on the basis of the above definitions, in respect of any non-cancellable lease, the lessee possess both an asset and a liability and that these should be reflected on the balance sheet. Hence, the report's recommendation that all non-cancellable leases should be capitalised is advanced on the grounds of both theory and pragmatism. This is normally a powerful combination but it remains to be seen whether the recommendation will be accepted by the ASB in its review of this topic.

Reflecting the substance of transactions

The vast majority of transactions of the vast majority of companies are simple and straightforward. A fixed asset or an item of stock is purchased for cash or on credit and the impact on the company's assets and liabilities can be easily assessed. But occasionally a company will enter a complex set of transactions that involve a series of different events that, if viewed in isolation, might give a misleading picture.

Let us suppose X Limited 'sells' some land to Y Bank for £1 000 000 with an option to reacquire it for, say, £1 080 000 in six months' time.

Is it a genuine sale or is it a device to borrow money, 'off the balance sheet', for six months? And, if it is the latter, would the financial statements show a more realistic picture if the asset were not treated as a sale, but retained as an asset with the corresponding recognition of the obligation to 'repay' the bank?

The task is to determine the substance of the transaction. The doctrine of 'substance over form' is found in many attempts to construct a conceptual framework of accounting. Many interpretations have been made of the phrase but it is perhaps most readily understood as the belief that financial statements should, when there is conflict, be based on economic (or commercial) reality rather than legal form.[18]

The capitalization of leases is an example of accounting for substance over form and this special case was the subject of SSAP 21. FRS 5 deals with the general issue.

---

[17] The countries represented were Australia, Canada, New Zealand, United Kingdom and the United States.

[18] For a comprehensive discussion on the subject *see* B.S. Rutherford, *The Doctrine of Substance over Form*, Certified Accountants Publications, London, 1988.

FRS 5 *Reporting the substance of transactions*

FRS 5 requires that the reporting entity's financial statements should report on the substance of the transaction into which it has entered (Para. 14).

FRS 5, as are many of the transactions to which it relates, is complex but there is a governing principle which is that, when determining the nature of a transaction, one needs to decide whether, as a result of the transaction, the reporting entity has created new assets or liabilities or whether it has changed any of its existing assets or liabilities (Para. 16). The standard hence adopts a strictly 'balance sheet' approach: identify the assets and liabilities and let the profit and loss account emerge.

In order to determine 'substance' FRS 5 emphasises the need to identify all aspects and implications of a complex transaction and points out that some aspects will be uncertain or contingent and that greater weight needs to be given to those aspects which are likely to have a commercial effect in practice. The standard suggests that the accountant needs to consider the expectations and motivation of all parties to the transaction and points out that, whatever is the substance of the transaction, it will normally have a commercial logic for all the parties and hence, if a transaction appears not to make sense, this might indicate 'that not all related parts of the transaction have been identified or that the commercial effect of some element of the transaction has been incorrectly assessed' (Para. 51). In other words it suggests that if the accountant digs deep enough the reality of the transaction will emerge.

The standard is relevant to those complex transactions whose substance is not readily apparent and whose commercial effect may not be fully reflected by their legal form. Common features of such transactions are:

(i)   the separation of legal title to an item from the ability to enjoy the principal benefits and exposure to the principal risks associated with it;

(ii) the linking of a transaction with one or more others in such a way that its commercial effect cannot be understood without reference to the series as a whole; and

(iii) the inclusion in a transaction of one or more options whose terms make it highly likely that the option or options will be exercised.

Scope of FRS 5

With certain exceptions, which are summarised in Table 6.4, the standard covers all transactions of all entities whose financial statements are intended to give a true and fair view of its financial position and profit or loss for a period. The standard is, for the most part, couched in pretty general terms and hence, when a transaction which would otherwise fall within the scope of the standard is also covered by another FRS, or a SSAP or specific statutory requirement, the standard or statute which contains the more specific provision or provisions should be applied (Para. 13).

Table 6.4 Transactions outside the scope of FRS 5 (unless part of a transaction that falls within its scope)

1   Forward contracts and futures

2   Foreign exchange and interest rate swaps

3   Contracts where a net amount will be paid or recieved based on the movement in a price or an index ('contracts for differences')

4   Expanditure commitments and orders placed, until the earlier of delivery or payment

5   Employment contracts.

The structure of FRS 5

The standard deals with the following main issues:

(a) the identification of assets and liabilities and tests for whether the asset or liability should be recognised in the balance sheet;
(b) transactions in previously recognised assets;
(c) options;
(d) assets which are separately financed and, in particular, the circumstances where 'linked presentation' should be used (linked presentation means that, on the face of the balance sheet, the finance should be deducted from the gross amount of the asset which it finances);
(e) the, very limited, circumstances when it is permissible to offset assets and liabilities;
(f) the treatment of 'quasi-subsidiaries', when the relationship between the two entities is effectively, but not legally, one as between a parent and its subsidiary.

We will examine the provisions of FRS 5 in the above order.

The identification of assets[19]

An asset is defined as:

> Rights or other access to future economic benefits controlled by an entity as a result of past transactions or events. (Para. 2)

Whilst in the context of an asset, control is defined as:

> The ability to obtain the future economic benefits relating to an asset and to restrict the access of others to those benefits. (Para. 3)

Although the existence of future benefits is an essential criterion for the identification of an asset, it is not implied that the asset should be valued by reference to those benefits, although the present value of the asset's expected future benefits will provide an upper limit to its carrying value.

All assets carry some risk and the allocation of that risk between the various parties to a transaction will usually be a significant indication of whether the transaction has resulted in the acquisition or disposal of an asset. Risk is the potential variation between the actual and expected benefits associated with the asset and includes the potential for gain as well as exposure to loss. Normally the party that has access to the benefits also has to face the risks, and in practice the question of whether an asset should be identified is often dependent on an assessment of where the risk falls.

Control in this context is related to the means by which an entity ensures that the benefits accrue to itself and not to others and must be distinguished from the day-to-day management of the asset. Although control normally rests on the foundation of legal rights, the existence of such rights is not essential as commercial, or even moral, obligations may be significant factors.

The existence of an asset depends on a past and not a future event. Thus, in straightforward transactions it is easy to draw a distinction between a right to immediate control over future economic benefits and a right to acquire such control in the future. Both rights can be regarded as creating assets, but in the second case the asset is simply the option. The position in linked transactions may be different. An option

---

[19]Although FRS 5 considerably predates the Revised Draft System of Principles there are no differences in substance between the key definitions of assets, liabilities, etc. provided in the two documents.

may be simply a device to ensure that effective control of future benefits will be retained by the party who ceases, temporarily, to be the legal owner. Then the terms of the option may be such that the costs of exercising it are negligible compared to the benefits; in other words it would be commercial madness not to exercise the option. In such a case the accounting treatment (is there an asset and if so what is it?) will have to be decided by reference to the rights and obligations (including those taking effect in the future) that result from the transactions as a whole.

The identification of liabilities

A liability is defined as:

> An entity's obligations to transfer economic benefits as a result of past transactions or events. (Para. 4)

Little is said in FRS 5 on the general issue of liabilities but what is said is consistent and does not go beyond our discussion of the subject in Chapter 4.

Recognition of assets and liabilities

Assets and liabilities, although identified in terms of the above, should only be recognised in the balance sheet if:

(a) there is sufficient evidence of the existence of the item (including, where appropriate, evidence that a future inflow or outflow of benefit will occur); and
(b) the item can be measured as a monetary amount with sufficient reliability.
(Para. 20)

An obvious example of an item which although identified may not be recognised in the balance sheet is a contingent liability.

The above general criteria for recognition are also to be found in Chapter 4 of the ASB's Revised Draft Statement of Principles, in which a more detailed discussion of the subject will be found.

Transactions in previously recognised assets

The basic principle is straightforward. If, as a result of a transaction involving a previously recognised asset, there is no significant change in either the reporting entity's access to benefits or exposure to the risks inherent in those benefits, then the asset should continue to be recognised. The asset should cease to be recognised if both the access to benefits and the exposure to risks are transferred to others (Para. 22).

The range of possible outcomes can be well illustrated by the factoring of trading debts. If the terms of the deal are such that, although the legal title to the debts has been transferred, the finance charge that the 'seller' of the debts will have to pay will depend on the speed at which debtors pay or the seller retains responsibility for whole or part of the bad debts, then the risk has not been transferred and the asset, debtors, should continue to be shown in the balance sheet as the total amount due from debtors. The amount received from the factors in respect of the debts that are still outstanding would be included in liabilities. (There is a possible exception that would arise if the transaction satisfies the condition for linked presentation, *see* pp. 195–6). On the other hand if the terms of the agreement are that the finance fee payable will be in no way affected by the future behaviour of the debtors then the whole of the risk has been transferred to the factors and the asset should cease to be recognised.

Special cases of transactions

Three special cases are mentioned in the standard:

(a) a transfer of only part of the asset;
(b) a transfer of all the item for only part of its life;
(c) a transfer of all the item for all its life but where the entity retains some significant rights to benefits on exposure to risks.

It may be helpful to provide some examples of the special cases:

1 The holder of a security might sell the right to receive the annual interest but retain the right to receive the principal.
2 The seller agrees to repurchase the asset it has sold after its use.
3 A company might sell its interest in a subsidiary but where the ultimate consideration depends in whole or in part on the future performance of the subsidiary.

The main point of the standard is pretty simple. In all cases an asset, albeit a different asset, continues to exist but its description and the amount at which it is included in the balance sheet will change, and it is, of course, possible that the 'new' asset will not pass the recognition tests to which we referred earlier.

Options

One of the characteristics of complex transactions is the existence of options[20] and, in deciding how to treat them, consideration needs to be given to all aspects of the series of transactions of which the option is part. If, after such consideration, it is decided that there is no genuine commercial possibility that the option will be exercised, the exercise of the option should be ignored whilst, if there is no genuine commercial possibility that the option will fail to be exercised, its future exercise should be assumed (FRS 5, Para. 61).

In assessing whether there is a genuine commercial possibility that an option will be exercised it should be assumed that the parties will act in accordance with their economic interests and that the parties will remain both liquid and solvent, unless it can reasonably be foreseen that either will not be the case. Thus, actions, which the party will take only in the event of a severe deterioration in liquidity or creditworthiness that is not currently foreseen, should not be taken into account.

There will be some circumstances that fall between the two certainties – the exercise or non-exercise of the option. In such a case the asset itself, which would appear in the balance sheet of the entity with the right to acquire, would be not the asset but the option to acquire the asset. Let us return to our simple example that involved X Limited 'selling' some land to a bank for £1m with an option to repurchase. If the price at which the option would be exercised is such that it is virtually certain to be less than the then market price, FRS 5 requires the transaction to be treated as a loan. If, conversely, the option price is virtually certain to be more than the prevailing market price then it would be presumed that the option would not be exercised and the transaction should be treated as a sale. But suppose there exists uncertainty, in that the option price lies within a range in which the market price of the land might reasonably be expected to fluctuate. In that case the asset that X Limited would show would be the option to reacquire the land, and the cost of that asset would be the extra finance costs that the borrower would incur in a transaction that involved an option as against a straightforward borrowing which did not include an option.

---

[20] The disclosure requirements relating to options and other derivatives are discussed in Chapter 5.

Linked presentation

A borrower can finance an item on such terms that the provider of finance has access only to the item financed and not to the entity's other assets. A well-known example of this is the factoring of debts. In some such arrangements, whilst the provider of finance has only recourse against the specified item, the 'borrowing' entity retains rights to the benefits generated by the asset, and can repay the finance from its general resources if it wishes to preserve those rights. In such situations the entity has both an asset and a liability and linked presentation would not be appropriate.

Linked presentation, which as we shall see involves the setting-off on the face of the balance sheet the liability against the asset, is only possible in situations where the finance has to be repaid from the benefits generated by the asset and the borrowing entity has no right to keep the item or to repay the finance from its general resources. The remaining conditions that have to be satisfied are set out in the standard (Para. 27); the essence of these conditions is that the borrower is under no legal, moral or commercial obligation to repay the loan other than from the benefits generated from the asset.

The question to be answered is 'What is the nature of the asset which is retained by the borrowing entity and, in particular, what rights and benefits are associated with that asset?' The issue is best explained by introducing the example used in FRS 5.

Suppose that an entity transfers title to a portfolio of high quality debts of 100 in exchange for non-returnable proceeds of 90 plus rights to a further sum whose amount depends on whether the debts are paid. If we assume that the 90 is under no circumstances repayable then there are three ways of presenting the position in the balance sheet:

(a) Show the asset as 100 and a liability, distinct and separate, of 90. The problem with this form of presentation is that it would not reflect clearly the fact that the 90 liability has no relevance to the remaining assets of the entity and would, in particular, give a misleading view of the security of the entity.
(b) Set off the two amounts and show 10 as an asset. This may appear to be the most sensible procedure but it is argued that because the eventual return to the entity depends on the behaviour of the whole portfolio of debts which has been factored the risks remaining are the normal risks which could be related to that total portfolio of debt.
(c) Use what FRS 5 describes as the 'linked presentation' method: that is to show on the face of the balance sheet both the gross asset of 100 less possibly a small deduction for the normal provision against doubtful debts, and a deduction of 90. It is claimed that this presentation shows both that the entity retains significant benefits and risks relating to the whole portfolio of debts and that the claims of the provider of the finance are limited solely to the funds generated by the debts.

The art of financial statement preparation is not well served by over-elaboration and the drawing of fine distinctions based on immaterial differences. The 'linked presentation' provision smacks of over-elaboration and its application would provide only marginal assistance to the users of accounts while adding the possibility of confusion. To take the ASB's own example, what is the asset, 100 or 10? Ignoring bad debts it is 10, the maximum that will be received in the future from the asset; 90 has been received but would in no circumstances have to be repaid, and so it is not a liability. Why suggest that it is? The obvious way of accounting for the transaction is to show the asset at 10 less an appropriate provision against doubtful debts. The fact that the provision is actually based on 100 rather than 10 can be explained in the notes if the fact is material.

However, the conditions that have to be satisfied if linked presentation is to be used are stringent and hence only apply to a small number of entities.

Offset

It is a general requirement of UK Company Law that assets and liabilities should not be netted of. The only exception is where the right of set-off exists between monetary assets and liabilities, such as, for example, bank balances and overdrafts with the same party. The provisions of FRS 5 are more stringent and more precise than those found in company law and include the unambiguous statement that 'assets and liabilities should not be offset' (Para. 29). However, it goes on to state, in the same paragraph, that 'debit and credit balances should be aggregated into a single net item where, and only where, they do not constitute separate assets and liabilities'.

The offset should only be made when the balances are fundamentally linked such that the reporting entity would not have to transfer economic benefit arising from the credit balance without being sure that it would receive the benefits reflected by the debit balance.

The conditions under which offset should and must be applied are set out in Para. 29 and may be summarised as follows:

(a) The items to be offset must be determinable monetary amounts denominated in either the same currency or in different but freely convertible currencies.
(b) The reporting entity has the ability to insist on a net settlement and that this ability is assured beyond doubt. This means, for example, that the debit balance matures no later than the credit balance and that the arrangement is such that it would survive the insolvency of the other party.

Disclosure

In the world of complex transactions some assets may differ in some ways from most other assets, and some liabilities, such as limited recourse finance, may differ from the generality of liabilities. A common example of a different form of asset is one that, while it is available for use in the trading activities of the enterprise, may not be available as security for a loan.

The disclosure requirements of FRS 5 are less specific than admonitory, urging that:

> Disclosure of a transaction in the financial statements, whether or not it has resulted in assets or liabilities being recognized or ceasing to be recognized, should be sufficient to enable the user of the financial statements to understand its commercial effect. (Para. 30)

> Where a transaction has resulted in the recognition of assets or liabilities whose nature differs from that of items usually included under the relevant balance sheet headings, the differences should be explained. (Para 31)

Quasi-subsidiaries

FRS 5 observes that there can be instances where, although the relationship between two companies may not constitute a parent/subsidiary relationship as defined by statute, the dominant company might have as much effective control over the assets of the other as would have been the case had the company been a subsidiary. A simple example is one where the dominant company holds less than 50 per cent of the equity of the other company but has an option to acquire additional shares which would take its holding over 50 per cent.

The standard refers to the controlled company as a quasi-subsidiary, which it defines as follows:

> A quasi-subsidiary of a reporting entity is a company, trust, partnership or other vehicle which, though not fulfilling the definition of a subsidiary, is directly or indirectly controlled by the reporting entity and gives rise to benefits for that entity that are in substance no different from those that would arise were the vehicle a subsidiary. (Para. 7)

The concept of substance over form requires that a company which is in effect a subsidiary should be treated as such and this is supported by Section 227(6) of the Companies Act 1985 as amended by the Companies Act 1989, which specifies that, if in special circumstances, compliance with any provisions of the Act with respect to the matters to be included in a company's group accounts or in the notes thereto is inconsistent with the true and fair view requirement, the directors shall depart from that specific provision to the extent necessary to give a true and fair view. FRS 5 points out that the nature of quasi-subsidiaries is such that their existence will usually constitute such special circumstances. Thus, they should be included in the group accounts in the same way as legally defined subsidiary undertakings. If the dominant company does not have any subsidiaries it should provide, in its financial statements, consolidated financial statements of itself and the quasi-subsidiary (Para. 35). In addition, the notes to the financial statements should include summaries of the financial statements of the quasi-subsidiaries (Para. 38).

The conditions under which subsidiaries are permitted or required to be excluded are set out in FRS 2 'Accounting for Subsidiary Undertakings', but the grounds for exclusion are not generally applicable to quasi-subsidiaries which by definition need to be included in the consolidation if a true and fair view is to be obtained. FRS 5 concludes that the only circumstances under which quasi-subsidiaries should be excluded are when the quasi-subsidiary is held only with a view to subsequent sale and has not previously been included in the entity's consolidated accounts (Para. 36).

One set of circumstances is identified in the standard where the accounting treatment of a quasi-subsidiary would differ from that of a fully-fledged subsidiary. This occurs when the quasi-subsidiary holds either a single item or a single portfolio of similar items that are financed in such a way as to require the use of linked presentation. In the case of a quasi-subsidiary, linked presentation should be used in the consolidated balance sheet if the requirements that need to be met can be satisfied by the group (Para. 32). The difference in the case of a legal subsidiary is that linked presentation should only be used on the consolidated balance sheet if it is also applicable to the subsidiary's own balance sheet; in other words, all the conditions need to be met by the subsidiary itself. This particular refinement is required in order to comply with the Companies Act under which the subsidiary is part of the group as legally defined, and hence its assets and liabilities are assets and liabilities of the group and need to be treated in the consolidation in the normal way (Para. 102).

The section of FRS 5 on quasi-subsidiaries does not incorporate any major items of principle, unless the point about linked presentation discussed above is regarded as such, but mainly provides guidance and authority on the use of the override principle of the Companies Act.

Summary of FRS 5

The main elements of the standard have been dealt with in the text but we will summarise the main points in the following list:

1 The substance of transactions should be recorded; greater weight should be given to aspects that are likely to have a commercial effect.

2 Complex transactions should be analysed to see whether the entity's assets or liabilities have been affected.

3 If assets and liabilities are identified then general tests need to be applied to see whether they should be recognised. Reference may also need to be made to other FRSs, SSAPs or statute.

4 Essentially there are four possible outcomes to the analysis:
   (a) record the asset and liability separately;
   (b) apply linked presentation;
   (c) offset (very rare);
   (d) ignore the transaction.

5 Adequate disclosure is required, in particular (i) where the asset or liability recognised in the financial statements differs in some respects from the generality of assets and liabilities, and (ii) where, although identified, assets or liabilities are not recognised in the primary and financial statements.

6 Quasi-subsidiaries should be treated in much the same way as legal subsidiaries.

FRS 5 application notes

There are five application notes covering: consignment stock; sale and repurchase agreements; factoring of debts; securitised assets; and loan transfers. Each application note has three sections: features which describe the nature of required transactions; analysis which analyses the transaction in terms of the framework of FRS 5; and required accounting which is the proposed standard covering recognition in the financial statement and disclosure in the notes. In addition each note contains tables and illustrations that are intended for general guidance and which do not form part of the proposed standard.

Compliance with International Accounting Standards

There is no International Accounting Standard on this subject.

Postscript to FRS 5

The provisions of FRS 5 are complex, as are the features of the transactions that it seeks to control. The provisions apply only to a small minority of financial statements but, where they do apply, their effect is often significant because complex transactions typically involve large amounts. The aim of the ASB in attempting to minimise off balance sheet financing is entirely laudable and the provisions of FRS 5 provide a set of principles that are sufficiently comprehensive and robust to cope with the increasing ingenuity of the capital market.

Recommended reading

T.M. Clark, *Leasing*, McGraw-Hill, Maidenhead, 1978.

The PricewaterhouseCoopers Leasing Team, *Leasing in the UK*, Tolley, Croydon, 1998.

B.A. Rutherford, *The Doctrine of Substance over Form*, Certified Accountants Publications Limited, London, 1988.

P. Weetman, *Assets and Liabilities: Their Definition and Recognition*, Certified Accountants Publications Limited, London, 1989.

7 Taxation: current and deferred

Overview   In this chapter we look first at the treatment of current taxation and then at accounting for deferred taxation. While the former is concerned with the presentation of corporation tax, income tax and overseas taxes in financial statements, the subject of deferred taxation involves measurement and is consequently more difficult and more controversial. Both topics are presently under review by the ASB.

SSAP 8 *The Accounting Treatment of Taxation under the Imputation Tax System in the Accounts of Companies* (last amended 1992) regulates the accounting treatment of current taxation in a set of financial statements. However, we explain why it now sits uneasily with a taxation system which has seen the abolition of Advance Corporation Tax. We examine briefly the proposals of FRED 18 *Current Taxation* (June 1999) for a replacement standard.

In the larger part of the chapter, we explain the need for deferred taxation and the main methods of accounting for it, namely the full provision and partial provision methods. SSAP 15 *Accounting for Deferred Taxation* (revised 1985) requires companies to account for deferred taxation using the partial provision method but this method has serious conceptual weaknesses, is open to manipulation and is out of line with international practice. We end by outlining the proposals of FRED 19 *Deferred Taxation* (August 1999) that we should move to a system of full provision in respect of most, but not all, timing differences.

Introduction

The treatment of taxation in financial statements is regulated not only by the Companies Acts but also by three statements of standard accounting practice: SSAP 5 *Accounting for Value Added Tax* (April 1974); SSAP 8 *The Treatment of Taxation under the Imputation System in the Accounts of Companies* (last amended 1992) and SSAP 15 *Accounting for Deferred Taxation* (October 1978, revised 1985).

Although the treatment of value added tax may require complex bookkeeping arrangements, it poses few conceptual problems and is therefore not dealt with in this book. The treatment of both current taxation and, more particularly, deferred taxation give rise to a number of difficulties which are addressed in this chapter.

SSAP 8 was published in 1977 'to establish a standard treatment of taxation in company accounts with particular reference to advance corporation tax and mainstream corporation tax'. Advance corporation tax was abolished from 6 April 1999 but there is as yet no replacement standard. The ASB has addressed the issue in a number of documents of which the latest is FRED 18 *Current Taxation* (June 1999).[1]

We shall explain the provisions of SSAP 8 and outline the proposals of FRED 18 in the next section of this chapter.

SSAP 15 was last revised in December 1985 and requires the use of the partial provision, rather than the full provision, method of accounting for deferred taxation. This partial provision method has serious conceptual weaknesses, is open to manipulation and is now out of line with international practice. In the Discussion Paper 'Accounting for Tax' (March 1995) and, more recently, in FRED 19 'Deferred Taxation' (August 1999), the ASB has made proposals for a change from partial to full deferred tax accounting. We explain the need to account for deferred taxation and the alternative approaches available. We conclude by outlining the proposals of FRED 19.

Current taxation

Readers are assumed to be aware of the law relating to the taxation of companies and we shall only explain the system to the extent necessary to provide an understanding of the accounting implications of that system. For simplicity, we shall assume that a company makes up its financial statements for a year, rather than any other period, and that the rate of corporation tax is 30 per cent, the rate applicable to companies with chargeable profits in excess of £1 500 000.[2]

The imputation tax system prior to 6 April 1999

When a company made a distribution prior to 6 April 1999, it had to pay Advance Corporation Tax (ACT), amounting to one-quarter of the distribution, to the Inland Revenue. It had to account for such ACT quarterly but could offset any tax credit in respect of any Franked Investment Income, that is distributions received from UK resident companies. For accounting purposes the year was divided into four quarters running to 31 March, 30 June, 30 September and 31 December respectively, although special rules were provided to cope with the situation where a company's accounting year did not end on one of these four dates. ACT had to be paid to the Inland Revenue within fourteen days of the end of the relevant period.

At the end of an accounting period, the corporation tax payable on profits for the period was computed. ACT in respect of distributions made during that accounting year, subject to an overriding maximum, was then set off against the corporation tax payable for the year. The balance, known as 'mainstream' corporation tax was then payable nine months and one day after the end of the accounting year or within 30 days from the date of assessment if this was later.

---

[1] The ASB issued a Discussion Paper 'Accounting for Tax' (March 1995) which dealt with both current taxation and deferred taxation. It subsequently issued an exposure draft of a 'Proposed Amendment to SSAP 8: Presentation of Dividend Income' (October 1997). More recently it has dealt with current taxation and deferred taxation separately by the issue of FRED 18 'Current Taxation' (June 1999) and FRED 19 'Deferred Taxation' (August 1999).

[2] This is the rate for the financial year 1999, the year from 1 April 1999 to 31 March 2000. There is also a small companies rate of 20 per cent for companies with chargeable profits not exceeding £300 000 and marginal relief for companies with chargeable profits which exceed £300 000 but do not exceed £1 500 000. It has also been announced that a new low rate of corporation tax, set initially at 10 per cent, will be introduced in the financial year 2000.

Where the distribution was large in relation to the taxable profits, then it was sometimes not possible to set off the full amount of the ACT against the corporation tax payable for the year. In such a case, a company had what was called 'surplus ACT'. Such 'surplus ACT' could be carried back and relieved against the corporation tax liabilities for the preceding six years or it could be carried forward and relieved against the corporation tax liability of future periods.

The imputation tax system since 6 April 1999

Advance Corporation Tax was abolished with effect from 6 April 1999. Hence the payment of a dividend, or any other distribution, by a company no longer triggers the need for the company to pay ACT to the Inland Revenue. In spite of this there is now a tax credit of one-ninth attached to the receipt of a dividend, or other distribution, from a UK resident company. For example, if a company receives a dividend of £90 000 from another UK resident company, there will be a tax credit of one-ninth of this amount, that is £10 000. The Franked Investment Income will therefore be £100 000 (£90 000 + £10 000). This is not subject to corporation tax, as it has come from profits of another company which have already borne corporation tax.

To ensure that regular cash inflows to the government continue, a large company, that is one which pays corporation tax at the full rate, must now pay its corporation tax for an accounting year in instalments.[3] These instalments are based on the company's own estimates of its corporation tax liability for the accounting year and, for a twelve-month accounting period, there are four equal annual instalments due on the 14th day of the seventh, tenth, thirteenth and sixteenth month after the start of the accounting year. If we ignore the transitional arrangements for phasing in this new system, then for an accounting year ended 31 December 2000, the corporation tax for the year would be due in four equal instalments payable on 14 July 2000, 14 October 2000, 14 January 2001 and 14 April 2001.

Although this system introduces many difficulties for companies in estimating their corporation tax liabilities, it simplifies quite considerably accounting for current taxation.

Where a company resident in the UK carries on activities overseas, the profits made overseas will usually be subject both to overseas taxation and UK corporation tax, although as we shall see, the UK tax payable may be reduced by all or part of the overseas tax payable.

With this background, let us turn to the provisions of the existing standard SSAP 8.

SSAP 8

This Statement of Standard Accounting Practice requires that the following items should be included in the taxation charge in the profit and loss account and, where material, separately disclosed.[4]

---

[3] The corporation tax of small companies is due, as before, in one amount payable nine months and one day after the end of the accounting period.
[4] SSAP 8, Para. 22.

    (a) The amount of United Kingdom corporation tax specifying:

        (i) the charge for corporation tax on the income of the year (where such corporation tax includes transfers between the deferred taxation account these should also be separately disclosed where material);

        (ii) tax attributable to franked investment income;

        (iii) irrecoverable ACT;

        (iv) the relief for overseas taxation.

    (b) The total overseas taxation, relieved and unrelieved, specifying that part of the unrelieved overseas taxation which arises from the payment or proposed payment of dividends.

We shall examine each of these items in turn, discussing both the treatment in the profit and loss account and the associated treatment in the balance sheet. Deferred taxation will be dealt with later.

Corporation tax

As we have seen, a large company must estimate its corporation tax liability for an accounting year and pay this amount in four equal instalments. If we assume an accounting year ended 31 December 2000 and ignore transitional arrangements, the first instalment will be paid by 14 July 2000 and the second by 14 October 2000. When we come to the end of the year, it is then necessary to make provision for the amount still outstanding. If previous estimates have been correct, the amount payable will be the two instalments due on 14 January 2001 and 14 April 2001.

In practice, estimates will not be so precise. Hence at the end of the year, it will be necessary to estimate the corporation tax payable for the year ended 31 December 2000, which will be charged in the profit and loss account or Statement of Total Recognised Gains and Losses as appropriate, and to provide for this amount less the payments on account already made. Although the balance sheet formats provide headings for 'other creditors including taxation and social security', the Companies Act 1985 specifically requires the disclosure of the amount for creditors in respect of taxation and social security separately from other creditors.[5]

Tax on franked investment income

Where a UK company receives dividends or other distributions from a UK resident company, those dividends now come with an associated tax credit of one-ninth. Thus a dividend received amounting to £90 000 comes with a tax credit of £10 000 so that the franked investment income is £100 000. As explained above, this franked investment income is not subject to corporation tax.

SSAP 8, Para. 13 requires that the franked investment income should be shown in the profit and loss account at the 'gross' amount with the tax credit being shown as part of the taxation charge. So, using the above example, receipt of the dividend would be disclosed in the profit and loss account as follows:

---

[5] Companies Act 1985, Schedule 4. Notes on the balance sheet formats (9).

	£	£
Income from investments		100 000
:		
less Taxation:		
Corporation tax	X	
Tax credit on franked		
investment income	10 000	X

In October 1997, the ASB issued an exposure draft with the title 'Amendment to SSAP 8: 'The Treatment of Taxation under the Imputation Tax System in the Accounts of Companies: Presentation of Dividend Income'. This proposed that there should be no grossing up of dividends in the profit and loss account. Rather, the amount of the dividend received should be shown as income. As we shall see later, this is also the treatment proposed in the subsequent FRED 18 'Current Taxation', which was issued in June 1999.

Irrecoverable advance corporation tax

As we have seen above, companies were able to offset ACT paid against the corporation tax liability for the year leaving only the mainstream corporation tax to pay. In the past, many companies have paid large dividends in relation to their taxable profits such that the set-off of ACT was restricted and, in extreme situations, some companies had no corporation tax liability against which to set the ACT paid at all. As we explained above this has given rise to what was known as surplus ACT.

Where such surplus ACT existed, it was necessary to consider whether or not any such ACT, a debit balance on an ACT recoverable account, should be regarded as an asset or instead written off to the profit and loss account as 'irrecoverable advance corporation tax'.

In considering this question it was important not to confuse the treatment of ACT recoverable for taxation purposes with its accounting treatment. For taxation purposes ACT unrelieved due to insufficient taxable profits for the accounting period could be carried back for six years or carried forward indefinitely. If carried back, then the ACT was of course recovered. If carried forward, then nothing that is done in the financial statements removes the right of ultimate set-off for taxation purposes. However, the ACT would only be recovered in future years if there were sufficient taxable profits in future years and, if the company was not expected to generate such taxable profits then it was argued that prudence dictated that the ACT recoverable should no longer be regarded as an asset but should instead be written off in the profit and loss account. This requirement to write off irrecoverable ACT did not apply where the ACT recoverable could be set off against an appropriate credit balance on deferred taxation account but only when it was shown as a separate deferred asset. SSAP 8 stated that it was prudent only to have regard to the immediate and foreseeable future and suggested that this should normally not extend beyond the next accounting period.[6]

Given the abolition of ACT from 6 April 1999, no new ACT payments will arise and hence there are likely to be few cases of irrecoverable ACT appearing in profit and loss accounts in future.[7]

---

[6] SSAP 8 Para. 6.

[7] There is, however, a system of 'Shadow ACT' in existence to deal with cases of unrelieved surplus ACT on 6 April 1999. As a consequence of this, it is possible for irrecoverable ACT to appear subsequently. Interested readers are recommended to consult the relevant section of a textbook on taxation such as Alan Melville's *Taxation*, published by Financial Times Prentice Hall annually.

Overseas taxation

A company resident in the UK is liable to corporation tax on all its profits whether they arise in the UK or overseas. As profits which have arisen overseas are usually subject to taxation in the relevant overseas country, they may therefore be subject to double taxation. Similarly, where a UK company receives dividends from the taxed profits of an overseas subsidiary, such dividends are neither franked investment income nor group income and hence are subject to UK corporation tax.

It is usually possible to obtain relief for such double taxation, although the precise nature of the relief depends upon the terms of any double taxation convention between the UK government and the relevant overseas government. Where there is no double tax convention, it is still possible to obtain unilateral relief for double taxation.

In some cases it is possible to obtain relief against UK corporation tax for the whole of the overseas taxation payable but, in other cases, some of the overseas taxation may be unrelieved. One example of the latter is where the rate of overseas taxation on overseas profits exceeds the rate of UK corporation tax on those same profits. To illustrate, let us suppose that a UK company has taxable profits of £300 000 overseas and an additional £2 000 000 in the UK. The rate of overseas corporation tax is 50 per cent while the rate of UK corporation tax is 30 per cent.

The corporation tax payable overseas is 50 per cent of £300 000, that is £150 000, while the corporation tax payable in the UK is 30 per cent of £(2 000 000 + 300 000), that is £690 000. As the UK corporation tax payable on overseas income is only £90 000 (30 per cent of £300 000) this is the maximum relief which may be given against the overseas taxation of £150 000.

Following the layout of Appendix 1 to SSAP 8, the taxation charge in the profit and loss account would therefore include the following:

	£000
Corporation tax on income – 30% of £2 300 000	690
less Relief for overseas taxation	90
	600
Overseas taxation	150
	750

We have now illustrated all the items which SSAP 8 requires to be disclosed in the profit and loss account or notes to the accounts. Of these, tax on franked investment income is likely to disappear following the issue of a new standard while Irrecoverable ACT is likely to disappear with the passage of time.

We shall conclude this section with a brief look at the proposals of FRED 18 'Current Taxation', issued in June 1999.

Towards a new standard: FRED 18

FRED 18 'Current Taxation' is a very short document which is concerned mainly with the way in which dividends and interest received and paid should be treated in the profit and loss account of a company when tax credits and withholding taxes are involved. Paragraph 2 of the exposure draft provides a number of definitions including the following:

Tax credit on dividends:
The credit attributable to the recipient of a dividend under UK tax legislation because the dividend received is paid out of income that has already been subject to tax in the company that earned it. The rate of tax credit is set by tax legislation.

Withholding tax:
Tax deducted from dividends received or other income, paid to the tax authorities wholly on behalf of the recipient.

An example of the former is the tax credit attributable to a dividend received from a UK company. Examples of the latter are income tax deducted at source from patent royalties or interest received from a UK company or foreign tax deducted at source from interest or dividends received from an overseas company.

The exposure draft considers the following three possible ways of disclosing receipts in the profit and loss account.

(i)   Dividends, interest and similar amounts received should not be grossed up but should be shown at the net amounts received.
(ii) Dividends, interest and similar amounts received should be grossed up for both tax credits and withholding tax deducted.
(iii) UK dividends received should not be grossed up for any tax credit but interest and similar amounts, as well as foreign dividends, received should be grossed up for any withholding tax deducted.

A majority of the ASB favour the third of these three alternatives although, given the lack of a sound criterion for choosing between the methods, there is support among members for each of the other methods as well.

FRED 18 proposes a consistent treatment of dividends, interest and similar amounts paid, grossing-up the actual payments for any withholding tax levied but not grossing-up dividends to UK companies for the attributable tax credit.

The exposure draft also stresses the need for consistency in reporting the taxation consequences of any gain or loss. Thus, where a gain or loss is recognised in the profit and loss account, then the taxation charge or credit should be reported there as well. Where, however, a gain or loss is recognised in the Statement of Total Recognised Gains and Losses, then the taxation charge or credit should be recognised in that statement too. An example of the latter would be the taxation consequences of an exchange gain or loss on foreign currency borrowing which hedge an equity investment in an overseas company.

Finally FRED 18 provides guidance on what rate of tax should be used where the rate of corporation tax has not been enacted for a relevant period:

> If the rate of corporation tax has not been enacted for the whole or part of the period covered by the accounts, the latest enacted rate should be used unless legislation setting a new rate has been substantively enacted by the balance sheet date. (Para. 12)

The proposals of the ASB on both of the above points seem eminently sensible although one wonders whether it is really necessary to include such obvious points in an accounting standard.

FRED 18 appears to be remarkably 'thin' on substance as a potential accounting standard so it is not surprising to read that FRED 18 'Current Taxation' and FRED 19 'Deferred Taxation' may be combined into one standard.[8]

---

[8] See Preface, Para 1, final sentence: 'The two resulting standards may eventually be combined.'

Accounting for deferred taxation

Timing differences

Although accounting profits form the basis for the computation of taxable profits in the UK, for most companies there are substantial differences between the two. Such differences may be divided into two categories: (a) permanent differences; (b) timing differences.

In the case of permanent differences, certain items of revenue or expense properly taken into account in arriving at accounting profit are not included when arriving at taxable profit. Examples are regional development grants received, amounts spent on entertainment, and depreciation of non-industrial buildings.

In the case of timing differences, the same total amount is added or subtracted in arriving at both accounting profits and taxable profits over a period of years, but it is added or subtracted in different periods. It is the existence of such timing differences which gives rise to the perceived need to account for deferred taxation.

There are a number of variations between accounting practice and taxation law which give rise to timing differences and, in the context of a single entity, the more important are:[9]

(a) short-term differences from the use of the receipts and payments basis in taxation computations and the accruals basis in financial statements; these differences normally reverse in the subsequent accounting period although they may be replaced by new originating differences;

(b) availability of capital allowances in taxation computations which are different from the related depreciation charges in financial statements;

(c) pension contributions payable allowed for tax purposes which differ from the pension cost determined in accordance with the provisions of SSAP 24;

(d) unrealised revaluation surpluses on fixed assets, for which a taxation charge does not arise until the gain is realised on disposal of the asset;

(e) realised surpluses on the disposal of fixed assets which are subject to rollover relief for taxation purposes;

(f) tax losses carried forward to be used against taxable profits which arise in the future.

One of the four fundamental accounting concepts listed in SSAP 2 is the 'accruals' concept, under which expenses are matched against the revenues recognised in a particular accounting year. While some accountants might argue that taxation is an appropriation of profit, the vast majority would classify it as an expense. If it is so regarded, then it follows that taxation is subject to the accruals concept and that the taxation charge should be matched against the accounting profit to which it relates.

To illustrate, let us consider an example of a short-term timing difference.

Hongbo plc makes up its financial statements to 31 December each year and has a profit, before making any provision for reorganisation costs, of £2 000 000 in both 20X1 and 20X2. During the year to 31 December 20X1 it made a provision for reorganisation costs amounting to £200 000 but these were not paid, and hence allowed

---

[9] We will not consider other timing differences which arise within the context of a set of consolidated financial statements. Examples of these are unrealised intergroup profits removed on consolidation and unremitted profits of associates and joint ventures recognised in the consolidated statements.

for tax purposes, until the following year 20X2. If we assume a 30 per cent rate of corporation tax and make no provision for deferred taxation, the profit and loss accounts for the two years 20X1 and 20X2 would appear as follows:

Profit and loss accounts for the years ended 31 December

	20X1	20X2
	£000	£000
Profit before provision	2 000	2 000
less Provision for reorganisation costs	200	–
Profit before taxation	1 800	2 000
less Corporation tax:		
20X1: 30% × 2 000 000	600	
20X2: 30% × (2 000 000 – 200 000)		540
Profit after taxation	1 200	1 460

The picture shown by these profit and loss accounts is, arguably, misleading: the payment of £200 000 for reorganisation costs in 20X2 brings with it a tax reduction of £60 000 (30 per cent of £200 000) but, while the provision is recognised in 20X1, the consequent tax reduction is recognised in 20X2.

If we follow the accruals concept, then the tax reduction should be recognised in the same accounting year as the expense and this is achieved by the use of a deferred taxation account as shown in the profit and loss accounts below:

Profit and loss accounts for the years ended 31 December

	20X1	20X2
	£000	£000
Profit before provision	2 000	2 000
less Provision for reorganisation costs	200	–
Profit before taxation	1 800	2 000
less Taxation:		
Corporation tax – as above		
30% of 2 000 000	600	
30% of (2 000 000 – 200 000)		540
Deferred taxation:		
On originating timing difference,		
30% of 200 000	(60)	
On reversing timing difference,		
30% of 200 000		60
	540	600
Profit after tax	1 260	1 400

In 20X1 the accounting profit is £200 000 less than the taxable profit while, in 20X2, the taxable profit is less than the accounting profit by that same amount. As may be seen above, the profit and loss account for 20X1 is credited with deferred tax on the originating timing difference so that deferred tax account is debited while in 20X2 the deferred tax asset account is credited and the profit and loss account debited with tax on the reversing difference. The end result is that the profit and loss account for 20X1 reflects both the provision for reorganisation costs and the consequent reduction in taxation.

We have implicitly assumed that there are no permanent differences or other timing differences so that the total tax charge in each year reflects exactly 30 per cent of the reported accounting profit:

	20X1		20X2	
Total tax charge	540	= 30%	600	= 30%
Accounting profit	1800		2000	

Few would quarrel with the use of a deferred taxation account in such simple circumstances. However, things are not always so simple, so let us now explore the timing differences which arise where capital allowances exceed depreciation.

FRS 15 'Tangible Fixed Assets' requires that relevant assets should be depreciated as 'fairly' as possible over the lives of those assets estimated on a 'realistic' basis. Subject to these parameters and, in particular, the opinions of its auditors, each company may select its own depreciation methods. A long-standing feature of the tax system is that the depreciation charge as shown in the financial statements is not an allowable charge in arriving at taxable profits. Instead, relief for tax purposes is given through capital allowances. The major reason for this has been the wish of governments to prevent companies from delaying the payment of tax by the adoption of unreasonably accelerated methods of depreciation. Conversely, at some times, the government has used the capital allowance system to encourage investment by granting generous capital allowances for expenditure on certain types of fixed assets.[10]

In respect of expenditure on plant and machinery, there is currently a writing-down allowance of 25 per cent applied on a reducing balance basis. Even though this is much less generous than at many times in the past, substantial timing differences still arise and it is instructive to examine the case of an asset with a five-year life.

Let us assume that, as before, Hongbo plc makes up accounts annually to 31 December. On 1 January 20X1 it purchases a machine for £500 000. The machine has an expected life of five years at the end of which its residual value is expected to be £120 000.[11]

The company uses the straight-line method so that the annual depreciation charge is £76 000 ((500 000 − 120 000) ÷ 5).

The depreciation charge and writing-down allowance are therefore as given in columns (ii) and (iii) of Table 7.1. Amounts are rounded to the nearest £1000.

Table 7.1 shows how the deferred tax account is built up. In years 1 and 2 there are originating timing differences: capital allowances exceed depreciation so that taxable profits are lower than accounting profits. The tax charge in the profit and loss account must be increased and there is a resulting credit balance on the deferred taxation account. In years 3 to 5 there are reversing timing differences: capital allowances are less than depreciation so that taxable profits exceed accounting profits. The tax charge in the profit and loss account is reduced, thus 'drawing down' and finally extinguishing the balance on the deferred taxation account.

If we assume that the company has a constant profit of £2m before depreciation and taxation and that there are no permanent differences or other timing

---

[10] For example, from 1972 to 1984, companies were allowed to claim a first year allowance of 100 per cent in respect of expenditure on plant and machinery, thus obtaining tax relief for the whole cost of such assets in the year of acquisition.

[11] For illustrative purposes, the expected residual value has been assumed to approximate the tax written-down value at the end of five years, namely £500 000 $(1 - 0.25)^5$ = £118 652 ≃ £120 000.

Table 7.1 Calculation of deferred tax account balance

(i) Year	(ii) Depreciation	(iii) Capital allowances	(iv) Difference (iii) – (ii)	(v) Tax on difference at 30%	(vi) Balance at year end on deferred tax a/c
	£000	£000	£000	£000	£000
20X1	76	125	49	15	15
20X2	76	94	18	5	20
20X3	76	70	–6	–2	18
20X4	76	53	–23	–7	11
20X5	76	38	–38	–11	–
	380	380	0		

differences, the consequences of accounting for deferred taxation may be seen in the profit and loss accounts.

Profit and loss account for the year to 31 December

	20X1	20X2	20X3	20X4	20X5
	£000	£000	£000	£000	£000
Profit before depreciation	2 000	2 000	2 000	2 000	2 000
Depreciation	76	76	76	76	76
	1 924	1 924	1 924	1 924	1 924
Taxation					
Corporation tax @ 30%[12]	562	572	579	584	589
Deferred tax – as per Table 7.1	15	5	(2)	(7)	(11)
	577	577	577	577	578
Profit after tax	1 347	1 347	1 347	1 347	1 346

The use of a deferred taxation account in this situation results in a tax charge which is 30 per cent of the accounting profit of each period. It is therefore possible to argue that the use of the deferred taxation account is necessary to comply with the accruals concept and that comprehensive tax allocation, that is the making of a full provision for deferred taxation, provides useful information. However, it is important to bear in mind the simplifications which have been made.

First, we have assumed that the rate of corporation tax is the same in each of the five years. Were the rate of tax to change, then it would be necessary to make a choice on whether to apply the 'deferral' method or the 'liability' method of accounting for deferred taxation.

Under the deferral method, all reversing timing differences in respect of an asset are, in principle, reversed at the same rate of tax as that applied to the originating timing difference on that asset. To apply this method to a multi-asset firm strictly involves extensive record keeping and hence, when it is used in practice, it is usual to

---

[12] Corporation tax payable for each year is calculated as follows (£000):
20X1 (2000 – 125) = 1875 × 30% = 562
20X2 (2000 – 94) = 1906 × 30% = 572
20X3 (2000 – 70) = 1930 × 30% = 579
20X4 (2000 – 53) = 1947 × 30% = 584
20X5 (2000 – 38) = 1962 × 30% = 589

apply an approximate 'net change' method. Thus, where there is a net originating difference for a group of assets in a particular year, it is dealt with at the current rate of tax. If, however, there is a net reversing difference in respect of those assets, it is reversed using some rule of thumb, such as FIFO or the average rate of tax on accumulated timing differences.

Under the liability method, whenever there is a change in the rate of tax, the balance on the deferred taxation account is adjusted to that current rate of tax on accumulated timing differences. The necessary adjustment is charged or credited to the profit and loss account and hence has an immediate impact on the shareholders' interest. Subsequent reversing differences are made at the new rate of tax. It follows that, to operate the liability method, it is not necessary to keep such detailed records as those required for the deferral method, as calculations may be made in total. To give one example: to calculate the balance on deferred taxation required because of the differences in capital allowances and depreciation on fixed assets, it is merely necessary to know the differences between the net book value and tax written-down value of the relevant assets and the current rate of tax on the balance sheet date. The liability method is therefore much simpler to apply than the deferral method and has been the more popular of the two methods.

The second simplification which we have made is to assume that Hongbo plc purchased one machine in 20X1 but made no further purchases in 20X2–20X5. We shall now explore the position where a company makes regular purchases by assuming that Hongbo plc purchases one machine each year at a constant cost of £500 000. The depreciation charges and writing-down allowances for tax purposes are then as shown in columns (*ii*) and (*iii*) of Table 7.2.

Table 7.2 Calculation of deferred tax account balance

(i) Year	(ii) Depreciation	(iii) Capital allowances	(iv) Difference (iii) – (ii)	(v) Tax on difference at 30%	(vi) Balance at year end on deferred tax a/c
	£000	£000	£000	£000	£000
20X1 (1 machine)	76	125	49	15	15
20X2 (2 machines)	152	219	67	20	35
20X3 (3 machines)	228	289	61	18	53
20X4 (4 machines)	304	342	38	11	64
20X5 (5 machines)	380	380	–	–	64
20X6 (5 machines)	380	380	–	–	64

From Table 7.2 it can be seen that the balance on the deferred tax account gradually builds up and that, eventually, a steady state is reached in 20X5. From 20X5 capital allowances and depreciation are equal and originating timing differences offset reversing timing differences. Thus, if Hongbo plc continues to invest a constant amount each year, there will be no net reversal of timing differences and the balance on the deferred tax account will remain constant at £64 000.

We could develop this theme further by assuming that the cost of the machine increased year by year and, in such a case, we would find again that there would be no net reversing differences, with the consequence that the balance on the deferred tax account would become larger and larger.

An examination of the accounts of companies which used comprehensive tax allocation in the 1970s, before practice changed in 1979, shows how rarely there was a draw-down (or reduction) in the deferred taxation balance from year to year and how large the balance on deferred taxation could become.[13]

Such a deferred taxation balance was normally disclosed as a separate item in the balance sheet of a company and certainly not as part of the shareholders' equity. If the balance was not part of the shareholders' equity, then a knowledge of elementary accounting would suggest that it was a liability. However, this may be questioned. As we have seen, for many companies it may well not have been payable in the foreseeable future and, in such cases, its inclusion in the balance sheet may therefore have been regarded as inconsistent with the going concern concept.

The inclusion of a full provision for deferred taxation in the balance sheet of a company undoubtedly posed problems of interpretation. If the amount is not part of the shareholders' equity, then it must presumably be included as part of other long-term capital in measuring gearing. This resulted in many UK companies appearing to be very highly geared!

As we shall see, problems such as these persuaded the ASC to change from a requirement for companies to make a full provision for deferred taxation to a requirement that they should make a partial provision. We shall also see that, partially, but not entirely, in response to subsequent changes in the taxation system, the ASB is attempting to move us back towards the use of a full provision.

Attempts at standardisation: ED 11 to SSAP 15

The Accounting Standards Steering Committee made its first attempt at a standard method of accounting for deferred taxation when it issued ED 11, 'Accounting for Deferred Taxation', in May 1973. This proposed that companies should adopt comprehensive tax allocation using the deferral method. The ensuing SSAP 11, which was published in August 1975, followed this approach, although it permitted companies to use either the deferral method or the liability method.

SSAP 11 came under such heavy criticism from industry that its starting date was postponed indefinitely and it was eventually withdrawn. The ASC was criticised for this withdrawal and many saw it as a manifestation of weakness, that is the ASC bending in the face of opposition rather than taking a strong line. Others saw it as an example of the ASC rightly responding to criticism, although even such supporters would argue that critics should make their views known during the exposure period rather than after a standard has been published.

ED 19, which was issued in May 1977, adopted a very different approach from SSAP 11. Instead of requiring comprehensive tax allocation, it permitted partial tax allocation in certain circumstances. Thus, instead of requiring companies to perform a mechanical calculation to provide for deferred taxation on all timing differences, it recognised that not all timing differences would reverse in the foreseeable future and consequently permitted a more subjective approach which took into account the circumstances of the particular company. Even where a company took advantage of this

---

[13] For example, the accounts of Thorn Electrical Industries for 1978 showed that deferred taxation was approximately one-third of its long-term capital. This fell enormously when the company adopted partial tax allocation in 1979.

permissive approach, it was still required to provide a note to the balance sheet showing the potential deferred taxation on all timing differences and this potential deferred taxation was to be calculated using the liability method.

SSAP 15 was originally issued in 1978 and reissued in a revised form in 1985, following the publication of an Exposure Draft (ED 33). The basic principle of SSAP 15 is to require companies to make a partial provision, using the liability method, with the amount of the potential deferred tax not provided for stated by way of note.

The current version of SSAP 15 differs from the original on the matter of the balance of proof. In the original version SSAP 15 started with the presumption that full provision should be made unless it could be shown that the liability (or asset) would not crystallise. The current version is more even-handed: if it is probable that the liability (or asset) will crystallise, then provide; if it is probable that it will not crystallise, then do not provide.

The approach of SSAP 15 (1985)

Under the provisions of SSAP 15, companies are required to account for timing differences to the extent that it is probable that a liability or asset will crystallise but not to account for timing differences to the extent that it is probable that a liability or asset will not crystallise (Paras. 25 and 26). The decision on whether deferred tax liabilities or assets will or will not crystallise involves looking into the future and should be based upon reasonable assumptions (Para. 27). Under such a partial tax allocation approach, only the liability method makes any sense and SSAP 15 requires that this be used (Para. 24).

The Standard requires the disclosure of the major components of both the amount provided (Para. 27) and the amount *unprovided* (Para. 40). It follows that accountants need to know not only how to calculate a partial provision but also how to calculate a full provision, so that the amount unprovided may be disclosed.

Whereas a full provision for deferred taxation may be made on the basis of the knowledge of what has happened in the past, in order to make a partial provision, it is necessary to look into the future. Thus, it is necessary to look at financial plans or projections covering a period of years sufficient to enable an assessment to be made of the likely pattern of future tax liabilities (Para. 28). The Appendix, which is for guidance only, states that this period may be relatively short – say, three to five years – where the pattern of timing differences is expected to be regular (Appendix, Para. 4). Where such regularity is not expected, it will be necessary to peer even further into the future.

Although the SSAP is silent on the matter, the Appendix also states that 'the combined effect of timing differences should be considered when attempting to assess whether a tax liability will crystallise, rather than looking at each timing difference separately' (Appendix, Para. 4). Given that the objective is to arrive at a meaningful provision in the circumstances faced by each particular company, such a global approach is undoubtedly sensible, although it does sometimes make it difficult to give the required analysis of the provision.

In spite of this requirement to look at the combined effect of timing difference we shall, for explanatory purposes, look first at each of the six major categories of timing difference identified earlier in this chapter. We shall assume a company which makes up accounts to 31 December and that we are deciding what, if any, provision is necessary at 31 December 20X1.

(a) Receipts and payments versus accruals

In order to decide whether or not to provide for deferred taxation at 31 December 20X1, it is necessary to look into the future to see whether or not a reversing difference is likely to occur.

Let us return to the example of Hongbo plc which made a provision of £200 000 for reorganisation costs in 20X1 which were not allowed for tax purposes until they were paid in 20X2. Whether or not it is necessary to account for deferred taxation at 31 December 20X1 depends upon whether the timing difference is likely to reverse in the foreseeable future without being replaced by a similar difference.

In the absence of further provisions for reorganisation costs in 20X2, there is no doubt that the difference will reverse when the reorganisation costs are paid in 20X2 and hence a deferred tax asset amounting to £60 000 (30 per cent of £200 000) must be created at 31 December 20X1. This recognises that, in the absence of any other timing differences, taxable profits in 20X2 will be lower than the accounting profits for that year.

(b) Capital allowances and depreciation

In the example of Hongbo plc, we have seen that where a company regularly purchases fixed assets eligible for accelerated capital allowances, new originating differences may exceed reversing timing differences. Thus, there may be a hard core of timing differences which are not expected to reverse while the company continues to operate under existing tax legislation. In such a case full provision for deferred tax is not necessary.

Where the expenditure on eligible fixed assets is erratic, then reversing timing differences may exceed future originating differences so that a net reversing difference occurs and a tax liability crystallises. In such a case, a provision for deferred taxation will be necessary, although there may be differences of opinion about the precise amount of the provision.

To illustrate the calculation of a partial provision, let us assume that Hongbo plc is calculating the necessary provision at 31 December 20X1 and that, taking into account expected capital expenditure, capital allowances and depreciation, it has produced the following forecast for the next four years:

Forecast for the years ended 31 December

	20X2	20X3	20X4	20X5
	£000	£000	£000	£000
Capital allowances	2 300	2 100	1 500	2 400
Depreciation	1 800	1 900	2 250	1 800
Net originating differences	(500)	(200)	–	(600)
Net reversing differences	–	–	750	–

In the year ended 31 December 20X4, the taxable profits are expected to exceed the accounting profits by £750 000 and, given that the rate of corporation tax is 30 per cent, the tax involved is 30 per cent of £750 000, which is £225 000. The most prudent partial provision on 31 December 20X1 would therefore be £225 000.

However, it may be argued that this is too prudent and that it is necessary to take a cumulative view of the position in future years. On this basis, the net reversing difference in the year to 31 December 20X4 is preceded by net originating differences in the years 20X2 and 20X3. Thus, it would be possible to make additional provisions in those two years so that the minimum amount to be provided at 31 December 20X1 may be calculated as follows:

	£000	£000
Net reversing difference expected in 20X4		750
less Future net originating differences		
20X2	500	
20X3	200	
		700
Minimum provision necessary at 31 December 20X1		50
30% × £50 000		15

If this approach is adopted, the provision at 31 December 20X1 will be £15 000. Assuming that forecasts are met, additional provisions of £150 000 (£500 000 × 30 per cent) and £60 000 (£200 000 × 30 per cent) will be made in 20X2 and 20X3 respectively. By the beginning of the year in which the net reversing difference occurs, 20X4, there will then be an accumulated provision equal to taxation on those net reversing differences, in this case £225 000.

SSAP 15 provides no guidance on how the partial provision should be calculated and this leaves considerable scope for variations in, and possible manipulation of, reported after tax results in practice.

(c) Pension contributions and pension costs

As we have explained in Chapter 5, the objective of SSAP 24, 'Accounting for Pension Costs', is to require companies to recognise the cost of providing pensions on a systematic and rational basis over the period during which they benefit from the services of the employees. This necessarily involves companies taking a long-term view.

Because tax law allows the pension contributions payable by the company as a tax expense, rather than the cost determined in accordance with SSAP 24, there is frequently a timing difference and hence the need to account for deferred taxation. However, if companies use the partial approach required by SSAP 15, they are providing deferred tax on differences which reverse in the foreseeable future, usually three to five years. It follows that the time horizon used to determine the deferred tax in respect of pension costs will usually be much shorter than that used in determining the pension cost itself.

The ASB addressed this inconsistency in 'Amendment to SSAP 15 Accounting for Deferred Tax', issued in December 1992. This amendment permits, but does not require, companies to use the same recognition criteria for the deferred tax applicable to pensions as it uses in determining the pension cost itself. Companies may therefore use either the full provision basis or the partial provision basis to account for the deferred tax implications of pensions and other post-retirement benefits. The ASB clearly recognised that this amendment provided only an interim solution to the inconsistency pending comprehensive reviews of both SSAP 15 and SSAP 24. The first stage of each of these reviews has led to the issue of a Discussion Paper by the ASB, 'Accounting for Tax' (March 1995) and 'Pension Costs in the Employer's Financial Statements' (June 1995). The former has then led to the issue of two exposure drafts FRED 18 'Current Taxation' (June 1999) and FRED 19 'Deferred Taxation' (August 1999), both of which are discussed in this chapter. The latter has led to the issue of a further Discussion Paper 'Aspects of Accounting for Pension Costs' (July 1998) which has been discussed in Chapter 5.

(d) Unrealised revaluation surpluses on fixed assets for which a taxation charge does not arise until the gain is realised on disposal

Taxation on a revaluation surplus only becomes payable when that surplus is realised, and then only if no rollover relief is available. It follows that a provision for deferred tax will only be necessary if the directors intend to sell the revalued asset in the foreseeable future in circumstances where it is not possible to take advantage of rollover relief. If such a sale is not expected, then no provision for deferred taxation is necessary. If such a sale is expected, then deferred tax should be provided and deducted from the revaluation surplus which is taken to the statement of total recognised gains and losses.

(e) Surpluses on disposals of fixed assets which are subject to rollover relief

As under (d) above, tax will only become payable on such a surplus if the replacement asset is sold and no rollover relief is possible at that time. Where such a sale is not envisaged in the foreseeable future, no provision for deferred taxation is necessary. Where such a sale is envisaged, then deferred tax should be provided and charged against the realised surplus on disposal.

(f) Tax losses carried forward

Where a company is unable to obtain a more immediate benefit from a tax loss, that loss may be carried forward to set off against future profits. It follows that such a tax loss, incurred in the past, is an asset in that it will reduce tax payable in one or more future periods. SSAP 15 specifically 'draws attention to the fact that such a loss for tax purposes is a timing difference'.[14]

Deferred tax relating to current trading losses may be treated as recoverable when:

(i)   the loss results from an identifiable and non-recurring cause; and
(ii) the enterprise, or predecessor enterprise, has been consistently profitable over a considerable period, with any past losses being more than offset by income in subsequent periods; and
(iii) it is assured beyond reasonable doubt that future taxable profits will be sufficient to offset the current loss during the carry-forward period prescribed by tax legislation.[15]

The tax on such recoverable tax losses would reduce the tax charge in the current profit and loss account, perhaps making it negative, and would normally be deducted from any relevant provision for deferred taxation in respect of the other timing differences which have been discussed above.

A global approach

We have now looked at each of the major categories of timing differences individually but, as explained above, it is in fact necessary to look at the combined effect of all timing differences when determining the amount of the necessary provision for deferred tax on a particular date. Hence it would be necessary to prepare a table incorporating the forecast timing differences expected by a particular company and if, for example, we bring together two of the income items discussed above, such a table might include the following:

---

[14] SSAP 15, Para. 19.
[15] Appendix to SSAP 15, Para. 14. Para. 15 contains similar rules in respect of deferred tax on capital losses.

Forecast timing differences

	20X2 £000	20X3 £000	20X4 £000	20X5 £000
Receipts and payments/accruals				
Reversing difference	200	–	–	–
Accelerated capital allowances				
Net originating differences	(500)	(200)	–	(600)
Net reversing differences	–	–	750	–
	(300)	(200)	750	(600)

In such a case, the minimum provision necessary on 31 December 20X1 would be calculated as follows:

	£000	£000
Net reversing differences in 20X4		750
less Net originating differences		
20X2	300	
20X3	200	500
		250
Minimum provision necessary at 31 December 20X1		
£250 000 @ 30%		75

The amount of the charge/credit to the profit and loss account in respect of deferred taxation for 20X1 will be the difference between £75 000, the required provision at the year end, and the opening balance on the deferred taxation account in respect of such income items.

As we have explained above, SSAP 15 requires a note to support the provision for deferred taxation shown in the balance sheet and a hypothetical example of such a note is as follows:[16]

Example of note to the financial statements

Deferred taxation	Amount provided £000	Amount unprovided £000
Accelerated capital allowances	240	360
Accruals and provisions	(30)	(–)
	210	360
Revaluation of fixed assets		
and gains on disposals	40	60
	250	420

The International Standard: IAS 12

Whereas the original IAS 12 'Accounting for Taxes on Income' (1979) permitted the use of either full or partial deferred tax accounting, the revised version 'Income Taxes' (1996) now requires the use of full deferred tax accounting, using the liability method. Hence the proposals of SSAP 15 for partial deferred tax accounting are now out of line with the international standard.

IAS 12 requires companies to account for deferred taxation not just on timing differences but on what it calls 'temporary differences'. This approach adopts a balance sheet

---

[16] For clarity, we have omitted comparative figures.

focus and requires deferred taxation to be provided in respect of differences between the carrying values of assets and liabilities in the balance sheet and their values for taxation purposes. While all timing differences are temporary differences, the latter term is wider. For example, it will include the taxation implications of fair value adjustments made on the acquisition of a subsidiary and of certain foreign exchange gains and losses.

As we shall see in the final section of this chapter, the ASB favours a move towards full provision of deferred taxation but rejects the use of the 'temporary differences' approach to deferred taxation.

Towards a new standard: FRED 19

As part of its review of SSAP 15, the ASB issued a Discussion Paper 'Accounting for Tax' in March 1995. Although this dealt with both current taxation and deferred taxation, the ASB has subsequently produced separate exposure drafts on each topic. FRED 19 'Deferred Tax' was published in August 1999.

FRED 19 proposes the abolition of the partial provision approach of SSAP 15 in favour of full provision. Partial provision may be seen as a pragmatic approach to the situation in the 1970s when, as a consequence of generous tax allowances in a period of high inflation, there were often very large differences between accounting and taxable profits. The theoretical foundations of partial provision have always been weak and the approach is inconsistent with other areas of accounting. Where else would we ignore creditors on a balance sheet date on the grounds that they will be replaced by other creditors in future?

The partial provision may also be criticised because of the subjectivity involved. Any calculation of the necessary provision requires management to forecast what is likely to occur in the foreseeable future taking into account its plans for that period. This clearly opens the door for the manipulation of the provision by unscrupulous directors.

A third reason to move away from partial provision is the fact that, as we have seen above, it is now rejected by the international accounting standard IAS 12, which requires the use of the full provision method. While it would be possible for the ASB to go it alone, as it has done in the case of goodwill[17], the ASB proposes that, in the case of deferred taxation, we should try to move in line with the international accounting standard by requiring full provision to be made. However it does not go the whole hog: it does not recommend the use of the 'temporary differences' approach of IAS 12 even though it may be argued that this method is consistent with the balance sheet focus proposed in its own draft Statement of Principles. Rather it favours a particular form of the timing differences approach.

The ASB proposes that deferred taxation be provided on all timing differences except for the following:[18]

- unrealised gains on the revaluation of assets;
- realised gains rolled over onto replacement assets or likely to be rolled over onto replacement assets; and
- unremitted earnings of subsidiaries, associates and joint ventures, that is the share of earnings recognised in the consolidated profit and loss account but not paid over to the investor company as dividends.

---

[17] *See* Chapter 8.
[18] Even here, the exposure draft draws attention to exceptions where deferred tax should be provided. For example, deferred tax should be provided on an unrealised gain on revaluation when the reporting entity has entered into a binding agreement to sell the asset in circumstances where no rollover relief will be available (*see* FRED 19, Para. 8).

For many companies, a change from partial provision to full provision would lead to substantial increases in provisions for deferred taxation but the effects of this would be mitigated if deferred taxation liabilities were to be discounted. Although not permitted by the IASC, discounting is favoured by the ASB and it suggests a possible approach. The full reversals of all relevant timing differences should be scheduled on a year-to-year basis. Tax on these reversing differences should then be discounted back to the balance sheet date using the post tax yields to maturity on government bonds with appropriate maturity dates for each amount. It remains to be seen whether the introduction of discounting proves to be politically acceptable in this context.

In addition to these fundamental changes in measuring deferred taxation, FRED 19 also proposes changes in disclosure. In particular, it proposes that companies should provide a note reconciling the tax charge which would be expected from applying the current corporation tax rate to the reported accounting profit before tax with the current tax charge shown in the profit and loss account. Such a note would undoubtedly provide useful information and might take the following form:

Reconciliation of tax charge

	20X2 £000	20X1 £000
Profit on ordinary activities before tax	2 200	2 000
Standard rate of tax of 30% applied to above profit	660	600
Effects of:		
Expenses not deductible for tax purposes, including unwinding of deferred tax liability	30	33
Capital allowances in excess of depreciation	(125)	(116)
Utilisation of tax losses	(19)	(17)
Changes in deferred tax discount rate	9	10
Current tax charge for period	555	510

It now seems highly likely that the financial reporting standard developed from FRED 19 will outlaw the partial provision approach of SSAP 15 and will, instead, require full provision of deferred taxation in respect of most, but not all, timing differences using the liability method. Whether or not it will require or permit discounting remains an open question.

Recommended reading

Anthony J. Arnold and Brian J. Webb, *The Financial Reporting and Policy Effects of Partial Deferred Tax Accounting*, ICAEW, London, 1989.

R. Munson, 'Deferred Tax', *Accountants Digest No. 174*, ICAEW, London, 1985.

I.P.A. Stitt, *Deferred Tax Accounting*, ICAEW, London, 1985.

P. Weetman (ed.), *SSAP 15 Accounting for Deferred Taxation*, ICAS, Edinburgh, 1992.

8 Business combinations and goodwill

Overview   We start this chapter by discussing the economic and business context of business combinations and by describing the ways in which such combinations may be effected. We then describe and evaluate the two methods of accounting for business combinations, the *acquisition* method and the *merger* method. The former is based on the premise that there is a purchase by a dominant partner whereas the latter assumes a coming together of more or less equal partners. In this section we deal with the standard FRS 6 *Acquisitions and Mergers* (September 1994).

We also outline the provisions of the international accounting standard and draw attention to current international thinking on this topic.

In the second section of the chapter, we turn to the thorny issue of accounting for goodwill. We explain why goodwill arises and then describe the attempts of the standard setters to arrive at an appropriate accounting treatment for this, often very valuable, phenomena. In this we draw upon the standard FRS 10 *Goodwill and Intangible Assets* (December 1997).

Because standard accounting practice for goodwill under FRS 10 now involves impairment reviews, we also revisit the standard FRS 11 *Impairment of Fixed Assets and Goodwill* (July 1998), which was introduced in Chapter 4.

We conclude with a brief look at relevant international accounting standards.

Business combinations

Introduction

Words such as merger, amalgamation, absorption, takeover and acquisition are all used to describe the coming together of two or more businesses. Such words do not have precise legal meanings and, as they are often used interchangeably, the American description 'business combinations' best describes the subject matter of this chapter.

A company may expand either by 'internal' or 'external' growth. In the former case it expands by undertaking investment projects, such as the purchase of new premises and plant, while in the latter case it expands by purchasing a collection of assets in the form of an established business. In this second case we have a business combination in which one company is very much the dominant party, acquiring control of that other business either with or without the consent of the directors of that business.

Where such 'external' growth is contemplated, it will be necessary to value the collection of assets it is proposed to purchase. It will usually be necessary to determine at least two values: (a) the value of the business to its present owners (this will determine the minimum price which will be acceptable); (b) the value of the business when combined with the existing assets of the acquiring company (this will determine the maximum price which may be offered). In some cases it may be possible to apply capital budgeting techniques to arrive at these values but often other methods of valuation, such as those discussed in Chapter 14, will be used.

In other circumstances two or more companies may both see benefits from coming together. Thus, two companies may consider that their combined businesses are worth more than the sum of the values of the individual businesses. For such a combination, the individual businesses must be valued to help in the determination of the proportionate shares in the combined business, although, of course, the ultimate shares will, to a considerable extent, depend upon the bargaining ability of the two parties.

Table 8.1 gives some indication of the importance of business combinations in the years 1989–98. It shows acquisitions and mergers of industrial and commercial companies in the UK by UK companies.[1]

Some reasons for combining

Purchase of undervalued assets

As we shall see in the chapter on valuation of securities and businesses (Chapter 14), the same collection of assets may have different values to different people. As a result, it is often possible for one business to purchase another business, that is a collection of assets, at a price below the sum of the values of the underlying assets. If we take limited companies, for example, the shares of a company may be standing at a relatively low price because the current management is making poor use of the assets or has not communicated good future prospects to the shareholders. Even though the acquiring company purchases the shares at a price higher than the existing market price, it may be able to acquire underlying assets which have a much higher value than the price paid. Indeed, as many asset strippers have shown, even the sale of assets on a piecemeal basis may generate a sum considerably in excess of the price paid for those assets.

Table 8.1 Acquisitions and mergers in the UK by UK companies: 1989 to 1998

Year	Number of companies acquired	Total	Consideration (£million)		
			Cash	Ordinary shares	Fixed interest securities
1989	1 337	27 250	22 356	3 520	1 374
1990	779	8 329	6 402	1 533	393
1991	506	10 434	7 278	3 034	121
1992	432	5 941	3 772	2 122	47
1993	526	7 063	5 690	1 162	211
1994	674	8 269	5 302	2 823	144
1995	505	32 600	25 524	6 617	459
1996	584	30 742	19 551	10 926	265
1997	506	26 829	10 923	15 583	323
1998	637	29 549	15 799	13 156	594

[1] This information has been taken from *Financial Statistics,* published monthly by the Office for National Statistics.

Economies of scale

The combination of two businesses may result in economies of scale, that is to say the cost of producing the combined output will be less than the sum of the costs of producing the separate outputs or, alternatively, the combined output will be greater for the same total cost. Such economies of scale may exist not only in production but also in administration, research and development and financing.

Concentrating first on production, economies of scale may arise for such reasons as the following: set-up costs and marketing costs may be spread over larger outputs; indivisible units of high cost machinery may become feasible at higher levels of output; where capacity is dependent on volume and cost is dependent on surface area, as in the case of storage tanks, such area–volume relationships may result in less than proportionate rises in costs.

When we turn to administration, a large organisation may attract and make better use of scarce managerial talent and enable the firm to employ specialists. Large organisations may also be able to attract suitable people to administer research and development programmes and to use the results of those programmes more effectively. In addition, the larger organisation is often in a position to raise and service capital more cheaply than a smaller organisation.

Economics textbooks devote considerable space to discussions of the theoretical bases for economies of scale, and governments have often encouraged and supported combinations on the grounds that they would improve the efficiency of British industry, in particular its competitiveness in international markets. For reasons discussed below, there is now less confidence that benefits will be obtained from combinations.

Various techniques have been developed to examine whether and to what extent economies of scale exist in practice. Although there appears to be scope for economies of scale in many industries, these do not appear automatically after a business combination, but have to be planned. A number of studies have found that the performances of many combined businesses have been rather disappointing. In particular there are diseconomies of large organisations, due mainly to the problems of administering large units, which may often outweigh the benefits afforded by economies of scale.

Elimination or reduction of competition

By eliminating or reducing competition, it may be possible for a company to make larger profits; combining with another business may be one means of achieving this end. Although integration may occur for many reasons, one reason may be that it is possible to reduce competition both by vertical integration, that is by combining with a firm at an earlier or later stage of the production cycle, or by horizontal integration, that is by combining with a firm at the same stage in the production cycle.

To illustrate, a firm at one stage of production may combine with a firm at an earlier stage of production, that is a supplier, thus ensuring a ready source of supply and perhaps putting it in a position to charge a lower price than competitors at the second stage, and hence squeeze them out of business. The extent to which this is possible would depend upon the structure of the market, that is the extent to which there are monopolistic or competitive elements present.

Combination with a firm at the same stage of production would reduce the number of competitors by one and again may give rise to higher profits as a result of the increased industrial concentration although much would depend upon the structure of the industry before and after the combination. The combination of two small firms in a very competitive industry might have little effect, whereas the combination of two giants might turn an oligopoly into a virtual monopoly.

Part 2 · Financial reporting in practice

There are obvious dangers to the public at large from mergers which reduce the level of competition and it is for this reason that we have legislation on monopolies and mergers.

Reduction of risk

By combining with a firm which makes different products, a business is often able to reduce risk. Thus one reason for a combination involving businesses in different industries may be a desire to generate an earnings stream which is less variable than the separate earnings streams of the two individual businesses. Such a reduction of risk is usually considered to be an advantage and will often lead to an increase in share values, although it may be argued that a shareholder may be better able to reduce risk by the selection of his or her own portfolio of shares.

Use of price/earnings ratios

In many business combinations, one company has been able to increase the wealth of its own shareholders by combining with a company which has a lower price/earnings ratio.

To illustrate let us take a simple example of two companies:

	Company A	Company B
Earnings	£10 000	£10 000
Number of ordinary shares	100 000	100 000
Earnings per share	10p	10p
Current market price	£1.50p	£1.20p
P/E ratio	15	12

Let us suppose that company A issues 80 000 shares valued at £120 000 (80 000 at £1.50) in exchange for 100 000 shares in company B valued at £120 000 (100 000 at £1.20). If there is no change in earnings after the combination, the earnings of the combined companies as reflected in the group accounts will be £20 000 and the earnings per share 11p, that is £20 000 divided by 180 000 shares in A. If the market continues to use the P/E ratio of company A, that is 15, the price of a share in company A after the combination will be £1.65. This is greater than £1.50, the price of a share in company A before the combination and hence advantageous to the original shareholders in the company. It is also advantageous to the original shareholders in company B who now hold 80 000 shares in company A valued at £132 000 compared with their former holdings of 100 000 shares in company B which were valued at £120 000.

It may be argued that the market is unlikely to apply the same P/E ratio to the combined earnings as it previously did to the earnings in company A as a separate company. An 'average' P/E ratio of 13.5, calculated as shown below, would perhaps be expected:

	Earnings	Values
Company A	£10 000	£150 000
Company B	£10 000	£120 000
Combined	£20 000	£270 000

The average P/E ratio is 270 000/20 000 = 13.5.

This does not appear to happen in practice, and the resulting P/E ratio is usually well above this 'average' P/E ratio because the market anticipates a better future.

Thus, even though benefits such as economies of scale and reduction of competition do not materialise, some companies have been able to increase the wealth of their shareholders by acquiring other companies with lower P/E ratios.

Managerial motives

Under traditional economic theory, the role of management is to respond in a rational, but more or less automatic way, to circumstances which present themselves. Thus if, for example, economies of scale are perceived to be likely if two businesses combine, such a combination will be pursued in order to maximise the wealth of shareholders.

A number of studies have suggested that the usual financial and economic reasons put forward for mergers were, in practice, not of prime importance. What seemed to be a more important determinant of mergers among large companies was the objectives of managers. In order to cope with increasing uncertainty, managers desired to increase their market power or to defend their market position. Although such activities could well further the interests of shareholders, they may have even greater benefits for the managers themselves. Thus, a less uncertain life, in particular less chance of the company itself being taken over, a larger empire and perhaps larger remuneration due to control of such an empire may be extremely important motivating forces.

Whatever the ultimate objective, managerial motives seemed to play a much larger role in merger activity than traditional economic theory allowed.

Methods of combining

In order to be able to account for combinations, we must first explore some of the methods which may be used to effect them. Such methods may best be classified as to whether or not a group structure results from the combination.

Let us take as an example two companies, L and M, and assume that the respective boards of directors and owners have agreed to combine their businesses.

Combinations which result in a group structure

Two such combinations may be considered.

In the first case, company L may purchase the shares of company M and thereby acquire a subsidiary company; alternatively company M may purchase the shares of company L.

The choice of consideration given in exchange for the shares acquired will determine whether or not the shareholders in what becomes the subsidiary company have any interest in the combined businesses. Thus, if company L issues shares in exchange for the shares of company M, the old shareholders in company M have an interest in the resulting holding company and thereby in the group, whereas, if company L pays cash for the shares in company M, the old shareholders in M take their cash and cease to have any interest in the resulting group.

In the second case, a new company, LM, may be established to purchase the shares of both L and M. Thus, the shareholders in L and M may sell their shares to LM in exchange for shares in LM. The resulting group structure would then be as shown in Figure 8.1. The shareholders in LM would be the former shareholders in the two separate companies and their respective interests would depend, as in all the examples in this section, upon the valuations placed upon the two separate companies, which would in turn depend in part upon bargaining between the two boards of directors.

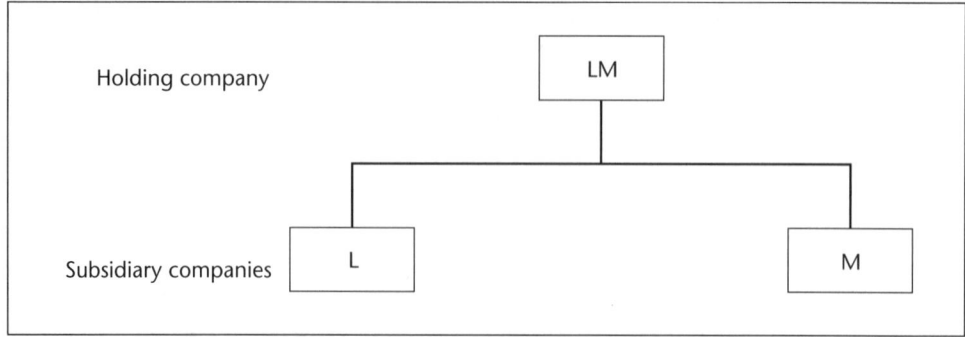

Fig. 8.1 Resulting group structure after combination

It is possible for company LM to issue not only shares but also loan stock in order to purchase the shares in L and M. It would be difficult for payment to be made in cash as LM is a newly formed company, although it could, of course, issue other shares or raise loans to obtain cash.

Combinations not resulting in a group structure

Again, two such combinations may be considered.

First, instead of purchasing the shares of company M, company L may obtain control of the net assets of M by making a direct purchase of those net assets. The net assets would thus be absorbed into company L and company M would itself receive the consideration. This would in due course be distributed to the shareholders of M by its liquidator.

As before, the choice of consideration determines whether or not the former shareholders in M have any interest in the enlarged company L.

Second, instead of one of the companies purchasing the net assets of the other, a new company may be formed to purchase the net assets of both existing companies. Thus, a new company, LM, may be formed to purchase the net assets of company L and company M. If payment is made by issuing shares in LM, these will be distributed by the respective liquidators so that the end result is one company, LM, which owns the net assets previously held by the separate companies and has as its shareholders the former shareholders in the two separate companies.

Preference for group structure

The above are methods of effecting a combination between two, or indeed more, companies although, in practice, virtually all large business combinations make use of a group structure, rather than a purchase of assets or net assets. Such a structure is advantageous in that separate companies enjoying limited liability are already in existence.

It follows that names, and associated goodwill, of the original companies are not lost and there is no necessity to renegotiate contractual arrangements. All sorts of other factors will be important in practice; some examples are the desire to retain staff, the impact of taxation and whether or not there is a remaining minority interest. A group structure also permits easy disinvestment by sale of one or more subsidiaries.

Choice of consideration

As discussed above, the choice of consideration will determine who is interested in the single business created by the combination and will therefore be affected by the intentions of the parties to the combination. It will also be affected by the size of the companies and by conditions in the market for securities and the taxation system in force.

The main possible types of consideration are cash, loan stock, ordinary shares, some form of convertible security or any combination of these.

Let us look at the effect of each of these before turning to some factors which influence the choice between them.

Cash

Where one company purchases the shares or assets of another for cash the shareholders of the latter company cease to have any interest in the combined businesses.

From the point of view of the selling shareholders, they take a certain cash sum and will be liable to capital gains tax on the disposal of their shares.

From the point of view of the purchasing company, its cash holdings will decrease. It has sometimes been suggested that the use of cash will give a better chance of success if opposition is anticipated and, providing the earnings of the company which is purchased are greater than the earnings which would be made by using cash in other ways, there will be an increase in the earnings per share.

Loan stock

In this case the selling shareholders, either directly or indirectly, exchange shares in one company for loan stock in another company. Hence an equity investment is exchanged for a fixed interest investment, which may or may not be an advantage, depending upon the relative values of the securities and the circumstances of the individual investor. Any liability to capital gains tax will be deferred until ultimate disposal of the loan stock.

From the point of view of the shareholders of the purchasing company, there may be an advantage in that the level of gearing will be increased. In addition, interest on the loan stock will be deductible for corporation tax purposes.

Ordinary shares

A share for share exchange is often the method used in combinations involving large companies. Here the shareholder simply exchanges shares in one company for shares in another company.

There are many potential benefits for the selling shareholders, although the extent to which they exist will depend upon the exact terms of the combination and the relative values of the shares. The selling shareholder continues to have an interest in the combined businesses with the benefits mentioned in the second section of this chapter and will not be subject to capital gains tax on the exchange. Against this the value of the security received is not certain but will depend upon market reaction to the combination.

From the point of view of the combined companies, a share exchange does not affect their liquidity. The extent to which it is beneficial for the existing shareholders of the company must depend upon the relative values of the shares.

Although shares were popular in the mid-1980s, cash has been the major part of the consideration in all but one of the ten years 1989 to 1998.[2]

Convertible loan stock

The issue of convertible loan stock has become more common and has sometimes been used in connection with business combinations. In such a case, the shareholders in one company exchange their shares for convertible loan stock in another company.

---

[2] See the statistics on p. 220 for an analysis of the total expenditure for each of the years 1989–98 between cash, ordinary shares and fixed interest securities.

From the point of view of a selling shareholder, an equity investment is exchanged for a fixed interest security, but one which is convertible into an equity investment at some time in the future. Thus, if in the future share prices move in his favour he will be able to take up his equity interest while, if they move against him, he will be able to retain his fixed interest investment. Again, any liability to capital gains tax is deferred until ultimate disposal of the convertible stock or equity shares issued in exchange.

From the point of view of the company issuing such securities, the interest on the loan stock is deductible for taxation purposes and the debt is self-liquidating if loan holders convert loan stock into ordinary shares. If loan holders do convert, the tax deductibility is, of course, lost and in addition there is a reduction in gearing and possible dilution of the existing shareholders' interest.

The choice in practice

As has been seen above, the various forms of consideration which may be used have advantages and disadvantages. The choice in any business combination will depend upon a large number of factors, some of which are discussed in this section.

It is convenient to distinguish between an agreed combination where the two sets of shareholders in the individual companies are to be shareholders in the new or enlarged company and a situation where one party is dominant and is seeking to obtain control of the other company as cheaply as possible.

In the first of these cases the major part of the consideration must obviously be equity shares although, if a situation of surplus cash or low gearing is expected after the combination, an opportunity may be taken to pay part of the consideration in cash or some form of loan stock.

In the second case the choice of consideration will be affected considerably by the nature of the companies involved and the market situation. Where the biddee company is small or opposition is expected, a cash bid may be preferred. Loan stock may be attractive where rates of interest are low and especially if they are expected to rise. Where, however, it is felt that the shares of the dominant company are overpriced relative to those of the other company, then a share issue is likely to be most attractive.

Accounting for business combinations

Accounting for business combinations is a topic which has been the cause of considerable controversy in many countries. The traditional method of accounting for combinations in the UK was the 'acquisition' or 'purchase' method but, in the 1960s, a new method began to find favour. This was the 'merger' or 'pooling of interests' method which had been extensively used in the USA. ED 3 'Accounting for Acquisitions and Mergers', which was published in 1971, attempted to define situations in which each method should be used but was never converted into a Statement of Standard Accounting Practice. Changes introduced by the Companies Act 1981 made it possible to make progress and SSAP 23 'Accounting for Acquisitions and Mergers' was issued in April 1985. This standard was the subject of considerable criticism and, in 1990, the ASC issued a revised version ED 48. The ASB then issued its own exposure draft, FRED 6 'Acquisitions and Mergers', in May 1993 and this was followed by FRS 6, with the same title, in September 1994. We shall explore these attempts at standardisation after we have distinguished between the 'acquisition' and 'merger' methods of accounting.

Acquisition and merger accounting

As stated above, the acquisition method has traditionally been used to account for business combinations and, where the consideration for shares or assets purchased is wholly cash or loan stock, this is agreed to be the correct method of accounting. However, where the consideration given is wholly or predominantly ordinary shares, many accountants would argue that the acquisition method is inappropriate. Here the shareholders in one company exchange their equity holding in that company for an equity interest in another company: a holding company if shares are purchased, or an enlarged company if net assets are purchased. In such circumstances, use of the acquisition method frequently produces inconsistencies in the treatment of the two combining companies. These inconsistencies are avoided by the use of the merger method but, as we shall see, consistency is obtained only at a price.

Under acquisition accounting, an investment in a subsidiary would normally be recorded at the fair value of the consideration given. Where the fair value of any shares issued exceeds their par value, a share premium account or merger reserve would normally be created in the parent company's accounts.[3] In the consolidated accounts, the investment would be replaced by the underlying separable assets and liabilities of the subsidiary at their fair values, representing their 'cost' to the group. Any difference between the cost of the investment and the sum of the values of the separable assets and liabilities is recorded as goodwill. Pre-acquisition profits of the subsidiary are no longer available for distribution and the results of this new subsidiary are only brought into the consolidated profit and loss account from the date of acquisition.[4]

Under the merger method of accounting, the investment in the subsidiary company would normally be recorded in the parent company's accounts as the aggregate of the nominal value of any shares issued plus the fair value of any other consideration. Thus, the carrying value of the investment would not be the fair value of the consideration given and no share premium account or merger reserve would be created.

In the consolidated accounts, the investment would be replaced by the underlying separable assets and liabilities, not at fair value, but at their book values in the subsidiary's own accounts subject to adjustments necessary to achieve consistency of accounting policies for the group. The pre-acquisition profits of the new subsidiary are not frozen but are aggregated with those of the parent company, and the results of the new subsidiary are brought into the consolidated profit and loss account for the whole period as if the companies had always been merged. No goodwill is recorded, and any difference between the nominal value of shares issued plus the fair value of any other consideration given and the nominal value of shares purchased is treated as an adjustment to 'other reserves' in the consolidated financial statements. FRS 6 also makes it clear that any share premium account or capital redemption reserve in the subsidiary's balance sheet should also be treated as a movement in 'other reserves' (Para. 18).

The essential differences between the two methods can be illustrated in a simple example involving a share for share exchange.

---

[3] The conditions for the creation of a merger reserve, rather than a share premium account, will be discussed below.

[4] The acquisition method of accounting is considered in much greater depth in the next chapter. FRS 7 'Fair Values in Acquisition Accounting', September 1994, provides guidance both on identifying assets and liabilities at the date of acquisition and on determining their fair values.

Example 8.1

Column 1 shows the summarised balance sheets of H Limited and S Limited before combination. H buys the shares in S in a share for share exchange. In order to concentrate on the essential differences between the two methods, we will assume that the current value of a share in both H Limited and S Limited is agreed to be £3. Hence H issues 800 shares in exchange for the 800 shares in S. We shall also assume that the sum of the fair values of separable net assets in H and S are £1800 and £1500, respectively.

Columns 2 and 3 show the parent company's balance sheet using the principles of the acquisition method and merger method respectively.[5]

Summarised balance sheets

	1 Before combination	2 After combination Acquisition method	3 After combination Merger method
	£	£	£
H Limited			
Net assets (Fair values £1800)	1 600	1 600	1 600
Shares in S Limited – at 'cost'		2 400	800
	1 600	4 000	2 400
£1 ordinary shares	1 000	1 800	1 800
Share premium/merger reserve		1 600	
Retained profits	600	600	600
	1 600	4 000	2 400
S Limited			
Net assets (Fair values £1500)	1 200	No change	
£1 ordinary shares	800	No change	
Retained profits	400		
	1 200		

If the acquisition method is used, the shares issued by H will be valued at their fair value at the date of issue, that is at £3 per share. The investment in subsidiary will be shown at a cost of £2400 while a share premium or merger reserve of £1600 will be recorded. Column 2 of the summarised balance sheets above reflects these entries.

If the merger method is used, the shares issued by H will be valued at their par value and the investment in subsidiary will be shown at a 'cost' of £800. This is shown in column 3 above.

We may now prepare the consolidated balance sheet of H Limited and its subsidiary S Limited using the acquisition and merger methods respectively.

---

[5] This is not strictly correct in that the treatment of the investment in the parent company's accounts is legally independent of what method of accounting is used in the consolidated accounts. Thus, if merger relief is available, H does not have to create a share premium/merger reserve in its own accounts even though such a merger reserve will be required to apply acquisition accounting in its consolidated accounts. What we have done is logically consistent with the subsequent treatment of the combination in the consolidated accounts.

Consolidated balance sheet of H Limited and subsidiary S Limited

	1 Acquisition method £	2 Merger method £
Net assets: H 1600 + S 1500	3 100	
H 1600 + S 1200		2 800
Goodwill on consolidation		
2400 – 1500	900	
	4 000	2 800
£1 ordinary shares	1 800	1 800
Share premium/Merger reserve	1 600	
Retained profits: H only	600	
H + S		1 000
	4 000	2 800

Column 1 shows the consolidated balance sheet immediately after the combination using the acquisition method. In preparing the consolidated balance sheet the excess of the cost of investment in the subsidiary (£2400) over the sum of the fair values of the separable assets and liabilities (£1500) is shown as goodwill on consolidation. The effect of using this method may be summarised as follows:

(a) *Retained profits*. Before the combination H had retained profits of £600 and S had retained profits of £400. However, the consolidated balance sheet only includes the retained profits of H and those of S have been frozen. Thus, if H receives a dividend from the pre-acquisition profits of S, this normally reduces the carrying value of the investment. The dividend received cannot be used as the basis for a dividend payment to the shareholders in H.

(b) *Net assets*. While the net assets of H are shown on the basis of their book values (£1600), those of S are included at their fair values (£1500).

(c) *Goodwill*. The goodwill in the consolidated balance sheet relates to S. None appears in relation to H.

Many would question whether this gives a true and fair view of the combination. After all, exactly the same people are interested in the net assets after the combination as before, although their proportionate interests will probably have changed as a result of the bargaining process. All that has happened is that the shareholders in S have exchanged their shares in S for shares in H, which now in turn owns S. Thus, two sets of shareholders have come together for their mutual benefit. Why then should the retained profits of one company be frozen while those of the other are not? Why should the net assets of one company be shown at fair values while those of the other are shown at their historical cost values? Why should we recognise goodwill for one company but not for the other?

A further criticism could be made of the method in that the consolidated balance sheet would look very different if, instead of the acquisition of shares in S by H, S had acquired the shares of H. This is a perfectly feasible alternative means of combination. The results produced will therefore vary depending upon what may in fact be an arbitrary choice of the holding company.

Consideration of questions like this have led to the development of merger accounting.

Under the merger method, shares issued in exchange for other shares are valued not at their fair value, but at their par value. Thus, using our simple example, the 800 shares issued by H would be valued at £1 each, that is £800, rather than at £3 each. Correspondingly, the investment in S would be shown at a 'cost' of only £800. Column 3 of the summarised balance sheets (p. 228) reflects this entry.

Column 2 of the consolidated balance sheets provides the resulting consolidated balance sheet. From this it may be seen that the precombination retained profits of the two individual companies are still available for dividend while the net assets of both companies are shown at their historical-cost-based valuation. It is as if the companies had been combined since the cradle and it follows that, in preparing the consolidated profit and loss account, the results of both companies would be included for the whole year irrespective of the date on which the combination occurred.[6] In preparing the consolidated accounts, necessary adjustments must, of course, be made to reflect uniform accounting policies throughout the group.

While the use of the merger method results in a consistent treatment of the profits and net assets of the two companies, it does, of course, have the result that all the assets are valued on the basis of old historical costs, which are arguably of little relevance to users of the accounts. Under the acquisition method, the assets of at least one company are shown at their fair values at the date of the combination, and to move from such a position to one where all assets are shown on the basis of their historical costs to the separate companies is regarded by some accountants as a step in the wrong direction.

One way to avoid this consequence of merger accounting would be for both companies to restate the carrying values of the separable assets and liabilities at their fair values at the date of combination so that the assets and liabilities of both companies would be shown on a consistent basis at fair value rather than at out-of-date values.

In the above example the par value of the shares issued by H was the same as the par value of the shares purchased. In most combinations this will not be the case and, in addition, the consideration may include cash and loan stock. Any difference between the par value of the shares issued plus the fair value of any other consideration and the par value of the shares purchased and any share premium account in respect of these shares would be dealt with as a movement on the consolidated reserves.

We have now explored the differences between acquisition accounting and merger accounting. Providing shares are used to purchase shares or net assets in another company, so that two sets of shareholders have an interest in the resulting combined business, we have the theoretical possibility of applying the merger method of accounting. We shall now explore the way in which the use of such a method has been regulated by some of the official pronouncements.

Development of an accounting standard

The Companies Act 1981

Prior to the Companies Act 1981, there were severe doubts about the legality of the merger method of accounting. Although the ASC had issued ED3 'Accounting for

---

[6] This is to be contrasted with the position using the acquisition method of accounting where the consolidated profit and loss account will only include the results of a new subsidiary from the date of acquisition. This topic is considered in some detail in the following chapter.

Acquisitions and Mergers' in 1971, it was unable to make progress in this area until the passage of the Companies Act 1981.

The Companies Act 1981 relieved companies from the need to create a share premium account in certain circumstances and these provisions are now contained in Companies Act 1985, Sections 131–134. This so-called merger relief is available when one company issues equity shares to purchase equity shares in another company and ends up with an equity holding of 90 per cent or more. In such circumstances, the company does not have to create a share premium account either in respect of the equity shares issued or any non-equity shares issued in exchange for non-equity shares.[7]

Thus, if one company issues equity shares to acquire 95 per cent of the equity shares of another company, it is not necessary to create any share premium account in respect of that transaction. If, however, one company already holds 20 per cent of the equity shares in another company and then purchases an additional 75 per cent of those shares, the relief from the need to create a share premium account applies only to the equity shares issued to obtain the 75 per cent holding, that is the purchase which takes the total holding to 90 per cent or above.

The main consequence of the above provisions was that they permitted, although they did not require, the subsequent use of merger accounting.

Once the merger method had been legalised, the ASC was able to turn its attention to the circumstances in which this method should be used. Before we look at the provisions of SSAP 23 (April 1985) and its successor FRS 6 (September 1994), we shall examine some of the matters which had to be considered and resolved.

Criteria for use of the merger method

Use of merger accounting would seem to offer certain advantages where there is a uniting of interests, that is where the equity shareholders in two separate companies pool their interests to become equity shareholders in a combined entity.

As described above, the Companies Act 1985 allowed (but did not require) the use of the merger method, providing at least 90 per cent of the equity shares of the acquired company were part of the pool or, to put it another way, even when up to 10 per cent of the equity shares did not become part of the pool. Within this legal framework, the ASC had to decide what conditions were necessary for the use of the merger method of accounting and whether, if those conditions were satisfied, use of the merger method should be obligatory or optional. In this section some of the factors that had to be considered are discussed briefly.

First, although there must be a uniting of interests, to what extent is it necessary to obtain the approval of the two sets of shareholders? Do all the shareholders in the two companies have to agree to the merger or only some minimum proportion? The law requires the holding in the offeree company to exceed 90 per cent but it says nothing about obtaining the agreement of the shareholders in the offeror company. Clearly it would be possible to impose much more stringent conditions here.

Second, there is the question of relative size. If one company is much smaller than the other then, even though all shareholders in both companies agree to a uniting of interests, the end result may well be a situation in which one set of shareholders is dominant in the combined entity with the other set of shareholders having

---

[7] Relief from the requirement to create a share premium account is also provided in the case of certain group reconstructions which involve the transfer of ownership of a company within a group (Companies Act 1985, Sec. 132).

insignificant influence. Is this really a uniting of interests or merely an 'acquisition' using equity shares as the consideration?

Third, in order for there to be a uniting of interests, the consideration must be equity shares. If the consideration is wholly cash or loan stock, resources leave the combining businesses and one set of shareholders ceases to have any equity interest in the combination and there is definitely no uniting of interests. A difficulty arises where the consideration consists mainly of equity shares but also partly of cash or loan stock. Does this disqualify the combination for treatment as a merger? If it does not do so in principle, then what is the maximum percentage of the consideration which may be given in a form other than equity shares?

These were the main questions to be answered in specifying the circumstances in which merger accounting could be used, although, as we shall see, the Companies Act 1989 has subsequently restricted the proportion of non-equity consideration which may be included in the total consideration. Given the nature of the questions, answers can only involve arbitrary choice and hence it is not surprising that the selection of a suitable set of criteria has posed problems for standard-setting bodies here and overseas.

The approach of SSAP 23

SSAP 23 permitted the use of merger accounting if all of the following conditions were satisfied:[8]

(a) the business combination results from an offer to the holders of all equity shares and the holders of all voting shares which are not already held by the offeror; and

(b) the offeror has secured, as a result of the offer, a holding of (i) at least 90 per cent of all equity shares (taking each class of equity separately) and (ii) the shares carrying at least 90 per cent of the votes of the offeree; and

(c) immediately prior to the offer, the offeror does not hold (i) 20 per cent or more of all equity shares of the offeree (taking each class of equity separately), or (ii) shares carrying 20 per cent or more of the votes of the offeree; and

(d) not less than 90 per cent of the fair value of the total consideration given for the equity share capital (including that given for shares already held) is in the form of equity share capital; not less than 90 per cent of the fair value of the total consideration given for voting non-equity share capital (including that given for shares already held) is in the form of equity and/or voting non-equity share capital.

If we concentrate on a situation in which two companies are combining by forming a holding company/subsidiary company relationship and we assume that both companies have only voting equity shares in issue, the conditions may be summarised in the following way.

Any initial holding of one company in the other could not exceed 20 per cent; the offer had to be made to all remaining shareholders and had to result in a total holding of 90 per cent or more. Not less than 90 per cent of the fair value of the total consideration given for shares, both in the present transaction and in past transactions, had to be in the form of voting equity shares.[9]

Where the initial holding exceeded 20 per cent, there was a presumption, albeit rebuttable, of significant influence requiring the use of the equity method of account-

---

[8] SSAP 23, Para. 11.

[9] As we shall see below, this last criterion has been tightened considerably by Companies Act 1989 which requires that the fair value of any consideration other than equity shares must not exceed 10 per cent of the nominal value of equity shares issued.

ing. The equity method, discussed in Chapter 9, is based on the principles of acquisition accounting and is therefore incompatible with the use of merger accounting.

The requirement that the total holding is 90 per cent or more was necessary to comply with the Companies Act condition for the use of merger relief, and the final condition that 90 per cent or more of the fair value of the total consideration was in the form of voting equity shares limited the non-share consideration to 10 per cent. Hence, there was a limit on the resources leaving the group.

The SSAP 23 conditions did not require the combination to be approved by the shareholders in the offeror company. Nor did it concern itself with the relative sizes of the two companies. Even when the conditions were satisfied, the use of merger accounting was not compulsory: acquisition accounting could still be used.

The use of these conditions in SSAP 23 led to a number of difficulties and has been superseded by new conditions for the use of merger accounting, inserted in the Companies Act 1985 by the Companies Act 1989.[10] We shall explore these difficulties and provisions before turning to the later thinking of the standard setters as embodied in FRS 6.

Experience of SSAP 23

If we compare the consequences of using acquisition accounting and merger accounting in our simple example above, it is not hard to see why a company may prefer to use the merger method if it is available for a particular business combination. Under the merger method, the balance sheet figures for separable net assets are lower and no amount emerges for goodwill. Subsequent reported profits will be higher as depreciation will be based on lower asset values and there will be no goodwill to amortise. Thus, the merger method will result in higher returns on capital employed in the company's subsequent accounts than would be disclosed if the acquisition method were used.

Given the desire of companies to report their affairs in the best possible light, it is perhaps not surprising that numerous attempts were made to exploit the conditions included in SSAP 23 in order to be able to apply merger accounting. Let us look at a few examples.

Under SSAP 23 it was not possible to use merger accounting if the purchasing company held 20 per cent or more of the equity shares in the other company immediately prior to the offer. Where one company held more than 20 per cent in the other, it was easily able to reduce the holding below 20 per cent by 'warehousing' shares with a banker or other third party. Thus, by temporarily selling enough shares to take the holding below 20 per cent and buying them back in the general offer, it was able to satisfy this particular condition.

Other rather blatant exploitations of the specific conditions were the so-called 'vendor placing' and 'vendor rights' schemes. These were used where one company wished to buy shares in another for cash, or some other non-equity share consideration, but also wished to use merger accounting. A payment in cash would mean resources leaving the group and would require the use of acquisition accounting. In order to avoid this, some companies made a share for share exchange but gave the shareholders in the acquired company the power to convert the shares which they received into cash immediately, either by placing them with a third party or by selling them back to the shareholders in the acquiring company. The former was a vendor placing and the latter a vendor rights scheme. The end result was that shares had been

---

[10] Companies Act 1985, Schedule 4A, Para. 10.

purchased for cash but in such a way that merger accounting could be used. While no resources left the group, there was certainly no pooling or uniting of shareholders' interests of the two companies!

It is quite clear that some companies applied the letter rather than the spirit of the standard and the above perceived abuses of the standard brought much criticism from commentators.

FRS 6 Acquisitions and Mergers

Following the Companies Act 1989, which implemented the EC Seventh Directive on consolidated accounts, conditions for the use of merger accounting have now been incorporated in the law, and these conditions differ somewhat from those included in SSAP 23. This change, together with the criticisms discussed above, necessitated a revision of SSAP 23.

The legal conditions for the use of merger accounting are contained in Schedule 4A to Companies Act 1985 and are listed in Table 8.2.[11]

Table 8.2 Legal conditions for use of merger accounting

1   At least 90 per cent of the nominal value of the relevant shares in the undertaking acquired is held by or on behalf of the parent company and its subsidiary undertakings

2   The proportion referred to in condition 1 was attained pursuant to an arrangement providing for the issue of equity shares by the parent company or one or more of its subsidiary undertakings

3   The fair value of any consideration other than the issue of equity shares given pursuant to the arrangement by the parent company and its subsidiary undertakings did not exceed 10 per cent of the nominal value of the equity shares issued

4   Adoption of the merger method of accounting accords with generally accepted accounting principles or practice.

Although the conditions in Table 8.2 do not fix a maximum shareholding immediately prior to the combination, condition 3, that the fair value of any non-equity consideration does not exceed 10 per cent of the nominal value of the shares issued, is much stricter than the SSAP 23 condition that it did not exceed 10 per cent of the fair value of the total consideration given. Whereas the purpose of the SSAP 23 condition was clear, the new legal condition appears to lack any economic validity whatsoever.

Condition 4 leaves it to the standard setters to specify any further criteria for the use of merger accounting and their thinking, developed in ED 48 and FRED 6, can now be found in FRS 6 'Acquisitions and Mergers', issued in September 1994.

The approach taken in FRS 6 owes much to the Canadian standard setters[12] and restricts drastically the circumstances in which merger accounting may be used. The objective of the standard (Para. 1) makes this quite clear:

> to ensure that merger accounting is used only for those business combinations that are not, in substance, the acquisition of one entity by another but the formation of a new reporting entity as a substantially equal partnership where no party is dominant; to ensure the use of acquisition accounting for all other business combinations; and to ensure that in either case the financial statements provide relevant information concerning the effect of the combination.

---

[11] Schedule 4A, Para. 10. Schedule 4A was inserted in Companies Act 1985 from Schedule 2 Companies Act 1989.

[12] See Canadian Institute of Chartered Accountants (CICA) Handbook, Sec. 1580, 'Business Combinations', 1973.

The relative sizes of the combining entities, considered unimportant in earlier definitions, now become extremely important in the FRS 6 definition of a merger:

> A business combination that results in the creation of a new reporting entity formed from
> the combining parties, in which the shareholders of the combining entities come together in
> a partnership for the mutual sharing of the risks and benefits of the combined entity, and in
> which no party to the combination in substance obtains control over any other, or is seen to
> be dominant, whether by virtue of the proportion of its shareholders' rights in the combined
> entity, the influence of its directors or otherwise.

The standard (Paras. 6–12) then lists five criteria for determining whether this definition of a merger is met and these are summarised in Table 8.3. Where these criteria
are met, merger accounting is compulsory. In all other circumstances, except certain
group reconstructions, acquisition accounting must be used.

Whether the combination is an acquisition or merger, the standard specifies minimum disclosure requirements to enable users to understand the effect of the
combination. For all combinations, this disclosure must include the names of the
combining entities, the date of the combination and whether merger accounting or
acquisition accounting has been used.

When merger accounting has been used, the required disclosure includes an analysis of the principal components of the profit and loss account and statement of total
recognised gains and losses into amounts related to the merged entity after the date of
the merger and, for each party to the merger, amounts relating to that party for the
period up to the date of the merger. Comparative amounts for the preceding financial
year are also required. The standard also requires disclosure of the aggregate book
values of the net assets of each party at the date of the merger and any adjustments
made to these to achieve consistency of accounting policies between the parties as
well as a statement of the adjustments made to consolidated reserves.

Few business combinations meet the criteria for the existence of a merger laid
down in FRS 6 and hence the use of merger accounting is extremely rare. As always,
most business combinations will be acquisitions and the appropriate method of
accounting will be acquisition accounting as discussed at length in Chapter 9,
'Investments, groups, associates and joint ventures'.

Table 8.3 Criteria used to identify a merger

1 No party is portrayed as acquirer or acquired by the board or management of either party

2 All parties participate in selecting the management structure and personnel of the new entity
by consensus rather than purely by the exercise of voting rights

3 Relative sizes of the combining entities are not so disparate that one party dominates the
combined entity

4 Equity shareholders in the combining entities receive, as consideration, primarily equity shares
in the combined entity. Any non-equity consideration must be an immaterial proportion of the
fair value received[13]

5 The equity shareholders in the combining entities must not retain a material interest in the
future performance of only part of the combined entity. However, a combining entity may
divest itself of a peripheral part of its business and still meet the the definition of a merger.

---

[13]As we have seen, the law restricts the non-equity consideration to 10 per cent of the nominal value of the
equity shares issued.

The international position

The relevant international accounting standard IAS 22 'Business Combinations', first issued in 1983, has been revised subsequently in 1993 and 1998. This standard distinguishes between two different types of combination, an acquisition and a uniting of interests, and specifies different methods of accounting for each of these.

A uniting of interests, what the ASB describes as a merger, only occurs when an acquirer cannot be identified.[14]

Where there is an acquisition, then acquisition accounting must be used. However, as we explain in the last section of Chapter 9, IAS 22 provides a choice in that it specifies both a benchmark treatment and an allowed alternative treatment. The difference between them is the way in which the share of any minority interest is valued.[15] Suffice it to say, at this stage, that FRS 6 adopts the allowed alternative treatment for acquisitions.

Where there is a uniting of interests, then the 'pooling of interests' method of accounting must be used. This is the same as the merger method of accounting specified in FRS 6.

While FRS 6 is consistent with IAS 22, there appears to be a move towards the abolition of the merger/pooling of interests method of accounting. The group of international standard setters G4+1 issued a Position Paper in 1998 and this has subsequently been published as a Discussion Paper by the ASB.[16] This paper considers whether there should be a single method of accounting for business combinations and, if so, what it should be. It comes to the conclusion that the purchase method, that is the acquisition method of accounting in British terminology, should be used for all business combinations. The authors would welcome such an approach on both theoretical and practical grounds and await further developments.

Goodwill

Introduction

Goodwill is the term used by accountants to describe the difference between the value placed on a firm and the sum of the fair values of the assets and liabilities of the firm which are identified and recorded separately in the accounting system. There are two reasons why these values will not be equal. First, most firms possess not only the predominantly tangible assets listed in a balance sheet but also such intangible assets as 'managerial ability', 'efficient staff' and 'regional monopoly' which contribute to the value of the firm and yet are not included in a balance sheet. Second, there is the simple economic fact that assets operating together frequently have a much higher value than the sum of the values of those same assets operating separately.

Goodwill is usually only recorded in an accounting system when a company purchases an unincorporated business or acquires a subsidiary or associated undertaking

---

[14] See IASC Standing Interpretations Committee, Interpretation SIC-9 'Business Combinations – Classification either as Acquisitions or Uniting of Interests', 1998.

[15] *See* Chapter 9, p. 292.

[16] G4+1 Position Paper 'Recommendations for Achieving Convergence on the Methods of Accounting for Business Combinations', FASB, 1998, and Discussion Paper 'Business Combinations', ASB, London, December 1998.

and prepares consolidated accounts. In the former case the goodwill arises in the accounts of the purchasing company itself whereas, in the latter case, the goodwill arises only in the consolidated accounts. In both cases the goodwill is described as 'purchased goodwill' to distinguish it from internally-generated goodwill.

In the past goodwill has sometimes been calculated as the difference between the price paid and the sum of the book values of the individually identified assets less liabilities in the books of the acquired firm or company. Although this may simplify calculations, it makes little economic sense, as the values in the books of the acquired firm or company are irrelevant in determining the historical cost of assets to the acquiring company or group. In accounting for an acquisition it is necessary for the acquiring company or group to value the individual assets and liabilities at their fair values, which determine their historical cost to the acquiring company or group.[17] Thus, the total cost of the collection of net assets, tangible and intangible, must be apportioned between those assets and liabilities which are to be identified separately in the accounting system and those which are not so identified. The latter group are recorded in the accounting system as a balancing figure which is described as goodwill. Such goodwill will normally be positive, but FRS 10 'Goodwill and Intangible Assets' takes the view that it may be negative.[18] This may occur when the price paid for the collection of net assets is less than the sum of the fair values of the separable net assets, although the standard warns us that, where such negative goodwill emerges, the amounts allocated to the separable net assets should be reviewed to ensure that their fair values have not been overstated.

Internally-created goodwill is not recorded, whereas goodwill which results from a market transaction is. It is therefore important to recognise that when a goodwill figure appears in a set of accounts, it does not relate to the whole reporting entity but merely to one segment which has been acquired by purchase.[19] Once the purchase has been made, that segment may be merged with the other assets of the enlarged entity and will then no longer be separately identifiable.

With this background we may proceed to examine the problem of accounting for goodwill, assuming for the most part that the goodwill figure is positive.

Accounting for goodwill

Some possibilities

At the date of acquisition, goodwill represents the cost of acquiring certain intangible assets. As such is the case, the accruals concept would seem to dictate that the cost should be carried forward and matched against revenues of the periods expected to benefit from the use of such intangible assets. However, the future benefits may be

---

[17] See Companies Act 1985, Schedule 4A, Para. 9, which requires the use of fair values when a subsidiary is acquired, and FRS 9, Para. 31(a), which requires a similar treatment in the case of an associate or joint venture. FRS 7 'Fair Values in Acquisition Accounting' (September 1994) specifies standard accounting practice in relation to both the identification of assets and liabilities at the date of acquisition and their valuation. We discuss this topic in Chapter 9.

[18] Many accountants would not admit this possibility, arguing that the price paid must place a ceiling on the sum of the 'costs' of the separable net assets. See later section of this chapter on the International position.

[19] An exception to this general position occurs when the net assets of one firm are purchased by a newly formed entity. An example is the conversion of a sole tradership or partnership into a limited company. Provided the limited company acquires only the net assets of the firm and owns no other assets, the goodwill figure will relate to the whole business.

extremely uncertain and there may be no way of determining which benefits arise from the particular collection of intangible assets. Hence, the prudence convention would appear to suggest that no asset should be recognised; rather that the amount paid for goodwill should be written off.

Given that there is a conflict between fundamental accounting conventions, it is not surprising to find that various methods of accounting for goodwill have been proposed. If we ignore the impractical suggestion that goodwill for the whole entity be revalued on each balance sheet date, the various proposals may be summarised as follows:

(a) Retain goodwill at cost, unless there is a permanent fall in the value.
(b) Write off (amortise) the cost of goodwill over a period of years, which could be (i) its useful life, or (ii) a specific number of years, or (iii) its useful life subject to a maximum number of years.
(c) Write off goodwill immediately against reserves.

Some writers have argued that, in view of the unique nature of goodwill, the amount under (a) or (b) should appear, not as an asset, but as a 'dangling debit', that is as a deduction from share capital and reserves. This treatment can be regarded as a 'half-hearted' adoption of options (a) or (b) in that the information is provided but in such a way as to cast doubt upon its relevance.

Let us look at each of the proposals in turn.

The retention of goodwill at cost would seem to be justified only if the asset has an indefinite life. It is expected that this would rarely be true in the case of the particular intangible assets purchased, although the purchased benefits may, of course, be replaced by subsequent activities. If the intangible assets acquired do not have an indefinite life, it is necessary to recognise the possibility of a fall in the value of goodwill, but the determination of whether or not such a permanent fall has occurred will be an extremely difficult, if not impossible, task. It will certainly be difficult where the segment of the business which gave rise to the goodwill is no longer separately identifiable.

The amortisation of goodwill over a period of years is also subject to difficulties. In the first case, it is usually very difficult, if not impossible, to determine the useful life of goodwill, a residual category of assets measured by a balancing figure. In the second case, the selection of a specific number of years such as 5 or 40 is merely arbitrary, although the selection of a long period has the advantage that the results of no one period are significantly affected. The third case merely combines the difficulty of the first with the arbitrariness of the second.

The third proposal recognises that, after the year of acquisition, the retention of a goodwill figure relating to part of the business is unlikely to provide information useful to those interested in the affairs of the entity. It therefore requires its removal from the balance sheet by an immediate write-off against reserves.

In view of the different proposals which have been made and their associated problems, it is not surprising that standard setters have experienced considerable difficulty in deciding upon an appropriate standard accounting practice.

The approach of SSAP 22

SSAP 22 'Accounting for Goodwill' was issued in December 1994 and revised in July 1989. It was replaced by FRS 10 'Goodwill and Intangible Assets', which we discuss below, in December 1997.

Unless it was prepared to use the true and fair override, the retention of goodwill at its cost was not an option available to the ASC in drafting the original SSAP 22.

The Companies Act 1985 stated clearly that, where goodwill is treated as an asset, it must be amortised systematically over a period not exceeding its useful economic life.[20] However, this still left the possibility of amortisation or of immediate write-off of goodwill against reserves for, in the latter case, goodwill is not treated as an asset and hence the legal requirement for amortisation does not apply.

While SSAP 22 preferred companies to write off goodwill immediately against reserves, it also permitted them to capitalise goodwill and to amortise it in arriving at the profit or loss on ordinary activities.[21] Both methods could be used simultaneously in respect of different acquisitions.

The preferred method had two major advantages. First, it avoided the difficult task of estimating the useful life of goodwill. Second, it resulted in a consistent treatment of purchased goodwill and internally-generated goodwill. Given that the law does not permit companies to include internally-generated goodwill in their balance sheets, the write-off of purchased goodwill results in the consistent position that no company shows goodwill in its balance sheet.

A major bias with the above requirements was that, if goodwill was capitalised and amortised, future profits and earnings per share would be reduced, whereas, if goodwill was written off against reserves, there would be no impact on the profit and loss account at all! Not surprisingly the vast majority of companies adopted the preferred method of accounting under SSAP 22, often taking some pretty extreme steps to be able to do so.

Experience of SSAP 22

Before we explore the ways in which companies responded to SSAP 22, it will, perhaps, be helpful if we illustrate how large goodwill may be in relation to the other net assets of a company at the date of acquisition. A good, but extreme, example was provided in the annual accounts of Saatchi and Saatchi Company plc, a consulting firm, for the year to 30 September 1986. The prices paid for subsidiaries, the tangible net assets acquired, and the resulting goodwill in respect of that year were as follows:

	£m
Cost of acquisitions	443.2
Net tangible assets	41.2
Goodwill	402.0

A more recent example is provided in the annual accounts of Thorn EMI plc for the year to 31 March 1993, a year in which Thorn EMI plc acquired the Virgin Music Group Limited from Richard Branson:

	Total	Virgin Music Group Ltd	Other
	£m	£m	£m
Cost of acquisitions	653.7	593.0	60.7
Fair value of net assets acquired	17.3	14.1	3.2
Goodwill	636.4	578.9	57.5

[20] Companies Act 1985, Sec. 4, Para. 21.
[21] SSAP 22, Paras. 32–35.

In both of these cases, goodwill dwarfed the identifiable net assets, as might be expected in any successful company or group where people are the most important assets.

Given that large amounts have been paid to acquire valuable goodwill, there was a considerable reluctance among many companies to write off that goodwill in accordance with SSAP 22. One response was to isolate an element of goodwill as 'brands' and to retain this in the balance sheet.[22] Such an approach raised considerable controversy and, in ED 52 'Accounting for Intangible Fixed Assets' (May 1990), the ASC attempted to outlaw separate accounting for brands. We shall examine the approach of the ASB later in this chapter.

Once faced with the need to account for goodwill in accordance with SSAP 22, it is perhaps not surprising to find that the vast majority of companies chose immediate write-off rather than amortisation through the profit and loss account with its consequent impact on earnings per share. The way in which many large companies did so makes interesting reading.

If a company wished to adopt the policy of immediate write-off, the first question which had to be answered, on which SSAP 22 was silent, was which reserves could be used for the purpose of writing off goodwill. There was widespread agreement that the balance on the profit and loss account and any merger reserve could be used for this purpose, but there was dispute over whether the law permitted the use of a revaluation reserve. Although there was a large body of opinion to the effect that a revaluation reserve could not be used for this purpose, many companies chose to ignore this opinion.[23]

The next problem arose when the 'available' reserves were too small to absorb a write-off of goodwill and here we found two major responses.

Some companies effectively used share premium accounts to write off goodwill. They applied to the courts for a reduction of capital in order to be able to comply with the preferred method of accounting under SSAP 22. The share premium accounts were effectively relabelled, perhaps as a special reserve, thus becoming available to absorb the goodwill write-off.[24]

The second response was to create an appropriate reserve, a 'goodwill write-off' reserve, with a zero balance. The purchased goodwill could be written off against this goodwill write-off reserve resulting in a debit balance, a negative reserve, which was deducted from the share capital and reserves in the consolidated balance sheet.[25]

As well as provoking the above responses, the preference of SSAP 22 for immediate write-off appears to have had certain other consequences. By understating the fair values of the identifiable assets and liabilities, groups have been able to increase the amount labelled as goodwill and, given that this goodwill is written off to reserves, future reported profits benefited from reduced depreciation charges on the identified tangible and intangible assets purchased.

---

[22] Some companies have gone further than this by including the values of internally-generated brands as well as those which have been purchased. Good examples of companies which accounted for brands are Rank Hovis McDougall and Grand Metropolitan.

[23] Since Companies Act 1989, the Revaluation Reserve is definitely not available for the write-off of goodwill, Companies Act 1985, Schedule 4, Para. 34.

[24] Examples of companies which employed such an approach are Saatchi and Saatchi in 1985 and 1986 and Blue Arrow plc in 1987. A capital redemption reserve could presumably also be used in this way.

[25] Examples of groups which have used this 'dangling debit disclosure' are Erskine House Group plc and TI Group plc.

Particular variants of this have involved the creation, at the date of acquisition, of a provision for reorganisation costs and sometimes even a provision for future losses. Such provisions reduce the identified net assets and again increase the goodwill written off against reserves. They are then available to absorb costs which would otherwise have to be charged to the profit and loss account, and any unused amount could, in due course, be credited to the profit and loss account. Although it is possible to justify the setting up of such provisions, some groups have undoubtedly set up excessive provisions. As we have seen in Chapter 5, FRS 12 'Provisions, Contingent Liabilities and Contingent Assets' now outlaws this approach as does FRS 7 'Fair Values in Acquisition Accounting', to which we return later in this chapter.

It was developments such as those outlined above which caused the ASC to issue a revised version of SSAP 22 in July 1989. The purpose of this standard was not to change the practice of accounting for goodwill, but to provide additional disclosure to help the users of accounts to understand what had been done.[26] Thus companies were required to show how goodwill had been dealt with and to provide the table, subsequently required by law, showing the book values and fair values of each major category of assets and liabilities, together with an explanation of reasons for differences. In addition, it required disclosure of movements on provisions related to acquisitions and of information relating to the treatment of disposals of previously acquired businesses or business segments.

Even as the revised SSAP 22 was being issued, the accounting treatment of goodwill was under review and this led to the very different proposals in ED 47 'Accounting for Goodwill', which was published in February 1990.

Towards a new standard

ED 47 took a very different view from SSAP 22. Whereas SSAP 22 favoured immediate write-off and permitted amortisation, ED 47 removed any choice and proposed that all goodwill should be amortised over its useful economic life. Whereas SSAP 22 attempted to achieve consistency between the treatment of purchased goodwill and non-purchased goodwill, ED 47 attempted to achieve consistency between the treatment of goodwill and other purchased intangible and tangible fixed assets. So, because buildings, machinery and trademarks are depreciated over their useful economic lives, it was argued that goodwill should be amortised.

ED 47 therefore proposed that positive goodwill should be amortised through the profit and loss account over its useful economic life using the straight-line basis or any other systematic basis which is more conservative and considered to give a more realistic allocation. However, it added the proviso that the useful economic life should not exceed 20 years, except in rare circumstances, and that the maximum life, even in those rare circumstances, should never exceed 40 years. These are provisions we do not find in standards dealing with tangible fixed assets! However, in common with similar provisions in respect of tangible fixed assets, ED 47 envisaged that there should be an annual review to ensure that the carrying value of goodwill was not excessive.

The exposure draft admitted the possibility of negative goodwill although, should such goodwill arise, it proposed a review of the fair values ascribed to the 'identifiable' assets and liabilities. Any negative goodwill remaining after such a review was to be credited to the profit and loss account over a suitable period.

---

[26] The additional disclosure requirements were contained in paragraphs 47–53 of the revised standard.

The accounting treatment of goodwill proposed in ED 47 was very different from the preferred treatment of SSAP 22 adopted by the vast majority of UK companies. Given the potential impact of the proposed approach on reported profits, it is perhaps not surprising that there was considerable opposition to ED 47 and, partly due to the demise of the ASC, it was never converted into an accounting standard. As we shall see, the subsequent proposals of the ASB are rather more sophisicated, although we shall argue that the resulting standard, FRS 10 'Goodwill and Intangible Assets', suffers from spurious sophistication.

ASB pronouncements

It was not until December 1993 that the ASB produced its first discussion paper on this subject entitled 'Goodwill and Intangible Assets'.

In its proposed treatment of intangible assets the discussion paper was clear: purchased intangible assets, such as brands, should be subsumed within purchased goodwill and accounted for accordingly, although purchased legal rights, such as patents, attaching to internally-created intangible benefits should be capitalised at their historical cost and amortised appropriately (Paras. 1.7 and 3.1.3).

When it turned to the subject of accounting for purchased goodwill there was much less certainty. The paper identified the six methods of accounting for goodwill shown in Table 8.4. Three methods involved the recognition of goodwill as an asset while three methods involved the elimination of goodwill.

Table 8.4 Methods of accounting for goodwill

A – Asset-based methods

1 *Capitalisation and amortisation over a predetermined* life subject to a maximum number of years, possibly 20, and subject to the usual test of recoverability at the end of each year.

2 *Capitalisation and annual review.* Under this approach, the value of goodwill is assessed at each balance sheet date using certain 'ceiling' tests described at length in Appendix A to the Discussion Paper. These involve comparing the present value of the cash flows from the relevant segment of the business with the sum of the fair values of the separable assets and liabilities of that segment to determine the value of goodwill. Amortisation through the profit and loss account is only necessary if the value so determined is less than the existing carrying value of the goodwill.

3 *Combination of 1 and 2* with 1 being the norm and 2 being used when the goodwill has an indeterminate life expected to be more than 20 years.

B – Elimination methods

1 *Immediate write-off against reserves,* the preferred method of SSAP 22.

2 *Creation of a separate goodwill write-off reserve* with disclosure as a 'dangling debit', a deduction from share capital and reserves. Under this approach no further adjustment would be made to the goodwill write-off reserve unless the acquired segment of the group to which it relates is disposed of or closed.

3 *Variant of 2* involving creation of a separate goodwill write-off reserve but with an annual assessment of recoverability to ensure that the goodwill write-off reserve is reduced if the value of the goodwill has fallen permanently.

Although the discussion paper provided extensive discussion of the merits and demerits of the various methods, it failed to identify any single proposed approach.

Indeed it identified two very different approaches which had support among Board members, namely methods A3 and B2 or B3. Method A3 is itself a combination of A1 and A2, while methods B2 and B3 both involve the creation of a separate goodwill write-off reserve, either with (B3) or without (B2) a recoverability test. In other words, the Board envisaged possible ways forward which might have been described by a cynic as anything other than the preferred method of SSAP 22 – B1!

It came as no surprise that no consensus emerged in the responses to the Discussion Paper, although there was considerable opposition to the proposal that all intangible assets should be subsumed within purchased goodwill. To move matters forward, the ASB issued a working paper in June 1995 entitled 'Goodwill and Intangible Assets' for discussion at public hearings, the first such hearings to be held in the UK. This working paper and associated public hearings paved the way for the issue of FRED 12 'Goodwill and Intangible Assets' in June 1996 and FRS 10, with the same title, in December 1997.

FRS10 'Goodwill and Intangible Assets'

The ASB follows the provisions of company law by specifying that purchased goodwill should be capitalised and shown on the face of the balance sheet or consolidated balance sheet while internally generated goodwill should not be capitalised.

It requires that an intangible asset purchased separately should be capitalised at its cost while an intangible asset acquired as part of a purchase of a business should only be capitalised separately from goodwill if its fair value can be measured reliably; otherwise such an intangible should be subsumed within the amount shown for purchased goodwill.

On the purchase of a business, the amount of purchased goodwill will therefore be calculated as the difference between two values:

	£
Price paid to acquire business	X
less Sum of fair values of assets and liabilities identified and to be recorded separately in the accounting system, including intangible assets which can be measured reliably	<u>X</u>
Purchased goodwill, including intangible assets which cannot be measured reliably	<u>X</u>

We will deal first with the normal situation where purchased goodwill is positive and turn to negative goodwill later in the chapter.

Having required their capitalisation, the standard then attempts to ensure that 'capitalised goodwill and intangible assets are charged to the profit and loss account in the periods they are depleted' (Para. 1(a)). In the view of the ASB, such depletion only occurs 'to the extent that the carrying value of the goodwill is not supported by the current value of the goodwill within the acquired business' (Summary Para. (e)). We shall argue that this approach is fundamentally unsound.

In spite of these general principles, the ASB envisages that in practice goodwill and intangible assets will be amortised over their useful economic lives. Recognising the inevitable subjectivity, some would say impossibility, involved in estimating such lives and the potential desire of directors to overestimate them in order to minimise the amortisation expense in the profit and loss account, the standard contains a presumption that the useful economic life of purchased goodwill and intangibles does not exceed twenty years. The presumption is rebuttable so the standard accepts that the useful economic life may exceed twenty years and even that it may, in some cases, be indefinite so that no amortisation will be necessary. The grounds for adopting a life greater than twenty years must be clearly explained and, where an indefinite life is envisaged, the company must disclose the fact that it is invoking the true and fair override and explain why it is doing so.

In accordance with the provisions of FRS 11 'Impairment of Fixed Assets and Goodwill', which we have explored in the context of tangible and intangible fixed assets in Chapter 4, it is necessary to ensure that the carrying values of goodwill and intangible assets do not exceed their recoverable amounts. This necessitates an impairment review but FRS 10 identifies two different triggers for an impairment review: where the estimated useful economic life does not exceed twenty years, an impairment review is required at the end of the first full financial year following the initial recognition and subsequently if events or changes in circumstances indicate that its carrying value may not be recoverable in full. We shall describe this as a 'prompted' impairment review. Where the estimated useful economic life is expected to exceed twenty years, the ASB requires companies to conduct an annual impairment review. Figure 8.2 summarises the requirements of FRS 10.

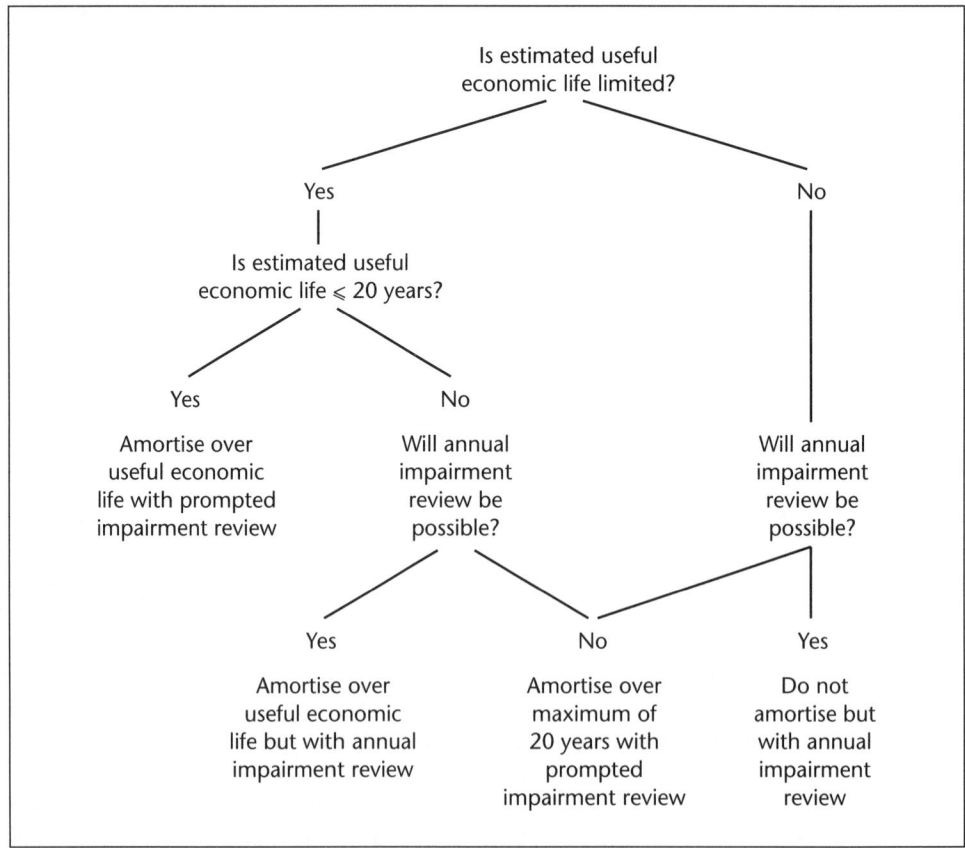

Figure 8.2 Treatment of positive goodwill and intangibles

Impairment reviews

Company law requires that provision be made for the diminution in value of any fixed asset when the diminution in value is expected to be permanent. Such impairment occurs when the recoverable amount of an asset falls permanently below its carrying value and, as we have seen in Chapter 4, FRS 11 'Impairment of Fixed Assets and Goodwill' attempts to standardise accounting practice in this area. As we shall demonstrate, it is more difficult to conduct an impairment review for goodwill than it is for other assets.

As we have explained, FRS 11 distinguishes between what we have described as a prompted impairment review and an annual impairment review but the conduct of the review is the same. To conduct an impairment review it is necessary to compare the carrying value of an asset with its recoverable amount. Recoverable amount is defined as shown in Figure 8.3.

Net realisable value is the proceeds which would be received from selling an asset less any direct selling costs, while the value in use is the present value of the estimated future cash flows which the asset is expected to produce. As we have seen in Chapter 4, the major problem of applying such reviews in practice is that it is rarely possible to estimate the cash flows produced by a single asset. Groups of assets are used to produce cash flows. FRS 11 therefore proposes that impairment reviews be undertaken for the smallest group of assets, defined as an income generating unit, which produce a largely independent income stream. In the case of purchased goodwill, the income generating unit is the business acquired which gave rise to the purchased goodwill and, as we shall see, this introduces conceptual and practical problems of a high order.

Let us assume first that the business acquired is not merged in any way with the business of the acquiring company but, rather, that it remains a separately identifiable business unit. According to FRS 11, an impairment review would require a comparison of the value of the acquired business on a subsequent balance sheet date with the sum of the carrying values of the assets and liabilities, including purchased goodwill, relating to that business unit on that same date. Provided the value of the business exceeds the sum of the carrying values there is no impairment whereas, if the reverse is the case, impairment must be recognised by writing down relevant assets.

If impairment on this basis has occurred then, if there is evidence that there is an impairment of any specific asset, that asset should be written down. Otherwise the impairment should be allocated as follows:

(a) first to any goodwill in the unit;
(b) thereafter to any capitalised intangible asset in the unit; and
(c) finally, to the tangible assets in the unit, on a prorata or more appropriate basis.
(FRS 11, Para. 48.)

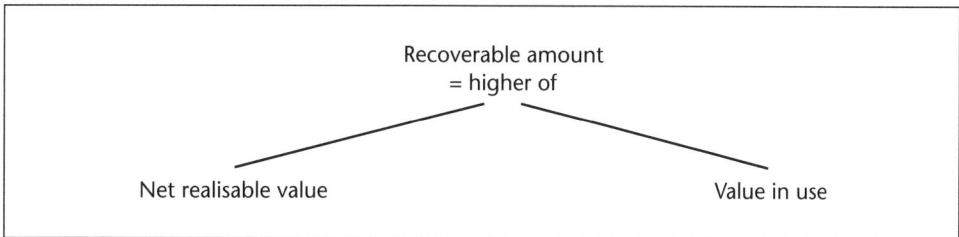

Fig. 8.3 Recoverable amount

Thus the more subjective values are written down first.

In our view, this approach is fundamentally flawed because the value of the business unit on any balance sheet date subsequent to the date of acquisition will reflect both goodwill created internally since the date of acquisition and any unrecognised gains and losses on the separable assets and liabilities shown in the balance sheet.

Let us explore this point in an example by supposing that a wholly owned subsidiary was acquired on 1 January 1991 and that it still exists as a separately identifiable unit ten years later on 31 December 2000. Positive purchased goodwill of £90 000 was recognised on acquisition and this is being amortised on a straight line basis over thirty years. To conduct an impairment review on 31 December 2000 it would be necessary to value the investment in the subsidiary, usually by discounting the expected future cash flows of the subsidiary, and to compare this value with the sum of the carrying values of assets and liabilities of the subsidiary plus the carrying value of the purchased goodwill:

	£000	£000
Value of investment in subsidiary – say		500
less Sum of carrying values:		
Separately identified assets and liabilities – say	400	
Purchased goodwill (90 000 – 10(3000))	60	
		460
Surplus		40

On the basis proposed by FRS 11, there is no impairment on the grounds that the carrying value of the purchased goodwill is supported by the current value of the goodwill within the acquired unit on 31 December 2000. However, the value of the investment on 31 December 2000 reflects goodwill generated internally since 1 January 1991 as well as any unrecognised gains and losses in respect of the tangible assets and liabilities. Let us suppose that we were to revalue the separately identified assets and liabilities to produce a sum of £420 000, rather than £400 000, and that we were able, in some magical way, to value the goodwill generated internally since acquisition at £50 000, the position would be as follows:

	£000	£000
Value of investment in subsidiary – as before		500
Sum of current values of separately identified assets and liabilities	420	
Carrying value of purchased goodwill	60	
Value of internally generated goodwill not recognised	50	
		530
Impairment		(30)

Given relevant information, there has clearly been an impairment and the carrying value of purchased goodwill should be written down by £30 000, from £60 000 to £30 000. The FRS 11 approach fails completely to pick this up.

We are not suggesting for one moment that this alternative approach is feasible but, rather, illustrating why the ASB approach fails to identify whether or not impairment has occurred.

In addition to this fundamental flaw, there is a further problem. It will often be the case that an acquired business, for which purchased goodwill has been recognised, will be merged with other businesses of the acquirer. This would mean that the acquired business unit would no longer be identifiable at a subsequent balance sheet date. Although a sensible accountant might be tempted to recognise this as a clear example of a situation where an impairment review was impossible, the ASB attempts to provide a means of conducting a review in such circumstances and also provides us with a fall-back position.

Let us suppose that A plc acquired an unincorporated business B on 1 January 1991 and recognised purchased goodwill of £300 000, which is being amortised on a straight line basis over its estimated useful life of 30 years. Let us also assume that the net assets of A plc and B have subsequently been merged to produce one income generating unit. How is it possible to conduct an impairment review after ten years on 31 December 2000?

Using the approach promulgated in FRS 11, we would first have to estimate the internally generated goodwill in A plc at the date of acquisition, 1 January 1991; we will assume that this was £600 000. On 31 December 2000 we would then have to value the income generating unit, A plus B, and compare this value with the sum of the carrying values of the assets and liabilities in the balance sheet, which include purchased goodwill, together with the unrecognised internally generated goodwill which we have estimated, suitably amortised. If we assume that an appropriate amortisation method for the internally generated goodwill in A plc is straight line over say twenty years, then the calculation might run as follows:

Impairment review on 31 December 2000

	£000	£000
Value of income generating unit (A+B) – say		2 000
Sum of carrying values of separately identified assets and liabilities	1 900	
Purchased goodwill in B, less amortisation (£300 000 – [10 × £10 000])	200	
Unrecognised goodwill in A, less amortisation (£600 000 – [10 × £30 000])	300	
		2 400
Impairment		(400)

FRS 11 requires that this impairment be allocated on a pro-rata basis to purchased and internally generated goodwill:

	£000
Impairment allocated to:	
Purchased goodwill 200/(200 + 300) × £400 000	160
Unrecognised goodwill 300/(200 + 300) × £400 000	240
	400

Only the amount allocated to purchased goodwill would be recognised in the financial statements. So the carrying value of purchased goodwill would be reduced by £160 000, from £200 000 to £40 000, and this amount would be charged to the profit and loss account.

While these calculations give the appearance of precision, the numbers produced are subjective and arbitrary and fundamentally flawed. Both the estimation of the internally generated goodwill in A plc on 1 January 1991 and the valuation of the income generating unit on 31 December 2000 are difficult tasks. But, even if reasonable estimates of these can be made, the approach suffers from the fundamental conceptual error that the valuation of the income generating unit on 31 December 2000 includes both unrecognised valuation changes in individual assets and liabilities as well as goodwill generated internally between 1 January 1991 and 31 December 2000.

While the ASB makes reference to extensive consultation and field testing of such impairment reviews, the conceptual and practical problems of conducting such reviews appear to be immense. We therefore take some consolation in the fall-back position that, where goodwill is not capable of continued measurement so that annual reviews are not feasible, the goodwill should be amortised over a maximum period of twenty years.

Even this suffers from conceptual problems. Where the expected useful economic life of goodwill does not exceed twenty years, what we have described as a prompted impairment review may become necessary. Such impairment reviews are necessary 'if events or changes in circumstances indicate that the carrying values may not be recoverable'. In an extreme situation where events or circumstances indicate that the value of the goodwill is zero, there will be no problem. However, in a less extreme situation, the FRS 11 approach puts us in an impossible position: an expected life not exceeding twenty years has been selected because it is impossible to conduct an impairment review but then an event or change of circumstances triggers the need for such a review! The logic of the ASB proposals here leaves much to be desired.

Purchased goodwill is the term used by accountants to describe a residual category of assets measured by a balancing figure. Given the difficulty of estimating the useful economic life of such a creature and the virtual impossibility of conducting sensible impairment reviews, we shall not be at all surprised to find that most companies amortise their positive purchased goodwill over a period of twenty years. Whatever they do, amounts attributed to goodwill in financial statements are likely to be rather short on economic meaning.

Negative goodwill

Let us turn next to the subject of negative goodwill, which occurs when the sum of the fair values of the individual assets and liabilities recognised on acquisition exceed the cost of the acquisition.

Given that accountants use fair values to determine the historical cost to the new owner of the individual assets and liabilities recognised at the date of acquisition, many accountants would argue that there can be no such phenomena as negative goodwill. This is certainly the position taken by Accounting Principles Board Opinion 16 in the USA, which makes it absolutely clear that the sum of the 'costs' of the individually identified assets and liabilities cannot exceed the cost of the business or investment purchased. Where negative goodwill appears on an initial calculation, APB Opinion 16 requires that the recorded costs of the non-monetary assets be reduced to eliminate that goodwill. In our view, this is the only approach which is compatible with the use of historical cost accounting.

FRS 10 does not accept this strict historical cost approach. The ASB envisages situations where negative goodwill may arise as, for example, when a bargain purchase has been made or where future reorganisation costs must be incurred consequential upon the acquisition but these costs do not satisfy the criteria for recognition as provisions at the date of acquisition. Where such negative goodwill emerges, the standard exhorts us to have a closer look at the values attributed to the identified assets and liabilities to see whether these should be amended.

Once having permitted, indeed required, the recognition of negative goodwill, FRS 10 then has to confront the problem of how to account for it. The standard takes the view that negative goodwill should be shown next to positive goodwill among the assets in a balance sheet and that it should be recognised through the profit and loss account over the period when the non-monetary assets acquired are used or sold. Given that there will probably be a large collection of non-monetary assets with varying lives, the determination of this relevant period is beset with problems and is bound to be arbitrary. As with positive goodwill, any figure which appear in a profit and loss account or balance sheet in respect of negative goodwill is almost certain to lack any economic meaning whatsoever.

Disclosure requirements
FRS 10 requires substantial disclosures concerning positive goodwill, negative goodwill and intangible assets. We have not attempted to summarise this disclosure but rather direct readers to the relevant paragraphs of FRS 10, namely paragraphs 52 to 64.

The international position
There are a number of International Standards relevant to the treatment of goodwill, namely:

IAS 22 'Business Combinations' (revised 1998);
IAS 36 'Impairment of Assets' (1998); and
IAS 38 'Intangible Assets' (1998).

IAS 38 prohibits the recognition of internally generated goodwill as an asset. IAS 22 requires that purchased goodwill should be recognised and accepts that it may be positive or negative.

Positive goodwill must be recognised as an asset and amortised, on a systematic basis, over its useful economic life. As under FRS 10, there is a rebuttable presumption that the useful economic life will not exceed twenty years. However, unlike FRS 10, IAS 22 takes the view that 'the useful life of goodwill is always finite' (Para. 51). IAS 36 requires impairment reviews similar to those required by FRS 11, and IAS 22 requires that, as a minimum, there must be an annual impairment review when goodwill has a life exceeding twenty years.

Like FRS 10, IAS 22 permits the recognition of negative goodwill and lays down rules to govern its recognition through the income statements. The carrying value of negative goodwill is to be treated as a deduction from assets under the same balance sheet classification as positive goodwill.

Conclusion
It is easy to be critical of the ways in which standard setters have dealt with goodwill but it is instructive to ponder why they have found the topic difficult and to suggest a different approach to the solution of the problem.

Under the conventional historical cost accounting system, purchased goodwill may be included in balance sheets but internally generated goodwill may not be included. As the ASB wisely points out, every method of accounting for this purchased goodwill is inconsistent with other aspects of financial accounting. If the purchased goodwill is recognised, this is inconsistent with the treatment of internally generated goodwill. If purchased goodwill is eliminated, this is inconsistent with the treatment of other fixed assets. While SSAP 22 preferred the elimination of purchased goodwill, FRS 10 has moved to the other end of the spectrum by requiring the recognition and amortisation of purchased goodwill.

As we have seen, FRS 10 even accepts that goodwill may have an indefinite life. The fundamental question here is whether after, say, fifty years of successful operations, the current goodwill is the original purchased goodwill or goodwill which has been created in the subsequent period. We have no doubts as to the answer to this question and are extremely sceptical of the view that goodwill can have an indefinite life. We therefore feel more comfortable with the view of IAS 22 that 'the useful life of goodwill is always finite'.

Even if we confine ourselves to a situation where the expected useful economic life of goodwill is finite, there must be severe doubts about any estimate of the useful economic life of this goodwill which is, after all, computed as a balancing figure representing a residual category of assets not recognised separately in the accounting system. Any estimate of the useful life of such a creature must be both subjective and arbitrary so that any figure for goodwill which appears in a balance sheet or profit and loss account is likely to be lacking in economic meaning.

The ASB seeks to ensure that the carrying value of goodwill does not exceed its recoverable amount but, as we have demonstrated, the FRS 11 approach to impairment reviews is conceptually unsound and may actually result in the inclusion of internally generated goodwill in the balance sheet in some circumstances.

In our view, the treatment of goodwill will remain an intractable problem while we continue to attempt to force all relevant financial information into an articulated set of financial statements. Even where individual assets and liabilities are shown at their current values, the financial statements of a business do not attempt to provide a valuation of the business. Goodwill usually derives from a past valuation of a part of the business. How can such different approaches possibly be reconciled?

Our preferred solution is quite simple. Given the impossibility of arriving at any meaningful figures for goodwill in the primary financial statements, all goodwill should be written off immediately. However, larger companies should then be required to present a separate statement which summarises and aggregates the current values of the individual assets and liabilities recognised in the financial statements on the balance sheet date and, in addition, provides an estimate of the valuation of the whole business, perhaps based on its market capitalisation. The difference between these two totals provides an indication of the value of goodwill of the company or group on the balance sheet date. Such a figure may be explained and discussed and would seem to sit comfortably with the ASB's attempt to deflect attention from any one number in the financial statements towards a larger set of relevant information.[27]

---

[27] As we explain in Chapter 18, a similar approach was proposed in the Discussion Document 'Making Corporate Reports Valuable', Institute of Chartered Accountants of Scotland, Kogan Page, London, 1988. Readers are referred to the proposed 'Assets and Liabilities Statement' discussed in Chapter 7 of that report.

The value for goodwill would, of course, be highly subjective but the subjectivity would be apparent and such an approach would be far from the spurious accuracy of the figures required by FRS 10.

We find it hard to imagine that FRS 10 will be the final word on accounting for goodwill and intangible assets.

Recommended reading

J.A. Arnold, D. Egginton, L. Kirkham, R.H. Macve and K. Peasnell, 'Goodwill and other intangibles', ICAEW, London, October 1992.

T.E. Cooke, *Mergers and Acquisitions*, Blackwell, Oxford, 1986.

M.C. Miller, 'Goodwill – an aggregation issue', *The Accounting Review*, April 1973.

M.A. Weinberg and M.V. Blank, *Takeovers and Mergers*, Vols 1 and 2, 5th edn by L. Rabinovitz, Sweet and Maxwell, 1989.

9 Investments, groups, associates and joint ventures

Overview Investments by one entity in another take many different forms, ranging from simple or passive investments at one end of the spectrum to investments which command control of the investee's activities, assets and liabilities at the other end of the spectrum.

This chapter is divided into four sections of which the first examines the treatment of investments in the financial statements of an investing company.

The second section deals with accounting for groups using the acquisition method of accounting and pays particular attention to the treatment of acquisitions and disposals. It therefore draws upon the relevant provisions of the following standards:

- FRS 2 *Accounting for Subsidiary Undertakings* (July 1992)
- FRS 6 *Acquisitions and Mergers* (September 1994)
- FRS 7 *Fair Values in Acquisition Accounting* (September 1994)

The third section deals with accounting for associates and joint ventures and, after exploring both proportional consolidation and the equity method of accounting as possible methods of accounting for such interests, it discusses the provisions of:

- FRS 9 *Accounting for associates and joint ventures* (November 1997)

The final section identifies relevant international accounting standards and focuses on major differences between UK and international standards.

Investments

Many companies hold investments in other entities and it is therefore necessary to determine how these investments are to be treated in the financial statements of the reporting entity. As we shall see, the treatment of investments in the financial statements of an individual company is relatively straightforward but, as soon as an investment is sufficient to give influence or control over the affairs of the investee, things become more complicated.

Investments may range from simple or passive investments, held to obtain dividends and potential capital growth, to those which give the investing company control over the activities, assets and liabilities of the investee. The revised exposure draft of the 'Statement of Principles for Financial Reporting' distinguishes four different categories of investment, as shown in Table 9.1.[1]

In drawing up this table, we have assumed that all four categories involve investments in entities but FRS 9 'Associates and Joint Ventures' (November 1997) also

---

[1] 'Statement of Principles for Financial Reporting', Revised Exposure Draft, ASB, London, March 1999: Chapter 8 'Accounting for interests in other entities'.

Table 9.1 Four categories of investment

Degree of influence	Control	Joint control	Significant influence	Lesser or no influence
Resulting categorisation	Subsidiary	Joint venture	Associate	Simple or passive investment

identifies a joint arrangement which is not an entity. We shall discuss accounting for all five types of interest in this chapter.

We start by examining the accounting treatment of investments in the individual financial statements of the investing company. This treatment is the same whatever the degree of control or influence it exercises over the investee.

We then move to the other end of the spectrum and, in the second section of the chapter, 'Accounting for groups', we focus on situations where the investment is large enough to give control. Where this occurs, the investee is a subsidiary undertaking and, subject to certain exceptions, the investing company must prepare group accounts. Since the enactment of the Companies Act 1989, these group accounts must be consolidated accounts[2] and relevant standard accounting practice is contained in FRS 2 'Accounting for Subsidiary Undertakings'. We examine the definition of a group and the possible exclusion of subsidiaries from the consolidated accounts before turning to some of the questions which must be answered in accounting for the purchase and sale of subsidiaries. As we have seen in Chapter 8, merger accounting is likely to be extremely rare in future and, in this chapter, we shall be concerned only with aquisition accounting.

In the third section of the chapter, we turn to the intermediate categories of investment which give partial influence over the investee, that is investments in associates and joint ventures, as well as joint arrangements that are not entities. We compare and contrast the two contenders as methods of accounting for such interests, namely the equity method of accounting and proportional consolidation. We then discuss the rather unhelpful legal provisions and the present source of standard accounting practice FRS 9 'Associates and Joint Ventures', which was issued in November 1997.

In the final section of the chapter, we examine the pronouncements of the International Accounting Standards Committee on the subject matter of this chapter and draw attention to the major differences which presently exist between these and the British standards.

Individual company financial statements

The key to determining the treatment of an investment in the shares of another company in the financial statements of the investing company is *intention*. If the investment is intended to be for the long term, it will be treated as a fixed asset; if for the short term, it will be treated as a current asset. In a traditional historical cost balance sheet, a fixed asset investment is shown at its historical cost unless its value has been impaired, in which case it is written down to its recoverable amount. A current asset investment is shown at the lower of cost and net realisable value. The carrying value used for an

---

[2] Companies Act 1985, Sec. 227, Para. 2.

impaired fixed asset investment will differ from that of a current asset investment when its value in use, or present value, exceeds its net realisable value and this sensibly reflects the management decision to retain, rather than to sell, the investment.

For both types of investment it is usual to take credit in the profit and loss account of the investing company for dividends received and receivable, although dividends receivable are only recognised to the extent that they are in respect of accounting periods ended on or before the accounting year-end of the investing company and have been declared prior to approval of the investing company's own accounts. Some companies are even more prudent and take credit only for dividends received in an accounting period.

The above accounting treatments provide limited information to users of the investing company's accounts and, in order to remedy this, some companies have taken advantage of the alternative accounting rules to show investments at their current value.[3] In such cases, any revaluation surplus must be taken to a revaluation reserve and any revaluation deficit must be taken to the revaluation reserve to the extent that that reserve contains a revaluation surplus in respect of the same investment but otherwise must be charged to the profit and loss account.

In its death throes in July 1990, the ASC issued Exposure Draft 55 'Accounting for Investments' and this made proposals in respect of both fixed asset and current asset investments. It proposed that, where a company adopts the alternative accounting rules to show fixed asset investments at a valuation, that amount should be kept up to date by an annual revaluation. However, its major proposal for change was in accounting for certain current asset investments, namely those which are 'readily marketable'. In the view of the ASC, such investments should be stated in a balance sheet at their quoted current value and any difference between that current value and the previous carrying value should be reflected in the profit and loss account. Hence the profit and loss account would reflect not only the dividends receivable but also any changes in the value of such an investment during an accounting year. In the view of the ASC any such change would be a realised profit or loss on the grounds that it has been reliably measured by reference to a quoted price.[4]

While many accountants applauded the ASC for attempting to ensure that such changes in value are reflected in a profit and loss account, there were severe doubts about the legality of the proposed method of accounting for readily marketable current asset investments.[5] The method which was proposed did not comply with the historical cost accounting rules, which require such current asset investments to be shown at the lower of cost and net realisable value, nor with the alternative accounting rules which require any revaluation surplus to be taken, not to the profit and loss account, but to a revaluation reserve. The ASC was well aware that its proposals could only be introduced by relying on the true and fair override or if there were to be a change of law.[6] These

---

[3] The rules on what is an acceptable current value differ for fixed assets and current assets respectively. (See Companies Act 1985, Schedule 4, Sec. C, Paras. 31(3) and 31(4).) Thus, a current asset investment may be shown at its current cost, while a fixed asset investment may be shown at its market value or any other value which the directors consider to be appropriate. In the latter case, the method of valuation adopted and the reasons for adopting it must be stated.

[4] ED 55 'Accounting for Investments', July 1990, Para. 43. As we have seen in Chapter 3, there are different ways of defining realisation. ED 55 took the view that a profit or loss made due to a change in value of a readily marketable current asset investment is realised because the value of that investment can be reliably measured. In its view, the investment did not have to be converted into cash by sale before the profit could be treated as realised.

[5] 'Investments: conceptual clarity v legal muddle', R. Macve, *Accountancy*, March 1991, pp. 84–5.

[6] ED 55, Preface, Paras. 1.17 and 1.18.

were, of course, the days before FRS 3 and the 'Statement of Total Recognised Gains and Losses' but, even with this help, the ASB has not yet been able to resolve the matter.

Accounting for groups

What is a group?

Subject to certain exceptions which we discuss below, any UK company which is a parent company at its year end must prepare group accounts in addition to its individual accounts. Since the Companies Act 1989, these group accounts must be a set of consolidated accounts for the parent company and its subsidiary undertakings.[7]

Prior to the Companies Act 1989, a subsidiary had to be a company, and a parent company/subsidiary relationship was defined as existing when the parent company was a shareholder and controlled the composition of the board of directors of the other company and/or when it held more than half of the equity share capital of that other company.[8]

This definition was thus based on both control and ownership and betrayed some confusion about why group accounts were required. While ownership and control usually go hand in hand, this is not always the case and, because the definition of 'equity share capital' was widely drawn, on some occasions one company was legally a subsidiary of two other companies at the same time!

In response to the EC Seventh Directive, which we discussed in Chapter 2, the Companies Act 1989 introduced a much clearer concept of a group for accounting purposes.

First, it required that consolidated accounts include the parent and all *subsidiary undertakings*. The latter is a new term which is not restricted to companies but includes partnerships and 'unincorporated associations carrying on trade or business with or without view to profit'.[9]

Second, it introduced a new definition of a parent/subsidiary relationship based not upon ownership but upon control. Thus the relationship between a parent undertaking and a subsidiary undertaking is now defined as follows:[10]

> ⋮
>
> (2) An undertaking is a parent undertaking in relation to another undertaking, a subsidiary undertaking, if –
>   (a) it holds a majority of the voting rights in the undertaking, or
>   (b) it is a member of the undertaking and has the right to appoint or remove a majority of its board of directors, or
>   (c) it has the right to exercise a dominant influence over the undertaking –
>   (i) by virtue of provisions contained in the undertaking's memorandum or articles, or
>   (ii) by virtue of a control contract, or
>   (d) it is a member of the undertaking and controls alone, pursuant to an agreement with other shareholders or members, a majority of the voting rights in the undertaking.
>
> ⋮

---

[7] Companies Act 1985 (as amended by Companies Act 1989), Sec. 227. Before the Companies Act 1989, consolidated accounts were just one possible form which group accounts could take.

[8] Companies Act 1985, Sec. 736.

[9] Companies Act 1985 (as amended by Companies Act 1989), Sec. 259.

[10] Companies Act 1985 (as amended by Companies Act 1989), Sec. 258.

(4) An undertaking is also a parent undertaking in relation to another undertaking, a subsidiary undertaking, if it has a participating interest in the undertaking and –

(a) it actually exercises a dominant influence over it, or

(b) it and the subsidiary undertaking are managed on a unified basis.

While paragraph (2) is concerned with the existence of legal power of control, the rather wider paragraph (4) reflects the very different definition of a group prevalent in Germany, namely a definition which rests on the existence of the *de facto* control rather than *de jure* control.

The more precise definition of a group introduced by the Companies Act 1989 helps us to keep clearly in our minds that the purpose of consolidated accounts is to show the assets and liabilities under common control and how these are being used. It will also help accountants to ensure that some of the many off balance sheet finance schemes which have exploited the previous definition of a subsidiary do now find their way onto the consolidated balance sheet. Indeed, as we have seen in Chapter 6, FRS 5 'Reporting the Substance of Transactions' has attempted to go even further than this in requiring the inclusion of quasi-subsidiaries in the consolidated accounts.[11]

The compass of group accounts

Group accounts must take the form of a set of consolidated accounts, the only exception now being where such a set of consolidated accounts would not give a true and fair view.[12] Thus a parent company must usually prepare a set of consolidated accounts showing the results and state of affairs of itself and all its subsidiary undertakings as a single economic entity.[13]

The law does, however, exempt the parent company from preparing group accounts in certain circumstances and permits the exclusion of subsidiary undertakings from the consolidated accounts in other circumstances. We shall deal with each in turn.

In view of the desire of successive governments to reduce the burdens on business, the law exempted a parent company from the need to prepare group acccouts where the group, provided that it is not an ineligible group.[14]

As with the definitions of small and medium-sized companies, the definitions for small and medium-sized groups are framed by reference to turnover, balance sheet total (assets) and number of employees.[15]

In addition to these exemptions based on size, a parent company does not have to prepare group accounts where it is itself an intermediate holding company with an immediate parent company in the European Union, provided consolidated financial statements are prepared at a higher level in the group. There are a number of conditions which must be satisfied if this exemption is to apply, in particular, the higher level consolidated accounts must be prepared in accordance with law based on the EC Seventh Directive and must be filed with the UK parent's individual accounts together with certified translations, where appropriate.[16]

[11] See Chapter 6, pp. 196–7.
[12] Companies Act 1985, Sec. 227.
[13] Companies Act 1985, Sec. 228.
[14] Companies Act 1985, Sec. 248. A group is ineligible if any of its members is a public company, a banking company, an insurance company or an authorised person under the Financial Services Act 1986.
[15] Companies Act 1985, Sec. 249.
[16] Companies Act 1985, Sec. 228.

Where a parent company is not able to take advantage of the above exemptions, it must prepare consolidated accounts for all the companies in the group which are under the control of the parent company. However, the law *permits* the exclusion of subsidiary undertakings from the consolidated accounts in the following circumstances:[17]

⋮

(3) . . . a subsidiary undertaking may be excluded from consolidation where –
   (a) severe long-term restrictions substantially hinder the exercise of the rights of the parent company over the assets or management of that undertaking, or
   (b) the information necessary for the preparation of group accounts cannot be obtained without disproportionate expense or undue delay, or
   (c) the interest of the parent company is held exclusively with a view to subsequent resale and the undertaking has not previously been included in consolidated group accounts prepared by the parent company.

⋮

(4) Where the activities of one or more subsidiary undertakings are so different from those of other undertakings to be included in the consolidation that their inclusion would be incompatible with the obligation to give a true and fair view, those undertakings shall be excluded from consolidation.

This subsection does not apply merely because some of the undertakings are industrial, some commercial and some provide services, or because they carry on industrial or commercial activities involving different products or provide different services.

FRS 2 takes a more restricted view and specifically states that neither disproportionate expense nor undue delay can justify excluding material subsidiary undertakings from the consolidated accounts. However, whereas the law *permits* the exclusion of subsidiary undertakings from the consolidated accounts, FRS 2 *requires* their exclusion in certain circumstances and specifies the required accounting treatment for such excluded subsidiaries (*see* Table 9.2, p. 258).[18] Thus, paragraph 25 of FRS 2 states that a subsidiary *should* be excluded from consolidation in three circumstances:

(a) where severe long-term restrictions substantially hinder the exercise of the rights of the parent company over the assets or management of the subsidiary undertaking;
(b) where the interest in the subsidiary undertaking is held exclusively with a view to subsequent resale and the subsidiary undertaking has not previously been consolidated in group accounts prepared by the parent company;
(c) where the subsidiary undertaking's activities are so different from those of other undertakings to be included in the consolidation that its inclusion would be incompatible with the obligation to give a true and fair view.

All three of these required exclusions follow from the legal provisions quoted above, except that the circumstances envisaged under (c) are in practice, extremely rare. In particular, the explanation to the standard emphasises that any differences between banking and insurance companies/groups and other companies/groups, or between profit and not-for-profit undertakings, is not sufficient of itself to justify non-consolidation.[19]

Having specified the circumstances under which subsidiary undertakings should be excluded, FRS 2 specifies the accounting treatment to be applied to such subsidiaries and the information to be disclosed. The required accounting treatment may be summarised as follows:[20]

---

[17] Companies Act 1985, Sec. 229.
[18] FRS 2 'Accounting for Subsidiary Undertakings', Paras. 25–30.
[19] FRS 2, Para. 78e.
[20] FRS 2, Paras 27–32.

(a) *Severe long-term restrictions.* If the parent company is denied control but retains significant influence over the excluded subsidiary, use the equity method of accounting. The equity method of accounting, which is the required method of accounting for associates, is described later in this chapter.

If the parent does not even retain significant influence, treat the excluded subsidiary as a fixed asset investment showing it at the carrying value at which it would have appeared if the equity method had been in use when the restrictions came into force.[21] Subsequently take credit only for dividends actually received.

In either case, it is essential to write down the investment if there has been impairment.

(b) *Subsidiary held exclusively with a view to resale.* This should be treated as a current asset and shown at the lower of cost and net realisable value.

(c) *Different activities.* In the rare circumstances where a subsidiary undertaking is excluded for this reason, the investment should be recorded in the consolidated financial statements using the equity method of accounting, and a separate set of financial statements for the subsidiary should be included with the consolidated financial statements.[22]

Table 9.2 Attitude to exclusion of subsidiary

	Companies Act 1985	FRS 2
Inability to exercise control	Permits	Requires
Disproportionate expense or undue delay	Permits	Forbids
Subsidiary acquired for resale	Permits	Requires
Different activities where inclusion would be incompatible with true and fair view	Permits	Requires*

*But extremely rare in practice

Changes in the composition of a group

Consolidated accounts for a group are prepared to show the results of the group as a single economic entity. It follows that, subject to the cancellation of intercompany balances and the removal of unrealised intercompany profit, the consolidated profit and loss account should include the profits or losses of all companies in the group for the relevant periods during which they were members of the group. The consolidated balance sheet should show the combined assets and liabilities of companies which are members of the group at the accounting year end. This simple requirement gives rise to many accounting problems where there is an acquisition or disposal of a subsidiary during the course of a year.

The first problem is to decide exactly when an acquisition or disposal occurs. The negotiations which lead to such an event are often long and drawn out, involving preliminary discussions, agreement in principle, a drawing up of terms, an offer, an

---

[21] This carrying value may be the cost of the investment if the restriction existed at the date of acquisition (FRS 2, Para. 27).

[22] Certain other disclosures are required in respect of subsidiaries, both included and excluded. Readers are referred to Companies Act 1985, Schedule 5 and to FRS 2, Paras 31–34.

unconditional acceptance and then payment of the consideration. In the 1970s various of these possible events were selected as fixing the date of acquisition or disposal and often the selection of the date appeared to have been influenced by a desire to show the largest possible profit in the consolidated accounts. Thus, when a new profit-making subsidiary is acquired, the earlier the selected date of acquisition, the greater the profits which will be included in the consolidated profit and loss account. Similarly, when the shares in a loss-making subsidiary are sold, the earlier the date of disposal, the less the losses which serve to reduce the consolidated profits.

In order to remove discretion about the choice of possible date, FRS 2 defines the effective date of acquisition or disposal as the date on which control is obtained or relinquished.[23] Control usually passes when an offer becomes unconditional and, in the case of a public offer of shares, this will be the date when the necessary number of acceptances has been obtained.

The consolidated profit and loss account must include the profits of any new subsidiary from the date of acquisition, as defined above, to the end of the accounting year and the profits or losses of any subsidiary sold from the beginning of the accounting year to the date of disposal. As we have seen in Chapter 6, FRS 3 'Reporting Financial Performance' specifically requires the disclosure of the aggregate results of continuing operations, acquisitions (as a component of continuing operations) and discontinued operations.[24]

Let us look first at the treatment of acquisitions and then consider some of the various types of disposal which may occur.

Treatment of an acquisition

Fair values and goodwill

When a company acquires a subsidiary undertaking, it pays a price to obtain control of the assets and liabilities of that subsidiary. In the balance sheet of the parent company it is necessary to record the investment at its cost while, in the consolidated balance sheet, it is necessary to recognise the individual assets and liabilities of that subsidiary.

When a subsidiary is acquired for cash, the determination of the cost of the investment is easy but, when shares in a subsidiary are acquired in exchange for an issue of shares or other securities in the parent company or where part of the consideration is deferred or contingent on some future event, the determination of the cost may not be so clear cut.

Where the consideration is an issue of shares, it is necessary to determine the fair value of the shares and, if this exceeds the nominal value of the shares, to record a share premium or, where merger relief is available, a merger reserve.[25]

Similarly, where other securities are issued, these should be valued at their fair value. Fair value is the market price of the securities when control is obtained or, if the securities are unquoted, the best approximation to the market price using the methods of valuation which we discuss in Chapter 14.

Where the consideration is deferred or contingent, a reasonable estimate of its fair value should be included.[26] This would be provided by the expected value of the amount payable, that is the present value of the amounts expected to be paid in future.

---

[23] FRS 2, Para. 45.
[24] FRS 3 'Reporting Financial Performance', ASB, October 1992, Para. 14.
[25] See Chapter 8, pp. 231–2.
[26] Further guidance is provided by FRS 7 'Fair Values in Acquisition Accounting', ASB, September 1994.

In preparing a consolidated balance sheet it is necessary to replace the investment in the subsidiary by the whole of the underlying assets and liabilities of the subsidiary showing any minority interest therein. Under the historical cost convention, these assets and liabilities must be included at their historical cost to the group and, for this purpose, the amounts at which they appear in the subsidiary's own balance sheet are, of course, irrelevant. Indeed the group may not recognise certain assets and liabilities which appear in the subsidiary's balance sheet and may recognise assets and liabilities which do not appear in the subsidiary's own balance sheet at all.

The difficulty which must be faced here is that the parent company has not bought the individual assets and liabilities of the subsidiary. It has paid a global price to obtain control over a collection of assets and liabilities and, in order to prepare a consolidated balance sheet, it is necessary to allocate the global price to the individual assets and liabilities using the concept of fair value.

The difference between the cost of the investment and the appropriate proportion of the sum of the fair values of the individual 'identifiable' assets and liabilities recorded will provide the amount of goodwill. The ASB follows the law in using the adjective 'identifiable' but, although we shall continue to use this adjective, it does seem to be rather inappropriate. Many assets such as a good management team, a considerable research potential or a regional monopoly may be identifiable but are not usually recognised in the consolidated accounts except as part of the goodwill figure.

FRS 7 'Fair Values in Acquisition Accounting' (September 1994) provides standard accounting practice for determining which assets and liabilities of the subsidiary should be recognised in the consolidated accounts and how they should be valued:

> The identifiable assets and liabilities to be recognised should be those of the acquired entity that existed at the date of acquisition. (Para. 5)

> The recognised assets and liabilities should be measured at fair values that reflect the conditions at the date of the acquisition. (Para. 6)

The standard makes it clear that certain assets and liabilities not recognised in the accounts of the subsidiary should be recognised at acquisition. Examples are pension surpluses and deficiencies, as well as contingent assets. However it also makes it quite clear that certain provisions which have sometimes been recognised in the past should not be made in future. This is in line with the thinking subsequently embodied in FRS 12 'Provisions, Contingent Liabilities and Contingent Assets', which we have discussed in Chapter 5.[27] The banned provisions include those for reorganisation and integration costs expected to be incurred as a result of an acquisition, as well as provisions for expected future losses (FRS 7, Para. 7). The existence of such provisions results in post-acquisition costs bypassing the profit and loss account and, as we have seen in Chapter 8, such provisions have been difficult to police in practice. There is considerable agreement that, in the case of some groups, excessive provisions appear to have been made and now all such provisions have been banned.

Once the identifiable assets and liabilities have been listed, it is then necessary to obtain their fair values. Fair values are defined as follows:

> The amount at which an asset or liability could be exchanged in an arms length transaction between informed and willing parties, other than in a forced or liquidation sale. (FRS 7, Para. 2)

---

[27] FRS 12 'Provisions, Contingent Liabilities and Contingent Assets', ASB, London, September 1998.

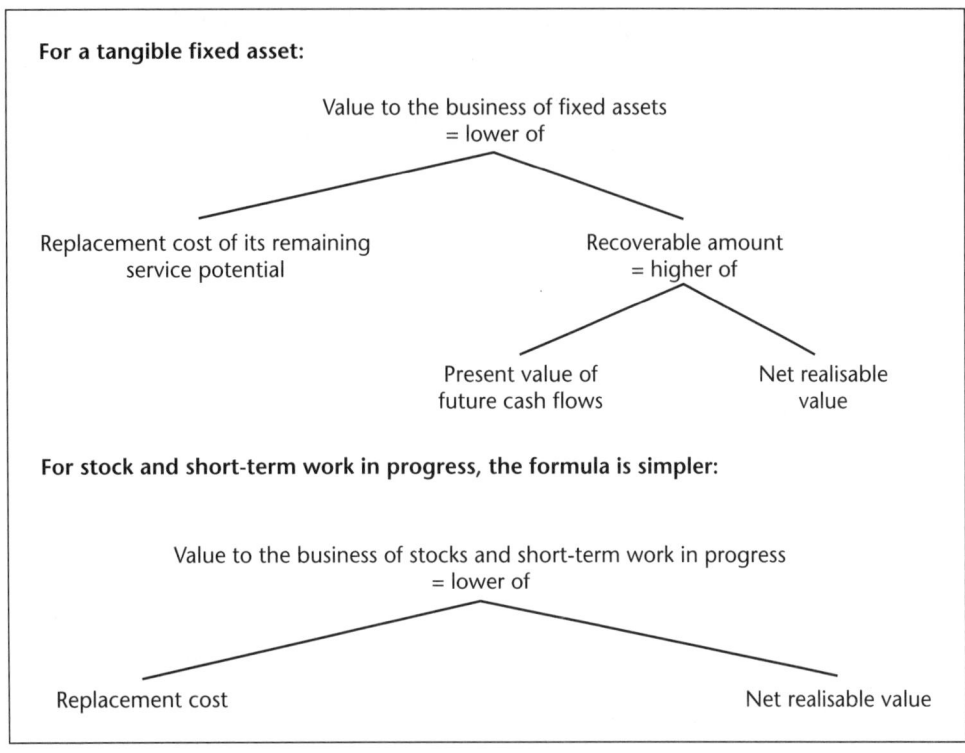

For a tangible fixed asset:

Value to the business of fixed assets
= lower of

Replacement cost of its remaining
service potential

Recoverable amount
= higher of

Present value of
future cash flows

Net realisable
value

For stock and short-term work in progress, the formula is simpler:

Value to the business of stocks and short-term work in progress
= lower of

Replacement cost

Net realisable value

Fig. 9.1 Determination of fair value

While this would imply the estimation of a value based upon an hypothetical transaction, the standard makes it clear that the fair value of tangible fixed assets and stocks and work in progress should not exceed their recoverable amounts. Recoverable amount is defined in turn as the greater of the net realisable value of an asset and, where appropriate, its value in use (Para. 2).

Although it does not use the term, FRS 7 sensibly requires us to include the assets acquired at their 'value to the business'. The value to the business of tangible fixed assets and stocks and work in progress, which has been discussed in Chapter 4, is given by the formulae shown in Figure 9.1.

The replacement cost of the remaining service potential of a fixed asset should be based upon the market value, if assets similar in type and condition are bought and sold on an open market, or at depreciated replacement cost, reflecting the acquired business's normal buying process and the sources of supply and prices available to it.[28]

Whereas the fair values of short-term and certain long-term debtors and creditors will be equal to their face values, it will be necessary to discount any long-term debtors and creditors which do not carry interest at the current market rate.

To help users of accounts to understand what has happened, Company Law requires companies to publish a table showing, for each class of assets and liabilities, the book values before an acquisition, the fair values at the date of acquisition, and an explanation for any significant adjustment made together with the goodwill on acquisition.[29]

---

[28] FRS 7, Para. 9.
[29] Companies Act 1985, Schedule 4A, Para. 12 (5).

An example of the table required by law is given in Table 9.3.

Table 9.3 Table required by Company Law

	Book value at acquisition	Fair value adjustments	Fair value to the group
	£000	£000	£000
Tangible fixed assets	420	140	560
Current assets	340	50	390
Creditors due within one year	(190)	–	(190)
Creditors due in more than one year	(200)	(30)	(230)
Provisions for liabilities and charges	(50)	(10)	(60)
	320	150	470
Goodwill			130
Consideration paid			600

FRS 6 requires that the fair value adjustments are analysed between (a) revaluations, (b) adjustments to achieve consistency of accounting policies and (c) any other significant adjustments.[30]

In practice, the identification and valuation of assets and liabilities may take some considerable time. FRS 7 stipulates that all adjustments to fair values and purchased goodwill should be fixed by the date when the consolidated accounts for the first *full* financial year following the acquisition are approved by the directors.[31]

Before we look at a more complete example of an acquisition, let us examine the further complication caused when a subsidiary undertaking is acquired in stages. To take an example, one company may purchase 10 per cent of the equity shares in another company and then purchase a further 70 per cent of the shares at a later date. As control is only obtained at the time the latter purchase is made, the law requires that the combined cost of the 80 per cent should be matched against that percentage of the sum of the fair values of the identifiable assets and liabilities to determine goodwill at the date on which control is obtained.[32]

This method will lead to a rather dubious figure for goodwill in that the price paid for the earlier purchase related to the fair value of the net assets and goodwill at the date of that purchase rather than their value at the much later date when control was obtained. However FRS 2 sees it as a practical means of applying acquisition accounting.[33]

The standard does recognise, however, that it will not always be appropriate and requires the use of the true and fair override to depart from the legal rule in certain circumstances. One example where this would be appropriate would be when the earlier purchase was sufficient to constitute the investee an associate for which equity

---

[30] FRS 6, Para. 25.
[31] FRS 7, Para. 25.
[32] Companies Act 1985, Sched. 4A, Para. 9.
[33] FRS 2, Para. 89.

accounting was appropriate. The application of the equity method of accounting requires the use of fair values at the initial purchase date and use of the legally specified approach at a subsequent purchase which means control would result in the post-acquisition profits and gains of the associate being reclassified as goodwill. In these circumstances, the standard requires that goodwill be calculated in stages, summing the differences between the cost of each purchase and the appropriate proportion of the fair value of the identifiable assets and liabilities at the date of each purchase. Such an approach would, of course, require the use of the true and fair override and the consequential disclosure that this had occurred.

The standard also deals with the situation where a company increases its stake in a subsidiary thus reducing or perhaps eliminating the minority interest.[34] In such a case it is essential to revalue the identifiable assets and liabilities in the subsidiary at the date of the increase in shareholding.

We have seen that the consolidated profit and loss account must include the results of a new subsidiary from the date of acquisition to the end of the accounting year and that the consolidated balance sheet must include the assets and liabilities of the new subsidiary which is a member of the group at the year end. This general statement is best explored in the context of an example.

Example 9.1

Let us take a company J Limited, which has many subsidiaries and makes up accounts to 31 December each year. J acquires a new wholly-owned subsidiary, K Limited, during the year to 31 December 20X1. Control is obtained on 1 July 20X1. Summarised consolidated accounts of the J group (excluding K) and accounts for K Limited are given below:[35]

Summarised profit and loss accounts for the year ended 31 December 20X1

	J Group £000	K Limited £000
Turnover	2 000	500
less Expenses	1 500	420
Profit from ordinary activities before tax	500	80
less Taxation	200	36
	300	44
less Minority interest	40	
	260	44
add Extraordinary profit (net of taxation and minority interest)	30	20
	290	64
less Dividends proposed	100	
	190	64

---

[34] FRS 2, Para. 90.

[35] While the authors appreciate that FRS 3 has resulted in the virtual disappearance of the extraordinary item, we have included extraordinary profits in this and later examples for completeness.

Summarised balance sheets on 31 December 20X1

	J Group £000	K Limited £000
Fixed assets		
Goodwill	100	–
Tangible fixed assets	500	156
Investment in K Ltd – 40 000 shares at cost	200	–
Net current assets	300	100
	1 100	256
less Long-term loans	170	50
	930	206
Share capital (£1 shares)	250	40
Revaluation reserve (created 1 July 20X1)	–	20
Retained profits	500	146
	750	206
Minority interests	180	–
	930	206

As K Limited was acquired on 1 July 20X1, the date on which control passed, it is necessary to value the identifiable assets and liabilities at their fair values on that date. In practice it is extremely helpful if their fair values are incorporated in the individual accounts of the subsidiary and this has been done in the balance sheet of K Limited to produce a Revaluation Reserve on 1 July 20X1 of £20 000.

The consolidated profit and loss account must include the results of K Limited from 1 July 20X1 to 31 December 20X1. If we assume that the sales and operating profit of K Limited accrued evenly over the year and that the extraordinary profit did not arise until October 20X1, the consolidated profit and loss account must include the following post-acquisition profits of K from 1 July 20X1 to 31 December 20X1:

	£000	Post-acquisition £000
Turnover	$500 \times \frac{1}{2}$	250
less Expenses	$420 \times \frac{1}{2}$	210
	80	40
less Taxation	$36 \times \frac{1}{2}$	18
	44	22
add Extraordinary profit	20	20
	64	42

The consolidated profit and loss account with relevant workings, will appear as follows:[36]

---

[36] We have assumed that the extraordinary profit of K Limited remains extraordinary within the context of the group.

Consolidated profit and loss account for the year ended 31 December 20X1

	£000	£000
Turnover		
J Group (excluding K)	2 000	
K, $\frac{1}{2} \times$ £500 000	250	2 250
Expenses		
J Group (excluding K)	1 500	
K, $\frac{1}{2} \times$ £420 000	210	1 710
Profit from ordinary activities before tax		540
less Taxation		
J Group (excluding K)	200	
K, $\frac{1}{2} \times$ £36 000	18	218
		322
less Minority interest (no change as new subsidiary is wholly owned)		40
		282
add Extraordinary profit (net of taxation and minority interest)		
J Group (excluding K)	30	
K (all post-acquisition)	20	50
		332
less Dividends proposed		100
Retained profit for the year		232

Movement on profit and loss account reserve for the year ended 31 December 20X1

	£000
Balance on 1 January 20X1 (old J Group only)	
(£500 000 – £190 000)	310
Retained profit for the year per consolidated profit and loss account	232
Balance on 31 December 20X1	542

Note that the retained profits brought forward do not include any profits in respect of K; after all, K did not become a member of the group until 1 July 20X1 so all retained profits before that date are pre-acquisition and represented by the net assets purchased on that date.

On the assumption that no major discontinuance is planned for K, the results of the new subsidiary will be included as part of the results of continuing operations and disclosed separately in accordance with the provisions of FRS 3.[37]

We next turn to the preparation of the consolidated balance sheet on 31 December 20X1. As K is a member of the group on that date, the balance sheet must include all of its assets and liabilities together with any goodwill on acquisition. In order to calculate the goodwill on acquisition we need to know the sum of the fair values of the identifiable assets and liabilities on 1 July 20X1. As these fair values have been incorporated in the accounts of K, they are equal to the sum of the share capital and reserves of K at the date of acquisition, which may be calculated as follows:

---

[37] FRS 3, Para. 14.

K Limited

Net assets on 1 July 20X1	£000	£000
Share capital		40
Revaluation reserve		20
Retained profits		
On 1 January 20X1	82	
1 January to 30 June 20X1, $\frac{1}{2} \times$ £44 000	22	104
		164

J Limited has paid £200 000 to acquire net assets which have an aggregate fair value of £164 000 on 1 July 20X1. Hence it has paid £36 000 for goodwill.

The consolidated balance sheet on 31 December 20X1, together with appropriate workings, will appear as follows:

J Group
Summarised consolidated balance sheet on 31 December 20X1

		£000	£000
Fixed assets			
Intangible			
Goodwill	– Old J group	100	
	K	36	136
Tangible	– Old J group	500	
	K	156	656
Net current assets	– Old J group	300	
	K	100	400
			1192
less Long-term loans	– Old J Group	170	
	K	50	220
			972
Share capital, £1 shares			250
Retained profits, per consolidated profit and loss account			542
			792
Minority interest, as before			180
			972

Now that we have examined the basic principles for dealing with the acquisition of a new subsidiary, readers should be in a position to cope with various complications. Thus, the acquisition of a loss-making subsidiary or one in which profits do not arise evenly over the period should give few problems. Similarly, the acquisition of a partially-owned subsidiary requires little modification to the approach we have adopted above.

Treatment of disposals

Just as companies acquire shares in subsidiaries, so too do they dispose of shares in subsidiaries. When we turn to disposals we may distinguish various categories of sales to outsiders[38] depending upon the shareholding, if any, which is retained:

(a) sale of total shareholding;
(b) sale of part of shareholding such that the investee company remains or becomes
    (i) a subsidiary;
    (ii) an associate;
    (iii) a simple investment.

In all cases it is necessary to recognise that different treatments are required in the individual accounts of the company making the sale and in the consolidated accounts.

We shall illustrate the principles involved in the context of a sale of the total shareholding and will then look briefly at partial disposals.

Sale of total shareholding

In the accounting records of the company which makes the sale, it is necessary to match the carrying value of the investment with the proceeds of sale to determine the profit or loss on disposal.

The disposal may, of course, have taxation consequences but, once the investing company has recognised the profit or loss and made any necessary provision for taxation, that is the end of the matter as far as that company is concerned.

When we turn to the consolidated accounts, matters are a little more complicated. In accordance with normal practice in the UK, post-acquisition profits of a subsidiary are credited to the consolidated profit and loss account year by year, whether or not they are distributed as dividend to the investing company. Hence, year by year, we recognise profits which are retained by the subsidiary company and so increase the net assets shown in the consolidated balance sheet by these amounts.

In the consolidated accounts, the profit or loss on disposal usually differs from that shown in the investing company's own profit and loss account. In the consolidated accounts the profit or loss on disposal will be the difference between the sale proceeds and the appropriate share of the underlying net assets of the subsidiary at the date of sale plus any goodwill on acquisition which has not been written off in the consolidated profit and loss account. Thus the difference between the profit on disposal shown in the investing company's records and in the consolidated accounts will depend on the change in the net assets of the subsidiary since acquisition. To the extent that the net assets of the subsidiary have grown, due to the profits made and retained between acquisition and disposal, these have been recognised in the consolidated profit and loss account as part of the group's results.

Let us start with a very simple example. L Limited has two wholly-owned subsidiaries, M Limited and N Limited. The respective summarised balance sheets on 31 December 20X1 are given below.

---

[38] Intra-group sales may also occur. In addition, a parent company may lose control of a subsidiary even without a sale of shares where, for example, a rights offer by the investee is taken up by other shareholders but not by the existing parent. FRS 2 describes such a loss of control as a 'deemed disposal' and the principles involved in such a case are the same as those described in the text.

Summarised balance sheets on 31 December 20X1

	L	M	N
	£	£	£
Net assets	110 000	60 000	70 000
Investments in subsidiaries, at cost			
20 000 shares in M Limited	45 000		
30 000 shares in N Limited	70 000		
	225 000	60 000	70 000
Share capital, £1 shares	100 000	20 000	30 000
Retained profits	125 000		
at date of acquisition		10 000	20 000
post acquisition		30 000	20 000
	225 000	60 000	70 000

If we assume that there are no fair value adjustments and that goodwill has not been written-off, the summarised consolidated balance sheet, with relevant workings, on 31 December 20X1, would appear as follows:

Summarised consolidated balance sheet on 31 December 20X1

	£	£
Goodwill		
M (£45 000–£30 000)	15 000	
N (£70 000–£50 000)	20 000	35 000
Other net assets		
(£110 000 + £60 000 + £70 000)		240 000
		275 000
Share capital, £1 shares		100 000
Retained profits		
L	125 000	
M post acquisition	30 000	
N post acquisition	20 000	175 000
		275 000

From this consolidated balance sheet we can see that the consolidated retained profits have been credited with £30 000 of post-acquisition profit retained by M and £20 000 post-acquisition profit retained by N. Thus, since acquisition, the net assets of these two companies have increased by £30 000 and £20 000, respectively, due to the making and retention of profits.

Let us now suppose that L sells its shareholding in M for £100 000 on 1 January 20X2. In the books of L it is necessary to compute the profit or loss on disposal by matching the carrying value of the investment, here its cost, against the sale proceeds. Sale proceeds are £100 000 and the cost was £45 000 so that the profit on disposal is £55 000.

In order to concentrate on principles, we shall postpone consideration of taxation until later in the chapter. The profit and loss account of L for the year ended 31 December 20X2 will therefore include the profit on disposal of shares in subsidiary amounting to £55 000.

As the investment in M was sold on the very first day of 20X2, we shall prepare the consolidated profit and loss account for the year ended 31 December 20X2 by aggregating the profit and loss account items of L and N, the two companies in the group for this year. Concentrating only on the essential figures, we may produce a draft consolidated profit and loss account as follows:

Profit and loss accounts – year to 31 December 20X2

	L	N	Total
	£	£	£
Operating profit	80 000	60 000	140 000
less Taxation	40 000	20 000	60 000
			80 000
add Profit on disposal of shares in M	55 000		55 000
			135 000
add Retained profits brought forward			
L	125 000		
N (post-acquisition)		20 000	145 000
Retained profits carried forward			280 000

Notice that the retained profits figure of £145 000 brought forward in this consolidated profit and loss account does not agree with the retained profits figure carried forward in the previous year's accounts and shown in the consolidated balance sheet on 31 December 20X1 as £175 000. The difference is, of course, the £30 000 post-acquisition retained profits of M Limited, which ceased to be a member of the group on 1 January 20X1. We cannot now say that this £30 000 never existed. What has happened is that we have previously taken credit for profits of £30 000 which are represented in the net assets of company M. Any proceeds received for the shares are in respect of the underlying net assets at the date of disposal. What we must do is to return our profits brought forward to £175 000 by adding £30 000 and correspondingly to reduce the profit on disposal:

Workings for consolidated profit and loss account – year to 31 December 20X2

	Total	Adjustment	Draft consolidated P and L account
	£	£	£
Operating profit	140 000		140 000
less Taxation	60 000		60 000
	80 000		80 000
add Profit on disposal of shares	55 000	−30 000	25 000
	135 000		105 000
add Retained profits brought forward	145 000	+30 000	175 000
Retained profits carried forward	280 000		280 000

Notice that we have not changed the retained profits carried forward. These relate to L and its subsidiary N, the only two companies in the group at the year end. All we have done is to rearrange the items in the consolidated profit and loss account in order to give a true and fair view of what has happened:

	£	£
Sale proceeds		100 000
less Net assets of M at date of disposal	60 000	
Goodwill on acquisition	15 000	75 000
Profit on disposal		25 000

For ease of exposition, we have assumed that purchased goodwill has not been amortised. If goodwill had been amortised in the consolidated profit and loss account, only the unamortised amount applicable to M would be deducted in calculating the profit on disposal. To the extent that goodwill has been amortised in the past, it has already reduced consolidated retained profits.

The consolidated balance sheet on 31 December 20X2 poses no problems. At that date L has one subsidiary N and hence the consolidated balance sheet will be an aggregation for those two companies only.

Let us now complicate the example by assuming that the disposal occurs not on 1 January 20X2 but during the year to 31 December 20X2, for simplicity on 30 June 20X2. Let us assume that the proceeds on that date are £110 000 producing profit on disposal in the profit and loss account of L amounting to £65 000. Let us also assume that the profits of M arise evenly throughout the year.

M Limited
Summarised profit and loss account for the year to 31 December 20X2

	£
Operating profit	44 000
less Taxation	20 000
	24 000
add Retained profits brought forward	40 000
Retained profits carried forward	64 000

As explained above, we must make adjustments in the consolidated accounts to show the results as far as the group is concerned. First, we must restore the retained profits brought forward to £175 000 and reduce the profit on disposal by £30 000, as we did before. However, we must, in addition, make a second adjustment. The operating profit and taxation figures included in the total column above relate only to L and N. However, the group consisted of L, N and M for the first six months of the year. The profits made and retained by M during those first six months should therefore be included in the group profits. Such profits are, of course, represented by net assets at the date of disposal and hence we must also reduce our profit on disposal. The appropriate adjustment will be as follows:

		£
Operating profits, $\frac{1}{2} \times$ £44 000	=	22 000
less Taxation, $\frac{1}{2} \times$ £20 000	=	10 000
		12 000

Our consolidated profit and loss account will therefore be arrived at as follows:

Draft consolidated profit and loss account of L Limited and its subsidiaries M Limited and N Limited for the year ended 31 December 20X2

	Total (L and N) as above	Adjustments	Draft consolidated P and L account
	£	£	£
Operating profit	140 000	+22 000	162 000
less Taxation	60 000	+10 000	70 000
	80 000	+12 000	92 000
add Profit on disposal of shares in subsidiary	65 000	−12 000 ⎱ −30 000 ⎰	23 000
	145 000		115 000
add Retained profits brought forward	145 000	+30 000	175 000
Retained profits carried forward	290 000		290 000

Notice again that the retained profit carried forward relates only to L and N, the companies in the group on 31 December 20X2. The profit on disposal amounts to £23 000 and may be explained as follows:

	£	£
Sales proceeds		110 000
less Net assets at date of disposal:		
On 31 December 20X1	60 000	
Increase in 6 months to 30 June 20X2	12 000	
	72 000	
Goodwill on acquisition	15 000	87 000
Profit on disposal		23 000

We have now examined the basic approach to the accounting treatment of disposals. Before we explore partial disposals, let us consider first the treatment of taxation and, second, the disclosure of the disposal in the consolidated profit and loss account.

Taxation

Under the UK taxation system, a chargeable gain or loss will occur when an investing company sells shares. Assuming that there is a gain, the profit in the accounts of the selling company will be reduced by taxation.

When we turn to the consolidated profit and loss account the treatment is, as in the examples above, a little more complicated.

Let us take the last example in the previous section and assume that company L faces a liability to taxation at 25 per cent on the chargeable gain. Thus, on the gain of £65 000 in the accounts of L, the taxation would be £16 250 so that our profit on disposal in the profit and loss account of L would be as follows:

	£
Profit on disposal of shares in subsidiary	65 000
less Taxation	16 250
	48 750

When we turn to the consolidated profit and loss account, an analysis of the component parts of the profit on disposal would be as follows:

	£
Sales proceeds	110 000
less Cost of investment	45 000
	65 000
Recognised in consolidated accounts:	
Post-acquisition profits retained:	
to 31 December 20X1	30 000
6 months to 30 June 20X2	12 000
	42 000
Profit on disposal	23 000
	65 000

What is happening is that, although the post-acquisition profits have already borne corporation tax, they are being taxed again as a result of the disposal. It may therefore be argued that we should recognise this by apportioning the taxation charge to the three components:

			£		£
Post-acquisition profit					
to 31 December 20X1		30 000	× 25%	7 500	
6 months to 30 June 20X2	12 000	× 25%	3 000		
Profit on disposal		23 000	× 25%	5 750	
		65 000		16 250	

The second and third elements of this tax charge relate to the current year and should be included as part of the taxation expense in the consolidated profit and loss account. The first element relates to the retained profits brought forward and some accountants would argue that it should be treated as an adjustment to reserves. However, such a treatment appears to be inconsistent with FRS 3 and, in the view of the authors, all three elements should be included as part of the tax charge in the consolidated profit and loss account. All three elements have arisen because of the disposal during the current year and should be reflected in the consolidated profit and loss account, even though this may result in a relatively high tax expense in relation to the profits included.

This could, if desired, be isolated as taxation related to discontinued operations although, as we shall see below, this is not actually required by FRS 3.

Disclosure
In order to provide the results of the group, it is necessary to include as part of the consolidated profits those relating to the subsidiary M from the beginning of the year to the date of disposal. It is also necessary to include the profit on disposal of the subsidiary.

FRS 3 requires certain disclosures in the consolidated profit and loss account, namely that:

> The aggregate results of each of continuing operations, acquisitions (as a component of continuing operations) and discontinued operations should be disclosed separately.[39]

The relevant analysis of turnover and operating profit must be included on the face of the consolidated profit and loss account but an analysis of other statutory format headings between turnover and operating profit must be included either on the face of the consolidated profit and loss account or in the notes to the accounts.

If we assume that the sale of M falls within the FRS 3 definition of discontinued operations, an appropriate presentation for the relevant part of the consolidated profit and loss account for the L group would be as follows:

Consolidated profit and loss account – year to 31 December 20X2

	Continuing operations £	Discontinued operations £	Total £
Turnover			
Expenses – in accordance with statutory format	Analysed appropriately		
Operating profit	140 000	22 000	162 000
Profit on disposal of discontinued operations	–	23 000	23 000
Profit on ordinary activities	140 000	45 000	185 000
Taxation	60 000		
(10 000 + 16 250)		26 250 }	86 250
Profit on ordinary activities after tax	80 000	18 750	98 750

FRS 3 does not require an analysis of the taxation charge between continuing operations and discontinued operations. We have included it for completeness.

Partial disposals

Where one company sells part of a holding in a subsidiary undertaking, the principles applied are the same as those illustrated above. However, the precise treatment depends upon the nature of the remaining investment. The investee may remain a subsidiary or the holding may be sufficient to make it an associate or a simple investment.

In all cases, it is essential to maintain a clear distinction between the entries in the accounting records of the selling company and those in the consolidation working papers.

In the records of the investing company it is necessary to match the appropriate proportion of the carrying value of the investment against the proceeds of disposal to produce a profit or loss on disposal. This may be subject to taxation but, now that we have explained the treatment of tax, we shall ignore it for the remainder of this chapter.

When we turn to the consolidated accounts, the position is somewhat different. We shall explore in detail the treatment where a subsidiary is retained and then look more briefly at the situation where an associate or simple investment is retained.

(1) Retention of subsidiary

At the beginning of the year the consolidated retained profit will include the post-acquisition profits of all subsidiaries based on the respective holdings of those

---

[39] FRS 3 'Reporting Financial Performance', ASB, October 1992, Para. 14.

subsidiaries at that particular date. In order to give a true and fair view of the operations of the year, the consolidated profit and loss account must include the appropriate portion of profits or losses of all companies which were members of the group during the year. The consolidated balance sheet at the end of the year will be an aggregation of the balance sheets of all companies in the group as at that date.

This is best illustrated with an example. P Limited acquired an 80 per cent interest in Q Limited many years ago when the reserves of Q were £20000. The summarised balance sheets of the two companies, together with a summarised consolidated balance sheet on 31 December 20X1, were as follows:

Summarised balance sheets on 31 December 20X1

	P £	Q £	Consolidated £
Goodwill on consolidation			32 000
Investment in Q Limited: 32 000 shares			
at cost	80 000		
Other net assets	220 000	100 000	320 000
	300 000	100 000	352 000
Share capital, £1 shares	100 000	40 000	100 000
Retained profits	200 000		232 000
At date of acquisition		20 000	
Post acquisition		40 000	
Minority interest			20 000
	300 000	100 000	352 000

P sells 4000 shares in Q on 30 June 20X2 for £16 000. This produces a profit in the records of P amounting to £6000, as shown below, and leaves P with a 70 per cent shareholding in Q.

Sale of shares in subsidiaries

20X2		£	20X2		£
June 30	Investment account, cost of shares sold $\frac{1}{8} \times £80\,000$	10 000	June 30	Sale proceeds	16 000
	Profit on disposal	6 000			
		16 000			16 000

The consolidated profit and loss account must include the result of Q as an 80 per cent owned subsidiary for the first six months of the year and as a 70 per cent owned subsidiary for the second six months. Our consolidated balance sheet on 31 December 20X2 will, of course, be based upon the 70 per cent holding at that date.

A simple approach is to prepare initially a consolidated profit and loss account on the basis of the holdings at the end of the year. Assuming that there are no unrealised profits on intercompany trading and that we have the individual profit and loss accounts as shown in the first two columns, we may proceed as follows:

Workings for consolidated profit and loss account for the year ended 31 December 20X2

	P	Q	Consolidated
	£	£	£
Operating profit	50 000	20 000	70 000
less Taxation	20 000	8 000	28 000
	30 000	12 000	42 000
less Minority interest, 30% × £12 000			3 600
			38 400
add Profit on disposal of shares in Q Limited	6 000		6 000
			44 400
add Retained profit brought forward	200 000		
Post-acquisition group share (70% × £40 000)		28 000	228 000
Retained profit carried forward			272 400

As in the previous section, we may now make adjustments to show what has happened as far as the group is concerned. First, we must restore the retained profits brought forward to the figure shown in the consolidated balance sheet on 31 December 20X1 by adding £4000 and reduce the profit on disposal accordingly. Second, we must recognise that the minority interest was 20 per cent rather than 30 per cent for the first half of the year. Thus we must reduce the minority interest figure and also reduce the profit on disposal figure by 10 per cent of the profits of the first six months, which have of course increased the net assets underlying the shares sold. Assuming that the profits of Q arose evenly, we must therefore reduce the minority interest by £600 (10% × $\frac{1}{2}$ × £12 000):

Workings for consolidated profit and loss account for the year ended 31 December 20X2

	Total based on 70% holding as above	Adjustment	Draft consolidated P and L account
	£	£	£
Operating profit	70 000		70 000
less Taxation	28 000		28 000
	42 000		42 000
less Minority interest	3 600	−600	3 000
	38 400		39 000
add Profit on disposal of shares in Q Limited	6 000	−600 −4 000	1 400
	44 400		40 400
add Retained profits brought forward	228 000	+4 000	232 000
Retained profits carried forward	272 400		272 400

Having made these adjustments, the operating profits of £39 000 after minority interest may be analysed as follows:

	£	£
Operating profit after taxation		
P (£50 000–£20 000)		30 000
Q		
6 months to 30 June 20X2, 80% × ($\frac{1}{2}$× £12 000)	4 800	
6 months to 31 December 20X2, 70% × ($\frac{1}{2}$× £12 000)	4 200	9 000
Per consolidated profit and loss account		39 000

With some rearrangement and additional information on turnover and expenses, readers should be in a position to prepare a consolidated profit and loss account for the group.

As before, the closing consolidated balance sheet poses no problems. At 31 December 20X2 P has one subsidiary, Q, in which it has a 70 per cent interest.

(2) Retention of an associate

Where a parent company sells shares in a subsidiary but retains a holding sufficient to give significant influence over the investee, it retains an associate. In the individual accounts of the parent we match the relevant proportion of the cost of the investment against the proceeds of disposal to produce a profit or loss on disposal which may attract a taxation liability.

In the consolidated profit and loss account, we must recognise that the group has a subsidiary for part of the year but an associate for the remainder of the year. Thus for the first part of the year we must include all of the relevant profits of the subsidiary, subject to deducting any minority interests, together with the profit or loss on disposal. For the second part of the year we must include the appropriate proportion of the profits of the associate using the equity method of accounting.[40]

In the consolidated balance sheet at the year end, the investment in the associate will appear at its cost, less goodwill written off, plus the appropriate share of post-acquisition retained profits of that associate.

(3) Retention of simple investment only

The treatment in the parent company's accounts is exactly the same as for other disposals. However, the consolidated profit and loss account must include the whole of the profits of the subsidiary up to the date of disposal, subject to any minority interest, together with the relevant profit or loss on disposal. Subsequently there is only a simple investment so credit should be taken only for dividends received and receivable and the investment should be shown at the same value at which it appears in the parent company's own balance sheet.

While this sounds straightforward, it does give rise to the need to remove from the consolidated profit and loss account reserve the share of post-acquisition retained profit included in relation to the simple investment retained.

To give an example, let us suppose that a parent company disposes of 90 per cent of the equity shares in a wholly-owned subsidiary, thus retaining a 10 per cent holding.

The consolidated profit and loss account reserve will have included 100 per cent of the retained profits of the subsidiary from the date of acquisition to the date of disposal

---

[40] The equity method of accounting is discussed later in this chapter.

and these will be reflected in the net assets of the subsidiary at the date of disposal. Whereas the post-acquisition retained profits relating to the 90 per cent holding sold will be taken into account in calculating the profit on disposal, those relating to the remaining 10 per cent holding must be removed if the investment is to be shown at its cost. Thus it would be necessary to have an adjustment to the consolidated profit and loss account reserve to remove the share of post-acquisition retained profits in respect of the remaining holding in a company which was previously a subsidiary.

In the consolidated balance sheet the investment would appear at its historical cost unless the directors had decided to revalue it at a higher amount or it had suffered impairment. As is the case with all disposals, preparation of the consolidated balance sheet poses few problems.

Having explored some of the major issues of accounting for groups, we now turn our attention to investments which give the investor significant influence but not control.

Accounting for associates and joint ventures

Investments giving significant influence

Before the issue of SSAP 1 'Accounting for the Results of Associated Companies' back in 1971[41], a long term investment in another company was treated in one of two ways. Either it was a simple investment, to be treated as a fixed asset investment, as discussed in the first section of this chapter, or it was an investment in a subsidiary, in which case it was normal to prepare a set of consolidated financial statements, as discussed in the second section of this chapter. SSAP 1 recognised an intermediate category of investment, an investment in an associated company, where a long-term investment was such as to give the investor company significant influence over the investee company. The term associated company included both a joint venture, where significant influence in the form of joint control was assumed, and a long-term investment which carried significant influence. Although it has proved difficult to develop a precise definition, the essence of the relationship was that the investing company or group participated in and had significant influence over the commercial and financial policy decisions of the associated company, including decisions on the level of distributions.

As we shall see later in this section, the Companies Act 1989 introduced a new term, an associated undertaking, which it defined in an extremely unhelpful way which made it difficult to improve standard accounting practice in this area. However, FRS 9 'Associates and Joint Ventures', which was issued in November 1997, now provides that standard practice.

The main methods of accounting which have been developed for investments which give the investor significant influence over the investee are proportional consolidation and the equity method of accounting. We shall explore the similarities and differences between these two methods of accounting before returning to examine the current regulatory framework later in the chapter.

---

[41] SSAP 1 'Accounting for the Results of Associated Companies', ASC, London, January 1971. This was issued as a revised SSAP 1, 'Accounting for Associate Companies', by the ASC in April 1982.

Possible methods of accounting

Where one company exercises significant influence over another company, it seems unreasonable to account for the investment in that company as a simple or passive investment. To take credit in the profit and loss account merely for dividends received and receivable is not sufficient where the directors of the investing company are able to influence the level of those dividends. To show the investment in the balance sheet at its historical cost gives no guide to what is happening to the underlying net assets, the use of which is influenced by the investing company's directors. In order to evaluate the stewardship of their directors, shareholders in the investing company require further information.

If treatment as a simple investment is inadequate, there would appear to be two closely related possibilities. The first is *proportional consolidation*, and the second is the *equity method* of accounting. We shall look at each of these possibilities in turn. In so doing we shall assume that the investee is an associate which is a company rather than an unincorporated body.

Using the method of proportional consolidation we would remove the investment in the associate from the investing company's balance sheet and replace it by the proportionate share of the assets and liabilities of that associate on a line-by-line basis together with any goodwill on acquisition. In the profit and loss account of the investing company we would remove any dividends received or receivable already credited and take credit, instead, for the appropriate proportion of the revenues and expenses of the associate on a line-by-line basis. The consolidated profits would then include the appropriate proportion of the post-acquisition profits retained by the associate.

Using the equity method of accounting we would value the investment in the balance sheet at cost plus the share of post-acquisition profits retained by the associate. Thus, the carrying value of the investment in the balance sheet would be increased by the appropriate proportion of the increase in net assets of the associate due to retained profits. The profit and loss account would be credited, not with dividends received and receivable, but with the appropriate proportion of the profits of the associate. Conversely, it would be debited with the appropriate proportion of any losses.

The net effect on the profit and loss account under both proportional consolidation and the equity method is the same but the way in which information is disclosed is different. Under proportional consolidation, the share of revenue and expenses of the associated company are added to those of the investing entity on a line-by-line basis. Under the equity method of accounting, as currently applied, it is usual to leave the revenues and operating expenses of the investing company or group unchanged and to then take credit for the share of the associate's operating profit as a separatre item including each subsequent item of income or expense on a line-by-line basis.

Let us explore a balance sheet using each method of accounting.

The summarised balance sheets of A Limited and B Limited on 31 December 20X1 are as follows:

Summarised balance sheets on 31 December 20X1

	A Limited £	B Limited £
Fixed assets		
Tangible assets	90 000	40 000
Investment in B Limited		
5000 shares at cost	22 000	–
Net current assets	10 000	24 000
	122 000	64 000
Share capital, £1 shares	50 000	20 000
Retained profits	72 000	44 000
	122 000	64 000

A purchased its 25 per cent holding in B Limited some years ago when the retained profits of B were £28 000. Providing there have been no changes in share capital, this tells us that B's summarised balance sheet at the date of acquisition was:

	£
Net assets	48 000
Share capital	20 000
Retained profits	28 000
	48 000

A purchased a 25 per cent interest in these net assets for £22 000 and hence paid £10 000 (i.e. £22 000 less 25 per cent of £48 000) for goodwill. As we explained above in the context of a subsidiary, the book values of the assets and liabilities of B at the date of acquisition should be replaced by their fair values, or more precisely their value to the business, at that date. However, for ease of exposition, we shall assume that the book values at the date of acquisition were equal to these values. We shall also assume, for the present, that goodwill has not been amortised.

Between the date of acquisition and 31 December 20X1, B has increased its retained profits by £16 000 (i.e. £44 000 less £28 000). A's share of this retained post-acquisition profit is 25 per cent or £4 000. We may therefore replace the asset 'Investment in B Limited' shown in the balance sheet of A at £22 000, by the following items:

	£
Fixed assets	
Tangible assets, 25% of 40 000	10 000
Goodwill	10 000
Net current assets 25% × 24 000	6 000
	26 000
less Retained profits (share of post-acquisition retained profits)	4 000
	22 000

Using proportional consolidation we would produce the following balance sheet, grouping like items for the investing company and associate together.

A Limited – Summarised balance sheet on 31 December 20X1 (using proportional consolidation)

	£	£
Fixed assets		
Intangible		
Goodwill		10 000
Tangible		
A Limited	90 000	
B Limited	10 000	
		100 000
		110 000
Net current assets		
A Limited	10 000	
B Limited	6 000	16 000
		126 000
Share capital (£1 shares)		50 000
Retained profits		
A Limited	72 000	
B Limited	4 000	
		76 000
		126 000

Using the equity method of accounting the investment is simply shown at cost plus the share of post-acquisition profits retained by the associate, that is at £26 000 (£22 000 plus £4000):

A Limited – Summarised balance sheet on 31 December 20X1 (using equity method of accounting)

	£	£
Fixed assets		
Tangible assets		90 000
Investment in associate (see below)		26 000
Net current assets		10 000
		126 000
Share capital, £1 shares		50 000
Retained profit		
A Limited	72 000	
B Limited	4 000	76 000
		126 000

The carrying value of the investment may be calculated in two ways:

Cost of investment	22 000
add Share of post-acquisition profits	
retained by B Limited	4 000
	26 000

or

Share of net assets of B Limited

25% of £64 000	16 000
Unamortised goodwill	10 000
	26 000

Comparison of the way in which the investment is shown using the equity method with the balance sheet using proportional consolidation makes it clear why the equity method is often referred to as a 'one-line consolidation'. The carrying value of the investment is equal to the appropriate proportion of the net assets of the associate plus any unamortised positive goodwill or less the balance of any negative goodwill.

As we have seen in the previous chapter, the provisions of FRS 10 'Goodwill and Intangibles' now usually result in the amortisation of goodwill. For ease of exposition we have not done this but the combined reserves of the two companies would be reduced by the amounts written off and only the net tangible assets and any unamortised goodwill would be represented in the balance sheet using either proportional consolidation or the equity method. It may be observed that proportional consolidation provides greater information about the underlying assets and liabilities and it is possible to argue that it is more useful, particularly when the associate is large in relation to the investing company or group.

The current regulatory framework

The legal background

Whereas the subject matter of SSAP 1 was associated companies, the Companies Act 1989 subsequently provided the following definitions of 'associated undertakings' and 'joint ventures':[42]

> An 'associated undertaking' means an undertaking in which an undertaking included in the consolidation has a participating interest and over whose operating and financial position it exercises a significant influence and which is not:
> (a) a subsidiary undertaking of the parent company, or
> (b) a joint venture dealt with in accordance with paragraph 19.
> Where an undertaking holds 20 per cent or more of the voting rights in another undertaking, it shall be presumed to exercise such an influence over it unless the contrary is shown.
> (Paras 20(1) and 20(2))

The above definition refers to 'a joint venture dealt with in accordance with paragraph 19'. The relevant part of this paragraph is as follows:

> Where an undertaking . . . manages another undertaking jointly . . . that other undertaking ('the joint venture') may, if it is not –
> (a) a body corporate, or
> (b) a subsidiary undertaking of the parent company,
> be dealt with in the group accounts by the method of proportional consolidation.
> (Para. 19)

---

[42] Companies Act 1985, Schedule 4A, Paras 19 and 20.

This is really rather bizarre drafting which posed considerable problems for the ASB as it attempted to prepare a sensible standard. While the legal definition of associated undertakings always includes an incorporated joint venture, it includes an unincorporated joint venture only if the venturer chooses to apply the equity method of accounting rather than proportional consolidation. Thus, under the provisions of the Companies Acts, if a venturer chooses to apply the equity method to an unincorporated joint venture, that joint venture is an associated undertaking while, if the venturer chooses to apply proportional consolidation to that unincorporated joint venture, it is not an associated undertaking. To define a joint venture by reference to the method used to account for it posed some difficulties in attempting to develop an appropriate accounting method for joint ventures!

FRS 9 *Accounting for Associates and Joint Ventures*
In developing standard accounting practice for associates and joint ventures, the ASB has developed an approach which distinguishes investments in entities from a joint arrangement that does not fall within its definition of an entity. The crucial definition here is the FRS 9 definition of an entity, which can only be described as arcane:

> A body corporate, partnership or unincorporated association carrying on a trade or business with or without a view to profit. The reference to carrying on a trade or business means a trade or business of its own and not just part of the trades or businesses of entities that have interests in it. (Para. 4)

Under this definition, a limited company, certainly an entity using any sensible definition of the word, may or may not be an entity under FRS 9. If the company carries on its own trade or business, it is such an entity while, if it merely carries on part of the trades or businesses of the investors, it is not such an entity.

The authors can only deplore such corruption of the definition of the word 'entity'. The distinction which the ASB makes can only lead to confusion and undoubtedly gives rise to problems in practice in deciding whether a body corporate, partnership or unincorporated association is carrying on its own trade or business or parts of the trades and businesses of the entities which have interests in it!

Nevertheless, on the basis of the above definition, FRS 9 distinguishes investments in entities, that is associates and joint ventures, from a 'joint arrangement that is not an entity'. Although the term is not used in the standard, the latter has, perhaps not surprisingly, attracted the acronym 'JANE'.

The standard provides definitions of the three categories of investment which it has identified and then clearly specifies the required accounting treatment for each category:[43]

> An *associate* is an entity (other than a subsidiary) in which another entity (the investor) has a participating interest and over whose operating and financial policies the investor exercises a significant influence.

> A *joint venture* is an entity in which the reporting entity holds an interest on a long term basis and is jointly controlled by the reporting entity and one or more other venturers under a contractual arrangement.

> A *joint arrangement that is not an entity* is a contractual arrangement under which the participants engage in joint activities that do not create an entity because it would not be carrying on a trade or business of its own. A contractual arrangement where all significant matters of operating and financial policy are predetermined does not create an entity because the policies are those of its participants, not of a separate entity.

---

[43] FRS 9 'Associates and Joint Ventures', ASB, London, November 1997, was preceded by a Discussion Paper and an Exposure Draft FRED 11, both with the same title, in July 1994 and March 1996 respectively. For definitions see FRS 9, Para. 4, and for required accounting treatment FRS 9, Paras 18–29.

The required accounting treatment for each of these is shown in Table 9.4.

Table 9.4 Required accounting treatment of associates, joint ventures and JANEs

Entities	Required treatment
Associate	Equity method
Joint venture	Gross equity method
Joint arrangement that is not an entity (JANE)	Account for share of assets, liabilities and cash flows

As we shall see, the difference between the gross equity method and the equity method is presentational in that the gross equity method provides more detailed disclosure of the share of the investee's turnover, gross assets and gross liabilities. The method specified for a JANE frequently, although not necessarily, produces the same results as proportional consolidation in practice.

To illustrate the approach of FRS 9, let us first take a situation where the investing company C Limited has subsidiaries and prepares consolidated financial statements. C has an associate D Limited in which it holds 30 per cent of the equity shares. Abbreviated consolidated financial statements for the group, together with the financial statements of D Limited for the year ended 31 December 20X1 are given below.

Summarised profit and loss accounts for the year ended 31 December 20X1

	C Limited Consolidated P&L a/c £	D Limited Associate P&L a/c £
Turnover	1 040 000	710 000
Cost of sales	670 000	230 000
Gross profit	370 000	480 000
Operating expenses	134 000	170 000
Operating profit	236 000	310 000
Dividend received from D Limited	24 000	–
	260 000	310 000
Interest payable	50 000	40 000
Profit from ordinary activities before tax	210 000	270 000
Taxation	80 000	60 000
Profit after tax	130 000	210 000
Minority interest	10 000	–
	120 000	210 000
Dividends paid and proposed	40 000	80 000
Retained profit for the year	80 000	130 000

Movement on reserves for the year ended 31 December 20X1

	£	£
Retained profits at 1 January 20X1	400 000	240 000
Retained profit for the year	80 000	130 000
Retained profits on 31 December 20X1	480 000	370 000

The profit and loss account of C Limited, and hence the consolidated profit and loss account, includes the dividend of £24 000 receivable from D Limited and this amount has been disclosed at the net amount in accordance with latest recommended practice.[44]

Summarised balance sheets on 31 December 20X1

	C Limited Consolidated Accounts £	D Limited Associated Company £
Fixed assets		
Goodwill on consolidation	70 000	–
Tangible assets	493 000	420 000
Investment in associate:		
45 000 shares (30%) at cost	97 000	–
Net current assets	280 000	360 000
	940 000	780 000
less Long-term loans	100 000	150 000
	840 000	630 000
less Deferred taxation	80 000	60 000
	760 000	570 000
Share capital £1 shares	200 000	150 000
Share premium	40 000	30 000
Retained profits	480 000	390 000
	720 000	570 000
Minority interests	40 000	–
	760 000	570 000

C Limited acquired its 30 per cent interest in D Limited on 1 January 20X1 when the reserves of D comprised a share premium account of £30 000 and retained profits of £60 000. On the basis of the simplifying assumption that book values were equal to fair values at the date of acquisition, goodwill of £25 000 would have been recognised:[45]

	£	£
Cost of investment		97 000
less Share of net assets:		
Share capital	150 000	
Share premium	30 000	
Retained profits	60 000	
30% of	240 000	72 000
Purchased goodwill		25 000

We shall assume that this goodwill had an expected useful economic life of five years and that it is being amortised over that period using the straight line method.

---

[44] See the Exposure Draft 'Amendment to SSAP 8 "The treatment of Taxation under the Imputation System in the Accounts of Companies: Presentation of Dividend Income"', ASB, London, October 1997.

[45] In addition to this simplifying assumption, we are implicitly assuming that there have been no changes to share capital or share premium since acquisition.

Let us focus first on the consolidated profit and loss account which, at present, includes £24 000 in respect of the dividend received or receivable from D. Using the equity method, this must be removed and replaced by the share of the associate's profit, whether or not this has been distributed. Under the provisions of FRS 9, the share of profit must be included after the group operating profit and then on a line by line basis.

	D Limited	30% share
	£	£
Operating profit	310 000	93 000
Interest payable	40 000	12 000
Profit from ordinary activities before tax	270 000	81 000
Taxation	60 000	18 000
Profit after tax	210 000	63 000

Inclusion of the share of these figures in the consolidated profit and loss account, together with the amortisation of goodwill, produces the following results:

Summarised consolidated profit and loss account for the year ended 31 December 20X1 (including results of associate)

	£	£
Turnover		1 040 000
Cost of sales		670 000
Gross profit		370 000
Operating expenses		134 000
Group operating profit		236 000
Share of operating profit of associate	93 000	
less Amortisation of goodwill	5 000	88 000
		324 000
Interest payable:		
Group	50 000	
Associate	12 000	62 000
Profit from ordinary activities before taxation		262 000
Taxation:		
Group	80 000	
Associate	18 000	98 000
		164 000
Minority interest		10 000
		154 000
Dividends paid and proposed		40 000
Retained profit for the year		114 000

We have brought in the share of profits amounting to £63 000 to replace the dividend receivable of £24 000. Thus we have taken credit for an extra £39 000, which is the share of the profit retained by the associate in respect of the year but this has, of course, been reduced by the amortisation of the goodwill of the associate.

When we turn to the movement on reserves, we must include the share of the post acquisition profits retained by the associate less the accumulated amortisation of goodwill. The following statement includes the relevant workings.

285

Movement on reserves for the year ended 31 December 20X1

	£	£
Retained profits on 1 January 20X1:		
Group		400 000
Share of post acquisition profits in associate –		
30% × (240 000 – 60 000)	54 000	
less Accumulated amortisation of goodwill – 1 year × 5000	5 000	49 000
		449 000
Retained profit for the year		114 000
Retained profits on 31 December 20X1		
Group	480 000	
Share of post acquisition profits in associate:		
30% × (370 000 – 60 000)	93 000	
less Accumulated amortisation of goodwill – 2 years × 5000	(10 000)	
	563 000	563 000

By the end of the year 20X1, we have therefore increased consolidated reserves by £83 000, the share of the post acquisition profits retained by the associate less the accumulated amortisation of purchased goodwill, and must increase the carrying value of the investment in the consolidated balance sheet by this amount to keep it in balance. The carrying value therefore becomes £180 000, which is the cost of £97 000 plus £83 000.

Summarised consolidated balance sheet on 31 December 20X1

	£
Fixed assets	
Goodwill	70 000
Tangible assets	493 000
Investment in associate	180 000
	743 000
Net current assets	280 000
	1 023 000
Long-term loan	100 000
	923 000
Deferred taxation	80 000
	843 000
Share capital	200 000
Share premium	40 000
Reserves: per Movement on reserves	563 000
	803 000
Minority interest	40 000
	843 000

The carrying value of the investment in the associate may be analysed as follows:

		£
Share of net assets in balance sheet of D: 30% × 570 000		171 000
Unamortised goodwill		
Cost of goodwill	25 000	
less Amortised – 2 years at 5000	10 000	15 000
		186 000

In order for the inclusion of these amounts to be meaningful, it is necessary for the accounting periods and policies of the associate to coincide with those of the group. In practice this may sometimes give rise to difficulties requiring adjustment to the results of the associate. As with full consolidation, adjustment will also be necessary to remove the effect of trading between the group and the associate.

Joint ventures and the gross equity method

As we have explained earlier in this section, FRS 9 requires the use of the 'gross equity method' for joint ventures. This method is defined as follows:[46]

> A form of equity method under which the investor's share of the aggregate gross assets and liabilities underlying the net amount included for the investment is shown on the face of the balance sheet and, in the profit and loss account, the investor's share of the turnover is noted.

Thus the method is exactly the same as the equity method except that a little more disclosure is required. The additional information required is illustrated in the following pro-forma consolidated profit and loss account and balance sheet incorporating both a joint venture and an associate. Headings relating to the joint venture are shown in italics.

Consolidated profit and loss account for the year ended 31 December 20X1

	£	£
Turnover: group and share of joint venture	X	
less Share of joint venture's turnover	X	
Group turnover		X
Cost of sales		X
Gross profit		X
Operating expenses		X
Group operating profit		X
Share of operating profit in:		
Joint venture	X	
Associate	X	X
		X
Interest payable		
Group	(X)	
Joint venture	(X)	
Associate	(X)	X
Profit on ordinary activities before tax (carried forward)		X

---

[46] FRS 9, Para. 4.

	£
Profit on ordinary activities before tax (brought forward)	X
Tax on profit on ordinary activities:	
Group, *joint venture* and associate	X
Profit on ordinary activities after tax	X
Minority interests	X
Profit on ordinary activities after tax	
and minority interests	X
Dividends	X
Retained profit for group and its share of	
joint venture and associate	X

Consolidated balance sheet on 31 December 20X1

	£	£	£
Fixed assets			
Tangible assets		X	
Investments			
Investment in joint venture:			
Share of gross assets	X		
Share of gross liabilities	(X)	X	
Investment in associate		X	X
Current assets			
Stock		X	
Debtors		X	
Cash at bank and in hand		X	
		X	
Creditors: amounts due within one year		(X)	
Net current assets			X
Total assets less current liabilities			X
Creditors: amounts due after more than one year			(X)
Provisions for liabilities and charges			(X)
			X
Capital and reserves			
Called up share capital			X
Share premium account			X
Profit and loss account			X
Shareholders' funds			X
Minority interests			X
			X

Approach where no consolidated accounts are prepared
In the above examples we have assumed that consolidated accounts have been prepared so that it was possible to apply the equity method or gross equity method of accounting in those accounts. It is, of course, possible for a company without a subsidiary to have an investment in an associate or joint venture. In such a case, it is not possible to apply the equity method or gross equity method in the investing company's accounts and yet there are no consolidated accounts available for that purpose.

In order to comply with FRS 9[47] the investing company:

---

[47] FRS 9, Para. 48.

... should present the relevant amounts for associates and joint ventures either by preparing a separate set of financial statements or by showing the relevant amounts, together with the effects of including them, as additional information to its own financial statements ...

In the former case, the treatment will be as illustrated above. In the the latter case, one or more supplementary notes to the company's own financial statements will be necessary. Thus there must be a note to the balance sheet showing what the carrying value of the investment would be using the equity method and, in the case of a joint venture, the share of the gross assets and gross liabilities making up that value. There must also be a note to the profit and loss account showing the effect of applying the equity method of accounting.

On the basis of the following summarised profit and loss accounts for the year ended 31 December 20X1 of E plc and F Limited, a possible note to the profit and loss account of E plc, which has 25 per cent of the shares in its associate F Limited, is illustrated below.

Summarised profit and loss accounts for the year ended 31 December 20X1

	E plc	F Ltd
	£	£
Operating profit	240 000	140 000
Dividends received and receivable from F Limited	10 000	–
	250 000	140 000
Taxation	80 000	60 000
Profit on ordinary activities after tax	170 000	80 000
Dividends paid and payable	100 000	40 000
Retained profit for the year	70 000	40 000

A possible note to the profit and loss account might run as follows:

Note to the profit and loss account of E plc
The effect of applying the equity method of accounting to the investment in the associate F Limited is as follows:

	£	£
Share of profit of associate		
25% of 140 000		35 000
Share of taxation of associate		
25% of 60 000		15 000
		20 000
add Profit of E plc		
Per profit and loss account	170 000	
less Dividends from associate	10 000	160 000
Profit from ordinary activities after taxation		180 000
less Dividends paid and payable		100 000
Retained profit for the year		80 000
Retained in investing company	70 000	
Retained in associate (25% × 40 000)	10 000	
	80 000	

Such a note could be easily expanded to provide the relevant disclosure for an investment in a joint venture.

Large investments in associates and joint ventures

In order to ensure that users have adequate information to interpret a set of financial statements, FRS 9 requires the disclosure of the name of each principal associate and joint venture, together with details of the proportional shareholding, its accounting period and an indication of the nature of its business. The equity method is then applied to all investments in associates and the gross equity method to all investments in joint ventures, either in the consolidated financial statements, where these are prepared, or as supplemenary information in the investing company's own financial statements.

Both the equity method and the gross equity method provide only very summarised information about the results, assets and liabilities of the investee entity and, hence, when the investee is particularly large in relation to the investing group or company, greater disclosure is required.

FRS 9 requires additional disclosure where certain thresholds are exceeded. These thresholds attempt to capture the relative size of the investee in the context of the investing group or company and require comparison between the investor's share of the investee with that of the investor of the following:

- gross assets
- gross liabilities
- turnover
- operating results on a three year average.

Additional disclosure is then required in three circumstances:

(i) where the *aggregate* of the investor's share in its associates exceeds a 15 per cent threshold;
(ii) where the *aggregate* of the investor's share in its joint venture exceeds a 15 per cent threshold;
(iii) where the investor's share in any *individual* associate or joint venture exceeds a 25 per cent threshold.

Because disclosures required under the equity method and the gross equity method are different, the additional disclosure required varies under each heading but includes such information as the investor's share of:

- turnover, if not already shown
- fixed assets
- current assets
- liabilities due within one year
- liabilities due after more than one year.

Readers are referred to the standard for precise details of the disclosure required in each case.[48]

Summary

We have seen that FRS 9 distinguishes between three categories of investment involving the exercise of significant influence over an investee by an investor: associates, joint

---

[48] FRS 9, Para. 58.

ventures and JANEs. In the case of associates and joint ventures, variants of the equity method are required, with slightly more information being provided in respect of joint ventures. In the case of the JANE, the investor must account directly for the share of assets, liabilities, results and cash flows. This will often produce the same result as proportional consolidation although this will not be the case when the venturer holds individual assets and liabilities in the joint arrangement in varying proportions.

Figure 9.2 provides a summary of the accounting treatment of fixed asset investments.

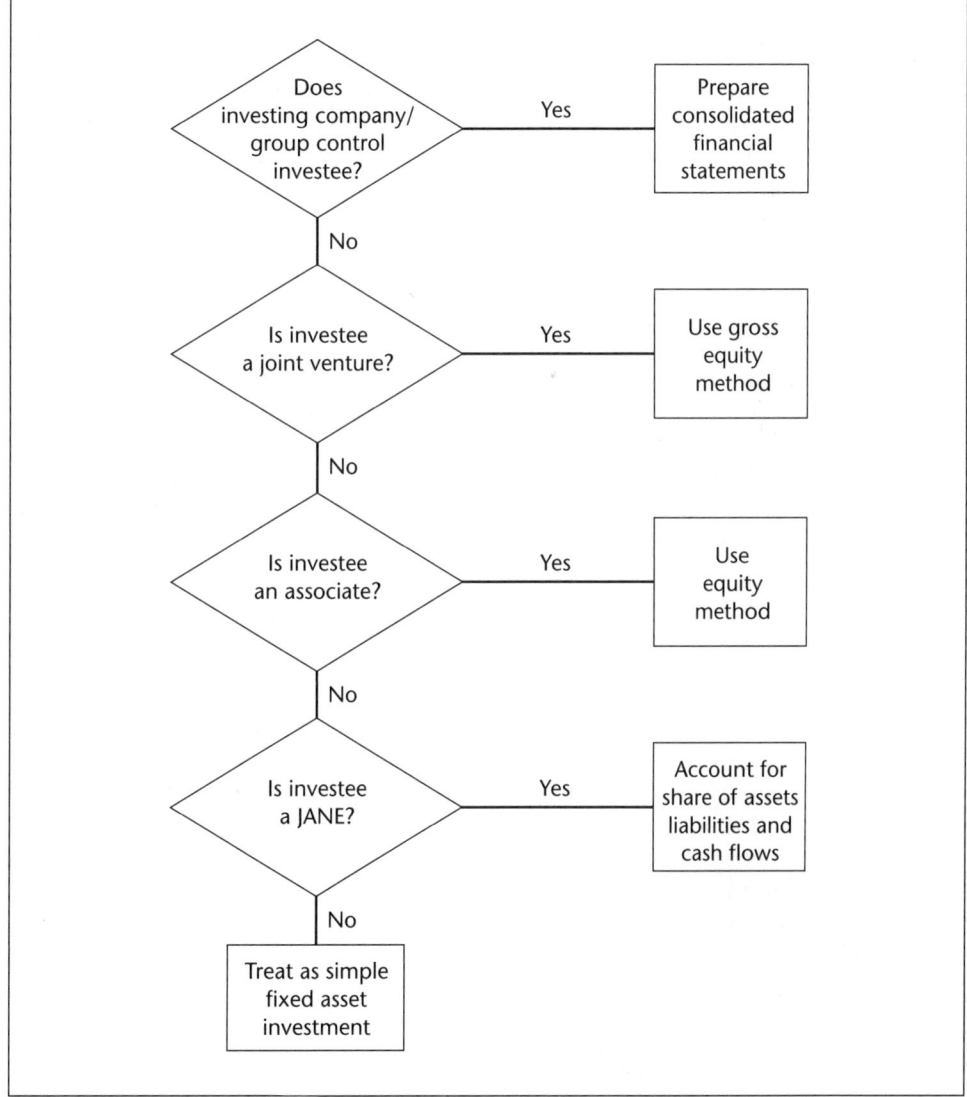

Fig. 9.2 Treatment of fixed asset investments

The international accounting standards

There are a number of international accounting standards which are relevant to the subject matter of this chapter:

IAS 25 *Accounting for Investments* (reformatted 1994)

IAS 27 *Consolidated Financial Statements and Accounting for Investments in Subsidiaries* (reformatted 1994)

IAS 22 *Business Combinations* (revised 1998)

IAS 28 *Accounting for Investments in Associates* (revised 1998)

IAS 31 *Financial Reporting of Interests in Joint Ventures* (revised 1998)

International accounting standards now specify a benchmark treatment but, in many cases, permit an alternative accounting treatment. While British standard practice is broadly consistent with international standards, there are a number of differences. In particular, there are cases where the ASB favours the alternative treatment rather than the benchmark treatment of the international accounting standard. We shall focus on three important differences.

Consolidated financial statements

In this chapter we have discussed the acquisition method of accounting and have, in particular, explained the need to use fair value or, more precisely, value to the business in order to arrive at the historical cost of the separately identified assets and liabilities of a subsidiary to be included in the consolidated financial statements. FRS 2 requires us to state all of the assets and liabilities of a subsidiary at their fair values and any minority interest in the subsidiary will be measured as the relevant proportion of the aggregate of those fair values.

While this is the allowed alternative treatment under IAS 22, it is not the benchmark treatment. The benchmark treatment requires the use of fair values to the extent to which the subsidiary is owned by the group but requires that the minority interest be based upon the book values of assets and liabilities in the balance sheet of the subsidiary at the date of acquisition. This is best illustrated by means of an example.

Let us suppose that S plc acquires a 90 per cent interest in T plc. The aggregate book value of the net assets in the balance sheet of T at the date of acquisition is £400 000 and the sum of the fair values of those net assets is £600 000.

In accordance with British practice and the allowed alternative treatment of the international accounting standard, the net assets would be shown at £600 000 and the minority interest would be shown at £60 000, that is 10 per cent of £600 000. However, under the benchmark treatment of IAS 22, the net assets and minority interest would be calculated as follows:

		£
Carrying value of net assets:		
S's interest	90% of £600 000	540 000
Minority interest 10% of £400 000		40 000
		580 000
Minority interest at date of acquisition		
10% of £400 000		40 000

This benchmark treatment results in strange carrying values for the individual assets and liabilities of the subsidiary in the consolidated financial statements and makes subsequent accounting for the group extremely complicated. However, it is the method which has long been part of US GAAP and became the benchmark treatment of IAS 22 in spite of considerable opposition from other countries.

Associates

IAS 28 and FRS 9 both require the use of the equity method of accounting for associates in consolidated financial statements. However, there is a difference when it comes to reporting investments in associates in the investor's own financial statements. IAS 28 permits a company to include an investment in an associate in its own accounts using cost or the equity method or a revaluation. FRS 9 does not permit the use of the equity method in the investor's individual financial statements.

Joint ventures

The definition of joint venture in IAS 31 is much wider than that of FRS 9: IAS 31 defines a joint venture in terms of contractual arrangements whereas FRS 9 restricts the term joint venture to an entity and deals separately with joint arrangements that are not entities.

The benchmark treatment of joint ventures under IAS 31 is proportionate, what we have called proportional, consolidation while the allowed alternative treatment is the equity method of accounting. Although FRS 9 requires the use of a method along the lines of proportional consolidation for joint arrangements which are not entities, it requires the use of the gross equity method for joint ventures. Here again the British standard requires application of the allowed alternative treatment, rather than the benchmark treatment, of the international accounting standard.

Recommended reading

G.C. Baxter and J.C. Spinney, 'A closer look at consolidated financial statement theory', *CA Magazine*, January and February 1975.

S.J. Gray and A.G. Coenenberg (eds), *International Group Accounting*, Croom Helm, NJ, 1988.

S.M. McKinnon, *Consolidated Accounts: The Seventh EEC Directive*, A.D.H. Newham (ed.), Arthur Young McClelland Moores, 1983.

C. Nobes, *Some Practical and Theoretical Problems of Group Accounting*, Deloitte Haskins & Sells, London, 1986.

A. Simmonds, A. Mackenzie and K. Wild, 'Accounting for subsidiary undertakings', *Accountants Digest No. 288*, ICAEW, London, Autumn 1992.

P.A. Taylor, *Consolidated Financial Reporting*, Paul Chapman, London, 1996.

10 Overseas involvement

Overview   International trade may be carried out by firms of all sizes and comes in many and various forms. A firm's involvement may be restricted to the purchase or sale of goods and services using a foreign currency but it could involve a foreign currency loan or an investment in a foreign subsidiary, associate or joint venture.

From an accounting point of view we need to separately identify two different situations:

1 Accounting for foreign currency transactions in the accounting records.
2 Translation of foreign currency financial statements as a preliminary to some form of consolidation.

We deal with each in turn.

We explore accounting for foreign currency transactions in the context of a number of examples. When we turn to the translation of foreign financial statements as a preliminary to aggregation, we concentrate on the translation of the financial statements of an overseas subsidiary and explore the two methods of accounting specified for this purpose in SSAP 20 'Foreign Currency Translation' (April 1983), namely the closing rate/net investment method and the temporal method.

Having first introduced the two methods, we discuss their strengths and weaknesses. We then explore a more complex example of the closing rate/net investment method, the method used by the vast majority of companies in the UK. We conclude with a brief look at the International Accounting Standard IAS 21 *The Effects of Changes in Foreign Exchange Rates* (December 1993).

The problems identified

Many firms based in the UK undertake transactions with firms in other countries and have branches and subsidiary and associated undertakings overseas.

Transactions undertaken between firms will often be expressed in foreign currencies and it will be necessary to translate these amounts into sterling in order to enter them in the accounting records of the UK firm. If the rate of exchange changes between the date of the transaction and the date of settlement it is necessary to decide how to deal with the resulting difference on exchange in the accounts of the UK company. If there is an intervening balance sheet date, then it is necessary to decide which rate of exchange should be used at the balance sheet date and how the resulting difference on exchange should be treated.

Where there is an overseas branch, subsidiary or associated undertaking, it is usual for the accounting records of the overseas unit to be kept in the local currency: indeed, the local law may require the preparation and publication of accounts in terms of the local currency. In order to combine the results of the overseas unit with the sterling results of the investing company and those of any similar UK and other overseas units, the accounts expressed in foreign currency must be translated into sterling.[1] When exchange rates between currencies fluctuate, this need for translation poses two problems. First, it is necessary to decide what rates of exchange are appropriate for the individual assets, liabilities, revenues and expenses in the accounts of the overseas unit. No matter how this question is answered, the translation process invariably gives rise to differences on exchange. As a second problem, it is therefore necessary to decide how these differences are to be dealt with in the aggregated financial statements.

Until the ASC attempted to standardise the accounting treatment of exchange differences in ED 16,[2] professional accountancy bodies in the UK had provided little guidance on how the above questions should be answered. Official pronouncements[3] tended to describe various methods and to emphasise that selection between them is a matter of professional judgement, without providing any guidance as to the principles on which that professional judgement should be based. As a result, many different methods have been used in practice.

In this chapter, we look first at accounting for transactions denominated in foreign currencies and then turn our attention to the more complex subject of translating the financial statements of an overseas unit for the purposes of aggregation. The accounting treatment of both topics is regulated by SSAP 20, *Foreign Currency Translation*, issued in April 1983.

Accounting for foreign currency transactions

A UK company may purchase fixed assets, stocks or services from an overseas company and may, in addition, sell such items to an overseas company. It may also raise loans denominated in a foreign currency and make investments in the shares of an overseas company. When the amounts involved are expressed in a foreign currency, it will be necessary to translate those amounts into sterling in order to incorporate them into the accounting records of the UK company. The approach which should be adopted is best illustrated by means of a number of examples.

Example 10.1

Let us consider a UK company, Han Limited, which makes up its accounts to 31 December each year. On 15 September 20X1 it purchased a fixed asset, a machine, from a German company for 30 000 Deutschmarks when the rate of exchange was DM3.00 to £1. It paid for this machine on 15 December 20X1 when the rate of exchange was DM3.30 to £1.[4]

At the date of purchase, 15 September 20X1, it is necessary to translate the foreign currency amount to record the cost of the machine and the corresponding creditor in sterling. In

---

[1] Following the American terminology introduced by ED 21, the term 'conversion' is restricted to the exchange of one currency for another.

[2] ED 16, 'Supplement to "Extraordinary items and prior year adjustments"', September 1975.

[3] *See*, for example, recommendation N 25 of the ICAEW, issued in February 1968.

[4] Although the currencies used in this and the following examples are often real currencies, the rates of exchange used are fictitious and movements are exaggerated to illustrate the principles involved. Exchange rates of European countries in the Economic and Monetary Union are now fixed against the Euro and hence against each other pending the withdrawal of the national currencies in 2002: Such countries include France and Germany but not, at present, the UK.

the absence of an agreed rate of exchange for settlement, in which case the German company would bear the risk of any exchange rate movement, or a forward exchange contract, the rate ruling on the date of purchase, that is DM3.00 to £1, should be used for this purpose.

20X1

Sept 15 *Dr* Machinery – at cost   £10 000
              Cr Creditor German company   £10 000

Purchase of machine for DM30 000 at exchange
rate of DM3.00 to £1

The sterling cost of the machine is £10 000 and it is this amount which will be depreciated over the expected useful life of the asset. No further adjustment to this cost is necessary whatever subsequently happens to the rate of exchange. However, if the asset is subsequently revalued, it is necessary to translate the revalued amount at the rate of exchange ruling on the date that the new valuation is established.

In order to pay for the machine, Han Limited must arrange with its bankers to convert sterling into Deutschmarks. If bank charges are ignored, the payment of DM30 000 on 15 December 20X1 will require an amount of £9091 in sterling given that the rate of exchange is DM3.30 to £1

20X1

Dec 15 *Dr* Creditor – German company   £9 091
              Cr Cash   £9 091

Payment of DM30 000 converted at DM3.30 to £1

The debt is now settled but when we look at the account in the records of Han Limited, it shows a credit balance of £909.

Creditor: German company

20X1		£	20X1		£
Dec 15	Cash	9 091	Sept 15	Machine	10 000
	Difference:				
	gain on				
	exchange	909			
		10 000			10 000

This is a difference on exchange, in this case a gain which arises because sterling has strengthened (that is become more valuable) against the Deutschmark between the date of purchase and the date of settlement. The gain is, of course, realised and SSAP 20 requires that it be credited to the profit and loss account in arriving at the profit or loss from ordinary activities for the accounting year ended 31 December 20X1.

Example 10.2

In Example 10.1 we assumed that there was no contractually agreed rate of exchange for settlement or forward exchange contract in existence. SSAP 20, Para. 48 states that, where appropriate, contractually agreed rates of exchange *should* be used and *permits* the use of rates of exchange fixed in related or matching forward contracts.

Let us assume that, as before, Han Limited purchased a machine from a German company for DM30 000 on 15 September 20X1. However, let us also assume that, on that date, Han Limited entered into a forward exchange contract with its bank to purchase DM30 000 for delivery on 15 December 20X1. Relevant rates of exchange are:

		DM to £1
20X1		
Sept 15	Spot rate	3.00
	Forward rate – 3 months	3.10

Under SSAP 20, the company may record the cost of the machine at one of two amounts:

Cost of machine:	£
Using spot rate – as in Example 10.1	10 000
Using forward rate – 30 000/3.10	9 677

Given that the subsequent payment will be made at the agreed forward exchange rate of DM3.10 to £1, the subsequent position will be as follows:

(i) Using spot rate

Creditor: German company

20X1		£	20X1		£
Dec 15	Cash	9 677	Sept 15	Machine	10 000
	Gain on				
	exchange	323			
		10 000			10 000

(ii) Using forward rate

Creditor: German company

20X1		£	20X1		£
Dec 15	Cash	9 677	Sept 15	Machine	9 677

Under the provisions of SSAP 20, Han Limited may choose to record the cost of the machine at either £10 000 or at £9677. Clearly this does little to standardise accounting practice in this area and reflects what may now be regarded as a rather naive approach by SSAP 20. The difference between the spot rate and the forward rate reflects differences between the interest rates in the two countries and it may be argued that the purchase of the machine and the forward exchange contract should be recognised as two different transactions. Under the more sophisticated approach adopted by the US Statement of Financial Accounting Standard 52 'Foreign Currency Translation', the cost of the machine would be calculated using the rate of exchange at the date of purchase, the forward exchange contract would be recorded separately and 'marked to market' and the discount or premium under the forward exchange contract would be taken to the profit and loss account as part of the finance charge over the period of the contract. The difference between the US approach and the UK approach will, of course, be more marked where the contracts extend over two or more accounting periods.

SSAP 20 is now becoming rather long in the tooth and, in addition to a number of problems which we address in this chapter, it fails to deal satisfactorily with the various purposes for which forward exchange contracts, currency swaps and currency options are used. However, the standard is unlikely to be reviewed until the ASB project on financial instruments has been completed and has settled some of the key issues relevant to foreign currencies.[5]

Example 10.3

The next complication which may arise is that the purchase and the payment occur in different accounting years. To illustrate this, let us assume that Han Limited purchased stock from a French company for 200 000 French francs on 20 November 20X1 when the rate of exchange was 8 francs to £1. It subsequently paid for the goods on 15 January 20X2 when the rate of exchange was 10 francs to £1. The rate of exchange on 31 December 20X1, the intervening balance sheet date, was 9.5 francs to £1. Following the principles explained in Example 10.1, the purchase would be recorded as follows:

```
20X1
Nov 20   Dr Stock                              £25 000
            Cr Creditor – French company                    £25 000
         Purchase of stock for 200 000 francs at 8 francs to £1.
```

The cost of stock is recorded at £25 000 and, as before, this figure is not affected by any subsequent changes in the exchange rate. If the stock is still held on 31 December 20X1 it is included in the balance sheet at the lower of cost and net realisable value. Cost will be determined in accordance with the company's normal accounting policy (e.g. FIFO, average cost, etc.).

When we turn to the creditor, a monetary amount, such an approach is not sensible and, in the absence of either contractually agreed exchange rates for settlement or forward exchange contracts, SSAP 20 requires that all monetary items are translated at the closing rate.[6] The closing rate is defined more precisely as follows:

> The closing rate is the exchange rate for spot transactions ruling at the balance sheet date and is the mean of the buying and selling rates at the close of business on the day for which the rate is to be ascertained.[7]

On 31 December 20X1 the amount payable to extinguish the creditor is not £25 000 but a lower amount of £21 053, that is 200 000 francs, translated at the closing rate of exchange on that day – 9.5 francs to £1. When the liability is adjusted to this figure, the result is a gain on exchange:

Creditor – French company

20X1		£	20X1		£
Dec 31	Balance c/d	21 053	Nov 20	Stock	25 000
	Profit and loss account				
	– gain on exchange	3 947			
		25 000			25 000
			20X2		
			Jan 1	Balance b/d	21 053

---

[5] The ASB made precisely this point when, in May 1999, it withdrew the brief exposure draft 'Amendment to SSAP 20 "Foreign Currency Translation"' on the grounds that more substantial changes to SSAP 20 are necessary.
[6] But *see* preceding example.
[7] SSAP 20, Para. 41.

The gain on exchange has occurred because the sterling value of the liability has fallen between 20 November 20X1 and 31 December 20X1 which is due to the strengthening of sterling against the French franc. SSAP 20 considers that, as there is objective evidence for the sterling value of the liability and, as such a gain on a short-term monetary item will shortly be reflected in cash flows, so the profit on exchange is a part of realised profit and hence should be included in the profit or loss from ordinary activities.

The gain recognised in 20X1 could, of course, be fully or partly offset by a loss in the subsequent year if sterling weakens against the franc between 31 December 20X1 and the date of settlement, 15 January 20X2. The treatment adopted is, of course, consistent with the accruals concept: the gain occurred in 20X1 and is reported in 20X1, while the loss would occur in 20X2 and be reported in 20X2.

In this particular example there is, of course, no loss in 20X2 but a further gain on exchange when settlement is made on 15 January 20X2. Ignoring bank charges, the amount payable in sterling is £20 000 (200 000 francs ÷ 10) so that the creditor's account appears as follows:

Creditor – French company

20X2		£	20X2		£
Jan 15	Cash	20 000	Jan 1	Balance b/d	21 053
	Profit and loss account – gain on exchange	1 053			
		21 053			21 053

As in 20X1, the gain on exchange is credited to the profit and loss account, this time for the year ended 31 December 20X2.

SSAP 20 requires similar adherence to the accruals principle in the case of long-term monetary liabilities although, as we shall see, the standard adopts a different stance on the realisation of gains on exchange on such long-term liabilities.

Example 10.4

Let us suppose that Han Limited raised a long-term loan of 400 000 French francs on 1 October 20X1 when the rate of exchange was 8 francs to £1. The loan will be recorded in the accounting records of Han Limited at a figure of £50 000:

```
20X1
Oct 1    Dr Cash                        £50 000
              Cr Long-term loan                      £50 000
         Being loan of 400 000 French francs
         translated at 8 francs to £1.
```

If, on 31 December 20X1, the rate of exchange is 9.5 francs to £1 then, under the provisions of SSAP 20, the liability must be translated into sterling at that rate to produce a figure of £42 105 (400 000 ÷ 9.5):

Long-term loan

20X1		£	20X1		£
Dec 31	Balance c/d	42 105	Oct 1	Cash	50 000
	Profit and loss				
	account – gain				
	on exchange	7 895			
		50 000			50 000
			20X2		
			Jan 1	Balance b/d	42 105

Restating the sterling liability at this figure produces a gain on exchange of £7895 and SSAP 20 requires that this be reported as part of the 'ordinary' profits of Han Limited.

Some accountants would argue that such a gain is realised on the grounds that there is objective evidence, in the form of an officially published exchange rate, that it actually occurred in 20X1. Others would argue that, because it relates to a long-term item which has not been repaid at the balance sheet date, the gain may be reversed by subsequent exchange rate movements before repayment and is therefore not realised at the balance sheet date. These two views reflect the lack of consensus on the precise meaning of realisation, which was discussed in Chapter 3.

Although SSAP 20 takes the view that exchange gains on unsettled short-term monetary items are realised, it takes the view that such gains on unsettled long-term monetary items are unrealised.[8] In the authors' view, this is an extremely uncomfortable position, for it may result in a situation where a gain on a short-term item will be treated as realised even though we may know, at the time of preparing the accounts, that it has subsequently been reversed, whereas a gain on a long-term item, where we have no such certain knowledge of reversal, will be treated as unrealised. The ASC appears to have adopted different definitions of realisation for short-term and long-term items. In the former case, the existence of an objective exchange rate seems crucial, no matter what happens to the exchange rate subsequently. In the latter case, the existence of the objective exchange rate seems unimportant and uncertainty about the ultimate cash payable appears to be dominant. Among such confusion, we should perhaps be thankful that, rightly or wrongly, there is little disagreement among accountants that exchange losses on unsettled monetary items, whether short-term or long-term, are realised.

Given the ASC's conclusion that exchange gains on unsettled long-term monetary items are unrealised, many accountants argue that the prudence concept dictates that such gains should not be included in the profit and loss account. Indeed, they may quote statutory support for their argument in that the Companies Act 1985 specifically states that: 'only profits realised at the balance sheet date shall be included in the profit and loss account'.[9] However, the law permits directors to depart from this principle if there are special reasons, providing that the notes to the accounts give particulars of the departure, the reason for it and its effect.[10] SSAP 20 considers that such a departure from the realisation principle is essential if exchange gains and losses are to be treated symmetrically in accordance with the accruals principle. Thus, in contravention of SSAP 2, SSAP 20 requires that the accruals concept takes precedence over the prudence concept.[11] Hence, in the same way that exchange losses on

---

[8] SSAP 20, Para. 65.
[9] Companies Act 1985, Schedule 4, Para. 12(a).
[10] Companies Act 1985, Schedule 4, Para. 15.
[11] SSAP 2, Para. 14(b): '. . . provided that where the accruals concept is inconsistent with the "prudence" concept, the latter prevails.'

long-term liabilities during the period are debited to the profit and loss account, so exchange gains for the period are credited to the profit and loss account.

Relevant disclosure must be made. In addition any such unrealised profits credited to the profit and loss account should be removed when calculating legally distributable profits.

Example 10.5

It is possible for a UK company to raise a foreign currency loan which it then invests in the shares of an overseas company. The loan and investment may be in the same currency or, alternatively, the loan may be raised in one currency while the investment is made in a country with a different currency. For ease of exposition we shall assume that only one currency is involved.

Let us assume that Han Limited raised a long-term loan of US $300 000 on 1 October 20X1 when the rate of exchange was US $1.5 to £1. It immediately invested the proceeds in the shares of a US corporation so that, if we ignore the receipt and payment of cash, the summarised journal entry will appear as follows:

20X1			
Oct 1	*Dr* Investment in US company	£200 000	
	Cr Long-term loan (US)		£200 000

Being loan of US $300 000 raised to finance investment in US company translated at $1.5 to £1.

The investment may constitute the US company a subsidiary, an associated undertaking or merely a simple investment. Whichever is the case, the treatment in the accounting records of Han Limited will be exactly the same, although the treatment in any consolidated accounts will differ.

Let us assume that the rate of exchange on 31 December 20X1 is $1.4 to £1. If Han Limited follows the rules explained in previous examples, certain difficulties will arise. Unless there had been a permanent fall in the value of the investment, the investment would be shown in the balance sheet at its cost of £200 000 while the loan, a monetary amount, would have to be translated at the closing rate of exchange and shown as a liability of £214 286 ($300 000 ÷ 1.4). Restating the loan at this amount produces a loss on exchange of £14 286 which would have to be charged to the profit and loss account.

Long-term loan – US dollars

20X1			20X1		
Dec 31	Balance c/d	£214 286	Oct 1	Cash	£200 000
			Dec 31	Profit and loss account – loss on exchange	14 286
		214 286			214 286

It may be argued that to make such a one-sided adjustment is misleading. Because of the adherence to historical cost accounting, the investment is retained at its historical cost in sterling while the liability is shown at its current sterling equivalent. SSAP 20 recognises the logic of this argument and *permits*, although it does not *require*, Han Limited to translate the investment at the closing rate of exchange rather than at the historical rate of exchange, thus:

Investment in US corporation

20X1			20X1		
Oct 1	Cost	£200 000	Dec 31	Balance c/d,	
				300 000 ÷ 1.4	£214 286
Dec 31	Gain on				
	exchange	14 286			
		214 286			214 286

This produces an absurd sterling figure for the investment, a figure which is neither the historical cost in sterling nor a current value in sterling, but what has been achieved is the creation of a gain on exchange which may be used to offset the loss on exchange on the long-term loan. In this case the gain on the investment is exactly equal to the loss on the long-term loan and one may be offset against the other without any need to charge any gain or loss to the profit and loss account. If the loan and investment were for different currency amounts or in different foreign currencies, this equality of gain and loss is unlikely to exist. In such a case SSAP 20 requires that any exchange gain or loss on the investment should be taken direct to reserves. Any loss or gain on the loan should then be offset against the gain or loss on the investment but, if the exchange loss/gain on the loan exceeds the gain/loss on the investment, then the excess must be charged/ credited to the profit and loss account.

The final problem addressed in this example is to what extent such an offset should be permitted. Should it be necessary to identify a particular loan with a particular investment? Should the offset be restricted to situations where the loan and investment are in the same currency? Where a large company has many loans denominated in various foreign currencies and many investments in various foreign currencies, should a global approach be permitted whereby any gains are set off against any losses? What criteria should be laid down to govern the use of this offset arrangement?

After receiving many different recommendations from those who commented on the offset arrangements included in ED 27, SSAP 20 specified the following conditions:[12]

(a) in any accounting period, exchange gains or losses arising on the borrowings may be offset only to the extent of exchange differences arising on the equity investments;

(b) the foreign currency borrowings, whose exchange gains or losses are used in the offset process, should not exceed, in the aggregate, the total amount of cash that the investments are expected to be able to generate, whether from profits or otherwise; and

(c) the accounting treatment adopted should be applied consistently from period to period.[13]

This must be recognised as a pragmatic solution to what is often a very difficult question to answer in practice: 'To what extent do foreign currency loans provide a hedge against foreign equity investments?'

Why the offset arrangement should apply to equity investments but not to other investments, such as a readily saleable property overseas, seems difficult to justify and displays the *ad hoc* nature of the ASC approach to standard setting.

---

[12] SSAP 20, Para. 51. Although ED 27, 'Accounting for Foreign Currency Translations', issued in October 1980, considered this topic within the context of consolidated accounts, it did not even mention such offset arrangements within the accounts of the individual company.
[13] SSAP 20, Para. 51.

Summary

The accounting treatment of foreign currency transactions may be summarised as follows:

1 Non-monetary assets shown on basis of historical cost

Non-monetary assets shown at an amount based upon historical cost should be translated at the exchange rate at the date on which the historical cost was established. However, if there is a contractually agreed exchange rate for settlement, this *should* be used and, if there are related or matching forward exchange contracts in respect of trading transactions, the rates of exchange specified in those contracts *may* be used. The cost of non-monetary assets purchased is not affected by subsequent changes in the exchange rate except where a company exercises the option to use the closing rate to translate the cost of foreign equity investments financed by foreign currency borrowings.

2 Non-monetary assets shown on basis of a revalued amount

Non-monetary assets which have been revalued, either upwards under the alternative accounting rules or downwards under the rules on impairment, should be translated at the rate ruling when the valuation was established.

3 Unsettled monetary items

Unsettled monetary items should be translated at the closing rate, unless there is a contractually agreed exchange rate for settlement, in which case the latter *should* be used. If there are related or matching forward contracts in respect of trading transactions, the rates of exchange specified in those contracts *may* be used.

4 Treatment of exchange gains and losses

All exchange gains and losses on settled and unsettled transactions should be credited or charged to the profit and loss account as part of the profit from ordinary activities (unless they relate to transactions which are treated as extraordinary items) but note that:

Gains on unsettled long-term monetary items are not regarded as realised and hence an adjustment should be made when calculating the legally distributable profit.

Translation of the financial statements of an overseas subsidiary

Where a UK company has an overseas branch, subsidiary or associated undertaking which keeps its records in a foreign currency, it is necessary to translate financial statements in order to be able to combine the figures with those of the UK company or group. In this chapter we assume that the overseas unit is a subsidiary, although readers will appreciate that similar principles are appropriate for a foreign branch or associated undertaking.

As explained in the first section of this chapter, when exchange rates are changing the existence of an overseas subsidiary requires us to answer two questions. Fir what rate of exchange should be used to translate the individual items in the acc of the overseas subsidiary? Second, how should the resulting differences on e be treated in the accounts?

Turning first to the balance sheet of the overseas subsidiary, there are rates of exchange which could be applied to each asset or liability. Th torical rate or the closing rate. The historical rate is the rate of exch date the transaction occurred or, where appropriate, the rate of exchange ruling at the date of a subsequent revaluation. The closing rate is the rate of exchange ruling on the balance sheet date.

The major methods of translation which have been used employ a combination of these rates, and Table 10.1 illustrates how four methods deal with the major categories of asset and liability.

Under the current/non-current method, current assets and liabilities are translated at the closing rate while fixed assets and long-term liabilities are translated at the appropriate historical rate.

Under the monetary/non-monetary method, monetary assets and liabilities are translated at the closing rate while non-monetary assets are translated at the historical rate.

Under the temporal method, which is discussed in more detail later in this chapter, the rate of exchange depends upon the basis of valuation used in the balance sheet of the overseas subsidiary. If items are shown at current value, which is automatically the case with monetary assets and liabilities, the closing rate is used.[14] Where items are shown at a figure based upon historical cost, an historical rate is appropriate, and where items are shown at a figure based on a valuation, the rate of exchange at the date of the valuation is used.

From Table 10.1, it can be seen that there is very little difference between the temporal method and the monetary/non-monetary method within the context of historical cost accounts. The most frequent instance of a difference occurs where stock is shown at net realisable value.

Under the closing rate method all assets and liabilities are translated at the closing rate of exchange.

Table 10.1 Major methods of translation

	Current/ non-current		Monetary/ non-monetary		Temporal		Closing rate	
	H	C	H	C	H	C	H	C
Assets								
Fixed assets								
At cost less depreciation	x		x		x			x
At current value	x		x			x		x
Current assets								
Stock								
At cost		x	x		x			x
At current value		x	x			x		x
		x		x		x		x
		x		x		x		x
	x			x		x		x
		x		x		x		x

sing rate.

nly true within the confines of traditional accounts. Arguably the current value of a uld be its present value, which takes into account interest for the time period until t.

303

When we turn to the profit and loss account, three possible translation rates may be distinguished: (a) historical rates, that is rates of exchange specific to each transaction; (b) average rate ruling during the year;[15] (c) closing rate on the balance sheet date. Under the first, the appropriate rate of exchange is that ruling on the date of the transaction. So, if depreciation is based upon an historical cost, the rate of exchange at the date of acquisition of the asset is appropriate. If depreciation is based upon a revalued amount, the rate of exchange at the date of revaluation is appropriate. Where revenues and other expenses arise on a particular day, the rate of exchange on that day is appropriate. In practice, for recurrent items such as wages, power, directors' remuneration etc., an average rate is used as an approximation to the historical or specific rate of exchange.

Under the second option, an average rate of exchange is used in its own right, whereas with the third approach the closing rate of exchange is used for all items in the profit and loss account.

When we consider rates of exchange applied to balance sheet items and profit and loss account items, the following combinations have been found:

Balance sheet	Profit and loss account
Current/non-current	Historical or average
Monetary/non-monetary	Historical or average
Temporal	Historical or average
Closing rate	Average or closing rate

Thus there has been a wide choice in practice as to the appropriate combinations of rates of exchange.

Whichever combinations are used, there will inevitably be differences on exchange and there are various ways of dealing with them in the consolidated accounts:

(i) Include as part of profit or loss from ordinary activities.
(ii) Treat as a movement on reserves.
(iii) Some combination of the above.

When the choice between relevant rates of exchange is coupled with the choice between the various ways of dealing with differences on exchange, there are a large number of possible combinations.

The SSAP 20 solution

ED 21, wrongly entitled 'Accounting for Foreign Currency Transactions',[16] was issued in September 1972 as the first comprehensive attempt towards standardising the accounting treatment of foreign currencies in the UK. It permitted companies to use either the temporal method or the closing rate method and laid down rules on the rates of exchange to be used for translation and the treatment of the differences on exchange.

---

[15] This should, of course, be an appropriate weighted average and not merely a simple average of the opening and closing rates.
[16] Wrongly entitled because it dealt almost exclusively with foreign currency translation and gave little attention to foreign currency transactions.

If ED 21 had become a Statement of Standard Accounting Practice, it would certainly have reduced the choice of methods available to companies by outlawing the use of the current/non-current and the monetary/non-monetary methods. However, when applied to historical cost accounts, the temporal method and the closing rate method usually produce very different results and, hence, the degree of standardisation proposed by ED 21 was limited and the Exposure Draft was heavily criticised.

The subsequent ED 27, 'Accounting for Foreign Currency Translations', issued in November 1980, and SSAP 20, 'Foreign Currency Translation', issued in April 1983, require the use of one method in most situations. The favoured method is now called the 'closing rate/net investment method' and this appears to be the method used by the majority of companies in the UK.

The words 'net investment' were added to the title of the method to indicate the view which the method implicitly takes of the investment in the overseas subsidiary. The majority of overseas subsidiaries are thought to have a certain amount of autonomy and to operate primarily within the economic environment of an overseas country using the currency of that country. Using the terminology of the Financial Accounting Standards Board (FASB) Statement No. 52, the 'functional currency' of the overseas subsidiary is usually that of the country in which it operates.[17] The holding company is therefore regarded as having an investment in the net assets of the subsidiary rather than in its individual assets and liabilities. It follows that only the net investment is at risk from movements in the exchange rate and, as we shall see, use of the closing rate/net investment method is consistent with this position.

In some cases, however, the overseas subsidiary may not have significant autonomy. Thus the affairs of the overseas company may be closely linked with those of the parent company, and its 'functional currency' may be sterling rather than the local currency. In such a case, SSAP 20 requires that the foreign accounts be translated using the temporal method so that the results are included as if the transactions had been undertaken by the parent company itself.

SSAP 20 provides little guidance on how to recognise situations where the temporal method is appropriate and, given the variety of situations found in practice, it has to be recognised that it will sometimes be extremely difficult to decide which method of translation to apply.

To summarise, under the provisions of SSAP 20, it is expected that the vast majority of companies should use the closing rate/net investment method while a small number of companies will be required to use the temporal method. It is therefore essential for us to look at both methods.

In the following two sections of this chapter we shall examine the principles of the closing rate/net investment and temporal methods using simple examples. We shall then compare and contrast the two methods before presenting, in the final section, a more complex example of the closing rate/net investment method.

Closing rate/net investment method

As we have seen, any method for translating the accounts of an overseas subsidiary must specify which rates of exchange are to be used for the various items in the accounts of that subsidiary and how the resulting differences on exchange are to be treated in the consolidated accounts.

---

[17] *See* Appendix A to Statement of Financial Accounting Standard No. 52 for factors which should be taken into account in determining the functional currency of an overseas subsidiary.

The SSAP 20 version of the closing rate/net investment method lays down the following rules:

(a) Assets and liabilities in the balance sheet of the overseas subsidiary are to be translated at the closing rate. This, of course, determines the amount of the shareholders' interest although, as we shall see, it is sensible to translate the share capital and components of reserves at various rates of exchange.

(b) Profit and loss account items are to be translated at either the average rate or the closing rate.[18]

(c) Differences on exchange arising on translation are to be taken direct to reserves.

When the rate of exchange between sterling and the overseas currency is fluctuating, a difference on exchange will arise in respect of the opening net assets of the subsidiary, which are translated at a different rate at the year end from that used at the beginning of the year. A second difference will arise if the average rate of exchange is used to translate profit and loss account items for, in such a case, the increase in net assets as shown by the retained profit or loss is translated at the average rate, whereas the resulting net assets are translated at the closing rate in the balance sheet. Both differences on translation are treated as movements on reserves.

Let us illustrate the method by means of a simple example.

Example 10.6

Widening Horizons Limited, a UK company which owns and rents out properties, established a wholly-owned overseas subsidiary, Foreign Venture Limited, on 31 December 20X1. Widening Horizons Limited subscribed £100 000 in cash for one million shares of 1 groucho each. On 31 December 20X1, the rate of exchange between currencies was 10 grouchos to £1.

Foreign Venture Limited immediately raised a long-term loan of 500 000 grouchos and purchased freehold land and buildings, suitable for renting, at a cost of 1 200 000 grouchos.

After these transactions, the opening balance sheet of the new subsidiary, in both foreign currency and sterling, is therefore as given below:

Foreign Venture Limited
Opening balance sheet on 1 January 20X2

	Grouchos	Rate of exchange (grouchos to £1)	£
Freehold land and buildings			
At cost	1 200 000	10	120 000
Short-term monetary assets			
Cash	300 000	10	30 000
	1 500 000		150 000
less Long-term loan	500 000	10	50 000
	1 000 000		100 000
Share capital			
1 000 000 shares of 1 groucho	1 000 000	10	100 000

---

[18] ED 27 proposed the use of the average rate for profit and loss account items and, although this is standard practice in the USA and Canada, the comments on ED 27 showed that there was considerable opposition to the exclusive use of an average rate in the UK.

At this date only one rate of exchange is appropriate; it qualifies as both the historical rate and the closing rate. Once the balance sheet is translated into sterling, it is possible to match the cost of the investment shown in the records of Widening Horizons Limited at £100 000 against the share capital of Foreign Venture Limited to produce neither positive nor negative goodwill on consolidation.

During the following year to 31 December 20X2, Foreign Venture Limited collects rentals and incurs expenses with the result that its profit and loss account for the year and balance sheet on 31 December 20X2 are as follows:

Foreign Venture Limited
Profit and loss account for the year ended 31 December 20X2

	Grouchos	Grouchos
Rentals received		400 000
less Expenses		
Management expenses	115 000	
Depreciation of buildings	50 000	
Interest on long-term loan	75 000	240 000
Profit before taxation		160 000
less Taxation payable		60 000
Retained profit for year		100 000

Balance sheet on 31 December 20X2

	Grouchos
Freehold land and buildings	
At cost	1 200 000
less Depreciation	50 000
	1 150 000
Short-term net monetary assets	
(debtors plus cash less creditors)	450 000
	1 600 000
less Long-term loan	500 000
	1 100 000
Share capital	
1 000 000 shares of 1 groucho each	1 000 000
Retained profit	100 000
	1 100 000

Assuming that the relevant rates of exchange between grouchos and sterling are as given below, we may proceed to translate the accounts in accordance with the closing rate/net investment method:

	Grouchos to £1
1 January 20X2	10
Average for year to 31 December 20X2	8
31 December 20X2	6

The average rate, rather than the closing rate, has been applied in the profit and loss account.

Foreign Venture Limited
Profit and loss account for the year ended 31 December 20X2

	Grouchos	Rate of exchange	£
Rentals received	400 000	8	50 000
less Expenses			
Management expenses	115 000	8	14 375
Depreciation of buildings	50 000	8	6 250
Interest on long-term loan	75 000	8	9 375
	240 000		30 000
Profit before taxation	160 000		20 000
less Taxation payable	60 000	8	7 500
Retained profit for year	100 000		12 500

Balance sheet on 31 December 20X2

	Grouchos	Rate of exchange	£
Freehold land and buildings			
At cost	1 200 000	6	200 000
less Depreciation	50 000	6	8 333
	1 150 000		191 667
Short-term net monetary assets	450 000	6	75 000
	1 600 000		266 667
less Long-term loan	500 000	6	83 333
	1 100 000		183 334
Shareholders' interest:			
Share capital	1 000 000	10(HR)	100 000
Retained profits	100 000	Per P and L a/c	12 500
	1 100 000		112 500
Difference on exchange	–	Balance	70 834
	1 100 000		183 334

Note: HR = historical rate.

The treatment of share capital merits special attention. It has been translated at the historical rate of exchange, that is the rate ruling at the date of acquisition.

If we assume for a moment that share capital had been translated at the closing rate of exchange of 6 grouchos to £1, this would have produced a sterling figure of £166 667 instead of the £100 000 shown. This would have reduced the difference on exchange, the balancing figure, by £66 667, but consideration must also be paid to the subsequent consolidation of the subsidiary's accounts with those of the parent company. In the consolidation workings the cost of the investment, £100 000, would be matched with the share capital of the subsidiary, £166 667, when translated at closing rate, to produce negative goodwill on consolidation of £66 667. This is clearly nonsensical since there was no goodwill on acquisition and the apparent negative goodwill would only have arisen because of the change in the exchange rate. In other words the £66 667 is a difference on exchange.

The wisdom of the method used in the example may now be seen. The application of the historical rate to share capital and, in a more general case, to pre-acquisition reserves as well, means first, that the total difference emerges in the translation of the subsidiary's balance sheet and, second, that there is no risk that an erroneous adjustment will be made to the goodwill on consolidation.

The total difference on exchange, a gain of £70 834, must be credited to consolidated reserves. It has arisen for two reasons. First, the opening net assets were translated at one rate on 1 January 20X2 and at a different rate on 31 December 20X2. Second, the increase in net assets, the retained profit, has been translated at one rate in the profit and loss account and at a different rate in the closing balance sheet. We may analyse the difference as follows:

Analysis of difference on exchange

	Grouchos	Opening balance sheet (10 grouchos to £1) £	Closing balance sheet (6 grouchos to £1) £	Difference £
Opening net assets				
Freehold land and buildings	1 200 000	120 000	200 000	80 000 (gain)
Cash	300 000	30 000	50 000	20 000 (gain)
	1 500 000	150 000	250 000	100 000
less Long-term loan	500 000	50 000	83 333	33 333 (loss)
	1 000 000	100 000	166 667	66 667

		£	£
Increase in net assets during year			
Retained profit for year			
Per profit and loss account, 100 000 grouchos at 8 grouchos to £1		12 500	
Per closing balance sheet (part of net monetary assets), 100 000 grouchos at 6 grouchos to £1		16 667	4 167 (gain)
Total gain on exchange			70 834

It is hoped that the above analysis helps to explain why the words 'net investment' have been added in the name 'closing rate/net investment' method. The loss on the opening long-term loan has effectively been offset against the gains on the opening assets so that it is only the gain on the opening *net* assets which is taken to reserves with the second part of the gain in respect of the retained profit for the year. If the closing rate had been used for profit and loss account items, this second part of the gain would not arise.

Let us assume that the accounts of the parent company are as given in the left-hand column below. Provided there are no unrealised intercompany profits or similar consolidation adjustments, we may proceed to consolidate by adding the figures for the parent company with the translated figures for the overseas subsidiary, treating the difference on exchange of £70 834 as a movement on reserves and disclosing it in the Statement of Total Recognised Gains and Losses.

Widening Horizons Limited
Workings for consolidated profit and loss account
for the year ended 31 December 20X2

	Widening Horizons Limited £	Foreign Venture Limited £	Consolidated £
Rentals received	500 000	50 000	550 000
less Expenses			
Management expenses	120 000	14 375	134 375
Depreciation	60 000	6 250	66 250
Loan interest	100 000	9 375	109 375
	280 000	30 000	310 000
Profit before taxation	220 000	20 000	240 000
less Taxation	100 000	7 500	107 500
	120 000	12 500	132 500
less Dividends proposed	60 000	–	60 000
Retained profit for year	60 000	12 500	72 500

Workings for movement on reserves for year to 31 December 20X2

	Widening Horizons Limited £	Foreign Venture Limited £	Consolidated £
Reserves on 1 January 20X2	420 000	–	420 000
add Retained profit for year	60 000	12 500	72 500
Gain on exchange	–	70 834	70 834
Reserves on 31 December 20X2	480 000	83 334	563 334

Consolidated statement of total recognised gains and losses
for the year ended 31 December 20X2

	£
Profit for the financial year	132 500
Gain on exchange	70 834
Total recognised gains for the financial year	203 334

Workings for consolidated balance sheet on 31 December 20X2

	Widening Horizons Limited £	Foreign Venture Limited £	Consolidated £
Freehold land and buildings			
At cost	2 000 000	200 000	2 200 000
less Depreciation	350 000	8 333	358 333
	1 650 000	191 667	1 841 667
Investment in Foreign Venture			
Limited – at cost	100 000	–	–
Goodwill on consolidation –			
at cost	–	–	–
Short-term net monetary assets	330 000	75 000	405 000
	2 080 000	266 667	2 246 667
less Long-term loan	1 000 000	83 333	1 083 333
	1 080 000	183 334	1 163 334
Share capital	600 000	100 000	600 000
Reserves	480 000	83 334	563 334
	1 080 000	183 334	1 163 334

Once the translation has been undertaken, preparation of the consolidated accounts poses only the normal problems faced when consolidating a UK subsidiary and preparing the accounts using the formats required by company law.

Temporal method

This method was first proposed by an American, Leonard Lorensen, in a study published by the American Institute of Certified Public Accountants.[19] It was the only method permitted by the US FASB in their standard on the subject, Financial Accounting Standard (FAS) 8, which was issued in October 1975. However, this standard attracted a great deal of criticism in the USA and has now been replaced by FAS 52, issued in December 1981, which, like SSAP 20, favours the closing rate method.

Under the temporal method, the rates of exchange to be used for translation are determined by the basis of measurement used for the various items in the financial statements of the overseas subsidiary.

In the balance sheet, assets which are shown at a figure based on historical cost are translated at the relevant historical rate; assets shown on the basis of a revalued amount at some past date are translated at the rate of exchange ruling when the revalued amount was established; assets and liabilities shown at a current value, which includes all monetary assets and liabilities, are translated at the closing rate.

In the profit and loss account the rate of exchange used is similarly determined by the underlying basis of measurement: depreciation based on historical cost is translated at the relevant historical rate; revenues and expenses which have accrued over the year are translated at an average rate; while revenues and expenses which relate to

---

[19] L. Lorensen, *Reporting Foreign Operations of US Companies in US Dollars*, Accounting Research Study No. 12, AICPA, New York, 1972.

amounts established in previous years or to merely a part of the current year are translated at a specific rate or an appropriate average rate.

It follows that more extensive records are necessary than those required for use of the closing rate/net investment method.

Under the SSAP 20 version of the temporal method, all differences on exchange are credited or charged to the consolidated profit and loss account as a part of the ordinary profits for the year.[20]

Let us examine the temporal method by applying it to the same simple facts used in the previous example.

Example 10.7

The opening balance sheet of Foreign Venture Limited, the new subsidiary established by Widening Horizons Limited, in both grouchos and sterling is repeated below:

Foreign Venture Limited
Balance sheet on 1 January 20X2

	Grouchos	Rate of exchange	£
Freehold land and buildings			
At cost	1 200 000	10	120 000
Short-term monetary assets			
Cash	300 000	10	30 000
	1 500 000		150 000
less Long-term loan	500 000	10	50 000
	1 000 000		100 000
Share capital	1 000 000	10	100 000

Widening Horizons Limited paid £100 000 for the investment and hence at the date of acquisition there is no goodwill on consolidation.

The accounts of Foreign Venture Limited for the year ended 31 December 20X2 are given below. The left-hand column gives the accounts in foreign currency while the right-hand column shows the results translated into sterling. For ease of reference, the relevant exchange rates are repeated:

	Grouchos to £1
1 January 20X2	10
Average for year to 31 December 20X2	8
31 December 20X2	6

In the profit and loss account the historical rate, that ruling when the buildings were purchased on 31 December 20X1, is applied to depreciation. For other items the average rate is an appropriate approximation to the historical rate. A simple average of the opening and closing rates would only be appropriate if the revenue and expenses arose reasonably evenly over the year and the rate of exchange moved reasonably evenly. Otherwise an appropriate weighted average would have to be used.

---

[20] Other variants of the temporal method exist. For example, the version of the temporal method required by the Canadian Institute of Chartered Accountants provides that unrealised gains and losses relating to long-term monetary assets and liabilities shall be amortised over the remaining life of the asset or liability.

Foreign Venture Limited
Profit and loss account for the year ended 31 December 20X2

	Grouchos	Rate of exchange (see note)	£
Rentals received	400 000	8(AR)	50 000
less Expenses			
Management expenses	115 000	8(AR)	14 375
Depreciation of buildings	50 000	10(HR)	5 000
Interest on long-term loan	75 000	8(AR)	9 375
	240 000		28 750
Profit before taxation	160 000		21 250
less Taxation payable	60 000	8(AR)	7 500
Retained profit for year	100 000		13 750

Note: AR = average rate, HR = historical rate.

In the balance sheet, the freehold land and buildings, shown at depreciated historical cost, are translated at the historical rate of exchange on 1 January 20X2 while all monetary assets and liabilities are translated at the closing rate.

As explained in the previous example, it is sensible to translate the share capital and, in a more general case, any pre-acquisition reserves at the historical rate in order to maintain the goodwill on acquisition at its 'historical cost' in the consolidated accounts. It is also necessary to translate the retained profit for the year at the same sterling figure as shown for retained profit in the profit and loss account. When this has been done the difference on exchange emerges as the balancing figure.

Balance sheet on 31 December 20X2

	Grouchos	Rate of exchange (see note)	£
Freehold land and buildings			
At cost	1 200 000	10(HR)	120 000
less Depreciation	50 000	10(HR)	5 000
	1 150 000		115 000
Short-term net monetary assets	450 000	6(CR)	75 000
	1 600 000		190 000
less Long-term loan	500 000	6(CR)	83 333
	1 100 000		106 667
Shareholders' interest:			
Share capital			
1 000 000 shares of 1 groucho each	1 000 000	10(HR)	100 000
Retained profit			
Per profit and loss account	100 000	Actual	13 750
	1 100 000		113 750
Difference on exchange	–	Balance	(7 083)
	1 100 000		106 667

Note: HR = historical rate, CR = closing rate.

As explained above, SSAP 20 requires any difference on exchange arising under the temporal method to be included in the ordinary profits and losses of the group.

If we assume that the accounts of the parent company are as given in the left-hand column below and that there are no consolidation adjustments for such matters as unrealised intercompany profits, we may proceed to consolidate. This requires adding the figures for the parent company with the sterling figures for the overseas subsidiary, treating the difference on exchange as part of the ordinary profits. We have not produced a Statement of Total Recognised Gains and Losses as there are no gains/losses except for the profit for the financial year.

Widening Horizons Limited
Workings for consolidated profit and loss account for the year ended 31 December 20X2

	Widening Horizons Limited £	Foreign Venture Limited £	Consolidated £
Rentals received	500 000	50 000	550 000
less Expenses			
Management expenses	120 000	14 375	134 375
Depreciation	60 000	5 000	65 000
Loan interest	100 000	9 375	109 375
	280 000	28 750	308 750
Revenue less expenses	220 000	21 250	241 250
less Loss on exchange	–	7 083	7 083
Profit before taxation	220 000	14 167	234 167
less Taxation	100 000	7 500	107 500
	120 000	6 667	126 667
less Dividends proposed	60 000	–	60 000
Retained profit for the year	60 000	6 667	66 667

Workings for movement on reserves for year to 31 December 20X2

	Widening Horizons Limited £	Foreign Venture Limited £	Consolidated £
Retained profits on 1 January 20X2	420 000	–	420 000
add Retained profit for year	60 000	6 667	66 667
Retained profits on 31 December 20X2	480 000	6 667	486 667

Workings for consolidated balance sheet on 31 December 20X2

	Widening Horizons Limited £	Foreign Venture Limited £	Consolidated £
Freehold land and buildings			
At cost	2 000 000	120 000	2 120 000
less Depreciation	350 000	5 000	355 000
	1 650 000	115 000	1 765 000
Investment in Foreign Venture Limited			
At cost	100 000	–	–
Short-term net monetary assets	330 000	75 000	405 000
	2 080 000	190 000	2 170 000
less Long-term loan	1 000 000	83 333	1 083 333
	1 080 000	106 667	1 086 667
Share capital	600 000	100 000	600 000
Retained profits	480 000	6 667	486 667
	1 080 000	106 667	1 086 667

From workings similar to the above, it is quite straightforward to produce the consolidated accounts for publication, although attention would have to be given to providing the more-detailed information in accordance with the formats prescribed by company law.

As would be expected in this case, there is no goodwill on consolidation. The loss on exchange is charged in the profit and loss account and would only be disclosed if it were an exceptional item.

There is no need to analyse the difference on exchange for the purposes of preparing the consolidated accounts. However, it is instructive to do so.

No difference on exchange relates to the freehold land and buildings. In the opening balance sheet of Foreign Venture Limited the freehold land and buildings were shown at cost and translated at 10 grouchos to £1. In the profit and loss account, depreciation of 50 000 grouchos was provided and this was translated at 10 grouchos to £1. In the closing balance sheet the asset is shown at cost less depreciation, again translated at 10 grouchos to £1.

The difference arises, first, because monetary assets and liabilities are translated at different rates in the opening and closing balance sheet and, second, because, for certain items, different rates are used in the profit and loss account and closing balance sheet. It may be analysed as follows:

Analysis of difference on exchange			£
1 Opening balance of short-term net monetary assets	300 000	grouchos	
In opening balance sheet, 10 grouchos to £1	£30 000		
In closing balance sheet, 6 grouchos to £1	£50 000		Gain 20 000
Carried forward			Gain 20 000

		£
Brought forward		Gain 20 000

2 Opening balance on long-term loan	<u>500 000</u> grouchos		
In opening balance sheet,			
10 grouchos to £1	£50 000		
In closing balance sheet,			
6 grouchos to £1	£83 333		Loss 33 333
3 Increase in short-term net	<u></u>		
monetary assets during year			
Per profit and loss account			
Retained profit	100 000 grouchos		
add Depreciation	<u>50 000</u> grouchos		
	150 000 grouchos		
At 8 grouchos to £1	£18 750		
Per closing balance sheet as part			
of short-term net monetary assets,			
at 6 grouchos to £1	£25 000		
	<u></u>		Gain 6 250
Net loss			<u>7 083</u>

The differences on exchange may therefore be understood by thinking in terms of a flow of net monetary items:

Movement in net monetary assets/liabilities for the year ended 31 December 20X2

	Grouchos	Grouchos	Rate	£
Opening balance of net				
monetary liabilities:				
Long-term loan		500 000		
Short-term monetary assets		<u>300 000</u>		
		200 000	10	20 000
less Source of net monetary assets				
Retained profit plus depreciation		150 000	8	18 750
				1 250
Difference on exchange –				
balance (loss)				7 083
Closing balance of net monetary liabilities				
Long-term loan	500 000			
Short-term monetary assets	<u>450 000</u>			
	50 000			
		50 000	6	8 333

A critical look at the two methods

Some substantial differences

We have now demonstrated the mechanics of the two methods of translation, using the same example but rather large movements in the hypothetical exchange rates.

When exchange rates between currencies change over time, the methods produce very different results from the same set of foreign currency accounts. Thus, if we compare the translated amount of the fixed assets of Foreign Venture Limited, in the simple examples in the two preceding sections, we find the following results:

Fixed assets of Foreign Venture Limited on 31 December 20X2

	Net book value £
Closing rate/net investment method	191 667
Temporal method	115 000

It is true that the rate of exchange moved from 10 grouchos to £1 at the beginning of the year to 6 grouchos at the end of the year, but there are substantial changes in practice in the exchange rates between currencies. Table 10.2 contains movements in the rate of exchange between sterling and a number of major currencies over a ten-year period.

To illustrate the effect of the differences between the two methods, let us suppose that a German subsidiary bought land in December 1988 and that this is shown in the balance sheet on 31 December 1998 as:

Land, at cost　　　　1 000 000 Deutschmarks

Under the closing rate/net investment method, this cost would be translated at the closing rate, while under the temporal method, it would be translated at the historical rate. Application of the two rates would produce very different sterling figures for the land:

Closing rate　　1 000 000 ÷ 2.77 = £361 011
Historical rate　1 000 000 ÷ 3.21 = £311 526

When we turn to differences on exchange, we again find substantial differences between the methods. Under the closing rate/net investment method differences on exchange are treated as a movement on reserves, while under the temporal method they are considered to be part of the ordinary profit or loss for the year.

Table 10.2 Movements in exchange rates over ten years

	Rates to £1 at end of December 1988	Rates to £1 at end of December 1998	Change as a percentage
US dollars	1.81	1.66	– 8.3
Belgian francs	67.40	57.16	–15.2
French francs	10.96	9.29	–15.2
German Deutschmarks	3.21	2.77	–13.7
Italian lire	2 362.00	2 743.43	+16.1
Japanese yen	226.00	187.67	–17.0

What then are the respective advantages and disadvantages of the two methods and why has SSAP 20 favoured the use of the closing rate/net investment method?

Advantages and disadvantages

In order to evaluate the two methods of translation, we must bear in mind how the translated figures are going to be used. If we were studying the accounts of an overseas company with a view to acquiring its shares, it might be useful to translate all items in the foreign currency accounts into sterling at the closing rate of exchange in order to produce figures which are meaningful in the home currency. Use of a constant rate of exchange for all items would maintain the same relationships in the sterling accounts as existed in the foreign currency accounts. Thus, for example, long-term liabilities would be the same proportion of fixed assets and the current ratio would be the same in sterling as in the foreign currency accounts.

However, when considering the translation of the accounts of a subsidiary company prior to consolidation, such a consideration would seem to be irrelevant. After all, we add the translated figures for the overseas subsidiary to those of the parent company and hence the relationship between items in the accounts of the overseas subsidiary will be completely lost. What would seem to be more important for meaningful aggregation in the consolidated accounts is that the bases of measurement used for the assets and liabilities are consistent.

If we accept the need to use consistent bases for consolidation then, in the context of historical cost accounting, it seems reasonable to aggregate the historical costs of the fixed assets and stocks of the subsidiary with the historical costs of the fixed assets and stocks of the parent company. Similarly, the amounts payable and receivable at the balance sheet date for both companies should be dealt with in a consistent manner.

Stated in this way, only the temporal method of translation is conceptually consistent with the historical cost basis of accounting and indeed any basis of accounting. The translation of an historical cost at an historical rate produces the historical cost in sterling, that is the amount which would have been incurred if a sum of money had been dispatched from the UK to purchase the asset. The translation of an historical cost at a closing rate would seem to produce a conceptual nonsense.

It was arguments such as these which led the US FASB to require the exclusive use of the temporal method in FAS 8. However, the temporal method is not without its problems.

First, there is the practical problem of keeping records. In order to translate fixed assets and stocks at historical rates of exchange, a detailed analysis of these items together with the respective rates of exchange has to be kept. Such a record is not required by those companies which use the closing rate/net investment method.

Second, the application of the method has caused large fluctuations in the reported profits of groups of companies from period to period, fluctuations which bear little relationship to the underlying operating performance of the overseas subsidiaries. Such volatility of reported earnings arises because of the requirement to include exchange gains and losses on long-term monetary items in the ordinary profits of the group, and the problem could be solved by taking these particular exchange gains or losses direct to reserve or by spreading them over a period of years.

Third, the method produces misleading differences on exchange, which may in turn have adverse behavioural implications.

Let us take as an example a UK company which has an overseas subsidiary. In the balance sheet of the overseas subsidiary, fixed assets and stocks are shown on the

319

basis of historical cost and these are usually financed by net monetary liabilities and an equity interest. During a particular year sterling is weakening against the overseas currency; that is, the other currency is becoming more valuable. In such a case the value of the overseas net assets to the UK company would be increasing and any potential dividends from the overseas subsidiary would be more valuable, as a given future dividend stream in the foreign currency would produce a greater amount of sterling. However, using the temporal method of translation, we would recognise no gains on the fixed assets but merely losses on the net monetary liabilities.

Thus, as a result of the movement in exchange rates, the overseas subsidiary is more valuable, but as a result of using the temporal method, the accounts show losses on exchange!

Under the provisions of both FAS 8 and SSAP 20, such losses on exchange reduced the profits from ordinary activities and hence the earnings per share. Given that boards of directors do not wish to undertake activities which reduce profits or produce losses in the accounts, evidence was produced to indicate that 'profitable' overseas projects had been rejected because of the subsequent accounting losses which resulted from the use of the temporal method of translation.[21]

The closing rate/net investment method does not produce these misleading differences. Because the closing rate is applied to non-monetary assets as well as monetary assets and liabilities, it is possible to set off exchange losses on foreign currency borrowings against exchange gains on real assets and therefore eliminate the need to charge such losses in the profit and loss account. The use of such a cover method is felt by many to reflect the reality of the situation where fixed assets and stocks are financed by money raised overseas. Indeed, under the offset arrangements included in SSAP 20, this cover method is extended to loans raised by the parent company or other companies in the group so that, where foreign currency borrowings have been used to finance, or provide a hedge against, group equity investments in foreign enterprises, exchange gains or losses on the borrowings may be set off against exchange differences arising on the retranslation of the net investment.[22]

Many would support the view that it is unhelpful to take into account exchange gains or losses on the monetary items without taking into account the exchange losses or gains on real assets. However, it is undoubtedly true that it would help users to understand what has happened and likely to happen if companies provided a list of net investments in foreign entities and related borrowings, whose exchange gains or losses are offset as reserve movements, according to the principal foreign currencies involved.[23]

To summarise, the temporal method has the advantage of producing translated figures which are conceptually consistent with the underlying basis of measurement used, whereas the closing rate/net investment method has the advantage of simplicity

[21] *See*, for example, D.P. Walker, *An economic analysis of foreign exchange risk*, ICAEW Research Committee Occasional Paper No. 14, ICAEW, London, 1978.

[22] SSAP 20, Para. 57 specifies the conditions under which this offset arrangement may be applied. As we shall see in the last section of this chapter, the exchange difference on the retranslation of the net assets in the consolidated accounts will usually differ from the exchange difference on the retranslation of the investment in the accounts of the parent company.

[23] It was to this end that the ASB published a brief Exposure Draft 'Amendment to SSAP20 "Foreign Currency Translation": Disclosure' in February 1999. This Exposure Draft was withdrawn shortly afterwards, in May 1999, on the grounds that more substantial changes to SSAP 20 are needed. The ASB proposes to issue a new Exposure Draft once its project on financial instruments is completed and has settled some of the key issues relevant to foreign currencies.

and manages to avoid the reporting of fluctuating profits and misleading differences on exchange by the use of one rate of exchange for both assets and liabilities.

The ASC had to balance the respective advantages and disadvantages of the two methods in producing SSAP 20. As we have seen, it favours the closing rate/net investment method for the majority of situations but requires the use of the temporal method where the trade of the foreign enterprise is more dependent on the economic environment of the investing company's currency than that of its own reporting currency. It does, however, recognise the limitations of the closing rate/net investment method where the foreign country suffers from hyper-inflation. In such a case it requires that the local currency financial statements be adjusted to reflect current price levels before the translation process is undertaken.[24]

In the view of the authors, the use of the closing rate/net investment method is inconsistent with the subsequent consolidation of the resulting sterling figures. In our view, the logic of the method should lead us to include the results of an overseas subsidiary in the consolidated accounts by using the equity method of accounting.[25] In this way the consolidated profit and loss account would include the appropriate proportion of the profit or loss of the subsidiary while the consolidated balance sheet would show a net investment in the overseas subsidiary. This is surely what the title of the closing rate/net investment method implies!

One aspect of a larger problem

We have seen that both of the major methods of translation have advantages and disadvantages and that it has been difficult to choose between them.

The difficulties which we face here may be seen as part of the much larger problem discussed in the early part of this book. In Chapter 3 we have seen, for example, that the addition of historical costs which have been incurred at different points in time results in an unhelpful total when the value of the pound has been changing over time. The movement of exchange rates between currencies presents us with similar problems and, given that we have not yet solved the problems of accounting where only one currency is involved, it is not surprising that there is considerable confusion when we introduce two or more currencies.

It might be suggested that the major stumbling-block is the traditional reliance on historical cost accounts, which are known to have so many defects. We cannot expect the choice of exchange rate to remedy these defects. If we were to depart from historical costs and instead to show assets and liabilities of the overseas company at their current values, only one rate of exchange would be appropriate. The closing rate is required by both the temporal method and the closing rate method and the resulting sterling figures may quite properly be aggregated with the current values of assets and liabilities of the parent company. It would still be necessary to determine the treatment of resulting differences on exchange but a major problem would have disappeared.

There would still, of course, be other problems in connection with foreign currencies. In all the examples, we have assumed that our UK parent company prepares consolidated accounts, so that sterling is the appropriate currency to use. Once we

---

[24] SSAP 20, Para. 26. This topic is addressed by IAS 29 'Financial reporting in hyper-inflationary economies' and UITF Abstract 9 'Accounting for operations in hyper-inflationary economies', June 1993. These specifically require adjustments where the cumulative rate of inflation over a three-year period is approaching or exceeds 100 per cent.

[25] See Chapter 9 for a comprehensive discussion of the equity method of accounting.

widen our horizons to look at a multinational company, which operates throughout the world and has shareholders in many countries, it is difficult to know even what the reporting currency should be, let alone what the resulting differences on exchange really mean.

To illustrate the sort of problem which we face, let us end this section with a very simple example:

Let us suppose that an individual habitually spends six months of every year in the UK and six months in the USA. On 1 January 20X2 he has wealth of $100 000 in the USA and £100 000 in the UK when the rate of exchange between the currencies is $2.0 to £1. During the year he lives on income arising in the respective countries and ends the year with exactly the same money wealth in each country when the exchange rate has moved to $1.5 to £1.

Let us compare his wealth at the beginning and end of the year in dollars and sterling, respectively:

	$	£
Opening wealth – 1 January 20X2		
(rate of exchange $2.0 to £1)		
UK, £100 000	200 000	100 000
USA, $100 000	100 000	50 000
	300 000	150 000
Closing wealth – 31 December 20X2		
(rate of exchange $1.5 to £1)		
UK, £100 000	150 000	100 000
USA, $100 000	100 000	66 667
	250 000	166 667
Gain during year	–	£16 667
Loss during year	$50 000	–

As can be seen, if we ignore changes in the purchasing power of the respective currencies, the translation process produces a loss of $50 000 or a gain of £16 667 during the year, even though our individual has the same money wealth at the end as he did at the beginning.

Problems such as those discussed above obviously bedevil the multinational company. Although such companies prepare consolidated accounts in the currency of the country where the parent company is situated, it must be admitted that the figures produced are of dubious significance to many shareholders.

A more complex example

Example 10.8 The closing rate/net investment method

(A) Some years ago, Home Country plc, a UK company, raised a long-term loan of $400 000 which it used to help purchase 80 per cent of the shares in Overseas Inc. at a total cost of $500 000.

(B) Relevant rates of exchange were as follows:

	Dollars to £1
At date of acquisition	5
On 31 December 20X1	4
On 31 December 20X2	3

(C) We shall first look at the treatment of the above transactions in the accounts of the parent company.

In accordance with the principles explained earlier in the chapter, the loan and investment would have originally been recorded at the following amounts:

Long-term loan ($400 000 ÷ 5)	£80 000
Investment in subsidiary ($500 000 ÷ 5)	£100 000

On 31 December 20X1 the loan would have been translated at the rate on that date and we shall assume that the company has also translated the investment at the closing rate at that date, as permitted by Para. 51 of SSAP 20. These items would have then appeared in the balance sheet as follows:

Home Country plc
Extract from balance sheet on 31 December 20X1
Long-term loan denominated in dollars
$400 000 ÷ 4	£100 000
Investment in subsidiary	
$500 000 ÷ 4	£125 000

The difference on exchange between the date of acquisition and 31 December 20X1 would have been credited to reserves in past years, namely:

Exchange gain on equity investment	
£125 000 – £100 000	£25 000
less Exchange loss on dollar loan	
£100 000 – £80 000	£20 000
Net gain	£5 000

When the balance sheet on 31 December 20X2 is prepared, the foreign currency amounts will be translated at the closing rate of $3 to £1:

Home Country plc
Extract from balance sheet on 31 December 20X2
Long-term loan denominated in dollars
$400 000 ÷ 3	£133 333
Investment in subsidiary	
$500 000 ÷ 3	£166 667

The difference on exchange to be treated as a movement on reserves in 20X2 in the accounts of the parent company is therefore as follows:

Home Country plc
Part of movement on reserves for 20X2

Exchange gain on equity investment	
£166 667 – £125 000	£41 667
less Exchange loss on dollar loan	
£133 333 – £100 000	£33 333
Net gain	£8 334

(D) The above figures for 20X2 are incorporated in the summarised accounts of Home Country plc for the year ended 31 December 20X2 which appear below:

Home Country plc
Profit and loss account for the year ended 31 December 20X2

	£
Profit before taxation	117 000
Dividend receivable from Overseas Inc. (net)	
(80% of £20 000)	16 000
	133 000
less Taxation	60 000
	73 000
less Dividends payable	30 000
Retained profit for year	43 000

Home Country plc
Movement on reserves for the year ended 31 December 20X2

	£
Balance on 1 January 20X2	133 666
Retained profit for year	43 000
Difference on exchange	8 334
Balance on 31 December 20X2	185 000

Home Country plc
Balance sheet on 31 December 20X2

	£	£
Fixed assets		
Tangible assets		400 000
Investment in subsidiary (80% holding)		166 667
Current assets		
Stocks	60 000	
Debtors	40 000	
Dividend receivable from Overseas Inc.	16 000	
Cash	5 666	
Carried forward	121 666	566 667

	£	£
Brought forward	121 666	566 667
less Current liabilities	70 000	51 666
		618 333
less Long-term loans:		
Denominated in dollars	133 333	
Denominated in sterling	100 000	233 333
		385 000
Share capital		200 000
Reserves		185 000
		385 000

(E) We may now turn our attention to the accounts of the overseas subsidiary.

The balance sheet of Overseas Inc. on 31 December 20X1 in dollars is given in the left-hand column while the relevant rates of exchange and resulting sterling amounts are given in the second and third columns, respectively. It has been assumed that the assets of Overseas Inc. were revalued at their fair values at the date of acquisition to produce a revaluation reserve of $150 000. Other reserves at the date of acquisition are assumed to have been $100 000.

Overseas Inc.
Balance sheet on 31 December 20X1

	$	Rate of exchange	£
Fixed assets			
At revalued amounts at date of acquisition and subsequent cost less depreciation	1 000 000	4(CR)	250 000
Current assets			
Stocks	300 000	4(CR)	75 000
Debtors	200 000	4(CR)	50 000
Cash	100 000	4(CR)	25 000
	600 000		150 000
less Current liabilities	400 000	4(CR)	100 000
Net current assets	200 000		50 000
	1 200 000		300 000
less Long-term loan	600 000	4(CR)	150 000
	600 000		150 000
Share capital	100 000	5(HR)	20 000
Revaluation reserve – at date of acquisition by Home Country plc	150 000	5(HR)	30 000
Reserves			
Pre-acquisition	100 000	5(HR)	20 000
	350 000		70 000
Post-acquisition	250 000	Balance	80 000
	600 000		150 000

Notice that in translating the balance sheet, the share capital and pre-acquisition reserves have been translated at the historical rate at the date of acquisition with the intention of maintaining the goodwill on consolidation at its 'cost'. This effectively treats the goodwill as a sterling asset, rather than a foreign asset, and appears to be the method envisaged by SSAP 20. While this articulated well with the regime of SSAP 22 under which goodwill was invariably written off immediately against reserves, it does not fit so comfortably with the FRS 10 approach under which goodwill continues to appear in consolidated balance sheets long after the acquisition of a subsidiary. If this goodwill is regarded as a foreign asset, rather than a sterling asset, then arguably it should be translated at the closing rate with any resulting difference on exchange being taken to reserves.

We shall continue to follow the former approach although we recognise that this may be changed in any successor to SSAP 20.

The balance of post-acquisition reserves, which is translated at £80 000, includes all exchange differences which have arisen since the date of acquisition. The size of these exchange differences depends upon when the post-acquisition reserves were earned and the rates of exchange prevailing at those dates. The less the fluctuation in exchange rates since acquisition, the lower will be the difference.

At first sight the use of historical rates for share capital and pre-acquisition reserves might be thought to be incorrect as far as the minority interest is concerned. However, the minority interest is 20 per cent of the net assets or total share capital and reserves, and the way in which the individual components of the share capital and reserves are translated has no effect on the total figure.

(F) The accounts of Overseas Inc. for the year ended 31 December 20X2 are given below. The left-hand column is in dollars, the centre column gives the relevant rate of exchange and the right-hand column gives the resulting sterling figures.

The profit and loss account has been translated at the closing rate rather than the average rate and, as we have seen earlier in the chapter, this avoids one difference on exchange.

Overseas Inc.
Profit and loss account for the year ended 31 December 20X2

	$	Rate of exchange (closing rate)	£
Operating profit	330 000	3	110 000
less Taxation	150 000	3	50 000
	180 000		60 000
less Dividends payable	60 000	3	20 000
Retained profit for year	120 000		40 000

Overseas Inc.
Balance sheet on 31 December 20X2

	$	Rate of exchange	£
Fixed assets			
At revalued amount or cost			
less depreciation	960 000	3	320 000
Current assets			
Stock	360 000	3	120 000
Debtors	240 000	3	80 000
Cash	160 000	3	53 333
	760 000		253 333
less Current liabilities			
(including dividend payable)	400 000	3	133 333
Net current assets	360 000		120 000
	1 320 000		440 000
less Long-term loan	600 000	3	200 000
	720 000		240 000
Share capital	100 000	5(HR)	20 000
Revaluation reserve			
(created at date of acquisition)	150 000	5(HR)	30 000
Reserves			
Pre-acquisition	100 000	5(HR)	20 000
Post-acquisition		Per balance	
at 1 January 20X2	250 000	sheet 31.12.20X1	80 000
(Net assets on 1.1.20X2)	600 000	4	150 000
Post-acquisition		Per P and L	
Current year – 20X2	120 000	account	40 000
	720 000		190 000
Difference on exchange	–	Balance	50 000
	720 000		240 000

Note that the balance sheet contains a suitable analysis of reserves and, in particular, that it is necessary to translate the post-acquisition reserves so that they agree with the previous year's accounts and with the profit and loss account balance for the year ended 31 December 20X2, respectively. An exchange gain of £50 000 emerges as the balancing figure. As the profit and loss account has been translated at the closing rate rather than the average rate, the whole of the difference on exchange relates to the opening net assets:

Difference on exchange

Opening net assets	$600 000	
Translation at beginning of year $600 000 ÷ 4		£150 000
Translation at end of year $600 000 ÷ 3		200 000
Gain on exchange		50 000

(G) In order to prepare consolidated accounts, it is necessary to provide the usual analysis of the shareholders' interest in Overseas Inc. and to decide how to deal with the difference on exchange. In practice there will usually be many other adjustments in respect of such matters as unrealised inter-company profits, but these are problems faced on any consolidation and are therefore not dealt with here.

The shareholders' interest in Overseas Inc. may be analysed as follows:

Overseas Inc.
Analysis of shareholders' equity on 31 December 20X2

	Total	Pre-acquisition	Group 80% Post-acquisition	Minority interest
	£	£	£	£
Share capital	20 000	16 000		4 000
Revaluation reserve	30 000	24 000		6 000
Other reserves				
Pre-acquisition	20 000	16 000		4 000
Post-acquisition				
At 1 January 20X2	80 000		64 000	16 000
Retained profit 20X2	40 000		32 000	8 000
Difference on exchange 20X2	50 000		40 000	10 000
	240 000	56 000	136 000	48 000
Cost of investment				
(original cost)		100 000		
Goodwill on consolidation		44 000		

(H) As shown in section (C), the accounts of Home Country plc for 20X2 include an exchange gain on the equity investment of £41 667 and an exchange loss on the dollar loan of £33 333, together producing a net gain of £8334 which has been credited to reserves.

When we turn to the consolidated accounts it is still possible to set the loss on the dollar loan, which appears in the parent company's accounts, against the gain on the investment as permitted by SSAP 20, Para. 57. However, the appropriate exchange gain in the consolidated accounts is the parent company's share of the exchange gain resulting from the translation of the subsidiary's accounts, in this case 80 per cent of £50 000 = £40 000.

This treatment is in line with the general principle of consolidation whereby the cost of the investment in the parent company's balance sheet is replaced by the underlying net assets of the subsidiary.

As a consequence of this, the net difference on exchange, which is to be treated as a movement on reserves in the consolidated accounts, will be:

	£
Gain on exchange in 20X2 in respect of Home Country's share of net assets in Overseas Inc., 80% of £50 000	40 000
less Loss on exchange in 20X2 in respect of dollar loan – per accounts of Home Country plc (see (C) above)	33 333
Net gain	6 667

(I) An adjustment similar to that discussed in (H) above is necessary to calculate the balance of consolidated reserves brought forward at 1 January 20X2.

It is insufficient just to add together the reserves of Home Country plc and 80 per cent of the post-acquisition reserves of Overseas Inc. As shown in Section (C), the reserves of Home Country plc on 31 December 20X1 include the following net exchange gain made since acquisition:

	£
Exchange gain on equity investment	25 000
less Exchange loss on dollar loan	20 000
Net gain	5 000

While the exchange loss on the dollar loan may be properly charged against consolidated reserves, the relevant exchange gain in the consolidated accounts is not that on the investment but the parent company's share of the gain on translating the subsidiary's accounts. We do not know the amount of this exchange gain but we do know that it is included in the figure of £80 000 for post-acquisition reserves shown in (E) above.

The balance of consolidated reserves on 31 December 20X1, that is brought forward on 1.1.20X2, may therefore be calculated as follows:

	£
Home Country plc	
Per company's own balance sheet (*see* (D))	133 666
less Exchange gain on equity investment included in above figure (*see* this section above)	25 000
	108 666
Overseas Inc.	
Share of post-acquisition reserves at 1.1.20X2 including exchange differences on net assets since acquisition, 80% of £80 000 (*see* (E))	64 000
	172 666

(J) We are now in a position to consolidate:

Home Country plc
Workings for consolidated profit and loss account for the year to 31 December 20X2

	£	£
Profit before taxation		
Home Country plc	117 000	
Overseas Inc.	110 000	227 000
less Taxation		
Home Country plc	60 000	
Overseas Inc.	50 000	110 000
		117 000
less Minority interest, 20% of (£110 000 – £50 000)		12 000
		105 000
less Dividends payable by parent company		30 000
Retained profit for the year		75 000

Workings for movement on reserves for year to 31 December 20X2

	£	£
Balance on 1 January 20X2 (per (I) above)		172 666
Retained profit for year – per consolidated profit and loss account above		75 000
Exchange gain (per (H) above)		
Gain on net assets	40 000	
less Loss on foreign currency borrowings	33 333	6 667
Balance on 31 December 20X2		254 333

Workings for consolidated balance sheet on 31 December 20X2

	£	£
Fixed assets		
Tangible assets – at net book value		
Home Country plc	400 000	
Overseas Inc. (see note (a))	320 000	720 000
Intangible assets		
Goodwill on consolidation – at cost per analysis of equity interest (see (G))		44 000
Net current assets (see note (b))		
Home Country plc	51 666	
Overseas Inc.	120 000	171 666
		935 666
less Long-term loans		
Home Country plc	233 333	
Overseas Inc.	200 000	433 333
		502 333
Share capital		200 000
Reserves – as above		254 333
		454 333
Minority interest, per analysis of equity interest		48 000
		502 333

Notes:
(a) Note that the revalued amount of the fixed assets of Overseas Inc. at the date of acquisition represents 'cost' to the group.
(b) An adjustment is necessary to cancel out the dividend receivable by Home Country plc. The amount is £16 000 but the effect on the total net current assets is, of course, nil.

It is now relatively straightforward to prepare the consolidated accounts for publication in the normal manner, although a greater amount of detail would be necessary to satisfy the disclosure requirements of company law and accounting standards. In order to simplify the example, goodwill on consolidation has not been written off.

The international accounting standard

Although IAS 21 'Accounting for the Effects of Changes in Exchange Rates', was first issued in 1983, it was reconsidered as part of the IASC comparability and improvements project and issued in a revised form as IAS 21 'The Effects of Changes in Foreign Exchange Rates' in November 1993. This revised version comes some ten years after the issue of SSAP 20 and some twelve years after the issue of the US Statement of Financial Accounting Standard number 95 'Foreign Translation' in December 1981. All three statements are based upon the same underlying principles although these are expressed rather differently. Inevitably, there are differences in detail.

In particular, IAS 21 makes it clear that it does not deal with hedge accounting except for items which hedge a net investment in a foreign entity; some guidance on hedge accounting has subsequently been provided in IAS 39 'Financial Instruments: Recognition and Measurement' (1998).

Leaving this on one side, IAS 21 requires the same method of accounting for foreign currency transactions as SSAP 20. Thus transactions are initially recorded at the actual rate of exchange. At subsequent balance sheet dates, non-monetary items must be translated at the historical rate, unless they are shown at a subsequent fair value, in which case the rate at the date on which the fair value was established must be used. Monetary assets and liabilities must normally be retranslated at the closing rate and any differences on exchange must be taken to the profit and loss account. The international standard does not have to concern itself with the thorny problem of whether exchange gains/losses are realised or unrealised, which bedevils discussion of this and many other topics in the UK. A cover method is required where a foreign currency liability is accounted for as a hedge of an enterprise's net investment in a foreign entity (see below) but the cumulative exchange differences relating to the investment should be recognised in the profit and loss account in the same period that the company recognises the gain or loss on disposal of the investment.

When we turn to the translation of foreign financial statements as a preliminary to aggregation, IAS 21 distinguishes between a foreign entity, the activities of which are not an integral part of those of the reporting enterprise, and a foreign operation that is integral to the operations of the reporting enterprise. It requires the use of the closing rate/net investment method for the former and the temporal method for the latter. Thus it adopts the basic approach of SSAP 20 although it uses different terminology. However, in the context of the closing rate method to be used for foreign entities, it specifically requires that income and expense items should be translated at the exchange rates at the dates of transactions rather than the average rate for the period or closing rate as required by SSAP 20. Given the conceptual deficiencies of the closing rate method, discussed earlier in this chapter, this would seem to achieve spurious accuracy.

IAS 21 specifically refers to the treatment of goodwill and fair value adjustments within the context of the closing rate method. It allows these to be translated either at the historical rate or at the closing rate. Thus, as we explained in Example 10.8 in the context of a UK parent, they may be treated either as a sterling asset or as a foreign currency asset.

The disclosure requirements of IAS 21 are more stringent than SSAP 20. In particular, the requirements of the international accounting standard include disclosure of:[26]

the amount of exchange differences included in the net profit or loss for the period; net exchange differences classified as equity as a separate component of equity, and a reconciliation of the amount of such exchange differences at the beginning and end of the period; the method selected . . . to translate goodwill and fair value adjustments arising on the acquisition of a foreign entity.

Recommended reading

I.J. Martin, *Accounting and Control in the Foreign Exchange Market*, 2nd edn, Butterworths, London, 1993.

C. Nobes, 'A review of the translation debate', *Accounting and Business Research Number 40*, ICAEW, London, Autumn 1980.

J. Pearcy, *How to Account for Foreign Currencies*, Macmillan, Basingstoke, 1984.

L. Revsine, 'The rationale underlying the functional currency choice', in *Accounting Theory and Policy*, R. Bloom and P.T. Elgers (eds), Harcourt Brace Jovanovich, Orlando, USA, 1987.

P. Wallace and B.D.G. Ogle, 'Foreign currency translation', *Accountants Digest Number 150*, ICAEW, London, 1983/84.

C.A. Westwick, *Accounting for Overseas Operations*, Gower, Aldershot, 1986.

---

[26] *See* IAS 21, Paras 42–47 for full disclosure requirements.

11 Expansion of the annual report

Overview   The size of the annual reports of companies, particularly those of listed companies, has grown substantially as directors have chosen to provide much greater information than that required by law. While much of this increased disclosure has been required or encouraged by the Stock Exchange and the Accounting Standards Board, much is provided voluntarily. In this chapter, we examine a number of statements with which accountants need to be familiar, namely:

- Cash Flow Statement
- Value Added Statement
- Operating and Financial Review
- Historical Summary
- Reporting about and to employees
- Summary Financial Statement

The Accounting Standards Board is also attempting to regulate other parts of the annual reporting package of listed companies and we shall conclude with a brief look at two recent ASB statements:

- Interim Reports
- Preliminary Announcements

Introduction

Traditionally a set of accounts, as financial statements used to be described, consisted of just two statements albeit supported by, often voluminous, notes. The balance sheet summarised the position at the end of an accounting year while the profit and loss account explained what had happened since the previous balance sheet. Neither document pretended to tell the whole story and, in particular, the profit and loss account was uncomfortable about reporting increases in value not caused by operations. We have seen, in earlier chapters, how accounting practice has developed to deal with some of the deficiencies of the traditional approach by the introduction of a new primary statement, the Statement of Total Recognised Gains and Losses, and a requirement for a Reconciliation of Movements in Shareholders' Funds. Such statements serve to provide a more coherent description of how things have changed but remain firmly based on the traditional reporting model.

In this chapter, we will discuss some different approaches to reporting. The differences come in varying forms. Some of the statements which we will consider, such as the Cash Flow Statement and Value Added Statement, try to provide a different perspective on what has happened during the year. Others, such as the historical summary and operating and financial review, provide a context for the current year's report while other statements, such as the simplified statements prepared for shareholders and employees, attempt to address the needs of particular user groups. Yet other reports, namely interim reports and preliminary announcements, seek to provide users with more timely information.

While the statements discussed in this chapter share the common feature that they are not required by company law, they are certainly not all produced with the same frequency. Some are found frequently because they are required by the Stock Exchange or the Accounting Standards Board; examples of these are Interim Reports and Cash Flow Statements. Some are produced by some companies but not by others; examples are historical summaries and simplified reports. While the Value Added Statement enjoyed a period of popularity in the 1970s and early 1980s, few companies now produce such a statement. However, these statements provide an important and different perspective on the activities of a company and are therefore all worthy of examination.

In broad terms the objectives of most additional statements are the same – to assist users of accounts to obtain a more comprehensive view of the progress and future prospects of the company. This broad objective can be served in a number of ways and it is helpful to have a framework within which the statements can be analysed. Essentially the statements can be seen as constituting two groups, depending on whether a statement:

(a) provides more data than is required by company law, or
(b) does not provide additional data but makes it easier to assimilate the data either by rearrangement of the figures or through the provision of simplified statements.

We might usefully refer to the first group as 'extended' statements and the second as 'rearranged and simplified' statements.

Extended statements include such documents as the Cash Flow Statement and Employment Report as well as the Operating and Financial Review.

Rearranged and simplified statements can be derived from the published accounts of the company, except in the case of smaller companies, and include such documents as the Value Added Statement, the simplified report to employees and the Summary Financial Statement which may be sent to the shareholders of listed companies.

It is interesting to question why companies should be required or choose to publish such rearranged and simplified statements. In part the reason may be behavioural in the sense that the publication of the document is intended to create better relations with employees and the community in general. Such an objective is clearly present in the case of simplified accounts prepared especially for employees. Another possible reason is the wish to remove the 'competitive advantage' possessed by investors and potential investors who have technical knowledge themselves or have ready access to professional advice.[1]

The first major developments in the drive towards the expansion of the annual report came in 1975 when the Accounting Standards Steering Committee issued both

---

[1] Supporters of the 'efficient market hypothesis' which, in its semistrong form, states that all available data relevant to the price of a share is immediately reflected in the market price, would presumably take the view that there is nothing to be gained from any requirement for companies to publish otherwise available data in a different form.

SSAP 10, 'Statements of Source and Application of Funds', and *The Corporate Report*.[2] SSAP 10 required all but very small enterprises to prepare a statement of source and application of funds as part of their audited financial accounts. It has since been superseded by FRS 1, 'Cash Flow Statements', first issued in September 1991 but subsequently revised in October 1996. *The Corporate Report* argued that the then current reporting practices did not fully meet the needs of the various users of accounts and recommended that all significant economic entities should publish the following additional statements:

(a) a statement of value added;
(b) an employment report;
(c) a statement of money exchanges with government;
(d) a statement of transactions in foreign currency;
(e) a statement of future prospects;
(f) a statement of corporate objectives.

The adoption of these recommendations would have resulted in the provision of substantially more information than that provided by the statutory financial accounts. While *The Corporate Report* remains an important document worthy of study, none of these recommendations have in fact been adopted by the ASC or ASB.

Even without legislative requirements, it is clear that the accountant must develop competence in producing and interpreting statements other than the traditional balance sheet and profit and loss account. This chapter concentrates on two of these, the Cash Flow Statement and the Value Added Statement. It then examines more briefly the Operating and Financial Review, the Historical Summary, the subject of reporting about and to employees and the Summary Financial Statement which listed companies may send to their shareholders instead of the full financial statements. Finally it examines the recent attempts of the ASB to regulate Interim Reports and Preliminary Announcements.

Cash flow statements

Background

It has long been recognised that the information provided by a balance sheet and profit and loss account gives users limited help in understanding how the liquidity of a company or group has been affected by its activities during a particular year. To remedy this, accounting standard setters in many countries have required companies to prepare 'funds statements', that is statements showing the sources and applications of funds. In the UK, SSAP, 10 'Statement of Source and Application of Funds', was first issued in July 1975 and required all companies with a turnover or gross income of £25 000 or greater to prepare such a statement.

One of the first difficulties which companies encountered in complying with SSAP 10 was that, although the statement defined net liquid funds as one component of funds, it did not actually define the term funds. As with profit, there are many possible definitions of funds including cash, working capital and all financial resources. The

---

[2] *The Corporate Report*, Accounting Standards Steering Committee, London, 1975.

choice of definition determines what the statement seeks to explain and hence what is shown as a source or application. To take a simple example, the receipt of cash from debtors is a source of funds if the cash concept is adopted, but merely a change in the constituent parts of funds if the working capital concept is used. As a second example, the issue of shares in exchange for the purchase of fixed assets is neither a source nor an application if either the cash or working capital concepts are used, but it certainly changes the financial resources of a company.

In the USA, the funds statement had long been the subject of criticism[3] and, in November 1987, the FASB replaced the requirement for US companies to produce a funds statement with a requirement for them to produce a statement of cash flows, Statement of Financial Accounting Standards number 95, 'Statement of Cash Flows', which requires relevant US companies to prepare a statement explaining the change in cash and cash equivalents by showing cash receipts and payments.

The UK accounting standard setters drew on this US standard in preparing FRS 1, 'Cash Flow Statements', the first standard to be published by the newly established Accounting Standards Board back in September 1991. However, FRS 1 was revised in October 1996 and, in the revised version, the ASB has moved some considerable way from the US and, indeed, international approach, which we shall outline later in the chapter.

FRS 1 requires all relevant British entities to prepare a Cash Flow Statement as one of its primary financial statements. The revised standard applies to all financial statements intended to give a true and fair view of financial position and profit or loss although exemptions are given to a number of entities including small companies, subsidiary undertakings where 90 per cent or more of the voting rights are controlled within the group, provided relevant consolidated accounts are publicly available, as well as to more specialised institutions such as pension funds and certain open-ended investment funds.[4]

We turn first to the preparation of a Cash Flow Statement for a single company.

FRS 1 and the individual company

The objective of FRS 1 is to ensure that the reporting entities falling within its scope:

(a) report their cash generation and cash absorption for a period by highlighting the significant components of cash flow in a way that facilitates comparison of the cash flow performance of different businesses; and

(b) provide information that assists in the assessment of their liquidity, solvency and financial adaptability.

(Para. 1)

To this end, it requires relevant entities to prepare a Cash Flow Statement explaining the change in cash balances during a period. In order to permit comparisons with other businesses, receipts and payments are to be analysed under the nine headings shown opposite:[5]

---

[3] *See*, for example, Loyd C. Heath, 'Let's scrap the funds statement', *Journal of Accountancy*, October 1978.
[4] FRS 1 'Cash Flow Statements' (Revised 1996), ASB, London, October 1996, Para. 5.
[5] FRS 1 (Revised 1996) required the use of eight headings but this has itself been revised by FRS 9 'Accounting for Associates and Joint Ventures', which was issued in November 1997. FRS 9 requires the insertion of a new heading 'Dividends received from associates and joint ventures'.

Cash flow statement for the year ended 31 December 20X1

	£
Net cash inflow/outflow from operating activities	X
Dividends received from associates and joint ventures	X
Returns on investment and servicing of finance	X
Taxation	X
Capital expenditure and financial investment	X
Acquisitions and disposals	X
Equity dividends paid	X̲
Cash inflow/outflow before use of liquid resources and financing	X
Management of liquid resources	X
Financing	X̲
Increase/decrease in cash during year	X̲̲

Cash is defined 'restrictively' as:

> Cash in hand and deposits repayable on demand with any qualifying financial institution, less overdrafts from any qualifying institution repayable on demand. Deposits are repayable on demand if they can be withdrawn at any time without notice and without penalty or if a maturity or period of notice of not more than 24 hours or one working day has been agreed. Cash includes cash in hand and deposits denominated in foreign currencies. (Para. 2)

In requiring companies to explain the change in cash during a period, the revised FRS 1 introduced the first true 'cash' flow statement. The original FRS 1, like the US standard 94 and the international standard IAS 7, had required companies to prepare a statement explaining changes in 'cash and cash equivalents'. As we shall explain later, the definition of cash equivalents gave rise to considerable problems in practice and the ASB was unable to develop a satisfactory definition to replace it.

In order to emphasise how the Cash Flow Statement articulates with the profit and loss account and balance sheet, FRS 1 requires that the statement be accompanied by two notes. The first provides a reconciliation with an item in the profit and loss account while the second provides a reconciliation with items in the opening and closing balance sheets.

Notes required:

1 Reconciliation of net cash inflow/outflow from operating activities with operating profit/loss.
2 Reconciliation of cash flows with the movement in net debt/net funds during the period.

Net debt is defined in paragraph 2 of the Standard, as:

> The borrowings of the reporting entity (comprising debt as defined in FRS 4 'Capital Instruments' (paragraph 6), together with related derivatives, and obligations under finance leases) less cash and liquid resources. Where cash and liquid resources exceed the borrowings of the entity reference should be made to 'net funds' rather than to 'net debt'.

With this framework, we shall examine the cash flows to be included under each of the nine main headings.

Net cash flow from operating activities

The net cash flow from operating activities is the cash flow relating to all those activities which are included in arriving at the operating profit of the entity. It may be calculated by the direct method (the gross method) or the indirect method (the net method) although only the resulting figure should be disclosed in the cash flow statement.

Direct method	
Cash receipts from customers	X
Cash payments to suppliers	(X)
Cash payments to and on behalf of employees	(X)
Net cash flow from operating activities	X
Indirect method	
Operating profit	X
Adjustments for items not involving a flow of cash:	
Depreciation	X
Increase in stocks	(X)
Increase in debtors relating to operating activities	(X)
Increase in creditors relating to operating activities	X
Net cash flow from operating activities	X

The direct method is undoubtedly easier for a non-accountant to understand but requires information which is not provided routinely by the accounting systems of many companies. The indirect method effectively reverses all the accruals adjustments which have been made in arriving at operating profit.

As we have explained above, FRS 1 requires companies to publish a note to the Cash Flow Statement reconciling the net cash inflow/outflow from operating activities to the operating profit. This provides the calculation of net cash flows using the indirect method and can be extremely confusing for non-accountants. While the original FRS 1 sensibly relegated this reconciliation to a note, the revised FRS 1 permits it to be given either adjoining the cash flow statement or as a note. However, it points out clearly that:

> The reconciliation is not part of the cash flow statement; if adjoining the cash flow statement, it should be clearly labelled and kept separate. (Para. 12)

In the view of the authors, this rather subtle point that the first part of a published Cash Flow Statement is a note, rather than a part of the Statement, is likely to be lost on the majority of users!

It should be noted that operating cash flows relating to provisions made in the past must also be included as part of the operating cash flow. So where a provision is made for a fundamental reorganisation or restructuring in the profit and loss account of one period but the cash payments take place in a later period, the cash outflows in that later period must still be included as operating cash flows (Para. 58).

Dividends received from associates and joint ventures

Following the issue of FRS 9 'Associates and Joint Ventures' in November 1997, it is now necessary to include dividends received from associates and joint ventures under this separate heading. Their proximity to the net cash flow from operating activities in the cash flow statement reflects the treatment of the share of the operating profit of such investees in consolidated profit and loss accounts or in the notes or supplementary profit and loss accounts prepared by individual companies.[6]

---

[6] See Chapter 9, pp. 282–91.

Returns on investments and servicing of finance

FRS 1 requires the separation of returns on investments and payments to service financing from the capital flows to which they relate. The cash flows under this heading should therefore include the following items:

- interest received, including any related tax recovered;
- interest paid, including any tax deducted therefrom and paid to the relevant tax authority (the standard specifically requires the inclusion of interest paid even if it is capitalised and, of course, requires the inclusion of the interest element of finance lease payments);
- dividends received, net of tax credits;
- dividends paid, on non equity shares.

Dividends paid on equity share capital are to be included under a separate heading 'Equity dividends paid' discussed below.

Taxation

The only amounts to be included under this heading are payments and receipts relating to tax on the company's revenue and capital profits. Thus this heading typically comprises payments of corporation tax and similar foreign taxes.

Taxes for which the company acts as a collecting agent for the government, such as VAT, would normally be dealt with as part of the operating activities of the company. Cash flows would then be shown net of any VAT and an adjustment would be made to reflect the change in the amount payable to or recoverable from the government.

Capital expenditure and financial investment

This heading comprises all payments and receipts in respect of the purchase or sale of fixed assets, whether tangible, intangible or investments in the loans or shares of other entities. It excludes payments and receipts in respect of acquisitions and disposals which must be included under the succeeding heading. However, it includes payments and receipts relating to any current asset investment which is not included in the company's definition of liquid resources. We shall discuss such liquid resources under the heading 'Management of liquid resources' below.

Some commentators had argued that the ASB should require companies to distinguish between capital expenditure incurred to maintain the size of the business and capital expenditure involving expansion. Not surprisingly, the ASB took the view that such a distinction would be both difficult to make and to police.

Acquisitions and disposals

This heading comprises receipts and payments in respect of acquisitions and disposals of trades and businesses as well as purchases and sales of investments in subsidiary undertakings, associates and joint ventures. As we shall see in a later section of the chapter, in dealing with the purchase or sale of subsidiary undertakings in consolidated financial statements, it will be necessary to show separately any balances of cash and overdraft of the subsidiary at the date of acquisition or disposal.

Equity dividends paid

The cash flows to be included here are the dividends paid on the reporting entity's equity shares.

Under the original FRS 1, such dividends were to be shown under the earlier heading 'Returns on investments and servicing of finance', which resulted in a consistent treatment of dividends received and paid as well as of interest received and paid. However, the revised FRS 1 requires that equity dividends paid, typically the dividends paid on ordinary shares, should be shown under this separate heading. The justification for this is presumably the fact that directors have a large measure of discretion over this payment in practice.

Management of liquid resources

Each company must decide and explain which current asset investments are regarded as 'liquid resources'. Liquid resources are defined as follows:

> Current asset investments held as readily disposable stores of value. A readily disposable investment is one that:
> (a) is disposable by the reporting entity without curtailing or disrupting its business;
> and is either
> (b) (i) readily convertible into known amounts of cash at or close to its carrying amount, or
> (ii) traded in an active market.
> (Para. 2)

As we have described earlier, the original FRS 1 required that a cash flow statement explained changes in 'cash and cash equivalents', terms which were defined as follows:

> Cash: Cash in hand and deposits repayable on demand with any bank or other financial institution. Cash includes cash in hand and deposits denominated in foreign currencies.

> Cash equivalents: Short-term, highly liquid investments which are readily convertible into known amounts of cash without notice and which were within three months of maturity when acquired; less advances from banks repayable within three months from the date of the advance. Cash equivalents include investments and advances denominated in foreign currencies provided that they fulfil the above criteria. (Original FRS 1, Paras 2 and 3)

Such a definition of cash equivalents attempted to ensure that the amounts receivable were not subject to fluctuations in value as a consequence of interest rate changes. However, the definition attracted an enormous amount of criticism. Many companies argued that it was too restrictive and out of line with their treasury management policies so that cash flow statements prepared using the definition failed to reflect their liquidity and financial adaptability. Although the ASB attempted to develop a new definition of 'cash equivalents', it was unable to develop one which was universally acceptable. Instead it decided to require a real cash flow statement and left it to individual companies to decide which investments they regarded as liquid resources. The revised FRS 1 requires companies to decide and explain which investments are regarded as liquid resources and then to show receipts and payments in respect of such investments under the heading 'Management of liquid resources'.

While this may have been the best approach achievable, it inevitably reduces comparability between companies. In the view of the authors, it is particularly unfortunate that the ASB has provided a definition of 'liquid resources' which excludes cash, the most liquid of all resources. The use of the term 'liquid investments' would surely have been more appropriate for its intended use!

Financing

This heading comprises the capital receipts from and payments to external providers of finance. Typical examples would be receipts from issuing shares or debentures and payments to repay loans and purchase or redeem share capital. However, the heading would also include receipts and payments in respect of short-term borrowing, except overdrafts, as well as payments of issue expenses and the capital element of finance lease rental payments.

The revised standard specifically permits the section for Financing to be combined with that for the Management of liquid resources, provided that separate sub-totals for each are provided.

With this summary of the cash flows to be included under each heading, we are now in a position to look at an example. We shall illustrate the preparation of a Cash Flow Statement supported by the two notes required by the revised FRS 1.

Example 11.1

Summarised accounts of a manufacturing company, Kamina plc, for the year ended 31 December 20X2, together with an opening balance sheet, are given below. The two right-hand columns by the balance sheet merely list differences between the opening and closing balances. The + column contains increases in assets and reductions in liabilities, while the – column contains reductions in assets and increases in both liabilities and the shareholders' interest.

Balance sheets on 31 December 20X1 and 20X2

	20X1	20X2	Change +	Change –
	£000	£000	£000	£000
Fixed assets				
Tangible at net book value (note (i)):				
Freehold properties	800	1 140	340	
Plant and machinery	1 100	1 400	300	
Investments at cost	100	110	10	
	2 000	2 650	650	
Current assets				
Stock	1 100	1 680	580	
Debtors (note (ii))	490	730	240	
Government securities – at cost	150	250	100	
Cash at bank	200	–		200
	1 940	2 660		
less Short-term creditors				
Bank overdraft	–	85		85
Creditors (note (iii))	735	970		235
Taxation payable (note (iv))	155	205		50
Proposed dividend	140	160		20
	1 030	1 420		
Net current assets	910	1 240		
	2 910	3 890		
less Long-term loans (note (v))	600	1 000		400
	2 310	2 890		
less Deferred taxation (note (vi))	380	479		99
	1 930	2 411		
Carried forward			1 570	1 089

341

	20X1	20X2	Change +	Change –
	£000	£000	£000	£000
Brought forward			1 570	1 089
Share capital and reserves				
£1 ordinary shares (note (vii))	1 000	1 100		100
Share premium (note (vii))	200	300		100
Retained profits	730	1 011		281
	1 930	2 411	1 570	1 570

Profit and loss account for the year ended 31 December 20X2

	£000	£000
Turnover		6 250
Cost of sales		3 750
Gross profit		2 500
Distribution costs	615	
Administrative expenses	1 064	1 679
Operating profit		821
Profit on sale of freehold property		40
		861
Dividend received		5
Interest received		12
		878
Interest payable (note (viii))		98
Profit on ordinary activities before tax		780
Taxation		
Corporation tax	180	
Deferred tax	99	279
Profit on ordinary activities after tax		501
less Equity dividends:		
Paid	60	
Proposed	160	220
Retained profit for the year		281

The following information is relevant:

(i) Fixed asset movements

	Freehold properties £000	Plant and machinery £000
Cost		
On 1 January 20X2	1 000	2 000
Additions	440	720
Disposal	(60)	–
On 31 December 20X2	1 380	2 720
Depreciation		
On 1 January 20X2	200	900
Disposal	(10)	–
Profit & loss account charge	50	420
On 31 December 20X2	240	1 320
Net book value 31 December 20X2	1 140	1 400
31 December 20X1	800	1 100

(ii) A freehold property was sold for £90 000 and, at 31 December 20X2, £75 000 of this amount is included in debtors.

(iii) Short-term creditors have been analysed as follows:

	31.12.20X1 £000	31.12.20X2 £000
Interest payable – £600 000 11% loan	33	33
£400 000 10% loan	–	10
Creditor for purchase of machinery	40	60
Trade and expense creditors	662	867
	735	970

(iv) Taxation payable has been analysed as follows:

	31.12.20X1 £000	31.12.20X2 £000
Corporation tax payable	80	95
Value added tax	75	110
	155	205

(v) Long-term loans

	31.12.20X1 £000	31.12.20X2 £000
11% loan	600	600
10% loan raised 1 April 20X2	–	400
	600	1 000

Interest on the 11 per cent loan is payable annually on 30 June while interest on the new 10 per cent loan is payable half yearly on 30 September and 31 March.

(vi) Deferred taxation

	31.12.20X1 £000	31.12.20X2 £000
Deferred taxation on timing differences other than chargeable gain	380	465
Deferred taxation on chargeable gain on sale of property	–	14
	380	479

(vii) Share issues

40 000 £1 ordinary shares were issued for cash of £80 000 on 5 December 20X2 while a further 60 000 £1 ordinary shares were issued on 12 December 20X2 to acquire a freehold property valued at £120 000.

(viii)   Interest payable is made up as follows:

	£000
Interest on long-term loans	
11% loan	66
10% loan (from 1 April 20X2 to 31 December 20X2)	30
	96
Interest paid on bank overdraft	2
	98

We shall now examine the workings for this example in detail. We shall assume that Kamina plc considers the current asset investment in government securities to be a liquid resource.

(A) Change in cash

	£000
Cash at bank on 1 January 20X2	200
Bank overdraft on 31 December 20X2	85
Decrease in cash	285

(B) Net cash inflow from operating activities using indirect method:

	£000	£000
Operating profit		821
Adjustments:		
Depreciation – freehold buildings (note (i))	50	
– plant & machinery (note (i))	420	470
Increase in stocks		(580)
Increase in debtors from operating activities:		
per balance sheet on 31 December 20X2	730	
less debtor for sale of property (note (ii))	75	
	655	
per balance sheet on 31 December 20X1	490	(165)
Increase in creditors from operating activities:		
Trade and expense creditors per note (iii) (867 – 662)	205	
VAT per note (iv) (110 – 75)	35	240
Net cash inflow		786

Note: It is not necessary to deduct the profit on sale of the freehold property as this has not been included in arriving at the operating profit shown in the profit and loss account.

(C) Returns on investments and servicing of financing

	£000
Interest paid (see notes (v) and (viii))	
On £600 000 11% loan	
Amount paid 30 June 20X2	(66)
(Check 33 000 + 66 000 – 33 000)	
On £400 000 10% loan	
Amount paid 30 September 20X2	
$\frac{1}{2} \times 10\% \times 400\,000$	(20)
(Check 0 + 30 000 – 10 000)	
Carried forward	(86)

	£000	£000
Brought forward	(86)	–
On bank overdraft (interest paid)	(2)	
		(88)
Interest received		12
Dividends received		5
Net payments		(71)

(D) Taxation – corporation tax

	£000	£000
Corporation tax paid during year		(165)
Check:		
Opening creditor per note (iv)	80	
Profit and loss account charge	180	
	260	
less Closing creditor	95	
	165	

(E) Investing activities

	£000	£000
Purchases of fixed assets using cash		
Freehold properties – additions per note (i)	(440)	
less Purchased by means of share issue per note (vii)	(120)	
Cash purchases		(320)
Plant and machinery – additions per note (i)	(720)	
less Increase in creditors for plant and machinery		
purchases per note (iii) (60 000 – 40 000)	20	
Cash purchases		(700)
		(1 020)
Sale of fixed assets – freehold property		
Net book value per note (i)		
(60 000 – 10 000)	50	
add Profit on disposal – per profit		
& loss account	40	
Proceeds as given in note (ii)	90	
less Debtor at 31 December 20X2	75	15
		(1 005)

(F) Equity dividends paid

	£000	£000
Dividend proposed at 31 December 20X1		140
add Dividends per profit		
& loss account:		
Paid	60	
Proposed	160	220
Carried forward		360

345

	£000	£000
Brought forward	–	360
less Dividend proposed at 31 December 20X2		160
Equity dividends paid		200

Check: Final dividend for 20X1	140
Interim dividend for 20X2	60
	200

(G) Management of liquid resources

	£000
Payment to acquire government securities	
(£250 000 – £150 000)	100

(H) Financing

	£000
Issue of ordinary shares for cash	
per note (vii)	80
New long-term loan – per note (v)	400
	480

(I) Change in net debt

The second note to the Cash Flow Statement must show why the net debt has changed, thus linking the cash flow statement to the opening and closing balance sheets. In our example, the note must therefore explain why the net debt has changed from £250 000 to £835 000, an increase of £585 000:

	31.12.20X1	31.12.20X2
	£000	£000
Long-term loans	600	1 000
Bank overdraft	–	85
less Cash at bank	(200)	(–)
Liquid resources	(150)	(250)
Net debt	250	835

There are three reasons for this change:

	£000
Decrease in the cash balance per (A)	285
New long-term loan per (H)	400
	685
less Purchase of liquid resources per (G)	(100)
	585

We are now in a position to prepare the cash flow statement and accompanying notes.

Kamina plc
Cash flow statement for the year ended 31 December 20X2

	£000	£000
Net cash inflow from operating activities		786
Returns on investment and servicing of finance:		
Interest received	12	
Interest paid	(88)	
Dividends received	5	(71)
Taxation:		
Corporation tax paid		(165)
Capital expenditure and financial investment:		
Payments to acquire tangible fixed		
assets	(1 020)	
Receipts from sales of tangible		
fixed assets	15	
Payment to purchase fixed asset		
investment (110 000 – 100 000)	(10)	(1 015)
Equity dividends paid		(200)
Cash outflow before use of liquid resources		
and financing		(665)
Management of liquid resources		
Purchase of government securities		(100)
Financing		
Proceeds from issue of ordinary shares	80	
Proceeds from new loan	400	480
Decrease in cash during the year		285

Notes to the cash flow statement

1 Reconciliation of operating profit to net cash flow from operating
activities (see Working (**B**)):

	£000
Operating profit	821
Depreciation of tangible fixed assets	470
Increase in stocks	(580)
Increase in debtors from operating activities	(165)
Increase in creditors from operating activities	240
Net cash inflow from operating activities	786

2 Reconciliation of net cash flow movement to movement in net debt:

	£000
Decrease in cash during the year	285
New long-term loan raised	400
Purchase of government securities	(100)
Increase in net debt resulting from cash flows	585
Net debt at 31.12.20X1 (see below)	250
Net debt at 31.12.20X2 (see below)	835

Net debt at 31 December	20X1	20X2
	£000	£000
Loans	(600)	(1 000)
Cash balances/overdrafts	200	(85)
Liquid resources	150	250
Net debt	(250)	(835)

The cash flow statement which we have prepared shows that, although there was a positive net cash inflow from operating activities of £786 000, there has been a net cash outflow before the use of liquid resources and financing amounting to £665 000. This is due to net interest paid, net dividends paid and corporation tax paid but, principally, to the fact that net payments to acquire fixed assets amounted to £1 015 000.

Kamina plc has raised £480 000 by issuing shares for cash and taking a new loan. However, it has invested £100 000 in liquid resources. The net effect is that cash balances have fallen by £285 000 during the year.

Now that we have explored the preparation of a cash flow statement for a individual company, we turn to the additional complications posed by the existence of subsidiaries, associates, joint ventures and foreign currencies.

Groups, associates and joint ventures

Groups

Where a company has subsidiary undertakings and prepares consolidated financial statements, the cash flow statement will reflect the cash flows of the group.

Following the normal consolidation techniques of acquisition accounting, which we have discussed in Chapters 8 and 9, a consolidated balance sheet includes the whole of the assets and liabilities of the parent undertaking and subsidiary undertakings even when those subsidiary undertakings are only partly owned. The cash flow statement will therefore explain changes in the cash of all the undertakings in the group as shown in the consolidated balance sheets. Inter-company cash flows, resulting from sales, management charges or dividend payments between group companies, are irrelevant although dividends paid to any minority interests will, of course, be shown as a payment under the heading 'Returns on investments and servicing of finance'.

Where the parent company uses the direct or gross method to determine the cash flows from operating activities of the group, it will be necessary to have in place a system to collect the relevant information from subsidiaries and to ensure that inter-group cash flows are eliminated. Where the indirect or net method is used, it will be possible to rely largely on the adjustments made during the consolidation process although, even in this case, certain additional information will be necessary. Examples of such additional information are analyses of group debtors and creditors, so that those relating to operating transactions can be identified and included, while those relating to non-operating transactions can be dealt with in computing receipts and payments included under the other headings in the cash flow statement.

When a company acquires a new subsidiary undertaking and acquisition accounting is used, the consolidated profit and loss account will include the profits or losses of that new subsidiary from the date of acquisition to the end of the period, and the consolidated balance sheet will include the whole of the assets and liabilities of the subsidiary, whether it is wholly or partly owned.[7] It follows that when we try to determine the reasons for differences between items in the opening and closing balance sheets, we find that part of the change will be due to the assets, liabilities and any minority interest of the subsidiary undertaking at the date of acquisition as well as to the payment made to acquire the subsidiary. So, for example, if we focus on the change in cash between the beginning and end of the year, we find that part of the change is due to any cash pay-

---

[7] *See* Chapter 9.

ment made by the parent company to acquire the new subsidiary, and a further part is due to the balance of cash held by the subsidiary at the date of acquisition. The cash payment which must be shown in respect of the purchase of subsidiary undertakings under the heading 'Investing activities' is therefore calculated as follows:

	£000
Cash consideration paid	x
less Cash of subsidiary undertakings	
at date of acquisition	x
Cash payment	x

Where a subsidiary is acquired for a consideration other than cash, all that will appear in the cash flow statement will be the cash balances of the subsidiary at the date of acquisition.

To enable users to understand what has happened, it is necessary to provide a note to the cash flow statement showing a breakdown of the assets and liabilities acquired, together with the consideration paid. Such a note would take the following form:

Purchase of subsidiary undertakings

	£000
Net assets acquired:	
Tangible fixed assets	16 000
Investments	40
Stocks	13 000
Debtors	5 000
Cash at bank and in hand	2 500
Bank overdrafts	(1 000)
Other creditors	(5 500)
Loans	(3 000)
Minority interests	(40)
	27 000
Goodwill	3 000
	30 000
Satisfied by:	
Shares allotted	25 000
Cash	5 000
	30 000

Analysis of net outflow of cash in respect of the purchase of subsidiary undertakings

	£000	£000
Cash consideration		5 000
Cash acquired		
Cash at bank and in hand	2 500	
Bank overdraft	(1 000)	1 500
Net payment		3 500

When a group disposes of a subsidiary undertaking the converse is the case. Any cash proceeds from the sale of shares in the subsidiary less any positive balance of cash of the subsidiary at the date of disposal will be recorded as a cash receipt under the heading 'Investing activities'. A note to the statement should then provide a list of the assets and liabilities of the subsidiary at the date of disposal together with the proceeds received and any profit or loss on disposal:

	£000
Net assets disposed of:	
Tangible fixed assets	5 000
Stocks	2 000
Debtors	3 000
Cash	1 000
Creditors	(4 000)
	7 000
Profit on disposal	1 000
	8 000
Satisfied by:	
Loan stock	4 000
Cash	4 000
	8 000

The net cash receipt from disposal of subsidiary would be:

Cash received	4 000
less Cash balances of subsidiary sold	1 000
	3 000

Associates and joint ventures

When an investing company purchases or sells its interest in an associate or joint venture, any payment or receipt of cash will be included under the heading 'Investing activities'.

As we have seen in Chapter 9, standard accounting practice requires the use of the equity method of accounting for associates and joint ventures. Under the equity method of accounting, an investing company takes credit in its consolidated profit and loss account for its full share of the profits or losses of the associate or joint venture. The consolidated balance sheet includes the investment but the individual assets and liabilities do not include relevant amounts in respect of the associated undertaking. Hence cash in the opening and closing consolidated balance sheets do not include the respective amounts for the associate or joint venture.

Apart from the purchase and sale of an investment and, perhaps, the making and repayment of a loan, the only recurrent receipt from an associate or joint venture will be the dividend received. This should be shown as a receipt under the separate heading 'Dividends received from associates and joint ventures', a heading which has been inserted into the Cash Flow Statement by FRS 9 'Associates and Joint Ventures', issued in November 1997.

Foreign currency differences

As we have seen in Chapter 10, exchange differences frequently arise both when a company engages in foreign transactions and when the accounts of an overseas entity are translated prior to the preparation of consolidated financial statements. We shall examine the treatment of such differences in the preparation of a cash flow statement. Where a company enters into a foreign currency transaction then, unless there is an agreed rate for settlement or a forward exchange contract, the foreign currency amount will be translated into sterling at the rate on the transaction date. Any difference arising on monetary items between the date of the transaction and the date of settlement will be taken to the profit and loss account as part of the operating profit. Where a debtor or creditor is outstanding at a balance sheet date, the foreign currency amount will be retranslated at the closing rate and again any resulting difference on exchange will be taken to the profit and loss account as part of operating profit.

As far as the cash flow statement is concerned, the cash flows to creditors or from debtors are the amounts actually paid and received in sterling and, if a company wishes to use the direct method to calculate the cash flow from operations, it must ensure that it has an adequate accounting system in place to collect this information. However, it is possible to use the indirect method although it will then be necessary to analyse the difference on exchange which has been included in arriving at operating profit. To the extent that the differences on exchange relate to operating activities, no adjustment is necessary. However, to the extent that differences relate to other activities, such as the purchase of fixed assets on credit or the retranslation of a foreign currency loan, this must be removed from the operating profit to arrive at the net cash flow from operating activities.

To illustrate, let us take examples of a settled transaction and an unsettled transaction, respectively. A company makes a purchase from an overseas supplier which is recorded in the accounting records at a sterling amount of £15 000. During the same accounting period, settlement is made of £16 500 resulting in a loss on exchange of £1500, which is deducted in arriving at the operating profit shown in the profit and loss account. The cash payment is, of course, £16 500 and this is the amount which has been deducted in arriving at operating profit, albeit in two parts:

	£
Purchase	15 000
Loss on exchange	1 500
	16 500

Turning to an example of an unsettled transaction, let us assume that a company makes a sale, denominated in foreign currency, to an overseas customer and that the foreign currency amount invoiced is translated at £24 000. If the amount is still due at the ensuing balance sheet date, it will be translated at the closing rate of exchange to produce a different amount of, say, £26 000. The gain on exchange of £2000 will be credited to the profit and loss account in arriving at the operating profit.

As far as the cash flow statement is concerned, there has been no receipt. If we take the operating profit and make the usual adjustment for the change in debtors, this is exactly what will be included in the net cash flow from operating activities:

	£
Operating profit (including gain on exchange)	
Sale	24 000
Gain on exchange	2 000
	26 000
less Increase in debtors	26 000
Cash flow from this transaction	–

Whereas no adjustment is necessary in respect of exchange differences relating to operating activities such as purchases and sales, adjustments to the operating profit will be necessary in respect of other exchange differences. So, for example, an exchange difference relating to the purchase of a fixed asset on credit or the retranslation of a long-term loan must feature as an adjustment in moving from operating profit to net cash flow from operating activities. In the latter case the exchange difference will also have to be included in the note reconciling the opening balance sheet value of the loan with its closing balance sheet value.

Let us now turn to the translation of the accounts of a foreign subsidiary or associate. Here FRS 1 makes it clear what should be done.

> Where a portion of a reporting entity's business is undertaken by a foreign entity, the cash flows of that entity are to be included in the cash flow statement on the basis used for translating the results of those activities in the profit and loss account of the reporting entity.[8]

The vast majority of companies in the UK use the closing rate/net investment method under which profit and loss account items are translated at average or closing rate and assets and liabilities in the balance sheet are translated at the closing rate. Differences on exchange are taken to reserves and these will relate to opening assets and liabilities and, where an average rate is used in the profit and loss account, to the increase in net assets which has occurred during the year. Such differences thus explain changes in the balance sheet amounts including the change in cash. The relevant parts of these differences on exchange must be included in the note reconciling opening and closing amounts for cash. Similarly, the relevant parts of the difference on exchange must be included in the note reconciling opening and closing net debt. The parts of the difference relating to such items as opening fixed assets, stocks, debtors and creditors will, of course, appear in relevant notes to the accounts but do not represent any receipt or payment of cash.

Where a company uses the temporal method of translation, exchange differences are taken to the consolidated profit and loss account and their treatment in preparing the cash flow statement will be exactly the same as that explained above for foreign currency transactions entered into by the company itself. After all, the purpose of the temporal method is to translate the foreign currency financial statements in such a way that the result is the same as if the investing company had itself entered into the transactions undertaken by the foreign entity.

Usefulness and limitations of the cash flow statement

Now that we have explored the preparation of a cash flow statement, it is time to explore briefly the usefulness and limitations of the statement.

---

[8] FRS 1, Para. 41.

As we have seen in Chapter 1, most users are concerned with the future performance of an entity and turn to the financial statements, as well as to other sources, for help in making a judgement about likely future performance. In assessing the cash flow statement, it is therefore necessary to ask how it helps users in that task.

The statement supplements the traditional accounts by focusing on changes in cash in a way which provides answers to many pertinent questions which a user might wish to ask. Examples of such questions are as follows: Has there been an increase or decrease in the cash balance? To what extent has cash been generated by the operations of the company? Are payments of interest, taxation and dividends covered by the net cash inflow from operations? Has cash been used to finance the purchase of fixed assets? To what extent has cash been raised to pay for an acquisition?

Answers to such questions as these undoubtedly help users to assess what has happened and what is likely to happen in future. However, like all the figures shown in a set of accounts, they cannot be used in isolation but must be interpreted as part of the whole collection of information. This may be illustrated by just one example. A user may look at a cash flow statement and find that there has been a substantial purchase of fixed assets out of cash balances. By itself, this may be a little worrying. However, the failure of long-term finance to cover the purchase of fixed assets in a particular year may merely reflect the fact that there were large cash balances at the opening balance sheet date, balances which have now been reduced to more appropriate levels!

The Cash Flow Statement is an enormous improvement on its predecessor, the Statement of Source and Application of Funds, and the Cash Flow Statement required by the revised FRS 1 (October 1996) improves still further that required by the original FRS 1 (September 1991). Its clear focus on changes in cash and its treatment of 'liquid resources' are to be applauded. However, it is not without some problems.

The focus of the revised FRS 1 on cash and its requirement to list cash flows under nine headings is even further out of line with the International Accounting Standard than the original FRS1. IAS 7 'Cash Flow Statements' (1992), like the original FRS 1, focuses on changes in cash and cash equivalents but requires flows to be analysed under three headings: Operating, Investing and Financing Activities. There is thus a lack of comparability of Cash Flow Statements in the international arena.

The need to include both receipts and payments under standard headings frequently results in a statement which is riddled with brackets and which may therefore be confusing to users.

Finally the authors have reservations about the introduction of a definition of 'liquid resources', which excludes cash, the most liquid of all resources! In our view, the term 'liquid investments' would better fit the bill.

Value added statements

Background

As we have seen in the introduction to this chapter, *The Corporate Report* recommended that all significant economic entities should publish a value added statement as part of their annual accounts. Contrary to the traditional legal position, but in keeping with many current organisational theories, such a statement regards the entity as being operated by and for the benefit of a team of interests. Such a team is usually taken to include employees, suppliers of long-term capital and the government, but to exclude other firms which supply goods and services. Thus, whereas the profit and loss account has traditionally shown the profit or loss of a period from the point of view of the equity shareholders, the value added statement shows the income of the larger entity and how this has been divided between the wider team of contributors.

The concept of value added

Once the team has been specified, the value added may be calculated as the difference between the value of the goods or services produced by the team, i.e. sales revenue, less the value of the goods and services purchased from outsiders, i.e. the cost of bought-in materials and services.

The value added statement is normally in two parts, the first of which shows the value added by the team, while the second shows how that value added has been divided between the team members. The illustrative layout proposed in *The Corporate Report* was as follows:

A manufacturing company
Statement of value added for the year to 31 December 20X1

	£	£
Turnover		x
Bought-in materials and services		x
Value added		x
Applied the following way		
To pay employees'		
wages, pensions and fringe benefits		x
To pay providers of capital		
Interest on loans	x	
Dividends to shareholders	x	x
To pay government		
Corporation tax payable		x
To provide for maintenance and expansion of assets		
Depreciation	x	
Retained profits	x	x
Value added		x

As may be seen from the above illustration, so far as large companies are concerned, the value added statement is largely a rearrangement of information disclosed elsewhere in the company's published accounts. For this reason many people consider it to be a mere cosmetic device to place less emphasis on the profit figure. Others would stress that presentation has an important role to play and that the arrangement of information in the value added statement provides a better means of understanding the contribution of a company to society. In particular, the inclusion of relevant percentages of value added by the side of items in the second part of the statement would make people aware of the respective shares of the various team members.

Simple company

Content of statement

For a manufacturing or trading company the first figure in the value added statement will usually be the turnover figure which appears in its profit and loss account. From this is deducted the cost of bought-in materials and services, which comprise the cost of materials and services consumed. Examples of such bought-in materials and services are raw materials, fuel costs, hire of computing facilities, printing and stationery and audit fees: these are all goods or services bought from non-team members. In practice the cost of bought-in materials and services will usually be calculated as a balancing figure.

Although the illustration in *The Corporate Report* does not deduct depreciation in arriving at value added, there is a very strong argument for doing so. The purchase of a fixed asset from another firm, a non-team member, is a bought-in item and it is only the fact that the asset has a long life which necessitates the charging of depreciation. Thus in arriving at value added, a preferred format would be:

	£	£
Turnover		x
less Bought-in materials and services	x	
Depreciation	x	x
		x

In order to avoid confusion it is perhaps sensible to talk of the illustration in *The Corporate Report* as a statement of gross value added and the illustration above as a statement of net value added. A similar distinction between gross national product and net national product is found in national income statistics.

In the lower part of the statement we need to show how the value added during the period has been shared between members of the team. Following the order in the illustrative layout of *The Corporate Report* we would start with amounts payable to all employees, that is gross pay, employers' National Insurance contributions, employers' pension contributions and pension payments and, to the extent that it is possible to arrive at them, fringe benefits. Theoretically we should disclose wages payable in respect of the sales of the year. However, most published statements have shown wages payable for the year and have ignored the changes in the labour content of work-in-progress or finished goods stock, thus losing the difference in the balancing figure for 'bought-in materials and services'.

Some companies showed as payable to employees merely the net pay of employees, grouping PAYE and both employers' and employees' National Insurance contributions under the heading 'To pay government'. Although one can understand companies wishing to emphasise how much is paid over to the government there seems a lot to be said for showing only corporation tax payable under the government heading for reasons which will be discussed below.

The second group of members of the team in the illustrative layout are providers of financial capital. Under this heading will be shown interest payable on loans and dividends payable to shareholders for the period. Where tax is deductible from interest payable, interest should be shown gross of tax, for the company is merely accounting for the recipient's income tax liability at the basic rate of taxation.

It is under the heading 'To pay government' that most variety has been found in practice. Some companies have merely shown corporation tax payable in respect of the period. Others have shown all taxes paid to the government whether paid over on behalf of others or not. In this case the heading 'To pay government' might include such taxes as the following: corporation tax, employees' PAYE, National Insurance contributions, taxation deducted from interest payable, VAT, local rates, motor vehicle license fees, Customs and Excise duties.

There seem to be arguments in favour of both treatments. To include just the figure for corporation tax payable avoids the need for arbitrary distinctions and time-consuming analysis of the accounts to ascertain the totals of the various taxes listed above. It also has the advantage of agreement with the profit and loss account figure. On the other hand, it may be argued that the inclusion of all taxes payable to the government would facilitate international comparison. The inclusion of only one direct tax, corporation tax, would make such international comparisons difficult in that countries have different mixes of direct and indirect taxes.

The final heading in the illustrative layout is 'To provide for maintenance and expansion of assets'. For the reasons stated above, depreciation is usually better classified as a bought-in cost. This leaves only retained profit, and some description such as 'available for investment' would then be more appropriate. Some people would argue that it is wrong to include such an abstraction as a member of the team, for, after all, retained profits belong to the equity shareholders.

Non-trading items

In the previous section we have examined the value added statement of a simple trading or manufacturing company. Most companies also have what may be loosely described as non-trading items, examples of which are investment income and, much more rarely, extraordinary profits and losses. Although it may be argued that investment income is a share of the value added distributable by another company rather than a part of the value added by the company with which we are concerned, that investment income is certainly a part of the value added available to share between team members. Indeed it is impossible to eliminate the investment income from the individual items in the second part of the statement and it must, therefore, either be deducted in total in the second part of the statement or, preferably, be included separately in the first part of the statement. A similar treatment is appropriate for extraordinary items and, if this treatment is adopted, the first part of the value added statement would appear as follows:

	£	£
Sales		x
less Bought-in materials and services	x	
Depreciation	x	x
Value added by the company		x
add Investment income	x	
Extraordinary profits	x	x
Value added available		x

Group of companies – minority interests

Where a company prepares consolidated accounts, the value added statement should be based upon the consolidated profit and loss account rather than the profit and loss account of the parent company. It will therefore show value added by the group. The minority interests in subsidiaries must therefore be treated as members of the team and their share of the value added included in the lower part of the statement. Two methods have been used in practice.

Some companies show, under the heading 'To pay providers of capital', the full share of minority interests in the current profits, whether or not these are distributable as dividends. Other companies split the share of profits applicable to minority interests, showing dividends paid and payable under the heading 'To pay providers of capital' and the retained profits applicable to the minority interest as a separate item under the heading 'Retained profits available for investment'. The latter would seem to be the better alternative as the treatment is consistent with that applied to the shareholders in the holding company.

Associates and joint ventures

Under FRS 9 companies are required to include in their consolidated profit and loss accounts their full share of profits and losses of associates and joint ventures. Such an item should therefore be included as a separate component of value added in the top part of the statement.

In the second part of the statement there must be shown the share of the corporation tax payable by the associated undertaking and the share of retained profits which will be held either by the investing company, to the extent that a dividend is payable by the associate undertaking, or in the associate undertaking itself. Tax payable should be shown under the heading 'To pay government', whereas the retained profits should be shown under the heading 'Retained to provide for investment'. Notice that no item appears under the heading 'To pay employees' because the figure we have included as value added is the share of profits in associated undertakings, after payment to employees.

The current position

As discussed above, some people considered the value added statement to be merely a cosmetic device to divert attention from the profit figure, while others considered it to be an instrument for improving industrial relations in the UK by emphasising the team nature of the entity.[9] Whatever the merits of the statement, it is clear that, although many large listed companies have, at some time, produced a value added statement as part of their annual reports, the proportion of such companies producing the statement has never exceeded 40 per cent and this proportion has declined 'drastically' in recent years.

The operating and financial review

As a consequence of changes in company law and of the work of the standard setters, the annual financial statements of companies have expanded out of all recognition over the past thirty years or so. While this has ensured that a large volume of mainly quantitative information is available to investors and other users of the statements, it has been argued that it would help users to understand this information if the

---

[9] See M.F. Morley, *The Value Added Statement*, Gee, London, 1978, Chapter 3.

directors were to put the information into context by explaining what is happening and by interpreting the financial statements for their benefit. After all, the directors have far more knowledge about the company than any outsider is ever likely to possess.

It was to this end that the ASB published the Statement 'Operating and Financial Review' in July 1993. This is not an accounting standard but a statement of best practice intended to encourage companies, particularly listed and large companies, to include an Operating and Financial Review as part of their annual report:

> 'The Operating and Financial Review (OFR) is a framework for the directors to disclose and analyse the business's performance and the factors underlying its results and financial position, in order to assist users to assess for themselves the future potential of the business.' (Para. 1)

Such an Operating and Financial Review may be provided as a stand-alone document but may be included as part of another statement, such as the Chairman's or Chief Executive's Report. Experimentation is encouraged and many approaches have been seen in practice.[10] The Statement lists the essential features of the review and then provides more detailed guidance on its contents.

The essential features of the Operating and Financial Review are listed as follows (Para. 3):

- it should be written in a clear style and as succinctly as possible, to be readily understandable by the general reader of annual reports, and should include only matters that are likely to be significant to investors;
- it should be balanced and objective, dealing even-handedly with both good and bad aspects;
- it should refer to comments made in previous statements where these have not been borne out by events;
- it should contain analytical discussion rather than merely numerical analysis;
- it should follow a 'top-down' structure, discussing individual aspects of the business in the context of a discussion of the business as a whole;
- it should explain the reason for, and effect of, any changes in accounting policies;
- it should make it clear how any ratios or other numerical information given relate to the financial statements;
- it should include discussion of:
  - trends and factors underlying the business that have affected the results but are not expected to continue in the future; and
  - known events, trends and uncertainties that are expected to have an impact on the business in the future.

The detailed guidance in the Statement is intended to help directors to implement these general principles in writing their review. Not surprisingly, such matters of detail are classified under two headings, Operating Review and Financial Review respectively. The former includes discussion of the operating results, the profit for the year and other gains and losses reported in the Statement of Total Recognised Gains and Losses, a discussion of the dynamics of the business and of the investments which have been made for the future. Discussion of investment should deal with not just capital investment but also revenue investment, such as expenditure on advertising

---

[10] *See*, for example, 'Operating and Financial Review: Experiences and Exploration', Pauline Weetman and Bill Collins, ICAS, Edinburgh, 1996.

and marketing, training and both pure and applied research. Such revenue investment affects future periods as well as the current financial year.

The Financial Review should be concerned to explain the capital structure of the company, its treasury policy and the dynamics of its financial position. Readers are referred to the Statement itself for greater detail of the suggested coverage.

The Statement recognises clearly that what is important to one company may not be important in the context of another company. It also recognises that, in deciding what should be disclosed, directors must weigh the benefits of disclosure against the possible danger of disclosing confidential or commercially sensitive information.

Clearly this is not a topic for regulation by an accounting standard but, rather, an area in which directors are encouraged to follow the spirit of the Statement within the context of their own company. It is inevitable that there will be some Boards of Directors who have difficulty in providing a review which is 'balanced and objective, dealing even-handedly with both good and bad aspects.'

The historical summary

As we explain in Chapter 13, it is usually difficult to draw conclusions about the performance and position of a company from a profit and loss account and balance sheet without some yardstick of comparison. Company law clearly recognises this in requiring the disclosure of corresponding amounts for the preceding financial year.[11] Thus the law ensures that, at a minimum, users are able to compare the performance and position in the current year with that of the previous year. Although such information is undoubtedly useful, comparative information for a longer period would be even more helpful in enabling users of the accounts to appreciate trends.

It was for this reason that, in the 1960s, the then Chairman of the Stock Exchange recommended that all listed companies should publish tables of relevant comparative figures for a ten-year period. Although this recommendation has never been incorporated into the Stock Exchange Regulations, nor into company law or accounting standards, it has become accepted practice for listed companies to provide a historical summary covering a five-year period. Five years has perhaps been chosen because this is the period specified for accountants' reports in prospectuses.

Given the lack of regulation, it is not surprising to find that the information included in a historical summary differs considerably from one company to another. While some companies only provide figures for turnover and profit for each of the five years, others provide summarised profit and loss accounts and balance sheets for the period. These are often supplemented by financial ratios, particularly earnings per share and dividend per share, and sometimes by a segmental analysis and/or non-financial information for the five-year period. Examples of the latter include the number of employees and the area of retail floor space available in each year. Readers familiar with the non-financial performance indicators published by utility companies will appreciate just how much detailed information of this type may be provided.

Given the lack of regulation and the fact that the historical summary is not subject to audit, it is, of course, possible for directors to choose to disclose those elements of a company's performance which show their company in the most favourable light. Thus, they may choose to disclose increasing amounts for turnover and operating profit while suppressing the fact that the profit before taxation and earnings per share

---

[11] Companies Act 1985, Schedule 4, Para. 4(1).

may have been declining. It is for this reason that some accountants have called for regulation of the content of the historical summary.[12]

In our view, the historical summary should include as a minimum the main headings and totals in the profit and loss account and balance sheet. The former would include turnover, operating profit, exceptional items, profit before taxation, profit after taxation, extraordinary items and dividends. The latter would include fixed assets, net current assets, borrowings and shareholders' interest. These should be supplemented by ratios for earnings per share, dividends per share and net assets per share.

In order to ensure comparability, in so far as this is possible, previously published figures should be adjusted to reflect changes in accounting policies and to correct any fundamental errors which have come to light. In addition, amounts shown for earnings per share, dividends per share and net assets per share should be adjusted to reflect any subsequent changes in the share capital such as bonus issues and rights issues. In order not to obscure trends, it is essential that both exceptional items and any extraordinary items should be disclosed separately. A brief description of these and of any major changes in the composition of the group should also be provided.

The main criticism which we would make of published historical summaries is that the vast majority are not adjusted for inflation. Although many users are able to make approximate adjustments for changes in the value of money by use of the published Retail Price Index, the trend shown by uncorrected information may be misleading for less sophisticated users.

To illustrate, let us assume that a company has reported its turnover for a five-year period as shown in the first line of Table 11.1. On the basis of the reported figures, turnover has been growing consistently over the five-year period. However, the second line of the table provides values for the average Retail Price Index each year and the third line provides the turnover for each year measured in average pounds for 1998.[13]

Whereas the unadjusted figures show a steadily increasing turnover, once we adjust for the fact that the value of the pound has been falling, the 'real' turnover has fallen consistently throughout the five-year period.

Table 11.1 Company's turnover for five-year period

Year to 31 December	1994	1995	1996	1997	1998
Turnover (£000)	600	610	620	630	640
Average RPI for year	144.1	149.1	152.7	157.5	162.9
Turnover measured in (£(1998)000)	678	666	661	652	640

---

[12] *See*, for example, R.M. Wilkins and A.C. Lennard, 'Historical summaries', in *Financial Reporting 1987–88*, L.C.L. Skerratt and D.J. Tonkin (eds), ICAEW, London, 1988. Wilkins and Lennard suggested that the Stock Exchange should consider introducing a requirement for historical summaries and that this should be supplemented by a SORP, giving practical guidance on the detailed information to be included and how problems areas should be handled. No such developments have occurred.

[13] To measure the turnover for each year in average pounds for 1998 – £(1998)s – it is merely necessary to multiply the turnover for each year by the average RPI for 1998 and to divide by the average RPI for the year to which the turnover relates. Hence the turnover for 1994 measured in £(1998)s, rounded to the nearest £1000, is calculated as £600 × 162.9/144.1 = £678. See Chapter 15 for a comprehensive coverage of Current Purchasing Power (CPP) accounting.

The ASC recommended that such simple adjustments be made.[14] In our view it is quite indefensible for companies to publish five-year historical summaries without incorporating changes in the value of the pound. The need for such adjustments is, of course, greater the higher the rate of inflation.

Reporting about and to employees

As we have seen in the introduction to this chapter, *The Corporate Report* favoured the expansion of the annual report to include an employment report.

Companies and other entities employ a large number of people who look to those entities for employment security and prospects while society at large expects employers to maintain certain standards of conduct in relation to its employees. *The Corporate Report* therefore took the view that significant economic entities should report employment information and recommended that the annual report should be expanded to include an employment report which should provide the following information:

(a) numbers employed, average for the financial year and actual on the first and last day;

(b) broad reasons for changes in the numbers employed;

(c) the age distribution and sex of employees;

(d) the functions of employees;

(e) the geographical location of major employment centres;

(f) major plant and site closures, disposals and acquisitions during the past year;

(g) the hours scheduled and worked by employees, giving as much detail as possible concerning differences between groups of employees;

(h) employment costs including fringe benefits;

(i) the costs and benefits associated with pension schemes and the ability of such schemes to meet future commitments;

(j) the cost and time spent on training;

(k) the names of unions recognised by the entity for the purpose of collective bargaining and membership figures where available or the fact that this information has not been made available by the unions concerned;

(l) information concerning safety and health including the frequency and severity of accidents and occupational diseases;

(m) selected ratios relating to employment.[15]

In the introduction to this chapter, we distinguished two types of statement. The employment report envisaged by *The Corporate Report* is an example of what we called an 'extended' statement. It is a general purpose statement to be included in the annual report of a company, which would provide much more information on employment than that required by company law. It should not be confused with another document, the employee report, which is an example of a 'rearranged and simplified' report, in this case a document separate from the annual report, intended for the use of employees.

---

[14] *See* the Discussion Paper 'Corresponding amounts and ten-year summaries in current cost accounting', ASC, 1982, and the Handbook 'Accounting for the effects of changing prices', ASC, 1986, Chapter 7.

[15] *The Corporate Report*, Para. 6.19. Appendix 3 to that document provides an example of the sort of employment report envisaged.

Employee reports usually contain a simplified set of accounts together with a narrative review of those accounts. The emphasis is on making the information as easy to understand as possible and such reports try to avoid technical language and frequently include charts and diagrams which might show, for example, the changes in sales or profits over a number of years or the distribution of value added between the team members.

In large companies the employees are primarily interested in a part, rather than the whole, of the entity and frequently employee reports are used to give more detailed segmental information about geographical areas, divisions or plants. They can thus be tailor-made for the particular company and can be improved in response to suggestions from the users, that is the employees, themselves.

Perhaps not surprisingly, companies have been reluctant to publish employment reports, especially given the fact that there has been little published work explaining which users find the particular pieces of information useful and for what purposes they may be useful. On the other hand, employee reports seem to be more widely used and these are often also issued to shareholders as a matter of course.

Summary Financial Statements

As we have seen in Chapter 2, company law has long required limited companies to send copies of their annual accounts, directors' reports and auditors' reports to every member and debenture holder of the company. However, the Companies Act 1989 introduced new provisions whereby a *listed* company may instead send members a Summary Financial Statement.[16] Such a statement must explain that it is a summary of the full accounts, inform members that they are entitled to the full accounts and carry a warning that the summary financial statement does not contain sufficient information to permit a full understanding of the results or position of the company or group. It must contain a report by the auditor that the statement is consistent with the full accounts and that it complies with the law. It must also include any qualified auditor's report together with details of certain types of qualification.

While the Companies Act 1989 introduced these general principles, the detailed regulations have been introduced by statutory instrument.[17] This specified the minimum content of the Summary Financial Statement which comprises certain information from the directors' report and the main headings and associated amounts from the profit and loss account and balance sheet.

With regard to the information in the directors' report, it is necessary to disclose the names of all directors who served during the financial year and either the whole or a summary of the fair review of results and position, of post balance sheet events and of likely future developments. With respect to the results and position it is necessary to give the minimum headings shown in Table 11.2. Given that almost all listed companies prepare group accounts, we have provided a list for a consolidated profit and loss account and balance sheet.

As will be seen from Table 11.2, the summary financial statement is indeed a highly simplified statement and, as the required warning states, it is unlikely to contain

---

[16] Companies Act 1985, Sec. 251.
[17] The Companies (Summary Financial Statement) Regulations 1990, SI 1990/515.

Table 11.2 Minimum content of summary profit and loss account and balance sheet

Summary consolidated profit and loss account

	£
Turnover	x =
Income from shares in associated undertakings	x =
Other interest receivable and similar income less interest payable and similar charges	x =
Profit (or loss) on ordinary activities before taxation	x
Tax on profit (or loss) on ordinary activities	x
Profit (or loss) on ordinary activities after tax	x
Minority interests	x
	x
Extraordinary items	x
Profit (or loss) for the financial year	x
Dividends paid and proposed	x
	x =
Directors' emoluments (total only)	x =

Summary consolidated balance sheet

	£	£
Fixed assets		x
Current assets	x	
Creditors: amounts falling due within one year	x	
Net current assets		x
Total assets less current liabilities		x
Creditors: amounts falling due after more than one year		x
		x
Provisions for liabilities and charges		x
		x =
Capital and reserves		x
Minority interests		x
		x =

sufficient information to allow for a full understanding of the group's performance and position.

However, given the increasing complexity of the main financial statements, such summary financial statements certainly have a role to play. In addition, they reduce substantially the cost to listed companies of sending full accounts to all shareholders.

Interim reports and preliminary announcements

So far in this chapter we have concentrated on the annual reports of companies and seen how these have grown in size in recent years. However, no matter how much information and how many statements are provided in such reports, annual reporting is unlikely to provide sufficient information for investors to make satisfactory investment decisions. More timely information is needed and it is to this end that the London Stock Exchange requires listed companies to publish half yearly, that is interim, reports as well as preliminary announcements of the full year's results as soon as this is possible.

The Stock Exchange rules on the contents of these documents are rather rudimentary and the ASB has issued two non-mandatory Statements to provide guidance on best practice in these areas: 'Interim Reports' was issued in September 1997 while 'Preliminary Announcements' was issued in July 1998.

Interim reports

In order to ensure that the information is timely, the Statement encourages companies to make their interim reports available within sixty days of the end of the period. In the UK the interim period is a half year while in other countries, such as the USA, the reporting period is a quarter.

The purpose of the interim report is to provide an update to the previous annual report and the Statement recommends that it include the following:

Management commentary

Summarised profit and loss account, including the analysis of turnover and operating profit required by FRS3 and accompanied by segmental information and one or more earnings per share figures

Statement of total recognised gains and losses, where material gains or losses, other than profit for the period, are recognised

Summarised balance sheet

Summarised cash flow statement, providing a summary of cash flows using the nine headings required by FRS1 and supported by the two notes required by that standard.

The management commentary should be a less comprehensive version of the Operating and Financial Review, discussed earlier in this chapter. It should highlight and explain what has happened since the previous annual report and is intended to help users to understand what has happened and to make judgements on what is likely to happen in future. The interim report will therefore provide both confirmatory and predictive information.

The Statement provides a list of the information which should be included in the summarised financial statements and Table 11.3 provides this listing for the profit and loss account and balance sheet. Comparative amounts are required.

The interim financial statements should normally be drawn up using the same accounting policies as those in the previous annual financial statements. The exception would be when it is intended to change these policies in the next annual financial statements when the new policies should be implemented in the interim statements and explained

For the accountant involved with such an interim report, there are two different approaches which could be adopted in preparing the financial statements. The first, the discrete method, regards the half year as a distinct reporting period. The second, the integral method, regards the half year as merely a part of the longer annual reporting period. The ASB Statement recommends the use of the discrete method which has the conceptual advantage that the elements included in the interim financial statements may be defined in the same way as they are for the annual financial

Table 11.3 Interim Report: Contents of summarised consolidated profit and loss account and balance sheet

Summarised consolidated profit and loss account

- Turnover
- Operating profit or loss
- Interest payable less interest receivable (net)
- Profit or loss on ordinary activities before tax
- Tax on profit or loss on ordinary activities
- Profit or loss on ordinary activities after tax
- Minority interests
- Profit or loss for the period
- Dividends paid and proposed

Summarised consolidated balance sheet

- Fixed assets
- Current assets
  - Stocks
  - Debtors
  - Cash at bank and in hand
  - Other current assets
- Creditors: amounts falling due within one year
- Net current assets (liabilities)
- Total assets less current liabilities
- Creditors: amounts falling due after more than one year
- Provisions for liabilities and charges
- Capital and reserves
- Minority interests

Note: Turnover and operating profit should be analysed as required by FRS 3 and there should be a separate identification of amounts relating to associates and joint ventures.

statements. However, it also recognises that this approach will not be appropriate for all items of revenue and expense and specifically draws attention to taxation as one such expense. The calculation of the corporation tax expense for a separate half-year period would often produce a meaningless figure. In such a case, it would be necessary to estimate the corporation tax payable for the full year and to apportion the relevant amount to the half year period. In practice, the preparation of the half yearly financial statements will inevitably involve a compromise between the use of both the discrete method and the integral method.

Preliminary announcements

In the UK, listed companies are required to notify the Stock Exchange of their preliminary statement of annual results and dividends as soon as possible after these are approved by the Board of Directors. At present these preliminary announcements are also distributed to financial analysts and institutional investors, rather than to shareholders at large. The ASB Statement 'Preliminary Announcements' encourages companies to distribute them more widely and, in particular, encourages companies to experiment with the use of electronic communication to achieve this end.

As with interim reports, the Stock Exchange requirements are minimal and rather out of date, so the ASB Statement is intended to lay down best practice in this area.

Given that both interim reports and preliminary announcements are providing new information to the market about the company's performance and position, it is not surprising that there is considerable overlap between the contents of the two statements. Thus the Statement recommends that the preliminary announcement include the same documents as the interim report, namely:

- Management commentary
- Summarised profit and loss account
- Statement of total recognised gains and losses
- Summarised balance sheet
- Summarised cash flow statement

The management commentary should provide a balanced coverage of developments since the last annual report and interim report. The ASB encourages directors to specifically refer to developments in the second half of the year, which might otherwise not be commented upon.

The contents of the summary financial statements should be the same as those in the interim report as discussed in the previous section and partially listed in Table 11.3.

A preliminary announcement can only be made once the preparation and audit of the, as yet unpublished, financial statements for the year are well advanced; approval of the preliminary statement of results by the Board and agreement of the auditors are required before publication. It follows that the preparation of the preliminary announcement for the year avoids many of the conceptual problems of preparing an interim report.

Recommended reading

Much useful information on current practice is included in *UK GAAP: Generally Accepted Accounting Practice in the United Kingdom*, 6th edition, Mike Davies, Ron Paterson and Allister Wilson, Macmillan, London 1999.

12 Capital reorganisation, reduction and reconstruction

Overview   While the law cannot prevent the reduction of permanent capital which occurs when a company makes losses, it seeks to protect the creditors and shareholders of a limited company by restricting the reduction of permanent capital in other circumstances. We have already explored an example of this in Chapter 3 where we saw that dividends may only be paid out of distributable profits. In this chapter, we discuss the circumstances where a reduction of capital is permitted and explain the strict procedures which must be followed in order to do so.

The law permits limited companies to purchase and cancel their own shares. While it is intended that public companies must keep their capital intact and may only make a 'purchase not out of capital', private companies may purchase their shares in a way which leads to a reduction of capital, a 'purchase out of capital'. We start this chapter with an explanation of both of these purchases.

We then turn to the legal rules which govern the reduction of capital in other circumstances and illustrate such capital reduction schemes. Finally we discuss the regulatory framework for a wide range of reconstruction schemes and provide an illustration of the design and evaluation of such a scheme.

Introduction

There are many reasons for making changes to a company's capital structure and these range from those which are virtually cosmetic to those where the company's capital base has almost disappeared.

At the cosmetic end of the spectrum is the bonus (or scrip) issue designed to tidy up a balance sheet which might otherwise show a large number of different reserves. At the other end of the spectrum is the capital reconstruction scheme entered into as the only possible alternative to liquidation of the company. In such a case, the value of the company's assets may be less than the value of its liabilities with the probable result that the company will be unable to meet its debts as they fall due. The company must then reach some agreement with its debenture-holders and other creditors about how their liabilities are to be treated. To achieve economic viability, it will often be necessary to raise new capital from existing shareholders and if, as is likely, the company has accumulated losses, the new shares would probably be unattractive to investors. The writing-down, or reduction, of share capital removes such losses from the balance sheet and brings a greater likelihood of earlier future dividends, thus making the shares more attractive.

Within this spectrum of reasons for a reorganisation of capital, there are numerous possibilities. A company may wish to raise new share capital and use a rights issue as a cheaper alternative to a general offer to the public; conversely it may wish to reduce its share capital in line with a smaller level of operations or perhaps to permit a shareholder director in a family company to retire. A capital reorganisation scheme may be used to effect a change in the relative rights of different classes of shareholders, perhaps when a company is involved in a business combination. Taxation considerations are important in leading a company to reorganise its capital so that its earnings may be distributed to members in a tax-efficient way.

In some cases the reason for the reorganisation is unique, that is it is only applicable in the circumstances of the particular company. A good example is the scheme of arrangement undertaken by European Ferries plc in 1984. Under this scheme, ordinary shareholders were permitted to convert their ordinary shares into preference shares and only those preference shares now carry the right to discounts on P & O ferries. The purpose of the scheme was to limit any future growth in the number of shareholders entitled to such discounts.

Changes in share capital such as bonus issues and rights issues are dealt with in more elementary textbooks on accounting. Here we concentrate on certain reorganisations of capital permitted under the provisions of the Companies Act 1985.

First, we look at the redemption or purchase of its own shares by a company under the provisions of the Companies Act 1985. We deal with both the purchase of shares other than out of capital, which may be made by any limited company with a share capital, and a purchase out of capital, which may only be made by a private limited company. In the following section we examine the more wide-ranging powers to reduce capital contained in the Companies Act 1985. Next we provide the background to other capital reorganisations including those which involve the alteration of creditors' rights. In the final section, we consider the design and evaluation of a capital reconstruction scheme to be undertaken as an alternative to liquidation.

Redemption and purchase of shares

Purchase not out of capital[1]

Until the Companies Act 1981, the only class of share that a company was able to redeem was redeemable preference shares. The Companies Act 1985 now permits limited companies both to issue redeemable shares of any class, and to purchase its own shares, whether or not they were issued as redeemable shares. The difference between a redemption and a purchase is that in the former case the shares will be reacquired on terms specified when the security was issued, whereas in the case of a purchase the amount payable will depend on conditions prevailing at the date of purchase. Apart from this, the rules governing redemption and purchase are the same and, in order to avoid repetition, we shall merely use the term purchase throughout this section. In both cases the purchased shares must be cancelled and cannot be reissued, although the government is considering whether companies should be permitted to retain uncancelled purchased shares as investments as part of their treasury management policies.[2]

---

[1] The relevant legal provisions are contained in the Companies Act 1985, Sections 159–170.

[2] *See* URN98/713, Department of Trade and Industry, May 1998. Retention of uncancelled purchased shares as treasury investments is permitted in many other countries including the USA.

The Act distinguishes two categories of purchase: a market purchase and an off-market purchase. The·market purchase is a purchase of shares quoted on a recognised investment exchange other than an overseas investment exchange. It follows that such a purchase may only be made by a public company which has shares quoted on the relevant market. The off-market purchase is any other purchase of shares under a contract and may be made by both public and private companies. In view of the possibility that one particular shareholder may be beneficially treated, the Act lays down more onerous conditions for an off-market purchase than for a market purchase. Thus, whereas the market purchase may be made in accordance with a general authority passed by an ordinary resolution in general meeting, the off-market purchase requires approval of a specific contract by a special resolution in general meeting.

Private companies are in certain circumstances allowed to reduce their permanent capital by the purchase of their own shares and we shall deal with these provisions later in the chapter. With this exception, the 1985 Act lays down very detailed rules to ensure that the permanent capital is maintained intact following the purchase. The general principle, which has applied for many years on the redemption of redeemable preference shares, is that the purchase must be made either out of distributable profits or out of the proceeds of a new issue of shares made for the purpose, or by a combination of the two methods.

In many instances the purchase will be made at a premium, i.e. the purchase price will exceed the share's nominal value. Any premium payable on purchase must be paid out of distributable profits unless the shares being purchased were originally issued at a premium,[3] in which case some or all of the premium may come from the proceeds of any new issue.

Where the purchase is made out of distributable profits, an amount must be transferred to a capital redemption reserve, which is treated as paid-up share capital of the company. It would appear that the intention of the Act is that the amount of the transfer should be such as to ensure that the permanent capital following the purchase is maintained at the original level. However, probably unintentionally, due to the particular wording used in the Act, circumstances can arise which could result in either an increase or a reduction in permanent capital. The circumstances might occur where shares are purchased at a premium out of the proceeds of a fresh issue of shares itself made at a premium and these will be illustrated in the examples which follow.

First, let us assume that a company purchases shares without making a new issue of shares. In such a case, the amount payable, including any premium, must come from distributable profits and, in order to maintain the permanent capital of the company, it is necessary to transfer an amount equal to the nominal value of the shares purchased from distributable profits to a capital redemption reserve, which is treated as paid-up share capital of the company. This is illustrated in Example 12.1.

---

[3] This means that where some of the shares in issue were issued at par with others having been issued at a premium it will be necessary to identify which particular shares are being purchased.

Example 12.1

Bratsk plc has the following summarised balance sheet:

	£
Net assets	1 500
Share capital – £1 shares	1 000
Share premium	200
(Permanent capital)	1 200
Distributable profits	300
	1 500

It purchases 100 £1 shares for £160 out of distributable profits.
Summarised journal entries together with the resulting balance sheet are as follows:

	£	£
Dr Share capital	100	
Premium on purchase	60	
Cr Cash		160
	160	160
Dr Distributable profits	160	
Cr Premium on purchase		60
Capital redemption reserve		100
	160	160

Summarised balance sheet after purchase of shares:

		£
Net assets	(1 500 – 160)	1 340
Share capital	(1 000 – 100)	900
Share premium		200
Capital redemption reserve		100
(Permanent capital)		1 200
Distributable profits	(300 – 160)	140
		1 340

Notice that the permanent capital of the company remains unchanged at £1200.

Next let us assume that a company purchases shares out of the proceeds of a new issue. In the absence of any premium payable on purchase, discussed below, the nominal value of the shares purchased is replaced by the nominal value of and any share premium received on the new issue.

Example 12.2

Chita Limited has the following summarised balance sheet:

	£
Net assets	1 500
Share capital – £1 shares	1 000
Share premium	200
(Permanent capital)	1 200
Distributable profits	300
	1 500

Chita purchases 100 £1 shares at their nominal value out of the proceeds of an issue of 80 £1 shares at a premium of 25p per share.

Summarised journal entries and the resulting balance sheet are as follows:

	£	£
Dr Cash	100	
Cr Share capital		80
Share premium		20
	100	100
Dr Share capital	100	
Cr Cash		100

Summarised balance sheet after purchase of shares:

	£
Net assets	1 500
Share capital (1000 + 80 − 100)	980
Share premium (200 + 20)	220
(Permanent capital)	1 200
Distributable profits	300
	1 500

Once again, the permanent capital has been maintained at £1200.

Frequently, as in the case of Bratsk (Example 12.1), a premium is payable on the shares purchased. Such a premium must be paid out of distributable profits except that, where the shares which are being purchased were originally issued at a premium, all or part of the premium now payable may be paid out of the proceeds of the new issue and charged against the share premium account. The amount which may be charged against the share premium account is the lower of:

(i) the amount of the premium which the company originally received on the shares now being purchased, and
(ii) the current balance on the share premium account, including any premium on the new issue of shares.

Example 12.3

Dudinka Limited has the following summarised balance sheet:

	£
Net assets	1 500
Share capital – £1 shares	1 000
Share premium	200
(Permanent capital)	1 200
Distributable profits	300
	1 500

Dudinka Limited purchases 100 £1 shares which were originally issued at a premium of 20p per share. The price paid is £180 and this is financed by the issue of 90 £1 shares at a premium of £1 per share.

Part of the premium payable may be financed from the proceeds of the new issue; the amount is the lower of the original share premium on the shares now being purchased and the balance of the share premium account, including the premium on the new share issue. In this case the amount is the lower of £20 (100 at 20p) and £290 (£200 + £90) and hence £20 may be debited to the share premium account. The balance must come from distributable profits.

Summarised journal entries and the resulting balance sheet are as follows:

	£	£
Dr Cash	180	
Cr Share capital		90
Share premium		90
	180	180
Dr Share capital	100	
Premium on purchase	80	
Cr Cash		180
	180	180
Dr Share premium	20	
Distributable profits	60	
Cr Premium on purchase		80
	80	80

Summarised balance sheet after purchase of shares:

	£
Net assets (1 500 + 180 – 180)	1 500
Share capital (1 000 + 90 – 100)	990
Share premium (200 + 90 – 20)	270
(Permanent capital)	1 260
Distributable profits (300 – 60)	240
	1 500

So, even where the proceeds of the new issue are exactly equal to the amount payable on purchase, the restriction on the amount of any premium payable which may be charged against the share premium account will often result in part of the premium payable being charged against distributable profits and a consequent increase in the permanent capital of the company.

In the final example in this section, we look at a company which purchases shares but raises only part of the finance by making a new issue of shares. We shall assume that the shares are purchased at a premium and that the new shares are issued at a premium. As we shall see, it is in this situation that a reduction in the permanent capital of the company may occur.

Example 12.4

Ivdel plc has the following summarised balance sheet:

	£
Net assets	1 500
Share capital – £1 shares	1 000
Share premium	200
(Permanent capital)	1 200
Distributable profits	300
	1 500

It purchases 100 shares which were originally issued at a premium of 50p per share. The agreed price is £180 and the company issues 40 shares at a premium of £1 per share to help finance the purchase.

The premium payable on purchase is £80 and part of this may come from the proceeds of the new issue and be charged to the share premium account. As explained above, this amount is the lower of the original premium (£50) and the balance on the share premium account after the new issue (£240). Hence £50 may be debited to the share premium account and the balance must be debited to distributable profits.

As part of the purchase price is being met from distributable profits, it is necessary to make a transfer to capital redemption reserve. Section 170(2) of the 1985 Companies Act requires the amount to be calculated by deducting the aggregate amount of the proceeds of the new issue from the nominal value of the shares purchased. In this case the amount of the transfer is therefore:

	£
Nominal value of shares purchased	100
less Proceeds of new issue	
(40 × £2)	80
Necessary transfer	20

Necessary journal entries and the resulting balance sheet are given below:

	£	£
Dr Cash	80	
Cr Share capital		40
Share premium		40
	80	80
Dr Share capital	100	
Premium on purchase	80	
Cr Cash		180
	180	180
Dr Share premium	50	
Distributable profits	30	
Cr Premium on purchase		80
	80	80
Dr Distributable profits	20	
Cr Capital redemption reserve		20

Summarised balance sheet after purchase of shares:

	£
Net assets (1 500 + 80 – 180)	1 400
Share capital (1 000 + 40 – 100)	940
Share premium (200 + 40 – 50)	190
Capital redemption reserve	20
(Permanent capital)	1 150
Distributable profits (300 – 30 – 20)	250
	1 400

In this case, the permanent capital has been reduced from £1200 to £1150 which does not appear to accord with the intended aim of maintaining permanent capital. The reason the reduction occurs is because the proceeds of the new issue are used to finance part of both nominal value and premium payable and yet this is not recognised in making the transfer to capital redemption reserve.

Let us illustrate: the proceeds of the new issue are £80 and, of this, £50 is used to finance the premium on purchase. This leaves only £30 to replace the nominal value of the shares issued. To maintain permanent capital of the company, the transfer to capital redemption reserve should be calculated as follows:

	£	£
Nominal value of shares purchased		100
less Net proceeds of new issue:		
Total proceeds	80	
less Utilised to finance part of premium payable	50	
		30
Transfer to capital redemption reserve		70

Such a transfer would maintain permanent capital at £1200 but it is not the transfer required by law. Section 170(2) makes no reference to 'net' proceeds and hence the law seems to permit such a reduction in capital for both public and private companies. In our view, the law has been poorly drafted with the consequence that it fails to achieve the objective of maintaining the company's permanent capital.

Purchase out of capital[4]

The permissible capital payment

Whereas failure to maintain capital in the circumstances discussed above may be an unintended effect of the legislation, the 1985 Act specifically permits a private, but not a public, company to purchase its shares out of capital. This provides such a company with a means for reducing its permanent capital without the formality and expense of undertaking a capital reduction scheme, which we discuss in the next section. Such an ability to purchase shares out of capital is of considerable benefit to, for example, a family-owned company where a member of the family wishes to realise his or her investment but no other member of the family wishes, or is able, to purchase it.

A purchase of shares out of capital results in a fall in the resources available to creditors and the 1985 Act therefore provides a number of safeguards to protect their interests. Before summarising these safeguards, we will explain the calculation of the permitted reduction in capital, what the Act describes as the 'permissible capital payment'.

The private company is not free to specify the amount of the payment out of capital. Rather the payment is restricted to the amount actually paid for shares less both the distributable profits and the proceeds of any fresh issue of shares made for the purpose of the purchase. Thus, a payment from capital may only be made when all distributable reserves have been utilised. Rules are laid down to ensure that the permanent capital of the company is not reduced by more than the permissible capital payment, although these rules may still not succeed due to the problem discussed in connection with Example 12.4.

If the total of the permissible capital payment and the proceeds of a fresh issue of shares is less than the nominal value of the shares purchased, there would be a reduction in permanent capital in excess of the permissible capital payment. To prevent this, the law requires that the difference be transferred to a capital redemption reserve. If the permissible capital payment together with the proceeds of any fresh issue of shares exceeds the nominal value of the shares purchased, the excess may be eliminated by writing it off against any one of a number of accounts, including accounts for capital redemption reserve, share premium, share capital or unrealised profits. This ability to write off the excess to any one of these named accounts or, indeed, to deal with it in some other way, provides a private company with considerable flexibility to design its own capital reduction scheme.

We shall illustrate the above rules with two examples of the purchase of shares by private companies.

In Example 12.5 the purchase of shares is made partly out of capital and partly out of distributable profits, whereas in Example 12.6 the purchase is, in addition, made partly out of the proceeds of a new issue of shares.

---

[4] The relevant legal provisions are contained in the Companies Act 1985, Sections 171–177.

Example 12.5

Kotlas Limited has the following summarised balance sheet:

	£
Net assets	1 250
Share capital – £1 shares	1 000
Distributable profits	250
	1 250

It purchases 200 £1 shares at a cost of £300. In the absence of a share premium account or a new issue of shares at a premium, the amount of the premium payable must be provided from distributable profits.

The permissible capital payment is:

	£
Amount payable	300
less Distributable profits	250
Permissible capital payment	50

As the permissible capital payment (£50) is less than the nominal value of the shares purchased (£200) it is necessary to make a transfer from distributable profits to a capital redemption reserve.

	£
Nominal value of shares purchased	200
less Permissible capital payment	50
Necessary transfer	150

Necessary journal entries and the resulting summarised balance sheet are given below:

	£	£
Dr Share capital	200	
Premium on purchase	100	
Cr Cash		300
	300	300
Dr Distributable profits	250	
Cr Premium on purchase		100
Capital redemption reserve		150
	250	250

Summarised balance sheet after purchase of shares:

	£
Net assets (1 250 – 300)	950
Share capital (1 000 – 200)	800
Capital redemption reserve	150
(Permanent capital)	950

The permanent capital of the company has been reduced from £1000 share capital to £950. It has fallen by the amount of the permissible capital payment.

Example 12.6

Nordvik Limited has the following summarised balance sheet:

	£
Net assets	1 250
Share capital – £1 shares	1 000
Share premium	200
(Permanent capital)	1 200
Distributable profits	50
	1 250

Of the £1 shares, 500 were issued at par when the company was formed and 500 were issued at a premium of 40p per share some years later.

Nordvik purchases 200 of the shares which were originally issued at par for an agreed price of £300 and finances the purchase in part by an issue of 50 shares at a premium of 60p per share.

As the shares purchased were not originally issued at a premium, no part of the premium payable may come from the proceeds of the new issue. The whole of the premium payable, that is the whole of the increase in value of these particular shares since their issue, must be charged against distributable profits.

In this case the permissible capital payment is:

	£	£
Amount payable		300
less Distributable profits	50	
Proceeds of new issue (50 × £1.60)	80	130
Permissible capital payment		170

In order to determine whether or not a transfer to capital redemption reserve is necessary, we must compare the proceeds of the new issue and the permissible capital payment with the nominal value of the shares purchased.

	£	£
Nominal value of shares purchased		200
less Permissible capital payment	170	
Proceeds of new issue	80	250
		(50)

In this case no transfer to capital redemption reserve is required. Rather the excess £50 may be charged to one of the accounts discussed above and we have chosen to debit it to the share premium account.

Necessary journal entries and the resulting summarised balance sheet are given below:

	£	£
Dr Cash	80	
Cr Share capital		50
Share premium		30
	80	80
Dr Share capital	200	
Premium on purchase	100	
Cr Cash		300
	300	300
Dr Distributable profits	50	
Share premium	50	
Cr Premium on purchase		100
	100	100

Summarised balance sheet after purchase of shares:

	£
Net assets (1 250 + 80 – 300)	1 030
Share capital (1 000 + 50 – 200)	850
Share premium (200 + 30 – 50)	180
(Permanent capital)	1 030
Distributable profits	–
	1 030

The permanent capital of the company has been reduced from £1200 to £1030 by the amount of the permissible capital payment of £170.

The safeguards

In view of the fact that there is a reduction in the permanent capital, that is a reduction in the net assets available to creditors and the remaining shareholders, the law provides a number of safeguards where a company wishes to make such a purchase of shares involving a payment out of capital. Thus, not only must the payment out of capital be permitted by the company's articles of association and authorised by a special resolution of the company, but the directors must also provide a statutory declaration of solvency to the effect that, having made a full enquiry into the affairs and prospects of the company, they have formed the opinion that the company will be able to pay its debts both immediately after the payment and during the following year. As the protection of creditors and shareholders rests on this continuing solvency of the company, the law requires that a report by the company's auditors on the reasonableness of the directors' opinion is attached to the statutory declaration.

After the payment out of capital has been authorised, the company must publicise it in an official gazette and either a national newspaper or by individual notice to each creditor. Any creditor, or any shareholder who did not vote for the special resolution, may then apply to the court for the cancellation of the resolution and the court may then cancel or confirm the resolution and may make an order to facilitate an arrangement whereby the interests of dissenting creditors or members are purchased.

If the directors' optimism subsequently proves not to have been well founded and the company commences to wind up within a year of the payment out of capital and is unable to pay all its liabilities and the costs of winding up, then directors and past shareholders may be liable to contribute. The directors who have signed the statutory declaration and/or past shareholders, whose shares were purchased, may have to pay an amount not exceeding in total the permitted capital payment.

Thus the Companies Act 1985 provides safeguards to protect creditors. The use of its provisions to make a purchase of shares partly out of capital is undoubtedly much cheaper and less burdensome than a reduction of capital under the provisions to which we turn next.

Capital reduction

The Companies Act 1985 gives companies a much wider power to reduce capital than that discussed above, but it also imposes the more onerous condition that any such reduction must be confirmed by the court.[5]

Providing it is authorised to do so by its articles of association, a limited company may reduce its share capital by passing a special resolution, which must be confirmed by the court. The Act gives a general power to reduce share capital but specifically lists three possible ways to reduce capital:[6]

(a) extinguish or reduce the liability on any of its shares in respect of share capital not paid up; or

(b) either with or without extinguishing or reducing liability on any of its shares, cancel any paid-up share capital which is lost or unrepresented by available assets; or

(c) either with or without extinguishing or reducing liability on any of its shares, pay off any paid-up share capital which is in excess of the company's wants.

A capital reduction for the first and third of the possible reasons listed is extremely rare. With regard to the first, few companies now have partly paid shares in existence and hence there is invariably no liability in respect of partly paid capital which could be reduced. With regard to the third, although it might make good economic sense for directors to return 'permanent' capital to shareholders where better investment opportunities exist outside of the company than within it, most directors have been loath to relinquish their control over such resources and have usually found some way to employ them within the company.

Both of these capital reductions ((a) and (c)) do, of course, result in a reduction in the potential net assets or actual net assets available to creditors. Thus, in the first case, there is a reduction in the liability of members and hence in the potential pool of net assets available to creditors on a liquidation. In the third case, resources actually

---

[5] The Company Law Review Steering Group has proposed the abolition of this requirement for confirmation by the Court and its replacement by a requirement for a declaration of solvency to be made by directors of the company. *See* Chapter 5.4 of *Modern Company Law for a Competitive Economy: The Strategic Framework*, A Consultative Document from the Company Law Review Steering Group, Department of Trade and Industry, February 1999.

[6] Companies Act 1985, Section 135.

leave the company, so directly reducing the pool of net assets to which the creditors have recourse. For these reasons the court must give any creditor an opportunity to object to the capital reduction and will usually only confirm the scheme if the debt of such a dissenting creditor is paid or secured.

The second of the three possible capital reduction schemes is the one most commonly found in practice. Thus, where a company has made losses in excess of previous profits, its net assets will be lower than its permanent capital. Given that such a position has been reached, it will often be sensible to recognise the fact by reducing the capital and writing off the losses so that a more realistic position is shown by the balance sheet and the company is allowed to make a fresh start. In particular, after such a scheme the company will be able to distribute realised profits without the need to first make good the accumulated realised losses and, in the case of a public company, net unrealised losses.[7]

The simplest way of carrying out such a capital reduction scheme is to reduce proportionately the nominal value of the ordinary shares outstanding. This has no effect whatsoever on the real value of the ordinary shareholders' interest since the same number of shares in the same company are held in the same proportions by the same people! Each shareholder has the same proportional interest in the net assets of the company after the scheme as before. This demonstrates the irrelevance of the par value and supports the argument that companies should be permitted to issue shares of no par value.[8]

To illustrate such a scheme, let us look at an example.

Example 12.7

Perm plc has the following summarised balance sheet:

	£
Net assets	1 200
Share capital	
1000 £1 ordinary shares, fully paid	1 000
500 £1 10% preference shares, fully paid	500
	1 500
Share premium	200
	1 700
less Accumulated losses	500
	1 200

The preference shares rank for dividend and repayment of capital in priority to ordinary shares. The company wishes to reduce its capital by an amount sufficient to remove the accumulated losses and to write down the net assets to a more realistic book value of £900. Thus it wishes to reduce permanent capital by £800, that is £(500 + (1200 – 900)).

For illustrative purposes we shall consider two possible capital reduction schemes, the first involving a reduction of ordinary share capital only and the second involving the reduction of both ordinary share capital and preference share capital.

---

[7] *See* Chapter 3.

[8] A government committee under the chairmanship of Mr Montague Gedge reported in favour of the issue of shares of no par value as long ago as 1954, Cmnd 9112/5, HMSO, London, 1954. A similar proposal in favour of no par value shares has been made, 35 years later, in Chapter 5.4 of *Modern Company Law for a Competitive Economy: The Strategic Framework*, Department of Trade and Industry, February 1999. No doubt a similar recommendation will emerge in 2034!

Scheme 1

As explained above, the total amount of the capital reduction is £800. However, for the purpose of a reduction of capital, a share premium account is to be treated as paid-up share capital of the company[9] so that £200 may be written off against the share premium, leaving £600 to reduce the ordinary share capital from £1000 to £400, that is from £1 to 40p per share.

The balance sheet after the capital reduction would therefore appear as follows:

Summarised balance sheet after capital reduction

	£
Net assets	900
Share capital	
1000 40p ordinary shares	400
500 £1 10% preference shares	500
	900

The interest of preference shareholders and ordinary shareholders in the liquidation value of the company has not altered. Preference shareholders would receive the first £500 while ordinary shareholders would receive the remainder. If the company continues to trade, both sets of shareholders gain in the sense that the company will be able to pay dividends as soon as profits are made without any need to make good the past losses.

Scheme 2

Given the fact that preference shareholders as well as ordinary shareholders benefit from the capital reduction scheme, ordinary shareholders might argue that preference share capital as well as ordinary share capital should be reduced. However, as we shall see, a reduction in the par value of a preference share has a much more serious effect than the reduction in the par value of ordinary shares. Indeed, a reduction in the par value of both preference shares and ordinary shares, with no other changes, will lead to a fall in the real value of the preference shares but a rise in the real value of the ordinary shares. This may be illustrated as follows.

As before, let us assume that the amount of the capital reduction is £800 and that, of this, £200 may be written off against the share premium account, leaving £600 to be written off against share capital. Given that the ordinary share capital is £1000 and that the preference share capital is £500, it might be thought that the amount of £600 should be written off in the ratio 2:1 which would produce a balance sheet as follows:

Summarised balance sheet after capital reduction

	£
Net assets	900
Share capital	
1000 60p ordinary shares	600
500 60p 10% preference shares	300
	900

Although this may initially appear to be fair, a little thought will make it clear that the preference shareholders have been unfairly treated.

Given that the par value of a preference share determines the amount of the preference dividend and the amount which the preference shareholders receive on a liquidation, prefer-

---

[9] Companies Act 1985, Section 130(3).

ence shareholders will have suffered a real loss. They are worse off after the scheme than before. Conversely, the ordinary shareholders are better off. Not only would they receive more on an immediate liquidation, as less would be paid to the preference shareholders, but they are also likely to receive higher future dividends, as a lesser dividend would be paid to the preference shareholders.

Careful attention must be paid to the likely effect of reducing the par values of different types of share capital. A capital reduction such as Scheme 2 is unlikely to be acceptable to the preference shareholders unless they are given some other benefit, such as a holding of ordinary shares, which will give them an opportunity to share in any future prosperity.

The legal background to other reorganisations

We have looked in some detail at the ways in which a company may reduce its share capital under the provisions of the Companies Act 1985. As we saw in the introduction to this chapter, there are many other ways in which a company may wish to reorganise its capital. For example, it may wish to alter the respective rights of different classes of shareholders, or, if it is in financial difficulties, it may need to reduce not only share capital but also the claims of creditors. In this section we look briefly at the legal background to such reorganisations.

First, it is necessary to clarify that although the term 'capital reduction' has a clear legal meaning, as discussed above, the terms 'capital reorganisation', 'capital reconstruction' and, indeed, 'scheme of arrangement' do not. These terms tend to be used interchangeably although there is, perhaps, a tendency to use the term 'capital reconstruction' for the more serious changes in capital structure; so in the final section of this chapter we look at a capital reconstruction scheme undertaken as an alternative to liquidation of the company. In the remainder of this section we will use the term reorganisation.

Any reorganisation which involves creditors will invariably be carried out in accordance with the procedures laid down in Sections 425–426 of the Companies Act 1985. These procedures are designed to protect the various parties involved by requiring court approval for the reorganisation. This sounds fine in theory but the courts have been reluctant to pass judgement on the economic merits and fairness of schemes and have tended to concern themselves with deciding whether the scheme satisfies the required legal formalities.[10]

Under Sections 425–426, the company applies to the court which will then direct meetings of the various parties affected to be held. The company must then send out details of the proposed scheme and, providing a majority agree – in number representing three-quarters in value of those attending the various meetings – and providing the scheme is sanctioned by the court, it will become binding on all parties once a copy is delivered to the Registrar of Companies.

Sometimes a reorganisation entered into in accordance with the above provisions will involve the transfer of the whole or part of an undertaking from one company to another. In such a case, Sec. 427 gives the court wide powers to make provision for the transfer of ownership of assets, liabilities, rights and duties to the transferee company.

---

[10] *See* L.C.B. Gower, *Gower's Principles of Modern Company Law*, 6th edn, edited by Paul L. Davies, with a contribution by Dan Prentice, Sweet & Maxwell, London, 1997, Chapter 28.

The above provisions may be used to effect a reorganisation even where there is no change in creditors' rights. However, alternative procedures are available in such cases which do not involve the formality and expense of going to court. Thus, it may be possible to vary the rights of two or more classes of shareholders by merely holding separate class meetings and obtaining the necessary majority votes, although a dissenting minority is given a right to object to the variation in an application to the court.

Another possible means of reorganisation is provided by Section 110 of the Insolvency Act 1986. Under this section, once a voluntary liquidation of the company is proposed, the liquidator may be given authority to sell the whole or a part of the undertaking to another company in exchange for shares or other securities in that other company. Thus, where it is desired to change the rights of two or more classes of its shareholders, the company may be put into voluntary liquidation and a new company may be formed with the desired mix of various classes of shares. The business of the transferor company may then be sold to the new company in exchange for the new shares, which may then be distributed to the shareholders in the transferor company to achieve the desired change. This procedure is much simpler than the use of a scheme under Sections 425–427 of the Act.

Invariably taxation considerations will be extremely important in most capital reorganisations and, in view of the complexity of the tax legislation, specialist advice is almost always necessary.

Capital reconstruction

In this section we shall concentrate on the design and evaluation of a capital reconstruction scheme for a company which is in severe financial difficulties. It will be assumed that, in the absence of a capital reconstruction scheme, the liquidation of the company would be inevitable. This assumption will affect both the design of the scheme and the way in which it will be evaluated by the interested parties.

As the alternative source of benefits to interested parties is the amount receivable on liquidation, it is essential for us to recall the order in which the proceeds from the sale of assets must be distributed by a liquidator.

Distribution on liquidation

It is the duty of a liquidator to sell the assets of a company as advantageously as possible and to pay costs, creditors and shareholders in the following order:

1 Debts secured by a fixed charge. These must be paid out of the proceeds of sale of the particular assets. In practice a receiver will usually be appointed to sell the assets which are the subject of the charge, and to pay the secured creditors the amounts due to them.

 It will rarely be the case that the proceeds of sale are exactly equal to the costs of the receiver and the amount of the debt. Any excess will be paid over to the liquidator of the company while, to the extent of any deficiency, the creditors are treated in the same way as other unsecured creditors.

2 Costs of the liquidation, in the order specified by law.

3 Preferential creditors. These are listed in Schedule 6 to the Insolvency Act 1986 and include income tax deducted from employees' emoluments under PAYE, value added tax, car tax, social security contributions, contributions to pension schemes

and remuneration of employees. There are limits to each of these categories so, for example, PAYE is preferential to the extent of one year's deductions, value added tax to six months, social security contributions up to one year and remuneration of employees up to four months. To the extent that only a part of a debt is preferential, the remainder will be treated as an unsecured creditor.

4 Creditors secured by a floating charge.

5 Unsecured creditors, including the amounts mentioned in 1 and 3 above.

6 Shareholders of the company in accordance with their rights as laid down in the company's articles of association. Preference shares will normally be paid before any amounts are paid to ordinary shareholders.

Where the amounts available are insufficient to pay any of the above groups in full, each member of the particular group receives the same proportion of the amount of his debt. This proportion is determined as the amount available for a particular group divided by the total amounts due to that group.

Design of a capital reconstruction scheme

Given that a company is in financial difficulties, the objective in the design of a capital reconstruction scheme will be to produce an entity which is a profitable going concern. In some cases the financial difficulties may be so severe that this is impossible for, no matter how skilfully a capital reconstruction scheme is designed, it is not possible to turn the sow's ear into a silk purse. Where the financial difficulties are less severe and the company is capable of operating profitably, a capital reconstruction scheme may have a high probability of success. In order to achieve that success, it will usually be necessary to relieve the company of its burden of immediate debts and will often be necessary to raise new finance, probably by a new issue of shares.

Any capital reconstruction scheme which affects the rights of creditors and shareholders will require the necessary majorities of votes in favour of the scheme as required by Section 425 of the Companies Act 1985, together with the sanction of the court. Hence, to stand any chance of success, the scheme must give each interested party the same amount or more than they would receive on liquidation of the company. In addition the scheme must be accepted as equitable by the various interested parties. It must ensure that no one class of creditor or shareholder is favoured at the expense of any other, so that all creditors and shareholders are treated – and feel that they are treated – fairly.

The design of a capital reconstruction scheme is illustrated in the following example, and the resulting scheme is evaluated in the final section of this chapter.

Example 12.8

A summarised balance sheet of Sakhalin plc on 31 December 20X1 is as follows:

Sakhalin plc
Balance sheet on 31 December 20X1

	£000	£000
Fixed assets at cost less depreciation		
Land and buildings	2 500	
Plant and machinery	1 000	3 500
Carried forward		3 500

	£000	£000
Brought forward		3 500
Current assets		
Stock and work in progress	1 000	
Sundry debtors	1 500	2 500
		6 000
less Current liabilities		
Bank overdraft	3 000	4 250
Trade creditors	1 000	
Arrears of debenture interest	250	
		1 750
Financed by		
10% secured debentures (note (a))		1 250
1 million authorised and issued £1		
5% preference shares	1 000	
2 million authorised and issued £1		
ordinary shares	2 000	
	3 000	
less Accumulated losses	2 500	500
		1 750

The following information is available:

(a) The debentures are secured on the office premises, the net realisable value of which is estimated to be £900 000.
(b) The other land and buildings are estimated to have a net realisable value of £1 900 000.
(c) The net realisable value of the plant and machinery is estimated to be £500 000, of the stock and work-in-progress £750 000, and the recoverable debts are now estimated to be £1 425 000.
(d) The preference dividend has not been paid for four years.
(e) The debenture interest is two years in arrears.
(f) The articles provide that, on liquidation, the preference shareholders rank for repayment at par prior to any distribution to the ordinary shareholders.

From preliminary meetings of the directors and soundings of the interested parties the following information has also been obtained:

(g) The debenture holders are prepared to agree to a reconstruction scheme providing the rate of interest is increased from 10 to 15 per cent p.a., and they are given a fixed security on the total land and buildings, rather than just the office premises, of the company. They are also willing to accept ordinary shares in lieu of £125 000, that is one of the two years' interest in arrears.
(h) The bank is prepared to agree to a reconstruction scheme provided its debt is secured by a floating charge over the assets of the company, thus improving its position vis-à-vis any other creditors of the reconstructed company. They would be willing to provide the same amount of finance for the medium term.
(i) The trade creditors are unlikely to agree to any reduction in their claims but are thought to be willing to supply the reconstructed company and to continue to grant credit on normal terms.

(j)   The preference shareholders would be willing to forego their arrears of dividend and to accept ordinary shares instead of preference shares.

(k)   The directors consider that, if the company is able to raise an additional £1 million in cash by a rights issue, it will be able to commence trading successfully. Expected annual earnings before debenture interest and dividends will then be at least £300 000 and, due to accumulated tax losses, no corporation tax will be payable in the foreseeable future.

(l)   Debenture holders, preference shareholders and ordinary shareholders are willing to subscribe for new ordinary share capital in the company.

(m) Costs of the reconstruction scheme are expected to be £60 000.

(n)   In the absence of a satisfactory scheme the company will have to be liquidated involving costs of £295 000.

From the above information it is possible to calculate the amount of the capital reduction required, namely:[11]

		£000
(a)	To correct the value of plant and machinery	500
(b)	To correct the value of stock and work in progress	250
(c)	To correct the value of debtors	75
(d)	To eliminate the adverse balance on the profit and loss account	2 500
(e)	To provide for the costs of the scheme	60
		3 385
(f)	Less surplus on revaluation of land and buildings	300
		3 085

In order to begin to decide who must bear this loss in the reconstruction scheme, we must first examine what each class of creditor and shareholder would receive if the company were to be liquidated.

The realisable value of the assets and the way in which they would be distributed are as follows:

	£000	£000
Office premises	900	
less Payable to debenture holders secured on office premises	900	–
Other premises		1 900
Plant and machinery		500
Stock and work in progress		750
Sundry debtors		1 425
		4 575
less Costs of liquidation		295
Available for unsecured creditors		4 280

[11] In a balance sheet, assets should be shown at their 'going concern value' rather than their net realisable value. In order to avoid complicating the example by the introduction of another set of values, the realistic going concern values, assets have been written down to their net realisable values.

	£000	£000
Unsecured creditors:		
Bank overdraft		3 000
Debenture holders		
Capital	1 250	
Interest	250	
	1 500	
less Paid out of security as above	900	600
Trade creditors		1 000
		4 600

For simplicity it is assumed that there are no preferential creditors.

There would be £4280 available to meet unsecured creditors of £4600 with the result that each of these creditors, including the debenture holders to the extent that they are unsecured, would receive 93p in the £1. The various parties would therefore receive the following amounts on liquidation of the company:

	£000
Bank (0.93 × £3 000 000)	2 790
Debenture holders (900 000 + 0.93 × 600 000)	1 460
Trade creditors (0.93 × 1 000 000)	930
Preference shareholders	0
Ordinary shareholders	0
	5 180

Thus all parties would lose on a liquidation and there is an incentive for them to agree to a suitable reconstruction scheme. It is clear that any losses under the scheme must fall most heavily on the shareholders.

One possible scheme of reconstruction would be as follows:

	Reduction £000
(a) 2 million £1 ordinary shares each to be reduced to 1p ordinary shares	1 980
(b) 1 million £1 preference shares to be cancelled in exchange for 1 million 1p ordinary shares	990
(c) The granting of an increased rate of interest of 15 per cent p.a. and a fixed charge on all premises to the debenture holders and the waiving of £125 000 of interest in arrears in exchange for 1 million 1p ordinary shares (£10 000)	115
(d) The granting of a floating charge on the debt due to the bank	–
(e) Consolidation of the 4 million 1p ordinary shares into 40 000 £1 ordinary shares	–
(f) The making of a rights issue of 25 £1 ordinary shares for each £1 ordinary share held, thus raising cash of £1 000 000. Thus finance would come from old ordinary shareholders (£500 000), old preference shareholders (£250 000) and old debenture holders (£250 000)	–
Total reduction achieved as required	3 085

After such a reconstruction scheme is carried into effect, the balance sheet would appear as shown below:

Sakhalin plc

Balance sheet after scheme	£000	£000
Tangible fixed assets – at valuation		
Land and buildings		2 800
Plant and machinery		500
		3 300
Current assets		
Stock and work-in-progress	750	
Debtors	1 425	
Cash	1 000	
	3 175	
less Current liabilities		
Bank overdraft (secured)	3 000	
Debenture interest (1 year)	125	
Trade creditors	1 000	
Cost of reconstruction	60	
	4 185	(1 010)
		2 290
less 15% Debentures (secured on land and buildings)		1 250
		1 040
Share capital		
1 040 000 £1 ordinary shares, fully paid		1 040

Note: The apparently poor current ratio is due to the fact that the bank overdraft is included in current liabilities, in accordance with normal practice, whereas it is in fact medium-term capital.

Evaluation of a capital reconstruction scheme

In evaluating a capital reconstruction scheme, as in designing it, the aim must be to establish the relative fairness of the changes in rights as a result of the scheme. In most cases, professional advisers are called upon by each class of member and creditor to evaluate the scheme from their point of view and, in order to do this, it is necessary to evaluate the scheme as a whole since the changes of relative rights will be extremely important.

The rights of participants fall into two classes: the capital repayment rights and the income participation rights. In order to make an appropriate comparison of these, it is helpful to set out the interest of the various parties in the company both before and after the proposed reconstruction.

In Example 12.9 we shall do this in respect of the scheme which has been proposed for Sakhalin plc in Example 12.8.

Example 12.9

Table 12.1 Evaluation of proposed scheme – comparison of interests

Original class	Interest prior to scheme	Interest after scheme
Bank	£3 000 000 unsecured overdraft	£3 000 000 secured overdraft
Debenture holders	£1 250 000 partly secured 10% debentures *plus* £250 000 arrears of interest	£1 250 000 fully secured 15% debentures *plus* £125 000 arrears of interest *plus* one-quarter of the ordinary shares
Trade creditors	£1 000 000 unsecured debt	£1 000 000 unsecured debt
Preference shareholders	£1 000 000 £1 5% preference shares	One-quarter of the ordinary shares
Ordinary shareholders	All ordinary shares	One-half of the ordinary shares

We have already considered the amounts each class would receive should the scheme be rejected and the company forced into an immediate liquidation. These amounts need to be compared with the position following the reconstruction and we shall do so by evaluating three alternative possible outcomes. First, we shall assume that, despite the scheme, the company goes into liquidation immediately following the end of the capital reconstruction. Second, we will assume that the earnings are as expected, about £300 000 per annum. Finally, we will assume that the earnings are more than anticipated; we will, for this purpose, assume a figure of £500 000 per annum.

If we assume that the costs of the reconstruction scheme are paid, the position on the subsequent liquidation would be as follows:

Position on liquidation after scheme

	£000	£000
Amount receivable from sale of premises		2 800
less Debentures		
Capital	1 250	
Interest	125	1 375
		1 425
Amount realised from other assets:		
Plant and machinery	500	
Stock and work-in-progress	750	
Debtors	1 425	2 675
Cash (1 000 000 – 60 000)		940
		5 040
less Costs of liquidation		295
		4 745
less Bank secured by floating charge		3 000
		1 745
less Trade creditors		1 000
Available for ordinary shareholders		745

Divisible:

Old debenture holders ($\frac{1}{4}$)	186
Old preference shareholders ($\frac{1}{4}$)	186
Old ordinary shareholders ($\frac{1}{2}$)	373
	745

So, on a liquidation subsequent to the scheme the original parties would receive the following amounts:

	£000
Bank	3 000
Debenture holders (1 375 000 + 186 000)	1 561
Trade creditors	1 000
Preference shareholders	186
Ordinary shareholders	373
	6 120

Debenture holders and preference shareholders have, of course, subscribed £250 000 each for new ordinary share capital while ordinary shareholders have subscribed £500 000.

Let us next examine the interests of the various parties in the expected earnings of the reconstructed company.

As we have seen in note (k) on p. 386, the annual earnings before debenture interest and dividends are expected to be at least £300 000 and no corporation tax is likely to be paid in the foreseeable future. It follows that these earnings may be divided:

	£	£
Old debenture holders		
Interest 15% × £1 250 000	187 500	
Share of balance $\frac{1}{4}$ (300 000 − 187 500)	28 125	215 625
Old preference shareholders		
$\frac{1}{4}$ (300 000 − 187 500)		28 125
Old ordinary shareholders		
$\frac{1}{2}$ (300 000 − 187 500)		56 250
		300 000

It is helpful to examine the position if earnings turn out to be higher or lower than expected and, for illustrative purposes, we look at the position if earnings are £500 000:

	£	£
Old debenture holders		
Interest − as above	187 500	
Share of balance $\frac{1}{4}$ (500 000 − 187 500)	78 125	265 625
Old preference shareholders		
$\frac{1}{4}$ (500 000 − 187 500)		78 125
Old ordinary shareholders		
$\frac{1}{2}$ (500 000 − 187 500)		156 250
		500 000

We are now able to set out in Table 12.2 the position of each party before and after the proposed scheme in order to draw conclusions about its acceptability:

Table 12.2 Positions of parties before and after proposed scheme

			Position after scheme		
Original class	Amount receivable on liquidation before scheme £000	New capital introduced £000	Amount receivable on liquidation after scheme £000	Share of earnings £300 000 £000	Share of earnings £500 000 £000
Bank	2 790	–	3 000	n/a	n/a
Debenture holders	1 460	250	1 561	215.625	265.625
Trade creditors	930	–	1 000	n/a	n/a
Preference shareholders	–	250	186	28.125	78.125
Ordinary shareholders	–	500	373	56.250	156.250

The scheme would appear to offer advantages to all parties:

The bank converts unsecured debt into secured debt and stands to receive more in a liquidation after the scheme than in one before it.

On an immediate liquidation the debenture holders would receive £1 460 000, whereas if they invest a further £250 000 they will obtain a higher rate of interest on their debentures, a higher level of security and one-quarter of the ordinary shares in the reconstructed company. Although they would only receive £1 561 000 on a liquidation after the scheme, their share in future earnings is attractive. If the level of future earnings is £300 000 their rate of return is approximately 12.6 per cent, that is £215 625 divided by the amount of £1 710 000 (1 460 000 + 250 000) effectively invested. If future earnings are £500 000, the rate of return rises to approximately 18.2 per cent.

Trade creditors would receive more in a liquidation after the scheme than in one before it.

Both preference shareholders and ordinary shareholders would appear to benefit considerably from the scheme. Although they would not receive back their new investment if a liquidation occurred immediately after the scheme, their potential earnings yield is high. If future earnings are £300 000, the yield is 11.25 per cent (28.125/250) while, if earnings are £500 000, the yield rises to 31.25 per cent (78.125/250).

If all the parties are happy with the scheme, they will vote in favour of it at their respective meetings. Provided it is then confirmed by the court, the scheme will become operative as soon as a copy of the court order is lodged with the Registrar. If any of the parties are unhappy with the scheme, it will be necessary to amend it. If, at the end of the day, agreement on a satisfactory scheme cannot be reached, the company will be liquidated.

Recommended reading

J.H. Farrar, N.E. Furey, B.M. Hannigan and O.P. Wylie, *Farrar's Company Law*, 4th edn, Butterworth, London, 1998.

L.C.B. Gower, *Gower's Principles of Modern Company Law*, 6th edn, edited by Paul L. Davies with a contribution from Dan Prentice, Sweet & Maxwell, London, 1997.

M. Wyatt, *Company Acquisition of Own Shares*, 4th edn, Financial Times Pitman Publishing, London, 1995.

M. Wyatt, 'Purchase of own shares', *Accountants Digest No. 376*, ICAEW, London, 1997.

PART 3

Interpretation and valuation

13 Interpretation of financial statements

Overview   As we have seen in Chapter 1, all sorts of people have an interest in the financial statements of limited companies but, as we have learned in other chapters, interpretation of such statements is rarely easy. We start by examining traditional univariate analysis, the study of successive ratios in conjunction with some yardstick of comparison in order to build up a tentative picture of a company's performance and position. We then look more briefly at a multivariate approach which combines a number of ratios to provide a particular score which can be used in an attempt to predict whether the company is likely to fail.

Interpretation of a set of financial statements is made more difficult if a company or group operates in several different markets or where that company or group is involved with related parties. We therefore examine the ways in which SSAP 25 'Segmental Reporting' and FRS 8 'Related Party Disclosures' try to ensure that adequate information is made available to users in these circumstances.

Introduction

As we saw in Chapter 1, there are many different groups of people who are interested in the affairs of a business entity and who are therefore likely to use its financial statements. Although the government as tax collector is interested mainly in the past, most users, including the government in other roles, are more interested in what is likely to happen in the future. Such people will therefore use the accounts for a past period to help them make a judgement on the likely future success or otherwise of the entity.

Relatively little is known about the way in which accounts are used in the process of decision making but, at a general level, it is clear that members of different user groups will place greater or lesser emphasis on particular aspects of a company's performance. To give an example, a potential long-term equity shareholder in a company will be interested in the potential returns and the riskiness of those returns in comparison with other investment opportunities, whereas a potential supplier of goods, that is a trade creditor, will be interested in the likelihood of receiving payment for goods supplied. Both users are interested in the future performance of the company but the emphasis of their interpretation will differ. When called upon to interpret a set of accounts, it is essential for the accountant to keep clearly in mind the purpose of the exercise.

Traditionally, textbooks on financial accounting have tended to concentrate on univariate analysis. Thus they examine and discuss one ratio at a time and show how it is possible to draw tentative conclusions by comparing the result for that ratio with some yardstick of comparison. By studying a number of ratios in this way, it is possible to piece together a picture of the company's performance and position. This is the predominant approach used in practice and occupies the second section of this chapter. In that section we shall assume that readers are familiar with the basic principles of ratio analysis.[1]

In the 1970s there was a move towards the use of multivariate analysis, that is a consideration of the impact of several ratios at the same time by using such statistical techniques as multiple regression analysis and discriminant analysis. The third section of the chapter examines this approach.

Two particular factors complicate the interpretation of a set of financial statements. First, many companies and groups of companies are diversified and, as a consequence, it may be difficult to draw conclusions from one set of accounts covering all such diverse activities. Second, the behaviour of a company may be influenced by the existence of 'related parties', and interpretation may be hampered without knowledge of the existence of such parties and transactions with them, which may not have been 'at arm's length'. The results of such transactions may not provide a good basis for the estimation of future profitability.

In the fourth section of the chapter, we examine the case for segmental reporting and outline some of the problems which must be faced in the provision of such information within the context of SSAP 25 'Segmental Reporting' (1990). In the final section, we examine the provisions of FRS 8 'Related Party Disclosures' (1995).

Univariate analysis

Accounting systems

In this section, we will concentrate on the interpretation of historical cost accounts although we will refer to some differences of approach which may be necessary where the alternative accounting rules have been applied. As we have seen in Chapter 4, these alternative accounting rules permit piecemeal revaluation in the historical cost accounts or the preparation of current cost accounts. FRS 15 'Tangible Fixed Assets' (February 1999) has attempted to introduce some consistency in the use of piecemeal revaluations.

When a company revalues its fixed assets in an upwards direction, the gains recognised in an accounting period will be shown in the Statement of Total Recognised Gains and Losses rather than in the profit and loss account. Hence, when we begin to examine the performance of a company, it is important to look at both of these primary statements.[2] While recognised revaluation surpluses may be very important, they will not usually have the same significance as the results of the company as reported in the profit and loss account. Of the latter, the results of continuing operations are likely to provide a better clue as to what is likely to happen in future.

---

[1] Readers who wish to revise this topic are referred to Ian Gillespie, Richard Lewis and Kay Hamilton, *Principles of Financial Accounting*, Prentice-Hall, London, 1997.

[2] As we have seen in Chapter 6 (pp. 167–70), the ASB Discussion Paper 'Reporting Financial Performance: Proposals for Change' (June 1999) proposes that the Profit and Loss Account and Statement of Total Recognised Gains and Losses be combined in one Performance Statement, which should report three components of financial performance:
(a) the results of operating activities
(b) the results of financial and other treasury activities
(c) other gains and losses.

Yardsticks of comparison

As readers will be aware, one figure in a set of financial statements, or a ratio based on two figures in those statements, are of little use unless the user has some yardstick of comparison. Although an internal user of accounts will have access to budgets as a possible yardstick, the external user, with whom this book is concerned, must have recourse to other yardsticks. These are usually the results of previous periods, the results of other similar companies, or industry averages for the same accounting period. Comparison with the results of previous periods is known as trend or time series analysis, and comparison with the results of other firms, either individually or in terms of industry averages, is known as cross-sectional analysis. Both need to be applied with caution.

When trend analysis is employed, the results of each year will usually have been arrived at using consistent accounting policies.[3] Even so, the fixed asset values shown in historical cost accounts and the depreciation charges based on these tend to become more and more out of date as time passes. In addition, comparisons are difficult when the value of the measuring rod, the pound, is changing over time. In financial statements which incorporate current values, the former of these problems is largely removed because fixed assets are shown at their value to the business; however, unless such a current value system incorporates adjustments for changes in the value of a pound, it is still difficult to compare results over time.

In addition to these difficulties caused by the accounting principles used, there is the more fundamental problem that the company's environment will change over time, with the result that performance which was considered satisfactory in the past may no longer be so. Thus, for example, a current ratio which might be considered to be acceptable in a period when additional short-term credit can be obtained cheaply and easily might be regarded as being dangerously low when short-term loans are very difficult to obtain.

When cross-sectional analysis is employed, even greater problems must be faced. First, there is the problem of finding a comparable business. This may be difficult as businesses may be diversified to a greater or lesser extent. Indeed, there can be substantial differences between businesses even when they operate within the same industry. Two examples will illustrate this point: (a) although two companies manufacture the same product, one company may own its own property while another company may rent its property; (b) two companies may manufacture a similar finished product but, whereas one company uses bought-in components, the other may manufacture all its components from raw materials.

In addition to these underlying differences, the fixed asset values which appear in a set of historical cost accounts tend to become more and more out of date as time passes. This, together with the ability of directors to revalue assets on a piecemeal basis, introduces biases which depend on the dates of purchase or revaluation of the assets. Such biases are, of course, removed in accounts which use current values.

To the above difficulties is added the wide choice of accounting policies available to reflect underlying business reality, with the result that one company may choose one set of policies while a second may choose a very different set.[4]

---

[3] When this is not so, as in the case of a change in accounting policies, suitable adjustments must be made to render the figures comparable.

[4] The Centre for Interfirm Comparison Limited, which conducts interfirm comparison schemes for firms in a number of industries, goes to considerable lengths to adjust the accounting data of participants to a common set of accounting policies. Although the Centre conducts schemes for the benefit of management rather than external users, its requirements for extensive adjustments indicate the difficulties of making comparisons if these adjustments have not been made.

As readers may imagine, it is usually very difficult for an external user to make any adjustments for these differences, although they must be borne in mind when interpreting a set of accounts. Probably the best warning that can be given is that one must not be too dogmatic when interpreting financial statements.

Aspects of performance

It is convenient to examine separately two aspects of performance of a company: profitability and liquidity. The continuance of a business depends both upon profitable operations and upon having enough cash to meet its commitments as they fall due. Although in the long run satisfactory profitability and liquidity are likely to accompany one another, in the short run it is quite possible for a company to be, on the one hand, profitable but illiquid or, on the other hand, liquid but unprofitable. In both cases there may be some doubt about the continuance of the business. Let us look at each of these aspects of performance in turn.

Profitability

Whether or not a company pursues profit maximisation as its objective, the majority of users of accounts will be interested in its profitability, that is how well the directors are using the resources at their disposal. Return on capital employed is frequently used as a measure of profitability, although it is necessary to exercise care in interpreting such a ratio. In particular, it is essential to be wary of undue reliance on a single ratio which attempts to summarise what may be an extremely complex business reality. The ASB took considerable pains to emphasise this point in FRS 3 'Reporting Financial Performance'.

If a profit and loss account shows that a company has made a profit of, say, £100 000, it is impossible to draw any conclusion from this one figure on whether the company has performed well or badly. The conclusion would differ if, on the one hand, assets worth £500 000 had been used and, on the other hand, assets worth £10 000 000 had been used to generate the profit. In the former case the return on assets or capital employed is 20 per cent while in the latter case it is only 1 per cent.

A ratio of a measure of profit to a measure of capital employed is a first step towards assessing the profitability of many, although not all, businesses. While such a ratio is extremely useful for companies whose assets are mainly tangible and hence recognised in the financial statements, it has less relevance for companies with a preponderance of intangible assets not so recognised. As neither historical cost accounts or current value accounts include a value for human capital employed, such a ratio would be particularly unhelpful for assessing the profitability of professional accountancy or consultancy firms.

Even where a return on capital has been calculated at, say 20 per cent, it is still impossible to draw any conclusion about profitability without reference to one of the yardsticks of comparison mentioned in the preceding section.

Bearing in mind this need for comparison, let us try to be a little more precise in what we mean by return on assets or capital employed. Should we take operating profit, profit before interest and tax, profit available for shareholders, or profit available for equity shareholders? Should we take gross assets or net assets, total capital employed whether short-term or long-term, long-term capital employed or just equity capital employed? Whichever of these capital figures we select, should we use opening balance sheet figures, closing balance sheet figures or some average for the year?

Many combinations are possible and each may be useful for a specific purpose and also in helping us to build up a picture of the business. **It is essential, however, that the numerator and denominator of each ratio are logically consistent.**

We shall examine three ratios which measure different aspects of the return on capital employed:

(a)
$$\frac{\text{Profit available to equity shareholders}}{\text{Equity shareholders' interest}}$$

Equity shareholders and potential equity shareholders will be interested in the return which is being earned on equity capital employed in the business. This ratio provides an indication of the overall efficiency of the management, not only in the operations of the business but also in arranging the financing position and taxation affairs of the company for the benefit of the equity shareholders.

When the ratio is calculated on the figures disclosed in historical cost accounts, the profit to be taken is that after deducting interest, taxation and any preference dividends. The equity shareholders' interest is not just the equity share capital but the sum of equity share capital and all reserves. As the profits are earned over a period of time, it is preferable to use an appropriate average figure for the denominator.

Such a ratio based upon historical cost accounts suffers from the fact that the figure for equity interest shown in the balance sheet is based on out-of-date historical costs rather than current values. Similarly, the profit figure is arrived at after charging out-of-date costs rather than current costs. These deficiencies are remedied to some extent where figures based on current values are used to calculate the ratio.

(b)
$$\frac{\text{Profit before interest on long-term loans and taxation}}{\text{Long-term capital employed}}$$

This ratio indicates the return on all long-term capital employed. Long-term capital comprises the equity shareholders' interest, preference share capital and any long-term loans. As profit is earned during a period an appropriate average figure should be employed for the denominator.

Difficulties may often occur with bank overdrafts which, although legally repayable on demand, are often in practice part of the long-term capital of a company. Here it is necessary to make a judgement upon whether or not overdrafts are long-term capital and then to frame the ratio accordingly. If bank overdrafts are considered to be part of long-term capital, the denominator will include the average overdraft and the numerator must therefore be the profit before charging interest on overdrafts. If they are not considered to be part of long-term capital, they will be excluded from the denominator and the numerator will be the profit after bank interest but before interest on long-term loans and taxation.

(c)
$$\frac{\text{Operating profit}}{\text{Operating assets employed}}$$

This ratio does not measure the overall success of the firm but abstracts from the financing and taxation position in order to measure what may be called operating efficiency. Thus it shows the rate of return which has been earned on the operating assets at the disposal of the directors, irrespective of how those assets have been financed.

The denominator should be an average of the operating assets employed by the firm, before the deduction of any current or long-term liabilities. The numerator should be the operating profit before interest on any sources of finance.

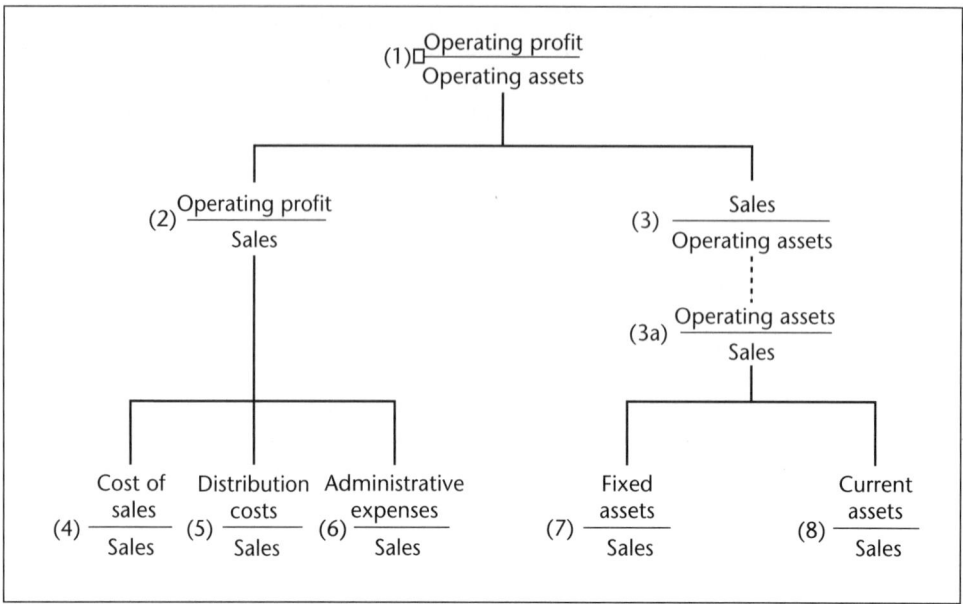

Fig. 13.1 Pyramid of ratios for manufacturing company

When a set of detailed financial statements is available, it is possible to carry out a systematic analysis using a pyramid of ratios like the one illustrated in Figure 13.1.[5] This is a pyramid for a manufacturing company but it is, of course, possible to design all manner of pyramids depending upon the circumstances of the particular company and the information required.

Ratio (1) provides the return on operating assets usually expressed as a percentage. This may be analysed by examining ratios (2) and (3). Ratio (2) is the net profit margin on sales, also usually expressed as a percentage, and ratio (3) is the asset turnover in times per year. The relationship between the three ratios is expressed as follows:

$$\frac{\text{Profit}}{\text{Assets}} = \frac{\text{Profit}}{\text{Sales}} \times \frac{\text{Sales}}{\text{Assets}}$$

i.e. Ratio (1) = Ratio (2) × Ratio (3)

To give an example, if the result for ratio (2) is 10 per cent and the result for ratio (3) is two times per year, the result for ratio (1) is 20 per cent.

If the net profit margin on sales (ratio (2)) has deteriorated compared with previous years or is poor in comparison with the corresponding ratio of other companies, it is possible to move down the left-hand side of the pyramid to determine why this is so. By examining the results for ratios (4), (5) and (6), it is possible to see which ratios are increasing and hence causing ratio (2) to fall. If we assume that all ratios are expressed as percentages, the relationship between ratios (2), (4), (5) and (6) is expressed as follows:

Ratio (2) + Ratio (4) + Ratio (5) + Ratio (6) = 100%[6]

---

[5] Such an analysis is only possible if companies adopt profit and loss account formats 1 or 3 specified in the Companies Act 1985, Schedule 4, Part 1.

[6] This must follow if operating profit is defined as sales less operating costs and operating costs comprise cost of sales, distribution costs and administrative expenses.

The higher the result for ratios (4), (5) and (6), the lower will be the result for ratios (1) and (2). Hence at this stage we may say that high results for ratios (4), (5) and (6) are undesirable although, as we shall see later in this section, even this statement will have to be modified when we consider the interrelationships between the two sides of the pyramid.

Turning now to the right-hand side of the pyramid, we may explore how well the firm is utilising its assets to achieve sales. Ratio (3) shows the asset turnover and, provided that ratio (2) is positive, the higher the result for this ratio the better. Many people find it conceptually difficult to think in terms of asset turnover, and it is therefore useful to express the same measures in a somewhat different way. Whereas ratio (3) shows sales divided by assets, ratio (3a), its reciprocal, shows the value of assets per pound of sales. A result of two times per year for ratio (3) would therefore be equivalent to a result of £0.5 for ratio (3a). If similarly expressed measures are used for ratios (7) and (8), we have the advantage, for analytical purposes, that:

$$\text{Ratio (7)} + \text{Ratio (8)} = \text{Ratio (3a)}$$

Again we may tentatively say that the lower the results for ratios (7) and (8) the better.

It is possible to extend the pyramid downwards. Thus the utilisation of the various categories of fixed assets and current assets may be explored. To take an example let us examine the utilisation of current assets (Figure 13.2).

Current assets may be analysed into stocks, debtors and any other current assets and an examination made to determine to what extent a high value for ratio (8) is due to high results for ratios (9), (10) and (11). This may be the best that can be done with the information available in published accounts. The figures for stocks and debtors will, at best, be averages of the opening and closing balance sheet figures, and such simple averages may not be good approximations to the average, in the sense of typical, values for the period. Similarly, ratios (9) and (10) are both logically inconsistent for the reasons given below and could be improved with better information.

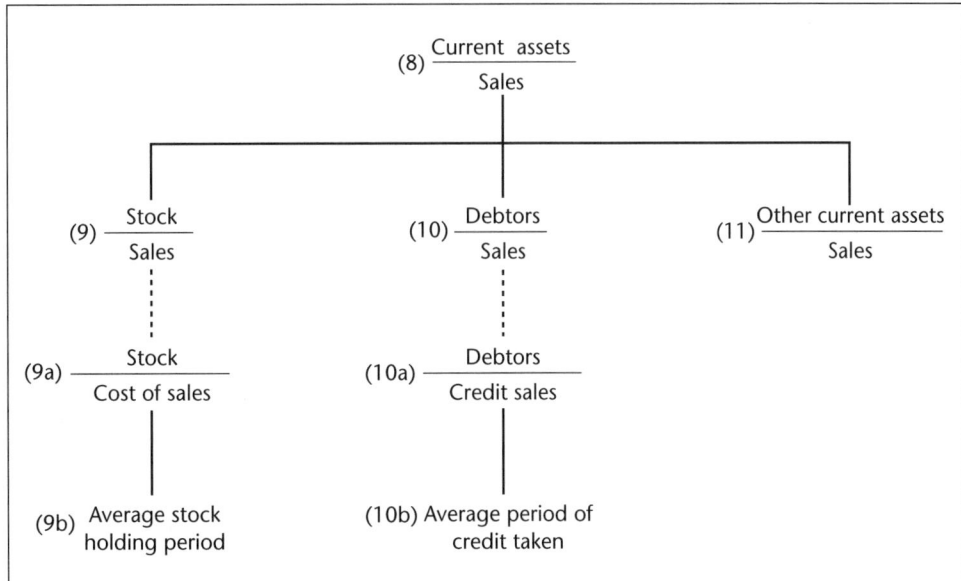

Fig. 13.2 Pyramid for examination of utilisation of current assets

Concentrating first on ratio (9), stocks are usually shown at cost whereas sales are at selling price. A consistent ratio would relate stocks to the cost of sales, as shown in ratio (9a), and from this we may arrive at the average stock-holding period in days (ratio (9b)):

$$\text{Average stock-holding period (Ratio (9b))} = 365 \times \frac{\text{Stock}}{\text{Cost of sales}}$$

A consistent ratio for (10) would relate debtors, not to total sales, but to credit sales. This is done in ratio (10a). Again we are able to arrive at an average period of credit taken by debtors, shown by ratio (10b):

$$\text{Average period of credit (Ratio (10b))} = 365 \times \frac{\text{Debtors}}{\text{Credit sales}}$$

We have now seen how, given sufficient data, it is possible to analyse performance in a systematic way. In addition we have seen that, looked at individually, high results for the cost ratios and for the asset utilisation ratios (3a), (7) and (8) are unfavourable. It is, however, most important not to be too dogmatic here and to bear in mind that there are links across the pyramid. To give an example, a high result for ratio (5), selling and distribution costs to sales, is by itself unfavourable. However, high expenditure on selling may increase sales with the result that it is possible to use assets more effectively and hence achieve favourable results for the asset utilisation ratios.

This emphasises that interpretation of accounts is an art by which we look for clues to performance. It is an art in which one should never be rigid in one's thinking.

Liquidity

Even a very profitable company may be forced into liquidation if it is unable to meet its debts and, in view of this, most users of financial statements are concerned with the liquidity of a company. To help users in this process, FRS 1 requires companies to prepare a cash flow statement. As we have seen in Chapter 11, the cash flow statement reports receipts and payments for a period under a number of standard headings and enables users to seek answers to a number of questions. However, as we have pointed out in that chapter, it is often impossible to draw firm conclusions from that statement alone. It must be interpreted within the context of the whole set of financial statements.

We will therefore look at a number of ratios which may be used to examine the liquidity position and solvency of a company.

The short-term liquidity position of a company has traditionally been assessed by looking at the relationship between current assets and current liabilities, or some components of current assets and current liabilities, on a balance sheet. These are essentially static measures, whereas debts are paid out of cash flows. A more recent tendency has been to look at ratios of a dynamic nature relating cash or funds flow to current liabilities. We shall look at these in turn, commencing with the static measures.

The current, or working capital, ratio relates current assets to current liabilities:

$$\text{Current ratio} = \frac{\text{Current assets}}{\text{Current liabilities}}$$

A result greater than 1 suggests that a company is able to pay its current liabilities out of current assets. However, the composition of the current assets is important; two companies may have the same result for the current ratio although in one case the major part of current assets is stock whereas, in the other case, the major part of current assets is debtors. Because of this it is usual to supplement the current ratio with a 'liquid' or 'quick' asset ratio, relating the more liquid current assets, such as debtors, cash and short-term marketable securities, to current liabilities:

$$\text{Liquid ratio} = \frac{\text{Debtors + Cash + Short-term marketable securities}}{\text{Current liabilities}}$$

A ratio in excess of 1 is a much clearer indication, although still not conclusive evidence, that a company is able to meet its short-term debts.

Once the above ratios have been calculated it is usually still very difficult to say whether the results are good or bad. Although high results for the current ratio and the liquid ratio suggest a sound liquidity position, they may also suggest that an excessive amount of money is tied up unprofitably in stocks, debtors and cash. In addition, in an inflationary era, a large amount tied up in monetary assets will lead to monetary losses, that is losses of purchasing power, which most companies will be keen to avoid.

The above ratios are essentially static in nature and hence only give us indications of the short-term liquidity position to the extent that they are typical and that no window dressing has taken place. Window dressing occurs when action is taken to manipulate certain figures which appear in a set of financial statements to produce more satisfactory results. The current ratio and liquid ratio are both particularly susceptible to such manipulation. This is best understood by recognising that if a ratio is greater than 1, the subtraction of the same amount from both numerator and denominator will make it larger whereas, if it is less than 1, the subtraction of the same amount from both numerator and denominator will make it smaller.[7]

Let us look at an example. A company forecasts that it will have a liquid ratio of 0.7 on its balance sheet date, calculated as follows:

$$\frac{\text{Liquid assets}}{\text{Current liabilities}} = \frac{700\,000}{1\,000\,000} = 0.70$$

The firm realises that this ratio is lower than that of previous years and considers that it is likely to have an adverse effect on the company's share price. It therefore delays the payment of creditors amounting to £300000 so that the liquid ratio based on the reported results becomes:

$$\frac{700\,000 + 300\,000}{1\,000\,000 + 300\,000} = 0.77$$

The possibility of such window dressing emphasises the dangers of assessing liquidity by taking the position at just one point in time. As current liabilities are paid out of cash flow, rather than out of a stock of current assets, analysts have developed ratios of a more dynamic nature. Two such ratios using cash flows are:

(a) $$\frac{\text{Net cash inflow from operating activities}}{\text{Current liabilities}}$$

---

[7] If $A/B > 1$, then $(A - x)/(B - x) > A/B$. Conversely, if $A/B < 1$, then $(A - x)/(B - x) < A/B$. $(B > x > 0.)$

(b) $$\frac{\text{Quick assets}}{\text{Daily outflow of cash on operations}}$$

The former relates the source of cash from operations, as shown in the cash flow statement, to the current liabilities at the close of a period. It therefore gives an indication of how long it takes to generate sufficient cash to pay off the stock of current liabilities. By dividing 365 days by the result for ratio (a), this information may be expressed in days. The second of the two ratios relates the quick assets, that is cash, debtors and marketable securities, to the average daily outlay of cash on operations. The former figure would be taken from the closing balance sheet while the latter would be approximated by taking the total operating expenses from the profit and loss account and deducting depreciation. It indicates how many days the firm would be able to continue operations if there were no further inflow of cash and is usually referred to as a 'defensive interval measure' or sometimes a 'no credit interval'. Neither of these ratios is without fault, but they do attempt to focus on the flows out of which debts are paid rather than on what may be an atypical position at one point in time. Of course they still suffer from the possibility that the current liabilities or quick assets included in the ratios may themselves be atypical.

We have so far focused on the short-term liquidity of a company. It is also important to consider the longer-term solvency, in other words the ability of the company to meet debts in the future.

Two ratios are of particular help here: the first is the gearing or leverage ratio, that is the relationship between debt and equity capital.

(a) $$\frac{\text{Long-term debt and preference share capital}}{\text{Long-term debt, preference share capital and equity interest}}$$

This ratio is often calculated on the basis of balance sheet values, although to have any economic meaning it should properly be based upon current values. The higher the result for this ratio, the greater the proportion of the assets which is financed by non-equity capital and hence the greater the risk of debt holders suffering a loss on a liquidation. In addition, the higher the result for this ratio, the greater the potential volatility of the earnings stream attributable to the equity shareholders.

Of course, this is a simple initial conclusion because, on the one hand, different forms of debt have different rights and security and, on the other hand, the realisable values of the assets on a liquidation may bear little relationship to their balance sheet values in either historical cost accounts or current cost accounts. Nevertheless it is frequently used to compare the financial position of one company with that of another.

The second ratio is commonly called 'times interest covered', that is the relationship between operating income and interest and preference dividends payable.

(b) $$\frac{\text{Operating income before interest and taxation}}{\text{Interest payments (before taxation) and preference dividends payable}}$$

This ratio tries to capture the same feature as ratio (a) above by looking at the proportion of the total operating income which goes to suppliers of long-term capital other than equity shareholders. The lower the ratio, the less certain are debt holders to receive their interest and preference shareholders their dividends; in other words, the greater the risk to lenders and preference shareholders.

In interpreting these ratios, it is, of course, essential to bear in mind the variability of the operating earnings. A company with stable earnings over time will be able to support a much higher level of gearing than a company with variable earnings over time.

We must stress the undesirability of attempting to draw definite conclusions from the liquidity and solvency ratios. Instead the ratios should be used to help build up a picture of the company's overall position. Thus, one should ask such questions as: Are the current and liquid ratios becoming larger or smaller over time? Is the gearing increasing or falling? How do the ratios of this company compare with those of other companies in the industry? If the ratios are out of line with those of other companies, what are the possible reasons?

Multivariate analysis

Introduction

In the preceding section we concentrated on the univariate approach to interpretation. Under this approach one particular ratio is examined, comparisons are made with the results of previous years or of similar companies, and tentative conclusions are drawn. This process is repeated in respect of another ratio and, gradually, by examining many ratios, a picture is built up of the position and likely future prospects of the company. The ratios are not combined together in any formal manner, but professional judgement is used to determine how much weight should be given to each of them.

A different approach involves considering several ratios simultaneously by means of multivariate analysis. Under this approach several ratios are combined by means of a formula to produce an index number and conclusions may be drawn by comparing that index number with the similar number for previous periods or for similar companies. One of the best documented areas in which such an approach has been applied is in the prediction of corporate failure and we shall concentrate on that particular application here.

The prediction of corporate failure

The failure[8] of a company will usually have serious repercussions for the individuals involved, such as shareholders, employees and creditors, and often for society at large. If it were possible to predict that a company was likely to fail, then it may well be possible for management to take steps to avoid failure and for other interested parties to take remedial action to mitigate the effects of failure in their own interests. A method which successfully predicts failure would therefore be very valuable, and considerable effort has been devoted to this problem by researchers.[9] Both univariate and multivariate approaches have been used, although we shall concentrate on the latter approach here. As will be seen, it is not possible to predict whether a particular company is going to fail. Rather it appears possible to say whether or not a particular company exhibits characteristics similar to other companies which have failed in the past.

---

[8] Failure may be defined (and has been defined) in many ways in different studies. This may include insolvency, entry into receivership, creditors' voluntary liquidation or compulsory liquidation, the need for a reconstruction or receipt of government aid as alternatives to liquidation.

[9] In this section we concentrate on methods of predicting failure based on information contained in a set of financial statements. These methods may be said to concentrate on the symptoms rather than on the more fundamental defects of the company and the mistakes of its management. John Argenti has developed an 'A' score, based on both accounting data and on qualitative judgments of management. Interested readers are referred to the extremely readable book, J. Argenti, *Corporate Collapse*, McGraw-Hill, New York. 1976.

Although the multivariate approach had been used in this context before, the most influential work on the prediction of failure was that of the American Professor E.I. Altman.[10] In a study published in 1968, he took a sample of 33 failed and 33 non-failed American manufacturing companies. He then examined many ratios to see which ratios taken together best discriminated between companies in the two groups. In the absence of any well-developed theoretical models which would explain why companies fail, he used a statistical technique known as 'multiple discriminant analysis'. By this means he found five ratios which could be combined to produce what is called a Z score, the level of which best captured differences between the failed and non-failed firms.

The discriminant function took the form:

$$Z = 0.012X_1 + 0.014X_2 + 0.033X_3 + 0.006X_4 + 0.010X_5$$

The five ratios were:

$$X_1 = \frac{\text{Working capital}}{\text{Total gross assets}}$$

$$X_2 = \frac{\text{Retained earnings}}{\text{Total gross assets}}$$

$$X_3 = \frac{\text{Earnings before interest and tax}}{\text{Total gross assets}}$$

$$X_4 = \frac{\text{Market value of equity}}{\text{Book value of debt}}$$

$$X_5 = \frac{\text{Sales}}{\text{Total gross assets}}$$

Thus the Altman Z score combined ratios covering aspects of liquidity, re-invested earnings, profitability, gearing and asset turnover. There is no obvious economic reason why these emerged; it was simply that, statistically, they gave the best results.

Having arrived at the above equation, Altman then found that all companies with a Z score greater than 2.99 were non-failed companies, whereas all companies with a Z score below 1.81 were failed companies.[11] It was impossible to be so categoric with companies which had a score between 1.81 and 2.99. Altman tested his statistical model on different samples of companies and found that, one year before failure, his model correctly classified companies to the failed or non-failed group accurately in 96 per cent of the cases. However, more generally he found that the percentage of correct classification declined considerably with data taken more than one year prior to failure.

It is important to bear in mind that Altman's researches and model relate to the manufacturing sector of the US economy in the period 1946–65. It therefore does not follow that his results would be applicable to other sectors or at other times; nor does it follow that his results would be relevant in the different conditions of the UK economy. What he did was to provide us with an approach to the prediction of failure which may be applied in other circumstances.

---

[10] *See*, for example, E.I. Altman, *Corporate Financial Distress*, John Wiley, New York, 1983.
[11] Strictly 'non-bankrupt' and 'bankrupt', respectively, using Altman's terminology.

R.J. Taffler and H. Tisshaw applied the approach to UK data and developed two 'Z scales', one for quoted manufacturing enterprises and one for non-quoted manufacturing enterprises with turnover above £$\frac{1}{2}$ million.[12] For the sample of quoted manufacturing enterprises, statistical analysis resulted in the following formula:

$$Z = C_0 + C_1 R_1 + C_2 R_2 + C_3 R_3 + C_4 R_4$$

C_0 to C_4 are coefficients and R_1 to R_4 are the following ratios:

$$R_1 = \frac{\text{Profit before taxation}}{\text{Current liabilities}}$$

$$R_2 = \frac{\text{Current assets}}{\text{Total liabilities}}$$

$$R_3 = \frac{\text{Current liabilities}}{\text{Total assets}}$$

$$R_4 = \text{No credit interval}$$

$$= \frac{\text{Immediate assets} - \text{Current liabilities}}{\text{Operating costs excluding depreciation}}$$

Thus, the four ratios combine together various aspects of profitability and solvency to produce a Z score. When they turn to the unquoted manufacturing enterprises the formula comprises not four but five ratios.

Taffler and Tisshaw claim very good results for their formula but, because of their proprietary interest, have not been willing to publish the coefficients for their equations. It has not therefore been possible for others working in the same area to test and comment on the particular models put forward.

In a general textbook on financial accounting we have only been able to provide a brief introduction to multivariate analysis. Such techniques are being used by various investment institutions and large accounting practices to determine whether or not the going concern concept is appropriate.

Segmental reporting and its problems

The financial statements of a company and the consolidated financial statements of a group summarise the results and financial position for the reporting entity as a whole. Thus, subject to the possible exclusion of one or more subsidiaries from consolidation in accordance with the provisions of FRS 2, the financial statements summarise all of the activities of the reporting entity, no matter how diverse these activities may be. Many companies and groups of companies operate in a number of different industries and in a number of different geographical areas, perhaps manufacturing in certain countries and supplying customers in other countries. The industrial and geographical segments of the entity may enjoy different levels of profitability, may be subject to very different risks and may have very different growth potentials. If users are to be able to assess past performance and to predict likely future performance of the entity

---

[12] A brief account of this work appears in R. J. Taffler, 'Z-scores: An approach to the recession', *Accountancy*, July 1991, pp. 95–7. Note that the ratios here differ from those which emerged in Altman's work.

as a whole, it may be argued that it is necessary for them to be provided with a detailed analysis in respect of the individual segments. The provision of such an analysis is known as segmental, analysed or disaggregated reporting.

Company law and the Stock Exchange have accepted the need for such segmental reporting for many years although, as we shall see, their requirements are limited. An international accounting standard was first issued on this subject in 1981 and subsequently reformatted in 1994. A revised version of IAS 14 'Segment Reporting' was issued in 1997 and this draws heavily on the US standard[13]. In particular, the revised IAS 14 provides more guidance on the identification of segments and increases the disclosure requirements. As a consequence, SSAP 25 'Segmental Reporting', which was issued in 1990, is now somewhat out of line with the revised IAS 14. Although the ASB considered possible changes to the standard in a Discussion Paper 'Segmental Reporting' in 1996, it has concluded that, as there is general satisfaction with the present segmental reporting requirements, no further action will be taken at this time.[14]

We shall look first at the requirements of company law and the Stock Exchange before turning to the provisions of SSAP 25.

So long as the disclosure of the information is not seriously prejudicial to the interests of the company, the Companies Act 1985 requires two analyses, the first where a company or group has carried on business of two or more classes that (in the opinion of the directors) differ substantially from one another and the second where a company or group has supplied geographical markets that (in the opinion of the directors) differ substantially from each other.[15]

In the former case, the law requires a description of each class of business together with the turnover and the profit or loss before taxation attributable to each class whereas, for the geographical segments, the law requires only an analysis of turnover. For listed companies, the Stock Exchange increased the amount of disclosure by requiring 'a geographical analysis of both net turnover and contribution to trading results of those trading operations carried on . . . outside the United Kingdom and the Republic of Ireland', although the analysis of contribution is only required if the profit or loss from a specific area is out of line with the normal profit margin.[16]

The above requirements ensure the provision of a minimum amount of segmental information but leave a great many questions unanswered.

Although some would question the wisdom of leaving the selection of reportable segments to directors, this would seem to be inevitable given the variety and complexity of modern businesses.[17] However, any segmental analysis provided may be highly misleading if there is substantial trading between segments, especially if this trading occurs at artificially determined prices, and yet the law and Stock Exchange do not require the disclosure of any inter-segment turnover nor the basis of inter-segment pricing. Where an analysis of profit or contribution is required, there is the problem of how to deal with common or joint costs which are not directly attributable to any one segment; examples would be interest cost and the cost of a head office. In addition, the segmental information would appear to be of limited use without some

---

[13] SFAS 131 'Disclosures about Segments of an Enterprise and Related Information', June 1997.
[14] *See* 98 Annual Review, Financial Reporting Council, p. 47.
[15] Companies Act 1985, Schedule 4, Para. 55(1) to 55(5).
[16] *See The Listing Rules.*
[17] SSAP 25, Para. 9 defines a reportable segment by reference to the relative size of the segment, namely 10 per cent or more of external turnover, results or net assets.

indication of the net assets employed in each segment but, immediately an attempt is made to provide such an indication of net assets, the accountant confronts the problem of how to deal with common or joint assets, that is assets used by more than one segment. We would expect to turn to the Accounting Standard for guidance on the above matters.

While the standard contains some provisions relating to the statutory segmental disclosure, which therefore apply to all companies, it also extends these requirements for any entity that:[18]

(a) is a public limited company or that has a public limited company as a subsidiary; or
(b) is a banking or insurance company or group . . .; or
(c) exceeds the criteria, multiplied in each case by 10, for defining a medium-sized company under section 247 of the Companies Act 1985, as amended from time to time by statutory instrument.

Thus, segmental disclosure required by statute is increased for public companies and certain specialised companies as well as for large private companies, although such a large private company does not have to provide the additional information if its parent provides the required information.

The extent of the increase in disclosure may be seen in paragraph 34 of the standard:

> If an entity has two or more classes of business, or operates in two or more geographical segments which differ substantially from each other, it should define its classes of business and geographical segments in its financial statements, and it should report with respect to each class of business and geographical segment the following financial information:
> (a) turnover, distinguishing between (i) turnover derived from external customers and (ii) turnover derived from other segments;
> (b) result, before accounting for taxation, minority interests and extraordinary items; and
> (c) net assets.

The geographical segmentation should be given by *turnover of origin*, that is the area from which products or services are supplied and for which results and net assets will be determined. However, it should also be given by *turnover of destination* where it is materially different.[19]

The division of turnover between external sales and inter-segment sales undoubtedly helps users to appreciate the interdependence of segments, although the effect of such interdependence on results will be impossible to ascertain without some knowledge of the way in which inter-segment prices are determined. While IAS 14 requires disclosure of the basis of inter-segment pricing, SSAP 25 does not require this.

The standard provides guidance on determining segmental results and increases the legal provisions by requiring the disclosure of net assets for each segment. As a consequence it should be possible to compute returns on capital employed for the different activities of the business.

Results are to be taken before taxation, minority interests and extraordinary items and normally before taking account of any interest receivable or payable. Net assets will normally be the non-interest earning operating assets less the non-interest bearing operating liabilities. Only if the interest income or expense is central to the business of the segment should it be included in arriving at the segmental result when, for consistency, the assets or liabilities to which it relates should be included in the segmental net assets.

---

[18] SSAP 25, Para. 41.
[19] SSAP 25, Para. 34.

Interest excluded and other common revenues and costs should be excluded from the segmental analysis but included in the total results. Similarly, common assets and liabilities should be excluded from the segment net assets but included separately as part of the total net assets. This is essential if the segmental analysis is to agree with the related totals in the financial statements of the company or group and, where such agreement is not apparent, a reconciliation must be provided.[20]

The Appendix to SSAP 25 contains an illustrative segmental report covering both classes of business and geographical segment. Table 13.1 illustrates the sort of segmental report envisaged for classes of business only, although, for simplicity, we have excluded comparative figures.[21]

Table 13.1 Illustrative segmental report (excluding comparative figures)

Classes of business	Industry A £000	Industry B £000	Group £000
Turnover			
External sales	700	250	950
Inter-segment sales	50	–	50
Total sales	750	250	1 000
Profit before taxation			
Segment profit	150	100	250
less Common costs			60
			190
Share of profit before taxation of associated undertakings	40	–	40
Net assets			
Segment net assets	1 500	400	1 900
Unallocated assets			100
			2 000
Share of net assets of associated undertaking	300	–	300
			2 300

From Table 13.1 it is possible to compare the profit margin on sales and the return on net assets for each segment. Thus, it can be seen that the smaller segment, that is industry B, has the higher profit margin and the higher return on capital employed:

Profit margin
Segment A $150 \div 750 = 20\%$
Segment B $100 \div 250 = 40\%$
Return on net assets
Segment A $150 \div 1\,500 = 10\%$
Segment B $100 \div 400 = 25\%$

---

[20] SSAP 25, Para. 37.

[21] Note that the illustration includes the aggregate share of the results and net assets of associated undertakings. This is required if such associated undertakings account for at least 20 per cent of its total results or 20 per cent of its total net assets (SSAP 25, Para. 36).

In practice such results could be compared with those for previous years to build up a picture of past trends and hence likely future progress. For example, given the results disclosed, an investor would be much happier if the involvement of the company or group in industry B were growing as a proportion of its total activity than if the involvement in industry A were growing.

By requiring the disclosure of inter-segment sales and of segmental net assets, the standard has certainly improved the usefulness of the legally required segmental disclosure. However, it will be more difficult to draw conclusions from a segmental report the higher the level of inter-segment sales and the greater the proportion of common costs/revenues and common net assets.

Although, potentially, the segmental information should be of considerable benefit to users, the inevitable discretion permitted to directors may reduce that benefit substantially in practice.

Related party disclosures

Under traditional economic theory, a company is assumed to act in the interests of its owners, the equity shareholders, but, as we have seen in earlier chapters, many people have an interest in the affairs of a company and often the interests of different groups and individuals will conflict with one another. Companies must be managed and, in practice, directors and managers have to learn how to deal with these conflicting interests. Indeed, the directors and managers may well find themselves in a position where decisions which have to be taken on behalf of the company may be of considerable relevance, and possibly benefit, to themselves in a private capacity. As has often been noted, it is a question of which hat is being worn, and the law and accounting standards try to ensure adequate disclosure of directors' interests and the benefits which they receive.

Another obvious example of a possible conflict of interest is where one company is controlled by an individual or another entity and enters into transactions with that 'related party' which are in the interest of the other party, rather than in the interest of the company itself.

The Department of Trade and Industry has investigated many cases involving related party transactions, including that of Pergamon Press Limited in 1969. The Chairman of Pergamon Press was Robert Maxwell and it is perhaps no coincidence that the impetus for related party disclosures stemmed from the scandal involving Robert Maxwell, Mirror Group Newspapers, Maxwell Communications Corporation and the Mirror Group Pension Funds which eventually surfaced in the early 1990s.

Various branches of the law, including company, trust and criminal elements, take more than a passing interest in the abuses which can flow from the existence of related party transactions, but our purpose is confined to the disclosure issues involved.

There are two reasons why disclosure is required:

1 If transactions are not at arm's length, the users of financial statements may be misled; in particular, the financial statements may not provide a satisfactory basis for the prediction of future results. This would, of course, affect both parties to the transaction with the results of one party being overstated and those of the other party being understated. Disclosure might indicate the extent to which those with a legitimate interest in the company have gained or lost as a consequence.

2 Even in the absence of transactions, knowledge of the existence of a related party which controls the reporting entity will warn users that they may be subject to the effects of such transactions in future.

ED 46 'Disclosure of Related Party Transactions', published by the ASC in 1989, proposed that companies should disclose abnormal transactions with related parties. By restricting the disclosure to abnormal transactions, it hoped to avoid lengthy disclosures. However, many commentators stressed the impossibility of distinguishing between normal and abnormal transactions and, when FRED 8 'Related Party Disclosures' was issued in 1994, it followed international practice by requiring disclosure of all related party transactions. Both IAS 24 'Related Party Disclosures' (reformatted in July 1994) and FRS 8 'Related Party Disclosures' (November 1995) adopt this approach.

FRS 8 has as its objective:

> ... to ensure that financial statements contain disclosures necessary to draw attention to the possibility that the reported financial position and results may have been affected by the existence of related parties and by material transactions with them. (Para. 1)

Thus it is a standard concerned with disclosure rather than measurement, although the existence of the standard may, of course, affect the amounts shown in the financial statements where the need for disclosure causes changes in the behaviour of the related parties.

The required disclosure may be summarised under two headings:

1 *Disclosure of existence and name of controlling party.* Where the reporting entity is controlled by another party, it is required to disclose the relationship and the name of the controlling party and, if different, that of the ultimate controlling party. This information is required whether or not any transactions have taken place between the controlling parties and the reporting entity in a particular year. Even if no transactions have occurred, the existence of a relationship which may give rise to such transactions in future is important information for those using the financial statements (Para. 5).

   For the purpose of FRS 8, control is defined as 'the ability to direct the financial and operating policies of an entity with a view to gaining economic benefits from its activities' (Para. 2.2).

2 *Disclosure of material transactions with related parties.* The reporting entity should disclose material transactions with a related party, irrespective of whether a price is charged, and this disclosure should include:

   (a) the names of the transacting related parties;
   (b) a description of the relationship between the parties;
   (c) a description of the transactions;
   (d) the amounts involved;
   (e) any other elements of the transaction necessary for an understanding of the financial statements;
   (f) the amounts due to or from related parties at the balance sheet date and provisions for doubtful debts due from such parties at that date;
   (g) amounts written off in the period in respect of debts due to or from related parties (Para. 6).

Related party transactions include purchases and sales of goods, purchases or sales of property, rendering or receiving of services, agency arrangements, licence agreements and management contracts. However, in order to avoid excessive detail, the standard normally permits transactions to be disclosed on an aggregated basis.

The definition of related parties

The purpose of the standard is clear; all that remains is to examine the definition of related parties. The key element in the definition is that the relationship between two or more parties is such that, either through influence or control, the interest of one of the parties may be subordinated to the interests of one of the other parties. In the words of FRS 8:

Two or more parties are related parties when at any time during the financial period:
(i) one party has direct or indirect control of the other party; or
(ii) the parties are subject to common control from the same source; or
(iii) one party has influence over the financial and operating policies of the other party to an extent that that other party might be inhibited from pursuing at all times its own separate interests; or
(iv) the parties, in entering a transaction, are subject to influence from the same source to such an extent that one of the parties to the transaction has subordinated its own separate interests.
(Para. 2).

The standard provides two lists of related parties. One list consists of those which are automatically deemed to be related parties; the other of those who are presumed to be related parties unless there is evidence that neither party has influenced the financial and operating policies of the other in such a way as to inhibit the pursuit of its own separate interests. The first list therefore consists of those who are automatically guilty, whereas the second consists of those who are presumed guilty unless they can prove their innocence, a task which seems, philosophically, rather difficult. The lists are summarised in Table 13.2.

The lists are long but a number of exemptions are granted. So, for example, parties which can influence the behaviour of the reporting entity through their economic or commercial relationship with it are excluded. Thus, Paragraph 4 of the standard makes it clear that disclosure is not required of transactions with providers of finance, utility companies, government bodies, customers and suppliers, even where there is economic dependence. It recognises that such relationships may be extremely important but only requires disclosure if the entities mentioned fall within the definitions of related parties.

Fellow group members are obviously related parties but it would be extremely burdensome to report in detail on transactions between group members. Hence Paragraph 3 allows a number of exemptions which may be summarised as follows:

(a) It is not necessary to disclose in consolidated financial statements any inter-group transactions which have been eliminated on consolidation although it is, of course, necessary to disclose transactions with other related parties;
(b) It is not necessary to disclose related party transactions in a parent company's own financial statements where these are presented with consolidated financial statements;

Table 13.2 Lists of related parties

Automatically related parties	Presumed related parties unless there is evidence to the contrary
Parent, subsidiaries and fellow subsidiaries	Key management of reporting entity or its parent
Associates and joint ventures	Person owning or able to control over 20 per cent of voting rights
Investors or venturers in respect of which the reporting entity is an associate or joint venture	Each person acting in concert in a way to exercise control or influence
Directors of the entity or its parent	An entity managing or managed by the reporting entity under a management contract
Pension fund for the benefit of employees in reporting entity or related party	
	Other presumed related parties Members of the close family of any individual deemed or presumed to be a related party. Partnerships, companies, trusts or other entities in which any individual or member of the close family deemed or presumed to be a related party has a controlling interest

Notes:
(a) Where the parent is itself a subsidiary, the references to parent include the ultimate parent as well as any intermediate parent.
(b) Close members of the family of an individual are those family members, or members of the same household, who may be expected to influence, or be influenced by, that person in their dealings with the reporting entity.

(c) Where a subsidiary undertaking has 90 per cent or more of its voting rights controlled within a group, it is not necessary to disclose transactions with group entities provided that consolidated financial statements including the subsidiary undertaking are publicly available.

It also includes two other more specific exemptions:

(d) It is not necessary to disclose pension contributions paid to a pension fund;
(e) It is not necessary to disclose emoluments in respect of services as an employee of the reporting entity.

There are no exemptions for small companies and it is perhaps not surprising that no such exemptions are envisaged.

Materiality

The definition of related parties is widely drawn and the potential disclosure under FRS 8 enormous. Are there ways of reducing the volume? The early approach of only reporting abnormal items was rejected but there still remains our old friend materiality which might be relied on to reduce some of the noise. FRS 8, Para. 20, specifically refers to materiality by stating that 'transactions are material when their disclosure might reasonably be expected to influence the decisions made by the users of general purpose financial statements'. This could be used to avoid reporting many transactions with related parties but there is a sting in the tail. Paragraph 20 goes on to state that materiality must be judged, not only in terms of the reporting entity, but also in relation to the other related party where that party is a director, a key manager or other person who can influence the entity, a member of their close family or an entity controlled by the individual or close family member. Thus an amount which is quite small from the point of view of the reporting entity might still have to be reported if it is judged to be large from the point of view of the other party!

Recommended reading

G. Foster, *Financial Statement Analysis*, 2nd edn, Prentice-Hall, Englewood Cliffs, N.J., 1986.

E. Hodgson, 'Segmental reporting', *Accountants Digest No. 248*, ICAEW, London, Summer 1990.

Geoffrey Holmes and Alan Sugden, *Interpreting Company Reports and Accounts*, 7th edn, Financial Times Prentice Hall, Harlow, 1999.

M. Pendlebury and R. Groves, *Company Accounts – Analysis, Interpretation and Understanding*, 4th edn, International Thomson, London, 1999.

14 The valuation of securities and businesses

Overview   The chapter opens with a discussion of the valuation of securities, a subject we approach from a number of directions including the use of the net present value model and the use of stock market indicators of various forms. The next section of the chapter is devoted to the valuation of businesses including the special considerations that affect valuations in the context of a merger of two or more enterprises.

The chapter concludes with an important appendix that deals with the basis of calculating the Earnings per Share (EPS) which when combined with the price of a security, provides one of the more widely used financial measures – the price to earnings ratio. It is in the appendix that we introduce the only accounting standard discussed in any detail in this chapter:

• FRS 14 *Earnings per Share* (October 1998).

Introduction

More than a passing reference has been made elsewhere in this book to the fact that conventional accounting based on the historical cost convention does not reflect the current economic value of either individual assets or the business as a whole. It might then appear to be somewhat paradoxical that the results disclosed by a business's financial statement loom so large in the way in which businesses and shares in businesses are valued.

We will in this chapter discuss the basic principles associated with the valuation of financial securities and businesses and consider the part played therein by accounting information.

The standard valuation model for any asset is based on the cash flows that will accrue to the owner as a result of his or her possession of that asset – the 'present value model', i.e.

$$V_0 = \sum_{j=1}^{\infty} \frac{C_j}{(1+k)^j}$$

where V_0 is the value of the asset at time t_0, C_j is the cash flow to the owner which will be generated in year j and k is the discount rate.

We will assume that the readers are familiar with the basic principles underlying present value calculations but we, nonetheless, emphasise two important assumptions that underlie the simple model presented above; one is that the discount rate k is constant, the other is that cash flows occur only at the end of each year.

It can be seen from the model that, in order to value an asset, estimates of C_j and k are required.

The valuation of securities

In this section we consider the valuation of holdings of securities which do not constitute a controlling interest in the enterprise. If the holding is sufficient to give a controlling interest, the focus of interest changes to the value of the business as a whole – a topic which will be covered in the second part of the chapter.

Ex post and ex ante valuations

It is convenient to distinguish between the *ex post* (after) and the *ex ante* (before) need to value securities although, as we will show, similar principles apply in each case. In an *ex post* valuation the purpose of the exercise is the determination of the value of the securities at a current or past date, whereas in an *ex ante* valuation the requirement is to estimate the value of the security at some future date.

Perhaps the most common reason for requiring an *ex post* valuation is taxation, particularly for inheritance and capital gains tax. The inclusion of investments in the balance sheet of the owner at current cost also gives rise to the need for an *ex post* valuation.

Ex ante valuations are also of considerable importance. The management of a company should consider the effect on the value of the company's securities of alternative courses of action when deciding upon such matters as the company's investment policy or capital structure. It is possible, for example, that diversification into a new area may influence the stock market's perception of the risk associated with the company's earnings. Thus, it seems reasonable that when management is contemplating such diversification it should consider the likely impact on security prices and not confine itself to an assessment of the change in the company's cash flow.

Valuation of fixed interest securities

Loans and preference shares are usually described as fixed interest securities even though the preference shareholders are entitled to a fixed rate of dividend rather than a fixed rate of interest.[1] Both may be irredeemable or redeemable at some specified date in the future.

In the case of fixed interest securities, the future cash flows are known and so the only problem is the selection of an appropriate discount rate. As discussed below, this is likely to be different for loans and preference shares in view of the different risks involved. For the moment, we shall assume that the discount rate is known.

Where a security is irredeemable, it will yield the same sum of cash each year for the indefinite future. If we assume that the interest or dividend is payable annually and that the first receipt will occur in one year's time, then the value of the security will be given by the following formula:

$$V_0 = \frac{s}{k}$$

where V_0 is the value at t_0, s is the annual cash receipt and k is the discount rate. So, for example, if we wish to value 10 per cent irredeemable debenture stock which pays interest annually, when the discount rate is 16 per cent, we would proceed as follows.

---

[1] Some preference shares may, of course, be participating preference shares and both loans and preference shares may be convertible into ordinary shares. The valuation of these participating and convertible securities is not dealt with in this book.

Let us value £100 of debenture stock. This produces a cash flow of £10 (10% × £100) per annum so the value of this perpetual flow of £10 per annum would be:

$$V_0 = \frac{£10}{0.16} = £62.5$$

Thus the value of £100 of this debenture stock would be £62.50.

Where the interest is payable half-yearly or quarterly, it is still possible to use the above formula but s would then represent the half-yearly or quarterly cash receipt, as appropriate, while k would be the appropriate half-yearly or quarterly discount rate.

Redeemable fixed interest securities will yield the same sum of money each period until their redemption date when a return of capital will take place on some pre-scribed basis.

Consider a security which will pay an annual sum of £s for n years at which time a return of capital of £C will be made. The first receipt will occur in one year's time.

Using a present value model, the value of this security would be given by:

$$V_0 = \sum_{j=1}^{n} \frac{s}{(1+k)^j} + \frac{C}{(1+k)^n}$$

Once the annual cash flow, the redemption date and value and a cost of capital are known, the actual calculations can be made painlessly, given the possession of a suitably programmed calculator or a set of compound interest tables.

In choosing an appropriate discount rate for fixed interest securities, it is important to distinguish between loans and preference shares. The payment of loan interest is a contractual liability of the company and must be paid whether or not profits are made, whereas preference dividends may only be paid if there are distributable profits available and the directors decide to pay such dividends. On a liquidation, loan hold-ers will be repaid before preference shareholders. Thus, it is clear that loan holders can be more certain of their income and capital than preference shareholders. Hence, loan holders are likely to apply a lower discount rate in arriving at the valuation of their securities than are the preference shareholders.

In general the appropriate discount rates will be derived from market comparisons. In the case of securities which are not listed on a stock exchange, a higher discount rate would be expected to compensate for the lack of marketability.

The valuation of ordinary shares

We will first consider the usually simple task of valuing quoted shares. We will then introduce a theoretical model and show how it may be applied to unquoted shares.

Quoted shares

In most circumstances the *ex post* valuation of quoted shares will present few difficulties as the valuation can be made by reference to the prices at which the shares were traded on the required valuation date. Typically, there will be a number of different prices quoted for any one day, since prices will fluctuate during the day and the normal practice, for valuation purposes, is to take the average of the highest and lowest prices marked.

There are circumstances when the Stock Exchange price will not give a reliable guide to the value of a holding of shares. This will occur when the block of shares to be valued is large compared with the number of shares which are actively traded on the Stock Exchange. Clearly, if the normal level of activity in a company share runs at about 10 000 shares per day, it is extremely likely that the hypothetical sale of 100 000 shares would only have been achieved at a lower price than that which actually prevailed on the appropriate date. Similarly, a purchase of a large block of shares would probably have to have been made at a higher price. Thus, in such circumstances, the realisable value of a large block of shares will be less than the product of the number of shares and the Stock Exchange price per share, whereas the replacement cost of the shares would be greater than that figure. Valuation of such large blocks of shares therefore requires a considerable element of subjective judgement about the circumstances leading to the need for evaluation and about the likely effect on the market of a transaction of unusual size.

True and market value

We will now consider whether it can be said that a share has a true or intrinsic value which may be different from its market value. There are different opinions on this matter. Some argue that there cannot be a difference between the two because (ignoring the problem of large blocks of shares) the value of a quoted share must be the same as the price at which it was traded and that it is not meaningful to talk of a 'true' value which differs from its market value. Advocates of this view believe that the price of a share is determined by the interaction of buyers and sellers, who are influenced by many factors including speculative motives, and that there is little point in attempting to analyse the results of any particular company in any great detail. The investment strategy of this school is to attempt to determine when share prices will change and to buy or sell depending upon whether they think that the share price will rise or fall. An extreme, and well-known, example of this approach is provided by the chartists, who claim that it is possible to identify patterns of past share price movements which may be used to determine whether the share price will rise or fall. It must be said that not everyone agrees that this is a valid approach.

An alternative view is that the share does have a true value based on the economic value of the company which, if the company is a going concern, will be based on the company's prospective dividends since they must ultimately be available to the shareholders. It is argued that due to differences in expectations and other market imperfections it is likely that the market price will not be the same as the true value but that over time the difference will be eroded as the participants in the markets come to share the same expectations. This view suggests that it would be profitable to attempt to identify and purchase those shares which are currently 'undervalued'.

We will concentrate on the second approach, not only because of its importance in its own right, but also because it provides a theoretical underpinning to the whole subject of the valuation of shares, whether quoted or unquoted.

Dividend valuation models

The first assumption we must make is that investors are only interested in the cash flows that will accrue to them as a result of their ownership of shares, i.e. we will assume that investors will ignore any non-pecuniary benefits (such as prestige from holding shares in the company or other perquisites available to shareholders).

We will consider initially a potential purchaser of a share who intends to hold that share for only a year and then to resell it. His outlay is the current purchase price; he will receive a dividend in one year's time and will then sell the share. We will assume at this stage that the purchaser could alternatively put his money in a risk-free bank account and leave it there to earn interest. There is, therefore, a cost to the individual that is the lost interest. We can consider this lost interest as his cost of capital.

Let us suppose that the price he pays to purchase the share is $£P_0$, the price for which he sells the share is $£P_1$, the dividend he receives at the year end is $£D_1$ and the cost of capital (expressed as a decimal) is k.

Now if the potential investor had deposited the purchase price in a risk-free interest-earning bank account at the beginning of the year (time t_0) he would at the end of the year (time t_1) have $£P_0(1 + k)$. Alternatively, if he purchases the share he would at time t_1 receive $£(P_1 + D_1)$. He will only purchase the share if he expects the purchase to make him at least as well off as his deposit in the interest-earning account, i.e. if $P_0(1 + k) < P_1 + D_1$ or $P_0 < (P_1 + D_1)/(1 + k)$.

Let us assume that the participants in the market all make the same estimates of P_1, D_1, and k. Then a share which is cheaply priced, i.e. where $P_0 < (P_1 + D_1)/(1 + k)$, will be purchased and the price will be bid up until equilibrium is achieved, when $P_0 = (P_1 + D_1)/(1 + k)$.

We have thus derived a simple present value model of the value of a share based on its expected dividend for the year and its expected price in one year's time.

If we consider the subsequent purchaser (who will hold the share for one year only), then the same considerations will apply at time t_1 so that we can say that P_1 will be given by $P_1 = (P_2 + D_2)/(1 + k)$, where P_2 is the selling price of the share at time t_2, and D_2 is the dividend to be paid at time t_2. Thus we could state that

$$P_0 = \frac{D_1}{1 + k} + \frac{D_2}{(1 + k)^2} + \frac{P_2}{(1 + k)^2}$$

and so, by extending the analysis for the whole life of the company,

$$P_0 = \frac{D_1}{1 + k} + \frac{D_2}{(1 + k)^2} + \frac{D_3}{(1 + k)^3} + \ldots + \frac{D_n}{(1 + k)^n}$$

$$= \sum_{j=1}^{n} \frac{D_j}{(1 + k)^j}$$

If, therefore, we can estimate the dividends to be paid out for the rest of the life of the company, including the final or liquidating dividend and also the cost of capital, we can make an estimate of the equilibrium value of the share.

This represents a laborious calculation, quite apart from the fact that it is a difficult forecasting problem. To simplify this, it is sometimes possible to assume that the dividend can be expected to grow at a constant rate (less than the cost of capital) each year.

Let the rate of growth of the dividend be g and the cost of capital be k, which is greater than g; also let the dividend at time t_0 be D_0. Then we can state that the value of the share at time t_0 will be given by the expression[2]

$$P_0 = \frac{D_0(1 + g)}{(k - g)}$$

Thus, if we use the assumption that the company will have a reasonably long life with dividends increasing at $100g$ per cent per year and has a constant cost of capital of $100k$ per cent, we can use the last declared dividend to estimate the value of a share.

---

[2] This expression may be derived from the formula for the sum of a geometric progression.

If, however, the rate of growth of the dividend is greater than the cost of capital, we must discount the forecast dividends for the desired time horizon in order to arrive at a value for the share.

Estimation of the variables

There remains the problem of estimating the growth rate (g) and the cost of capital (k). Of these g is the simpler to estimate as it is usually possible to examine past data for the company and so estimate its past dividend growth rate. This, of course, assumes that the past rate will provide a good estimate of future growth. If other information about the expected future dividend pattern is available, extrapolation from past data may not be necessary.

Care should be taken to ensure that the dividends per share are adjusted to take account of any rights issue or other capital changes that may have taken place in the period under review.

Example 14.1

Consider a company which has paid the following dividends:

Year	Dividend (pence per share)
1992	6.0
1993	6.2
1994	6.4
1995	6.8
1996	6.8
1997	7.2
1998	7.3
1999	7.5
2000	7.8

Graphically the above can be represented as shown in Figure 14.1.

Mathematical techniques are available which can be used to estimate the average percentage growth in dividends for the period, but we will describe a simple and quick method which will often give a reasonable first approximation.

We can see that dividends have increased from 6.0p per share in 1992 to 7.8p per share in 2000. A visual inspection of the graph indicates that these observations are reasonably close to the trend and it therefore seems safe to use them. The average increase in dividends is $1.8/8 = 0.22$p per year, but we are seeking the average percentage growth g, which can be calculated as follows:

$$D_0 (1 + g)^8 = D_8$$

where D_0 is the 1992 dividend and D_8 is the 2000 dividend, i.e

$$6.0(1 + g)^8 = 7.8$$
$$\frac{1}{(1 + g)^8} = \frac{6.0}{7.8} = 0.77$$

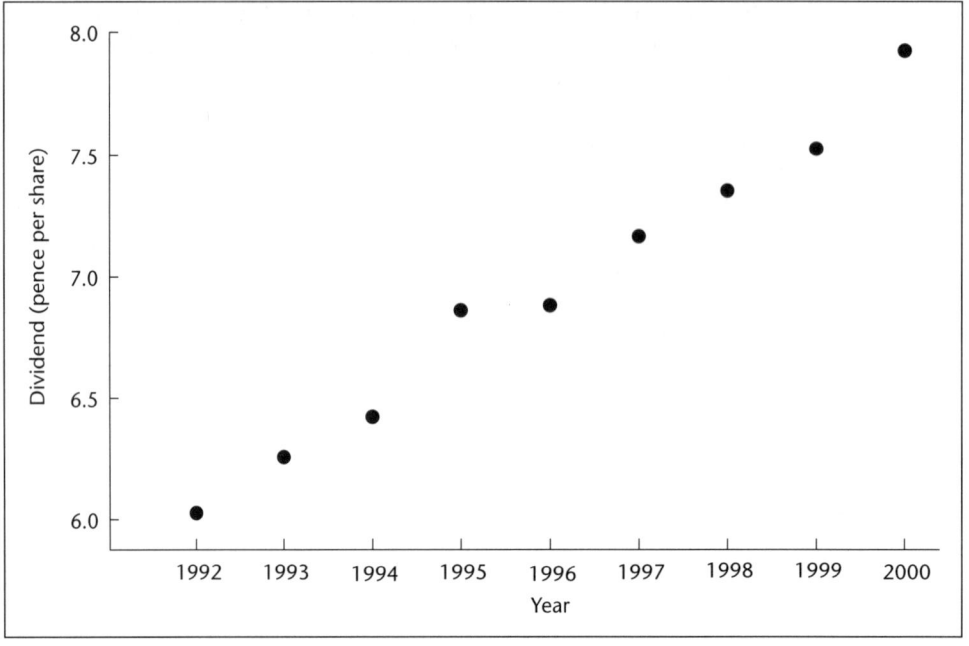

Fig. 14.1

$(1 + g)^8$ and hence g can be calculated by the use of logarithms, but an easier way is to make use of present value tables which give the value of $1/(1 + g)^n$ for different values of g and n. If we use the tables where $n = 8$ we find the following:

g	Present value
0.02	0.853
0.03	0.789
0.04	0.731

We can see that g lies between 0.03 and 0.04 and we could probably accept an estimate of say 0.035 ($3\frac{1}{2}$%). Given the other problems of estimation there seems little point in interpolating between 0.03 and 0.04 to find a more exact figure.

Where, however, the growth rate of the annual dividend is not constant in the period under consideration, some approximation must be made, such as taking a geometric mean[3] of the growth rates in the period under consideration.

Alternatively it may be possible to identify a cyclical trend in the dividend pattern and this could be used to forecast the dividends for the next five years, using a mean

---

[3] The geometric mean of n items is the nth root of the product of those items, e.g. the geometric mean, g, of the growth rates for periods 1 and 2, g_1 and g_2, is given by $g = \sqrt{g_1 \times g_2}$. This mean is appropriate for our analysis since the mean g for which we are searching is such that

$$D_0 (1 + g)^n = D_0(1 + g_1)(1 + g_2) \dots (1 + g_n)$$

$$= D_0 \prod_{j = 1}^{n} (1 + g_i)$$

growth rate thereafter. In this way it is often possible to obtain a reasonable estimate of value from the dividend valuation model, i.e.

$$P_0 = \frac{D_1}{(1+k)} + \frac{D_2}{(1+k)^2} + \frac{D_3}{(1+k)^3} + \frac{D_4}{(1+k)^4} + \frac{D_5 + D_5 \dfrac{(1+g)}{(k-g)}}{(1+k)^5}$$

(Since $P_5 = D_5[(1+g)/(k-g)]$ this is simply the discounting of expected cash flows over a five-year time horizon.)

Throughout the analysis which has been carried out so far it has been assumed that the cost of capital can be determined, and the proposition that it is the return which could be achieved by investment in a bank deposit account has not been retracted. It will, however, be clear that, in the absence of unexpected inflation, an investment in a deposit account with a sound bank can be regarded as a risk-free investment while it is evident that investment in the shares of a limited company is not risk free.

The risk associated with investment in the shares of a limited company can be explained in two main ways. First, the interest element, or dividend for ordinary shares, is not guaranteed but may fluctuate with the fortunes of the company and the whim of the directors. Second, the ability to recover one's capital at the end of the 'investment period' is dependent upon the sale of those shares. Since the sale of shares requires a market transaction, the recovery of capital is dependent upon the state of the market and is by no means guaranteed.

It therefore seems reasonable that an investor will require a higher return from a risky investment compared with a risk-free investment. Strictly, this depends on the assumption that the investor is risk averse, i.e. that he would prefer the certainty of receiving £X rather than enter an arrangement whereby he has a 50 per cent chance of receiving £(X + Y) and a 50 per cent chance of receiving £(X − Y). A risk preferer might favour the risky prospect and therefore expect a lower rate on a risky investment because he enjoys the uncertainty and is attracted by the possibility of higher returns. Most investors may be assumed to be risk averse, an assumption that is evidenced by the taking out of insurance policies to reduce the level of risk experienced in life.

The introduction of risk into this analysis makes the estimation of the cost of capital more difficult. In practice the problem is often tackled by inflating the cost of capital based on a risk-free investment by a premium determined on some subjective basis, depending on the investor's view of the riskiness of the investment. There are theoretical objections to this approach which are based upon the subjectivity of the risk assessment, and theoretical models have been formulated relating the premium to some objective measure of the risk of the proposed investment.

The best-known model is the Capital Asset Pricing Model which relates the expected return on a share to its risk in the following way:[4]

$$Ex_j = r + (Ex_m - r)\beta_j$$

This states that the expected return on share j (Ex_j), that is the appropriate cost of capital or discount rate, is a function of the risk-free rate of interest (r) and a risk

---

[4] This model (CAPM) is described in finance texts such as Richard A. Brealey and Stuart C. Myers, *Principles of Corporate Finance*, 5th edn., McGraw-Hill, 1996, and J.F. Weston and T.E. Copeland, *Managerial Finance*, 2nd UK edn., adapted by A.F. Fox and R.J. Limmack, Continuum Publishing, 1988.

premium. The risk premium depends upon the excess of the expected return on the market as a whole over the risk-free rate of interest ($Ex_m - r$) and the beta value of the particular share (β_j). This beta is a measure of what is called the systematic or non-diversifiable risk of the share. It is a measure of the riskiness of the share in relation to the market as a whole. The beta value for the market as a whole is defined as 1 so that, if a particular share has a beta value of 2, it is twice as risky as the market and hence demands twice the risk premium. Conversely, if the beta value for another share is 0.5, that share is half as risky as the market and requires half of the risk premium of the market. Beta values for UK companies and industry sectors are published by various sources.[5]

The Capital Asset Pricing Model rests on a large number of simplifying assumptions but, in spite of its elegance, the model enjoys only limited support from empirical studies. Use of the model to obtain a discount rate in practice requires the identification of the particular industry sector in which a company operates, so that an appropriate beta value may be obtained. This process becomes difficult where a particular company has diversified into different industry sectors for which different beta values are appropriate. Here, again, a large element of subjective judgement will be involved.

A further complicating factor in determining the cost of capital is that of a changing price level. If the price level of goods and services, which would otherwise be bought with the capital that is invested, is subject to change, then the value of the capital invested by the individual will change as its purchasing power will change. There are basically two ways of dealing with inflation in the valuation model.

The first is to adjust all items to real terms by expressing all cash flows in terms of purchasing power of a common, usually the current, date. However, if this is done then the cost of capital should also be measured in real terms to ensure that inflation is not counted twice.

The real cost of capital (for an investment of given level of risk), r, can be estimated as follows.

Let k be the 'nominal' cost of capital (i.e. the actual rate of return which is required on an investment of the given level of risk) and let m be the annual rate of inflation. Assume that £1.00 is invested at the start of the year; this is equivalent to an investment of $£1(1 + m)$ in year-end pounds. However, at the year end the investor will receive $£1(1 + k)$. Therefore the real rate of interest, r, is given by the equation

$$£1(1 + m)(1 + r) = £1(1 + k)$$

or

$$1 + m + r + mr = 1 + k.$$

If we assume that mr is very small, since it is the product of two small numbers, both much less than 1, then we can state that $r = k - m$.

The estimate, therefore, of the real cost of capital is the nominal cost less the expected change in the price index.

The second alternative for valuing the investment in ordinary shares is to express all the cash flows which have been predicted in money terms at their expected price levels and to discount these cash flows at the money ('nominal') cost of capital. This method is probably simpler to understand since money figures will be used

---

[5] One such listing is published by the London Business School.

throughout the analysis, reducing the conceptual problems of identifying 'real' monetary units.

The determination of the cost of capital does, in the final analysis, depend upon the opportunity cost approach. The opportunity cost of an investment is the best alternative return which has been foregone by selecting this specific investment. This approach to determining the cost of capital is one of the most useful approaches available to those involved in the valuation of securities, since it enables an estimate of the cost of capital to be made by comparison with other available investments. When such a comparison is being made it is important that the risk characteristics of the alternative investments are sufficiently alike to make the comparison meaningful.

This opportunity cost method of comparison is then the dominant approach used by market participants in their valuation calculations, especially in the case of shares in unquoted companies or in the search for underpriced shares in quoted companies. The typical procedure that would be followed would be to identify a comparable quoted company and to obtain its dividend yield (*see below*) which represents the first approximation to the opportunity cost of capital. This dividend yield will then be adjusted upwards by about a quarter to a third to reflect the lack of marketability of the unquoted shares. Additional adjustments will usually be made to reflect other differences between shares in the quoted company and those in the unquoted company. These might include differences in dividend cover, asset backing or growth prospects. The adjusted dividend yield will then be used as the cost of capital in order to capitalise the dividends of the unquoted share.

The opportunity cost method is therefore theoretically justifiable and applicable in practice: there are, however, two main practical problems inherent in this approach. There is the problem that no two companies are exactly alike, and great care must be taken when selecting a company with which comparisons are to be made. Ideally companies being compared should be in the same industry, be of approximately the same size and operate in the same market as a company whose shares are being valued. It is unlikely that the ideal company will be found. The other problem is that comparison can be made in respect of more than one aspect of a company's performance. It is rather like the problem faced by a judge in a music competition. Most people would not rank the participants in terms of only one of their attributes; they are likely to consider technique, expression, presence, etc., and balance these factors in their own minds before coming to a ranking decision. Similarly, when comparing the results of two companies, one would have to consider a number of factors in addition to the level of dividends upon which we have concentrated so far. These factors would be the assets and earnings of the companies because these will influence the expectation of future dividends. Only if the companies have sufficient earnings will they be able to maintain their dividend pay out.

The valuation of unquoted shares

In this section of the chapter we will first consider the main stock exchange indicators which provide a basis for comparison of companies. We will then present an example dealing with the valuation of the shares of an unquoted company.

In order to discuss the main stock exchange indicators we will make use of a hypothetical quoted company whose summarised accounts for the year t_0 to t_1 are given below:

Profit and loss account for the period t_0 to t_1

	£000
Turnover	2 000
Earnings	200
less Corporation tax (at 33% of taxable profit)	80
	120
Dividends paid	60
Unappropriated earnings for the period	60
Retained earnings at t_0	400
Retained earnings at t_1	460

Balance sheets

	t_0 £000	t_1 £000
Assets *less* current liabilities	1 000	1 060
less 9% debentures 2010	100	100
	900	960
Capital and reserves:		
1 million 50p ordinary shares	500	500
Reserves	400	460
	900	960

At time t_1, the company's shares are quoted at £1.50. For the period t_0 to t_1, tax of 10 per cent is withheld from dividends.

In this section we will examine five ratios: the dividend yield, the dividend cover, the earnings per share, the price/earnings ratio and the earnings yield. Four of these ratios include the price of the company's shares and thus can be used to make a direct comparison between one share and another; the dividend cover ratio is different in that it serves as an indicator of risk associated with the dividend as well as giving some indication of the management's distribution policy.

Dividend yield

The dividend yield provides a measure of the return that the investor will receive on an investment. It is calculated on a pre-tax basis (for the recipient) and hence the dividend figure included in the calculation will be the gross dividend, i.e. the net cash payment received by the shareholder plus the tax credit.

In our example, the net dividend per share is given by £60 000/1 000 000 = 6p and, as the tax credit is 10 per cent, the gross dividend is 6.6. The dividend yield is then given by:

$$\text{Dividend yield} = \frac{\text{Gross dividend per share}}{\text{Market price per share}} \times 100\%$$

$$= \frac{6.6}{150} \times 100 = 4.4\%.$$

Dividend cover

The purpose of this ratio is to help assess the likelihood that management will not have to reduce the dividend from its current level. The dividend cover is the ratio between the profit, excluding extraordinary items, attributable to the ordinary shareholders (i.e. profit after tax and any preference dividends) and the current dividend.

In the case of our example, profit attributable to shareholders is £120 000 and the dividend declared is £60 000. Therefore dividend cover = 120 000/60 000 = 2.

In the USA the reciprocal of the dividend cover, the payment ratio, is a more commonly used statistic.

Earnings per share

The earnings per share ratio is one that is very simple in concept, but which is often difficult to calculate in practice. The basic concept is that the earnings of the company for the year should be apportioned to the ordinary shares in issue to give an indication of the amount of earnings which would be available to the holder of one ordinary share. This simple concept thus enables the earnings associated with holding an ordinary share in one company to be compared with those associated with holding an ordinary share in another company.

It is, however, on this matter of comparability that complications can and do arise. If the ratio is to be used meaningfully, then it must be calculated on a similar basis for every company, and the earnings must be representative of the company's earnings potential. It is clear that the earnings stated in companies' reports are not necessarily comparable with one another because different accounting policies may have been applied and there may have been differing levels of earnings from non-trading transactions which will not be representative of the companies' earnings potentials.

In order to increase comparability, the earnings per share figure should be calculated on the consolidated profit of the period (after tax and after deducting minority interests and preference dividends) divided by the average number of equity shares in issue and ranking for dividend in respect of the period.[6]

Hence, if the earnings for the year attributable to the ordinary shareholders is £120 000 and the number of shares in issue is 1 000 000, then the earnings per share is 12p.

Some of the other problems which may occur in the calculation of the earnings per share, and a discussion of SSAP 3, will be found in the appendix to this chapter.

Price/earnings ratio

While the security valuation model developed so far rightly concentrates upon the dividend to be expected, consideration is given in practice to the company's earnings. This has been found to be useful because earnings represent an upper limit for dividend distribution.

The most common valuation tool based on earnings is the price/earnings (P/E) ratio, which is calculated as follows:

$$\text{P/E ratio} = \frac{\text{Price per share}}{\text{Earnings per share}}$$

---

[6] FRS 14, Para. 11.

In the case under examination, the earnings per share is 12p, as we showed above, and the share price is £1.50. Hence:

$$P/E = \frac{150}{12} = 12.5$$

The P/E ratio shows the investor the numbers of years' earnings that he will purchase with his investment and enables him to compare this investment with alternatives. The flaw in the argument is, of course, that the P/E ratio is based on the last known earnings figure while the investor is 'buying' future earnings. Thus, the shares of a company whose earnings are expected to grow will, all other things being equal, have a higher P/E ratio than the shares of a company whose earnings are not expected to increase. Similarly, a company whose earnings are considered by the market to be risky will have shares with a lower P/E ratio than a company with a more certain earnings stream.

Earnings yield

The earnings yield is an alternative way of relating the company's earnings to its share price and is given by:

$$\text{Earnings yield} = \frac{\text{Earnings per share}}{\text{Share price}} \times 100\%$$

Unfortunately, the value of earnings per share most commonly used in such calculations is based on different assumptions from the value of earnings per share used to calculate the P/E ratio. For the purposes of calculating the earnings yield, the earnings per share figure is the maximum dividend that could have been declared from the profits for the year, i.e. the grossed-up earnings to allow for the tax credit. It is therefore necessary to determine whether the figure being used for valuation purposes is gross or net of tax so that consistent comparisons may be made.

Example 14.2: Valuation of the shares of an unquoted company

The basic principle is that the value is the price that the shares would fetch if sold on the open market on the date in respect of which the shares are being valued. As was stated earlier, this is done by looking at the price of shares of quoted, but otherwise similar, companies.

X Limited is an unquoted company whose accounts for the last four years disclosed the following:

Balance sheets

End of year	1	2	3	4
	£000s	£000s	£000s	£000s
Net assets	850	1 000	990	1 110
Share capital				
£1 ordinary shares	500	500	500	500
Retained earnings	200	300	390	510
Loans	150	200	100	100
	850	1 000	990	1 110

Results	Year 1	Year 2	Year 3	Year 4
	£000s	£000s	£000s	£000s
Earnings after tax	150	160	180	220
Dividend	50	60	90	100

We will attempt to place a value on the shares of X Limited as at the end of year 4 on the assumption that the shares being valued represent only a small proportion of the total issue.

There are two quoted companies, A plc and B plc, which appear to be similar to X Limited. The *Financial Times* listing at the end of year 4 shows the following:

Price	+ or −	52 week		Volume	Yield	P/E
		High	Low	000s		
130	+2	135	100	115	4.7	10
80	−1	90	60	165	3.9	8

The price is the price of the share, quoted in pence, at the end of the day's business while the next column shows the change from the closing prices at the end of the previous day. The 'high' and 'low' are the highest and lowest prices achieved over the last year, adjusted, if necessary, for changes in the capital structure. Volume indicates the number of securities traded in the day, while the yield is net, i.e. after the deduction of tax, and the PE ratio is based on the lastest annual report updated, where possible, for interim results.

We will now calculate the earnings per share and dividend per share for X Limited for the last four years:

	Year			
	1	2	3	4
Earnings per share	30p	32p	36p	44p
Dividends per share, net	12.5p	15.0p	22.5p	25.0p

We can see that both the earnings and dividends per share have grown steadily over the period. These are expressed in monetary terms and in a full analysis we should attempt to eliminate the effect of inflation. However, we will assume that the figures for year 4, which will be used in the comparison, are not unrepresentative of the period.

First we will make an estimate of the share value using a dividend yield approach.

The dividend per share for X Limited is 25.0p. The dividend yield for A plc is 4.7 per cent. In order to adjust the figure for X Limited being an unquoted company we might increase it by about a third, giving a level of comparison of about 6.25 per cent. Thus we could produce a value for the shares of X Limited of £(0.25/0.0625) = £4.00. Alternatively, if we compare X Limited with B plc we would expect a dividend yield of about 5.2 per cent (3.9% × 1.33). Thus we would produce a value for the shares of X Limited of £(0.25/0.052) = £4.81.

The dividend valuation approach therefore gives values of £4.00 and £4.81.

We may similarly attempt to carry out a valuation using an earnings approach. Again we must adjust the P/E ratios of the quoted companies by about one-third to allow for the fact that X Limited is unquoted. In using P/E ratios, such an adjustment involves a reduction to reflect the fact that the shares in the unquoted company are less valuable than those in the quoted company. Thus we would apply P/E ratios of about 7.0 and 5.5 in comparison with the ratios of 10 for A plc and 8 for B plc.

The earnings per share of X Limited is 44p, thus the application of an earnings-based approach gives valuations for X Limited's shares of £3.08 (44p × 7) and £2.42.

We would also look at the asset backing of X Limited's shares. This can be done using the net book value of the assets as disclosed by the historical cost accounts:

Net book value of assets at the end of year 4	=	£1 110 000
Loans outstanding	=	£100 000
Net book value of assets less loans	=	£1 010 000
Number of shares	=	500 000
Net book value per share	=	£2.05

If the shares are being valued on the assumption that the business is a going concern then the above figure may be of dubious value, but it might give some indication of the lowest possible share valuation. An examination of the current value of the assets may also be of interest, but this is likely to be of much greater relevance to a potential purchaser of a controlling interest in the business, which will be discussed later in the chapter.

Thus, we have five possible valuations of a share in X Limited:

(a)	book value per share	£2.05
(b)	comparison with A plc	
	(i) on dividend yield	£4.00
	(ii) on P/E ratio	£3.08
(c)	comparison with B plc	
	(i) on dividend yield	£4.81
	(ii) on P/E ratio	£2.42

These figures represent a large range and it may, on further investigation, be discovered that one of the two quoted companies provides a closer comparison to X Limited. If that company is found to be A plc, and the possibility of X Limited being broken up is discounted, then the value of X Limited's shares would seem to fall between £3.08 and £4.00.

While it is often necessary to value unquoted shares by reference to the market value of otherwise comparable quoted shares, it must be noted that the method does suffer from many severe limitations in that (a) the dividend policies of unquoted companies tend to be different from and less stable than those of their quoted counterparts; (b) the asset base and its financing of unquoted companies is likely to be different from the quoted companies with which they will be compared, the quoted companies being on the whole less volatile; (c) the value of quoted companies' shares is dependent upon the market and therefore will be volatile and not necessarily equal to the shares' intrinsic worth.

The valuation of shares cannot be made simply by application of formulae. The valuer must balance the information derived from an analysis such as that described above with other information and, ultimately, apply his or her intuition and judgement before arriving at a conclusion.

Some, but by no means all, of the other factors which might be considered are as follows: (a) whether there are any restrictions upon the transfer of shares and the nature of any such restrictions; (b) the history and prospects of the company and the industries in which it operates; (c) the nature and quality of the company's management; (d) the prospects of a takeover or a merger; (e) the impact of inflation; (f) the results of a more detailed analysis of the company's accounts, as discussed in Chapter 13.

The valuation of shares for statutory purposes

In valuing shares for statutory purposes, such as the calculation of the liability of an individual to capital gains tax or inheritance tax, an agreement of valuation must be reached with the Shares Valuation Division of the Inland Revenue. This body has shown that it tends to calculate the value of an unquoted shareholding by comparison with the value of shares in similar quoted companies, making allowance for the differing circumstances of the companies and also discounting the share price so derived by between 10 per cent and 35 per cent on the basis of the restrictions of the articles of association of the company and the size of the shareholding in question.

In negotiations for the statutory valuation of shares it is necessary to consider the possibility of capital appreciation in addition to the points made in the preceding section. Potential capital appreciation will be taken into account in the statutory valuation when it can be shown that it is likely to occur; such would be the case if, for example, the directors were already considering a new issue of shares at a higher price than the current valuation.

It must be remembered that the requirement for the valuation of shares for capital gains tax, as laid down in Schedule 10 of the Finance Act 1975, is that the value is the assumed price of an arm's length transaction given all the information a prudent purchaser might reasonably acquire. This is open to many interpretations and serves to illustrate the large range of values which could be maintained in the negotiations for the statutory valuations of shares in unquoted companies.

Readers who are faced with the problem of statutory valuation are urged to make reference to recent appeals dealt with by the Special Commissioners and the High Court to acquaint themselves with current precedent. These are frequently reported in the weekly and monthly accounting journals.

The valuation of a business

Introduction

A business is an asset, and the same theoretical underpinnings can be applied to the valuation of a business as are applied to the valuation of individual assets. There is, however, one very important difference between a single asset and a business: this is that a single asset usually represents only a small proportion of the owner's wealth. It is unlikely that this will be so in the case of a business and hence its valuation will depend in part on the other assets owned by the person or group on whose behalf the valuation is being made. In other words, the value of a business could be said to be given by: the value of the owner's total stock of assets on the assumption that the business is owned *less* the value of the owner's total stock of assets without the business.

The significance of the effect of the potential or existing owner's other assets can be seen by considering the example of valuation of a pharmaceutical business. Let us suppose that there are two potential purchasers – a photographic company and an engineering company. It is likely, all other things being equal, that the photographic company would place a higher value on the business than the engineers if, as is probable, the pharmaceutical and photographic businesses have common outlets which would enable the photographic company to use the same representatives to sell both types of product. This is an example of what is called positive *synergy*, i.e. the

431

interaction of assets so that the combined earnings of two or more assets will exceed the sum of their potential separate earnings.

The bases of valuation of a business will be dependent on the circumstances in which the valuation is being made, and we should therefore consider the reasons why a valuation of a business is required.

Taxation

Tax legislation dictates that a business will have to be valued for the purposes of inheritance tax and capital gains tax when the proprietor of a business dies or transfers part or all of his or her interest in the business during his or her life.

Insurance

A prudent management will wish to insure its business. This is often done by reference to the tangible assets of the business only, and the problem then reduces to deciding on the value to be attached to the business's tangible assets, a subject which is dealt with in some detail elsewhere in this book.

There are, however, many businesses where such an approach would result in a significant undervaluation of the business because tangible assets constitute only a small proportion of its assets. Examples of such enterprises include management consultancies, advertising agencies and firms of accountants. In these and similar cases, the major asset of the business is the skill and enterprise of its owners and employees and in many, especially smaller, concerns the greater proportion of these assets is provided by the owners themselves. If this is the case, owners should carefully consider the amount of life and disability insurance required to ensure that the value of their assets, or of their estate, will not decline should they be unable, by death or otherwise, to continue to work. In theory the amount of the insurance, the insurable risk, should, if we ignore the contribution of employees and other elements of 'goodwill', be equal to the value of the business less the value of the tangible assets.

Transfer of ownership

Both the potential vendor and the potential purchaser of a business will require valuation from their own particular standpoint and would, for the purposes of negotiation, wish to estimate the value which is in the minds of the other party to the transaction. We will discuss this topic in detail later in the chapter, but at this stage we will point out the particular problems faced by the potential purchaser.

A potential purchaser cannot be sure of retaining the trained labour force and management which are currently part of the business. Also, the potential purchaser may not be interested in the business as a whole but only in a part of it which she/he intends to keep as a going concern, selling off the other assets. In contrast, she/he may not wish to persist with any part of the business and may only be interested in one or a number of the assets of the business which she/he would find more expensive to acquire in any other way.

There is also the question of synergy to be considered; thus the degree of interaction between the business being acquired and the purchaser's present business may be such that the value of the business to the purchaser bears little relation to the value of the business on its own. The potential purchaser also faces the practical problem that she/he may not be able to obtain all the necessary information.

In addition to the above circumstances, which apply to most forms of business enterprise, a number of special factors apply in the cases of partnerships and companies.

Partnerships

If the business is a partnership, the problems of valuation may be acute and frequent. Whenever there is a change in the partnership arrangements a valuation of both the 'old' and 'new' partnerships is required, for the ongoing partners will give up a share in the old partnership in return for a share in the new partnership. In practice the difficult problems involved are often dealt with, in so far as the valuation of the old partnership is concerned, by the addition to the tangible assets of a figure for goodwill based on such arbitrary formulae as x years' purchase of the average profits of a past period. Such an approach is theoretically unsound because it is based on past results rather than future expectations, but the method is usually easy to apply and will reduce the possibility of disagreement arising between the partners.

The contribution of the partners to the new partnership is dealt with in the first instance by the selection of a profit-sharing agreement based on the capital and labour inputs of the partners, but this will, of course, only encompass the profits recognised by the accounting system and will ignore changes in the valuation of assets, especially goodwill. Thus, when there is next a change in the partnership arrangements, the problem of the valuation of the business will again have to be faced.

Companies

When a company requires new capital and proposes to raise this by the issue of new shares it will be necessary to value the company in order that an appropriate and equitable price will be derived for the new issue. Often, when a company is faced with a takeover bid, it will be advantageous to obtain a valuation in order that either the bid may be defended or a fair price be agreed for the company's shares.

In addition, there is also a need for the shareholders of the company to have some indication of the current value of the company in order that they may judge the stewardship of the directors by reference to the rate of return which they obtain on their investment. Indeed, it is argued that this knowledge should be in the possession of all investors on the grounds that the most efficient use of the nation's resources will be achieved if investment is steered towards those companies which offer the greatest return.

A valuation model based on earnings

The present value model which discounts future cash flows to their net present value, which has already been introduced, provides what most people would regard as the correct theoretical approach to the valuation of a business. However, in practice it is often difficult to make or obtain all the necessary data required and hence other approaches of varying degrees of crudity are often used.

We will start this section by discussing an earnings-based model, and, in particular, investigate the circumstances under which the differences between models based on cash flows and reported earnings may not be all that significant.

The standard valuation model may be presented thus:

$$V_0 = \sum_{j=0}^{\infty} \frac{Y_j - X_j}{(1 + k)^j}$$

where V_0 is the value of the asset at time t_0, k is the discount rate, Y_j is the cash receipts generated by the asset in year j, X_j is the cash expenses associated with the asset in year j.

Now if C is the expenses of the business in year j on an accruals basis and R is the revenue of the business in year j on an accruals basis, then the profit of the business in year j is given by

$$P_j = R_j - C_j$$

Over the life of the business the cash receipts from sales must be the same as the revenue accrued (if bad debts and discounts are ignored), i.e.

$$\sum_{j=0}^{\infty} Y_j = \sum_{j=0}^{\infty} R_j$$

and the cash payments must be the same as the expenses calculated on an accruals basis (again ignoring bad debts and discounts), i.e.

$$\sum_{j=0}^{\infty} X_j = \sum_{j=0}^{\infty} C_j$$

If the net expenditure on fixed assets per year is approximately the same as the annual depreciation charge, and if the business investment in net current assets is approximately constant, then it follows that

$$Y_j \simeq R_j \text{ and } X_j \simeq C_j$$

The valuation model can then be restated as follows:

$$V_0 = \sum_{j=0}^{\infty} \frac{Y_j - X_j}{(1 + k)^j}$$

and thus

$$V_0 \simeq \sum_{j=0}^{\infty} \frac{R_j - C_j}{(1 + k)^j} = \sum_{j=0}^{\infty} \frac{P_j}{(1 + k)^j}$$

Therefore the value of the firm can be stated in terms of the discounted value of the expected profits to be earned over the firm's lifetime.

The nature of the discounting process is such that the later terms in the series have less impact on the overall valuation V_0 than the earlier terms. In other words, for a given P_j and k, $P_j/(1 + k)^j$ becomes smaller as j becomes larger. Thus, the importance of the assumptions referred to above relating to the purchase of fixed assets and investment in working capital is reduced as the years pass.

It might be argued that this formulation overstates the value of the business because not all the profit is paid to the proprietor, but some is reinvested in the business. Thus, the cash flow to the proprietor is less than the profit flow to the business. This is generally true, but the recognition of this point leads us to modify but not abandon our approach. A rational proprietor with a discount rate k would only reinvest the profits of the business where the expected rate of return on that investment was greater than k. Consider, for example, the reinvestment of I from the profits in year 1. Then the profit paid to the proprietor falls from P_1 to $P_1 - I$. However, this investment must earn at least rate k, so the profits in year 2 must be increased from P_2 to at least $P_2 + I(1 + k)$ if this was a one-year investment.

Thus, in place of the valuation

$$V_0 = P_0 + \frac{P_1}{1 + k} + \frac{P_2}{(1 + k)^2} + \dots + \frac{P_n}{(1 + k)^n} + \dots$$

we have, if it is assumed that the amount invested earns a return of k (i.e. that profits of year 2 are $P_2 + I(1 + k)$), a value, V_0', which is given by

$$V_0' = P_0 + \frac{P_1 - I}{(1 + k)} + \frac{P_2 + I(1+k)}{(1 + k)^2} + \dots + \frac{P_n}{(1 + k)^n} + \dots$$

$$= P_0 + \frac{P_1}{(1 + k)} + \frac{P_2}{(1 + k)^2} + \dots + \frac{P_n}{(1 + k)^n} + \dots$$

$$= V_0$$

The same analysis can be applied to investments made in later years.

If it is assumed that the amounts invested will earn a greater return than k then the value V_0 can be regarded as providing a lower limit of the range of values of the business.

We have thus established a theoretical model for the valuation of a business as a going concern, based upon the discounted value of the future earnings of the business.

Valuation of a business as a going concern

Initially, we will confine the discussion to the case of a business which is being valued as a going concern, and the management and assets of which will be unchanged as a result of the circumstances leading to the requirement for a valuation.

The direct application of our theoretical model poses several problems. The first and most obvious problem is that the model requires us to forecast earnings for the business for the remainder of its life. This, it will readily be recognised, is an impossible task. The second problem arises in the estimation of the discount rate, k, which should be used to carry out this calculation. Thus, in practice, the theoretical model is rarely applied as we have derived it, but rather various rule-of-thumb approximations are used to establish a range of values for the business which experience has shown might be indicated by the theoretical model, were we able to use it.

The asset valuation approach

Our first approach to the problem of valuation will be an asset valuation approach. It can be argued that if a business is acquiring or retaining an asset, then the value of that asset to the business must, in the case of acquisition of the asset, be greater than the cost of that asset and, in the case of retention of the asset, be greater than the net realisable value of the asset. If, therefore, all the assets of the business are valued at their net realisable values, then the sum of those values will clearly be less than their value to the business and can be regarded as providing the lower bound to the range of values based on the asset valuation approach. This point is not as simple as it appears because of the difficulty in determining the net realisable value of assets and, as described in Chapter 3, the net realisable value of an asset depends on the circumstances under which it is assumed that the asset will be sold.

The upper bound of the range of assets will be the sum of the replacement costs of the company's assets so long as it is recognised that the assets include intangibles such as goodwill. The determination of the replacement cost of both tangible and, in particular, intangible assets does produce substantial practical difficulties.

Discounted earnings approaches

These approaches are related to the present value method, but contain a number of simplifying assumptions which facilitate their use. There is, however, a danger that the crudity of the assumptions may in certain circumstances mean that the links between the methods described and the present value method become tenuous.

A common theme of the simplified approaches is that one figure is selected as representing what is termed the *maintainable profit* of the business. This figure is sometimes based on the average profit for the recent past, in which case adjustments need to be made for changes in capital employed, inflation, etc. Alternatively, the profits of the most recent year or the forecast profit of the current year may be used to provide a first estimate of the maintainable profit. The first estimate, however derived, may then be adjusted on a more or less subjective basis by the valuer. The valuer might feel that the current year, or recent past, does not provide a reasonable indication of the future and may, therefore, inflate or deflate the first estimate depending on his/her view of the likely future trend in profits.

The valuer will, especially in the case of smaller businesses, have to consider the extent to which profit is being distributed by way of remuneration. For example, the directors of a family-owned limited company may be paid a great deal more than the economic value of their services, and part of their remuneration should be regarded as profit. In such an instance, the reported accounting profit is understated in the sense that – all other things being equal – a higher profit could have been obtained if the family directors were replaced by professional managers paid at the market rate.

Sometimes an adjustment will have to be made in the opposite direction, for it is not uncommon, especially at the start of a company's life, for directors to pay themselves less than the market rate of remuneration. We are now in a position to consider a simple discounted earnings approach.

Let us assume that an estimate of the maintainable profit has been obtained. The next step is to determine the capitalisation rate which will be necessary to fix the current value of an anticipated stream of future earnings. This is usually done by comparing the business concerned with a similar business of which the current value is known and for which maintainable profit can be estimated. The capitalisation rate derived from the relationship between current value and earnings in this case can be applied, after making any necessary adjustments, to the business which is to be valued.

One very convenient basis of comparison is the share price and earnings of a publicly quoted company undertaking a similar type of business, since this will give a readily available price to earnings (P/E) ratio which can be applied to the earnings of the business. It is usual to apply a lower P/E ratio to the earnings of the business being valued than is currently applied to the earnings of a publicly listed company, and the discount to cover the lack of marketability would usually be in the region of 25 to 33 per cent. In addition, it will be necessary to make suitable adjustments to this P/E ratio to take into account differences, in such matters as asset backing and earnings growth, between the quoted company and the unquoted business.

One disadvantage of this approach is that the P/E ratio derived from the market is based on marginal transactions, i.e. the price which is associated with the transfer of a relatively small proportion of the shares in issue. This price is not obviously applicable for the valuation of the business as a whole because, on the one hand, the purchase of the business would mean that a larger parcel of shares was acquired (which would suggest that a lower P/E ratio should be used), while on the other hand the purchaser would be gaining control of the whole business (which might justify the use of a higher P/E ratio).

The above approach, together with the asset valuation method, is illustrated in Example 14.3. The data of this example will be used as the basis of a running example which will appear later in the chapter.

Example 14.3

ABC Limited is an unquoted company which has been trading for 10 years in an inflation-free environment and has been earning profits consistently. It is required, for some reason for which tax effects and influence upon the path of the business will be negligible, to arrive at a valuation for the business. The following information is known about the business as at 31 December 20X9:

Profits for ABC Limited			
20X0	£1 000	20X5	£15 000
20X1	£2 000	20X6	£14 000
20X2	£5 000	20X7	£16 000
20X3	£8 000	20X8	£14 000
20X4	£12 000	20X9	£17 000

The book values of the assets of the business in 20X0 were £10 000 and are now £70 000.

The book values of the assets of the business are believed to be reasonable approximations to their net realisable values, apart from the business premises, which have a book value of £20 000 but an estimated net realisable value of £60 000.

The net realisable value of ABC's assets is thus £70 000 + £(60 000 – 20 000) = £110 000 which, as argued above, might be regarded as the lower band of the range of values based on an asset valuation approach.

The maintainable profit of the business could be based on the average of the last five years' profits, which appear to be reasonably stable; hence the maintainable profit is £15 200.

Let us assume that the quoted shares of a similar business sell at a P/E ratio of 10 and that it is appropriate to discount this figure by 25 per cent to take account of the reduced marketability of the shares of ABC Limited, i.e. the P/E ratio would be 0.75 of 10 = 7.5.

The simple discounted earnings method valuation of the business is then 7.5 × £15 200 = £114 000.

Super-profits method

It is sometimes suggested that the earnings stream of a business can be divided into two elements: the first is the expected return on the value of the tangible assets employed in the business; the second is an additional amount known as the *super-profit*. The super-profit is therefore the difference between the maintainable profit and the expected return on the tangible assets employed. The essence of the super-profit method is that the additional profits are regarded as riskier than the expected return and that the super-profit should therefore be capitalised at a lower multiple (or higher capitalisation rate) than the expected return.

A number of arguments can be advanced to support the view. One is based on the standard economic theory that, in a perfectly competitive market, profits that are higher than the norm for the type of assets employed in the business will be eroded away because the existence of excess profits will encourage new entrants into the market. The new firms will drive down the price until the excess profits are eliminated. The strength of this argument does depend on the structure of the market involved and it has to be recognised that there may be barriers to entry whereby a monopolist can continue to reap excess profits in the long term.

The super-profits method has also been justified by reference to the transient nature of goodwill. It can be argued that the super-profits represent the profits generated by the existence of goodwill. Consider a new business which has tangible assets of £800 000 and that the normal return on assets of the type employed by the business is 12 per cent. Then the expected profit is £96 000. An existing business with identical tangible assets may be earning a profit of £120 000. The difference between the two profits, which may be regarded as the super-profit, is due to the fact that the existing business has created 'goodwill', e.g. has established good relationships with customers, a skilled workforce, etc. Now by its very nature, goodwill will disappear if no steps are taken to ensure its survival. Thus, new employees will have to be trained, customers will have to be provided with satisfactory service, and so on. When an existing business is acquired, its goodwill will gradually disappear and it will, in effect, have to be replaced by the activities of the new owners. This view, if accepted, can be used as an argument for applying a lower multiple to the super-profits.

The theoretical weakness of the super-profits method is that the separation of maintainable profits into the two elements is artificial. The associated practical difficulty is the determination of the expected rate of return on assets of the type employed in the business. All businesses have some goodwill (although in very badly-run firms goodwill may be negative) and thus it is unlikely that reference to similar businesses will yield the required return. It is sometimes suggested that the expected return might be related to the return on government securities, but an investment in a business will carry a greater risk and it will therefore be necessary to adjust for this difference.

The super-profits method is perhaps superficially attractive, but on more detailed consideration it is clear that it suffers from severe theoretical and practical shortcomings. Given its difficulties, a valuer might well be advised to use the present value approach described earlier in the chapter, which would mean that he/she would not be confined to one figure of maintainable profit. He/she could estimate the future trend of profits, which would enable the consideration of the possibility of growth. The required discount rate could be obtained from an examination of similar businesses and would avoid the need to make the artificial distinction between normal and super-profits.

The mechanics of the super-profits method are illustrated in Example 14.4.

Example 14.4

Data are the same as in Example 14.3.

Let us suppose that the 'normal' rate of return on assets of the type used by ABC Limited is 10 per cent. The 'super-profits' can then be calculated as follows:

	£
Expected maintainable profits (from Example 14.3)	15 200
less Normal return, 10% of £110 000	11 000
Super-profits	4 200

Let us assume that it is believed that the super-profits should be valued at four years' earnings, i.e. a multiple of four or a capitalisation rate of 25 per cent should be applied to the figure of £4200. It should be noted that one of the major defects of the super-profits method is that it is by no means clear how the required multiple should be determined.

The value of ABC Limited would then be determined as follows:

	£
Value of tangible assets	110 000[7]
Value of super-profits 4 × £4 200	16 800
	126 800

Valuation of a business for amalgamation with another

The valuation of a business which is to be amalgamated with another business is a more complex process because it cannot be made in isolation. From the point of view of potential purchasers, the maximum price that they would be prepared to pay is the difference between the value of the combined businesses and the value of their existing business.

If the amalgamation gives rise to positive synergy, the value of the amalgamated business will be greater than the sum of the values of the individual businesses taken in isolation. The basic principle can be simply stated, but the practical problems are immense in that the purchaser has to place a value on a business which has yet to be established. The purchaser will usually not only have to consider the tangible assets, which can be valued with relative ease, but also the intangible assets which may be particularly influenced by the synergical effect of the amalgamation.

In many amalgamations some of the assets of the acquired business will not be retained in the new business. The first step, therefore, in valuing a business for acquisition will be to determine the asset structure of the business and identify the assets which will not be required in the future. These assets must be valued at their net realisable value at the time at which they are expected to be sold and these figures discounted to the present time to ascertain the present value of the superfluous assets. In many cases, the sale of the superfluous assets will take place immediately and therefore no discounting will be necessary. The value of these assets may be considered to be a deduction from the purchase price of the business.

In practice the valuation figure must be the net realisable value of the surplus assets which are to be sold plus the present value of the additional earnings which will accrue to the acquiring business as a result of the acquisition. It is of course apparent that a major problem arises in determining the rate of interest at which the earnings of the business must be discounted, and this has already been discussed.

We will consider an example in order to assist with the explanation of this analysis.

Example 14.5

ADG is a business which produces and sells to retailers a certain range of fashion clothes. It has made the following estimates of potential earnings for the next 10 years:

Year no.	1	2	3	4	5	6	7	8	9	10
Earnings (£000)	120	140	170	200	210	220	240	260	280	300

---

[7] This is of course equivalent to capitalising the expected return of £11 000 at 10 per cent.

439

XYZ is a business which owns a number of boutiques in a certain locality. The boutiques buy clothes from various suppliers and retail them. Each boutique has a manager and an assistant but all purchasing and policy decisions are taken centrally by the owner and her staff.

XYZ independently estimates its earnings for the next 10 years to be:

Year no.	1	2	3	4	5	6	7	8	9	10
Earnings (£000)	10	15	20	25	28	31	33	34	35	35

The net assets of XYZ have a book value of £100 000, which includes 10-year leases on retail shops valued at about £60 000, a freehold shop and office valued at £20 000, stock worth £20 000 at retail prices, on which £12 000 is owing to suppliers.

ADG is interested in acquiring XYZ in order to provide some additional retail outlets. If it were to do this, it would retain most of the shops with their staff, but would not retain the owner, nor her staff, nor the freehold shop and offices. It would use the shops to sell only its own clothes, and so improve its turnover and profit margin.

ADG has made the following estimates of costs and earnings if it were to acquire XYZ. Initially, it would sell the freehold shop and office for £20 000 and the leases on two of the shops for a further £10 000. This would entail the dismissal of 10 staff who would need to be compensated for loss of employment, which would cost ADG about £25 000. The entire stock of the shops would be sold as quickly as possible and replaced with clothing supplied by ADG. The estimated trading earnings of ADG with XYZ for the next 10 years are as follows:

Year no.	1	2	3	4	5	6	7	8	9	10
Earnings (£000)	125	150	200	230	255	270	280	300	320	350

Thus, ADG can assess the differences between its performance without XYZ and with XYZ. These differences are:

Year no.	1	2	3	4	5	6	7	8	9	10
Difference in earnings (£000)	+5	+10	+30	+30	+45	+50	+40	+40	+40	+50

Additional gains to ADG would be the sale of the freehold and the leasehold shops (£30 000) and of the stock (£20 000) less the liabilities due to suppliers (£12 000) and the cost of laying off the excess employees (£25 000): an immediate net gain of £13 000.

It is assumed that all other assets of the business would be retained. Thus, the figures to be discounted to give a present value for the acquisition are as follows:

Year no.	0	1	2	3	4	5	6	7	8	9	10
Earnings (£000)	13	5	10	30	30	45	50	40	40	40	50

In practice it may be difficult to decide upon the appropriate discount rate. The problem may be overcome by considering a range of discount rates within which it is likely that the appropriate rate will fall. We will assume that the selected range is 15–20 per cent.

The present values of the earnings stream are £157 620 when discounted at 15 per cent and £127 063 when discounted at 20 per cent, while the present values of the earnings of XYZ for the next 10 years, should it continue as an independent business, are £116 926 when discounted at 15 per cent and £93 598 when discounted at 20 per cent. The value of the business of XYZ on its own can therefore be seen to be less than its value to ADG at any given discount rate between 15 and 20 per cent; therefore agreement should readily be reached as to a purchase price since it will be advantageous for the owner of XYZ to sell at £117 000 or above and for ADG to buy at £127 000 or below, given that 15 per cent and 20 per cent represent the extremes of the possible discount rates applicable to this type of business.

As can be seen in the example, if the business can be put to a more profitable use by the new management, and if there is not a substantial difference between the discount rates used by the parties, it is likely that a price for the business will be agreed. If we retain the assumption about the comparability of the discount rates, it is clear that the converse holds, in that if the business were to be employed less profitably by the potential purchaser it is not likely that agreement could be reached, as the business would be worth more to the potential seller than it is to the potential buyer. If the parties employ widely different discount rates the above conclusions may not apply.

Suppose, for example, that the owner of XYZ was content with a return of 10 per cent on capital. Then, discounting the earnings stream of XYZ at 10 per cent, this would produce a present value of £149 606. If ADG expected a 20 per cent return on its investment then the value it would put upon the acquisition of the business would be £127 064. In such a case it would be impossible to fix a price which would not lead to a worsening of the perceived positions of one or both parties.

The value of control of a business

For a sole proprietor there is no question of ownership of a business without control, but for a partnership or a company it is possible to share in the ownership of a business without having control of the business. In using the word 'control' in this context we mean that the individual in question is able to determine the business policy or any particular action of the business without resort to persuading other owners of the business that this course of action is desirable.

When a business is jointly owned, the value of the business to the controlling owner is in most cases greater, proportionately to the holding, than to the other owners. This has been clearly established in law in valuing shares for capital transfer tax purposes where a controlling interest in a company was recognised as carrying a higher proportionate value than a minority interest. The law, however, merely follows upon observed fact, since the valuation is based upon what a potential purchaser would be likely to pay for the holding being valued, given that there was access to all the information that would be available to a prudent potential purchaser. Thus, we must examine the underlying reasons for which a controlling interest in a business is proportionately more valuable than a minority interest.

The most obvious reason for this higher valuation is that the controlling interest enables the owner of that interest to arrange the affairs of the business in a way that best suits his/her own circumstances. This may appear to offend the profit maximising principle which is assumed to apply to businesses, but it does take us one further step in the analysis and certainly explains why, as we have seen in Chapter 13, FRS 8 requires disclosure of the existence of and transactions with related parties. The assumption of profit maximisation for a business is an extension of the principle of the maximising of utility for the individual. These two criteria do not necessarily coincide, but provided there are many owners with many preferences, it is a practicable solution to suggest that if maximum profit is available then the individuals will be able to get the most utility from spending it. However, the crux of the problem can be illustrated by supposing there is only one owner and examining the maximising of the owner's utility and the profit of the firm separately.

Assume that there are two possible paths for the business to follow, producing the following dividend flows given differing reinvestment patterns:

Year no.	1	2	3	4	5
Path 1 dividends (£000)	5	7	12	17	20
Path 2 dividends (£000)	11	11	11	11	11

If the cost of capital to the business is 10 per cent then the present value of these dividends will be £43 376 if path 1 is followed and £41 700 if path 2 is followed. The profit maximisation assumption would indicate that path 1 should be followed.

Suppose, however, that the owner of the business requires more money in the early years and, if she is not able to take this money from the business, she must borrow it at 25 per cent interest and is prepared to do so. This means that the owner's discount rate is 25 per cent and therefore the present value of the dividends stream to her is £28 140 if path 1 is followed and £29 580 if path 2 is followed. She will choose to follow path 2.

Thus, the value to this individual from controlling the business, and thereby directing the business to follow path 2 rather than path 1, is £29 580 − £28 140 = £1440.

Now it is clear that if this business was owned by many shareholders and run by a professional manager it should follow path 1 because the manager could show that by reinvesting profits at a high rate in the early period the firm would be better off by £43 376 − £41 700, i.e. by £1676 in present value terms, whereas the individual we have considered would be worse off by £1140 if she were the sole recipient of these dividends.

Thus, we have shown that the net present value of the dividends stream from the business is dependent upon the rate at which the stream is discounted. Therefore the value which will be placed by an individual upon a business will depend upon her expected income stream and her own time preference rate. The control of a firm enables an individual to co-ordinate the discount rate used by the firm with that which optimises her own welfare.

There are, of course, other advantages to having control of a business, which are concerned with status and the ability to use the business to help to achieve personal goals, but the difference in value between a minority and controlling interest stems from the difference between the individual's utility maximising position and profit maximisation. The difference will, in nearly all cases, make a controlling interest in a business proportionately more valuable than a minority interest.

The valuation of a business represents, therefore, much the same type of problem as does the valuation of other assets, but because the business is a complex asset and its ownership is often diverse the estimation involved is even more difficult.

Appendix: FRS 14 'Earnings per share'

The importance of the earnings per share (EPS) measure and the uses to which it is put have been discussed in the main body of this chapter. It is therefore not surprising to find that one of the first statements of standard accounting practice issued by the ASC covered this topic. The standard was SSAP 3 *Earnings per Share*, that was issued in 1972. While the calculation of Earnings per Share has had to change over the years, in particular because of changes in tax law and because of the gradual elimination of the special treatment of extraordinary items, the basic principles underlying SSAP 3 have survived remarkably well. In fact in the section dealing with the development of its successor, FRS 14, also called, *Earnings per Share*, the ASB accepts that SSAP 3 is operating reasonably effectively and that the only reason for revising it are international developments in the area.[8]

The debate about whether the earnings measure used in the EPS should, or should not, include extraordinary items is no longer an issue with the virtual elimination of these items, while the removal of Advance Corporation Tax means that the level of taxation no longer could be dependent on the level of dividends and hence this particular complication, in deciding what should be the numerator in the EPS calculation, is no longer relevant.

Since the only reason why the reporting of EPS is of such importance is its use in calculating a security's Price Earnings ratio, FRS 14 covers only those entities whose ordinary shares or potential ordinary shares are publicly traded and those entities that are in the process of issuing ordinary or potential ordinary shares in public security markets. Potential ordinary shares are financial instruments or rights that may entitle the owner to ordinary shares, these include convertible preference shares, options and rights granted under employee share plans.

The earnings to be used in the calculation are the net profit or loss for the period attributable to ordinary shareholders after deducting dividends and other appropriations in respect of non-equity shares. In the case of cumulative preference shares the amount to be deducted is the maximum dividend for the period irrespective of whether or not the full dividend was declared.

The definition of earnings is pretty straight forward, the complications arise with the denominator, the number of shares and these relate to actual and possible changes in the capital structure that have, or may change, the number of equity shares in issue.

We will first discuss the treatment of actual changes in capital structure, which we shall do by considering the following hypothetical examples.

Assume that MM plc's earnings attributable to equity shareholders for 20X5 is £2.0 million and that at 1 January, the start of its financial year, it had in issue 20 million ordinary shares at 25p each and that on 1 October it issued a further 4 million 25p ordinary shares. What is the EPS for 20X5? The answer depends on the nature of the issue, specifically whether it was a scrip (or bonus) issue or whether the issue was for cash (or other consideration) and, if for cash, etc., whether the issue was at, or below, the market price.

Scrip issue

A scrip issue does not raise extra cash and merely represents a rearrangement of he equity interest in a company in that a transfer is made from reserves to equity share capital. There are simply more shares in issue at the end of the year than there were at the beginning and, hence, to show the EPS appropriate to the new capital structure, all that is required is to apportion the earnings over the shares in issue at the year end, 24 million, and thus the EPS is (£2 000 000 ÷ 24 000 000) × 100 = 8.3p.

To assist comparability, the EPS for the corresponding period should be adjusted accordingly. Similar considerations apply if shares are split into shares of a smaller nominal value.

---

[8] FRS 14, p. 48.

Issue at full market price

Let us now assume that the issue of shares was made at the full market price, while recognising that in practice such an issue is nowadays a rare event, as most issues for cash take the form of rights issues to existing shareholders at a price below that which prevails on the market. To calculate the EPS where there has been an issue at the full market price all that is necessary is to calculate the weighted average number of shares in issue in the course of the year and divide the result into the total earnings of the year. The average is weighted to take account of the timing of the share issue.

In this case the company had 20 million shares in issue for 9 months and 24 million for 3 months. The appropriate weightings to be applied are hence $\frac{3}{4}$ and $\frac{1}{4}$ and the weighted average is $\frac{3}{4} \times 20\,000\,000 + \frac{1}{4} \times 24\,000\,000 = 21\,000\,000$ with the new EPS $(£2\,000\,000/21\,000\,000) \times 100 = 9.5\text{p}$.

It will be noted that this figure exceeds the 8.3p per share in the scrip issue example and it will be instructive to consider why this is so. A company which makes a scrip issue raises no extra resources and hence, all other things being equal, will not increase its earnings. Thus, the only effect of the scrip issue is to divide the earnings over a greater number of shares. In contrast, if shares are issued for cash, extra resources are obtained which, it is hoped, will increase earnings in the future. If the new investment generates the same rate of return as the existing assets of the business, then, all other things being equal, the EPS after an issue at the full market price will be the same as that which prevailed before the issue. However, in practice it will take some time to deploy the additional resources and in the first instance the additional cash will earn a small or even a negative return, hence the issue of shares for cash will normally reduce the EPS (from that which applied before the issue) until the new investment comes on stream.

Rights issue

A rights issue lies somewhere between the two extremes of a scrip issue and an issue at the full market price in that it combines elements of both, since while additional cash is raised the original shares lose some of their value.

In order to distinguish between the two elements of a rights issue it is necessary to find what is called the *theoretical ex-rights price*. This is the price per share following the issue which would make the stock market value of the company immediately after the rights issue equal to the sum of the market value before the announcement of the issue and the proceeds of the rights issue.[9] Once the theoretical ex-rights price is determined, the EPS calculation can be made on the assumption that there were two transactions: a scrip issue followed by an issue at the new market price.[10]

Let us assume that a company, RIG plc, has in issue 12 000 shares which had a market price of £2 and 8 months after the start of the year makes a rights issue of 1 for every 3 shares held (a 1 for 3 issue) at a discount of 25 per cent, i.e. 4000 shares were issued at a price of £1.50 each so raising £6000. The theoretical ex-rights price, x, is given by:

$$16\,000\,x = 12\,000 \times £2 + 4000 \times £1.5$$
$$16\,000\,x = £24\,000 + £6000$$
$$x = £1.875$$

---

[9] The actual price per share following the issue is not likely to be equal to the theoretical ex-rights price as the actual price is likely to be affected by the market's expectations of future results and dividend policy. It might, for example, be thought that the total dividend per share would at least be held constant following the issue.

[10] Or the other way round.

We need to find the size of a hypothetical scrip issue which would, all other things being equal, have reduced the market price per share from £2 to £1.875.

Let X be the number of shares in issue following the scrip issue

$$\text{then } X \times £1.875 = 12\,000 \times £2$$

$$\text{or } X = 12\,000 \times \frac{£2}{£1.875} = 12\,800$$

Thus the scrip issue would be such as to increase the number of shares in issue from 12 000 to (12 000 × 2/1.875). We should note that the factor 2/1.875 is the:

$$\frac{\text{Actual market price (or fair value) before the issue}}{\text{Theoretical ex-rights price}}$$

We can now divide the rights issue into its two elements (a) the scrip issue and (b) the issue at the market price (or, in this case, at the theoretical ex-rights price).

Thus:

(i)   The company started with 12 000 shares.
(ii) The hypothetical scrip issue increased the shares to 12 000 × 2/1.875 or an additional 800 shares.
(iii) The hypothetical issue of 3200 shares at £1.875 raised £6000.

Thus the company finished with 16 000 shares.

To calculate the EPS it is necessary to remember that, in the case of a scrip issue, the earnings were simply divided by the number of shares ranking for dividend at the end of the year (irrespective of the date of the scrip issue), whereas in the case of an issue at market price the average number of shares was used (weighted on the basis of the time of the issue). To combine these two methods we draw a line after the hypothetical scrip issue and say that at the end of 8 months there were 12 800 (12 000 × 2/1.875) shares in issue but, as the increase was due to a scrip issue, we will calculate the EPS on the assumption that the company had 12 800 shares for the whole of the 8-month period. Thus, the weighted average number of shares will be calculated on the basis that the company had 12 000 × 2/1.875 shares for 8 months and 16 000 shares for 4 months. The weighted average number of shares is then:

$$12\,000 \times \frac{2}{1.875} \times \frac{2}{3} + 16\,000 \times \frac{1}{3} = 13\,867$$

and, if the earnings for the year were £1664, the EPS would be 12p.

The method described above is that set out in Para. 24 of FRS 14 that states that the factor which should be used to inflate the number of shares prior to the issue to adjust for the bonus element should be:

$$\frac{\text{Fair value per share immediately before the exercise of the rights}}{\text{Theoretical ex-rights value per share}}$$

In order to aid comparability, the EPS figure for the prior year needs to be adjusted to take account of the hypothetical scrip issue. If 12 000 shares were in issue for the whole of the preceding year then, for the purposes of restating the EPS, this figure be increased to 12 800, i.e. to 12 000 × (fair value)/(theoretical ex-rights price). Actually, a short cut can be taken as the same result can be obtained by multiplying the original EPS by the recipocal of the above ratio, i.e. by (theoretical ex-rights price)/(fair value).[11]

Dilution

If, at the balance sheet date, the company has contracted to issue shares at some time in the future, the effect may be to dilute (reduce) the EPS in future. The same might happen if at the balance sheet date the company has already issued shares which have not yet ranked for dividend (and hence which have been excluded from the EPS calculation) but which may do so in the future. In such cases FRS 14 requires that the fully diluted EPS be shown on the face of the profit and loss account together with the basic EPS. In addition:

(a) equal prominence should be given to both the basic and fully diluted EPS;
(b) the basis of calculation of the basic and diluted EPS figure should be disclosed.

Examples of financial instruments that might be converted to ordinary shares include options, warrants and convertible preference shares.

Note the use of the word *diluted*, if the potential change in the capital structure will lead to an increase in the EPS there is no need to calculate and display a different EPS figure. The test of whether a potential ordinary share is dilutive can be illustrated by reference to the conversion of preference shares.

There are two impacts on the EPS figure of such a change. The profit available to equity shareholders will increase because of the elimination of the preference dividend and this will increase the EPS but, as a result of the operation, there are more equity shares in issue and this will reduce the EPS. It will all depend on where the balance falls as to whether the convertible preference shares need to be treated as *dilutive potential ordinary shares*. Consider the following example.

Suppose that a company has a net profit available to ordinary (equity) shareholders of £2 million and has £5 million shares outstanding. The EPS is 40 pence.

Further suppose that the company has in issue £3 million convertible 15% preference shares that are convertible:

case 1, at one ordinary for one preference;
case 2, at one ordinary for three preference.

In either case the conversation would increase the net profit attributable to ordinary shareholders by £0.45 to £2.45 but in case 1 the number of ordinary shares would increase to 8 million and the EPS would become 31 pence, while in case 2 the number of ordinary shares would only increase to 6 million which would produce an EPS of 41 pence.

Hence, only in case 1 do we have dilutive potential ordinary shares and would be required to disclose a full diluted EPS alongside the basic EPS.

In determining whether potential ordinary shares are, or are not, dilutive the yardstick to be used is the profit or loss from continuing operations. Since by definition discontinued operations have ceased they are not relevant to the question of whether or not the issue of the shares will of itself reduce EPS.

---

[11] Let P be the original EPS, P' the restated EPS, E the earnings, S the orginal number of shares in issue and F the ratio of the cum rights to the theoretical ex-rights price. Then:

$$P = \frac{E}{S} \quad \text{and} \quad P' = \frac{E}{SF} = P \times \frac{1}{F}$$

If a company has more than class of potential ordinary in existence the order in which the exercise is done may effect the outcome. Therefore, in order to maximise the dilution of basic earnings per share, each issue or series of potential ordinary shares is considered in sequence from the most dilutive to the least dilutive (FRS 14, Para. 61).

Contingently issuable share

As the name suggests *contingently issuable shares* are those which will be issued depending on the outcome of a single or series of events. The standard makes it clear in a number of places that the EPS measure that emerges from the application of the rules of FRS 14 is a historical measure and not a prediction about the future. To give an example, suppose that a group of senior executives are offered shares if the average profit of a three year period exceeds £40 million (assume for the sake of simplicity that a loss of any amount would be treated as zero for the purposes of the calculation) and that the profits for the first two years of the period amount to £115 million that is £5 million short of the target. It does seem pretty certain that, short of an unexpected disaster, the goal will be achieved and the shares issued, but FRS 14 would not take these shares into account as it treats the end of the reporting period as the end of the contingency period. The ASB accepts that there are arguments for adopting a different approach based on a projection of the future, but comes down against mainly, it seems, because it is not the method chosen by the IASC.

It will not come as a surprise to learn that there are no fundamental differences between FRS 14 and its international equivalent IAS 33 *Earnings per share*.

Recommended reading

N. Eastway, H. Booth and K. Eamer, *Practical Share Evaluation*, 4th edn. Butterworths, London, 1998.

C.G. Glover, *Valuation of Unquoted Companies*, 2nd edn, Gee & Co., London, 1992.

C.G. Glover, 'Valuation of unquoted shares', *Accountants' Digest No. 299*, Accountancy Books, London, 1993.

A. Gregory, *Valuing Companies: Analysing Business Worth*, Woodhead-Faulkner, Hemel Hempstead, 1992.

PART 4

Accounting and price changes

15 Accounting for inflation

Overview   The traditional historical cost system of accounting has serious shortcomings when prices are changing. While these shortcomings are extremely serious when the rate of inflation is high, they do not disappear when the inflation rate is low nor are they corrected in any systematic way by piecemeal revaluations. The cumulative effect of a low annual rate of inflation may be highly significant and, even with an inflation rate close to zero, the rate of change of specific prices may be high.

Accountants in the UK experimented with different methods of accounting for price change in the 1970s and 1980s. We outline these experiments in the first part of this chapter before examining, in some depth, the system of Current Purchasing Power (CPP) accounting.

CPP accounting requires the adjustment of historical cost accounts for changes in the value of money as measured by a general price index such as the Retail Price Index in the UK. The system has the advantages of measuring all assets, liabilities, revenues and expenses in the same currency, £s on the balance sheet date, and of measuring and disclosing gains and losses from holding monetary liabilities and assets in an inflationary or, indeed, deflationary period.

The figures for non-monetary assets which emerge in a CPP balance sheet are usually far from the current values of those assets and this perceived defect led to experimentation with Current Cost Accounting (CCA) to which we turn in the ensuing chapters.

Introduction

In Chapter 3 'What is profit?' we suggested that the traditional system of accounting, based on historical cost asset measurement and financial capital maintenance, suffers from numerous shortcomings when tested against the purposes which financial reporting might sensibly be regarded as serving. This observation is not a new one[1] but the case for reforming accounts to reflect price changes was not widely accepted in the UK, especially by accountants, until the 1970s.

The high rate of inflation which was a feature of the UK economy of that period highlighted the limitations of the conventional accounting model and, when the annual rate of inflation rose to 25 per cent in 1974, it was no longer possible for accountants and governments to ignore the phenomena.

---

[1] *See* Sir R. Edwards, 'The nature and measurement of income', originally published as a series of articles in *The Accountant*, July–October 1938; reprinted in *Studies in Accounting*, W.T. Baxter and S. Davidson (eds.), ICAEW, London, 1977, pp. 96–140. This is only one, and by no means the earliest, of many references that could have been selected. In this classic paper Sir Ronald Edwards, an accountant who was both a university professor and successful businessman, clearly outlined many of the problems inherent in conventional accounting and discussed many important matters which are still controversial issues.

A striking example of the consequences of inflation on historical cost accounts was provided by the ASC in its 1986 publication *Accounting for the Effects of Changing Prices: a Handbook*, which will henceforth be referred to as the ASC Handbook. The example compared dividend distributions expressed as a percentage of (a) historical cost profit and (b) a measure of profit based on current cost principles. The results were derived from large samples of companies and covered the period 1980 to 1984, a period in which the UK had significantly lower inflation than in the 1970s. The results are shown in Table 15.1.

Table 15.1 Dividend distribution expressed as percentages of profit derived on (a) historical cost and (b) current cost principles

	Historical cost (%)	*Current cost (%)*
1980	37	97
1981	40	111
1982	48	130
1983	50	94
1984	52	64

Note that using an historical cost perception it appeared that company directors had on average pursued prudent distribution policies, but the results based on current costs indicate that in some years the average dividend exceeded the amount required to be retained in the business to sustain its existing scale of operations.

So it seems that in periods of high inflation business financial results based on historical cost asset valuations and money financial capital maintenance paint a misleading and distorted picture of the financial progress of companies. But does the case for accounting reform disappear in periods when inflation is low? It is certainly true that support for reform on the part of most businesspeople and professional accountants does depend on the rate of inflation. When inflation is high there is a strong pressure for change and exposure drafts and standards are issued, whereas when inflation falls the advocates of the status quo gain supremacy and the exposure drafts and standards are withdrawn. But the case for reform does not disappear.[2]

In its 1986 Handbook the ASC stated, 'The limitations of historical cost accounts exist not only in periods of relatively rapid price changes but also when prices are changing more slowly.'[3] Three reasons were advanced to support this view:

(a) Even with low annual rates of inflation, the cumulative effect of inflation over time is significant; for example, with 5 per cent inflation, prices double every 14 years.
(b) The accounting effects of previous high rates of inflation persist over a number of years.
(c) Rates of change of specific prices may be substantial even when the rate of inflation is relatively low.

[2] Michael Mumford, 'The end of a familiar inflation accounting cycle', *Accounting and Business Research*, Vol. 9, No. 34, Spring 1978, pp. 98–104.
[3] *Accounting for the Effects of Changing Prices: a Handbook*, ASC, London, 1986, p. 11.

The progress of accounting reform

The path towards accounting reform was both long and tortuous and, so far, unsuccessful. As far as Britain is concerned, the path is outlined in Figure 15.1 (see p. 454), which can be used as a guide to this and subsequent chapters.

There are two lines shown in Figure 15.1. One represents the current purchasing power (CPP) method, which takes account of general price changes but which ignores specific price changes; in terms of the analysis presented in Chapter 3 it is a system of accounting based on the combination of the adjusted historical cost asset valuation basis and the maintenance of real financial capital. A detailed exposition of CPP accounting is provided later in this chapter. The other line represents an approach generally known as current cost accounting (CCA) which, in the United Kingdom, combines a variant of the replacement cost approach to valuation with either the operating or the real financial capital maintenance concepts. This approach will be discussed in more detail in Chapter 16.

CPP accounting retains most of the significant features of historical cost accounting, and the only real change is the replacement of the money unit of measurement by the purchasing power unit. It will be seen that when compared to a system which attempts to measure current values the CPP model involves a far less radical departure from the conventional method, and it is perhaps not surprising that the first tentative steps on the path to accounting reform taken by the British accountancy profession were on the CPP route; much the same occurred in the United States and Australia.[4]

In 1968 the Research Foundation of the ICAEW published *Accounting for Stewardship in a Period of Inflation*. The title is instructive in that it suggests a far more restrictive view of the objectives of financial accounts than is accepted nowadays and does illustrate the extent of the changes that have since taken place. The methods outlined in that document were not original. They had been described in English by Sweeney in 1936[5] and his book was itself based on work done in Germany during the period of hyperinflation which followed the First World War. The significance of the publication was that it was produced by a body associated with a leading professional accounting institute and indicated that that body was apparently prepared to initiate reform. The seeds took a long time to germinate, and the world had to wait until 1973 for the publication of ED 8 by the ASSC. ED 8 proposed that companies should be required to publish, along with their conventional accounts, supplementary statements which would, in effect, be their profit and loss accounts and balance sheets based on CPP principles. ED 8 was followed by the issue of Provisional Statement of Standard Accounting Practice (PSSAP) 7, in May 1974. The inclusion of the word 'provisional' in the title of this standard (the only occasion on which this was done by the ASSC) reflected the uncertainties in the mind of the accountancy profession on this matter, since it meant that companies were requested rather than required to comply with the standard.

---

[4] For example, in the United States the FASB (the US equivalent of the British ASB) produced an Exposure Draft in December 1974 which was similar in content to ED 8, but the Securities Exchange Commission (a US Government Agency) in 1976 called for the disclosure by larger companies of additional information concerning the replacement costs of fixed assets and stock. The subsequent US standard, FAS No. 33 'Financial reporting and changing prices', September 1979, required supplementary disclosure of both types of information, but this statement was superseded by FAS No. 89, with the same title, in December 1986. This encouraged, rather than required, such disclosure.

[5] F.N. Sweeney, *op. cit.*

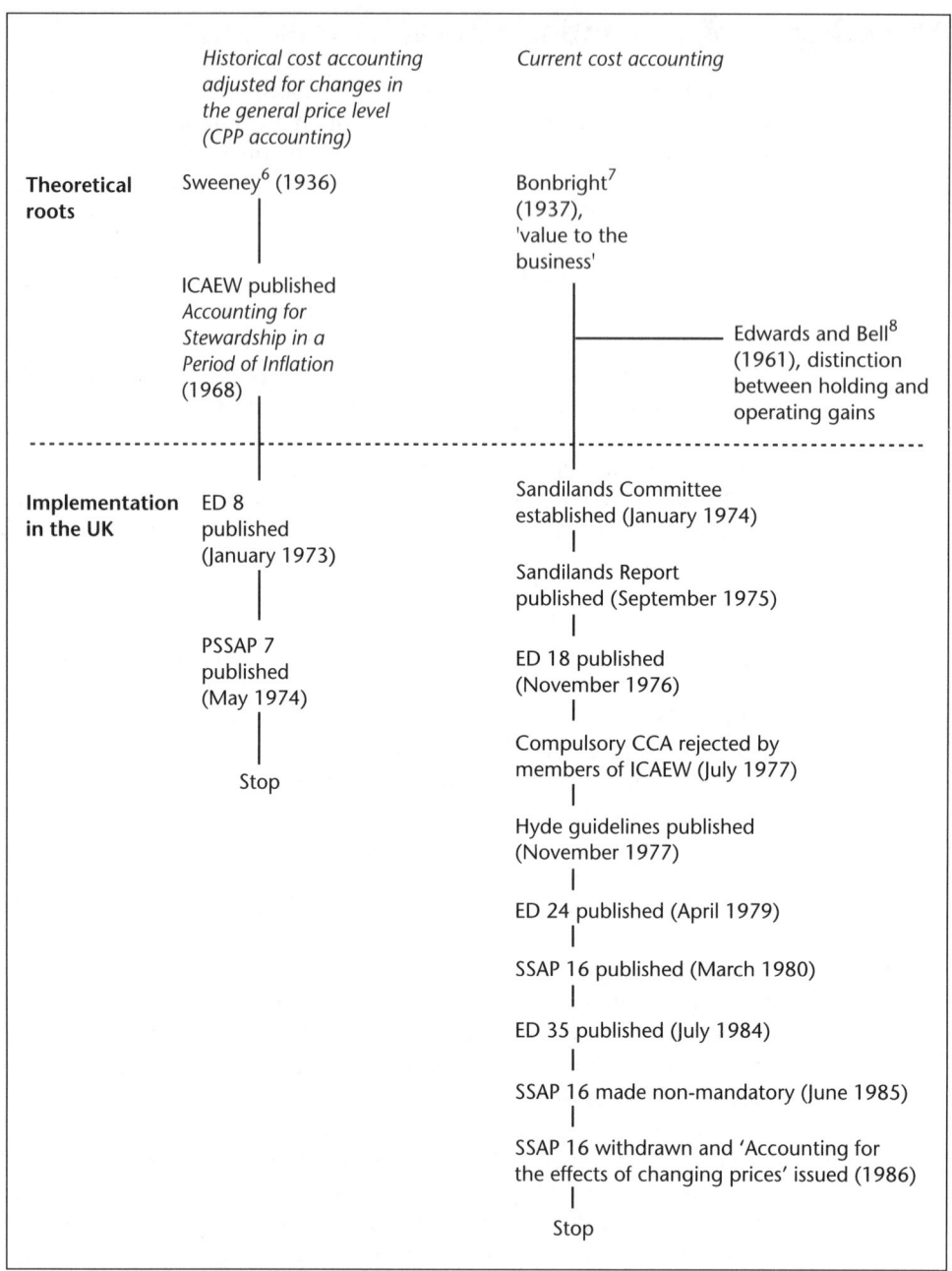

Fig. 15.1 The path towards account reform

[6] F.N. Sweeney, *Stabilized Accounts*, Harper, New York, 1936 (reprinted by Arno Press, New York, 1977).

[7] J.C. Bonbright, *The Valuation of Property*, Michie, Charlottesville, Va., 1937 (reprinted 1965).

[8] E.O. Edwards and P.W. Bell, *The Theory and Measurement of Business Income*, University of California Press, Stanford, Calif., 1961.

Many users of accounting reports, including the government, were dissatisfied with this approach. Consequently, the government established its own committee of enquiry into inflation accounting in January 1974, i.e. after the issue of ED 8. The committee was chaired by Sir Francis Sandilands, and its report (usually referred to as the Sandilands Report) was issued in September 1975.[9] The committee recommended the adoption of a system of accounting known as 'current cost accounting' which is, as will be shown later, a very different creature from CPP accounting. As a result of the publication of the Sandilands Report, the ASC abandoned its own proposals and set up a working party, the Inflation Accounting Steering Group (IASG) to prepare an initial Statement of Standard Accounting Practice based on Sandilands' proposals. The outcome of this group's labours was ED 18, 'Current Cost Accounting', which was published in November 1976. This publication came under a good deal of attack from many quarters, including those who supported the main principles of current cost accounting (CCA). The Exposure Draft was considered by many to be unnecessarily complicated and to deal with too many subsidiary issues. The draft was also attacked by many rank and file – some would say backwoods – members of the ICAEW, and their efforts resulted in the passing of a resolution in July 1977 by members of the Institute which rejected any compulsory introduction of CCA.

This did not halt the advance of CCA. The government, in a discussion document issued in July 1977 (*The Future of Company Reports*), reiterated its support for the adoption of CCA, while in November 1977 the accountancy profession issued a set of interim recommendations to cover the period until a revised set of detailed proposals could be formulated. These recommendations were called the Hyde guidelines after the name of the chairman of the committee responsible for the recommendations. A second Exposure Draft, ED 24, was published in April 1979 and was followed by the issue of SSAP 16 in March 1980. It was intended that SSAP 16 would prevail for three years while the effect of the introduction of CCA was evaluated.

With certain exceptions, SSAP 16 applied to all companies listed on the Stock Exchange and to large unlisted companies. Such companies were required to publish current cost accounts together with historical cost accounts or historical cost information. The intention was that primacy should be given to the current cost accounts although, as we shall see, things did not turn out in the way intended by the ASC.

Current cost accounts did not replace the historical cost accounts and they were often presented, and perhaps even more often regarded, as being supplementary to the main or, as many no doubt believed, the 'real' accounts. Many companies simply failed to comply with the provisions of SSAP 16, and although auditors were obliged to refer to the absence of current cost accounts in the audit report, such references were not regarded as important qualifications and the companies concerned did not seem to suffer as a consequence of their non-compliance.

Following the evaluation of the impact of SSAP 16, ED 35 was published in July 1984. The basic principles of CCA were maintained, albeit with some modifications, but ED 35 proposed that companies should only be required to produce one set of accounts, based on historical costs with notes showing the effect of changing prices. The proposals of ED 35 were not implemented but instead SSAP 16 was made non-mandatory in June 1985. This was, however, not the end of the matter, for in 1986 SSAP 16 was withdrawn and the ASC published its Handbook, *Accounting for the*

---

[9] *Report of the Inflation Accounting Committee*, Cmnd 6225, HMSO, London, 1975.

Effects of Changing Prices. At that time the Presidents of the five leading accountancy bodies in the UK issued a joint statement endorsing the view of the ASC that companies should appraise and, where material, report the effect of changing prices. In addition the Presidents supported the view that accounting for the effect of changing prices is of great importance and agreed that a suitable accounting standard should be developed. Numerous reasons can be advanced to explain why it has not proved possible to introduce a generally acceptable system of current cost accounting. Prominent among them is the lack of agreement on the part of those advocating change as to how to account for changing prices, and the associated problem that very many businesspeople and accountants do not understand the basic principles underlying current cost accounting.

We shall continue this chapter with a discussion of the CPP method and will return to current cost accounting in Chapter 16.

Current purchasing power (CPP) accounting

Introduction

The elements of CPP accounting were introduced in Chapter 3 – that is the adjusted historical cost basis of valuation coupled with profit measurement based on the maintenance of real financial capital. Before describing how these can be combined to produce a coherent accounting model it is necessary to consider how, and from whose point of view, the purchasing power of money should be measured.

The prices of different goods and services change by different amounts, and the problem faced by those responsible for measuring changes in the purchasing power of money is to find a suitable average value to reflect the different individual price changes which have taken place during the period under review. This could be done by considering all the different goods and services which are traded in the country during the period and to compare their prices with those prevailing in the comparison or base period. This is a massive task, but it is possible to arrive at the required answer by indirect methods, as is done in the United States in the calculation of the gross domestic product implicit price deflator.

An alternative approach is to select a sample of goods and services, measure the changes in their prices, and then average them. This method is used to construct the Index of Retail Prices (RPI), which is based on the price changes which affect 'middle income' households. In order to construct the index it is necessary to assign weights to the various price changes to take account of their relative importance. These weights are based on the spending patterns of a sample of householders which is drawn so as to exclude households with incomes which are significantly higher and significantly lower than the average.

One of the major provisions of PSSAP 7 was the stipulation that changes in the purchasing power of money should be measured by reference to the RPI. The consequence of this proposal was that changes in purchasing power were not to be measured from the point of view of the individual firm or even all firms but from the point of view of individual consumers. Thus it was the intention that CPP accounts should not be regarded as providing proxies to current value accounts, but rather as restatements of the conventional historical cost accounts in terms which attempted to adjust for the effect of inflation on shareholders and other individuals.

The basic principle underlying CPP accounts is that all monetary amounts should be converted to pounds of CPP in a manner which is analogous to the way in which sums expressed in different foreign currencies are translated to a common base. Assume that we are attempting to measure the CPP profit for a transaction which involved the purchase of goods for £2000 in January 1998 and their sale for £3000 in December 1998. The RPI was 159.5 at the date of purchase and 164.4 at the date of sale. If we wish to measure the profit in terms of purchasing power at December 1998 we would need to convert the £2000, which represented January 1998 purchasing power, in terms of December 1998 purchasing power. In order to carry out such calculations it will be helpful if we use symbols which indicate the purchasing power associated with the monetary amount; we will do this by specifying that £(Jan 98) means January 1998 pounds, and so on.

The calculation of CPP profit for the above transaction could then be shown as follows:

		£(Dec 98)
Sales		3 000
Purchases, £(Jan 98) 2 000 × $\frac{164.4}{159.5}$		2 061
		939

The equation:

$$£(\text{Jan 98})\ 2\,000 \times \frac{164.4}{159.55} = £(\text{Dec 98})\ 2\,061$$

means that a consumer would require £2061 in December 1998 in order to be able to command the same purchasing power as was available from the possession of £2000 in January 1998.

The consequence of the extension of the basic CPP principle to the profit and loss account is that all items will be expressed in terms of current (i.e. year-end) purchasing power, and the same will be true in the balance sheet. Thus, all items in the balance sheet will have to be converted in terms of year-end purchasing power except the so-called monetary assets and liabilities which are automatically expressed in such terms. Example 15.1 illustrates the preparation of CPP accounts in the absence of monetary assets and liabilities. To provide clear illustrations in this and subsequent examples, we will assume rates of inflation higher than those which have been experienced in the very recent past.

Example 15.1

Bell Limited's historical cost and CPP balance sheets at 31 December 19X6 (on which date a hypothetical RPI was 120) are given below:

Bell Limited
Balance sheet as at 31 December 19X6

	Historical cost £	Note	CPP £(31 Dec X6)
Fixed assets			
Cost	10 000	(a)	12 000
Accumulated depreciation	4 000	(b)	4 800
Carried forward	6 000		7 200

457

	Historical cost	Note	CPP
	£		£(31 Dec X6)
Brought forward	6 000		7 200
Stock	3 300	(c)	3 356
	£9 300	£(31 Dec 19X6)	10 556
Share capital	4 000	(d)	4 800
Retained earnings	5 300	(e)	5 756
	£9 300	£(31 Dec 19X6)	10 556

Notes:

(a) The fixed assets were purchased for £10 000 on 1 January 19X3 when the RPI = 100:

$$£(1 \text{ Jan X3}) \ 10\,000 \times \frac{120}{100} = £(31 \text{ Dec X6}) \ 12\,000$$

(b) Bell Limited depreciates its fixed assets on a straight-line basis over 10 years (assuming a zero scrap value). Thus, at the end of 19X6, four-tenths of the asset has been written off and the accumulated depreciation figure is thus:

$$4/10 \text{ of } £(31 \text{ Dec X6}) \ 12\,000 = £(31 \text{ Dec X6}) \ 4800$$

(c) The company's stock was purchased for £3300 on 30 September 19X6 when the RPI was 118:

$$£(30 \text{ Sep. X6}) \ 3300 \times \frac{120}{118} = £(31 \text{ Dec. X6}) \ 3356$$

(d) The share capital consists of 4000 £1 ordinary shares which were issued on 1 January 19X3 when the RPI was 100:

$$£(1 \text{ Jan. X3}) \ 4000 \times \frac{120}{100} = £(31 \text{ Dec. X6}) \ 4800$$

(e) Had CPP accounts been prepared in the past, the CPP retained earnings would have emerged in the same way that retained earnings emerge in the historical cost accounts. In this case the CPP retained earnings is found by treating it as the balancing figure in the CPP balance sheet. It is not possible to find the CPP retained earnings from its historical cost equivalent as the relationship between them depends on the aggregate of the differences between the CPP and historical cost figures of all the balance sheet items.

During 19X7 Bell Limited engaged in the following transactions:

(A) On 31 March 19X7 it sold half its stock for cash of £(31 Mar X7) 5500. £(31 Mar X7) 4400 of the proceeds were used to purchase additional stock while the balance was paid out as a dividend.

(B) On 1 July 19X7 one-quarter of the 1 January 19X7 stock was sold for £(1 July X7) 2750; the proceeds were used to pay for overhead expenses which may be assumed to accrue evenly over the year.

The RPI moved as follows:

Date	Index
1 January 19X7	120
31 March 19X7	121
1 July 19X7 (which may be assumed to be the average value for the year)	132
31 December 19X7	143

The CPP profit and loss account for the year ended 31 December 19X7 is given below:

Bell Limited
Profit and loss account

	£(31 Dec X7)	£(31 Dec X7)
Sales, £(31 Mar X7) $5500 \times \dfrac{143}{121}$	6 500	
Sales, £(1 July X7) $2750 \times \dfrac{143}{132}$	2 979	9 479
less Cost of sales		
Opening stock,		
£(30 Sep X6) $3300 \times \dfrac{143}{118}$	3 999	
Purchases,		
£(31 Mar X7) $4400 \times \dfrac{143}{121}$	5 200	
	9 199	
less Closing stock,		
£(30 Sep X6) $825 \times \dfrac{143}{118}$		
+ £(31 Mar X7) $4400 \times \dfrac{143}{121}$		
	6 200	2 999
Gross profit		6 480
less Overheads		
£(1 Jul X7) $2750 \times \dfrac{143}{132}$	2 979	
Depreciation,		
£1(1 Jan X3) $10\,000 \times \dfrac{1}{10} \times \dfrac{143}{100}$	1 430	4 409
Net profit		2 071
less Dividends paid		
£(31 Mar X7) $1100 \times \dfrac{143}{121}$		1 300
		771
Retained earnings, 1 Jan X7,		
£(1 Jan X7) $5756 \times \dfrac{143}{120}$		6 859
Retained earnings, 31 Dec X7		7 630

Bell Limited
CPP balance sheet as at 31 December 19X7

	£(31 Dec X7)	£(31 Dec X7)
Fixed assets:		
Cost, £(1 Jan X3) $10\,000 \times \dfrac{143}{100}$	14 300	
Accumulated depreciation,		
£(1 Jan X3) $5000 \times \dfrac{143}{100}$	7 150	7 150
Stock:		
£(30 Sep X6) $825 \times \dfrac{143}{118}$	1 000	
£(31 Mar X7) $4400 \times \dfrac{143}{121}$	5 200	6 200
		13 350
Share capital,		
£(1 Jan X3) $4000 \times \dfrac{143}{100}$		5 720
Retained earnings		
(from the profit and loss account)		7 630
		13 350

Example 15.1 illustrates the necessity of identifying the dates on which the different transactions took place in order to determine the denominator of the conversion factor (i.e. the RPI at the date of the transaction): the numerator is always the same – the RPI at the balance sheet date. In the example it was practicable to deal with each sale separately, but in practice it would usually be found necessary to make some simplifying assumption, e.g. that the sales accrued evenly over the year, which would mean that the average value of the RPI would be taken as the denominator in the conversion factor. A similar approach would usually be taken in respect to purchases and overhead expenses.

The treatment of depreciation merits special attention. Note that in Example 15.1 the conversion factor used in the calculation of the depreciation expense in the profit and loss account and the fixed asset items in the balance sheet is 143/100. The denominator, 100, is the RPI at the date on which the fixed asset was acquired. It is sometimes suggested that when calculating the depreciation expense the denominator should be the average value of the RPI for the year on the grounds that 'depreciation is written off over the year'. This is indeed so, but the vital point which is missing in this argument is that the pound of depreciation which is being written off in 19X7 is a pound of 1 January 19X3, because it was pounds with a 1 January 19X3 purchasing power which were given up in exchange for the asset.

Monetary assets and liabilities

A common feature of inflation is that debtors gain in purchasing power while creditors lose.[10] And, because free lunches are not a common feature of our economy, it

---

[10] It is possible for the contracts between lenders and borrowers to be drawn up in terms of purchasing power instead of monetary units. These are often called index-linked agreements.

is – to use the terminology of game theory – a zero-sum game; the debtors' gains equal the creditors' losses. In other words, all other things being equal, one effect of inflation is to transfer purchasing power from creditors to debtors.

The reason for this is that if a person borrows money in a period of inflation, they will repay it in pounds of lower purchasing power (value) than those which were obtained when the loan was granted. The longer the loan then, so long as the inflation continues, the greater will be the difference between the values of the pounds borrowed and of the pounds repaid.

It is, of course, possible for creditors to protect themselves in some cases by increasing the interest rate to take into account the expected rate of inflation. If this is done, the market rate of interest will be based upon the market's view of the likely future rates of inflation. Thus, a quoted rate of interest may be broken down into two parts: one, which we may term the 'real' interest rate, is that which would have been charged in the absence of inflationary expectations; the balance represents the inflation premium. This point has a good deal of relevance to some important questions about the treatment of gains and losses on monetary items. We will return to this point later.[11]

If the above analysis is extended to a company, it can be said that a company will lose purchasing power in a period of inflation if, taking the year as a whole, it holds net monetary assets (in simple terms if its cash plus debtors exceeds its creditors). Conversely, it will gain in purchasing power if, on average, it is in a net monetary liability position. The calculation depends on the meaning of monetary assets and liabilities.

In PSSAP 7 monetary items were defined as 'assets, liabilities, or capital, the amounts of which were fixed by contract or statute in terms of numbers of pounds regardless of changes in the purchasing power of the pound'.[12]

Let us first consider the distinction between monetary and non-monetary liabilities. A non-monetary liability would be one in which the payment of interest, or the return on capital, or both, are not subject to a limit expressed in terms of a given number of pound coins. Such liabilities are rare in the private sector of the economy, but the British Government has issued a number of securities in which the returns are dependent on movements of the RPI. In contrast, the obligations on the part of the borrower of a monetary liability are fixed and are not affected by changes in purchasing power.

We will now turn to the distinction between monetary and non-monetary capital. Preference shares which do not entitle their owners to a share of any surplus on liquidation of the company are clearly monetary items in that the rights associated with them – the annual dividend and the repayment of principal – are subjected to upper limits which are expressed in monetary terms. Conversely, equity capital is a non-monetary item because no limits are placed on the amounts that can be paid to the owners of this type of capital. The effect of inflation on the relationship between equity and preference shareholders is similar to that on the relationship between debtors and creditors, i.e. equity shareholders will gain in purchasing power at the expense of preference shareholders because the latter's interests are fixed in money terms and will decline with a fall in the value of money. This point will be illustrated in Example 15.3.

---

[11] *See* pp. 472–3.
[12] PSSAP 7, 'Accounting for changes in the purchasing power of money', Para. 28.

Monetary assets are those assets the values of which are fixed in monetary terms, e.g. cash and debtors. Non-monetary assets, such as stock and fixed assets, are those assets the values of which may be expected to vary according to changes in the rate of inflation. Consider as examples debtors and stock, and suppose that a company has £100 invested in each of these assets. Assume that as a result of some catastrophe the RPI increases by 100 per cent (or the purchasing power of money falls by 50 per cent) overnight. The violent change in the RPI will not affect the debtors' figure in that the asset will still only realise 100 £1 coins, but it is highly probable that it will have an effect on the stock figure as the cost of the stock will be likely to rise. In other words, it would take (100 + x) £1 coins to buy the stock using the less valuable pounds.

The classification of investments into monetary and non-monetary categories often appears to be difficult, but this is not really so because we can employ the same analysis as was used in our discussion of capital. If the investment is in a fixed interest security where the dividend or interest and the repayment of principal is fixed in monetary terms, then it is a monetary item. An investment in equity shares where there is no limit on the amount that can be received is a non-monetary item.

The computation of gains and losses on a company's net monetary position

We showed earlier that one effect of inflation is to transfer purchasing power from creditors to debtors; we will now show how the amount of the creditors' loss and debtors' gains can be calculated. We will at this stage concentrate on interest-free credit and hence ignore the possibility of creditors reducing or eliminating their loss by incorporating an inflation premium in the rate of interest charged.

Suppose that A Limited borrowed £(1 Jan X4)300 from B Limited on 1 January 19X4 which is repaid on 30 September 19X4. The year end for both companies is 31 December 19X4. Assume that the RPI moved as follows:

Date:	1 January X4	30 September X4	31 December X4
Index no.:	120	150	160

We will first consider the position from A Limited's point of view. The company borrowed 300 £1 coins when the index was 120 and repaid the same number of £1 coins when the index was 150. In order to calculate the gain on purchasing power involved we need to convert one or other of the pounds borrowed or repaid so that the comparison can be made in terms of common purchasing power. We will convert the pounds borrowed in terms of 30 September 19X4 purchasing power. The calculation could then be made as follows:

	£(30 Sep X4)
Purchasing power acquired,	
£(1 Jan X4) 300 × $\frac{150}{120}$	375
Purchasing power given up on repayment of the loan	300
Gain	75

The gain in purchasing power, expressed in 30 September 19X4 purchasing power, is thus £(30 Sep X4) 75. If the company's year end is 31 December, then for the purpose of the annual accounts the gain will have to be converted to 31 December 19X4 purchasing power:

$$\text{Gain} = £(30 \text{ Sep X4}) \, 75 \times \frac{160}{150}$$

$$= £(31 \text{ Dec X4}) \, 80$$

Note that the analysis has been confined to the borrowing made by A Limited. If A Limited has used all or part of the borrowing to invest in monetary assets (which would include keeping the cash in a bank) it would experience a loss in purchasing power due to the holding of a monetary asset in a period of inflation.

If we consider the creditor, B Limited, a similar analysis will show that its loss of purchasing power resulting from the loan is £(31 Dec X4) 80. In making the loan, B Limited gave up purchasing power amounting to £(1 Jan X4) 300 or £(30 Dec X4) 400. The repayment of the loan increased B Limited's purchasing power by £(30 Sep X4) 300 or £(31 Dec X4) 320. Thus its loss of purchasing power is £(31 Dec X4) 80.

The above analysis can be generalised as follows.

Suppose that a monetary asset of £(1)A was acquired at time 1 when the RPI was I_1, was sold at time 2 when the RPI was I_2 and that the year end is considered to be time 3 when the RPI was I_3. Then the purchasing power given up by virtue of the investment in the monetary asset is given by:

$$£(1)A = £(2)A \frac{I_2}{I_1}$$

The purchasing power regained from the disposal of the asset is given by £(2)A. The loss of purchasing power in time 2 purchasing power is:

$$£(2)A \frac{I_2}{I_1} - £(2)A = £(2)A \left(\frac{I_1}{I_2} - 1 \right)$$

and the loss of purchasing power in time 3 (year end) purchasing power is:

$$£(3)A \left(\frac{I_2}{I_1} - 1 \right) \frac{I_2}{I_2} = £(3)AI_3 \left(\frac{1}{I_1} - \frac{1}{I_2} \right)$$

In the special case where the asset is still in existence at the year end, $I_2 = I_3$ and the loss can be stated as follows:

$$\text{Loss} = £(3)AI_3 \left(\frac{1}{I_1} - \frac{1}{I_3} \right) = £(3)A \left(\frac{I_3}{I_1} - 1 \right) \tag{15.1}$$

If £A is replaced by −£A the above approach can be used to calculate the gain in purchasing power resulting from holding a monetary liability in a period of rising prices.

In the above analysis we concentrated on a single monetary item, but in practice a company's net monetary position will fluctuate on a daily basis. The foregoing method can be adapted to deal with this problem in the following way.

Suppose that a company starts the year on 1 January with net monetary assets of £200, reduces its net monetary assets by £280 on 1 April and finally increases its net monetary assets by £100 on 1 October. If this were the case, the company would have held net monetary assets of £200 for three months (January–March), net monetary liabilities of £80 for the next six months (April–September) and been a net monetary creditor of £20 for the last three months of the year. An alternative way of viewing the position, which we will use to calculate the total loss or gain on the company's monetary position, is to say that it: (a) held a monetary asset of £200 for the whole of the year; (b) held a monetary liability of £280 for the nine-month period from April to December; (c) held a monetary asset of £100 for the three-month period from October to December.

Assume that the appropriate index numbers are:

Date:	1 January	1 April	1 October	31 December
Index no.:	100	140	150	180

The loss or gain on each of the three hypothetical items can then be calculated by substituting the appropriate values in equation (15.1) as follows:

$$\text{(a)} \quad \text{Loss} = \pounds(31 \text{ Dec}) \; 200 \times \left(\frac{180}{100} - 1 \right)$$

$$\text{(b)} \quad \text{Loss} = - \pounds(31 \text{ Dec}) \; 280 \times \left(\frac{180}{140} - 1 \right)$$

$$\text{(c)} \quad \text{Loss} = \pounds(31 \text{ Dec}) \; 100 \times \left(\frac{180}{150} - 1 \right)$$

The total loss is given by:

$$\pounds(31 \text{ Dec}) \left\{ 200 \left(\frac{180}{100} - 1 \right) - 280 \left(\frac{180}{140} - 1 \right) + 100 \left(\frac{180}{150} - 1 \right) \right\}$$

$$= \pounds(31 \text{ Dec}) \left\{ -200 + 280 - 100 + 200 \times \frac{180}{100} - 280 \times \frac{180}{140} + 100 \times \frac{180}{150} \right\}$$

$$= \pounds(31 \text{ Dec}) \left(200 \times \frac{180}{100} - 280 \times \frac{180}{140} + 100 \times \frac{180}{150} \right) - \pounds(31 \text{ Dec}) \; 20$$

Note that the second term in the right-hand side of the above expression, $\pounds(31 \text{ Dec})$ 20, is the balance of the company's net monetary assets at the year end. We can now see that it is possible to calculate a company's total gain or loss by first converting all changes to the company's net monetary assets to year-end purchasing power (this gives us the first term on the right-hand side of the expression) and then subtracting the actual balance of net monetary assets.

The loss in this case will be:

$$\pounds(31 \text{ Dec}) \; 120 - \pounds(31 \text{ Dec}) \; 20 = \pounds(31 \text{ Dec}) \; 100$$

The above result may be interpreted as follows. If the company had been in a position to arrange its affairs so that cash, debtors and creditors had been in the form of non-monetary items of values which had changed exactly in step with inflation, it would have had 'net monetary assets' of £120 at the year end. It could have achieved this result had it been able to get its debtors to agree that they would repay the company with pounds which represented the same purchasing power as was represented by the amount of the debt at the date at which it was established, and had made a similar arrangement with its creditors. The company's bank balance is a special case of a creditor or debtor depending on whether or not the account is overdrawn.

The hypothetical £120 is then compared with the actual closing balance of £20 and it can be seen that the company's policy of holding net monetary assets over the year has resulted in a loss of purchasing power of $\pounds(31 \text{ Dec})$ 100.

The above argument can be generalised in the following fashion:

Let a_1 be the opening balance of net monetary assets plus the increases in net monetary assets for the first day of the year and let a_j, $j = 2, ..., 365$, be the increases in net monetary assets for day j. Then the loss of the holding of net monetary assets expressed in terms of year-end purchasing power, $\pounds(\text{day } 365)$, using equation (15.1) on page 463, is given by:

$$\text{Loss} = \pounds(\text{day } 365) \left[a_1 \left(\frac{I_{365}}{I_1} - 1 \right) + a_2 \left(\frac{I_{365}}{I_2} - 1 \right) + a_3 \left(\frac{I_{365}}{I_3} - 1 \right) + \ldots + a_{365} \left(\frac{I_{365}}{I_{365}} - 1 \right) \right]$$

$$= \pounds(\text{day } 365) \left(I_{365} \sum_{j=1}^{365} \frac{a_j}{I_j} \sum_{j=1}^{365} a_j \right)$$

Note that $\sum_{j=1}^{365} a_j$ represents the actual closing balance of net monetary assets which we can call A. Therefore:

$$\text{Loss} = \pounds(\text{day } 365) \left(I_{365} \sum_{j=1}^{365} \frac{a_j}{I_j} - A \right)$$

The use of computing facilities makes the above approach feasible in practice, but in preparing CPP accounts it was customary to take averages and assume that, depending on the circumstances, the increases in net monetary assets due to sales took place evenly either over the year as a whole or over each month or quarter, etc. If the annual assumption were made, the increase in net monetary assets would be assumed to have taken place at a date on which the general price index was at the average value for the year. If the calculation were done on a quarterly basis, the average values of the general price index for the quarters would be used.

Example 15.2 shows how one can calculate the loss or gain on a company's net monetary position.

Example 15.2

On 1 January 19X8 Match Limited's monetary items were as follows:

	£
Balance at bank	8 000
Trade debtors	2 000
Trade creditors	6 000
Proposed dividend	1 000

A summary of the company's cash book for 19X8 revealed the following:

		£			£
1 Jan	Opening balance	8 000	1 Jan	Purchases of	
Jan–Jun	Cash sales	5 000		fixed assets	50 000
	Trade debtors	18 000	Jan–Jun	Trade creditors	16 000
1 July	Issue of ordinary		1 July	Payment of 19X7	
	shares	30 000		dividend	1 000
July–Dec	Cash sales	8 000	July–Dec	Trade creditors	20 000
	Trade debtors	24 000	31 Dec	Closing balance	6 000
		£93 000			£93 000

Credit sales for the year were

January–June	£21 000
July–December	£28 000

Credit purchases for the year were

January–June	£14 000
July–December	£21 000

The values of a suitable general price index at appropriate dates were

Date:	1 January	Average Jan–Jun	1 July	Average July–Dec	31 December
Index:	140	148	160	162	165

We must identify the changes in the company's net monetary balances. Note that the sale of goods results in an immediate increase in the company's net monetary assets regardless of whether the sale was made for cash or credit. If the sale was made on credit, the increase in debtors will increase the company's net monetary assets, but the consequence of this is that the payment of cash by debtors will not affect the total net monetary position of the company. Similarly, the payment of the proposed dividend does not affect the net monetary position of the company. It merely reduces cash and the liability of proposed dividends, both of which are monetary items.

The changes in the company's net monetary assets may be summarised as follows:

		Increase £	Decrease £	Net £	Balance £
1 Jan	Opening balance				
	Bank	8 000			
	Debtors	2 000			
	Creditors		6 000		
	Proposed dividend		1 000		
		£10 000	£7 000	£3 000	3 000
1 Jan	Reduction in cash				
	(purchase of fixed assets)		£50 000	£(50 000)	(47 000)
Jan–Jun	Increase in cash				
	(cash sales)	5 000			
	Increase in debtors				
	(credit sales)	21 000			
	Increase in creditors				
	(credit purchases)		14 000		
		£26 000	£14 000	£12 000	(35 000)
1 July	Increase in cash				
	(issue of shares)	£30 000		£30 000	(5 000)
July–Dec	Increase in cash				
	(cash sales)	8 000			
	Increase in debtors				
	(credit sales)	28 000			
	Increase in creditors				
	(credit purchases)		21 000		
		£36 000	£21 000	£15 000	£10 000[13]

---

[13] The closing balance of the net monetary assets is made up as follows:

	£
Bank	6 000
Debtors	9 000
	15 000
less Creditors	5 000
	10 000

The company's loss or gain on its monetary position can now be found by converting all changes in net monetary items to year-end purchasing power.

		Conversion factor	Increase £	Decrease £
1 Jan	Opening balance	165		
	£(1 Jan X8) 3000	140	3536	
1 Jan	Decrease	165		
	£(1 Jan X8) 50000	140		58929
Jan–Jun	Increase	165		
	£(Jan–Jun) 12000	148	13378	
1 July	Increase	165		
	£(1 July X8) 30000	160	30938	
July–Dec	Increase	165		
	£(July–Dec) 15000	162	15278	
31 Dec	Balance			4201
			63130	63130

	£(31 Dec X8)
Actual balance of net monetary assets	10000
Balance from above	4201
Gain £(31 Dec X8)	5799

Note that the company gained in purchasing power even though it disclosed positive net monetary assets in both the opening and closing balance sheets because it was, over the year as a whole, a net monetary debtor.

Example 15.3 combines the features of Examples 15.1 and 15.2 in that it demonstrates how a set of CPP accounts can be produced in a case where a company holds net monetary items. It also shows how a set of historical cost accounts can be 'converted' into CPP accounts.

Example 15.3

(A) Parker Limited's historical cost and CPP balance sheets as at 1 January 19X5 (when the value of a hypothetical RPI was 150) are given overleaf:

Parker Limited
Balance sheets as at 1 January 19X5

	Historical cost		Notes, conversion factors	CPP	
	£	£		£(1 Jan X5)	£(1 Jan X5)
Fixed assets					
Net book value		8 000	(a) $\frac{150}{100}$		12 000
Current assets					
Stock	1 200		(b) $\frac{150}{140}$	1 286	
Debtors plus cash	600	1 800	(c)	600	1 886
		9 800		£(1 Jan X5)	13 886
Share capital					
£1 10% preference shares	2 000		(c)	2 000	
£1 ordinary shares	4 000	6 000	(d) $\frac{150}{80}$	7 500	9 500
Reserves		2 400	(e)		2 986
Owners' equity		8 400			12 486
15% debentures		1 000	(c)		1 000
Current liabilities		400	(c)		400
		£9 800		£(1 Jan X5)	13 886

Notes:
(a) The fixed assets were acquired when the RPI was 100.
(b) The stock was purchased over a period for which the average value of the RPI was 140.
(c) Monetary items.
(d) The ordinary shares were issued on a date at which the RPI was 80.
(e) The 'CPP reserve' is the balancing figure in the CPP balance sheet.

(B) During 19X5, Parker Limited issued 2000 £1 ordinary shares at a premium of 25 pence per share on 1 April when the RPI was 160 and purchased fixed assets of £(1 Sept X5) 3000; the RPI on 1 September 19X5 was 175.

Parker Limited's historical cost profit and loss account for 19X5 is given below:

Parker Limited
Profit and loss account

	£	£
Sales		12 000
less Opening stock	1 200	
Purchases	7 000	
	8 200	
less Closing stock	1 600	6 600
Gross profit (carried forward)		5 400

	£	£
Brought forward		5 400
less Sundry expenses	1 450	
Debenture interest	150	
Depreciation (20% reducing balance)	2 200	3 800
		£1 600

No dividends were declared during the year.

A full year's depreciation has been provided on the fixed assets purchased on 1 September 19X5.

(C) In order to prepare the CPP accounts it is necessary to make certain assumptions about the dates on which the various transactions took place. It will be assumed that sales, purchases, expenses and debenture interest all accrued evenly over the year and that the average RPI for the year was 170. It will further be assumed that the average age of the closing stock was two months and that the RPI on 31 October 19X5 was 178. The RPI at the year end will be taken to be 180.

For convenience the RPI at appropriate dates are summarised below:

Date	Index
Issue of original ordinary shares	80
Purchase of original fixed assets	100
Purchase of opening stock	140
1 January 19X5	150
1 April 19X5 (issue of 2000 ordinary shares)	160
Average for 19X5	170
1 September 19X5 (purchase of fixed assets)	175
31 October 19X5 (purchase of closing stock)	178
31 December 19X5	180

(D) We will now calculate the losses or gains resulting from the company's monetary position. The loss or gain on short- and long-term items will be calculated separately. The calculations are usually done separately because of the different factors which give rise to a company's holding of short-term and long-term monetary items. The short-term items depend on the company's policy regarding its investment in working capital; in most cases the short-term items are equivalent to a company's net current assets excluding stock. The longer-term position is a consequence of the company's overall financing strategy and depends on the level of gearing at which the company operates.

The short-term position may be calculated as follows:

		Actual		Conversion	Year-end pounds	
		+	–	factor	+	–
1 Jan	Opening balance	200		$\dfrac{180}{150}$	240	
1 Apr	Issue of shares	2 500		$\dfrac{180}{160}$	2 812	
Average for year	Sales less purchases, expenses + interest	3 400		$\dfrac{180}{170}$	3 600	
1 Sept	Purchase of fixed assets		3 000	$\dfrac{180}{175}$		3 086
31 Dec	Closing balance		3 100			3 566
					(31 Dec X5)	(31 Dec X5)
		£6 100	£6 100		£6 652	£6 652

The company's actual balance of short-term monetary items is £3100, but had the company been able to maintain the purchasing power of these items it would have had £3566. Hence, the loss on holding short-term monetary items for the year is:

$$£(31 \text{ Dec X5}) \ [3566 - 3100] = £(31 \text{ Dec X5}) \ 466.$$

The company's long-term monetary liabilities consist of the preference shares and the debentures. The opening balances for these items are:

	£(1 Jan X5)
Preference shares	2 000
Debentures	1 000
£(1 Jan X5)	3 000

The above balance is equivalent in year-end pounds to:

$$£(31 \text{ Dec X5}) \left[3000 \times \frac{180}{150} \right] = (31 \text{ Dec X5}) \ 3600$$

However, since we are dealing with monetary items, these values are not affected by the changes in the price level and the value at the year end is £(31 Dec X5) 3000.

The company has therefore gained in purchasing power from holding monetary liabilities and the gain is given by:

$$£(31 \text{ Dec X5}) \left[3000 \times \frac{180}{150} - 3000 \right] = £(31 \text{ Dec X5}) \ 3000 \left[\frac{180}{150} - 1 \right]$$

$$= £(31 \text{ Dec X5}) \ 600$$

(E) We are now in a position to prepare the CPP profit and loss account and balance sheet.

Parker Limited

CPP profit and loss account for the year ended 31 December 19X5

	£(31 Dec X5)	£(31 Dec X5)
Sales, $12\,000 \times \dfrac{180}{170}$		12 706
less Opening stock, $1200 \times \dfrac{180}{140}$	1 543	
Purchases, $7000 \times \dfrac{180}{170}$	7 412	
	8 955	
less Closing stock, $1600 \times \dfrac{180}{178}$	1 618	7 337
Gross profit		5 369
less Sundry expenses, $1450 \times \dfrac{180}{170}$	1 535	
Debenture interest, $150 \times \dfrac{180}{170}$	159	
Depreciation,		
$0.20 \times 8000 \times \dfrac{180}{100}$	2 880	
$0.20 \times 3000 \times \dfrac{180}{175}$	617	5 191
Net trading profit		178
Gain on long-term monetary items	600	
less Loss on short-term monetary items	466	134
Profit for the year	£(31 Dec X5)	312

CPP balance sheet as at 31 December 19X5

	£(31 Dec X5)	£(31 Dec X5)
Fixed assets		
Net book value:		
$(8000 - 1600) \times \dfrac{180}{100}$	11 520	
$(3000 - 600) \times \dfrac{180}{175}$	2 469	13 989
Current assets		
Stock, $1600 \times \dfrac{180}{178}$	1 618	
Cash *plus* debtors less creditors	3 100	4 718
	£(31 Dec X5)	18 707
Share capital		
£1 10% preference shares	2 000	
£1 ordinary shares:		
$4000 \times \dfrac{180}{80}$	9 000	
$2000 \times \dfrac{180}{160}$	2 250	11 250
		2 000
Carried forward		13 250

	£(31 Dec X5)	£(31 Dec X5)
Brought forward		13 250
Reserves		
Share premium account,		
$500 \times \dfrac{180}{160}$	562	
Reserves, 1 January 19X5,		
$2986 \times \dfrac{180}{150}$	3 583	
Profit for 19X5	312	4 457
Owners' equity		17 707
15% Debentures		1 000
	£(31 Dec X5)	18 707

The nature of the loss or gain on a company's net monetary position

One of the more important features of a set of CPP accounts is its disclosure of the loss or gain arising from the company's net monetary position. It attempts to show the results, from the point of view of the equity shareholders, of the financing policy adopted by the company in a period of changing prices.

The figures disclosed by CPP accounts have, however, been criticised on a number of grounds. One cause for criticism stems from the observation that the nominal interest normally includes some compensation for the fact that, in a period of rising prices, debtors will discharge their debts in pounds of a lesser value than the pounds which they borrowed. If, at the time the debt was issued, the market correctly assessed the future course of inflation, the 'gain' which apparently accrues to the borrower will be equal to the compensation for inflation which is included in the nominal rate of interest. If this were the case, it would seem sensible to set off the gain against the interest payable in the accounts of the borrower and to set off the corresponding loss against the interest receivable in the accounts of the lender. If this were done, the accounts would disclose the 'real' interest payable and receivable.

In practice the market will not be correct in its assessment of the future course of inflation and there will be a real loss or gain arising from the company's net monetary position. The loss or gain will depend on the difference between the anticipated and actual rates of inflation and thus, so far as interest-bearing loans are concerned, the debtor will not automatically gain nor the creditor automatically lose. The debtor will only gain if inflation turns out to be greater than that which was anticipated when the borrowing was made.

Suppose that £10 000 debentures were issued at a nominal rate of interest at 12 per cent and let us suppose that it is known that the market believed that prices would rise by 9 per cent each year for the period of the loan. It could thus be argued that the real rate of interest is 3 per cent.

Assume that the actual rate of inflation in 19X7 was 15 per cent. The items relating to the loan which would appear in the CPP profit and loss account for 19X7 would be:

Interest payable, 12% of £10 000	£1 200[14]
Gain on long-term borrowing, £10 000 $\left(\dfrac{115}{100} - 1\right)$	£1 500

It could, however, be argued that the following would provide a more realistic description of what in fact took place:

Interest payable, 3% of £10 000	£300
Gain on long-term borrowing,	
£10 000 $\left(\dfrac{115}{100} - 1\right)$ − 9% of £10 000	£600

In practice it is not possible to break down the nominal interest rate into the two elements – the real interest rate and the compensation for anticipated inflation – and hence it is not possible to present the CPP accounts in the above manner. However, it is clear that in the case of interest-bearing loans the loss and gain on the company's net monetary position will be overstated in the CPP accounts of the borrower and lender. There is thus a strong case for the suggestion that the loss or gain should be shown in the same section of the CPP profit and loss account as interest payable or receivable, and that the criticism referred to above is more concerned with the format of the CPP profit and loss account as proposed in PSSAP 7 than with the principles involved.

It must be emphasised that the above discussion refers only to interest-bearing items. The CPP profit and loss account will not overstate the loss or gain on such items as cash at bank on current account or trade creditors.

It has also been argued that it is misleading to measure the loss or gain by reference to changes in the RPI, as this assumes that the alternative of putting, say, £10 000 into a bank account is the payment of a dividend of that amount. In reality only a very small proportion of the cash generated by a company is used to pay dividends; the greater proportion is recirculated in the business and is used to purchase stock and fixed assets and to pay wages and other overheads. It has been suggested that the loss in purchasing power experienced if a company deposited £10 000 in a bank account for one month should be measured by reference to the increase in prices of those items which will be purchased by the company.

The above argument can be countered by the assertion that the purpose of business activity is to increase future consumption and that physical assets are not acquired for their own sake. The objective of CPP accounts is to show the effect of changing prices on the consumption opportunities of the equity shareholders and not on the potential asset purchases of the firm.

Suppose that a slothful company starts the year with £100 000 in the bank and does nothing until the end of the year when it purchases assets the cost of which have increased by 10 per cent over the year. Let us also assume that the RPI has increased by 15 per cent over the same period. Is the loss on holding money £10 000 or £15 000? From the point of view of the equity shareholders it is £15 000. Had the £100 000 been distributed at the beginning of the year the shareholders could have consumed goods and services amounting to £100 000. As prices had on average gone

---

[14] For simplicity it has been assumed that interest is paid at the year end and the question of whether the interest should be deemed to have accrued evenly throughout the year, which would require the interest payment to be converted to pounds of year-end purchasing power, has been ignored.

up by 15 per cent over the year they would have required £115 000 at the year end to purchase an equivalent bundle of goods and services.

At the year end the directors of the company must decide how best to maximise the total potential consumption over time of their shareholders. If the directors decide to invest the whole of the £100 000 in assets it must be on the basis of the belief that such action will be more beneficial to the shareholders than would the distribution of the cash. The shareholders would sacrifice immediate consumption in return for what is hoped will be greater consumption opportunities in the future.

It can be seen that there are two steps in the argument. First, the potential consumption opportunities of the shareholders have fallen by £15 000 (measured in year-end pounds) over the year. Second, a sacrifice of the consumption opportunity of £100 000 at the year end is required if the investment is to be made.

To show the loss on holding money as £10 000 would not reflect the fact that the potential consumption opportunity of the equity shareholders had fallen by £15 000 over the year.

Strengths and weaknesses of the CPP model

As we pointed out in Chapter 3, an accounting model can be appraised in terms of the selected capital maintenance test and asset valuation basis. We will now evaluate the CPP model in this way.

The real financial (money) capital maintenance test appears to be a sensible choice. Money is not of itself a valuable commodity – its utility depends on what can be done with it or, in other words, what it can buy either now or in the future. Thus, given that the purchasing power of money does vary over time, it seems reasonable to suggest that it is more helpful for many purposes to use a benchmark based on the maintenance of real money capital rather than money capital. In particular, the use, in CPP accounting, of a price index based on changes in consumer prices does seem to be the appropriate basis for the preparation of financial statements which serve to show the impact of an entity's operations on the economic welfare of its owner. The case for the use of the real financial capital test in such circumstances can be highlighted by the presentation of a simple example.

Suppose that a sole trader conducts all his/her business on a cash basis such that his/ her only business asset is cash and that the business has no liabilities. Assume that he/she starts the year with £10 000 and has £12 000 at the end of the year, during which time he/she has neither introduced nor withdrawn any cash.

The profit which would be disclosed by the conventional accounting method which uses the money capital test is £2000, but does this represent the owner's increase in 'well-offness' over the year? The question cannot be answered in the absence of any knowledge of the change in the purchasing power of money over the year. If the rate of inflation was less than 20 per cent, then it seems reasonable to suggest that the owner was better off at the end of the year than at the beginning of the year in the sense that more goods and services could be purchased. Similarly, if the rate of inflation was more than 20 per cent the owner would be worse off.

Let us now turn to the CPP basis of asset valuation. It is here that the CPP model is weak. As has already been stated, the CPP model does not purport to show the current economic value of assets since the basis of valuation is historical cost. With CPP accounting it is money and not the asset which is 'revalued'. Thus, the CPP model suffers from much the same limitations as historical cost accounting which were outlined in Chapter 3, and most authorities appear to agree that the CPP approach is not an adequate response to the criticisms of the conventional method.

Given the obvious usefulness of the real money capital test and the weakness of the CPP asset valuation basis, many people, including the authors, believe that it would be sensible to combine the profit measure based on real financial capital maintenance with a basis of asset valuation which does reflect current values. We will introduce such an approach in Chapter 17 but in Chapter 16 we will first introduce CCA.

Recommended reading

See end of Chapter 18.

16   Current cost accounting introduced

Overview   The rejection of Current Purchasing Power Accounting (CPP) by the Sandilands Report in 1975 led to the development of a system of Current Cost Accounting. In this chapter, we look first at the theoretical roots of such a system, namely:

- The distinction between holding and operating gains – Edwards and Bell.
- The concept of deprival value – Bonbright and Baxter.

We then explore the basic elements of CCA discussing the valuation of assets in a current cost balance sheet and the capital maintenance concept to be used in the measurement of current cost profit. There are two basic capital maintenance concepts to choose from:

- Operating capital maintenance.
- Financial capital maintenance.

We explain the following four adjustments which were developed to measure profit on the basis of operating capital maintenance:

- Cost of sales adjustment (COSA).
- Depreciation adjustment.
- Monetary working capital adjustment (MWCA).
- Gearing adjustment.

We also explain how the financial capital maintenance concept can be applied using money capital or real capital, that is inflation adjusted capital, as the benchmark.

Introduction

With the rejection of Current Purchasing Power Accounting (CPP) by the Sandilands Report in 1975, the ASC turned its attention to the development of the very different system of accounting, Current Cost Accounting (CCA), recommended in that report. The Sandilands Committee envisaged that Current Cost Accounts would replace Historical Cost Accounts but this proved politically unacceptable and SSAP 16 'Current Cost Accounting' (1980) required listed and large unlisted companies to prepare current cost accounts as well as historical cost accounts or historical cost information.

While SSAP 16 was withdrawn in 1986, the attempts to develop a system of Current Cost Accounting, both in the UK and in several other English speaking countries, remains one of the most interesting experiments in the attempts to reform accounting. We describe the basic elements of the system in this chapter and develop these further in Chapter 17.

We start by discussing the two theoretical roots of CCA identified in Figure 15.1, the contributions made by Edwards and Bell, and by Bonbright.

We discuss first the ideas of Edwards and Bell, whose seminal work *The Theory and Measurement of Business Income*[1] was published in 1961. This book represented a major advance in the development of current value accounting and its particular contribution to the CCA model was the recognition of the distinction between holding gains and operating gains; we will concentrate on this aspect of their work.

Theoretical roots

The distinction between holding and operating gains

For the purposes of determining business profit[2] Edwards and Bell divided the activities of a company into holding intervals and sales moments – the latter being assumed to be instantaneous (*see* Figure 16.1). A sales moment is the instant in time when the company sells goods while a holding interval is the interval between successive sales moments.

Suppose that a company starts an accounting period with assets with a replacement cost of £40, and that at the end of the first holding period its assets have a replacement cost of £60. These are not necessarily the same assets, as the company might well have exchanged assets during the period. Thus a manufacturing company might have reduced its cash and increased its holding of raw materials, work-in-progress and finished goods. Since, by definition, the company has made no sales during the holding interval, the change in the value of the assets must be due to an increase in the replacement cost of assets owned by the company.

Immediately after the first sales moment, the replacement cost of the company's assets equals £90. These assets will consist of the receipts from sales plus those of the company's assets which were not sold. The total business profit so far (assuming that no capital has been introduced or withdrawn) is £50: the difference between the replacement cost of the assets immediately after the first sales moment and the equivalent value at the start of the accounting period.

The total business profit of £50 can be divided into two elements. Part of the profit, £20, is due to the increase in the replacement cost of the assets during the holding period. This, Edwards and Bell called the realisable cost saving, although other terms used to describe it are holding gain and revaluation surplus. We will use the term holding gain. The replacement cost of assets at the moment of the first sale was £60, but as they were acquired with assets which had a current cost of £40, the company has gained, or saved, £20 by virtue of acquiring or manufacturing the goods sold in advance of the date of sale.

The remainder of the business profit, £30, is termed the *current operating profit*. This is the difference between the replacement cost of the assets before and after the

---

[1] E.O. Edwards and P.W. Bell, *The Theory and Measurement of Business Income*, University of California Press, Stanford, Calif., 1961.

[2] Edwards and Bell, *op. cit.*, used the phrase 'business profit' to refer to the profit measurement related to assets valued at current cost. As defined by Edwards and Bell, an asset's current cost is usually (but not always) the same as its replacement cost. For simplicity, we will assume that there is no difference between current cost and replacement cost.

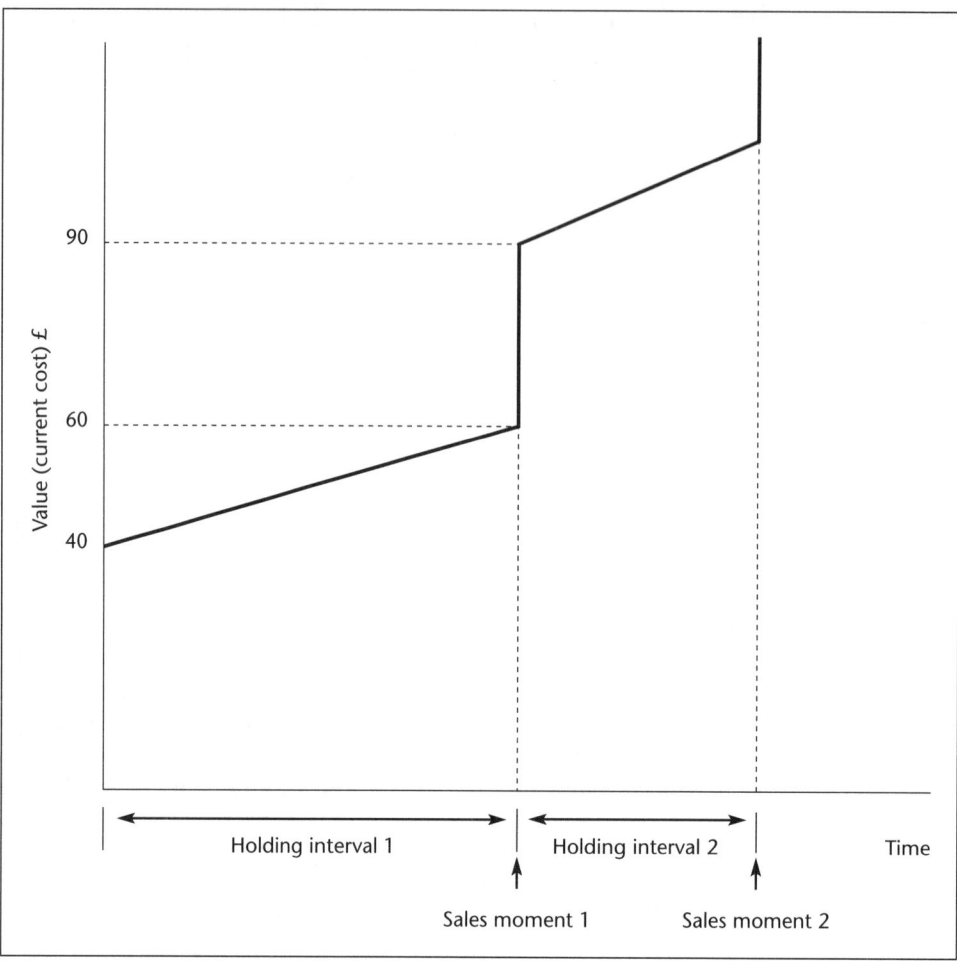

Fig. 16.1 Holding intervals and sales moments of a company

sales moment. Now many of the company's assets will remain unchanged during the sales moment (i.e. will not be sold) and the current operating profit can be stated in terms of the assets that do change. Thus, the current operating profit can be said to be equal to the receipts from sales less the replacement cost of assets used up (or exchanged) in the sales moment.

The same approach can be used for each sales moment and, if we consider the accounting period as a whole, then, if it is assumed that no capital is introduced or withdrawn,

Business profit for period = Replacement cost of assets at end of period – Replacement cost of assets at beginning of period
= Sum of current operating profits for all sales moments + Sum of holding gains for all holding intervals.

The approach described above is illustrated in Example 16.1.

Example 16.1

Bow Limited started the year with the following assets:

		£
Stock, at replacement cost		600
Cash		400
		£1 000

and finished the year with

		£
Stock, at replacement cost		900
Cash		500
		£1 400

It will be assumed that the company has no operating expenses and that no capital was introduced or withdrawn. The total business profit is thus: £1400 – £1000 = £400.

The company's activities for the year were as follows:

				Stock £	Cash £
First holding interval	1 Jan	Opening balances		600	400
	17 Feb	Purchased stock for £200		200	(200)
		Stock had a RC of £900			
	31 Mar	at 31 March	HG	100	
				900	200
First sales moment	31 Mar	Stock with a RC of £300 sold for £450 (COP = £150)		(300)	450
				600	650
Second holding interval	1 Apr	Stock had a RC of £680 on 30 June	HG	80	
	30 Jun			680	650
Second sales moment	30 Jun	Stock with a RC of £280 sold for £300 (COP £20)		(280)	300
				400	950
Third holding interval	1 July				
	30 Sep	Purchased Stock for £450		450	(450)
		Stock had a RC of £900 at 31 Dec (the year end)	HG	50	
	31 Dec	Closing balances		£900	£500

where RC is the replacement cost, HG is the holding gain and COP is the current operating profit.

The total business profit of £400 can be analysed as follows:

Current operating profits	£	£
First sales moment £(450 – 300)	150	
Second sales moment £(300 – 280)	20	170
Holding gains		
First holding interval £(900 – 800)	100	
Second holding interval £(680 – 600)	80	
Third holding interval £(900 – 850)	50	230
Business profit		£400

We will discuss the problems involved in distinguishing between holding and operating gains later when we introduce the CCA model. However, it might be useful if we commented that a company's holding gains might be argued to give some indication of its success in the acquisition or manufacture of inputs, e.g. the extent to which it benefited by purchasing stock before a price increase. In contrast, the current operating profit might be said to provide information about the company's success as a seller of goods – the extent to which, because of its efficiency or position in the market, it can sell goods for a price which is greater than the current cost of replacing them.

The distinction between realised and unrealised holding gains

The total holding gain for a period may be split into two elements: the realised holding gain (RHG) and the unrealised holding gain (UHG). The RHG is that part of the total which is associated with the assets which have been used up or consumed in the period; that is, the RHG is the difference between the current value of the asset at the date at which it is consumed (e.g. the date of sale in the case of stock) and the historical cost of the asset. Conversely, the UHG arises from the increase in value of the assets which remain on hand at the end of the period and is equal to the difference between the current value of the assets at the end of the period and their historical cost or, in the case of assets owned at the beginning of the period, their value at that date.

The position is complicated slightly when we consider the consumption of assets which were owned at the beginning of the period because part of the RHG is effectively the realisation of part or the whole of the UHG of earlier periods.

Example 16.2 illustrates these points.

Example 16.2

Clive purchased 100 units of stock for £10 each on 1 December 19X7. No sales were made in December 19X7 and the RC of the units at 31 December 19X7 (Clive's year end) was £11 each.

Clive sold 60 units for £18 each on 30 June 19X8, at which date the RC of each unit was £13. No more sales were made in 19X8 but Clive purchased 20 units for £5 each on 10 October. The RC of stock on 31 December 19X8 was £16 per unit.

In 19X7 the only element of business profit is the UHG of £1 per unit or £100.

Now let us consider the year 19X8. Clive's assets at the start of the year, measured at RC, amounted to 100 units at £11 each or £1100. His assets at the end of the year were:

	£
Cash (60 × 18) – (20 × 15)	780
Stock 60 units at £16	960
	£1 740

Clive's business profit for 19X8 was therefore £1740 – £1100 = £640. Clive's COP for the year is given by:

	£
Sales 60 x £18	1 080
less RC of stock at the date of sale, 60 x £13	780
COP	£300

His RHG is given by:

	£
RC of stock at the date of sale	780
less Historical cost of stock, 60 x £10	600
RHG	£180

But of the above RHG of £180 a part represents the realisation of a portion of the 19X7 UHG, the amount involved being 60 x £1 = £60.

Clive's UHG in 19X8 is given by:

	£	£
RC at year end of closing stock of 60 units		960
less RC at 1 January of unsold closing stock held on 1 January, 40 × £11	440	
Historical cost of stock purchased in the year, 20 × £15	300	740
UHG		£220

The total business profit (BP) for the year is given by:

BP = COP + RHG + UHG – (that part of the RHG which was
included in the UHG or previous years)

Substituting the monetary values, we have:

BP = £(300 + 180 + 220 – 60) = £640

The relationship between historical cost profit and business profit

The relationship can be easily seen if we resort to some simple algebra.

Let R be the revenue from sales, C be the current value of assets used up in generating sales, and H be the historical cost of those assets. Then the COP is given by $R – C$ while the RHG is equal to $C – H$.

The historical cost profit (HCP) is of course the difference between revenue and the historical cost of the assets consumed or, to use the above symbols:

$$HCP = R - H$$
$$= (R - C) + (C - H)$$
$$= COP + RHG.$$

In other words the historical cost profit is the sum of the current operating profit and the realised holding gains.

Let us now consider the implications of the above statement. The following discussion will serve as an introduction to the CCA model which will be developed later, as well as providing further evidence of the weaknesses of the historical cost accounting model.

It can be seen that historical cost profit has, when compared with business profit, two possible defects. First, historical cost profit combines two arguably distinct elements, COP and RHG, and the conventional accounting model makes no attempt to separate them. Second, the historical cost approach ignores UHG, i.e. it takes no account of the current value of the assets held at the end of the period.

The significance of these two observations depends on the view that is taken of the most suitable concept of capital for the purposes of profit determination. If the view is taken that the enterprise should be able to replace its assets as they are used up if it is to maintain its wealth or capital, i.e. the operating capital maintenance approach, then it might be argued that RHG should not be regarded as being part of the profit for the period.

Of course if one takes a different view of what constitutes 'well-offness' then it might be that RHG could be regarded as being part of profit. Such a view is implicit in the historical cost approach. However, it might still be argued that one of the defects of historical cost accounting is its failure to disentangle COP and RHG. This argument is based on the view that a company's COP and RHG are the result of different circumstances, and knowledge of the two elements might help the user of accounts to understand how the company obtained its historical cost profit. In particular, it might assist users to estimate future profits. For example, it might be that in a given year a company makes a very much greater profit than it had achieved in previous years because of the existence of RHGs. Those wishing to predict future profits would then no doubt consider the extent to which they believe that the opportunities to achieve RHGs will continue in the future.

To the extent that accounting practice in the UK and other countries allows companies to revalue assets for balance sheet purposes, UHGs are to be found in what are otherwise historical cost accounts. The recognition of UHGs in historical cost accounting has been partial, irregular (in the chronological and not moral sense) and has generally depended on the whim of the directors. Even after the issue of FRS 15 'Tangible fixed assets' (1998), directors will still enjoy considerable freedom as to which classes of assets are shown at current values.[3] Most adherents of current cost accounting would not wish to include UHGs as part of a company's profit. Even so, there is still a strong case for valuing assets at the current value, or in other words, systematically recognising UHGs. In CCA *all* UHGs on stocks and fixed assets are systematically recorded and reflected in the accounts.

The purpose of this section is to discuss the contribution of Edwards and Bell to the development of CCA. This can perhaps best be understood by noting that CCA makes a sharp distinction between current cost operating profit and holding gains.

---

[3] *See* Chapter 4.

It must, however, be noted that not all authorities agree that it is possible to make a clear and sharp distinction between operating profit and holding gains or that, even if it were possible, it would be desirable to do so. The distinction between operating and holding gains is clear in those cases when stock is replaced by more or less identical items. However, many traders do not act in this way but instead are prepared to switch from one line to another if they sense the opportunity of making greater profits. A trader might, for example, start the period with a warehouse full of carpets but use the cash flow generated from their sale to purchase refrigerators. In such a case it might be argued that it would not be realistic to include in the calculation of the trader's operating profit the replacement cost of carpets which the trader does not intend to replace. The designers of current cost accounting systems have been forced to include special provisions to deal with such cases.

Some would go further and argue that even if stock is to be replaced, the distinction between holding and operating gains is artificial. Such advocates would say that the decision to carry on a business of necessity involves holding stock and hence most price changes in the stock holding period are just as much a part of the operations of the firm as the differences between current revenue and the current cost of goods sold.[4]

Which 'current value'?

In Chapter 3 we pointed out that there are several ways of valuing an asset, each of which is of relevance in the determination of periodic accounting profit. In other words there is not one unique measure of profit but a whole set, depending on the basis of asset valuation employed and the selected capital maintenance concept.

Let us for a moment ignore the problems associated with the choice of the capital maintenance concept and accept the argument that the present value approach to asset valuation should be rejected for the theoretical and practical reasons outlined in Chapter 3. We are then – if we are to use current values – left with the choice between the replacement cost and net realisable value approaches.

Clearly both are of relevance and a strong case can be made for requiring companies, or at least larger companies, to publish multi-columnar accounts which show both the replacement costs and the net realisable values of their assets and, possibly, their historical costs. Thus, companies would be required to report profit on more than one basis. Against this, the view has been expressed that the approach would be too costly for the producers of accounts and too complicated for the users of accounts.

The cost argument is not wholly convincing because if assets are to be employed properly businesspeople will need to be aware of both the replacement cost and net realisable values of their assets. In addition, as will be seen, knowledge of both is required for the variant of current cost accounting which was favoured by the ASC. The second line of argument can – at least in the authors' view – be dealt with almost as easily. If it can be shown that there are a number of ways of measuring profit, then it surely is confusing and misleading to imply that there is only one. Considerations of practicability must limit the number of different profit figures which are reported, but it does seem reasonable to suppose that users of accounts should be able to cope with and benefit from the publication of two or three views of a company's results.

---

[4] *See* D.F. Drake and N. Dopuch, 'On the case for dictomising income', *Journal of Accounting Research*, Autumn 1965, and P. Prakash and S. Sunder, 'The case against separation of current operation profit and holding gain', *The Accounting Review*, January 1979.

The foregoing argument was not accepted by those charged with the task of reforming accounting practice except to the extent that it was advocated that both current cost and historical cost accounts should be published. Conventional wisdom decreed that one set of current value accounts was enough. The question of which asset valuation method should be adopted was therefore central to the current value accounting debate.

The net realisable value (NRV) approach possesses a number of virtues. The total of the net realisable values of a company's assets does provide some measure of the risks involved in lending to or investing in the company, in that the total indicates the amount that would be available for distribution to creditors and shareholders should the business be wound up. This point is, of course, dependent on the problems associated with the determination of net realisable values which were discussed in Chapter 3, and in particular the assumptions that are made about the circumstances surrounding the disposal of the assets. It has also been argued, notably by Professor R.J. Chambers, that the profit derived from a variant of the net realisable value asset valuation basis,[5] shows, after adjusting for changes in the general price level, the extent to which the potential purchasing power of the owners of an enterprise has increased over the period. However, the potential would only be realised if all the assets were sold, and it must be noted that in reality companies do not sell off all their assets at frequent intervals.

Advocates of net realisable value were, in the past, mostly to be found in academia but support for this view emerged from a professional accountancy body in the form of a discussion document issued by the Research Committee of the Institute of Chartered Accountants of Scotland.[6] The model advocated by the committee and their arguments in favour of the net realisable value approach will be discussed in a little more detail in Chapter 18.

The general view of the supporters of current cost accounting is that, in practice, companies continue in the same line or lines of business for a considerable time, making only marginal changes to the mix of their activities. It is therefore argued that if only one current value profit is to be published then it should be based on the replacement cost approach. For if it is assumed that a company is going to continue in the same line of business then it should only be regarded as maintaining its 'well-offness' if it has generated sufficient revenue to replace the assets used up. Thus, replacement cost was the preferred choice of those groups in the UK and most overseas countries which recommended the introduction of current value accounting. A strict adherence to the use of replacement cost, however, would not allow accounts to reflect the fact that companies do change their activities or the manner in which they conduct their present activities and that all the assets owned at any one time would not necessarily be replaced. Thus, some modification of the replacement cost approach is required.

Deprival value (value to the business)

A suitable basis of asset valuation, which would lead to the use of replacement cost in those circumstances where the owner would – if deprived of the asset – replace it and the use of a lower figure if the asset was not worth replacement, was suggested by Professor J.C. Bonbright in 1937. Professor Bonbright wrote, 'The value of a property

[5] A method known as Continuously Contemporary Accounting (CoCoA).
[6] *Making Corporate Reports Valuable*, Kogan Page, London, 1988.

to its owner is identical in amount with the adverse value of the entire loss, direct and indirect, that the owner might expect to suffer if he were deprived of the property.'[7]

Professor Bonbright's main concern was with the question of the legal damages which should be awarded for the loss of assets. He was not concerned with the impact of asset valuation on the determination of accounting profit. Others, notably Professor W.T. Baxter in the UK, recognised the relevance of this approach to accounting and developed the concept in the context of profit measurement. Professor Baxter coined the term 'deprival value', which neatly encapsulates the main point that the value of an asset is the sum of money which the owner would need to receive in order to compensate him/her exactly if he/she were deprived of the asset. It must be emphasised that the exercise is of an hypothetical nature; the owner need not be physically dispossessed of the asset in order for its deprival value to be determined. This approach was proposed in the Sandilands Report and, renamed 'Value to the Business' or 'Current Cost', it became the asset valuation basis of CCA. Thus, in a current cost balance sheet, assets would be shown at their deprival value, while a current cost profit and loss account would show the current operating profit, determined as the difference between the revenue recognised in the period and the deprival values of the assets consumed in the generation of revenue.

As we have seen in earlier chapters,[8] the ASB has moved, in its more recent publications, to the acceptance of the view that the value-to-the-business model provides the most appropriate way of measuring the current value of an asset.

Before turning to a discussion of CCA, it might be helpful if we explored the meaning of deprival value in a little more detail. Ignoring non-pecuniary factors, the deprival value of an asset cannot exceed its replacement cost, for if the owner were deprived of an asset, he or she could restore their original position through the asset's replacement. The owner might of course incur additional costs (e.g. a loss of potential profit) if there was any delay in replacement – the indirect costs referred to in Professor Bonbright's original definition. There may be circumstances where these additional costs may be so substantial that they will need to be included in the determination of the replacement cost, but generally these additional factors are ignored.

The owner might not feel that the asset was worth replacing, in which case the use of the asset's replacement cost would overstate its deprival value. Suppose that a trader owns 60 widgets, the current replacement cost of which is £3 per unit. Let us also assume that the trader's position in the market has changed since he acquired the widgets, that he will only be able to sell them for £2 each, and that this estimate can be made with certainty. The trader's other assets consist of cash of £100.

The trader's wealth before the hypothetical loss of the widgets is £220 (actual cash of £100 plus the certain receipt of £120). Let us now assume that the trader is deprived of his widgets. It is clear that he would only need to receive £120 in compensation, i.e. the net realisable value of the widgets, to restore his original position. If the trader were paid £180 (the replacement cost) he would end up better off.

In order for an asset's deprival value to be given by its net realisable value, the net realisable value must be less than its replacement cost. Otherwise a rational owner (and in this analysis it is assumed that owners are rational) would consider it worthwhile replacing the asset.

---

[7] J.C. Bonbright, *The Valuation of Property*, Michie, Charlottesville, Va., 1965.
[8] *See*, particularly, Chapters 1, 4 and 9.

We must now consider a different set of circumstances under which the owner would not replace the asset but has no intention of selling it. The asset may be a fixed asset which is obsolete in the sense that it would not be worth acquiring in the present circumstances of the business. The asset is still of some benefit to the business and it is thought that this benefit exceeds the amount that would be obtained from its immediate sale, i.e. its net realisable value. This benefit will, at this stage, be referred to as the asset's 'value in use'.

An example of this type of asset might be a machine which is used as a standby for when other machines break down. The probability of breakdowns may be such that it would not be worth purchasing a machine to provide cover because the replacement cost is greater than the benefit of owning a spare machine. It must be emphasised that the relevant replacement cost in this analysis is the cost of replacing the machine in its present condition and not the cost of a new machine. The machine may have a low net realisable value (which may be negative if there are costs associated with the removal of the machine) which is less than its value in use. In such circumstances an asset's deprival value will be given by its value in use, which would be less than its replacement cost but greater than its net realisable value.

As will be seen, the determination of an asset's value in use often proves to be a difficult task. In certain circumstances it may be possible to identify the cash flows that will accrue to the owner by virtue of his/her ownership of the asset and thus, given that an appropriate discount rate can be selected, its present value can be found. In other instances the amount recoverable from further use may have to be estimated on a more subjective basis. However, this estimate will approximate to the asset's present value and hence we will, at this stage, use the term present value (PV) for simplicity.

The above discussion is summarised in Figure 16.2.

In the case of a fixed asset, the replacement cost is the lowest cost of replacing the services rendered by that asset rather than the cost of the physical asset itself. The replacement cost of stock will depend on the normal pattern of purchases by the business and thus it will be assumed that the usual discount for bulk purchases will be available.

The net realisable value of work-in-progress which would, in the normal course of business, require further processing before it is sold needs careful interpretation. The

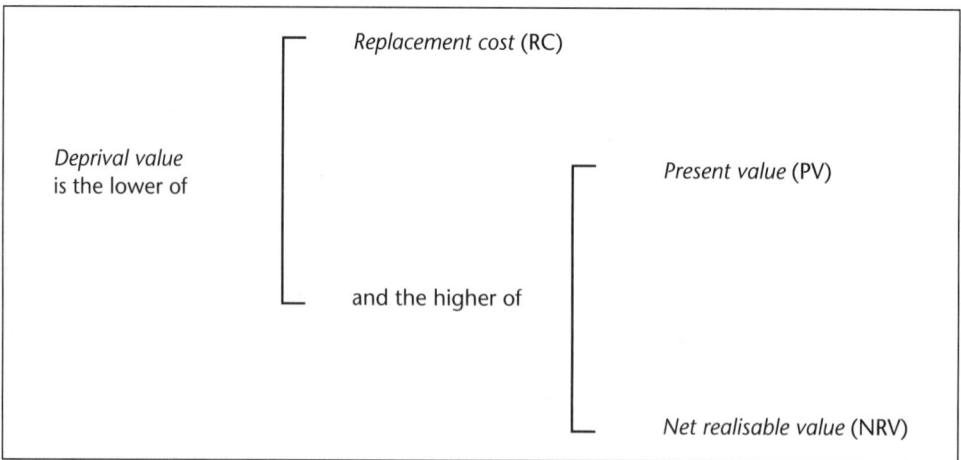

Fig. 16.2 A definition of deprival value

conventional definition of net realisable value in relation to stock is the 'actual or estimated selling price (net of trade but before settlement discounts) less (a) all further costs to completion and (b) all costs to be incurred in marketing, selling and distributing'.[9] There is an alternative definition which is the amount that would be realised if the asset were sold in its *existing* condition less the cost of disposal. For the purposes of determining the asset's deprival value, the higher of the two possible net realisable values will be taken.

Assume that a business holds an item of work-in-progress which could be sold for £200 in its existing condition, but which could, after further processing costing £30, be sold for £250. Also assume that its replacement cost is £350 and thus its replacement cost does not yield its deprival value.

In this case the asset's deprival value is £220 so long as the period required to complete and market the stock is brief enough for us to be able to ignore the effect of discounting. It is clear that, before the hypothetical deprival of the asset, the business would expect to receive £220 from its sale after taking account of the additional processing costs. If, on the other hand, the increase in the sales proceeds that would be expected if the asset were processed was less than the additional manufacturing costs, a rational owner would sell the asset in its existing condition and the net sales proceeds under these circumstances would give its deprival value.

In the context of Figure 16.2, six different situations can be envisaged:

1 RC < NRV < PV; then the deprival value is given by the RC. In this case the asset's RC is less than both its NRV and PV. It is worth replacing and because its PV is greater than its NRV it is likely that the asset involved is a fixed asset which will be retained for use within the company.
2 RC < PV < NRV; then the deprival value is given by the RC. As (1) except that as the asset's NRV exceeds its PV the asset will be sold and is probably part of the trading stock of the business.
3 PV < RC < NRV; then the deprival value is given by the RC. The asset would be replaced and then sold. It is almost certain to be part of the trading stock.
4 NRV < RC < PV; then the deprival value is given by the RC. This is likely to be a fixed asset. It is worth replacing since its PV is greater than its RC.
5 NRV < PV < RC; then the deprival value is given by the PV. This asset is not worth replacing, but given that it is owned it will be retained since its PV is greater than its NRV. This is likely to be a fixed asset which would not now be worth purchasing but is worth retaining because of its comparatively low NRV.
6 PV < NRV < RC; then the deprival value is given by the NRV. This is the second case where the asset's value to the business is not its RC. The asset is not worth replacing nor is there any point in keeping it. It is obviously an asset which should be sold immediately. It might be an obsolete fixed asset whose scrap value is now greater than the benefit that would be obtained from its retention. Alternatively, the asset might be an item of trading stock in respect of which there has been a change in the business's place in the market, i.e. it can no longer acquire or manufacture the stock for an amount which is less than its selling price net of expenses.

It is clear that the deprival value of a fixed asset can only be given by its replacement cost or present value. The deprival value of an asset is based on its net realisable value only when it would be in the interest of the business to dispose of the asset.

---

[9] SSAP 9, 'Stocks and Long-term Contracts'. Revised September 1988.

Thus, following the conventional definition of a current asset – an asset which will be used up within a year of the balance sheet date or within the operating cycle of the business, whichever is the longer – an asset whose deprival value is given by the net realisable value should be classified as a current asset.

The trading stock of a business is, by definition, an asset which is held for sale and hence its deprival value will either be its replacement cost or its net realisable value but not its present value (although in the case of stock which will not be sold for a considerable time its net realisable value may itself be based on the present value of future cash flows).

The deprival value of other current assets may be any of the three possible figures. Consider, as an example, the case of an unexpired insurance premium. Its deprival value is the loss which would be suffered if the insurance company could no longer honour its obligations. If the business felt that it was worth replacing the asset and would take out a new policy to cover the risk, the asset's deprival value would be given by its replacement cost. But suppose that it was believed that the cost of the new policy would outweigh the benefits that would be afforded by the policy. If the perceived benefits from the policy exceed the amount that could be obtained if the business surrendered the policy, the asset's deprival value would be its 'present value' (or value in use), which would be an amount which is less than the replacement cost but greater than its net realisable value (or surrender value of the policy). It may be that the net realisable value exceeds the perceived benefit that would flow from the retention of the policy. In this instance the deprival value of the asset is its net realisable value but, if this was indeed the case, the business should in any event surrender the policy.

The basic elements of current cost accounting

We are now in a position to introduce the basic elements of current cost accounting. In order to be able to concentrate on the principles involved we shall first use very simple examples. A more detailed example will be provided in Chapter 17 together with a discussion of the thinking of the ASC as reflected in its Handbook.

The current cost balance sheet

In a current cost balance sheet both assets and liabilities should in principle be shown at current cost, that is at deprival value or value to the business.

The current cost of short-term monetary assets will be the same as the amounts at which they appear in historical cost accounts. Hence, the assets which will appear at a different amount in a current cost balance sheet will be non-monetary assets, usually tangible fixed assets, investments and stocks.

In theory, liabilities should also be stated in terms of their 'current costs'. To do this we need to turn the definition of current cost around and ask how much the debtor would gain if he or she were released from the obligation to repay the debt. Clearly, all other things being equal, the longer the period before the debt is due, the less the gain from the extinction of the debt.

The 'current cost' or 'relief value' of a liability could be calculated by reference to its present value. Thus, if we ignore interest costs, the balance sheet figure for a debt of £100 000 repayable next month would be higher than a debt of the same nominal value repayable in ten years' time, the difference between the two figures depending on the discount rate.

Although a strong case can be made for revaluing substantial longer-term liabilities, in practice it is rarely done and liabilities are usually shown at their nominal values.

The total owners' equity in a current cost balance sheet is, as in a historical cost balance sheet, the difference between the assets and liabilities, but part of it will be treated as a reserve reflecting the amounts needed to be retained within the business to deal with the effect of changing prices. The size of the reserve, and its appropriate description, will depend on the selected capital maintenance concept (*see* Chapters 3 and 17).

The current cost profit and loss account

A current cost profit and loss account includes a number of items not found in one based on the historical cost convention. The actual number will depend on the chosen capital maintenance concept which may be 'operating capital maintenance' or 'financial capital maintenance'. We shall look at each in turn.

Operating capital maintenance

We will first examine a current cost profit and loss account based on the maintenance of operating capital. Operating capital may be defined in a number of ways, but it is usual to think of it as the productive capacity of the company's assets in terms of the volume of goods and services capable of being produced. Thus, from this standpoint, a company will only be deemed to have made a profit if its productive capacity at the end of a period is greater than it was at the start of the period after adjusting for dividends and capital introduced and withdrawn.

The most convenient way of measuring a company's operating capital is by using, as a proxy, its *net operating assets*. So, a company will only be deemed to have made a profit if it has maintained the level of its net operating assets. As we shall see later, it is difficult to reach agreement as to what constitutes net operating assets. At this stage we will regard net operating assets as a company's fixed assets, stock and all monetary assets less current liabilities.

As explained in Chapter 3, if the company is partly financed by creditors, the profit attributable to the equity holders is different from, and in periods of rising prices greater than, the entity profit (current cost operating profit) on the assumption that part of the additional funds needed to maintain the operating capital is provided by creditors.

There are four 'current cost adjustments' which might appear in a current cost profit and loss account and which may be regarded as 'converting' a historical cost profit into a current cost profit. The first three are the 'current cost operating adjustments' and the fourth is the gearing adjustment:

1 *Cost of sales adjustment* (COSA): This is the difference between the current cost of goods sold and the historical cost.
2 *Depreciation adjustment*: This is the difference between the depreciation charge for the year based on the current cost of the fixed asset and the charge based on its historical cost.
3 *Monetary working capital adjustment* (MWCA): Monetary working capital may be defined as cash plus debtors less current liabilities. In order to operate, most companies need to invest in monetary working capital as well as in fixed assets, thus they might need to hold a certain level of cash and sell on credit but will also be able to buy on credit. All other things being equal, an increase in prices will mean that a company will have to increase its investment in monetary working capital, and the purpose of the MWCA is to show the additional investment required to cope with price increases. Of course some companies can operate with negative working capital, for example a supermarket chain which buys on credit but sells for cash. In such

instances an increase in prices will result in a reduction in monetary working capital and the MWCA would then be a negative figure reflecting that reduction.

4 *The gearing adjustment*: The gearing adjustment is the link between the current cost operating profit and the current cost profit attributable to the equity shareholders. It depends on the assumption that part of the additional funds required to be invested in the business as a result of increased prices will be provided by long-term creditors.

These adjustments are illustrated below.

Since X Limited started trading all prices have remained constant; hence the balance sheet as at 1 January 19X2, shown below, satisfies both the historical cost and current cost conventions.

Balance Sheet as at 1 January 19X2

	£		£
Share capital and		Fixed assets	
reserves	4 500	purchased 31 Dec XI	3 600
Loan (interest free)	4 500	Stock (200 units)	2 000
		Debtors	2 400
		Cash	1 000
	£9 000		£9 000

X Limited buys for cash and sells on one month's credit.

The company incurs no overhead expenses.

The fixed asset is to be written off over three years on a straight-line basis.

The mark-up is constant at 20 per cent on historical cost determined using the first-in first-out method of stock valuation.

Stock is held constant at 200 units: the monthly sales are 200 units. The cost of stock at the end of the previous month was £10 per unit; the cost of purchases increased by 10 per cent at the beginning of the month. The replacement cost of the fixed asset increased by 50 per cent on that date. Thereafter all prices held constant.

All profits are paid out by way of dividend at the end of each month.

We will first present the historical cost accounts for January 19X2:

Historical cost profit and loss account for the month of January 19X2

	£	£
Sales, 200 × £10 × 1.2		2 400
less Opening stock	2 000	
Purchases, 200 × £10 × 1.1	2 200	
	4 200	
Less Closing stock	2 200	2 000
		400
Less Depreciation 1/36 of £3 600		100
Profit for month		300
less Dividend		£300

Historical cost balance sheet as at 31 January 19X2

Fixed assets	3 500
Stock	2 200
Debtors	2 400
Cash £(1000 + 2 400 − 2 200 − 300)*	900
	£9 000

	£
Share capital and reserves	4 500
Loan (interest free)	4 500
	£9 000

[*] Opening balance plus cash collected from debtors less purchases less dividends.

We will now look at the four adjustments on the assumption that the current cost of the assets is given by their replacement cost.

Cost of sales adjustment (COSA)

	£
Replacement cost of the 200 units sold	
200 x £10 x 1.1	2 200
Historical cost of goods sold	2 000
COSA	£200

Depreciation adjustment

	£
Depreciation charge for month based on the current cost of the fixed assets	
$1/36 \times £3600 \times 1.5$	150
Depreciation charge based on historical costs	100
Depreciation adjustment	£50

Note that in this simple introductory example we have assumed away the problem of the valuation of part-used assets, i.e. there is no prior or backlog depreciation. We shall discuss the question of depreciation in more detail in Chapter 17.

Monetary working capital adjustment (MWCA)

The company's opening monetary working capital consists of a cash balance of £1000, which represents half its monthly purchases (at the old prices) and debtors of £2400 (one month's sales). Hence, if it is assumed that for operational reasons the company will need to maintain the same relative position, an increase in the cost of purchases of 10 per cent will mean that the company's investment in working capital will also need to increase by 10 per cent.

Its opening monetary working capital was £3400;[10] hence the MWCA is 10 per cent of £3400 = £340.

---

[10] Debtors include the profit on the sales. Strictly the profit element should be eliminated from the calculation of the MWCA as follows:

	£
Cost of stock with debtors	
$\frac{10}{12} \times £2400$	2 000
Cash balance	1 000
MWC	£3 000
MWCA 10% of £3000	£300

We shall, however, ignore this complication at this stage.

The current cost operating profit and operating capability

Before turning to the gearing adjustment it is instructive to see what has happened so far. We started with a profit on the historical cost basis of £300 and have made three adjustments, the cumulative effect of which is:

	£	£
Historical cost profit		300
less COSA	200	
Depreciation adjustment	50	
MWCA	340	590
Current cost operating loss		£290

This example is based on the maintenance of operating capital, and the current cost operating loss of £290 can be related to the company's operating capacity as measured by its holding of net operating assets in the following way.

In order to be in the same position at the end of the month as it was at the beginning the company would need to:

(a) be able to replace that part of the fixed asset that has been consumed during the period (we will assume for the sake of the argument that the asset can be replaced in bits). At current prices it will need to set aside £150 to replace one thirty-sixth of the asset ($1/36 \times £5400 = £150$);

(b) hold stocks of £2200;

(c) carry debtors equal to one month's sales at the new price, £2640 (£2400 + 10% of £2400);

(d) hold a cash balance of £1100 (half the cost of one month's purchases).

We can now compare the required holding of assets with that which actually exists.

Required holding of assets

	£	£
Fixed assets		
remaining		3 500
required for replacement		150
Stock		2 200
Debtors		2 640
Cash		1 100
		9 590
Assets available at the end of the month		
Fixed assets	3 500	
Stock	2 200	
Debtors	2 400	
Cash	900	9 000
Shortfall		590

The shortfall can be explained by two factors

	£
Dividend paid	300
Current cost operating loss	290
	590

Thus, it appears that, if it is the company's intention to maintain its operating capital, it should not have paid the dividend, but even if the dividend had not been paid, the company's operating capital would have been reduced by £290.

Many advocates of CCA would say that the above line of argument is unduly prudent because it ignores the fact that part of the company is financed by long-term creditors. They would include a gearing adjustment of some kind.

The gearing adjustment

The purpose of the gearing adjustment is to show how much of the additional investment required to counter the effects of increased prices would be provided by longer-term creditors[11] on the assumption that the existing debt-to-equity ratio, in this example 1:1, will be maintained.

Unfortunately, the gearing adjustment is another example of a failure to agree on the most appropriate method and there are at least two ways of calculating the gearing adjustment. The most commonly used, the so-called restricted or partial gearing adjustment, was based on the assumption that the current cost profit attributable to shareholders should bear the burden of only that part of the cost of sales, depreciation and monetary working capital adjustments financed by the shareholders, in this case 50 per cent. Thus, the restricted gearing adjustment is a credit to current cost operating profit of 50 per cent of the total of the three adjustments, i.e.:

	£
COSA	200
Depreciation adjustment	50
MWCA	340
	£590

Gearing Adjustment, 50% of £590 = £295.

Putting all this together, the current cost profit attributable to shareholders can be determined as follows:

	£	£
Historical cost profit		300
less COSA	200	
Depreciation adjustment	50	
MWCA	340	590
Current cost operating loss		290
Add Gearing adjustment		295
Current cost profit attributable to shareholders		£5

---

[11] Short-term creditors, such as trade creditors, have been ignored in this example. In practice, short-term creditors were included in monetary working capital.

Thus, the company could pay a dividend of £5 and still maintain its operating capital so long as the long-term creditors provide (or will provide if asked at some stage in the future) £295.

Some argue that this gearing adjustment is unduly restrictive because it fails to take into account unrealised holding gains (UHG) which will be reflected in a current cost balance sheet and which will reduce the debt-to-equity ratio thus affording the opportunity for further borrowings. In this case the unrealised holding gain on the fixed asset is 50 per cent of 35/36ths of £3600 = £1750.

The alternative, the natural or full[12] gearing adjustment, is based on the sum of the UHG and the current cost adjustments – in this case 50 per cent of (£590 + £1750) = £1170, and thus the current cost profit attributable to shareholders becomes £880.

The use of the full gearing adjustment is based on the assumption that creditors would be prepared to lend the company an additional £1170 which would maintain the existing debt-to-equity ratio.

The current cost accounts

The current cost profit and loss account for January, using the restricted gearing adjustment, can be presented as follows:

Current cost profit and loss account for the month of January 19X2

	£	£
Sales		2400
Cost of goods sold:		
Historical cost	2000	
COSA	200	2200
		200
Depreciation:		
Historical cost	100	
Depreciation adjustment	50	150
		50
MWCA		340
Current cost operating loss		290
Gearing adjustment (restricted)		295
Current cost profit attributable to shareholders		5
Dividend, assumed equal to Profit		£5

A distinction can be made between the three current cost operating adjustments. One, the depreciation adjustment, represents the restated value of the cost of an asset consumed during the period and will thus be credited to the provision for depreciation. The other adjustments relate to the additional investments required to maintain operating capability and will be credited to a *current cost reserve account*.

Another adjustment is required in the balance sheet in respect of the fixed asset. At the beginning of the month the fixed asset's current cost (equal in this instance to its

---

[12] In its Handbook the ASC refers to the restricted (partial) gearing adjustment as a Type 1 adjustment and the full (natural) version as a Type 2 adjustment.

historical cost) was £3600. This increased by 50 per cent to £5400 on the first day of the month. However, the decision to depreciate the asset on a straight-line basis assumes that one thirty-sixth of the asset is used up in the month and hence 1/36 of the total gain of £1800, £50, is realised and the balance unrealised.

The total gain of £1800 is debited to the fixed asset account and credited to the current cost reserve account.

The gearing adjustment is debited to the current cost reserve account.

The current cost balance sheet as at 31 January 19X2 is therefore:

	£	£
Fixed assets at current cost	5 400	
less Provision for depreciation	150	5 250
Stock		2 200
Debtors		2 400
Cash (assuming a dividend of £5)*		1 195
		£11 045
Share capital and reserves		4 500
Current cost reserve account (see below)		2 045
		6 545
Loan (interest free)		4 500
		£11 045
Current cost reserve		
Gain on fixed assets		1 800
COSA		200
MWCA		340
		2 340
less Gearing adjustment		295
		£2 045

*1000 + 2400 − 2200 − 5

If we had used the full gearing adjustment, £1170, the current cost profit attributable to shareholders, and in this case the dividend, would be £880, thus reducing the assets to £10170 and the current cost reserve to £1170. These figures illustrate the argument in favour of the full gearing adjustment because if the creditors did increase their loan by the amount of this gearing adjustment, £1170, the original debt-to-equity ratio of 1:1 would be maintained. The introduction of funds equal to the restricted gearing adjustment would not have the same effect because of the failure to recognise the unrealised holding gain.

The consequences of using the different approaches are illustrated in the following summary balance sheets which assume that additional borrowings, equal to the appropriate gearing adjustment, are obtained.

	Restricted gearing adjustment		Full gearing adjustment	
	£	£	£	£
Sundry assets		9 850		9 850
Cash		1 195		320
		11 045		10 170
Additional cash generated by fresh borrowings		295		1 170
		£11 340		£11 340
Share capital and reserves		4 500		4 500
Current cost reserve account		2 045		1 170
		6 545		5 670
Original loan	4 500		4 500	
Additional loan	295	4 795	1 170	5 670
		£11 340		£11 340
Debt-to-equity ratio		1:1.36		1:1

Financial capital maintenance

We will now consider current cost accounts in which profit is measured on the basis of financial capital maintenance. The focus here is on the shareholders and whether their interest in the company has increased or not. There are two versions of financial capital maintenance, one based on monetary units and the second based upon purchasing power units. While the former ignores inflation, the latter takes into account inflation, as measured, say, by the Retail Price Index, and hence attempts to show whether or not the interest of the shareholders in the company has increased in 'real' terms. For the remainder of this chapter, we shall confine ourselves to this real terms version of financial capital maintenance.

If it is assumed that no capital is introduced or withdrawn during the period, the 'real terms' profit can be found as follows:

(a) Measure the shareholders' funds at the beginning of the period based on the current cost of assets.
(b) Restate that amount in terms of pounds of purchasing power at the balance sheet date by use of a relevant index of general prices (such as the Retail Price Index (RPI)).
(c) Compare the restated amount from (b) with the shareholders' funds at the end of the year, based on the current cost of assets. If shareholders' funds at the end of the period exceed the restated figure for the beginning of the period, a 'profit' has been made; which in the ASC Handbook is described as 'total real gains'.

Using our earlier illustration and assuming that on average prices increased by 20 per cent over one month and that no dividends were paid, we can calculate the total real gain as follows:

(a) Shareholders' funds based on current costs as at 1 January 19X2, £4500.
(b) If prices increased on average by 20 per cent over the month, shareholders' funds would need to amount to £5400 (£4500 × 1.20) if real financial capital is to be maintained.

(c)   **Calculation of total real gain**

	£
Shareholders' funds at 31 January 19X2	
at current cost	
Fixed assets	5 250
Stock	2 200
Debtors	2 400
Cash (before dividend)	1 200
	11 050
less Loan	4 500
Funds at 31 January 19X2	6 550
Funds at 1 January 19X2, restated in terms of	
31 January 19X2 purchasing power	5 400
Total real gains for January	£1 150

The above calculation gives no indication of how the gain was achieved. There are many ways of presenting a profit and loss account based on the maintenance of financial capital. One simple version based on our illustration is given below.

It starts in a similar fashion to the profit and loss account based on the maintenance of operating capital, in that it shows a current cost operating profit but without the inclusion of the monetary working capital adjustment which, along with the gearing adjustment, is inconsistent with the approach taken to monetary items in a system which does not seek to indicate the additional finance required to sustain a given level of net operating assets.

To the modified current cost operating profit are added the holding gains, distinguished between realised and unrealised. The cost of sales and depreciation adjustments are realised holding gains, which means that they are debited in the first part of the statement but are added back, or credited, in the second section.

The sum of the modified current cost operating profit and the total holding gains is described as the 'total gains'.

Finally, the 'inflation adjustment' is deducted from the total gains to give the total real gains.

Profit and loss account for January 19X2
'Real terms' (based on the maintenance of financial capital)

	£	£
Sales		2 400
Cost of goods sold : historical cost	2 000	
: COSA	200	
Depreciation : historical cost	100	
: depreciation adjustment	50	2 350
Current cost operating profit		50
add Realised holding gains:		
Cost of sales adjustment	200	
Depreciation adjustment	50	
	250	50
Unrealised holding gains: fixed asset	1 750	2 000
Total gains carried forward		2 050

	£
Total gains brought forward	2 050
less Inflation adjustment	900
Total real gains	£1 150

Recommended reading

See end of Chapter 18.

17 Current cost accounting developed

Overview   In this chapter, we explore in more detail the system of Current Cost Accounting which has been introduced in Chapter 16.

We first explore some of the different ways of determining the current costs of assets in practice, focusing on tangible fixed assets and stocks.

We then turn to the calculation of profit based on the maintenance of operating capital where we focus on the adjustments in respect of monetary working capital (MWC) and gearing. While there is general agreement on the need for a depreciation adjusment and a cost of sales adjustment, the MWCA and gearing adjustments are much more controversial and can be made in different ways. We explore the controversies and provide examples.

We end the chapter with a comprehensive example of the preparation of current cost accounts with profit measured, first, on the basis of operating capital maintenance and. second, on the maintenance of 'real' financial capital.

Introduction

In Chapter 16, we introduced and placed in context the ASC publication *Accounting for the Effects of Changing Prices: a Handbook*, henceforth referred to in this chapter as the Handbook. This Handbook was not an accounting standard and was neither mandatory nor prescriptive. Rather it was a publication to explain and discuss the methods for accounting for the effects of changing prices which may be adopted and to identify those which the ASC considered most appropriate. In short, it was a contribution to the debate on accounting for changing prices.

Although the Handbook was issued in 1986 it remains valid in that it encourages companies to appraise and, where material, report the effects of changing prices. Its basic message is still appropriate today: 'Please do something and, if you do something, this is probably the best way of doing it.'

The ASB undoubtedly favours the use of more current values in financial statements and was even accused of attempting to introduce a system of CCA by the backdoor in the first draft Statement of Principles. However, as we shall see in Chapter 18, the Board now seems to have thrown in the towel by accepting something much nearer the status quo, a mixed measurement system, in its revised exposure draft.[1]

---

[1] *See* the discussion of the two draft Statements of Principles in Chapter 1, and the discussion of the ASB current approach in Chapter 18.

The preferred method

The ASC view was that, of the various methods available, the most appropriate way of accounting for changing prices is an approach based upon:[2]

- current cost asset valuation with either
  - operating capital maintenance or
  - 'real' financial capital maintenance, and
- the nominal pound as the unit of measurement.

We have already discussed the current cost basis of asset valuation and the two capital maintenance concepts and will return to consider these in more depth later in the chapter. The selection of the nominal pound as the unit of measurement can be seen as a rejection of the constant purchaseing power unit used in CPP accounting.

The rejection of CPP

As we have shown in Figure 15.1, the first serious attempt to account for changing prices in the UK was CPP accounting. However, as we have explained, the approach was rejected in the report of the Sandilands Committee.[3]

This committee rejected the CPP unit of measurement on a number of grounds including the view that it is not possible to measure inflation except on an individual basis because inflation is a personal matter depending on an individual's particular pattern of consumption. They wrote:

> Inflation does not exist as a quantifiable phenomenon independent of the price movement in any specific group of goods and services or of the spending pattern of any specific group of individuals or entities and is not a phenomenon capable of independent and objective measurement, affecting all individuals and entities in the same way. The rate of inflation will vary for different individuals and entities in the country according to the selection of goods and services which they buy.[4]

Sandilands' proposals therefore eschewed the use of any broadly-based price index.

To this one might respond that the estimate of the effect of inflation provided by the RPI is probably a better estimate of the experience of all shareholders, and everybody else, than the estimate of zero which is implied by the complete rejection of any attempt to take account of changes in general purchasing power.

Another reason why the Sandilands Committee rejected CPP accounting in its pure form was that it does not disclose the current value of assets. This is a good reason but, as we have already seen in Chapter 16, it is possible to show the effects of changes in the general price levels in a system which reports the current cost of assets.

The re-emergence of some features of CPP

Although the ASC preferred the nominal pound as the unit of measurement, it sensibly recognised the role which could be played by the constant purchasing power unit of CPP. Thus one of its two recommended capital maintenance concepts, the 'real' financial capital maintenance concept, is based on the measurement of the effects of

---

[2] *Accounting for the Effects of Changing Prices: a Handbook*, ASC, London, 1986, Para. 1.11.
[3] *Report of the Inflation Accounting Committee*, Cmnd 6225, HMSO, London.
[4] *Ibid.*, p. 13.

changes in general price levels on the equity shareholders' interest. The opening share-holders' interest is restated in terms of closing purchasing power, using the Retail Price Index, and this is compared with the closing shareholders' interest, which is automatically measured in closing purchasing power. The profit measures the increase or decrease in shareholders' purchasing power which has occurred during the year.

While there may be a weak case for ignoring the effect of inflation for one year where it is not excessive, the same is certainly not true over longer time periods. Here again the ASC recognised the contribution which could be made by the CPP unit by proposing that corresponding amounts for the previous years and the figures in historical summaries should be remeasured in closing purchasing power units. We have already explored such adjustments in our discussion of historical summaries in Chapter 11 and will return to them later in this chapter.

The choice between the two capital maintenance concepts

The choice can be considered from two aspects: (a) the nature of the business and (b) the different interests of the various users of the accounts.

It is suggested that if it is possible to apply both concepts to a particular business then it would be helpful to produce information based on both concepts, but there are certain types of business, value-based companies, where it may not be possible or, if possible, sensible to apply the maintenance of operating capital test.

Value-based companies

The phrase 'value-based companies' is used to describe those companies where all or most of the profit is, by intention, derived from holding assets which increase in value, i.e. holding gains, rather than from trading. Examples of value-based companies include commodity traders, insurers, banks and investment trusts.

The problem of applying the operating capital maintenance test to value-based companies can be seen by examining the cost of sales adjustment. It will be found that either there is no meaningful cost of sales adjustment which can be calculated because the assets used up will not be replaced, or, if one can be calculated, it will eliminate the whole of the profit because the company's prime objective is the making of holding gains.

To judge the success of a value-based company, the best test is to see whether it has earned 'real' profits over and above inflation, and this can only be determined by applying the financial capital maintenance concept.

Different aspects of business performance

Let us now consider businesses, other than value-based companies, where it is possible to think in terms of the maintenance of operating capacity. If one has to select between the two concepts, the decision should rest on what particular aspect of the company's performance it is most useful to report or, to put it in a slightly different way, from whose standpoint profit should be measured. We will consider two extreme cases.

A shareholder might be interested only in the return on his or her investment and would expect management to maximise the return by switching resources from one type of business to another whenever profitable opportunities arise. Such shareholders would be much more interested in knowing whether their investment has been maintained in real terms than in knowing about whether the company has maintained its operating capacity, and are therefore likely to be more interested in a profit measure based on financial capital maintenance than one based on operating capital maintenance.

The other extreme is an employee who is interested in the continuity of his or her employment or a shareholder/owner of a company whose desire is to sustain it in its existing business. They will be particularly interested in a profit measure based on the maintenance of operating capital.

Although we have presented extremes it is likely that all the parties would also be interested in the 'other' capital maintenance test and hence the ASC suggested that some companies may wish to provide information based on both concepts.

The Handbook: detailed treatment of assets

We have already discussed the principles underlying the preparation of current cost accounts and will now discuss their application based on the methods of accounting for the effect of changes in prices as advocated in the Handbook.

Fixed assets

Plant and machinery

The current cost of a fixed asset is normally its *net current replacement cost*. The exception is where there has been a permanent diminution in its value when the asset will be written down to its recoverable amount.

The net current replacement cost of an asset is normally based on its gross current replacement cost (i.e. the replacement cost of a new asset) and the proportion of the asset that has been deemed to be used up. Thus, assume that an asset has a *gross current replacement cost* of £20 000 and, as at 31 December 19X1, that 40 per cent of it has been used up (say, for example, it has been depreciated at 10 per cent per annum on a straight-line basis for four years assuming a zero scrap value).

Its net current replacement cost will be £12 000 and it will be included in a current cost balance sheet at 31 December 19X1 as follows:

	£
Gross current replacement cost	20 000
less Accumulated depreciation	8 000
Net current replacement cost	£12 000

Generally the most convenient way of finding the gross current replacement cost is by applying a relevant specific index adjustment to the cost; the index used need not be highly specific and the same index could be applied to the blocks of similar assets. The indices could be those prepared by government agencies[5] or be generally recognised privately produced indices or even indices compiled by a company on the basis of its own purchasing experience.

There may be circumstances where the use of an index of asset prices may not be appropriate; in such cases the gross current replacement cost should be based on expert opinion or other evidence of the current cost of assets. A particular example is

---

[5] The Office for National Statistics publishes *Price Index Numbers for Current Cost Accounting* monthly.

where the speed of technological change is such that it would be unwise to rely on the use of any index of changes in specific prices. The problem is that we may not be comparing like with like. An index will disclose, say, that the average cost of machinery used in a particular industry has increased by, say, 60 per cent over the same period but will not show that its operating costs of the machinery was cut by, say, 40 per cent over the same period.

The unthinking use of an index could lead to misleading results. Its use without correction would mean that the value of an asset would be overstated and the current cost operating profit for the period would be understated because it would be charged with both a high depreciation charge (which would be based on a machine with low operating costs) and the higher operating costs associated with the old machine.

It may be possible to overcome the problem by using a more broadly based index but, in material cases, it may be necessary to address the issue directly by an analysis such as the following:

Original cost of asset	£100 000
Price index	
(a) at date of acquisition of asset	100
(b) at the date of valuation	225
Gross current replacement cost of asset based on the movement	
of the price index, £100 000 × 225/100	£225 000
Estimated total life of machine	5 years

However, let us suppose that the current cost of a modern asset which may be deemed to be a modern equivalent of the asset being valued is £250 000 and also suppose that the annual operating costs of the new machine are £16 000 a year less than the old machine and that the life of the new machine is five years.

On a comparable basis the value of the asset is clearly less than £250 000. The difference is the capital value which is attributable to the saving of £16 000 per year in operating costs. If conventional discounting theory is used, the capital value is the present value of £16 000 per year discounted at the appropriate rate of discount. Let us suppose that the rate of discount is 15 per cent, then using annuity tables the capital value is £16 000 × 3.3522 = £53 635. Thus the gross current replacement cost of the asset under review is £196 365 (£250 000 – £53 635).

The net current replacement cost will depend on the proportion of the asset which has been considered to have been used up; this will depend on the asset's estimated life and the enterprise's accounting policy for depreciation.

Depreciation (including backlog depreciation)

Under CCA the depreciation charge is based on the value to the business of that part of the asset used up in the period. In principle the value to the business should be measured by reference to the value at the date of consumption, i.e. on average current costs, but it is normally acceptable to use year-end values.

CCA does present one complication: *backlog depreciation*. This arises from the need to revalue accumulated depreciation, i.e. that part of the asset which has already been written off. This may appear to be a strange and unnecessary procedure, but it is required because the value of the asset is based in the first instance on the restatement of the gross current replacement cost of the asset. In so far as part of the asset has been used up, the increase in gross current replacement cost of the asset will overstate the holding gain made in the year. A deduction must therefore be made in respect of that part of the asset which has already been used up. Thus, the accumulated depreciation at the start of the period must also be 'revalued' and the increase in this value (backlog depreciation) must be deducted from the increase in the gross current replacement cost to give the net holding gain for the period.

To illustrate the point, suppose that an asset was purchased for £10 000 on 1 January 19X2 when the appropriate price index was 100. Let us also suppose that: (a) the index remained constant until 31 December 19X4 when it rose to 120; (b) the asset is depreciated on a straight-line basis over five years with a zero scrap value, i.e. 20% of the asset is assumed to be used up each year; (c) the company's year end is 31 December. The book value of the asset on 31 December 19X3 is as follows:

Gross current replacement cost (which is also the historical cost)	£10 000
Less Accumulated depreciation (2 years)	£4 000
Net current replacement cost	£6 000

The gross current replacement cost of the asset at 31 December 19X4 is £10 000 × 120/100 = £12 000. Given that sales revenue has accrued throughout the year, the current cost depreciation should be calculated using average values of the fixed assets. However, the Handbook permits the use of closing values as an approximation to this and in this illustration we shall use the closing value.

The CCA depreciation charge for 19X4, if based on the end of year value, is 20 per cent of £12 000, i.e. £2400. The value to the business, or net current replacement cost, of the asset at 31 December 19X4 is two-fifths of £12 000, i.e. £4800, as two-fifths of the asset remains to be used at that date.

Consider that portion of the asset which was deemed to be in existence at the beginning of the year (three-fifths of the original asset). Its value at the start of the year was £6000 and, since the index increased by 20 per cent, its year-end value was £7200. Thus the company experienced a holding gain or revaluation surplus of £1200 and this is the amount which is to be credited to the current cost reserve account.

The gross current replacement cost of the asset increased by £2000 (£10 000 to £12 000) and to take this amount, without adjustment, to the current cost reserve would be to overstate the gain.

The difference of £800 between £2000 and £1200 is the increase in value of that part of the asset which had been used up at the start of the year, i.e. two-fifths of £2000 = £800.

The argument can be illustrated graphically if it is assumed that the asset was made up of five equal blocks, one of which is used up each year. The position at 1 January 19X4 was:

Gross replacement cost, £10 000

2000	2000	2000	2000	2000

Accumulated depreciation, £4000 | Net replacement cost, £6000

The position at 31 December 19X4 *before* recording the depreciation charge for 19X4 was:

Gross replacement cost, £12 000

2400	2400	2400	2400	2400

Accumulated depreciation, £4800

Net replacement cost, £7200

	£
Increase in gross replacement cost, £12 000 – £10 000	£2000
less Backlog depreciation, £4800 – £4000	800
Net surplus on revaluation	£1200

The position at 31 December 19X4 *after* recognising the depreciation charge for the year was:

Gross replacement cost, £12 000

2400	2400	2400	2400	2400

Accumulated depreciation, £7200

Net replacement cost, £4800

In practice a convenient way of calculating backlog depreciation is to follow the steps set out below:

1 Estimate the asset's gross current replacement cost at the year end.
2 Calculate the depreciation charge for the year.
3 Calculate the required balance on the accumulated depreciation account at the year end – $x\%$ of (1) where $x\%$ is the proportion of the asset which has been assumed to have been used up.
4 Backlog depreciation is then the difference between (3) and the sum of the opening accumulated depreciation and the depreciation charge for the year.

Land and buildings

The current cost of land and buildings will in principle be their open market value. A distinction is drawn between specialised and non-specialised buildings. Specialised buildings are those which by their nature are rarely sold except as part of the sale of the business in which they are used. Non-specialised buildings are, by contrast, generally sold as units in their own right. Although it is easy to classify certain types of building – oil refineries are clearly specialised buildings, whereas office blocks are usually non-specialised – there are many instances where it will be difficult to make the distinction between the two types of building.

It is suggested that specialised buildings should be valued in the same way as plant and machinery[6] but that the underlying land should be valued on the same basis as non-specialised buildings.

---

[6] An exception to this rule is suggested in the case of buildings such as hotels, petrol filling stations and public houses which are conventionally recorded in the historical cost accounts at figures which include 'inherent trading potential' (or goodwill element). It is suggested that these buildings should be treated as non-specialised buildings because the method of valuation suggested for such buildings is a better basis of valuation of the goodwill element.

Non-specialised buildings, such as the majority of offices, shops and general industrial units, are those which are commonly bought and sold as one unit, together with the underlying land. Since the normal method of acquiring such assets is purchase in the open market, it is suggested that their net current replacement cost should be valued by reference to the estimated cost of purchasing the property on the open market and not by reference to the updated value of the cost of the building plus the current cost of the land. The use of indices is considered to be inappropriate because the market value of properties will often move in an individual way depending on their location, and the use of the individual valuations is therefore called for. In the case of land and buildings which will continue to be used by the business, their value can be increased by the cost of acquisition and adaptation, although adaptation costs should be valued on the same principles as plant and machinery. In contrast, land and non-specialised buildings which are surplus to the present and future needs of the business should be valued at their open market value less costs of disposal, i.e. at their net realisable value.

Valuation need not be made annually, but it is expected that not more than five years should elapse between valuations, which should be made by professionally qualified and experienced valuers who could be in the employ of the company owning the asset.

It should be noted that because the values of non-specialised buildings and land are found by reference to their existing condition, only the net current replacement cost is shown in the current cost balance sheet, i.e. the gross current cost and accumulated depreciation are not recorded.

Depreciation of non-specialised buildings

In accordance with the provisions of FRS 15, depreciation must be provided on buildings.

The Handbook does not provide an example showing how to depreciate non-specialised buildings but the following example is based on the guidance manual to ED 18.[7]

Suppose that XYZ Limited owned buildings which had a net current replacement cost of £550 000 on 1 January 19X3 and an estimated life of 21 years from 1 January 19X3. Let us assume that the buildings were revalued on 31 December 19X3, at which date a value of £600 000 was placed on the buildings but no change was made in the estimated life of the asset.

The depreciation charge is calculated by dividing the depreciable amount (estimated value of the buildings) by the life of the asset from the year end. The life is measured from the year end rather than the beginning of the year because the buildings were valued on the basis of their condition at the end of the year (i.e. after depreciation for the period).

The depreciation charge is thus £600 000/20 = £30 000. If the net current replacement cost of the buildings at 31 December 19X3 is £600 000 then the figure before charging depreciation for the year is £630 000. As the net current replacement cost at 1 January 19X3 was £550 000, the transfer to the current cost reserve is £80 000.

These adjustments can be conveniently summarised as follows:

---

[7] *Guidance Manual on Current Cost Accounting*, Inflation Accounting Steering Group, Tolley/ICAEW, London, 1976.

	£
Debit land and buildings	50 000
Debit profit and loss account (depreciation expense)	30 000
Credit current cost reserve	80 000

Let us assume that the buildings are not revalued in 19X4. The depreciation charge for 19X4 will thus be the same as in 19X3, £30 000. The figure can be obtained by dividing the asset's net current replacement cost at the beginning of the year by the buildings' life measured at that date. This method can be used for all periods in which there is not a revaluation of the asset. Thus, if there is no revaluation in 19X5, the depreciation charge for the year is given by:

$$\frac{\text{Net current replacement cost at 1 January 19X5}}{\text{Estimated life as at 1 January 19X5}} = \frac{£570\ 000}{19} = £30\ 000$$

Investments

A company which is a parent company of a group should present information on the effects of changing prices in respect of the whole group (*see* Handbook, Appendix 7). There will normally be no need for it to provide current cost information for itself as a single company.

Investments included as fixed assets should be included in the balance sheet at the directors' estimate of current cost. Investments carried as current assets should be shown at the lower of their current replacement cost and net realisable value.

Stocks

A distinction is made between stock which is, or is not, subject to the cost of sales adjustment (COSA). The distinction, however, is not clearly made, and the classification will in many instances depend heavily on judgement. A more detailed discussion of stock not subject to COSA will be provided later, but in general such stock may be said to consist of items for which replacement costs cannot be determined and those where such a valuation would be inappropriate because there is no intention to replace them by the purchase of substantially similar items.

Stock subject to a COSA

The value to the business of an item of stock is the lower of its current replacement cost and the recoverable amount (in the case of stock, its net realisable value).

The Handbook suggests that when stock is valued on a 'first-in first-out' basis and the average age is short, less than three months, it would generally not be misleading if stock is shown in the balance sheet at historical cost.

The current replacement cost may be obtained from any of a number of sources, including suppliers' price lists and the use of indices. In appropriate cases, use can be made of standard costs updated where necessary by the allocation of price variances. The current replacement cost of work-in-progress and finished goods is obtained by calculating the current replacement costs of the inputs (raw materials, labour and overheads) which have been required to bring the asset to its condition at the date of valuation. The existence of a suitable standard costing system would obviously help this process.

The problem of deciding whether stock should be written down to its net realisable value is little different from that which is experienced under historical cost accounting when the decision as to whether stock should be written down from cost to net realisable value has to be made. Strictly, each item of stock should be considered individually, but in practice the assessment might have to be made on the basis of the different categories of stock. If stock is written down to its recoverable value, the difference should be charged to the current cost profit and loss account and not debited to the current cost reserve account.

COSA

The COSA is the difference between the value to the business of the stock sold and its historical cost (i.e. the realised holding gain).

In principle the current cost profit and loss account should be charged with the value to the business of each item of stock sold, measured at the date of sale. The informational needs, if this were to be done for any but the smallest entities, would be enormous, so in practice proxy measures are normally used. In most instances the assumption is made that the objective of charging the profit and loss account with the current cost of replacement will be adequately served by charging the profit and loss account with the average cost for the year.

If the volume of stock has remained reasonably constant over the year, or has changed at a more or less constant rate, the average cost for the period can be used. If these conditions do not hold, perhaps because stock is purchased or manufactured at a fairly constant rate while sales are made in large parcels at infrequent intervals, the calculations should be based on shorter periods, e.g. monthly.

The averaging method

The averaging method is commonly employed to calculate the COSA because it is simple to calculate and requires the minimum of additional data over and above that which is part of the historical cost system. In essence, with the averaging method, the opening and closing stocks (based on the first-in first-out (FIFO) convention) are expressed in terms of average prices for the period. No adjustment is made to the purchases figure on the grounds that this is automatically expressed in terms of the average prices for the period. Thus, the three elements in the cost of goods sold expense (opening stock, closing stock and purchases) are all expressed in terms of the average cost for the period.

In order for the averaging method to be used, the stock volume must have been either constant or increased (or decreased) at a constant rate over the period for which the calculation is made. The average purchase price may be calculated by using a simple average of the period's prices selected at regular intervals. The use of the averaging method is illustrated below.

Suppose that the following historical cost of stock information is available (based on the FIFO convention): opening stock, £30 000; purchases, £140 000; closing stock, £40 000. Let us also assume that the appropriate price indices for the stock in question were as follows: opening stock 100; average for the year, 130[8]; closing stock,

---

[8] The average for the year will be the average value of a series of index numbers for a number of dates spaced at regular intervals over the year. It is not necessarily the simple average of the indices applicable at the beginning and end of the year.

150. The cost of goods sold expense, based on both historical cost and current cost principles, is shown below:

	Historical cost		Current cost
	£		£
Opening stock	30 000	(£30 000 × 130/100)	39 000
Purchases	140 000		140 000
	170 000		179 000
less Closing stock	40 000	(£40 000 × 130/150)	34 667
	£130 000		£144 333

The COSA is then £144 333 − £130 000 = £14 333.

Note that the COSA does not depend on knowledge of the purchases figure and that it can be found by simply adjusting the opening and closing stocks as long as the three price index numbers are available.

The opening stock element of the COSA is

$$£30\,000 \times \frac{130}{100} - £30\,000 = £9000$$

i.e. the difference between the opening stock valued at average price and its historical cost. Similarly, the closing stock element is

$$£40\,000 - £40\,000 \times \frac{130}{150} = £5333$$

i.e. the difference between the historical cost of closing stock and its value based on the average price for the period.

In times of rising prices the historical cost of closing stock will be greater than the closing stock figure based on average prices because, using FIFO, the units comprising the closing stock will have been deemed to have been purchased at more recent prices, which will be higher than the average. However, since closing stock is deducted in order to arrive at the cost of goods sold, the reduction in the value placed on closing stock will add to the COSA.

The formula for calculating the COSA can be expressed as follows. Let S_1 and S_3 be the historical cost (based on the FIFO convention) of opening and closing stock, respectively. Let P_1, P_2 and P_3 be the price indices applicable to opening stock, the average cost for the period and closing stock, respectively. The COSA is then given by:

$$\text{COSA} = S_1\left(\frac{P_2}{P_1}\right) - S_1 + S_3 - S_3\left(\frac{P_2}{P_3}\right)$$

$$= \frac{S_1}{P_1}(P_2 - P_1) + \frac{S_3}{P_3}(P_3 - P_2)$$

The above formula is also applicable in periods when prices are falling. In this case the COSA will represent a realised holding loss which will be credited to the current cost profit and loss account and debited to the current cost reserve account.

In principle the indices applied to both opening and closing stocks should relate to the date on which the stock was acquired (or more precisely to the date on which stock would have to have been ordered for delivery on the date of acquisition).

However, the Handbook suggests that the year-end indices can be used if the results so derived are not significantly different from those which would be obtained from the use of the indices applicable to the dates of acquisition.

In the above example the COSA was calculated for the year as a whole. This is acceptable if the volume of stock remains approximately constant or increases or decreases gradually. If the volume of stock is subject to severe fluctuations, the calculations should be made at more frequent intervals, possibly monthly.

It must be emphasised that the averaging method is only one method which can be used to arrive at the COSA. In the case of large units it may be possible to identify the value to the business of specific items when they are sold. In other cases the LIFO method may be used to arrive at the charge to the profit and loss account, but this method should not of course be used to find the balance sheet value of stock.

Stock not subject to a COSA

The discussion of stock has so far been based on the assumptions of a simplistic world in which stock when sold is replaced by more or less identical items. In such instances it is possible to make a clear distinction between a realised revaluation surplus (which is represented by the COSA) and an operating gain.[9] However, there are many situations where it would either be impossible or misleading to make such a distinction. An obvious example of a case where the use of a COSA would not be appropriate is provided by a trader who does not deal with a limited range of goods but instead is prepared to switch from one line to another whenever the opportunity arises of making greater profits.

As discussed earlier (p. 501), a company which is primarily concerned with stock which will not be replaced – value-based companies – will probably decide to use the financial capital maintenance approach which does not *require* the calculation of a COSA. The purpose of including a COSA in a financial capital maintenance current cost profit and loss account is to give some indication of how the total gains for the year were derived; the COSA will not affect the total gain reported as the debit in arriving at the current cost operating profit is exactly offset by the credit of the realised holding gain.

If the operating capital maintenance concept is used, then stock not subject to a COSA could be included with monetary working capital and hence any related price changes might be accounted for through the monetary working capital adjustment.

Whatever capital maintenance concept is selected, all stock should be shown on the balance sheet at its current cost, which may be derived from the use of price indices or by reference to market prices.

---

[9] It may be argued that this approach does not really arrive at the operating gain. After all, the decision to operate of necessity involves holding stock, and hence price changes in the period of stock holding are just as much a part of the operations of the firm as the differences between sales and revenue and the current cost of goods sold. For a consideration of this point readers are referred to D.F. Drake and N. Dopuch, 'On the case for dichotomising income', *Journal of Accounting Research*, Autumn 1965, and P. Prakash and S. Sunder, 'The case against separation of current operating profit and holding gain', *The Accounting Review*, January 1979.

Operating capital maintenance – two, three or four current cost adjustments?

The ASC recognised that there was, and still is, no consensus about the best way of applying the operating capital maintenance test. There is general agreement about the need for a depreciation adjustment and a cost of sales adjustment, but different views are taken on the need for the monetary working capital and gearing adjustments. Hence, in respect of the latter adjustments, the Handbook is not dogmatic but simply describes how they might be calculated should the company decide that they should be included in the current cost accounts.

Monetary working capital adjustment

The decision whether to include an MWCA depends on the view taken as to the composition of net operating assets, the proxy measure of operating capital. A list of the most commonly used definitions is provided in Paragraph 3.6 of the Handbook, which is reproduced below in Table 17.1.

Table 17.1 Net operating assets – commonly used definitions

(a) Fixed assets and stock

(b) Fixed assets, stock and monetary assets (excluding fixed or long-term monetary assets)

(c) Fixed assets, stock and all monetary assets

(d) Fixed assets, stock and all monetary assets less all liabilities

(e) Fixed assets, stock and all monetary assets less liabilities (excluding long-term borrowings)

(f) Fixed assets, stock and monetary assets (generally excluding cash) less short-term liabilities (generally excluding bank overdrafts)

The authors believe that in so far as it is necessary for a company to maintain a positive balance in net monetary assets, or is in a position to be financed in part by 'negative net monetary assets', then, if the company uses the operating capital maintenance concept and financial statements are to reflect the effect of changing prices, it is necessary to include an MWCA. This should be based on those net monetary assets which are required for the day-to-day operations of the business, hence excess cash holdings which may be used for dividend or for major capital investment should be excluded.

Probably the most useful definition of monetary working capital was that provided in SSAP 16, which defined monetary working capital as the aggregate of:

(a) trade debtors, prepayments and trade bills receivable, plus
(b) stock not subject to a cost of sales adjustment, less
(c) trade creditors, accruals and trade bills payable,

in so far as they arise from the day-to-day operating activities of the business as distinct from transactions of capital nature.[10]

The standard went on to point out that bank balances and overdrafts may fluctuate with the volume of stock or the items in (a), (b) and (c) above. It was argued that

---

[10] SSAP 16, Para. 44.

the part of bank balances or overdrafts arising from those fluctuations should be included in monetary working capital together with any cash floats required to support day-to-day operations.

One obvious example of a situation where bank balances or overdrafts should be included in monetary working capital is provided by a business which, because of the seasonal nature of activities, exhibits considerable fluctuations in its holding of stock and its investment in debtors. The most likely consequence of the business's net reduction in its investment in stock plus debtors less creditors is an increase in its bank balance (or a reduction in its overdraft). If prices rise in the period during which the business's bank balance is high, the business will only be able to purchase a lesser quantity of stock, etc., unless additional working capital is obtained. In such an example the temporary increase in the bank balance should be included as part of the monetary working capital and a MWCA should be calculated by reference to the total amount of working capital required in the circumstances of the business, irrespective of its composition.

Calculation of the MWCA

The MWCA is calculated in the same way as the COSA and the averaging method described on pp. 508–9 is usually found to be the most convenient approach. If the averaging method is used, the calculation will be based on the opening and closing balances of items included in monetary working capital, appropriate price indices relating to the beginning and end of the period and the average price index for the period.

The calculations can be done for the year as a whole or separate calculations may be made for lesser periods. It is important to ensure that the MWCA is calculated by reference to the same periods as the COSA. The reason for this is the relationship between stock and the remaining elements of working capital. In general, if stock is decreased, the other elements of working capital are increased and vice versa.

In principle, separate index numbers should be used to calculate the various elements of the MWCA. The index for debtors should be based on the movements of the costs of the goods and services sold which gave rise to the debtors.

In many cases the index used for the stock of finished goods will be suitable for debtors, but adjustments may be required if, for example, certain products are sold primarily for cash while others are sold on credit, since it is the costs of the inputs used in the manufacture of the goods sold on credit which are relevant to the debtors adjustment. Strictly, the calculation should be based on the debtors figure less the profit element, but the total debtors could be used where this gives a fair approximation.

The index for creditors should be based on movements of the items which are financed by creditors. Thus, changes in wage rates which should in general be included in the debtors index will often be immaterial so far as the index for creditors is concerned. Despite the fact that these two indices will normally reflect different price movements, where the percentage changes in debtors and creditors indices over the period are similar, a single index can be used.

As is the case with the COSA, regard must be paid to the average age of the debtors and creditors when applying the index if to do so would yield a materially different adjustment than would be obtained by the index numbers relating to the ends of the periods over which the calculation is made. Thus, if, for example, the average age of debtors is one month, the value of the appropriate index number at 30 November should be applied to the closing balance of debtors if the business has a 31 December year end.

If stock not subject to a COSA is included in monetary working capital, the appropriate index should be based on price changes most appropriate to the stock in question and the general nature of the business. In the absence of a more suitable index a general index should be applied.

If cash or overdrafts are included in monetary working capital, the index should be based on the price movements of the items which will be purchased by the cash.

If a business's monetary working capital is a net liability and if the net liability exceeds the value of stock subject to a COSA, the excess is not regarded as financing working capital and should be excluded from the MWCA calculation. The excess is included in the net borrowing figure and will therefore affect the gearing adjustment (*see below*).

We will now present an example to illustrate the calculation of both the COSA and MWCA.

Example 17.1

Suppose that Fowl Limited's current assets and current liabilities at 1 January and 31 December 19X5 are as follows:

	1 January		*31 December*	
	£	£	£	£
Current assets				
Stock at historical cost		60 000		90 000
Trade debtors		20 000		65 000
Prepayments		1 200		1 400
Cash in hand		2 000		2 200
		83 200		158 600
less Current liabilities				
Trade creditors	30 000		80 000	
Accrued expenses	5 000		7 000	
Dividends payable	16 000		20 000	
Corporation tax	20 000		44 000	
Bank overdraft	22 000	93 000	15 000	166 000
Net current assets		£(9 800)		£(7 400)

Assume:

(a) that the price movements relevant to stock, debtors and creditors follow the same path, thus enabling us to use the same index for all these items;

(b) that in view of the rapid turnover of stocks, debtors and creditors the index numbers at the beginning and end of the period can be used;

(c) that the business is not subject to any seasonality and that the COSA and MWCA can be calculated for the year as a whole;

(d) that the company's bank overdraft does not fluctuate with the level of stock, trade debtors and creditors and that it does not require cash floats to support its day-to-day operations. Thus, cash and overdrafts are excluded from the MWCA calculation;

(e) that the appropriate index numbers referred to in paragraph (a) are: 1 January, 120; average for the year, 125; 31 December, 140.

Under these assumptions, the cost of sales adjustment using the formula for the averaging method given on p. 509 is:

$$\text{COSA} = \frac{£60\,000}{120}\,(125 - 120) + \frac{£90\,000}{140}\,(140 - 125) = £12\,143$$

On the basis of the definition of monetary working capital given on p. 511 and the above assumptions, monetary working capital at 1 January and 31 December is:

	1 January		31 December	
	£	£	£	£
Trade debtors		20 000		65 000
Prepayments		1 200		1 400
		21 200		66 400
less Trade creditors	30 000		80 000	
Accrued expenses	5 000	35 000	7 000	87 000
		£(13 800)		£(20 600)

Note that the cash, dividends payable, corporation tax and the bank overdraft have not been included.

At both 1 January and 31 December the monetary working capital is a net liability, but, as the net liabilities are less than the stock subject to the COSA at both dates, nothing has to be added to net borrowings (*see below*).

Using the averaging method the MWCA is given by:

$$\text{MWCA} = \frac{-£13\,800}{120}\,(125 - 120) + \frac{-£20\,600}{140}\,(140 - 125) = -£2782$$

As the MWCA is negative, £2782 will be credited to the current cost profit and loss account and debited to the current cost reserve account.

In a case such as this, when the same index numbers are used in the COSA and MWCA calculations, the combined figure of £9361 (£12 143 – £2782) could be shown in the current cost profit and loss account.

The gearing adjustment

We have already described the rationale for a gearing adjustment and the fact that the Handbook describes two types: the restricted and full adjustments described in the Handbook as Type 1 and Type 2 adjustments, respectively (*see* p. 494). The Handbook does not state any preference between the two, or indeed whether there should be a gearing adjustment at all. The authors believe that in the context of current cost accounts based on the maintenance of operating capital, the gearing adjustment does provide useful information and, of the two versions presented in the Handbook, the full adjustment is the more logical in that it attempts to measure the effect of all relevant price changes.

In this section we will concentrate on the technical aspects of the topic and will first consider the measurement of *average net borrowing* and the *gearing ratio* which are required to calculate either type of gearing adjustment.

Average net borrowing

Net borrowings can be defined as:

(a) the aggregate of all liabilities and provisions fixed in monetary terms (including preference share capital, convertible debentures and deferred tax but excluding proposed equity dividends), other than those included as part of monetary working capital and those which are, in substance, equity capital; less

(b) the aggregate of all current assets other than those subject to a cost of sales adjustment and those included as part of monetary working capital.

(*Handbook*, Para. A5.10)

The average net borrowing may be calculated by using a simple average of the opening and closing balance sheets, unless there have been substantial changes during the year, in which case a weighted average would be more appropriate.

If, unusually, net borrowing is negative, then no gearing adjustment is made.

In summary, net borrowing will, in most cases, be made up of all those monetary items which are not part of the equity shareholders' interest (preference shares are part of net borrowing) or monetary working capital.

The gearing ratio

The gearing ratio (R) is the ratio of the average net borrowing during the period (L) to the sum of average net borrowing and average equity shareholders' interest (including proposed dividends) (S), i.e.

$$R = \frac{L}{L + S}$$

Some readers, having noted that one needs the shareholders' interest from the current cost balance sheet in order to calculate the gearing adjustment, may be puzzled about how to proceed given that one needs the gearing adjustment in order to complete the current cost balance sheet. The answer to this apparent paradox is that the gearing adjustment simply represents a transfer between the current cost reserve account and the profit and loss account, which are both part of the shareholders' interest. It is therefore necessary initially to prepare draft current cost accounts without the gearing adjustment in order to find the shareholders' interest and net borrowing; the inclusion of the gearing adjustment will then be a final adjustment which will change the composition but not the total of shareholders' interest.

Example 17.2

Suppose that the current cost balance sheets (before the calculation of the gearing adjustment in the case of 19X7) at 31 December 19X6 and 19X7 are as follows:

	19X6		19X7	
	£000	£000	£000	£000
Fixed assets		11 200		12 300
Net current assets				
Stock	3 000		4 300	
Monetary working capital	500		2 200	
Carried forward	3 500	11 200	6 500	12 300

	£000	£000	£000	£000
Brought forward	3 500	11 200	6 500	12 300
Proposed dividends	(200)		(300)	
Other current liabilities (incl. tax)	(600)	2 700	(400)	5 800
		13 900		18 100
Debentures	(4 000)		(4 000)	
Deferred tax	(600)	(4 600)	(700)	(4 700)
		£9 300		£13 400
Share capital and reserves				
Ordinary shares		5 000		6 000
Share premium		–		500
Current cost reserve		3 200		4 100
Other reserves		1 100		2 800
		£9 300		£13 400

Movement on current cost reserve

	£000
Balance 1.1. 19X7	3200
add COSA and MWCA	600
Increase in current cost of fixed assets	300
Balance 31.12.19X7	£4100

In order to calculate the gearing adjustments it will be helpful to recast the balance sheets to show net borrowing and equity shareholders' interest.

	£000	£000
Equity shareholders' interest:		
Share capital and reserves	9 300	13 400
Proposed dividends	200	300
Total equity shareholders' interest	£9 500	£13 700
Net borrowing:		
Other current liabilities	600	400
Debentures	4 000	4 000
Deferred tax	600	700
Total net borrowing	£5 200	£5 100

The average net borrowing is given by:

$$L = \frac{£5200 + £5100}{2} = £5150$$

and the average equity shareholders' interest by:

$$S = \frac{£9500 + £13\,700}{2} = £11\,600$$

The gearing ratio is then given by:

$$\frac{L}{L + S} = \frac{£5150}{£5150 + £11\,600} = 0.31$$

The two gearing adjustments are then:

Restricted – Type 1

Gearing ratio × current cost operating adjustments

$$0.31 \times £600 = £186$$

Full – Type 2

Gearing ratios × all holding gains in 19X7

$$0.31 \times £(600 + 300) = £279$$

Corresponding amounts and trend information

'For yet another year, sales have reached a new high' is the sort of statement which used to appear far too frequently in chairpersons' reports. Inflation made it easy for companies to present their results with a rosy glow when, in reality, the failure of the company to keep in step with the fall in the value of money should have been the cause for great concern.

The ASC recognised this and suggested that, to avoid distortion, adjustments should be made both to the corresponding amounts and figures for the previous period, which are required by the Companies Acts, and to any historical summaries, typically for a five- or ten-year period, which although not required by law are a common feature of financial statements.

If the corresponding amounts are restated into units of constant purchasing power, it is still necessary to show the figures before adjustment in order to comply with the Companies Acts.

Comprehensive example

We will conclude this chapter by providing a comprehensive example based, first, on the maintenance of operating capital and, second, on the maintenance of real financial capital.

Example 17.3 Operating capital maintenance

The historical cost and current cost balance sheets of Ant Limited as at 31 December 19X4 are given below:

	Historical cost £	Current cost £	Difference £
Fixed assets			
Cost	180 000	212 400	
less Accumulated depreciation	18 000	21 240	
Carried forward	162 000	191 160	29 160

	£	£	£
Brought forward	162 000	191 160	29 160
Current assets			
Stock	50 000	52 174	2 174
Debtors	60 000	60 000	
Current liabilities			
Creditors and accrued expenses	(30 000)	(30 000)	
Dividends payable	(5 000)	(5 000)	
Overdraft	(50 000)	(50 000)	
	187 000	218 334	31 334
Long-term liabilities			
10% debentures	(60 000)	(60 000)	
	£127 000	£158 334	£31 334
Share capital			
£1 ordinary shares	100 000	100 000	
Current cost reserve	–	36 466	36 466
Profit and loss account	27 000	21 868	–5 132
	£127 000	£158 334	£31 334

Ant Limited started trading on 1 January 19X4. As a current cost balance sheet has been prepared at the end of its first year of trading, the balance on the current cost reserve account at 31 December 19X4 can be analysed as follows:

	£	£
Unrealised surpluses		
Fixed assets	29 160	
Stock	2 174	31 334
Realised surpluses – the cumulative total of		
the current cost adjustments that have been		
passed through the profit and loss account		
including the gearing adjustment		5 132
		£36 466

Normally when current cost accounts are prepared for the first time the current cost reserve will include only unrealised surpluses at the date of introduction of the system and it would not be possible to identify past realised surpluses.

Ant Limited's historical cost trading and profit and loss account for the year ended 31 December 19X5 and balance sheet as at that date are given below:

Ant Limited
Trading and profit and loss account for the year ended 31 December 19X5

	£	£
Sales		500 000
less Opening stock	50 000	
Purchases	390 000	
	440 000	
less Closing stock	90 000	350 000
Gross profit carried forward		150 000

	£	£
Gross profit brought forward		150 000
less Sundry expenses	56 000	
Debenture interest	6 000	
Depreciation	28 000	90 000
Profit before taxation		60 000
less Corporation tax		16 000
		44 000
less Dividends		
Paid	8 000	
Proposed	15 000	23 000
		21 000
Retained profits 1 January 19X5		27 000
Retained profits 31 December 19X5		£48 000

Balance sheet as at 31 December 19X5

	£	£	£
Fixed assets			
Cost		380 000	
Accumulated depreciation		46 000	334 000
Current assets			
Stock		90 000	
Debtors		100 000	
Balance at bank		9 000	
less Current liabilities		199 000	
Creditors	50 000		
Accrued expenses	4 000		
Dividends payable	15 000		
Corporation tax	16 000	85 000	114 000
			448 000
10% debentures			60 000
			£388 000
Share capital			
£1 ordinary shares			300 000
Share premium account			40 000
Profit and loss account			48 000
			£388 000

Notes:

(a) On 1 July 19X5 the company issued 200 000 £1 ordinary shares at a premium of 20 pence per share.

(b) On 1 July 19X5 the company purchased fixed assets costing £200 000. There were no sales of fixed assets in the year. The company depreciated its fixed assets at 10 per cent per annum on a straight-line basis assuming a zero scrap value.

The workings required in order to prepare the current accounts will be organised in the following sections:

(A) Fixed assets and depreciation
(B) COSA and stock
(C) MWCA
(D) Gearing adjustment
(E) Movement on the current cost reserve account

(A)   Fixed assets and depreciation

(A1) The appropriate price index for fixed assets moved as follows:

Date:	1 January 19X5	1 July 19X5	31 December 19X5
Index:	118	132	144

(A2) An analysis of the fixed assets held on 1 January 19X5 revealed that they had all been purchased on 1 January 19X4 at a cost of £180 000.

(A3) The gross replacement cost of fixed assets at 31 December 19X5 is:

	£
Opening balance per current cost balance sheet,	
£212 400 × 144/118	259 200
Assets purchased on 1 July 19X5, £200 000 x 144/132	218 182
	£477 382

(A4) The current cost depreciation charge for 19X5 based on the average gross current replacement cost is:

	£
On fixed assets held on 1 January 19X5,	
10% of $\frac{1}{2}$ (£212 400 + £259 200)	23 580
On fixed assets purchased on 1 July 19X5,	
5% of $\frac{1}{2}$ (£200 000 + £218 182)	10 455
	£34 035

(A5) The depreciation adjustment is then

	£
Current cost depreciation	34 035
less Historical cost depreciation	28 000
Depreciation adjustment	£6 035

(A6) Required balance on accumulated depreciation at December 19X5:

	£
Fixed assets held on 1 January 19X5 (and purchased on	
1 January 19X4), 20% of £259 200	51 840
Fixed assets purchased on 1 July 19X5, 5% of £218 182	10 909
	£62 749

(A7) Backlog depreciation:

	£	£
Accumulated depreciation at 31 December 19X5		62749
less Accumulated depreciation		
(per current cost accounts)		
at 1 January 19X5	21240	
CCA depreciation charge for 19X5	34035	55275
Backlog depreciation		£7474

(A8) The CCA balance sheet figures are then

	£
Gross replacement cost (A3)	477382
less Accumulated depreciation (A6)	62749
Net replacement cost	£414633

(A9) The net credit to the current cost reserve is

	£
Increase in gross replacement cost	
Assets held on 1 January 19X5, £259 200 – £212 400	46800
Assets purchased on 1 July 19X5, £218 182 – £200 000	18182
	64982
less Backlog depreciation	7474
Net credit	£57508

(B)   COSA and stock

(B1) Assume (i) that all the stock is subject to a COSA; (ii) that the averaging method can be used and that the adjustment can be made for the year as a whole (note that this can only be done if similar assumptions can be made about the MWCA); (iii) that the average age of stock is three months; (iv) that the appropriate price index for stock moved as follows:

Date:	1 October 19X4	Average for 19X5	1 October 19X5	31 December 19X5
Index:	115	128	140	150

(B2) The COSA for 19X5 is given by:

$$\text{COSA} = \frac{£50\,000}{115}(128 - 115) + \frac{£90\,000}{140}(140 - 128) = £13\,366$$

(B3) The unrealised revaluation surplus on the stock held on 31 December 19X5 is given by:

	£
Current replacement cost at 31 December 19X5,	
$£90\,000 \times \dfrac{150}{140}$	96429
less Cost of stock	90000
Unrealised surplus	£6429

(B4) The credit to the current cost reserve account is:

	£	£
Realised surplus, i.e. COSA		13 366
Increase in unrealised surplus		
Unrealised surplus at 31 December 19X5	6 429	
Unrealised surplus at 1 January 19X5	2 174	4 255
		£17 621

(C) MWCA

(C1) Assume (i) that the overdraft and balance at bank do not fluctuate with the level of stock, debtors or creditors, and hence should not be included in monetary working capital; (ii) that the ages of debtors and creditors can be ignored and the year-end index numbers can be used in the calculation; (iii) that the appropriate price indices are as follows:

Date	1 January 19X5	Average for 19X5	31 December 19X5
Debtors index	120	133	146
Creditors and accrued expenses index	115	125	135

(C2) The MWCA is then given by

$$\text{Debtors,} \quad \frac{£60\,000}{120}\,(133-120) + \frac{£100\,000}{146}\,(146-133) = 15\,404 \quad £$$

Creditors and accrued expenses,

$$\frac{-£30\,000}{115}\,(125-115) - \frac{£54\,000}{135}\,(135-125) = \begin{array}{r} -6\,609 \\ \hline £8\,795 \end{array}$$

(D) Gearing adjustment

(D1) In order to calculate the gearing ratio it is necessary to construct a draft CCA balance sheet as at 31 December 19X5. It will be helpful if we first summarise the adjustments that have been made to the current cost reserve and the profit and loss account:

	£
Balance current cost reserve 1 January 19X5	36 466
add Increases for 19X5	
Fixed assets (A9)	57 508
Stock (B4)	17 621
MWCA (C2)	8 795
Balance before gearing adjustment at 31 December 19X5	£120 390

The balance on the CCA profit and loss account as at 31 December 19X5 (before making the gearing adjustment) is:

	£	£
Balance on CCA profit and loss account at 1 January 19X5		21 868
Increase in retained earnings in 19X5, historical cost profit and loss account	21 000	
Carried forward	21 000	21 868

	£	£	£
Brought forward		21 000	21 868
less Current cost adjustments			
Depreciation adjustment (A5)	6 035		
COSA (B2)	13 366		
MWCA (C2)	8 795	28 196	(7 196)
Balance of CCA profit and loss account			
at 31 December 19X5 before the gearing			
adjustment			£14 672

(D2) A draft CCA balance sheet (before the gearing adjustment) can now be prepared. For convenience the balance sheet will be arranged so as to disclose the totals of net operating assets, shareholders' interest and net borrowing.

CCA balance sheet as at 31 December 19X5 (before making the gearing adjustment for 19X5)

	£	Workings
Net operating assets		
Fixed assets	414 633	A8
Stock	96 429	B3
Debtors	100 000	
Creditors	(50 000)	
Accrued expenses	(4 000)	
	£557 062	
Shareholders' interest		
Share capital	300 000	
Share premium	40 000	
Profit and loss account	14 672	D1
Current cost reserve	120 390	D1
Proposed dividends	15 000	
	£490 062	
Net borrowing		
Balance at bank	(9 000)	
Corporation tax	16 000	
Debentures	60 000	
	£67 000	

Only the shareholders' interest and net borrowing are required to calculate the gearing proportion. In practice it will often be simplest to calculate the net operating assets and net borrowing, thus deriving shareholders' interest as the balancing figure.

(D3) As the gearing ratio is based on average values it is necessary to analyse the opening balance sheet to derive the required totals:

Analysis of CCA balance sheet as at 1 January 19X5

	£
Net operating assets	
Fixed assets	191 160
Stock	52 174
Debtors	60 000
Creditors	(30 000)
	£273 334

Shareholders' interest	£
Share capital	100 000
Current cost reserve	36 466
Profit and loss account	21 868
Proposed dividends	5 000
	£163 334
Net borrowing	
Overdraft	50 000
Debentures	60 000
	£110 000

(D4) The required averages are then calculated as follows:

Shareholders' interest $(S) = 0.5\ (163\,334 + 490\,062) = £326\,698$;

Net borrowing $(L) = 0.5\ (110\,000 + 67\,000) = £88\,500$.

The gearing ratio is then given by:

$$\frac{L}{L + S} = \frac{88\,500}{88\,500 + 326\,698} = 0.21$$

(D5) The total of the current cost adjustments (see D1) is £28 196 and the Type 1, restricted, gearing adjustment is therefore $0.21 \times £28\,196 = £5921$.

(E)   Movements on the current cost reserve

(E1)   The Handbook suggests that a full set of financial statements based on the current cost convention should include a statement showing the movement in current cost reserve distinguishing between the realised and unrealised elements.

(E2)   The balance on the current cost reserve account at 31 December 19X5 is:

	£
Balance (excluding gearing adjustment) from D1	120 390
less Gearing adjustment (D5)	5 921
Balance at 31 December 19X5	£114 469

(E3)   The above balance can be analysed in the manner described below, which will enable the realised and unrealised elements to be identified. Special reference needs to be made to the treatment of the depreciation adjustment for the year, i.e. the difference between the current cost and the historical cost depreciation charges. The excess depreciation is credited to the accumulated depreciation account and not the current cost reserve. It does, however, have an impact on the current cost reserve as it represents a transfer from the unrealised to the realised section of the account. This is because depreciation is a measure of the consumption of an asset and hence is a measure of the surplus on the fixed assets which has been realised during the year.

	Unrealised £	Realised £
Fixed assets		
Line 1: Balance at 1 January 19X5	29 160	
Line 2: Increase for year (A9)	57 508	
Line 3: Depreciation adjustment (A5)	(6 035)	6 035
Carried forward	80 633	6 035

	Unrealised £	Realised £	Total £
Brought forward	80 633	6 035	–
Stock			
Line 4: Balance at 1 January 19X5	2 174		
Line 5: Increase in unrealised surplus (B4)	4 255		
Line 6: COSA (B2)		13 366	
Line 7: Realised surpluses at			
1 January 19X5		5 132	
Line 8: MWCA (C2)		8 795	
Line 9: Gearing adjustment (D5)		(5 921)	
	£87 062	£27 407	£114 469

(E4) Using the above table a suitable statement can be prepared:

Current cost reserve	£	£	£
Balance at 1 January 19X5			
(Lines 1, 4 and 7)			36 466
Revaluation surpluses			
reflecting price changes			
Fixed assets (Line 2)	57 508		
Stocks and work-in-progress			
(Lines 4, 5 and 6)	17 621	75 129	
MWCA (Line 8)		8 795	
Gearing adjustment (Line 9)		(5 921)	78 003
			£114 469
Of which:			
Realised			27 407
Unrealised			87 062
			£114 469

We can now present the current cost accounts; to save space we will not reproduce all the notes which are suggested in the Handbook.

Ant Limited
Current cost profit and loss account for the year ended 31 December 19X5, based on the operating capital maintenance concept

	£	£	Workings
Turnover		500 000	
Cost of sales		(350 000)	
Gross profit		150 000	
Distribution costs and administrative			
expense		(84 000)	
Historical cost operating profit		66 000	
Current cost operating adjustments			
(Note (1))		(28 196)	D1
Current cost operating profit		37 804	
Interest payable	(6 000)		
Gearing adjustment	5 921	(79)	D5
Carried forward		37 725	

	£
Current cost profit on ordinary activities before taxation (brought forward)	37 725
Tax on profit on ordinary activities	(16 000)
Current cost profit for the year	21 725
Dividends paid and proposed	23 000
Current cost loss retained	£(1 275)

Note (1) Current cost operating adjustments

	£
Cost of sales	13 366
Monetary working capital	8 795
Working capital	22 161
Fixed assets (depreciation)	6 035
Current cost operating adjustments	£28 196

Current cost balance sheet as at December 19X5, based on the operating capital maintenance concept

	£	£	Workings
Fixed assets			
Tangible assets		414 633	A8
Current assets			
Stocks	96 429		B3
Debtors	100 000		
Cash at bank and in hand	9 000		
	205 429		
Creditors: Amounts falling due within one year:			
Trade creditors	(50 000)		
Other creditors			
sundry	(4 000)		
taxation	(16 000)		
proposed dividend	(15 000)		
	(85 000)		
Net current assets		120 429	
		535 062	
Creditors: Amounts falling due after more than one year			
10% Debentures		(60 000)	
		£475 062	
Capital and reserves			
Called-up share capital		300 000	
Share premium account		40 000	
Other reserves (Note (2))		135 062	
		£475 062	

		Workings
Note (2) Other reserves		
	£	
Current cost reserve	114 469	E4
Profit and loss account (£21 868 – £1275)	20 593	
	£135 062	

We will now present accounts based on the maintenance of real financial capital.

Example 17.4 Real financial capital maintenance

Facts are as in Example 17.3 with the following additional information.
Assume that the index of retail prices moved as follows:

Date:	1 January 19X5	30 June 19X5	31 December 19X5
Index:	150	172	188

Note that the assets and liabilities will be shown at the same figures, irrespective of whether the balance sheet is based on the maintenance of operating capital or financial capital. The only difference is the composition, but not the total, of owners' equity. In an 'operating capital' balance sheet, owners' equity includes a current cost reserve, whereas in a 'financial capital' balance sheet it will include a financial capital maintenance reserve.

We will assume that as at 31 December 19X4 the relevant figures in the 'financial capital' balance sheet were:

	£
Financial capital maintenance reserve	30 000
Profit and loss account	28 334
	£58 334

£58 334 is the sum of the current cost reserve (£36 466) and the profit and loss account balance (£21 868) shown on the 'operating capital' balance sheet appearing on p. 518.

Most of the workings required for this example have already been presented in Example 17.3 and references will be made to that example. The only new working is that required to calculate the inflation adjustment.

(F) Inflation adjustment to shareholders' funds

There was a share issue on 1 July 19X5 and hence there need to be separate adjustments for the opening balance and the proceeds of the share issue.

(F1) *Inflation adjustment*

	£
Opening capital £158 334 (188/150 – 1)	40 111
Share capital issued on 1 July 19X5	
£240 000 (188/172 – 1)	22 326
	£62 437

There are a number of ways of presenting the current cost profit and loss account based on the maintenance of financial capital. The virtue of the format used in this example is that it provides a detailed analysis of the holding gains.

Ant Limited

Current cost profit and loss account for the year ended 31 December 19X5 based on the maintenance of financial capital

	£	£	Workings
Historical cost profit for year before interest and taxation		66 000	
Interest		(6 000)	
Tax on profit		(16 000)	
Historical cost profit for year		44 000	
Cost of sales adjustment	(13 366)		
Depreciation adjustment	(6 035)	(19 401)	
Current cost retained profit		24 599	
Unrealised holding gains arising during the year (Note (a))	63 937		
Realised holding gains	19 401		
Realised holding gains previously recognised as unrealised (Note (b))	(8 209)		
Total holding gains	75 129		
Inflation adjustment to shareholders' funds	(62 437)		F1
Real holding gains		12 692	
Total real gains		37 291	
Dividends, paid and proposed		23 000	
Amount retained		£14 291	

Note (a) Unrealised holding gains arising during the year:

	£	Workings
Fixed assets	57 508	A9
Stock	6 429	B4
	£63 937	

Note (b) Realised holding gains previously recognised as unrealised:

	£	Workings
Depreciation adjustment	6 035	A5
Stock, unrealised holding gain at 1 January 19X4	2 174	B4
	£8 209	

Current cost balance sheet as at 31 December 19X5 based on the maintenance of financial capital

The assets and liabilities of the company will be shown at the same amounts as those shown in the current cost balance sheet on p. 526 totalling £475 062. However, the shareholders' interest, in particular the reserves, will be different:

	£
Net assets as before	475 062
Capital and reserves	
Called-up share capital	300 000
Share premium account	40 000
Financial capital maintenance reserve (Note (c))	92 437
Profit and loss account reserve (Note (c))	42 625
	£475 062

Note (c) Movement on reserves during the year:

	Financial capital maintenance reserve	Profit and loss reserve
	£	£
Balance at 1 January 19X5	30 000	28 334
Increase during year	62 437	14 291
Balance at 31 December 19X5	£92 437	£42 625

Recommended reading

See end of Chapter 18.

18   Beyond current cost accounting

Overview   In the previous two chapters we examined the attempts of the ASC to design a system of Current Cost Accounting (CCA) to replace or supplement the traditional historical cost accounts. In this chapter, we start by assessing the virtues of this CCA system for some of the main purposes for which periodic financial statements are used.

We then explore an alternative system, real terms current cost accounting, which combines useful features of both Current Purchasing Power accounting (CPP) and CCA.

The Institute of Chartered Accountants of Scotland publication *Making Corporate Reports Valuable*[1] took a much more revolutionary approach to the reform of accounting and we outline the major features of this report which include a call for further study of a system of accounting based upon the valuation of assets at their net ralisable values rather than at current cost.

Finally we explore the evolution of the ASB's approach to dealing with changing prices, an approach which undoubtedly reflects the reduced interest in such changes during the era of low inflation rates experienced in the last decade of the twentieth century. The ASB approach has severe limitations even in a period of low inflation but lays good foundations to cope with the situation when the merits of an approach to financial reporting based on a systematic use of current values becomes more widely accepted or, of course, when inflation rates begin to rise again.

The utility of current cost accounts

In Chapter 3 we identified some of the main purposes served by the publication of periodic financial statements and examined the extent to which traditional historical cost financial statements served those purposes. Here we assess the extent to which current cost accounts would satisfy those same purposes, namely control, taxation, consumption and valuation.

Control

Current cost accounts are likely to be more helpful than historical cost accounts or current purchasing power accounts in helping shareholders and others to assess how well or badly the directors have employed the resources which have been entrusted to them, especially through the use of such measures as return on capital employed. The current cost accounts attempt to show the current values of the assets of the company and whether or not the net assets have increased during a period after allowing for

---

[1] P.N. McMonnies (ed.), *Making Corporate Reports Valuable*, Institute of Chartered Accountants of Scotland and Kogan Page, London, 1988.

either specific or general price changes depending upon which capital maintenance concept is applied. Thus, it may be argued that the current cost accounts would provide a better vehicle for the exercise of control by shareholders and others.

There are obvious weaknesses with the ASC Handbook's current cost model, notably the complete absence of regard to changes in the general price level found in the operating capital maintenance variant, and the partial treatment provided by the financial capital maintenance approach.

Taxation

If one makes the not unreasonable assumption that a government would only wish to levy taxation on any surplus that is generated after the substance of the business has been maintained, then it can be seen that CCA is likely to provide a better basis for taxation than the historical cost or CPP methods.

It must be recognised that the amount of taxation payable by a company depends not only upon the way in which its taxable profit is calculated, but also upon the nominal tax rate applied to that taxable profit. Even if the government were to adopt current cost profits, rather than historical cost profits, as the basis for the computation of taxable profits, it might still wish to raise the same amount from the taxation of business profits. If such were the case, there would be a redistribution of the tax burden within the business sector, with no change in the total burden on that sector.

Current cost accounting does *prima facie* seem to provide a suitable basis for taxation, but since equity and clarity are desirable characteristics of any system of taxation much more will have to be done if taxes are to be based on current cost accounting. In particular, the degree of choice allowed to companies, especially with regard to the capital maintenance concept, would need to be reduced. It is unlikely that the Inland Revenue would accept the degree of subjectivity involved in any system of current cost accounting which has yet been developed.

The treatment of the gearing adjustment would also require careful consideration. It is reasonable to include the gearing adjustment in arriving at the profit subject to taxation, as it does offset the cost of interest which is charged to the accounts, so only the real cost of interest as opposed to the nominal charge would be allowed against tax. However, if this were done, there would be a strong case for not taxing the whole of the interest payments received by lenders, thus allowing them some relief from inflation. Such a change would have significant consequences for the whole of the tax system – both personal and corporate – and is unlikely to be made without a good deal of discussion.

Consumption

As is the case with taxation, the extent to which financial statements assist in the making and monitoring, by shareholders and others, of the consumption or dividend decision depends on the concept of capital which is to be 'maintained'. Although at its present state of development there is no general agreement as to the most suitable capital maintenance concept for CCA, it does not seem unreasonable to suggest that both the operating and financial capital bases provide more useful information than that provided by the historical cost model which, as we have argued at various places in this book, can be extremely dangerous in that dividends may be paid unwittingly out of capital.

In developing the CCA model its advocates have placed considerable emphasis on the dividend decision, but in some respects this aim has resulted in a degree of complexity which has hindered the acceptance of current cost accounting. The gearing adjustment is perhaps the most striking example. Such complexity may be inevitable in a system of accounting which does attempt to reflect reality – for reality is rarely simple. To take the dividend decision as an example, the desires of a short-term shareholder and a director/shareholder interested in security of employment will, as we argued at p. 501, be very different. If CCA is complex because it tries to present information which will be of value to both groups, should such complexity be condemned?

In developing CCA the emphasis has been placed on the needs of larger companies but it is often in the humbler parts of the business world that we find disasters caused by a level of consumption (through drawings or dividends) which is not supported by profits. If those responsible for the conduct of small and medium-sized enterprises are presented, as they are, with historical cost accounts which indicate they have generated a healthy profit, can one be surprised if some of them 'blow the lot', rather than intuitively estimating the cost of sales and other adjustments in order to see how much of that apparent profit needs to be retained to keep the business operating at its existing level?

If it is not yet possible to devise a suitable method for applying CCA principles in a way which would be appropriate to the circumstances of smaller enterprises, then, at the very least, the traditional historical cost accounts should carry a health warning.

Valuation

The sum of the values of the assets less liabilities of a business as shown in a current cost balance sheet will not, other than in the simplest of cases, be the same as the value of the businesses as a whole, but it is likely that the current cost total will give a better approximation to this value than the figures that are disclosed by the historical cost accounts.

It is not necessary at this stage to spell out the reasons why there is a difference between the total of the values of the individual assets less liabilities and the value of the business as a whole, as the subject of the valuation of a business was discussed earlier. The main reason for the difference is that which is covered by the concept of goodwill, which recognises that an existing business will usually possess substantial intangible assets such as reputation, established relationships with suppliers and customers, and managerial skills, which are not recorded in a balance sheet.

The liabilities section of the balance sheet provides another possible reason for the difference. It must be remembered that, under present proposals, liabilities are included at their nominal amounts and not at their current values.

The above discussion of goodwill was based on the assumption that the value of the business was greater than the total of the values of the assets less liabilities. The reverse can also be true, and a potential weakness of the CCA model is that it can overstate the value of the assets in particular because of the existence of interdependent assets. This problem arises from the fact that assets will be valued at their replacement cost unless a permanent diminution in value has been recognised. If each asset is considered individually and the values aggregated, it may be seen that they are collectively not worth replacing and thus that a value less than the sum of their replacement values should be placed on them. A hypothetical example of this situation is that of a railway line which runs through two tunnels. Assume that the present value of the railway line is £400 000 and the replacement cost of each tunnel is £250 000. If each tunnel is considered in isolation, it is clear that if either were destroyed it would be worth replacing, and thus would be valued for CCA purposes at £250 000. However, it is clear that if both tunnels were simultaneously destroyed they would not be replaced because the total replacement cost would exceed the benefit that would be derived from the action.

The above example is highly artificial, but the principles can obviously be extended to more complex and practical examples. The sum of the replacement costs of machines and other assets situated in a factory may easily be greater than the price that would be paid for the factory as a whole.

It is true that the position described above can and does exist under historical cost accounting. Accountants are reasonably good at ensuring that there is a write-down in the book value of individual assets, where their recoverable value falls below their net book value, but often fail to make the corresponding adjustment when there is a severe decline in the fortunes of the business as a whole. The questioning of the applicability of the going concern concept is relevant in those instances where the ability of the company to continue in business is an issue, but such questioning does not cover the intermediate position where the business can still survive but where its value has fallen below the total book value of the assets less liabilities. Clearly, given the fact that the total of the assets is likely to be higher in current cost accounts, this particular problem is likely to occur more frequently than is the case with historical cost accounting.

Thus, while it will generally be true that the current cost balance sheet totals will provide a closer approximation to the value of the business than historical cost information, there will still be substantial differences between the two values. This is not to be taken as a criticism of CCA in that the designers of the system did not set this as one of the objectives of CCA. However, it is likely that many laypeople will not fully appreciate this point, and there may well be some confusion on the part of the general public, who may believe that a system of current cost accounts should tell them how much a business is worth.

Interim summary

CCA is certainly not the perfect system of accounting in that there is more than one way of reflecting the activities of a business. Neither is it a perfect system of accounting in that, even within its own parameters, it is capable of improvement. The important practical question which had to be addressed was whether the benefits of current cost accounts exceeded the costs of developing the system and of preparing those accounts.

Attempts were made to try to answer this question, including studies commissioned by the ASC on the implementation of SSAP16. The general conclusion was that there were some advantages to be gained from the publication of current cost information in that its availability provided a better basis for decision making than a complete reliance on historical cost accounts.

The fact that current cost accounts are no longer required suggests that either the benefits did not exceed the costs or that those parties on which the costs fell, the companies and auditors, have much more political clout with the standard setters than the users, who would be expected to benefit from the information.

CPP and CCA combined

The relationship between accounting for changes in specific prices and accounting for changes in general prices has always been uneasy. As described in Chapter 15, the early moves to reform in the UK tended to polarise the position – the reformed models were either based on CPP or CCA ignoring inflation. Later, the financial capital maintenance variant of the ASC Handbook's CCA model included an 'inflation adjustment' applied to opening shareholders' funds but, in a sense, this was not accounting for inflation but an expedient to deal with the particular problem of value-based companies which could not be easily accommodated by the operating capital maintenance concept.

So why not combine the best features of CCA and CPP? Such an approach has been advocated by a number of accountants, mostly of the academic variety.[2] The change in shareholders' equity derived from a set of fully stabilised[3] financial statements based on 'value to the business' asset valuation is the same as that derived from the ASC Handbook's approach, but there is an important difference because of the treatment of price changes during the year and because of the treatment of monetary items. A fully-stabilised set of financial statements will, for example, show the loss or gain on holding monetary assets.

The basic principles can be illustrated in the following example.

Example 18.1

Guy started a business on 1 January 19X3 with £1000 which he used to purchase 100 units of stock for £10 each. Trading was not overactive during the year and the only sales were 60 units for £18 each on 31 December 19X3.

For simplicity we will assume that he incurred no overheads during the year. Let us suppose that the general price level increased by 10 per cent over the year while the replacement cost of stock increased by 15 per cent. Then Guy's only sales transaction can be analysed as follows:

	£
Cost of sales	600
Inflation increase	60
Cost of sales restated in current pounds (at 31.12.19X3)	660
Price increase in excess of inflation	30
Replacement cost at date of sale	690
Sales	1 080
Profit	£390

Now if we had prepared a standard CCA profit and loss account we would also have shown a profit of £390, as this is the difference between the sales proceeds and the current cost of the stock consumed. The major difference between the CCA approach and the above is that, in the latter, the CCA cost of sales adjustment of £90 has been broken down into two elements: (a) £60, which represents the amount by which the cost of the stock held needed to increase in

---

[2] *See*, for example, W.T. Baxter, *Accounting Values and Inflation*, McGraw-Hill, London, 1975.
[3] Fully stabilised means that all items are expressed in forms of a constant purchasing power, usually the unit of purchasing power on the balance sheet date.

order to keep step with inflation, and (b) £30, the amount by which the increase in the current cost of the stock exceeded inflation. The justification for disaggregating the CCA cost of sales adjustment in this way is that, if account is taken of the fall in the value of money, then the whole of £90 cannot be regarded as a realised holding gain, as £60 merely represents that which is required to keep step with inflation and is not a 'real gain'. In consequence, that element of the nominal gain which is required to keep step with inflation (£60 in this case) is sometimes known as the *fictitious holding gain*, whereas the *real realised holding gain* (or loss) is the difference between the current cost of the asset at the date at which it is consumed and the restated historical cost (i.e. the historical cost adjusted for the change in the general price level).

If we now turn our attention to the closing stock the same approach can be used, i.e.:

	£	£
Current cost of closing stock £400 x 1.15		460
Historical cost of closing stock	400	
Inflation adjustment (fictitious unrealised holding gain) 10%	40	440
Real unrealised holding gain		£20

Opening financial capital was £1000 and if real financial capital is to be maintained this amount must be enhanced by 10 per cent to take account of the fall in the value of money.

On the basis of the above considerations, Guy's accounts for 19X3 would appear as follows:

Profit and loss account 19X3

	£
Sales	1080
Current cost of goods sold	690
Operating profit	£390

Statement of gains/losses 19X3

	£
Operating profit	390
Realised real holding gain	30
Unrealised real holding gain	20
	£440

Balance sheet as at 31 December 19X3

	£	£
Capital 1.1.X3	1000	
Inflation adjustment 10%	100	1100
Reserves		
Realised gains		
Operating	390	
Holding	30	420
Unrealised gains		20
		£1540
Stock at current cost (40 items @ £11.50)		460
Cash (60 @ £18)		1080
		£1540

The capital and reserves section of the balance sheet well illustrates the different views that may be taken with regard to distribution. If it is accepted that capital is maintained if assets less liabilities at the balance sheet date equal opening capital after adjusting for inflation, then the maximum that could be distributed without diminishing capital is £440. If it is argued that only realised profits should be distributed then the dividend should be restricted to £420. If it is argued that the business must retain sufficient funds to maintain the same level of activity (i.e. be able to replace the 60 units sold) the maximum dividend is equal to the realised operating gain of £390.

This last line of argument brings us to the current cost account approach that it is the operating capability of the business that must be kept intact if capital is to be maintained. Thus, it can be seen that within the combined CCA/CPP approach it is possible to focus on a profit calculated on the basis of physical capital maintenance. The authors, along with most other writers on the subject, would not, however, advocate this be done, as they believe that the concept of 'operating capability' is unclear and ambiguous. However, even if the maintenance of real financial capital is taken to be the benchmark used to measure profit, it may still be of value to show what proportion of the operating profit has been paid out by way of dividend so that users can see the extent to which the reserves of the business have increased or decreased after setting aside a sum to allow for increases in specific prices over the rate of inflation. The formulation used in the above simple example would allow this assessment to be made as well as showing the extent to which the total gains are realised.

Before turning to a slightly more complex example, we will discuss those issues which we were able to sidestep in our very simple example – the monetary working capital and gearing adjustments.

The monetary working capital and gearing adjustments arise from the attempts to measure changes in operating capability. The first attempts to show the increased investment required in monetary working capital, and the second strives to show the extent to which the increased investment in stocks, fixed assets and monetary working capital would be provided by creditors. These adjustments are not required in a stabilised accounting system based on the maintenance of real financial capital. In such a system, the impact of inflation on monetary items is the loss or gain on both the business's short- and long-term monetary positions measured in the way described in Chapter 15.

Example 18.2 illustrates one way of combining current cost asset valuation with the maintenance of real financial capital.

Example 18.2

Suppose that Park Limited started business on 1 January 19X2. On that date the company issued 12 000 £1 shares and £4000 of debentures and purchased fixed assets for £12 000 and stock of £6000. The purchases were partly financed by an overdraft of £2000.

Park's balance sheet at 1 January 19X2 is then

	£		£
Share capital	£12 000	Fixed assets	£12 000
Debentures	4 000	Stock (100 units)	6 000
		Overdraft	(2 000)
	£16 000		£16 000

We will assume that all transactions took place on 1 July 19X2. On that date Park Limited purchased another 400 units for £75 (total £30 000) and sold 380 units for £36 000. Closing stock at FIFO cost is thus £9000.

Overhead expenses, including debenture interest, all paid for cash on 1 July 19X2, amounted to £5000. On 1 July the company paid its suppliers £27 000 and received £31 000 from its customers; thus trade creditors at 31 December 19X2 amounted to £3000 and trade debtors equalled £5000. The company's overdraft at the year end was

	£
Overdraft at 1 January 19X2	2 000
add Paid to suppliers	27 000
Paid for overheads	5 000
	34 000
less Received from customers	31 000
Overdraft at 31 December 19X2	£3 000

Depreciation is to be provided at 20 per cent per annum on a straight-line basis.

Assume that the appropriate price indices moved as follows:

Date	1 January	1 July	31 December
General price index	90	100	110
Stock price index	80	100	120
Fixed asset price index	95	100	105

Note that the stock price index increased by more than the rate of inflation while the fixed asset price index rose by less (i.e. the price of the fixed assets fell in real terms).

In order to see clearly how certain elements of CCA can be combined with a set of CPP accounts, it is helpful to prepare first the CPP accounts. These will appear as follows:

CPP accounts

Profit and loss account for 19X2	£(31 Dec)	£(31 Dec)	Workings
Sales, 36 000 × 110/100		£39 600	
less Opening stock,			
£6000 × 110/90	7 333		
Purchases,			
£30 000 × 110/100	33 000		
Carried forward	40 333	39 600	

	£(31 Dec)	£(31 Dec)	Workings
Brought forward	40 333	39 600	
less Closing stock,			
£90 000 × 110/100	9 900	30 433	
Gross profit		9 167	
less Overheads,			
£5000 × 110/100	5 500		
Depreciation,			
£2400 × 110/90	2 933	8 433	
		734	
Gain on short-term monetary items	344		A1
Gain on long-term monetary items	889	1 233	A1
CPP profit for the year		£1 967	

Balance sheet as at 31 December 19X2

	£(31 Dec)	£(31 Dec)
Fixed assets		
Cost		
£12 000 × 110/90	14 667	
less Accumulated		
depreciation,		
£2400 × 110/90	2 933	11 734
Current assets		
Stock, £900 × 110/100	9 900	
Debtors	5 000	
Current liabilities	14 900	
Creditors	(3 000)	
Overdraft	(3 000)	8 900
		20 634
Debentures		4 000
		£16 634
Share capital,		
£12 000 × 110/90		14 667
Retained profits		1 967
		£16 634

CPP workings

(A1) Loss on short-term monetary items is given by

		Actual £		Conversion factor	£(31 Dec)	
1 Jan	Opening balance		2 000	110/90		2 444
1 July	Sales	36 000		110/100	39 600	
	Purchases		30 000	110/100		33 000
	Overheads		5 000	110/100		5 500
31 Dec	Closing balance	1 000			1 344	
		£37 000	£37 000		£40 944	£40 944

Gain on short-term monetary items is £(31 Dec) (1344 − 1000) = £(31 Dec) 344.
Gain on long-term monetary liabilities is

$$£(31 \text{ Dec}) \ 4000\left(\frac{110}{90} - 1\right) = £(31 \text{ Dec}) \ 889$$

Real holding gains

Four adjustments need to be calculated, the realised and unrealised real gains (or losses) on stock and fixed assets expressed in closing pounds.

(a) *Real realised gain on stock (the cost of sales adjustment)* Stock with an historical cost of £27 000 was sold on 1 July by which date the stock price index had moved to 100, i.e. the replacement cost at date of sale was:

Opening stock, £(1 Jan) 6000 × 100/80	£(1 July)	7 500
1 July purchases	£(1 July)	21 000
	£(1 July)	28 500

These are 1 July pounds and have to be converted to year-end pounds;

£(1 July) 28 500 × 110/100	£(31 Dec)	31 350
Cost of goods sold per CPP profit and loss account	£(31 Dec)	30 433
Cost of sales adjustment	£(31 Dec)	917

(b) *Real realised loss on fixed assets (depreciation adjustment)*

	£(31 Dec)
Depreciation charge based on movement in specific prices, £2400 × 105/95	2 653
Depreciation charge per CPP accounts	2 933
Depreciation adjustment (loss)	(280)

Note:
(i) Depreciation is based on year-end prices.
(ii) The loss means that the cost of the asset consumed (deemed to be 20% of the fixed assets) increased by less than the rate of inflation.

(c) *Real unrealised gain on stock*

	£(31 Dec)
Closing stock	
At replacement cost, £9000 × 120/100	10 800
At adjusted historical cost £900 × 110/100	9 900
Real unrealised gain	900

(d) *Real unrealised loss on fixed assets*

	£(31 Dec)
Net book value at 31 Dec	
At replacement cost 80% of £12 000 × 105/95	10 611
At adjusted historical cost (per CPP accounts), 80% of £12 000 × 110/90	11 734
Real unrealised loss[4]	(1 123)

---

[4] Since this is the first year in the life of the assets and as depreciation is based on year-end values, there is no backlog depreciation.

We are now in a position to present the accounts, which we will do in summarised form:

Profit and loss account

	£(31 Dec)	£(31 Dec)
Sales		39 600
less: Current cost of goods sold	31 350	
Overheads	5 500	
Depreciation	2 653	39 503
Current cost operating profit		97

Statement of gains and losses

	£(31 Dec)	£(31 Dec)
Current cost operating profit		97
Gains/losses on assets		
Realised		
Gain on stock	917	
Loss on fixed assets	(280)	637
Unrealised		
Gain on stock	900	
Loss on fixed assets	(1123)	(223)
Gains on monetary items (per CPP accounts)		
Short term	344	
Long term	889	1233
		1744

Balance sheet 31 December

	£(31 Dec)	£(31 Dec)
Fixed assets, net current replacement cost		10 611
Current assets		
Stock at replacement cost	10 800	
Debtors	5 000	
	15 800	
Current liabilities		
Creditors	(3 000)	
Overdraft	(3 000)	9 800
		20 411
Debentures		(4 000)
		16 411
Share Capital		
Issued	12 000	
Inflation adjustment[5]	2 667	14 667
Reserves		1 744
		16 411

[5] In years other than the first, the inflation adjustment would be applied to the opening balance of shareholders' equity. In this case the inflation adjustment is £12 000 (110/90 – 1) = £2667.

A real alternative – making corporate reports valuable

Even a casual perusal of the earlier chapters of this book would lead the reader to conclude both that most accountants (both theoretical and practical) who have thought seriously about the issues agree that historical cost accounting is unhelpful and in periods of rapid price changes positively dangerous, and that the current cost accounting path to reform has proved difficult to travel and may not bring us to the promised land. Perhaps we should approach the problem from another direction? Is there a real alternative? Some, but as yet very few, accountants believe that there is. For some years a number of theoreticians, notably Professors Chambers in Australia and Sterling in the United States,[6] have advocated the use of the net realisable value basis for asset valuation. In 1998 their proposals received a powerful stimulus in the UK from the publication of the report of a major research project undertaken by the Research Committee of the Institute of Chartered Accountants of Scotland, entitled *Making Corporate Reports Valuable*.[7] The report is extremely stimulating and challenging and is an important contribution to the debate on accounting reform. It succeeds in its attempts to challenge preconceived ideas and is revolutionary rather than evolutionary. The revolutionary nature of its proposals is reflected in the committee's decision to reject traditional terms such as profit and loss account, balance sheet and auditor, which are replaced by phrases such as operations statement, assets and liabilities statement and independent assessor.

The report deals both with matters which could be addressed in the reasonably short term and those which could only be implemented in the longer term. We will not attempt to summarise the whole of the 108-page document but focus on three aspects: the desirability of providing more contextual information; the incorporation in financial statements of the company's market capitalisation; and the longer-term proposals about a radically different form of financial reporting based on net realisable values.

More contextual information

In *Making Corporate Reports Valuable* (which will from now on be referred to as *MCRV*) four users groups are recognised: equity investors, loan creditors, employees and business contacts. It is suggested that the fundamental information needs of these external users are:

(a) information on an entity's objectives and its performance towards achieving them;
(b) a comparison of an entity's total wealth now as against that at the previous reporting date and the reasons for the change;
(c) the entity's likely future status, performance and resources;
(d) the present and projected environment of the entity; and
(e) information on the ownership and control of the entity and on the background of its management.[8]

---

[6] *See* R.J. Chambers, *Accounting, Evaluation and Economic Behaviour*, Prentice-Hall, NJ, 1966; R.J. Chambers, *Second Thoughts on Continuously Contemporary Accounting*, Abacus, September 1970; R.R. Sterling, *Theory of the Measurement of Enterprise Income*, University Press of Kansas, 1970.
[7] *Op. cit.*
[8] *Op. cit.*, Para. 9.9.

In order to satisfy these needs, *MCRV* advocates the provision of a substantial amount of structured descriptive data to accompany the quantitative data.

Market capitalisation

Equity shareholders are very interested in the price at which they could sell their shares but the aggregate figure, i.e. the share price multiplied by the number of shares in issue, or market capitalisation, is traditionally not thought to be of great relevance to statements about the financial success of the company. The conventional view is that the market price is a marginal price reflecting deals between the seller and purchaser of a small parcel of shares, and hence a poor guide to the value of the company as a whole, and is affected by changes in the market which do not relate specifically to the company concerned. In response to this traditional view, *MCRV* makes an important empirical observation when it suggests that it is believed that there is only one case on record in which the premium on a successful bid for a company quoted on the London Stock Exchange was negative.[9] Thus, it is suggested that the market capitalisation provides an estimate of the value of the entity which is consistently at or below the true value. The report goes on to suggest that the underestimation of the true value is likely to be in the region of 15–20 per cent on the grounds that this range covers the average amount of takeover premiums and that such an error is likely to be far less than that derived from a comparison of true value with the balance sheet net worth based on the historical cost convention. Thus *MCRV* suggests that the market capitalisation figure should have a prominent place in the financial statements and that directors should be required to explain the reasons for significant changes between the differences between market capitalisation and the reported figure for net identifiable assets.

A net realisable value accounting model

MCRV argues that the two main criteria for selecting a basis for asset and liability valuation should be additivity and reality.[10] By additivity is meant the quality that when all the numbers in a statement are added together, the sum should have the same meaning as each of the numbers taken on their own; *MCRV* reminds us of the old adage of the undesirability of adding apples and pears. The meaning placed on reality is that numbers in the accounts should reflect as closely as is practical one or more economic facts with which most skilled observers would agree, and not conjectures where there can justifiably be a considerable difference of opinion even amongst reasonable and skilled people.

In the view of *MCRV* both current replacement cost (the main element of current cost accounting) and net realisable value pass the additivity and reality tests, albeit with some difficulties.[11]

A number of reasons why NRV is preferred to current replacement cost are advanced, of which the following are perhaps the most important:

---

[9] *Op. cit.*, Para. 6.16.
[10] *Op. cit.*, Para. 6.4.
[11] *Op. cit.*, Para. 6.11.

(a) NRV is a value which is readily understandable by investors and other users of accounts. *MCRV* points to evidence that some external users believe that this is the value which is actually disclosed by financial statements. Thus, it is suggested that the use of NRV would go some way to reducing the 'expectation gap' in financial reporting.[12]

(b) The use of current replacement cost still includes the making of 'arbitrary decisions' about such matters as depreciation. NRV is in this context far more elegant and simple for there is no need to allocate costs to different accounting periods. Assets are simply valued by reference to the market place, and their total value is the sum that would be obtained if all the assets were sold in an orderly fashion (i.e. not as a forced sale) – very additive and very realistic.

Of course the second of the two reasons given above can be turned round and used as a strong argument against NRV as a basis for valuation. An asset which is highly specific to the needs of a particular company may have a very low value in the market place, irrespective of its value to the company.

MCRV's answer is to question the definition or rather the delineation of the asset to be valued. A highly specific asset may, in the market place, be worthless in isolation but have a value when combined with other assets. To return to the railway example (see p. 532), the market value of a tunnel may be very low (depending primarily on its use for growing mushrooms or storing wine) but *MCRV* would argue that it is more meaningful to value the business unit of which the tunnel is a part.[13]

The question of whether the focus of asset valuation can be moved from the individual asset to the business unit is perhaps the key issue to be resolved if a practical and acceptable system of accounting based on NRVs is to be established. As we have seen in Chapters 4 and 8, the ASB now certainly envisages, indeed requires, the use of such a focus on business units in the conduct of impairment reviews.

MCRV's structure for financial systems

As part of its longer-term proposals, *MCRV* suggests that there should be four main statements:

(a) Assets and liabilities statement
(b) Operations statement
(c) Statement of changes in financial wealth
(d) Distribution statement.

Assets and liabilities statement

This should show the entity's assets and liabilities at the end of the period, each stated at net realisable value. Trade creditors would normally be shown at their nominal value but, if the liabilities include securities which are traded, then that element could be included at market value.

For companies whose shares are traded, the statement would include its market capitalisation together with a statement from the directors explaining what they think are the main reasons for the difference, normally positive, between the market capitalisation and the total of the net identifiable assets.

---

[12] *Op. cit.*, Para. 6.20(b).
[13] *Op. cit.*, Para. 6.8.

A possible structure of an Assets and Liabilities Statement is:

Market value of assets (listed individually)		x
Debtors		x
Cash		x
		x
less Market value of long-term loans	x	
Creditors	x	
Deferred taxation	x	x
Net identifiable assets		x
Market capitalisation		x

Operations statement

The operations statement shows the financial wealth created by trading. It differs from a profit and loss account in the following ways:

(a) no depreciation charge;
(b) stock would be shown at NRV;
(c) only exceptional and extraordinary items of a revenue nature would be included; exceptional or extraordinary gains or losses relating to fixed assets would be included in the Statement of Changes in Financial Wealth.[14]

An operations statement might be constructed as follows:

Sales		x
less Opening stock at market value	x	
Purchases	x	
Closing stock at market value	x	
	x	
Operating costs	x	x
		x
add Dividend income		x
Income from unusual events		x
		x
less Taxation		x
Financial wealth added by operations		£x

Statement of changes in financial wealth

This statement would show the change in the wealth of the business analysed into the main components; for example, change due to operations and changes due to movements in the market value of assets and liabilities.

It might appear as follows:

---

[14] *MCRV* predates the issue of FRS 3 (1992) which has effectively abolished extraordinary items.

Financial wealth added by operations		x
Increase in value of quoted investments		x
Reduction in debenture liability		x
Increase in value of stock		x
		x
less Decrease in value of plant	x	
Decrease in value of vehicles	x	x
Distributable change in financial wealth		x
less Distributions		x
		x
New share capital		x
Change In financial wealth		£x
Movement in market capitalisation		£xx

Perhaps one of the weaker aspects of the report is the *MCRV's* treatment of changes in the general price level. It is not that the issue is ignored but more that its impact on the *MCRV* model is not explained clearly. The change in financial wealth shown by the statement is effectively measured on the basis of money capital maintenance but *MCRV* suggests that, in times of significant inflation, an adjustment should be made to reflect the effect of changes in in the Retail Price Index.[15] Such an adjustment would be required in respect of the opening net identifiable assets and the proceeds of any share issue made during the year and would result in the disclosure of the change in financial wealth in real terms.

Distributions statement
This statement would articulate with the previous statement in that it starts with the distributable change in financial wealth for the year and then shows the undistributable surpluses brought forward, from which any distributions made or proposed would be deducted. The statement could also include an inflation adjustment derived from the application of the retail price index to the value of shareholders' contributed capital at the start of the year; in addition an entity which wishes to maintain its operating capability in physical terms could make a further appropriation to maintain its asset portfolio.

The statement might be shown as follows:

Distributable change in financial wealth for the year		x
less Inflation adjustment	x	
Appropriation to maintain operating capability	x	x
		x
add Undistributed surpluses brought forward		x
less Dividends		x
Paid	x	
Proposed	x	x
Undistributed surpluses carried forward		£x

Additional statements
In addition to the above four main elements, *MCRV* advocates the publication of cash flow statements showing the inflow and outflow of cash analysed into its main

---

[15] *Op. cit.*, Para. 7.25.

components, both historical for the year past and projected for, say, the next three years. Segmental reporting is also regarded as being of importance. Where the amounts are significant it is suggested that the statements should be split:

(a) by type of product;
(b) by manufacturing location;
(c) geographically;
(d) by currency.

In the longer term, *MCRV* proposes the publication of much more descriptive information about such matters as innovation, the economic environment and staff resources.[16]
    The longer-term proposals of *MCRV* are illustrated in Example 18.3.

Example 18.3

Egghead Limited is a management consultancy business which occupies its own premises. It has a small computer services division which has for the last 15 months been engaged in the production of a suite of software under contract for a company in the furnishing industry.
    Egghead's summarised historical cost balance sheets as at 1.1.19X2 and 31.12.19X2 and its profit and loss account for the year ended 31.12.19X2 are shown below:

Balance sheets

	1.1.19X2 £000	1.1.19X2 £000	31.12.19X2 £000	31.12.19X2 £000
Fixed assets				
Freehold property				
Cost	1 000		1 000	
Acc. depr.	200	800	220	780
Vehicles and equipment				
Cost	400		440	
Acc. depr.	250	150	300	140
Investments, cost		200		200
		1 150		1 120
Current assets				
Work-in-progress	30		310	
Trade debtors	100		200	
Balance at bank	10		110	
	140		620	
Current liabilities				
Trade creditors	50		70	
Proposed dividends	30		80	
	80	60	150	470
		1 210		1 590
10% Debentures		500		500
		£710		£1 090
Share capital		400		400
Unappropriated profits		310		690
		£710		£1 090

[16] *Op. cit.*, Para. 7.44.

Profit and loss account, year ended 31.12.19X2

	£000	£000
Fees		1 200
Increase in work-in-progress		280
		1 480
less		
Sundry expenses	900	
Depreciation		
Property	20	
Vehicles and equipment	50	
Debenture interest	50	1 020
		460
less Proposed dividend		80
Unappropriated profits for year		380
P and L account balance 1.1.19X2		310
P and L account balance 31.12.19X2		£690

(A) Additional information

1 The net realisable values of the fixed assets at 1.1.19X2 and 31.12.19X2 were   as follows:

	1.1.19X2	*31.12.19X2*
	£000	*£000*
Freehold property	900	945
Vehicles and equipment	190	205
Investments	400	480

2 The only material work-in-progress relates to the computer services division's contract. The work done under the terms of the contract had a negligible value at 1.1.19X2 but it is estimated that the software developed under the terms of the contract could have been sold for £500 000 at 31.12.19X2.

3 The market values of the debentures were:

| 1.1.19X2 | £400 000 |
| 31.12.19X2 | £370 000 |

4 The shares of the company are traded on the AIM. The market capitalisation figures were:

| 1.1.19X2 | £3 000 000 |
| 31.12.19X2 | £2 900 000 |

(B) Taxation and changes in the general price levels will be ignored.

We can now prepare the four main statements proposed by MCRV.

Assets and liabilities statement as at 31.12.19X2

	£000
Market value of:	
Freehold property	945
Vehicles and equipment	205
Investments	480
Work completed by computer services division	500
Trade debtors	200
Balance at bank	110
Carried forward	2 440

	£000	£000
Brought forward		2 440
Less		
Market value of debentures	370	
Trade creditors	70	
Proposed dividend	80	520
Net identifiable assets		£1 920
Market capitalisation		£2 900

Notes:

The directors would be required to comment on the possible reasons for the difference between the value of the net identifiable assets and the market capitalisation.

A case could be made for excluding proposed dividends from the above statement on the grounds that it is not a liability until approved by the shareholders.

Operations statement for the year ended 31.12.19X2

	£000	£000
Fees from services		1 200
Increase in value of work done by computer services division		500
		1 700
less		
Operating expenses	900	
Debenture interest	50	950
Wealth added by operations		£750

Note:

Because the increase in the value of the contracts undertaken by the computer services division is due primarily to the work undertaken by that group during the year, the increase in value has been included in the operations statement. If, in contrast, much of the work had been completed in 19X1 and the increase in value was due primarily to changes in the market value for such software, the increase of wealth would not be included in the operations statement but shown separately in the statement of changes in financial wealth.

Statement of changes in financial wealth for the year ended 31.12.19X2

	£000
Wealth added by operations	750
Increases in value of freehold property	45
Increase in value of investments	80
Decrease in value of debentures consequent upon an increase in interest rates	30
	905
less Decrease in value of vehicles and equipment (see Note (b))	25
Distributable change in wealth	880
less Distribution	80
Change in financial wealth	£800
Change in market capitalisation	£(100)

Notes:
(a) The directors would be required to comment on the reasons for the difference between the change in financial wealth and the change in market capitalisation.
(b) The fall in value of vehicles and equipment is found as follows:

	£000
NRV at 1.1.19X2	190
Cost of assets acquired during the year	40
	230
NRV at 31.12.19X2	205
	£25

Distribution statement for the year ended 31 December 19X2

	£000
Distributable change in financial wealth for the year	880
Undistributed surpluses brought forward (note (i))	720
Surplus available for distribution	1 600
less Proposed dividend	80
Undistributed surpluses carried forward (note (ii))	£1 520

Notes:
(i) The undistributed surpluses brought forward may be derived thus:

	£000	£000
Assets, at NRV, at 1.1.19X2		
Freehold property		900
Vehicles and equipment		190
Investments		400
Trade debtors		100
Balance at bank		10
		1 600
less MV of debentures	400	
Trade creditors	50	
Proposed dividend	30	480
		1 120
less Share capital		400
Undistributed surplus at 1.1.19X2		£720

(ii) The articulation of the statements can be demonstrated by showing how this figure is derived:

	£000
Net identifiable assets at 31.12.19X2, per the assets and liabilities statement	1 920
less Share capital	400
Undistributed surplus at 31.12.19X2	£1 520

In the example we have ignored the effects of changes in the general price level, the treatment of which we have already identified as a weakness in the report. Further thought is needed on ways of accounting for changes in the general price level within the *MCRV* model. In other respects the example does indicate the virtues of the approach. The statement of assets and liabilities is based on a clear and easily understandable principle. It indicates how much the assets would realise if sold in an orderly fashion. In contrast, a conventional balance sheet is, as we argued, vague in its concept and not readily understandable by users, especially laypeople.

The *MCRV* operations statement reflects not only its fees and expenses but what, for this company, has been an important event, the success of the programme of work for the design of software. The profit and loss account, on the other hand, fails to recognise the event and hence gives only a partial picture of what actually occurred during the year.

The obvious concern about the *MCRV* approach is its subjectivity. The NRV of individual assets cannot always be ascertained with reasonable confidence but the estimation of NRV of 'business units' which are probably unique is even more difficult.

Two points can, however, be made in mitigation:

(a) The *MCRV* proposals which include the requirement for directors to provide systematic contextual information, including historical and projected cash flow statements, would enforce some discipline on those responsible for making the estimates. Wild guesses unsupported by reasoned arguments would be difficult to sustain in an *MCRV* system.

(b) The second point is related. The market would become suspicious of companies which habitually made wrong estimates. It may be that companies could for a year or two fool the market but, eventually, as chickens come home to roost, so estimates are converted into actual cash flows. If that suggests that the market should place less reliance on one year's figures, and in particular one year's 'bottom line,' and take a longer view, then that would be no bad thing. The UK securities market does tend to take a short-term view and moves which would reduce the tendency would help the economy.

The *MCRV* approach remains fresh and imaginative and it seems to provide an excellent basis for further thought and experimentation. The ICAS published an annual report for a company, Melody Plc, based on the ideas in *MCRV* and expressed the hope that other companies will be prepared to adopt and experiment with this approach.

The evolution of the ASB's thinking

Since its formation in 1990, the ASB has shown considerable enthusiasm for the greater use of current values in financial statements. However, in view of the earlier experience of the ASC with the introduction of current cost accounting, it is not surprising that the ASB has chosen not to move too fast.

In its discussion paper 'The Role of Valuation in Financial Reporting', issued in March 1993, the ASB clearly recognised the unsatisfactory nature of modified historical cost accounting. Nevertheless it proposed to retain the system but with more consistent revaluations of certain limited classes of assets for which supplementary information was already required by law and which were traded on a ready market. The assets to be shown at their current values were:

(a) properties;
(b) quoted investments; and
(c) stock of a commodity nature and long-term stock where a market of sufficient depth exists.

By the time it issued the first exposure draft of the 'Statement of Principles for Financial Reporting' in November 1995, the ASB was considerably more enthusiastic about the use of current values. In Chapter 5 of that exposure draft, it compares the use of current values with the use of historical costs:

> Current values *sometimes* lack the attribute of reliability. Furthermore the costs of obtaining current values *may* outweigh the benefits of their use. On the other hand, the lack of relevance of the historical cost system is a *serious* deficiency . . .
>
> (Para. 5.10 but with italics added by the authors.)

It proceeds to outline its favoured system, which may be summarised as follows:

Assets: The appropriate current value is that given by the 'value to the business' rule. (Para. 5.35)

Liabilities: The use of the value to the business rule here is an unnecessary complication because the various values will converge to a single current value and thus market values may be used. (Para. 5.36)

Capital maintenance concept: The use of a real terms capital maintenance system with the disclosure of real holding gains and losses. (Para. 5.37)

Readers will observe that this is the real terms current cost accounting system which we have illustrated in Example 18.1, and the ASB provided a simple illustration in the appendix to Chapter 5 of the Draft which is, in all fundamental respects, identical to that example.

By the end of Chapter 5, the ASB is quite clear in its preference for current values:

> The Board therefore believes that practice should develop by evolving in the direction of greater use of current values to the extent that this is consistent with the constraints of reliability and cost. (Para. 5.37)

Such a clear statements was, perhaps not surprisingly, interpreted by many commentators as an attempt by the ASB to reintroduce a system of Current Cost Accounting. As we have seen in Chapter 1, criticism of this and other matters led to the withdrawal of the exposure draft and its replacement by a revised exposure draft Statement of Principles in March 1999.

In the revised exposure draft, the ASB is much less willing to state it its preference for current values. It now proposes that we continue to use the 'mixed measurement' or 'modified historical cost' system, the system used by most quoted companies in Britain at the present time. Where current values are used, the ASB continues to favour the use of 'Value to the Business' (Para. 6.28). In measuring profit, it favours the use of the financial capital maintence concept with no adjustment for general or specific price change even though it clearly recognises that this approach is only satisfactory under conditions of stable prices (Para. 6.41–6.43).

It is clear from this revised exposure draft that the ASB is not planning revolutionary change. However, as we have seen in earlier chapters, it is certainly achieving evolutionary changes necessary for the introduction of any system of current value accounting.

In Chapter 6 we discussed the Statement of Total Recognised Gains and Losses, which collects together the profit or loss for the year with other gains and losses recognised during the year. Such a statement already records unrealised holding gains and losses when assets are revalued and could readily be used to record holding gains or losses recognised under a full blown current value system of accounting.

In Chapter 4 we explained how, in FRS 15, the ASB has introduced some order into the use of revaluations, as an alternative to historical costs, within the mixed measurement system. In particular, all assets within a particular class must be revalued and the measurement of assets at out-of-date current values has been outlawed. Where companies chose to show their assets at current values rather than at historical costs, they are required to use 'value to the business' as their valuation concept. As a consequence, more and more accountants will become familiar with this powerful concept and it will not seem as strange in future as it did when Current Cost Accounting was first introduced in the 1970s.

There are many areas of accounting where it is only possible to provide meaningful information using current values. As we have seen in Chapter 5, one such area is accounting for financial instruments. The greater use of current values which must inevitably occur in such cases will also increase the exposure of accountants to the use of current values.

Some of the building blocks which have been put in place will make the reform of accounting possible in due course as higher rates of inflation stimulate both the need for and political desire for reform.

Conclusion

Most married couples are only too aware that there is more than one way of perceiving and describing the facts. The same can be said of business: there is more more than one way of telling what has happened.

At various stages in the debate on accounting reform, it has been suggested that financial statements should include two or more values for assets and liabilities and two or more profit figures based upon different capital maintenance concepts. This so-called multi-column approach has been rejected on the ground that it would confuse the users of financial statements. In our view, if more effort had been devoted to explaining that there is more than one way of explaining the results of complex businesses, we might be in a much better position than we are now. The ASB clearly recognises the limitations of any one bottom line figure and consistently encourages users to look at the whole package of information, both numerical and discursive, which is provided. However, it still advocates the one column, rather than the multi-column, approach to the measurement of assets, liabilities and profit.

It may be that, in due course, the models presented in this chapter will provide the basis for more relevant financial reporting. Both the real terms CCA and the *MCRV* models of financial reporting provide information which is relevant to the needs of users and there seems no reason, other than the cost of producing the information, why they should not appear in a company's financial statements. As we have argued in the previous section, there is certainly now a framework in existence to facilitate a move towards a real terms current cost accounting system.

In the meantime, despite the many weaknesses and limitations of the modified historical cost accounts, recognised by professional accountancy bodies as well as by academic accountants, these accounts continue to be regarded as the 'real' accounts. While this continues, it is difficult to argue with the old adage that an accountant is someone who prefers to be precisely wrong than approximately right!

Recommended reading

Accounting Standards Committee, *Accounting for the Effects of Changing Prices: a Handbook*, ASC, London, 1986.

W.T. Baxter, *Inflation Accounting*, Philip Allan, Deddington, 1984.

Institute of Chartered Accountants of Scotland, *Making Corporate Reports Valuable*, P.N. McMonnies (ed.), Kogan Page, London, 1988.

D.R. Myddleton, *On a Cloth Untrue*, Woodhead-Faulkner, Cambridge, 1984.

D. Tweedie and G. Whittington, *The Debate on Inflation Accounting*, Cambridge University Press, Cambridge, 1984.

G. Whittington, *Inflation Accounting: an Introduction to the Debate*, Cambridge University Press, Cambridge, 1983.

Appendix: Questions

The following questions have been selected from past examination papers of the Association of Chartered Certified Accountants, the Chartered Institute of Management Accountants and the Institute of Chartered Accountants in England and Wales. We gratefully acknowledge the permission of these three bodies to reproduce their questions although we are disappointed that the Association of Chartered Certified Accountants will not permit us to include questions set after December 1997.

The pace of change in accounting in recent years makes it impossible to include professional questions which refer only to current standards. We suggest that, in answering questions, readers should do so either on the basis of the position at the date the question was set or on the basis of up-to-date tax law and standards. Use of the latter approach may occasionally mean that some parts of a question (for example an instruction to write off purchased goodwill immediately to reserves) might need to be ignored. We hope that adopting lecturers setting questions for their students will provide those students with guidance on which basis should be used.

Answers to questions are included in the **Solutions Manual** which is published separately and is available to lecturers adopting this textbook. Answers have been prepared by *John Wyett, Brian Pain* and *John Blakemore*.

1 The search for principles

1.1 The ASB's Statement of Principles sets out the concepts which underpin its development of financial reporting standards.

Required
Discuss why the ASB has adopted this conceptual approach and whether any difficulties may be encountered.

ICAEW, Financial Reporting, November 1994   (10 marks)

1.2 *The Corporate Report* states that accounting information should be useful.

Required
(a) **Identify the characteristics of useful information and discuss each briefly.**   (10 marks)
(b) **Explain whether or not you consider that identification of desirable characteristics helps to improve financial reporting.**   (6 marks)
(c) **It has been suggested that corporate reports which possess these desirable characteristics sometimes recognise the economic substance of a transaction in preference to its legal form.**
    Describe two examples of where this may occur.   (4 marks)

ACCA The Regulatory Framework of Accounting, June 1983   (20 marks)

2 Sources of authority

2.1 Your managing director has approached you saying that he is 'confused at all the different accounting bodies that have replaced the old Accounting Standards Committee'.

You are required to draft a memorandum to your managing director explaining the purpose, a description of the type of work and, where applicable, examples of the work to date of the following:

(a) Financial Reporting Council   (3 marks)
(b) Accounting Standards Board   (4 marks)
(c) Financial Reporting Review Panel   (5 marks)
(d) Urgent Issues Task Force   (3 marks)

CIMA Advanced Financial Accounting, May 1993   **(15 marks)**

2.2 'It is fundamental to the understanding and interpretation of financial accounts that those who use them should be aware of the main assumptions on which they are based.'

Requirement
Explain how Statement of Standard Accounting Practice 2, Disclosure of accounting policies, seeks to achieve this understanding.

ICAEW Financial Accounting 1, May 1987   **(15 marks)**

2.3 The Accounting Standards Committee (ASC) was criticised heavily prior to its replacement by the Accounting Standards Board (ASB). The principal intention of the ASC was to create greater uniformity in the preparation of financial reports in order that there should be more comparability between the results of different companies. Many commentators felt that the ASC failed to achieve their intentions and criticised the role of the ASC because of the following reasons:

(i)   A failure to develop an agreed conceptual framework and to specify user needs.
(ii) The composition of the ASC. The ASC had little representation from independent user groups, with the majority of its members coming from the accounting profession.
(iii) The inadequate enforcement of standards. Some writers criticised the ASC for limiting the enforcement of standards to the qualification of the audit report.
(iv) The ASC was too open to pressure from various interested groups who had a direct interest in the work of the committee. This led to political interference in the standard setting process.
(v)   A failure to respond quickly to emerging issues.

When the Dearing Committee's recommendations on a whole new structure to replace the ASC were adopted, it was hoped that the new structures would lead to the elimination of the above criticisms. However, there are those who feel that there is no need for a standard setting body, and that there is no need for accounting standards. In contrast, others feel that standards should be set by the government and be incorporated in the law.

Required
(a) Explain why there is a need for regulation of financial information in the form of accounting standards.   (7 marks)
(b) Discuss to what extent you feel that the criticisms of the Accounting Standards Committee set out above apply also to the new structure for regulating accounting standards.   (12 marks)
(c) Discuss whether you feel that FRS 1 'Cash-flow Statements' has fulfilled the objective of creating greater uniformity in the preparation of cash-flow statements.   (6 marks)

ACCA Accounting and Audit Practice, June 1994   **(25 marks)**

2.4 Before the introduction of accounting standards, accounting practices varied from enterprise to enterprise – there was inconsistency and occasionally practices were inappropriate. Intercompany and inter-period comparisons were difficult as enterprises changed accounting policies and resorted to, for example, 'window-dressing' and 'reserve accounting'.

Discuss the extent to which the publication of more than 20 accounting standards has overcome these problems. Illustrate your discussion by reference to specific accounting standards.

ICAEW Financial Accounting 2, July 1993   **(12 marks)**

2.5 'At their simplest, accounts comprise a summary of cash receipts and payments. Concepts such as accruals and substance over form lead to increased complexity and may make it difficult for a user to interpret the results and financial position of a company. The key focus of future accounting standards and legislation should be simplification, not increased disclosure and more complex rules.'

Using examples, illustrate the complexities which may make it difficult for the various users to understand published accounts. Comment on any recent action taken by the Accounting Standards Board or the Government which has affected the complexity of accounts and discuss, reaching a conclusion, whether simplification of company accounts should be a key objective for the Accounting Standards Board and the Department of Trade and Industry.

ICAEW, Auditing and Financial Reporting, final exam, July 1996 **(12 marks)**

2.6 'In recent years, there has been growing interest in, and efforts directed towards, the harmonisation of international accounting.' *Advanced Financial Accounting* by Taylor and Underdown (CIMA/Butterworth Heinemann).

You are required to explain this statement.

CIMA Advanced Financial Accounting, November 1993 **(15 marks)**

3 What is profit?

3.1 Some commentators on financial reporting practices argue that financial statements produced under the historic cost convention do not provide relevant information to users of those statements in times of rising prices.

Requirements
(a) **Identify the main limitations of historic cost accounting, explaining the nature of those limitations.** (5 marks)
(b) **Discuss how the use of other capital maintenance concepts to that applied under historic cost accounting might provide more useful information to users of financial statements.** (5 marks)

ICAEW, Financial Reporting, May 1995 **(10 marks)**

3.2 (a) **Give a brief summary of the current value replacement cost accounting system (entry values).** (6 marks)
(b) **Give a brief summary of the current value net realisable value accounting system (exit values).** (6 marks)
(c) **To what extent do you consider it would be useful to prepare financial statements which used entry values for the profit and loss account and exit values for the balance sheet and why?** (8 marks)

ACCA Level 2 The Regulatory Framework of Accounting, December 1989 **(20 marks)**

3.3 Three unrelated companies, Tower plc (a public company), Book Ltd (a private company) and Holdings plc (a quoted investment company) have summarised balance sheets, as on 30 June 1985, as set out below with relevant additional information.

(a) *Tower plc*

	£m		£m
Share capital	2.0	Fixed assets	3.3
Share premium account	0.5		
Revaluation reserves	1.0	Net current assets	2.7
Profit and loss account	2.5		
	6.0		6.0

(1) A partial revaluation of fixed assets took place during the year with the following result:

	£m
Surplus on land	0.65
Surplus on buildings	0.35
Surplus on plant and machinery	0.10
Deficit on fixtures and fittings	(0.10)
	1.00

The directors consider that the value of the remaining fixed assets not revalued is equal to their net book amounts.

(2) Depreciation is provided at 2% on buildings, 15% on plant and machinery, and 20% on fixtures and fittings. All fixed assets are depreciated for the full year on the cost or revalued amounts.

(3) Fixed assets comprise:

	£m
Land	1.2
Buildings	0.8
Plant and machinery	0.8
Fixtures and fittings	0.3
Development costs	0.2
	3.3

(b) *Book Ltd – Current Cost Balance Sheet*

	£000		£000	£000
Share capital	45	Fixed assets		50
Current cost reserve	40	Investment in Worm Ltd		40
Retained profit	55	Current assets		
		Stock	10	
		Long-term work in progress	30	
			40	
		Cash	10	50
	140			140

(1) No provision has yet been made for the losses of the subsidiary, Worm Ltd. It is estimated that the net assets of Worm Ltd in which Book Ltd has an interest of 60% are £50 000.

(2) The current cost reserve comprises:

	£000
CCA adjustments passed through profit and loss account	13
Uplift of fixed assets to CCA values	27
	40

(3) Long-term work in progress includes a profit element of £6000 calculated in accordance with SSAP 9.

(c) *Holdings plc*

	£000		£000	£000
Share capital	650	Fixed assets		
Share premium	325	Tangible		20
Reserves	4 380	Investments		5 647
		Current assets		
		Debtors	98	
		Investments	2 436	
		Cash	147	
			2 681	
		Less creditors falling due		
		within 1 year	1 793	888
				6 555
		Creditors falling due in		
		more than 1 year		(936)
		Provisions		(264)
	5 355			5 355

Reserves consist of:

	£000
Unrealised capital losses	(48)
Unrealised revenue profits	140
Unrealised revenue losses	(17)
Realised capital profits	2 890
Realised capital losses	(1 241)
Realised revenue profits	2 666
Realised revenue losses	(10)
	4 380

Requirements

(a) State concisely for each of the three types of company mentioned, the principles for calculating distributable profits under the Companies Act 1980 (now part of the Companies Act 1985). (5 marks)

(b) Calculate for each of the three companies the maximum legally distributable profits. (7 marks)

(c) Discuss the reasons why it is not normally commercially or practically desirable to make the maximum distribution. (7 marks)

ICAEW Financial Accounting II, December 1985 **(19 marks)**

3.4 The balance sheet of Omega as at 30 September 1992 contained the following balances and notes:

		£000
Share capital		10 000
Reserves:		
Share premium	*Note 1*	1 000
Revaluation reserve	*Note 2*	1 780
Other Reserves:		
Merger reserve	*Note 3*	550
Profit and loss account – 1992	*Note 4*	1 940
Profit and loss account b/f		(200)
Capital and reserves		15 070
Liabilities		15 070
Total assets		30 140

Note 1 The share premium arose on the issue of shares on 1 October 1989.

Note 2 The revaluation reserve arose as a result of a revaluation of certain of the fixed assets on 1 October 1991. It comprises a gain of £2 000 000 on the revaluation of plant and machinery, which is the balance remaining after the transfer to the profit and loss account of £200 000 representing the depreciation on the revaluation surplus; and a loss of £220 000 arising from the revaluation of office premises. The directors propose to revalue the remaining fixed assets which currently appear at historic cost in a subsequent financial year.

Note 3 The merger reserve represented the premium of £1 450 000 on shares issued on the acquisition on 1 October 1991 of a subsidiary, Alpha plc, in accordance with the merger provisions of the Companies Act 1985 less goodwill of £900 000 arising on a separate transaction. The goodwill has an estimated useful economic life of 15 years.

Note 4 The profit and loss account balance is the balance after:
(i) Writing off the total acquisition goodwill of £400 000 arising on the acquisition on 1 October 1991 of an unincorporated business carried on by Beta Associates. The estimated useful economic life of the goodwill is 10 years.
(ii) Creating a provision of £1 200 000 representing a permanent diminution in the value of a subsidiary, Gamma plc.
(iii) The transfer of the £200 000 mentioned in Note 2 from the revaluation reserve to the profit and loss account representing the amount by which the total depreciation charge for the year exceeded the amount that would have been provided if the plant had not been revalued.
(iv) Crediting an exchange gain of £38 000 that arose on the translation of a long-term loan taken out in French francs on 1 October 1991. The loan was taken out to use in the United Kingdom because the interest rate was favourable at the date the loan was raised.

Required
(a) **Calculate the amount of distributable profit for Omega on the basis that it is:**
  (i) **A public company.**
  (ii) **An investment company.** (10 marks)
(b) **Explain briefly:**
  (i) **The disclosure requirements relating to distributable profits in a single company and group context.**
  (ii) **The effect on the distributable profits of the holding company if the group has sufficient distributable profits in aggregate to make a distribution to the holding company's shareholders but the holding company itself has insufficient distributable profits.**

(iii) The effect on the distributable profits of the holding company if the holding company has sold one subsidiary company to another subsidiary for a consideration that exceeds the carrying value of the investment in the holding company's accounts.

(iv) The effect on the distributable profits of the holding company if a subsidiary company which has a coterminous accounting period declares a dividend after the end of the holding company's year end. (10 marks)

ACCA Advanced Financial Accounting, December 1992 (20 marks)

4 Assets

4.1 The valuation and depreciation of fixed assets are covered by both mandatory accounting standards and the Companies Acts as sources of authority.

Requirement
Identify the main accounting issues involved in the valuation and depreciation of fixed assets and discuss to what extent these are addressed in the above sources of authority.

ICAEW, Financial Reporting, November 1995 (10 marks)

4.2 The managing director of your company has always been unhappy at depreciating the company's properties because he argues that these properties are in fact appreciating in value. Recently he heard of another company which has investment properties and does not depreciate those properties.

You are required to write a report to your managing director explaining

(a) the consequence of not depreciating the company's existing properties; (2 marks)
(b) the meaning of investment properties; (5 marks)
(c) the accounting treatment of investment properties in published financial statements.
(8 marks)

CIMA Advanced Financial Accounting, May 1991 (15 marks)

4.3 In accounting for physical fixed assets, the use of 'cost' as a valuation basis is well established.

You are required to outline the difficulties that arise in applying the cost principle, and to justify the solutions normally adopted, in cases where:

(a) physical fixed assets are acquired OTHERWISE THAN for a single cash payment (or on short-term credit) with IMMEDIATE transfer of the legal title to the assets; and
(12 marks)
(b) more than one separately identifiable item of physical fixed assets is acquired in the same transaction for a global sum of money, or for other valuable consideration that cannot be precisely apportioned. (4 marks)

ACCA Advanced Financial Accounting, June 1983 (16 marks)

4.4 X Ltd is a retail supermarket chain which regularly constructs its own superstores. During the year ending 31 December 1995, X Ltd began work on a new site.

On 1 January 1995, a leasehold interest in the site (of 50 years) was purchased for £20 million.

It was considered that a further £10 million would be required to build and fit the superstore. £6 million of the additional £10 million would be spent on the construction of the building and £4 million on fixtures and fittings. Past experience has led the management of X Ltd to believe that the fixtures and fittings would have an average useful economic life of ten years from first use before requiring replacement.

On 1 January 1995, X Ltd borrowed £30 million to finance the project. The £30 million carries no interest but is repayable on 31 December 1997 at a premium of £9.93 million (i.e. £39.93 million is to be repaid in total).

The superstore is to be brought into use on 1 January 1996.

Requirements

(a) **Set out the arguments for and against the capitalisation of borrowing costs on constructed fixed assets.** (9 marks)

(b) **Assuming that borrowing costs ARE capitalised where appropriate, calculate**
   (i) **the total amount to be included in fixed assets in respect of the development at 31 December 1995, and**
   (ii) **the total amount to be charged to the profit and loss account in respect of the development for the year ending 31 December 1996.** (11 marks)

Present value factors are shown below

Years t		Present value of £1 to be received after t years:	
	5%	10%	15%
1	0.952	0.909	0.870
2	0.907	0.826	0.756
3	0.864	0.751	0.658
4	0.823	0.683	0.572
5	0.784	0.621	0.497

CIMA Financial Reporting, November 1995 (**20 marks**)

4.5 C & R plc is a large company which operates a number of retail stores throughout the United Kingdom. The company makes up financial statements to 30 September each year.

On 1 October 1996 the company purchased two plots of land at two different locations, and commenced the construction of two retail stores. The construction was completed on 1 October 1997.

Details of the costs incurred to construct the stores are as follows:

	Location A £000	Location B £000
Cost of land	500	700
Cost of building materials	500	550
Direct labour	100	150
Site overheads	100	100
Fixtures and fittings	200	200

The construction of the stores was financed out of the proceeds of issue of a £10 million zero coupon bond on 1 October 1996. The bond is redeemable at a price of £25 937 000 on 30 September 2006. This represents the one and only payment to the holders of the bond.

Both stores were brought into use on 1 October 1997. The store at Location A was used by C & R plc but, due to a change of plan, the store at Location B was let to another retailer at a commercial rent.

It is the policy of C & R plc to depreciate freehold properties over their anticipated useful life of 50 years, and to depreciate fixtures and fittings over 10 years. The cost of such properties (including fixtures and fittings) should include finance costs, where this is permitted by the regulatory framework in the United Kingdom.

Requirements

(a) Compute the amounts which will be included in fixed assets in respect of the stores at Locations A and B on 30 September 1997.

Give full explanations for the amounts you have included. (11 marks)

(b) Compute the charge to the profit and loss account for depreciation on the fixed assets at the two locations for the year to 30 September 1998, stating clearly the reasons for your answers. (9 marks)

CIMA, Financial Reporting, November 1997 (Total Marks = 20)

4.6 G Ltd is a company specialising in the construction of sophisticated items of plant and machinery for clients in the engineering industry. Details of two contracts outstanding at 30 September 1995 (the balance sheet date) are as follows:

Contract with H Ltd

This contract was started on 1 January 1995 and is expected to be complete by 31 March 1996. The total contract price was fixed at £20 million and the total costs to be incurred originally estimated at £15 million, occurring evenly over the contract. The contract has been certified by experts as being 60% complete by 30 September 1995. Due to inefficiencies caused by industrial relations difficulties in the summer of 1995, the actual costs incurred on the contract in the period 1 January 1995 to 30 September 1995 were £10 million. However, the management is confident that these problems will not recur and that the remaining costs will be in line with the original estimate. In accordance with the payment terms laid down in the contract, G Ltd invoiced H Ltd for an interim payment of £10 million on 31 August 1995. The interim payment was received from H Ltd on 31 October 1995.

Contract with I Ltd

This contract was started on 1 April 1995 and was expected to be complete by 31 December 1995. The total contract price was fixed at £10 million and the total contract costs were originally estimated at £8 million. However, information received on 15 October 1995 suggested that the total contract costs would in fact be £11 million. The contract was certified by experts as being two-thirds complete by the year end and the costs actually incurred by G Ltd in respect of this contract in the period to 30 September 1995 were £7.5 million. No progress payments are yet due under the payment terms specified in the contract with I Ltd.

Requirements

(a) Explain the principles which are used to establish the timing of recognition of profits/losses on long-term contracts.

You should assume that recognition of profits/losses takes place in accordance with the provisions of SSAP 9 Stocks and long-term contracts, and should refer to fundamental accounting concepts, where relevant. (10 marks)

(b) Compute, separately for each of the contracts with H Ltd and I Ltd,

   (i) The amount of turnover and cost of sales that will be recognised in the profit and loss account of G Ltd for the year ended 30 September 1995.

   (ii) The contract balances (including nil balances, if appropriate) that will be shown at 30 September 1995 on the following accounts:
   - long-term contract work-in-progress
   - amounts recoverable on contracts
   - provision for losses
   - trade debtors. (10 marks)

CIMA Financial Reporting, November 1995 (20 marks)

4.7 Lewis plc specialises in bridge construction and had two contracts in progress at its year end, 30 April 1999.

Stornoway Bridge

Construction on this contract started in May 1997. Contract details extracted from the company's costing records as at 30 April 1999 were:

	£m
Total contract selling price	350
Work certified to date	210
Costs to date	175
Estimated costs to completion	75
Progress payments received	250

Work certified to date as at 30 April 1998 was £140 million and the appropriate amount of profit was recognised for the year ended 30 April 1998. No changes to the above total estimated contract costs have occurred since 30 April 1998.

On 11 May 1999 the customer's surveyor notified Lewis plc of a fault in one of the bridge supports constructed during a severe frost in February 1999. This will require remedial work in June 1999 at an estimated cost of £20 million.

Harris Link Bridge

Construction on this contract started in July 1998. Contract details extracted from the company's costing records as at 30 April 1999 were:

	£m
Total contract selling price	400
Work certified to date	45
Costs to date	40
Estimated costs to completion	395
Progress payments received	25

The company calculates attributable profit on the basis of work certified for all contracts.

Requirements

(a) **Calculate the amounts to be included in the financial statements of Lewis plc for the year ended 30 April 1999, preparing all relevant extracts of the financial statements excluding accounting policies notes and any disclosures relating to cash flows.**

(15 marks)

(b) **Explain how the requirements of SSAP 9, Stocks and long-term contracts, apply the prudence and accruals concepts to accounting for long-term contracts.** (5 marks)

ICAEW, Financial Reporting, June 1999 **(20 marks)**

4.8 MWT plc is a company involved in the design and manufacture of aircraft. During the year ended 31 March 1995, the company had commenced the following projects.

A. **Project Alpha** involves research into the development of a lightweight material for use in the construction of aircraft. To date, costs of £175 000 have been incurred, but so far the material developed has proved too weak.

B. **Project Beta** involves the construction of three aircraft for a major airline at a total contract price of £75 million. Costs incurred to 31 March 1995 amounted to £21 million, and payments on account received, relating to £20 million of those costs, amounted to £24 million. It is estimated that the contract will cost another £40 million to complete.

C. **Project Gamma** involves the development of a new engine for an overseas customer for a total contract price of £7 million. The total cost of the project is estimated to be £5 million. Only £1.4 million had been incurred to 31 March 1995. Payments on account, relating to those costs, of £2.4 million have been received.

D. **Project Delta** involves the refurbishment of a fleet of ten aircraft for another major airline. The total contract price is £30 million. To 31 March 1995, costs of £24 million have been incurred, and, because of materials shortage, it is estimated that it will cost another £12 million to complete. Although £20 million had been invoiced to 31 March 1995, relating to cost incurred to that date, only £19 million had been received at that date.

E. **Project Epsilon** commenced in February 1995 involving the production of light aircraft for a flying school for a total contract price of £18.2 million. Costs incurred to 31 March 1995 amounted to £1 million of a total estimated contract cost of £17 million. Invoices raised to 31 March 1995 amounted to £3 million of which £2.6 million had been received by that date.

Requirement
(a) **Explain, with appropriate figures, how each of the above projects should be treated in the financial statements of MWT plc.** (15 marks)
(b) **Show the relevant extracts from MWT plc's profit and loss account and balance sheet for the year ended 31 March 1995.** (5 marks)

CIMA Financial Reporting, May 1995 (20 marks)

4.9 Forfar plc is an innovative engineering company with a substantial research and development budget. It is company policy to capitalise all expenditure relevant to development work wherever possible and the following projects were in progress at the year end, 30 November 1998:

Project A100

The company incurred costs of £200 000 in the year ended 30 November 1998 to exploit research into the production of engineering equipment with reduced energy requirements. The company has produced a prototype model but commercial production is not expected for several years. No other feasibility studies have been carried out. The company also incurred expenditure of £100 000 on computer equipment to assist in testing and analysis and this is expected to have a useful economic life of five years.

Project A401

The company incurred technical research costs of £50 000 in November 1998 on behalf of a customer who commissioned Forfar plc to investigate the feasibility of high energy battery cells. Forfar plc expects to recover the costs incurred plus a mark-up of 20% from their customer for this work. Market research costs of £20 000 have also been incurred by Forfar plc in November 1998 but these will be reimbursed, at cost by the customer and an invoice was raised for this in December 1998. None of the technical research work has yet been invoiced though the project is successful and the work will be completed by January 1999.

Project C900

The company had capitalised development expenditure of £500 000 by 30 November 1997 on this project and incurred a further £70 000 during the year ended 30 November 1998. Commercial production of the new product started on 1 June 1998 and the company anticipates sales as follows:

Year ended	£
30 November 1998	250 000 actual
30 November 1999	300 000 budget
30 November 2000	500 000 budget
each year thereafter	600 000 budget

The company expects competitors will move into this market by 30 November 2002 and the product will no longer be profitable after that date.

In addition to the above costs, the company spent £150 000 on plant in December 1995 to assist with this project and has been depreciating this over five years to date. The plant has no further use once the product is developed.

Project G150

The company's technical director considers that there is the possibility of producing new generation computer-controlled engineering equipment. £400 000 was spent in the year ended 30 November 1998 to investigate the likelihood of a viable research project. In addition, technical staff costs on this project amounted to £55 000 in the year.

Project B105

This project was started in December 1994 to develop a new generation solar power panel. Costs capitalised to 30 November 1997 amounted to £550 000 Market research carried out in July 1998 at a cost of £25 000 indicated demand would reach 5000 panels per annum; the company's finance director has calculated 7500 panels per annum would need to be sold in order to break even.

Requirements

(a) Briefly identify and explain the appropriate accounting treatment required for the year ended 30 November 1998 for each of the above projects. (6 marks)
(b) Calculate and disclose the appropriate amounts for the financial statements of Forfar plc for the year ended 30 November 1998. (14 marks)

(20 marks)

Note: You are not required to produce any information for the directors' report, accounting policies or cash flow statement.

ICAEW Financial Reporting, December 1998

4.10 Amesbury plc produces and distributes computer-controlled machinery. As accountant for the company, you have been provided with the following information regarding the company's activities in researching and developing products in the year ended 31 October 1993:

(1) Expenditure on developing a new computerised tool for a long-established customer has amounted to £150 000. The work is now well advanced and the customer is likely to authorise the start of commercial production within the next 12 months. The customer is reimbursing, Amesbury plc's costs plus a 10% mark-up. To date the company has received £70 000 having invoiced £100 000 for agreed work done.
(2) A review of the company's quality control procedures has been carried out at a cost of £100 000. It is considered that the new procedures will save a considerable amount of money in the testing and analysis of existing and new products.
(3) The development of Product M479 has reached an advanced stage. Costs in the year ended 31 October 1993 amounted to £400 000. In addition there has been expenditure on fixed assets required for the development of this product amounting to £120 000 of which £60 000 was incurred in the year ended 31 October 1992. The fixed assets have a five-year life with no residual value and are depreciated on the straight-line basis with a full year's depreciation in the year of acquisition.

Market research, costing £20 000, has been carried out and this indicates the product will be commercially viable although commercial production is unlikely to start until April 1994. The company expects that Product M479 will make a significant contribution to profit.

(4) Commercial production started on 1 June 1993 for Product A174. The costs of developing this product had been capitalised as follows:

	£
Development expenditure capitalised as on 31 October 1992	200 000
Expenditure incurred in the year ended 31 October 1993	50 000
	250 000

The company has taken out a patent which will last for ten years. The associated legal and administrative expenses amounted to £10 000.

Actual and estimated sales for Product A174:

Year ended 31 October	£
1993	250 000
1994	750 000
1995	1 000 000
1996	500 000
1997	250 000

After 31 October 1996 the company's market share and profitability from the product are expected to diminish significantly due to the introduction of rival products by competitors.

(5) It is company policy to capitalise development expenditure wherever possible.

Requirement
Prepare all relevant extracts of the published financial statements for the year ended 31 October 1993 in accordance with current accounting standards and legislation, explaining your treatment of items (1) to (4).

Note: You are not required to prepare extracts of the cash flow statement or the directors' report.

ICAEW Financial Reporting, November 1993 (15 marks)

4.11 Global plc, which prepares accounts to 31 January each year, operates in several different countries and has recently obtained government financial assistance both in the UK and abroad:

(1) A foreign government has granted £4m to cover the establishment of a new factory. The factory and associated plant installation were completed in November 1992 at a cost of £10m for the land and buildings (land element – £2m) and £5m for the plant. Asset lives were estimated at 50 years for the premises and 10 years for the plant; a full year's depreciation is charged in the year of acquisition.

The grant was dependent on an inspection by government officials and the company retaining ownership of the factory for the next five years. The grant was released by the foreign government on 27 March 1993 following their inspection in January 1993.

The country in which the factory is situated has had a turbulent history with frequent changes of government but has enjoyed a period of relative stability over the past three years. No previous governments have granted assistance to foreign companies.

(2) A local authority in the UK has provided a grant of £130 000 which covers the total initial establishment costs of a new training programme for company staff. The grant is dependent on the company expanding its existing training unit and increasing the number of trainees in direct production areas within the local factory by 20 per cent. The increased number of trainees would have to be sustained for at least three years.

The grant was received in January 1993. Expected costs of the complete programme are £300 000 of which £100 000, relating to initial establishment costs, has been incurred to date.

Actual and projected trainee numbers provided by the production director are:

| | *Years ending 31 January* | | | |
	1993	*1994*	*1995*	*1996*
Welding shop	9	10	9	10
Lathe area	7	9	11	11
Computer controlled machinery	11	14	13	14
Trainee general managers	3	2	2	2
	30	35	35	37

Requirement

Calculate the amounts which should be included in the financial statements for the year ended 31 January 1993, preparing all relevant notes in accordance with SSAP 4, Government grants.

ICAEW Financial Reporting II, May 1993 (8 marks)

5 Liabilities and related issues

5.1 You are the management accountant of Short plc. On 1 October 1993 Short plc issued 10 million £1 preference shares at par, incurring issue costs of £100 000. The dividend payable on the preference shares was a fixed 4% per annum, payable on 30 September each year in arrears. The preference shares were redeemed on 1 October 1998 at a price of £1.35 per share. The effective finance cost of the preference shares was 10%. The balance sheet of the company on 30 September 1998, the day before the redemption of the preference shares, was as follows:

	£ million
Ordinary share capital (non-redeemable)	100.0
Redeemable preference shares	13.5
Share premium account	25.8
Profit and loss account	59.7
	199.0
Net assets	199.0

Requirements

(a) Write a memorandum to your assistant which explains

- how the total finance cost of the preference shares should be allocated to the profit and loss account over their period of issue;
- where in the profit and loss account the finance cost should be reported;
- where the preference shares should be disclosed in the balance sheet;
- the nature of any supporting information which is required to be disclosed in the notes to the financial statements regarding the preference shares.

Your memorandum should refer to the provisions of relevant Accounting Standards.

(8 marks)

(b) Calculate the finance cost in respect of the preference shares for EACH of the five years ended 30 September 1998. (7 marks)

(c) ASSUMING NO CHANGES OTHER THAN THOSE CAUSED BY THE REDEMP-TION OF THE PREFERENCE SHARES, prepare the balance sheet of Short plc at the end of 1 October 1998. You should give an explanation for any changes to any of the headings or any new headings which are required. (5 marks)

CIMA, Financial Reporting, November 1998 (Total Marks = 20)

5.2 Your managing director has recently read an article which referred to Financial Reporting Standard 4 (FRS 4) – Capital instruments. He has requested a report from you about FRS 4.

Requirement
Write a report to the managing director explaining the nature of capital instruments, giving *three* examples of capital instruments together with their required accounting treatment as specified in FRS 4.

CIMA Financial Reporting, May 1995 (20 marks)

5.3 Brora plc has prepared draft financial statements for the year ended 30 September 1997 and the Board of Directors has asked you, the group's financial accountant, to provide guidance on the following outstanding matters:

(1) The company borrowed £3 million from an associated company on 29 September 1997. It is anticipated that the company will repay this shortly after the year end. The directors of Brora plc have informed you that this cash was borrowed to improve the apparent liquidity of the group at the year end.

(2) A fire in one of tile company's warehouses on 5 October 1997 has reduced stock with a cost of £1.5 million to a net realisable value of £1 million. The company has a policy of selfinsurance and does not hold any insurance cover.

(3) An overseas subsidiary, with net assets of £750 000, has been nationalised by its local government on 10 October 1997. There has been no offer of compensation from the overseas government.

(4) The company is facing litigation for damages from a customer for the supply of faulty goods and consequent losses from the subsequent manufacturing process. The claim is for £1.4 million and was received on 1 October 1997. The directors, after consulting with legal and technical advisers, consider that a claim against Brora plc's suppliers is appropriate to reflect their contribution to the difficulties encountered by the company's customer and, accordingly, a claim of £1.2 million was sent to the suppliers on 9 October 1997.

Requirement
Advise the board of directors of Brora plc on the appropriate accounting treatment and disclosure for the above items in the financial statements for the year ended 30 September 1997, referring to appropriate accounting standards and legislation. (10 marks)

Note: You are not required to prepare extracts of the financial statements.

ICAEW, Financial Reporting, November 1997

5.4 Diverse plc has established a defined benefit pension scheme for all the company's full-time employees. The scheme receives contributions from the company and the participating employees. The scheme was originally established on 31 December 1991 and was actuarially valued at 31 December 1994. The scheme showed a deficit of £6 million. This deficit was caused by a reassessment of the original actuarial assumptions (an experience deficiency). No change to contribution levels was made as a result of the 1994 valuation. However, the deficit was funded by a one-off lump sum payment of £6 million into the scheme on 30 June 1995. The result of the 1994 valuation was not available when the 1994 financial statements of Diverse plc were approved by the Directors.

The scheme was actuarially valued for the second time at 31 December 1997. The results of this second valuation showed a surplus of £4 million. The actuaries advised that £3 million of this surplus was caused by a significant reduction in the number of scheme members because of a redundancy programme. The result of the 1997 valuation was not available when the 1997 financial statements of Diverse plc were approved by the Directors. No change was made to the normal contribution levels for 1998. Total contributions payable to the scheme for 1998 were £5 million. The average remaining service lives of participating employees in the scheme was estimated to be 20 years at the date of inception of the scheme. This estimate is reckoned to continue to be applicable in the medium term as older employees retire and younger employees join.

Requirements

(a) Explain the principles outlined in SSAP 24 – *Accounting for Pension Costs*, under which the profit and loss account charge for pension costs is determined in the financial statements of employing companies. You should indicate why the computation of the pension cost is more complicated in the case of defined benefit schemes than defined contribution schemes. (7 marks)

(b) Compute the charge in the profit and loss account of Diverse plc in respect of the pension costs for the year to 31 December 1998. (6 marks)

(c) Compute the pension asset or liability which would appear in the balance sheet of Diverse plc at 31 December 1998 and explain how it would be disclosed on the balance sheet. (7 marks)

CIMA Financial Reporting, November 1999 (Total Marks = 20)

5.5 You are the financial controller of C Ltd, a company which has recently established a pension scheme for its employees. It chose a defined benefit scheme rather than a defined contribution scheme.

C Ltd makes payments into the pension scheme on a monthly basis as follows:

- Employer's contribution of 12% of the gross salaries of the participating employees.
- Employees' contribution (via deduction from salary) of 6% of gross salary,
- Payments are made on the twentieth day of the month following payment of the salary.

C Ltd makes up financial statements to 31 December each year. On 30 June 1995 the scheme was subject to its first actuarial valuation. The valuation revealed a deficit of £2.4 million. The deficit was primarily caused by a change in the assumptions made by the actuary since the scheme was originally established. The deficit was extinguished by a one-off lump sum payment of £2.4 million into the scheme by C Ltd on 30 September 1995. The annual salaries of the scheme members for the year ended 31 December 1995 totalled £15 million, accruing evenly throughout the year.

Requirements

(a) Write a memorandum to your Board of Directors which explains
- the difference between a defined contribution scheme and a defined benefit scheme,
- the accounting objective set out in SSAP 24 – Accounting for Pension Costs – concerning the determination of the charge for pension costs in the profit and loss account of the employing company,
- why the accounting objective is more difficult to satisfy for an employer with a defined benefit scheme. (12 marks)

(b) Determine the total charge in the profit and loss account for pensions (EXCLUDING amounts deducted from employees' gross salaries) AND any balance sheet amounts in respect of pensions, explaining clearly where exactly on the balance sheet the amounts would be included.

Assume the provisions of SSAP 24 are followed by C Ltd.

You ascertain that at 30 June 1995 the average remaining service lives of the employees who were members of the pension scheme at that date was 24 years. (8 marks)

Ignore deferred taxation.

CIMA, Financial Reporting, May 1996 (Total Marks = 20)

5.6 Court plc has a defined benefits pension scheme for all its employees. Based on actuarial advice the company has previously made contributions of £2 million per annum to the pension fund, being 10% of pensionable earnings. The average remaining service lives of the company's existing employees is ten years and pensionable earnings will continue at their present level.

An actuarial valuation of the fund as at 1 January 1991 has revealed a surplus of £3 million (i.e. the actuarial value of the pension fund's assets exceeds the actuarial value of the liabilities). The surplus has arisen solely because the investment performance of the pension fund has been better than anticipated. The actuary has suggested to the company the following funding options:

(a) Reduce contributions from 10% to 7.5% for the next ten years; or
(b) Have a one year pension holiday and reduce contributions to 9% in the following nine years; or
(c) Receive a refund of £3 million now and retain the 10% contribution.

All of these options can be assumed to comply with the requirements of the Taxes Acts (including Finance Act 1986) concerning pension fund surpluses.

In advance of a board meeting, the finance director of Court plc wishes to consider the impact of the various options on the accounts of the company and has asked you to prepare appropriate analyses building up to the average annual profit and loss account charge in accordance with SSAP 24 under each option for the next ten years. Also for each option the finance director wishes to know the balance sheet effect, if any.

Requirements
Note: In parts (i) and (ii), ignore taxation and the interest effect in respect of pension contributions advanced or deferred.

(i) Calculate the average annual charge to the profit and loss account of Court plc in respect of pension costs for the ten years commencing 1 January 1991 under each of the above options (a), (b) and (c).
    For each option, (a), (b) and (c), detail the balance sheet effects of accounting for pension costs. (6 marks)
(ii) Assume that Court plc follows option (b) above with effect from 1 January 1991 and that a further actuarial valuation as at 1 January 1996 leads the actuary to recommend reducing the pension contribution to 8% for 1996 only (with continuing contributions at 9%); under these assumptions calculate the profit and loss account charge for pension costs in each of the fifteen years commencing 1 January 1991, and the balance sheet provision at the end of each of those fifteen years. The average remaining service lives of existing employees can be assumed to remain at ten years. (6 marks)
(iii) Set out, in note form, the practical accounting and presentational considerations, including taxation, which you would recommend the board of directors to take into

571

account when deciding on an appropriate course of action in relation to the pension fund surplus as at 1 January 1991. (6 marks)

ICAEW Financial Accounting 2, December 1991 (**18 marks**)

6 Financial statements – form and content

6.1 The introduction of FRS 3, Reporting Financial Performance, has resulted in a considerably expanded profit and loss account with related disclosures and a new primary statement. The standard is intended to be based on the 'all-inclusive' concept of income.

Requirements
(a) **Discuss why FRS 3 was introduced and whether it has achieved its objectives.**
(7 marks)
(b) **Describe how the standard has implemented the 'all-inclusive' concept of income.**
(3 marks)

ICAEW, Financial Reporting, November 1994 (**10 marks**)

6.2 The stated objective of FRS 3 is to 'require reporting entities failing within its scope to highlight a range of important components of financial performance to aid users in understanding the performance achieved by a reporting entity in a period and to assist them in forming a basis for their assessment of future results and cash flows'.

Discuss, giving your reasons, which components of financial performance are of particular importance and consider whether accounts prepared in accordance with the Companies Acts and Accounting Standards achieve all parts of the stated objective. Your discussion should not be confined only to those statements specifically identified by FRS 3.

ICAEW, Auditing and Financial Reporting, July 1994 (**12 marks**)

6.3 **Discuss whether the range of information provided by the implementation of FRS 3, Reporting financial performance, is helpful to users of published financial statements.**

ICAEW, Financial Reporting, Intermediate Examination, May 1998 (**10 marks**)

6.4 One of your clients. Sanna Ltd, has prepared a draft set of financial statements and submitted them to you for your advice:

Balance Sheet
as on 30 April 1994

	£'000	£'000	£'000
Fixed assets			
Intangible assets			
Development costs	50		
Goodwill	20		
		70	
Tangible assets			
Land and buildings	625		
Plant and machinery	500		
Fixtures and fittings	250		
		1 375	
			1 445
Carried forward			1 445

	£'000	£'000	£'000
Brought forward			1 445
Current assets			
Stocks		250	
Debtors		240	
Cash at bank and in hand		180	
		670	
Current liabilities			
Bank overdraft	60		
11% Loan stock 2010	490		
Trade creditors	220		
Accruals	50		
Proposed dividends	50		
		(870)	
Net current liabilities			(200)
Provision for liabilities and charges			
Deferred taxation			(90)
			1 155
Capital and reserves			
Share capital			890
Share premium			95
Reserves			170
			1 155

Profit and Loss Account for the year ended
30 April 1994

	£'000
Sales	5 728
Cost of goods sold	(4 475)
	1 253
Staff costs	(573)
Depreciation	(145)
Other operating charges	(30)
Distribution costs	(82)
	423
Interest payable	(110)
Profit before taxation	313
Taxation	(110)
Profit after taxation	203
Extraordinary items	(50)
Revaluation reserve transfer	20
	173

Additional information

(1) The reserves note drafted by the company shows:

	Revaluation Reserve £'000	Profit and Loss £'000	Total £'000
Balance as on 1 May 1993	37	30	67
Revaluation reserve realised	(20)	–	(20)
Retained profit for year	–	173	173
Proposed dividends	–	(50)	(50)
	17	153	170

(2) Development costs have arisen as a result of developing a product for a major customer. It is considered that the product will be a commercial success and the customer is reimbursing all of Sanna Ltd's costs plus a 15% mark-up.

(3) The freehold property was revalued three years ago. The company has been transferring the annual depreciation charged to the profit and loss account from the revaluation reserve to retained earnings as the company believes it is now a realised profit.

(4) Extraordinary items comprise:

	£'000
Closure of factory	90
Disposal of factory premises	(63)
Rationalisation of production processes	50
Attributable taxation	(27)
	50

The closure of the factory and the related disposal of the factory premises comprised a significant business segment of the company which had contributed £750 000 to turnover and accounted for 15% of the costs charged in arriving at operating profit.

The company's rationalisation costs above were necessarily incurred as a result of the closure of the factory.

(5) Staff costs comprise 70% production employees, 20% general and clerical employees and 10% sales and marketing employees. The company sub-contracts all its transport function.

(6) Other operating charges relate to losses on disposal of plant and machinery fixed assets.

(7) Depreciation of plant and machinery is £90 000 in the year ended 30 April 1994.

(8) As a change in accounting policy, goodwill is to be written off to reserves rather than amortised. The goodwill arose in the year ended 30 April 1993, amounted to £30 000 and had an estimated useful life of three years. No amortisation has been charged in the 1994 draft accounts.

Requirement

Prepare the profit and loss account, balance sheet and a reconciliation of movements in shareholders' funds for Sanna Ltd for the year ended 30 April 1994 in accordance with FRS 3, Reporting financial performance, and relevant legislation.

ICAEW, Financial Reporting, May 1994   (15 marks)

6.5 Brachol plc is preparing its accounts for the year ended 30 November 1992.

The following information is available from the previous year's balance sheet: At 30 November 1991 there were credit balances on the share premium account of £2 025 000, the revaluation reserve of £4 050 000, and the profit and loss account of £2 700 000.

During 1992 the following transactions occurred:

1. One million shares of £1 each were issued in exchange for net assets that had a fair value of £3 755 000.
2. A factory property that had been revalued from £500 000 to £1 310 000 in 1990 was sold for £2 525 000.
3. A fixed asset investment was revalued from £ 1 305 000 to £900 000.
4. There was a currency translation loss of £270 000 arising on foreign currency net investments.
5. A warehouse property was revalued from £1 000 000 to £1 540 000.

A prior period adjustment of £1 350 000 was required which had arisen from a change in accounting policy that had overstated the previous year's profit.

The profit and loss account for the year ended 30 November 1992 showed a profit attributable to members of the company of £810 000 and a dividend of £675 000.

Required
(a) (i) Draft a note showing the movements on reserves as at 30 November 1992.
    (ii) Draft a statement of total recognised gains and losses to show the net deduction from or addition to net assets as at 30 November 1992. (6 marks)
(b) Explain briefly
    (i) the purpose of the statement of total recognised gains and losses; and
    (ii) the extent to which a user of the accounts will be better able to make decisions by referring to a statement of total recognised gains and losses rather than the statement of movements on reserves that is produced to comply with the Companies Act 1985.
(c) Explain briefly (7 marks)
    (i) the nature of the adjustments that would be required to reconcile the profit on ordinary activities before tax to the historical cost profit; and
    (ii) the possible use that can be made of such information by a potential investor.
(7 marks)

ACCA Advanced Financial Accounting, June 1993 (**20 marks**)

6.6 A Ltd is a company which specialises in the processing of canned beans and canned spaghetti for sale to retail shops. The canned beans are processed from beans bought in directly from UK farmers. The canned spaghetti is processed from pasta which is purchased from suppliers in Italy. Processing and canning take place at one of two factories in the United Kingdom, one factory dealing with beans and one with spaghetti. Each factory maintains separate financial statements in order to produce a monthly operating report for Head Office.

Once canned, the products are transferred to one of four distribution centres (two centres per factory). The distribution centres (which also maintain their own individual financial statements) are used to transfer the products to shops and supermarkets following orders for sales. The accounting year end of the company is 31 December.

On 30 November 1995, a decision was made to rationalise the business. Due to adverse exchange rate movements it was decided to discontinue the processing and sale of canned spaghetti, and concentrate exclusively on canned beans. The consequence of this decision was that the factory which processed pasta into spaghetti and one of the associated distribution centres would be sold, and the majority of the personnel employed at these locations made redundant. It was decided to commence running down the processing operations and the distribution operations in the factory and the distfibution centre to be closed on 15 January 1996, with an expectation to complete the closure by 31 March 1996. Apart from carrying out extensive negotiations with relevant Trades Unions regarding redundancy packages, no other closure activities were to be commenced before 15 January 1996.

On 30 November 1995, A Ltd also decided to rationalise its distribution operation. The rationalisation included closing one of the four centres (as noted above) and redefining the areas covered by the remaining centres (so that the three remaining centres took on the distribution formerly carried out by the four centres, with the work relating only to baked beans). The timetable for the rationalisation of the distribution operation in the three remaining centres was identical to that for the closure of the factory and the fourth centre (rundown of spaghetti distribution and reallocation of beans distribution commencing 15 January 1996, rationalisation complete by 31 March 1996).

You are the Chief Accountant of A Ltd, and one of the directors has recently visited you to discuss the accounting treatment of the rationalisation. The director is unsure as to whether the rationalisation will have any impact on the financial statements for the year ended 31 December 1995 given that the programme did not actually commence until 15 January 1996. The director is aware that there is an accounting standard which deals with the issue of discontinued operations but is unaware of any relevant details. The 1995 financial statements are currently in the course of preparation and are expected to be formally approved by the directors at the April 1996 board meeting. For the purposes of this question, you should assume that today's date is 29 February 1996.

Requirement
Write a memorandum for the Board of Directors which

(a) explains how a discontinued aperation is defined in FRS 3; (6 marks)

(b) outlines the accounting treatment (if any) of the decision to close the factories and one of the distribution centres and to rationalise the operations of the remaining distribution centres, in the financial statements of A Ltd for the year ended 31 December 1995.

Your explanation should encompass the treatment in the balance sheet and profit and loss account and any additional information which is required in the notes to the financial statements. (14 marks)

CIMA, Financial Reporting, May 1996 (Total Marks = 20)

6.7 During the completion of the financial statements of Angus plc for the year ended 28 February 1997, the following matters have been brought to your attention.

(1) On 1 March 1996, the company revalued its freehold land and buildings (for the first time) to £20 million (land element £4 million) and the accounting records were adjusted to this value. The property originally cost £16 million on which annual depreciation of £280 000 had been charged. Accumulated depreciation to 29 February 1996 was £2.8 million. Depreciation of £400 000 has been charged to the profit and loss account for the year ended 28 February 1997.

(2) [*This part of the question is no longer applicable.*] The company's accounting policy on goodwill has been to capitalise the cost and amortise this over 10 years. On 1 March 1996, when goodwill of £1.5 million was held as an intangible fixed asset, this policy was changed to immediate write off of goodwill against reserves.

(3) The company announced the intended closure of its European operations on 31 January 1997 when a formal closure plan was approved and adopted. On 10 March 1997, the company contracted to terminate various operating leases and sell other fixed assets. The fixed assets had a net book value of £10.5 million and an agreed sale value of £9 million. The lessors of the assets held under operating leases agreed to terminate the contracts for a payment of £350 000. The European operations contributed 10% of turnover and profit.

(4) As a result of the closure in (3) above, the company will need to carry out a fundamental reorganisation of its other activities at a cost of £1.25 million.

(5) After accounting for the above items, the company's draft financial statements show turnover of £200 million, profit before taxation of £18 million and a tax charge of £6 million. The company has proposed a dividend of £2 million. Shareholders' funds at 1 March 1996 were £500 million.

Requirement

Prepare the following statements, suitable for publication, for Angus plc for the year ended 28 February 1997:

(i) Profit and loss account
(ii) Statement of total recognised gains and losses
(iii) Reconciliation of movements in shareholders' funds
(iv) Note of historical cost profits and losses.

ICAEW Financial Reporting, May 1997   (14 marks)

6.8 Glamis plc manufactures, distributes and retails glassware. The following matters relate to its financial statements for the year ended 31 July 1998:

(1) On 25 June 1998, one of the company's factories sustained damage from a freak storm. The cost of repairs in July 1998 was £500 000 and this has been provided for in the financial statements. The company's insurance does not cover this repair.

(2) The company disposed of a fixed asset for £1 million in June 1998. The asset cost £850 000 in August 1994 and had an expected life of five years. The asset was revalued to £900 000 in the financial statements on 1 August 1996; no change to its total useful economic life was recommended. The company does not charge depreciation in the year of disposal of an asset and has based the profit on disposal in the profit and loss account on the carrying value of the asset.

(3) The board of directors decided to close the company's retailing division on the basis of a formal plan submitted by the sales director. The company had accepted a firm offer of £3 million for the retail premises by 31 July 1998. The net book value of the premises was £2 million. Half of the staff involved in the retailing division were made redundant by 31 July 1998 at a cost of £500 000; the remaining staff were redeployed and retrained at a cost of £200 000. All these transactions have been included in the financial statements.

(4) The directors decided to change the accounting treatment of development costs to immediate write-off against profit as costs are incurred. This change has not yet been reflected in the draft financial statements. The balance on the development costs account at 31 July 1998 was £250 000 of which £200 000 was incurred by 31 July 1997.

The company's draft summarised profit and loss account shows:

	£'000
Turnover	5500
Cost of sales	(3100)
Gross profit	2400
Distribution costs	(1100)
Administrative expenses	(500)
Profit before taxation	800
Taxation	(240)
Profit after taxation	560
Dividends	(100)
	460

Opening shareholders' funds as on 1 August 1997 were £1.2 million, as previously reported.

Requirements

(a) **Advise the board of directors of Glamis plc on the most appropriate accounting treatment and disclosure for each of the above matters, preparing all necessary calculations. You should refer to relevant accounting standards and legislation as appropriate.**

(10 marks)

Note: You are not required to prepare extracts of the financial statements.

(b) **Prepare the following extracts of the financial statements for Glamis plc:**
   (i) **Statement of total recognised gains and losses**
   (ii) **Note of historical cost profit and losses**
   (iii) **Reconciliation of movements on shareholders' funds.**   (9 marks)

Note: You should provide comparative figures as far as you can from the information available.

ICAEW Financial Reporting, September 1998   **(19 marks)**

6.9 Shiny Bright plc was incorporated in 1980 to provide cleaning services for hotel, hospital and catering clients; it diversified into hotel ownership in the 1990s. In the early 1990s the company acquired a chain of 20 country hotels from Retort Hotels Ltd, a company then in receivership. Fifteen of the hotels were located in the South of England and five were located in Ireland. Since 1994 the directors have been preparing to seek a listing on the Alternative Investment Market and part of their strategy has been to dispose of operations that did not achieve an adequate return on capital employed.

At a recent seminar on reporting financial performance attended by the Managing Director, the seminar leader had briefly explained that exceptional items needed to be disclosed by virtue of their size or incidence, emphasised the importance of the operating profit figure and commented that it seemed that the market was often too easily misled by some companies' innovative use of FRS 3's layered approach to the profit and loss account to divert attention from the overall total result for which management was accountable.

When Shiny Bright plc was finalising its accounts for the year ended 31 October 1996 the Managing Director requested the Finance Director to make a brief presentation to the Board explaining exceptional items and innovative uses of the layered approach for the profit and loss account and advising on the accounting treatments that would produce the highest operating profit and on the presentation format that would concentrate attention on the EPS figure that was most favourable to the company.

The operating profit was £4 million from continuing operations and £0.1 million from its hospital cleaning services, which were discontinued in 1996, before taking account of the following information.

1 The company had acquired a restaurant in Central London for £1 million in 1991. It was revalued at £1.5 million in 1993. No depreciation had been provided on the property as it was company policy to maintain properties to a high standard.

The restaurant was sold on 30 September 1996 for £2.5 million.

2 All of the hotels acquired from Retort Hotels Ltd which were located in Ireland were sold on 31 August 1996 for £12.5 million. They were the only hotels operated by the company in Ireland and the directors decided that they were too distant for them to exercise effective management. They had been acquired for £16 million at the date they were purchased from the receiver. No depreciation has been provided by the company.

3 Shiny Bright plc has incurred costs of £1.4 million arising from the reorganisation of the hotel administration. This comprised £0.5 million for the centralisation of the accounting and booking function, £0.3 million for refurbishing the reception area to a common plan, £0.4 million for retraining staff and £0.2 million for redundancy payments.

4 The fixed assets used for cleaning were estimated to have fallen in value by £0.75 million following the discovery that cleaning equipment had suffered damage due to staff failing to follow the manufacturers' instructions.

5 There was an item on the agenda for the October 1996 Board meeting proposing the closure in the following financial year of a loss-making hotel. The Finance Director had prepared estimates for the following year for this hotel showing turnover £350 000, cost of sales £400 000, write down of equipment £50 000 and redundancy costs £40 000. The proposal was to complete the closure by May 1997.

Required
Assuming that you are the Finance Director, you are required to

(a) (ii) Explain the terms *size* and *incidence* in relation to exceptional items and the major difficulties in applying these terms.   (4 marks)

   (ii) Explain how companies might be able to make use of FRS 3's layered approach to the profit and loss account to direct attention to a result other than the overall total result for which management was accountable.   (4 marks)

(b) (i) Describe the accounting treatments in the profit and loss account for the year ended 31 October 1996 that would produce the highest operating profit figure, giving reasons to support your advice in respect of items 1–5 above.

   (ii) Calculate the operating profit from continuing and discontinued operations for 1996 assuming that your advice was followed.

   (iii) Describe the presentation of profit and loss account that would best direct attention to the profit figure most favourable to the company.   (12 marks)

ACCA Financial Reporting Environment, December 1996   **(20 marks)**

6.10 You are the financial director of Pilgrim plc, a listed company. Your new group managing director, appointed from one of Pilgrim plc's overseas subsidiaries, is reviewing the principal accounting policies and is having difficulty understanding the accounting treatment and disclosure of assets leased by Pilgrim plc as lessee, of which there are a substantial number (both finance and operating leases).

Requirement
Prepare a memorandum for your managing director explaining, in simple terms, the basics of accounting for leased assets in the accounts of listed companies (in full compliance with the relevant accounting standards and the Companies Acts). Your memorandum should be set out in sections as follows:

(a) Outline the factors which can influence the decision as to whether a particular lease is a finance lease or an operating lease.   (4 marks)

(b) As an example, taking the following non-cancellable lease details:
   – fair value (as defined in SSAP 21): £100 000
   – lease payments: five annual payments in advance of £20 000 each
   – estimated residual value at the end of the lease: £26 750 of which £15 000 is guaranteed by Pilgrim plc as lessee
   – interest rate implicit in the lease: 10%
   demonstrate whether the lease falls to be considered as a finance lease or an operating lease under the provisions of SSAP 21, explaining the steps in reaching a conclusion.
                          (4 marks)

(c) Explain briefly any circumstances in which a lessor and a lessee might classify a particular lease differently, i.e. the lessee might classify a lease as an operating lease whilst the lessor classifies the same lease as a finance lease or vice versa.   (3 marks)

(d) **Explain briefly any circumstances in which the requirements of SSAP 21 with regard to accounting for operating leases by lessees might result in charges to the profit and loss account different from the amounts payable for the period under the terms of a lease.**

(3 marks)

(e) **Draft a concise accounting policy in respect of 'Leasing' (as a lessee only) suitable for inclusion in the published accounts of Pilgrim plc and comment on the key aspects of your policy to aid your managing director's understanding.** (4 marks)

(f) **List the other disclosures Pilgrim plc is required to give in its published accounts in respect of its financial transactions as a lessee.** (3 marks)

Note: Ignore taxation

ICAEW Financial Accounting 2, December 1992 **(21 marks)**

6.11 Holmes Ltd, which has a year end of 30 September, is considering the replacement of its now outdated mainframe computer on 1 October 1988. The replacement computer has a cost of £2 120 000 and its useful economic life is estimated at 7 years. After negotiations with a leasing company, Duff Ltd, and other financial institutions, the directors of Holmes Ltd have identified three options available to them for consideration:

Option A
Enter a 4-year lease with Duff Ltd for total lease payments of £2 000 000 payable in four equal instalments, the first instalment being due on day 1 of the leasing period. Under this arrangement Duff Ltd would have responsibility for upkeep and maintenance and has negotiated a guaranteed repurchase by the manufacturer at the end of the lease term. The interest rate implicit in the lease is 10%.

Option B
Enter a 4-year lease with the same rental payment arrangements as Option A, but at the end of four years, commence a secondary rental period which provides for 3 annual payments of 60%, 40% and 20% respectively of annual rental payments in the primary period. Under the terms of this lease, Holmes Ltd would be responsible for the maintenance and upkeep. The interest rate implicit in the lease is 10.25%.

Option C
Purchase the new computer outright by issuing sufficient £100 debentures at a price of £55. The debentures would carry a coupon of 2% and would be redeemable at par, 7 years after the date of issue.

Required
(a) **With regard to Option A, demonstrate whether the arrangement should be treated as a finance or operating lease in the accounts of Holmes Ltd.** (4 marks)

(b) **With regard to Option B, calculate the amounts to be shown in the profit and loss account of Holmes Ltd for each of the years ending 30 September 1989 and 1990. Also calculate the amounts to be disclosed in the balance sheet at 30 September 1989 and draft the related notes thereto.** (6 marks)

(c) **Identify the principles underlying the treatment recommended in SSAP 21 with regard to the accounting for finance leases in the books of the lessor.** (5 marks)

(d) **Describe and assess the alternative methods of accounting in the books of Holmes Ltd for the financing arrangements outlined in Option C.** (5 marks)

ICAEW Financial Accounting II, July 1988 **(20 marks)**

6.12 Flow Ltd prepares financial statements to 31 March each year. On 1 April 1998, Flow Ltd sold a freehold property to another company, River plc. Flow Ltd had purchased the property for £500 000 on 1 April 1988 and had charged total depreciation of £60 000 on the property for the period 1 April 1988 to 31 March 1998.

River plc paid £850 000 for the property on 1 April 1998, at which date its true market value was £550 000.

From 1 April 1998 the property was leased back by Flow Ltd on a ten-year operating lease for annual rentals (payable in arrears) of £100 000. A normal annual rental for such a property would have been £50 000

River plc is a financial institution which, on 1 April 1998, charged interest of 10.56% per annum on ten-year fixed rate loans.

Requirements

(a) Explain what is meant by the terms 'finance lease' and 'operating lease' and how operating leases should be accounted for in the financial statements of lessee companies.

(7 marks)

(b) Show the journal entries which Flow Ltd will make to record
- its sale of the property to River plc on 1 April 1998,
- the payment of the first rental to River plc on 31 March 1999.

Justify your answer with reference to appropriate Accounting Standards.   (13 marks)

CIMA, Financial Reporting, May 1999   (Total Marks = 20)

6.13 Financial Reporting Standard 5 'Reporting the Substance of Transactions' requires an entity's financial statements to report the substance of transactions into which it has entered. The FRS sets out how to determine the substance of a transaction and whether any resulting assets and liabilities should be included in the balance sheet. The FRS came about partly as a result of concern over arrangements made by companies whereby assets and liabilities were omitted from the balance sheet.

Required

(a) Explain the reasons why companies may wish to omit assets and liabilities from their balance sheets.   (5 marks)

(b) Explain the reasons why the Accounting Standards Board felt it necessary to introduce FRS 5 'Reporting the Substance of Transactions'.   (5 marks)

(c) Discuss the proposed treatment of the following items in the financial statements:

(i) Beak plc sells land to a property investment company, Wings plc. The sale price is £20 million and the current market value is £30 million. Beak plc can buy the land back at any time in the next five years for the original selling price plus an annual commission of 1% above the current bank base rate. Wings plc cannot require Beak plc to buy the land back at any time.

The accountant of Beak plc proposes to treat this transaction as a sale in the financial statements.   (7 marks)

(ii) A car manufacturer, Gocar plc, supplies cars to a car dealer, Sparks Ltd, on the following terms. Sparks Ltd has to pay a monthly fee of £100 per car for the privilege of displaying it in its showroom and also is responsible for insuring the cars. When a car is sold to a customer, Sparks Ltd has to pay Gocar plc the factory price of the car when it was first supplied. Sparks Ltd can only return the cars to Gocar plc on the payment of a fixed penalty charge of 10% of the cost of the car. Sparks Ltd has to pay the factory price for the cars if they remain unsold within a four month period. Gocar plc cannot demand the return of the cars from Sparks Ltd.

The accountant of Sparks Ltd proposes to treat the cars unsold for less than four months as the property of Gocar plc and not show them as stock in the financial statements.   (8 marks)

ACCA Accounting and Audit Practice, December 1994   (25 marks)

6.14 FRS 5 – Reporting the Substance of Transactions – requires that a reporting entity's financial statements should report the substance of the transactions into which it has entered. FRS 5 states that in order to determine the substance of a transaction it is necessary to identify whether the transaction has given rise to new assets or liabilities for the reporting entity and whether it has changed the entity's existing assets or liabilities.

You are the management accountant of D Ltd which has three principal activities. These are the sale of motor vehicles (both new and second-hand), the provision of spare parts for motor vehicles, and the servicing of motor vehicles.

During the financial year ended 31 August 1996, the company has entered into a type of business transaction not previously undertaken. With effect from 1 January 1996, D Ltd entered into an agreement whereby it received motor vehicles on a consignment basis from E plc, a large manufacturer. The terms of the arrangement were as follows:

(i) On delivery, the stock of vehicles remains the legal property of E plc.

(ii) Legal title to a vehicle passes to D Ltd either when D Ltd enters into a binding arrangement to sell the vehicle to a third party or six months after the date of delivery by E plc to D Ltd.

(iii) At the date legal title passes, E plc invoices D Ltd for the sale of the vehicles. The price payable by D Ltd is the normal selling price of E plc *at the date of delivery*, increased by 1% for every complete month the vehicles are held on consignment by D Ltd. Any change in E plc's normal selling price between the date of delivery and the date legal title to the goods passes to D Ltd does not change the amount payable by D Ltd to E plc.

(iv) At any time between the date of delivery and the date legal title passes to D Ltd, the company (D Ltd) has the right to return the vehicles to E plc *provided they are not damaged or obsolete*. D Ltd does not have the right to return damaged or obsolete vehicles. If D Ltd exercises this right of return then a return penalty is payable by D Ltd as follows:

Time since date of delivery	Penalty as a percentage of invoiced price*
Three months or less	50%
Three to four months	75%
More than four months	100%

* i.e. the price that would otherwise be payable by D Ltd if legal title to the vehicles had passed at the date of return.

(v) E plc has *no right to demand* return of vehicles on consignment to D Ltd unless D Ltd becomes insolvent.

The managing director suggests that the vehicles should be shown as an asset of D Ltd only when title passes, and the purchase price becomes legally payable.

Requirement
Write a report to the managing director which

(a) explains how (under the principles established in FRS 5) an asset or liability is identified, and when an asset or liability should be recognised and should cease to be recognised, in the financial statements of a business; (12 marks)

(b) evaluates, in the light of the principles you have explained in (a), the correctness, or otherwise of the managing director's suggested accounting treatment for the new transaction. (8 marks)

CIMA, Financial Reporting, November 1996 **(Total Marks = 20)**

6.15 FRS 5 – *Reporting the substance of transactions* – requires that a reporting entity's financial statements should report the substance of the transactions into which it has entered.

You are the management accountant of S Ltd. During the most recent financial year (ended 31 August 1998), the company has entered into a debt factoring arrangement with F plc. The main terms of the agreement are as follows:

1 On the first day of every month S Ltd transfers (by assignment) all its trade debts to F plc, subject to credit approval by F plc for each debt transferred by S Ltd.
2 At the time of transfer of the debtors to F plc, S Ltd receives a payment from F plc of 70% of the gross amount of the transferred debts. The payment is debited by F plc to a factoring account which is maintained in the books of F plc.
3 Following transfer of the debts, F plc collects payments from debtors and performs any necessary follow-up work.
4 After collection by F plc, the cash received from the debtor is **credited** to the factoring account in the books of F plc.
5 F plc handles all aspects of the collection of the debts of S Ltd in return for a monthly charge of 1% of the total value of the debts transferred at the beginning of that month. The amount is debited to the factoring account in the books of F plc.
6 Any debts not collected by F plc within 90 days of transfer are regarded as bad debts by F plc and re-assigned to S Ltd. The cash previously advanced by F plc in respect of bad debts is recovered from S Ltd. The recovery is only possible out of the proceeds of other debtors which have been assigned to S Ltd. For example, if, in a particular month, S Ltd assigned trade debts having a value of £10 000 and a debt of £500 was identified as bad, then the amounts advanced by F plc to S Ltd would be £6650 [70% × £10 000 – 70% × £500].
7 On a monthly basis, F plc debits the factoring account with an interest charge which is calculated on a daily basis on the balance on the factoring account.
8 At the end of every quarter, F plc pays over to S Ltd a sum representing any credit balance on its factoring account with S Ltd at that time.

Requirement
Write a memorandum to the Board of Directors of S Ltd which outlines

(a) **how, under the principles set out in FRS 5, the substance of a transaction should be determined;** (10 marks)
(b) **how the debt factoring arrangement will be reported in the financial statements of S Ltd.** (10 marks)

CIMA, Financial Reporting, November 1998   (**Total Marks = 20**)

6.16 You are the management accountant of Prompt plc, a UK company which prepares financial statements to 31 March each year. The financial statements for the year ended 31 March 1998 are due to be formally approved by the board of directors on 15 June 1998.

Your assistant has prepared a first draft of the financial statements. These show a turnover of £200 million and a profit before taxation of £18 million. Your assistant has identified a number of transactions [(a), (b) and (c) overleaf] for which he is unsure of the correct accounting treatment. For each transaction, he has indicated the treatment followed in the draft financial statements. You have reviewed the transactions highlighted by your assistant.

Requirement
Draft a memorandum to your assistant which explains the correct accounting treatment for each transaction. Where the treatment adopted by your assistant in the draft financial statements is incorrect, your memorandum should indicate the reasons for this. For each transaction, your memorandum should refer to relevant provisions of company law and Accounting Standards.

Transaction (a)

During the year ended 31 March 1998, Prompt plc entered into an arrangement with a finance company to factor its debts. Each month 90% of the value of the debts arising from credit sales that month was sold to the factor, who assumed legal title and responsibility for collection of all debts. Upon receipt of the cash by the factor, the remaining 10% was paid to Prompt plc less a deduction for administration and finance costs. Any debtor who did not pay the factor within three months of the debt being factored was transferred back to Prompt plc and the amounts advanced by the factor recovered from Prompt plc. In preparing the draft financial statements, your assistant has removed the whole of the factored debts from trade debtors at the date the debts are factored. The net amount receivable from the factor has been shown as a sundry debtor. (5 marks)

Transaction (b)

On 15 March 1998, Prompt plc decided to close one of its three factories. This decision was taken because the product (called product X) which was manufactured at the factory was considered obsolete. A gradual run down of the operation commenced on 15 April 1998 and was expected to be complete by 15 June 1998. The factory produced monthly operating statements detailing turnover, profits and assets, and the turnover for the year ended 31 March 1998 was £35 million. Closure costs (including redundancy) were estimated to be £2.5 million. Your assistant has made no entries in the draft financial statements in respect of the closure since it took place in the year ending 31 March 1999. (12 marks)

Transaction (c)

On 30 June 1997, Prompt plc issued 100 million £1 debentures. The issue costs were £100 000. The debentures carry no interest entitlement but are redeemable on 30 June 2007 at a price of £259 million. Your assistant has included the nominal value of the debentures (£100 million) as part of shareholders' funds since they represent long-term finance for the company. The issue costs of £100 000 have been charged to the profit and loss account for the year, and your assistant suggests that the difference between the issue price and the redemption price should be dealt with in 2007 when the debentures are redeemed. (8 marks)

CIMA, Financial Reporting, May 1998 (Total Marks = 25)

7 Taxation: Current and deferred

7.1 In connection with SSAP 15 *Accounting for Deferred Taxation*:

(a) Write a description of accounting for deferred taxation which includes all of the main items in the Standard. The description should be appropriate for inclusion in the statement of accounting policies in a company's annual financial report, in accordance with SSAP 2 *Disclosure of Accounting Policies*. (6 marks)

(b) Prepare an example of a note on deferred taxation which includes all of the main items in the Standard. The note should be appropriate for inclusion in a company's financial statements and you should use your own figures to illustrate your answer. (You need not show comparative figures and you may assume that the company is not part of a group of companies.) (8 marks)

(c) Do you consider that the liability method adopts a balance sheet rather than a profit and loss account perspective? Contrast this with the deferral method. State your reasons. (6 marks)

ACCA Level 2 The Regulatory Framework of Accounting, June 1989 (20 marks)

7.2 Harmonise plc is a plastic toy manufacturer. Its toy sales have been adversely affected by imports and it has been changing towards the supply of plastic office equipment. Profits are expected to continue to fall for the next four years when they are expected to stabilise at the 1999 level. There will be a regular programme of plant renewal.

The following information is available:

Year ended 30 April	Profit before depreciation and tax	Capital allowances	Depreciation
	£	£	£
1996	1 250 000	400 000	80 000
1997	1 200 000	80 000	160 000
1998	1 100 000	80 000	240 000
1999	1 000 000	560 000	160 000

Assume a corporation tax rate of 33%. On 1 March 1995 there was a nil balance on the deferred tax account.

Required

(a) (i) Prepare the profit and loss and balance sheet extracts for corporation tax and deferred taxation for the four years 1996–1999 using the following methods
  (1) Flow-through
  (2) Full provision [*This part of the question is no longer applicable.*]
  (3) Partial provision
  Notes to the profit and loss account and balance sheet are *not* required.
  (ii) Calculate the deferred taxation using the partial provision method for the balance sheet as at 30 April 1996 arising from the following information on debentures.
  Harmonise plc had £1 million 10% debentures in issue at 30 April 1996 on which interest was payable half yearly in arrears on 1 May and 1 November each year. The company proposes to repay £400 000 on 30 April 1998 with all interest due and a further £200 000 on 30 April 1999 with all interest due.

(10 marks)

(b) Discuss arguments for and against each of the three methods in (a) (i) above.

(6 marks)

(c) Assuming that all of the shares in Harmonise plc were acquired for cash by Grab plc on 1 May 1995, explain the factors that would be taken into account in determining the fair value of deferred tax as at the date of acquisition. Grab plc applies the partial provision method. (4 marks)

ACCA Financial Reporting Environment, June 1996 **(20 marks)**

7.3 UK Ltd is the wholly-owned subsidiary of a US parent, US Inc. US Inc has a number of subsidiaries located in the US and in Europe. All group companies prepare financial statements to 31 December.

For the year ended 31 December 1996 the accounting profit before taxation of UK Ltd was £5 million. Depreciation charged for the year was £1.2 million on plant and machinery and £400 000 on retail premises. UK Ltd claimed capital allowances for the year of £1.5 million on the plant and machinery but no capital allowances were available on the retail premises. Apart from capital allowances and depreciation, there were no differences between accounting profit and taxable profit for the year.

UK Ltd accounts for deferred taxation using the partial provision method laid down in SSAP 15. The provision which was included in the balance sheet under this method at 31 December 1995 was £160 000. UK Ltd has produced the following estimates of capital allowances and depreciation for the next five years:

Year ending 31 December	Estimated capital allowances £000	Estimated depreciation on plant £000	Estimated depreciation on premises £000
1997	1 600	1 250	400
1998	1 200	1 300	400
1999	1 000	1 350	400
2000	800	1 400	400
2001	1 500	1 400	400

In the longer term, the level of capital expenditure is such that capital allowances on plant and machinery are likely to be equal to, or exceed, depreciation on plant and machinery.

The provision for mainstream corporation tax, which was included as a creditor in the balance sheet of UK Ltd at 31 December 1995, was £900 000. On 1 October 1996 the company paid the mainstream corporation tax for 1995, which was finally agreed at £920 000. The rate of corporation tax on profits which is appropriate for UK Ltd for 1995 AND 1996 is 33%.

Requirements
(a) Calculate the taxation charge that will be included in the profit and loss account of UK Ltd for the year ended 31 December 1996. (10 marks)
(b) Calculate the taxation charge that would be included in the profit and loss account of UK Ltd for the year ended 31 December 1996 if deferred taxation had been provided under the full provision method. (4 marks)
(c) Explain why SSAP 15 prefers the partial provision method to the full provision method. (6 marks)

Note: All computations in this question should be performed to the nearest £000.

CIMA, Financial Reporting, May 1997   (Total Marks = 20)

7.4 You are the management accountant of Construct Ltd, a private company which has as its main business activity the construction of houses for sale in the domistic sector. For its year ended 31 December 1998, the company charged depreciation of £700 000 and claimed capital allowances of £600 000. For the next five years, the capital allowances and depreciation for Construct Ltd are expected to be as follows:

Year ending	Capital allowances £000	Depreciation £000
31 December 1999	500	700
31 December 2000	450	720
31 December 2001	600	740
31 December 2002	800	780
31 December 2003	950	820

At 1 January 1998, the net book value of fixed assets which qualified for capital allowances exceeded their tax written-down value by £1.4 million. Construct Ltd follows the provisions of SSAP 15 – *Accounting for Deferred Tax* – and accordingly a provision for deferred tax of £225 000 was made in the 1997 financial statements. The rate of corporation tax which is appropriate for Construct Ltd is 31%.

Requirements
(a) Calculate the charge or credit to the profit and loss account for deferred tax for the year ended 31 December 1998 and the balance on the deferred tax account at 31 December 1998
  (i) under the accounting policy followed by Construct Ltd; (6 marks)
  (ii) under the full provision method. (4 marks)

(b) Explain why the Accounting Standards Board is currently reviewing SSAP 15 and may well produce a revised Financial Reporting Standard which requires the use of the full provision method. (10 marks)

CIMA, Financial Reporting, May 1999 (Total Marks = 20)

7.5 The Accounting Standards Board (ASB) currently faces a dilemma. IAS 12 (revised), 'Income Taxes' published by the International Accounting Standards Committee (IASC) recommends measures which significantly differ from current UK practice set out in SSAP 15 'Accounting for Deferred Tax'. IAS 12 requires an enterprise to provide for deferred tax in full for all deferred tax liabilities with only limited exceptions whereas SSAP 15 utilises the partial provision approach. The dilemma facing the ASB is whether to adopt the principles of IAS 12 (revised) and face criticism from many UK companies who agree with the partial provision approach. The discussion paper 'Accounting for Tax' appears to indicate that the ASB wish to eliminate the partial provision method.

The different approaches are particularly significant when acquiring subsidiaries because of the fair value adjustments and also when dealing with revaluations of fixed assets as the IAS requires companies to provide for deferred tax on these amounts.

Required
(a) Explain the main reasons why SSAP 15 has been criticised. (8 marks)
(b) Discuss the arguments in favour of and against providing for deferred tax on:
    (i) fair value adjustments on the acquisition of a subsidiary
    (ii) revaluations of fixed assets. (7 marks)
(c) XL plc has the following net assets at 30 November 1997.

	£000	Tax value (£000)
Fixed assets		
Buildings	33 500	7 500
Plant and equipment	52 000	13 000
Investments	66 000	66 000
	151 500	86 500
Current assets	15 000	15 000
Creditors: Amounts falling due within one year		
Creditors	(13 500)	(13 500)
Liability for health care benefits	(300)	–
	(13 800)	
Net current assets	1 200	
Provision for deferred tax	(9 010)	(9 010)
	143 690	78 990

XL plc has acquired 100% of the shares of BZ Ltd on 30 November 1997. The following statement of net assets relates to BZ Ltd on 30 November 1997.

	£000 Fair value	£000 Carrying value	£000 Tax value
Buildings	500	300	100
Plant and equipment	40	30	15
Stock	124	114	114
Debtors	110	110	110
Retirement benefit liability	(60)	(60)	–
Creditors	(105)	(105)	(105)
	609	389	234

587

There is currently no deferred tax provision in the accounts of BZ Ltd. In order to achieve a measure of consistency XL plc decided that it would revalue its land and buildings to £50 million and the plant and equipment to £60 million. The company did not feel it necessary to revalue the investments. The liabilities for retirement benefits and healthcare costs are anticipated to remain at their current amounts for the foreseeable future.

The land and buildings of XL plc had originally cost £45 million and the plant and equipment £70 million. The company has no intention of selling any of its fixed assets other than the land and buildings which it may sell and lease back. XL plc currently utilises the full provision method to account for deferred taxation. The projected depreciation charges and tax allowances of XL plc and BZ Ltd are as follows for the years ending 30 November:

	£000 1998	£000 1999	£000 2000
Depreciation (Buildings, plant and equipment)			
XL plc	7 010	8 400	7 560
BZ Ltd	30	32	34
Tax allowances			
XL plc	8 000	4 500	3 000
BZ Ltd	40	36	30

The corporation tax rate had changed from 35% to 30% in the current year. Ignore any indexation allowance or rollover relief and assume that XL plc and BZ Ltd are in the same tax jurisdiction.

Required
Calculate the deferred tax expense for XL plc which would appear in the group financial statements at 30 November 1997 using:

(i) the full provision method incorporating the effects of the revaluation of assets in XL plc and the acquisition of BZ Ltd.
(ii) the partial provision method. (10 marks)

(25 marks)

(Candidates should not answer in accordance with IAS 12 (Revised) 'Income Taxes').

ACCA Financial Reporting Environment, December 1997

8 Business combinations and goodwill

8.1 In connection with merger accounting:

(a) Since the issue of FRS 6 'Acquisitions and mergers', under what circumstances may a business combination be accounted for as a merger? (6 marks)
(b) What are the differences between acquisition and merger accounting, as may be seen from a consolidated balance sheet? (6 marks)
(c) The balance sheet of Beta plc at 31 December was:

	£
Ordinary share capital (nominal £1)	200
Revaluation reserve	250
Profit and loss account	350
	800
Net assets (at fair values)	800

Alpha plc merges with Beta plc and Alpha plc issues 800 ordinary shares (nominal value 5p) to acquire 200 shares in Beta plc.

(i) Calculate the merger reserve.
(ii) Under what circumstances could this merger reserve be regarded as realised and available for distribution to Alpha plc's shareholders? (8 marks)

ACCA The Regulatory Framework of Accounting, June 1993 (updated) (20 marks)

8.2 '*Accounting standards should narrow differences in reporting yet acquisition accounting and merger accounting result in significantly different results in the year of combination and thereafter.*'

You are required to discuss the above statement stating, with reasons, whether there is a need for two different methods.

CIMA Advanced Financial Accounting, May 1994 (15 marks)

8.3 A merger is 'a business combination that results in the creation of a new reporting entity formed from the combining parties, in which the combining entities come together in a partnership for the mutual sharing of the risks and benefits of the combined entity, and in which no party to the combination in substance obtains control over any other, or is otherwise seen to be dominant . . .' FRS 6 'Acquisitions and Mergers'. The continuity of ownership, control and the sharing of risks and benefits in the combined entity are seen as crucial to a combination being accounted for as a merger. There are certain criteria under FRS 6 which can be verified and substantiated in order to determine whether there is continuity of ownership. Similarly there are certain criteria in FRS 6 which could be said to be circumstantial or implied evidence of a merger and which cannot be exactly determined. This type of evidence is somewhat subjective. Finally FRS 6 has invoked certain criteria which attempt to prevent a company creating the superficial or cosmetic appearance of the occurrence of a merger.

Required
(a) Analyse and describe the criteria that a business combination must meet under FRS 6 for it to be accounted for as a merger under the following classes:
    (i)   verifiable and substantive signs of a merger
    (ii) implied or circumstantial evidence of a merger
    (iii) terms which prevent superficial mergers (anti–avoidance criteria). (9 marks)
(b) The following abridged financial statements relate to Merge plc and Acquire plc for the year ended 30 November 1997.

Profit and Loss Account Year Ended 30 November 1997

	£000 Merge plc	£000 Acquire plc
Turnover	21 285	18 000
Cost of sales	(16 950)	(14 450)
Gross profit	4 335	3 550
Distribution and administrative expenses	(3 310)	(2 730)
Operating profit	1 025	820
Income from investments (including tax credit)	200	100
Profit before taxation	1 225	920
Taxation	(365)	(274)
Dividends	(208)	(148)
Retained profit for year	652	498

Balance Sheet at 30 November 1997

	£000	£000
	Merge plc	*Acquire plc*
Fixed assets	4099	3590
including cost of investment in Acquire plc)		
Current assets	5530	4350
Creditors: Amounts falling due within one year	(2502)	(2530)
Net current assets	3028	1820
Total assets less current liabilities	7127	5410
Capital and reserves		
Called up share capital –		
ordinary shares of £1	2500	1250
Share premium account	400	250
Revaluation reserve	75	185
Other reserves	100	–
Profit and loss account	4052	3725
	7127	5410

(i) During the year the entire share capital of Acquire plc was acquired following a recommended offer by merchant bankers on 30 April 1997. Ordinary shares were issued to those shareholders of Acquire plc who accepted the offer and at the same time £36000 was paid in cash to shareholders who took the cash alternative. The offer was made on the basis of six shares in Merge plc for every five shares in Acquire plc. A fully underwritten cash alternative of £2.25 per share was offered to the shareholders of Acquire plc. The offer became unconditional on 31 May 1997 when the market value of shares in Merge plc was £2.50 per share. On 31 August 1997 Merge plc compulsorily acquired 8000 shares of Acquire plc for cash from shareholders who had not accepted the initial offer under the Companies Act 1985. The above transactions had been incorporated in the financial records of Merge plc at their nominal value.

(ii) Merge plc incurred £156000 of expenses in connection with the acquistion of Acquire plc. This figure included issue costs of shares of £58000 and has been included in administrative expenses.

(iii) Acquire plc paid dividends of £48000 on 31 March 1997 and has proposed a final dividend of £100000. Merge plc's dividends are all proposed. The proposed dividend of Acquire plc has been taken into account in Merge plc's financial statements. Assume that ACT (rate of 1/4) has been correctly dealt with on these items in the financial statements.

(iv) The acquisition fulfils all of the criteria in the Companies Acts and FRS 6 for merger accounting except for the criteria relating to the purchase consideration which has not been tested.

(v) There is no group election for tax purposes in force.

Required
Prepare the group profit and loss account for the year ended 30 November 1997 and the balance sheet as at 30 November 1997 for the Merge Group plc. (16 marks)

ACCA Financial Reporting Environment, December 1997 (**25 marks**)

8.4 Growmoor plc has carried on business as a food retailer since 1900. It had traded profitably until the late 1980s when it suffered from fierce competition from larger retailers. Its turnover and margins were under severe pressure and its share price fell to an all time low. The directors formulated a strategic plan to grow by acquisition and merger. It has an agreement to be able to borrow funds to finance acquisition at an interest rate of 10% per annum. It is Growmoor plc's policy to amortise goodwill over ten years.

1. *Investment in Smelt plc*

On 15 June 1994 Growmoor plc had an issued share capital of 1 625 000 ordinary shares of £1 each. On that date it acquired 240 000 of the 1 500 000 issued £1 ordinary shares of Smelt plc for a cash payment of £164 000.

Growmoor plc makes up its accounts to 31 July. In early 1996 the directors of Growmoor plc and Smelt plc were having discussions with a view to a combination of the two companies.

The proposal was that:

(i) On 1 May 1996 Growmoor plc should acquire 1 200 000 of the issued ordinary shares of Smelt plc which had a market price of £1.30 per share, in exchange for 1 500 000 newly issued ordinary shares in Growmoor plc which had a market price of £1.20p per share. There has been no change in Growmoor plc's share capital since 15 June 1994. The market price of the Smelt plc shares had ranged from £1.20 to £1.50 during the year ended 30 April 1996.

(ii) It was agreed that the consideration would be increased by 200 000 shares if a contingent liability in Smelt plc in respect of a claim for wrongful dismissal by a former director did not crystallise.

(iii) After the exchange the new board would consist of 6 directors from Growmoor plc and 6 directors from Smelt plc with the Managing Director of Growmoor plc becoming Managing Director of Smelt plc.

(iv) The Growmoor plc head office should be closed and the staff made redundant and the Smelt plc head office should become the head office of the new combination.

(v) Senior managers of both companies were to re-apply for their posts and be interviewed by an interview panel comprising a director and the personnel managers from each company. The age profile of the two companies differed with the average age of the Growmoor plc managers being 40 and that of Smelt plc being 54 and there was an expectation among the directors of both boards that most of the posts would be filled by Growmoor plc managers.

2. *Investment in Beaten Ltd*

Growmoor plc is planning to acquire all of the 800 000 £1 ordinary shares in Beaten Ltd on 30 June 1996 for a deferred consideration of £500 000 and a contingent consideration payable on 30 June 2000 of 10% of the amount by which profits for the year ended 30 June 2000 exceeded £100 000. Beaten Ltd has suffered trading losses and its directors, who are the major shareholders, support a takeover by Growmoor plc. The fair value of net assets of Beaten Ltd was £685 000 and Growmoor plc expected that reorganisation costs would be £85 000 and future trading losses would be £100 000. Growmoor plc agreed to offer four year service contracts to the directors of Beaten Ltd.

The directors had expected to be able to create a provision for the reorganisation costs and future trading losses but were advised by their Finance Director that FRS 7 required these two items to be treated as post-acquisition items.

Required

(a) (i) Explain to the directors of Growmoor plc the extent to which the proposed terms of the combination with Smelt plc satisfied the requirements of the Companies Act 1985 and FRS 6 for the combination to be treated as a merger; and

   (ii) If the proposed terms fail to satisfy any of the requirements, advise the directors on any changes that could be made so that the combination could be treated as a merger as at 31 July 1996. (8 marks)

(b) Explain briefly the reasons for the application of the principles of recognition and measurement on an acquisition set out in FRS 7 to provisions for future operating losses and for re-organisation costs. (3 marks)

(c) (i) Explain the treatment in the profit and loss account for the year ended 31 July 1996 and the balance sheet as at that date of Growmoor plc on the assumption that the acquisition of Beaten Ltd took place on 30 June 1996 and the consideration for the acquisition was deferred so that £100 000 was payable after one year, £150 000 after two years and the balance after three years. Show your calculations.

   (ii) Calculate the goodwill to be dealt with in the consolidated accounts for the years ending 31 July 1996 and 1997, explaining clearly the effect of deferred and contingent consideration.

   (iii) Explain and critically discuss the existing regulations for the treatment of negative goodwill.

                                                                  (9 marks)

ACCA Financial Reporting Environment, December 1996   **(20 marks)**

8.5 The balance sheets of A plc and its investee undertakings, B Ltd and C Ltd, at 30 September 1996 (the accounting date of all three companies) are given below:

	A plc £000	A plc £000	B Ltd £000	B Ltd £000	C Ltd £000	C Ltd £000
Fixed assets (*notes 1 and 3*):						
Tangible assets	9 100		9 000		8 000	
Investments	8 900		–		–	
		18 000		9 000		8 000
Current assets (*note 3*):						
Stocks	4 000		3 000		2 500	
Debtors	3 000		2 500		2 000	
Cash in hand	800		700		600	
	7 800		6 200		5 100	
Current liabilities (*note 3*):						
Trade creditors	2 500		2 000		1 700	
Taxation	600		500		450	
Proposed dividend	600		500		–	
Bank overdraft	3 200		2 800		2 450	
	6 900		5 800		4 600	
Net current assets		900		400		500
Long-term loans (*note 3*)		(8 000)		(2 000)		(2 000)
		10 900		7 400		6 500
Capital and reserves:						
Called-up share capital (£1 shares)		5 000		4 000		4 000
Profit and loss account		5 900		3 400		2 500
		10 900		7 400		6 500

Note 1: On 15 June 1978 (the date of incorporation of B Ltd) A plc subscribed for 3.2 million shares in B Ltd at par. No new shares have been issued by B Ltd since its incorporation.

Note 2: On 1 June 1996 A plc purchased 3 million shares in C Ltd at an agreed value of £1.90 per share. The purchase was financed by an additional issue of loan stock, carrying an interest rate of 10%.

Note 3: C Ltd produced interim financial statements, drawn up as at 1 June 1996, in connection with the acquisition by A plc. The balance sheet of C Ltd at that date showed the following:

	£000		£000
Tangible fixed assets (*note 4*)	7 875	Trade creditors	1 600
Stocks (*note 5*)	2 000	Taxation	300
Debtors	1 450	Bank overdraft	1 825
Cash in hand	600	Long-term loans (*note 6*)	2 000
		Share capital (£1 shares)	4 000
		Profit and loss account	2 200
	11 925		11 925

Note 4: The following information relates to the tangible fixed assets of C Ltd at 1 June 1996:

	£000
Gross replacement cost	14 220
Net replacement cost	8 295
Economic value	9 000
Net realisable value	4 000

The fixed assets of C Ltd at 1 June 1996 had a total purchase cost to C Ltd of £13.5 million. They were all being depreciated at 25% per annum pro rata on that cost. This policy is also appropriate for the consolidated financial statements of A plc. No fixed assets of C Ltd which were included in the interim financial statements drawn up as at 1 June 1996 were disposed of by C Ltd prior to 30 September 1996. No fixed asset was fully depreciated by 30 September 1996.

Note 5: The stocks of C Ltd which were shown in the interim financial statements at cost to C Ltd of £2 million would have cost £2.1 million to replace at 1 June 1996 and had an estimated net realisable value at that date of £2.4 million. Of the stock of C Ltd in hand at 1 June 1996, goods costing C Ltd £1.5 million were sold for £1.8 million between 1 June 1996 and 30 September 1996.

Note 6: The long-term loan of C Ltd carries a rate of interest of 10% per annum, payable on 31 May annually in arrears. The loan is redeemable at par on 31 May 2000. The interest cost is representative of current market rates. The accrued interest payable by C Ltd at 30 September 1996 is included in the trade creditors of C Ltd at that date.

Note 7: On 1 June 1996 A plc took a decision to rationalise the group so as to integrate C Ltd. The costs of the rationalisation (which were to be borne by A plc) were estimated to total £1.5 million and the process was due to start on 1 December 1996. No provision for these costs has been made in any of the financial statements given in this question.

Requirements
(a) Compute the goodwill on consolidation of C Ltd that will be included in the consolidated financial statements of the A plc group for the year ended 30 September 1996, explaining your treatment of the items mentioned in *Notes 2 to 7*. You should refer to the provisions of relevant Accounting Standards. (12 marks)
(b) Write a memorandum to a trainee accountant, explaining how the goodwill you have calculated in (a) should be dealt with in the consolidated financial statements of A plc. The trainee believes that since the goodwill is unlikely to fall in value for the foreseeable future, it should be retained in the accounts as a permanent item with no adjustments. You should refer to the provisions of relevant Accounting Standards, as appropriate. (10 marks)
(c) Prepare the consolidated balance sheet of the A plc group at 30 September 1996, assuming that A plc deals with investment income on an accruals basis and does not

wish to show goodwill on consolidation as an asset in the consolidated financial statements. (18 marks)

Note: All your numerical workings can be rounded to the nearest £000.

CIMA, *Financial Reporting, November 1996* (Total Marks = 40)

8.6 FRS 10 – *Goodwill and Intangible Assets* – was issued in December 1997. At the same time, SSAP 22, the previous Accounting Standard which dealt with the subject of accounting for goodwill, was withdrawn. SSAP 22 allowed purchased goodwill to be written off directly to reserves as one amount in the accounting period of purchase. FRS 10 does not permit this treatment.

Invest plc has a number of subsidiaries. The accounting date of Invest plc and all its subsidiaries is 30 April. On 1 May 1998, Invest plc purchased 80% of the issued equity shares of Target Ltd. This purchase made Target Ltd a subsidiary of Invest plc from 1 May 1998. Invest plc made a cash payment of £31 million for the shares in Target Ltd. On 1 May 1998, the net assets which were included in the balance sheet of Target Ltd had a fair value to Invest plc of £30 million. Target Ltd sells a well-known branded product and has taken steps to protect itself legally against unauthorised use of the brand name. A reliable estimate of the value of this brand to the Invest group is £3 million. It is further considered that the value of the brand can be maintained or even increased for the foreseeable future. The value of the brand is *not* included in the balance sheet of Target Ltd.

For the purposes of preparing the consolidated financial statements, the Directors of Invest plc wish to ensure that the charge to the profit and loss account for the amortisation of intangible fixed assets is kept to a minimum. They estimate that the useful economic life of the purchased goodwill (or premium on acquisition) of Target Ltd is 40 years.

Requirements
(a) Outline the key factors which lay behind the decision of the Accounting Standards Board to prohibit the write off of purchased goodwill to reserves. (11 marks)
(b) Compute the charge to the consolidated profit and loss account in respect of the goodwill on acquisition of Target Ltd for its year ended 30 April 1999. (5 marks)
(c) Explain the action which Invest plc must take in 1998/99 and in future years arising from the chosen accounting treatment of the goodwill on acquisition of Target Ltd. (4 marks)

CIMA, *Financial Reporting, November 1999* (Total Marks = 20)

8.7 Islay plc has acquired the following unincorporated businesses:

(1) 'Savalight', a business specialising in the production of low-cost, energy efficient light bulbs, acquired on 1 June 1996 for £580 000. The identifiable assets and liabilities of the business had a book value of £550 000 and were valued at £500 000 on 1 June 1996. The company estimated the useful economic life of the goodwill arising at five years and has been amortising this through the profit and loss account. It was anticipated that the goodwill would have a residual value of £20 000.

(2) 'Green Goods', a business specialising in the distribution of a range of environmentally friendly products, acquired on 1 June 1997 for £1.8 million. The identifiable assets and liabilities of the business had a book value of £1.1 million and were valued at £1.3 million on 1 June 1997, including goodwill of the business of £150 000. The company estimated the useful economic life of goodwill arising at 25 years and has been amortising this through the profit and loss account.

(3) 'Smart IT', a business specialising in the distribution of computers, acquired on 1 June 1998 for £900 000 The identifiable assets and liabilities of the business had a book value of £1 million and were valued at £1.2 million on 1 June 1998. Assume the major non-monetary assets in these amounts have a useful economic life of 15 years.

Islay plc revalued its tangible fixed assets during the year ended 31 May 1999 and created a revaluation reserve of £600 000. In addition, the company believes the goodwill arising on the purchase of 'Savalight' is now worth £350 000 and intends to reflect this in the financial statements for the year ended 31 May 1999.

The company's capital and reserves (**before reflecting any adjustments for the above acquisitions**) in the draft financial statements as at 31 May 1999 show:

Capital and reserves	£'000
Called up share capital (5 000 000 ordinary shares of £1 each)	5 000
Revaluation reserve	600
Profit and loss account (£200 000 for the year ended 31 May 1999)	700
	6 300

Requirements

(a) Calculate and disclose the amounts for goodwill to be included in the financial statements for Islay plc for the year ended 31 May 1999, providing the following disclosures:

> Balance sheet extracts
> Disclosure note for goodwill
> Disclosure note for movements on reserves. (13 marks)

(b) Explain the accounting treatment you have adopted for any goodwill arising in acquisitions (1) to (3) above, referring to the provisions of FRS 10, 'Goodwill and Intangible Assets', and noting any current or future action Islay plc will have to take on goodwill recognised. (4 marks)

ICAEW Financial Reporting, June 1999 (**17 marks**)

8.8 'Much of the true value of a business is reflected not in its balance sheet but in intangible factors such as brands, customer loyalty and the skill of its work-force.'

Required

Discuss, reaching a conclusion, whether factors such as those listed above should be reflected in a company's annual report and accounts, and how this could be achieved in practice.

ICAEW, Auditing and Financial Reporting, December 1994 (**12 marks**)

9 Investments, groups, associates and joint ventures

9.1 The accountancy profession has developed a range of techniques to measure and present the effects of one company owning shares in another company.

Briefly describe each of these techniques and how the resulting information might best be presented.

(The Companies Act 1985 disclosure requirements are **not** required.)

ACCA Level 2 The Regulatory Framework of Accounting, December 1986 (**20 marks**)

9.2 You are group financial accountant of a diverse group of companies. The board of directors has instructed you to exclude from the consolidated financial statements the results of some loss-making subsidiaries as they believe inclusion will distort the performance of other more profitable subsidiaries.

You are required to write a memorandum to the board of directors explaining the circumstances when a subsidiary can be excluded and the accounting treatment of such excluded subsidiaries.

CIMA Advanced Financial Accounting, November 1993   **(15 marks)**

9.3 Fair value is a concept underlying external financial reporting.

You are required
(a) to explain why fair value accounting is required;   (4 marks)
(b) to explain how the fair value concept is applied;   (5 marks)
(c) to list three areas of application of fair value accounting.   (6 marks)

CIMA Advanced Financial Accounting, November 1991   **(15 marks)**

9.4 Relevant balance sheets as at 31 March 1994 are set out below:

	£ 000 Jasmin (Holdings) plc	£ 000 Kasbah plc	£ 000 Fortran plc
Tangible fixed assets	289 400	91 800	7 600
Investments			
Shares in Kasbah (at cost)	97 600		
Shares in Fortran (at cost)	8 000		
	395 000		
Current assets			
Stock	285 600	151 400	2 600
Cash	319 000	500	6 800
	604 600	151 900	9 400
Creditors: amounts falling			
due within one year	289 600	238 500	2 200
Net current assets	315 000	(86 600)	7 200
Total assets less current liabilities	710 000	5 200	14 800
Capital and reserves			
Called up share capital			
Ordinary £1 shares	60 000	20 000	10 000
10% £1 Preference shares		4 000	
Revaluation reserve	40 000		1 200
Profit and loss reserve	610 000	(18 800)	3 600
	710 000	5 200	14 800

You have recently been appointed chief accountant of Jasmin (Holdings) plc and are about to prepare the group balance sheet at 31 March 1994.

The following points are relevant to the preparation of those accounts.

(a) Jasmin (Holdings) plc owns 90% of the ordinary £1 shares and 20% of the 10% £1 preference shares of Kasbah plc. On 1 April 1993 Jasmin (Holdings) plc paid £96 million for the ordinary £1 shares and £1.6 million for the 10% £1 preference shares when Kasbah's reserves were a credit balance of £45 million.

(b) Jasmin (Holdings) plc sells part of its output to Kasbah plc. The stock of Kasbah plc on 31 March 1994 includes £1.2 million of stock purchased from Jasmin (Holdings) plc at cost plus one third.

(c) The policy of the group is to revalue its tangible fixed assets on a yearly basis. However the directors of Kasbah plc have always resisted this policy preferring to show tangible fixed assets at historical cost. The market value of the tangible fixed assets of Kasbah plc at 31 March 1994 is £90 million. The directors of Jasmin (Holdings) plc wish you to follow the requirements of FRS 2 'Accounting for Subsidiary Undertakings' in respect of the value of tangible fixed assets to be included in the group accounts.

(d) The ordinary £1 shares of Fortran plc are split into 6 million 'A' ordinary £1 shares and 4 million 'B' ordinary £1 shares. Holders of 'A' shares are assigned 1 vote and holders of 'B' ordinary shares are assigned 2 votes per share. On 1 April 1993 Jasmin (Holdings) plc acquired 80% of the 'A' ordinary shares and 10% of the 'B' ordinary shares when the profit and loss reserve of Fortran plc was £1.6 million and the revaluation reserve was, £2 million. The 'A' ordinary shares and 'B' ordinary shares carry equal rights to share in the company's profit and losses.

(e) The fair values of Kasbah plc and Fortran plc were not materially different from their book values at the time of acquisition of their shares by Jasmin (Holdings) plc.

(f) Goodwill arising on acquisition is amortised over five years.

(g) Kasbah plc has paid its preference dividend for the current year but no other dividends are proposed by the group companies. The preference dividend was paid shortly after the interim results of Kasbah plc were announced and was deemed to be a legal dividend by the auditors.

(h) Because of its substantial losses during the period, the directors of Jasmin (Holdings) plc wish to exclude the financial statements of Kasbah plc from the group accounts on the grounds that Kasbah plc's output is not similar to that of Jasmin (Holdings) plc and that the resultant accounts therefore would be misleading. Jasmin (Holdings) plc produces synthetic yarn and Kasbah plc produces garments.

Required

(a) **List the conditions for exclusion of subsidiaries from consolidation for the directors of Jasmin (Holdings) plc and state whether Kasbah plc may be excluded on these grounds.** (4 marks)

(b) **Prepare a consolidated balance sheet for Jasmin (Holdings) Group plc for the year ending 31 March 1994. (All calculations should be made to the nearest thousand pounds.)** (18 marks)

(c) **Comment briefly on the possible implications of the size of Kasbah plc's losses for the year for the group accounts and the individual accounts of Jasmin (Holdings) plc.** (3 marks)

ACCA Accounting and Audit Practice, June 1994   (25 marks)

9.5 Balmoral plc acquired 75% of the ordinary share capital and 30% of the preference share capital of Glenshee Ltd for £2 million on 1 November 1994. The draft profit and loss accounts for the companies for the year ended 31 October 1998 were:

	Balmoral plc £'000	Glenshee Ltd £'000
Turnover	2 500	800
Changes in stocks of finished goods and work in progress	200	(100)
Own work capitalised	150	–
Raw materials and consumables	(1 000)	(300)
Staff costs	(400)	(50)
Depreciation	(350)	(110)
Profit before taxation	1 100	240
Taxation	(340)	(70)
Profit after taxation	760	170

Additional information

(1) The share capital and reserves of Glenshee Ltd at 1 November 1994 were:

	£'000
Ordinary shares of £1 each	1 500
10% preference shares of £1 each	500
Share premium account	100
Profit and loss account	400

There have been no subsequent changes to the share capital.

(2) The share capital of Balmoral plc comprises £2 million of 50p ordinary shares.

(3) The fair value of Glenshee Ltd's fixed assets was £200 000 higher than their net book value at 1 November 1994 and they have a useful economic life of 10 years.

(4) On 31 July 1998, Glenshee Ltd sold goods to Balmoral plc for £50 000 on the basis of cost plus a mark-up of one third. By 31 October 1998, £40 000 of the goods remained in Balmoral plc's stock.

(5) Neither company has paid dividends in the year but both have proposed a final ordinary dividend of 5p per share and Glenshee Ltd proposes to pay the preference dividend in full. These proposed dividends are yet to be accounted for.

(6) Any goodwill arising is to be amortised over 10 years.

Requirements

(a) **Prepare the consolidated profit and loss account of Balmoral plc for the year ended 31 October 1998.** (10 marks)

(b) **Discuss the benefits of consolidated accounts to the users of published financial statements.** (5 marks)

ICAEW, Financial Reporting, December 1998 (**15 marks**)

9.6 Highland plc owns two subsidiaries acquired as follows:

1 July 1991   80% of Aviemore Ltd for £5 million when the book value of the net assets of Aviemore Ltd was £4 million.

30 November 1997   65% of Buchan Ltd for £2 million when the book value of the net assets of Buchan Ltd was £1.35 million.

The companies' profit and loss accounts for the year ended 31 March 1998 were:

	Highland plc £'000	Aviemore Ltd £'000	Buchan Ltd £'000
Sales	5 000	3 000	2 910
Cost of sales	(3 000)	(2 300)	(2 820)
Gross profit	2 000	700	90
Net operating expenses	(1 000)	(500)	(150)
Other income	230	–	–
Interest payable and similar charges	–	(50)	(210)
Profit/(loss) before taxation	1 230	150	(270)
Taxation	(300)	(50)	–
Profit/(loss) after taxation	930	100	(270)
Dividends proposed	(200)	(50)	–
	730	50	(270)

Additional information

(1) On 1 April 1997, Buchan Ltd issued £2.1 million 10% loan stock to Highland plc. Interest is payable twice yearly on 1 October and 1 April. Highland plc has accounted for the interest received on 1 October 1997 only.

(2) On 1 July 1997, Aviemore Ltd sold a freehold property to Highland plc for £800 000 (land element – £300 000). The property originally cost £900 000 (land element – £100 000) on 1 July 1987. The property's total useful economic life was 50 years on 1 July 1987 and there has been no change in the useful economic life since. Aviemore Ltd has credited the profit on disposal to 'Net operating expenses'.

(3) The fixed assets of Buchan Ltd on 30 November 1997 were valued at £500 000 (book value £350 000) and were acquired in April 1997. The fixed assets have a total useful economic life of ten years. Buchan Ltd has not adjusted its accounting records to reflect fair values.

(4) All companies use the straight-line method of depreciation and charge a full year's depreciation in the year of acquisition and none in the year of disposal.

(5) Highland plc charges Aviemore Ltd an annual fee of £85 000 for management services and this has been included in 'Other income'.

(6) Highland plc has accounted for its dividend receivable from Aviemore Ltd in 'Other income'.

(7) It is group policy to amortise goodwill arising on acquisitions over ten years.

Requirement
Prepare the consolidated profit and loss account for Highland plc for the year ended 31 March 1998.

ICAEW Financial Reporting, May 1998 (13 marks)

9.7 The summarised balance sheets of A plc and its two subsidiaries, B Ltd and C Ltd, at 31 December 1992 are shown below:

Summarised balance sheets at 31 December 1992

	A plc £000	B Ltd £000	C Ltd £000
Investment in subsidiaries:			
A plc in B Ltd	1 164		
A plc in C Ltd	1 120		
Other net assets	2 516	1 260	1 400
	4 800	1 260	1 400

	A plc £000	B Ltd £000	C Ltd £000
Ordinary share capital (£1 shares)	1 500	500	400
Revenue reserves	3 300	760	1 000
	4 800	1 260	1 400

The summarised profit and loss accounts for A plc and B Ltd for the year ended 31 December 1993 are as follows:

	A plc £000	B Ltd £000
Operating profit	1200	250
Taxation	360	60
Profit after tax	840	190
Dividends paid	50	20
Retained profit for year	790	170
Retained profit b/fwd	3300	760
Retained profits c/fwd	4090	930

Additional information:
(i) A plc acquired 80% of the ordinary share capital of B Ltd on 1 January 1984 when the reserves of B Ltd were £420 000.
(ii) A plc acquired 90% of the ordinary share capital of C Ltd on 1 January 1985 when the reserves of C Ltd were £320 000.
(iii) It is the policy of A plc to write off goodwill to profit and loss over five years.
(iv) On 1 January 1993, A plc disposed of 350 000 shares in C Ltd for £1 925 000. The relevant profit on sale has **not** been included in the profit and loss account of A plc.
(v) Assume a rate of corporation tax on capital gains of 25%.
(vi) A plc accounts for dividends on a received basis.
(vii) There were no changes in the issued share capital of the subsidiaries since acquisition by A plc.

Requirements
(a) **Prepare the consolidated profit and loss account and balance sheet of the A plc group at 31 December 1993.** (24 marks)
(b) **Prepare a reconciliation of opening and closing consolidated reserves.** (6 marks)
Show all your workings.

CIMA Specimen Question Paper Financial Reporting, 1995 Syllabus (30 marks)

9.8 You are the management accountant of Complex plc, a listed company with a number of subsidiaries located throughout the United Kingdom. Your assistant has prepared the first draft of the financial statements of the group for the year ended 31 August 1999. The draft statements show a group profit before taxation of £40 million. She has written you a memorandum concerning two complex transactions which have arisen during the year. The memorandum outlines the key elements of each transaction and suggests the appropriate treatment.

Transaction 1
On 1 March 1999, Complex plc purchased 75% of the equity share capital of Easy Ltd for a total cash price of £60 million. The Directors of Easy Ltd prepared a balance sheet of the company at 1 March 1999. The total of net assets as shown in this balance sheet was £66 million. However, the net assets of Easy Ltd were reckoned to have a fair value to the Complex group of £72 million in total. The Directors of Complex plc considered that a group reorganisation would be necessary because of the acquisition of Easy Ltd and that

the cost would be £4 million. This reorganisation was completed by 31 August 1999. Your assistant has computed the goodwill on consolidation of Easy Ltd as follows:

	£ million	£ million
Fair value of investment		60
Fair value of net assets	72	
Less: reorganisation provision	(4)	
	68	
Group share		(51)
Goodwill relating to a 75% investment		9
Goodwill relating to a 25% investment ($\frac{25}{75}$)		3

Your assistant has recognised total goodwill of £12 million (£9 million + £3 million). The goodwill attributable to the minority shareholders (£3 million) has been credited to the minority interest account. The reorganisation costs of £4 million have been written off against the provision which was created as part of the fair value exercise.

Transaction 2
On 15 May 1999, Complex plc disposed of one of its subsidiaries – Redundant Ltd. Complex plc had owned 100% of the shares in Redundant Ltd prior to disposal. The goodwill arising on the original consolidation of Redundant Ltd had been written off to reserves in line with the Accounting Standard in force at that time. This goodwill amounted to £5 million.

The subsidiary acted as a retail outlet for one of the product lines of the group. Following the disposal, the group reorganised the retail distribution of its products and the overall output of the group was not significantly affected.

The loss on disposal of the subsidiary amounted to £10 million before taxation. Your assistant proposes to show this loss as an exceptional item under discontinued operations on the grounds that the subsidiary has been disposed of and its results are clearly identifiable. The loss on disposal has been computed as follows:

	£ million
Sales proceeds	15
Share of net assets at the date of disposal	(25)
Loss on disposal	(10)

Your assistant has noted that unless the goodwill had previously been written off, the loss on disposal would have been even greater.

Requirements
Draft a reply to your assistant which evaluates the suggested treatment and recommends changes where relevant. In each case, your reply should refer to the provisions of relevant Accounting Standards and explain the rationale behind such provisions.

The allocation of marks is as follows:

Transaction 1	(10 marks)
Transaction 2	(8 marks)
CIMA, Financial Reporting, November 1999	(Total Marks = 18)

9.9 Mull plc acquired shares in two companies as follows:

Skye Ltd
Ordinary shares – 8 million acquired on 1 June 1996 for £4.50 each.

Preference shares – £500 000 8% redeemable preference shares acquired, at par, on 1 June 1996.

At the date of acquisition the retained profits of Skye Ltd were £10 million.

Arran Ltd

Ordinary shares – 1 million acquired on 1 June 1998 for £6 each.

At the date of acquisition the retained profits of Arran Ltd were £5 million and the revaluation reserve was £11 million.

The draft balance sheets for the above companies at 31 May 1999 show:

	Mull plc £'000	Skye Ltd £'000	Arran Ltd £'000
Fixed assets			
Freehold property	40 000	20 000	10 000
Plant and equipment	–	–	5 700
Fixtures and fittings	10 500	5 900	5 200
Investment in Skye Ltd	36 500	–	–
Investment in Arran Ltd	6 000	–	–
	93 000	25 900	20 900
Current assets			
Stock	19 000	13 000	11 000
Debtors	22 500	7 000	10 000
Cash in hand and at bank	1 000	570	780
	42 500	20 570	21 780
Creditors: amounts falling due within one year			
Bank overdraft	5 600	–	8 400
Creditors	18 400	9 600	7 500
Corporation tax payable	4 000	5 400	2 300
Proposed dividends	2 000	1 500	–
	30 000	16 500	18 200
Net current assets	12 500	4 070	3 580
Net assets	105 500	29 970	24 480
Capital and reserves			
Called up share capital			
Ordinary shares of £1 each	50 000	10 000	4 000
8% Redeemable preference shares	–	2 000	–
Revaluation reserve	10 600	–	11 000
Profit and loss account	44 900	17 970	9 480
	105 500	29 970	24 480

Additional information

(1) Skye Ltd has continued to account for its assets at their book value though their fair values on 1 June 1996 were:

Freehold land   – £2.5 million above book value
Fixtures and fittings – £1.5 million below book value with an estimated remaining
                                    useful economic life of 5 years

The fair values of all other assets and liabilities for both Skye Ltd and Arran Ltd approximated to their book values.

(2) Skye Ltd's corporation tax payable at 31 May 1999 includes £1.4 million related to its year ended 31 May 1996. The company had originally provided £500 000 as the

estimated liability as at 31 May 1996. Mull plc incorporated this estimate when establishing the fair values of Skye Ltd's net assets on acquisition. However, following a protracted Inland Revenue investigation, the final liability was agreed on 31 May 1999 at £1.4 million, £900 000 higher than the estimate.

(3) Skye Ltd paid its preference dividend during the year. All proposed dividends relate to ordinary shares. Mull plc has not yet accounted for any dividends receivable.

(4) Any goodwill arising is amortised over 10 years on the straight-line basis.

Requirements

(a) **Prepare the consolidated balance sheet of Mull plc as at 31 May 1999.**   (11 marks)

Note: **You are not required to produce any disclosure notes.**

(b) **Briefly explain your accounting treatment of items (1) and (2) above, referring to the provisions of FRS 7, Fair values in acquisition accounting, where appropriate.**

(4 marks)

ICAEW, Financial Reporting, June 1999   (15 marks)

9.10 The balance sheets of A plc and its investee companies B Ltd and D Ltd, and of B Ltd's investee company C Ltd at 31 March 1998 (the accounting date for all four companies) are given below:

	A plc		B Ltd		C Ltd		D Ltd	
	£m	£m	£m	£m	£m	£m	£m	£m
Fixed assets								
Tangible assets	450		220		250		250	
Investments	850		280		–		–	
		1 300		500		250		250
Current assets								
Stocks	200		145		120		120	
Debtors	100		90		90		80	
	300		235		210		200	
Current liabilities								
Trade creditors	50		40		40		40	
Taxation	20		15		12		10	
Dividends	15		10		10		10	
Bank overdraft	50		40		30		30	
	135		105		92		90	
Net current assets		165		130		118		110
10% debentures		(200)		(90)		(80)		(80)
		1 265		540		288		280
Capital and reserves								
Share capital (£1 shares)		700		400		200		180
Share premium account		200		80		40		40
Profit and loss account		365		60		48		60
		1 265		540		288		280

Notes to the financial statements

1. Investments by A plc and B Ltd were as follows:
   - On 31 March 1996, A plc bought 300 million shares in B Ltd for £500 million. On the same date, A plc acquired all the debentures of B Ltd at par. The profit and loss account of B Ltd showed a balance of £52 million at that date. Apart from its investment in **the shares** of C Ltd, the net assets of B Ltd at 31 March 1996 had a fair value which was the same as their book value. The investment in **the shares** of C Ltd at 31 March 1996 had a fair value of £240 million.
   - On 31 March 1993, B Ltd bought 160 million shares in C Ltd for £200 million. On the same date, B Ltd acquired all the debentures of C Ltd at par. The profit and loss account of C Ltd showed a balance of £10 million at that date and a balance of £40 million at 31 March 1996. At 31 March 1993 and 31 March 1996, all of the net assets of C Ltd had a fair value which was the same as their book value.
   - On 31 March 1997, A plc bought 72 million shares in D Ltd for £140 million. On the same date, A plc acquired all the debentures of D Ltd at par. The profit and loss account of D Ltd showed a balance of £50 million at that date. At 31 March 1997, all of the net assets of D Ltd had a fair value which was the same as their book value. The board of directors of D Ltd had nine members and, because of the influence A plc was able to exercise over D Ltd through its trading relationship (see *note 3* below), six of the nine were appointees of A plc, including the chairman and the managing director.
   - On 15 April 1996, A plc acquired a 9% stake in E Ltd for £40 million. Another corporate investor holds 65% of the shares in E Ltd.
2. Premiums on acquisition are amortised over their estimated useful economic life of 10 years. Debenture interest is payable six monthly on 31 March and 30 September each year. The payments are made to the registered holders of debentures on the 25th of the month in which they take place.
3. D Ltd's main business is the manufacture of a component used by A plc (but not by B Ltd or C Ltd). The turnover of D Ltd for the year ended 31 March 1998 was £150 million, and £120 million of this represented sales to A plc, which were invoiced at cost plus 20%. At 31 March 1998, the stocks of A plc included £30 million in respect of goods purchased from D Ltd. At 31 March 1998 the debtors of D Ltd and the creditors of A plc included £20 million in respect of goods purchased from D Ltd by A plc.
4. A plc and B Ltd deal with investment income on an accruals basis. All shares in issue in all companies are equity shares.

Requirements

(a) **Explain how B Ltd, C Ltd, D Ltd and E Ltd will be dealt with in the consolidated balance sheet of A plc at 31 March 1998. Give reasons for your answer in each case. You may assume that equity shares in all companies carry one vote per share at general meetings.** (10 marks)

(b) **Prepare the consolidated balance sheet of the A plc group at 31 March 1998. You should perform all calculations to the nearest £0.1 million.** (30 marks)

CIMA, Financial Reporting, May 1998 (Total Marks = 40)

9.11 You are the accountant responsible for the Rag group consolidation. The profit and loss accounts of Rag plc, Tag Ltd and Bobtail Ltd for the year ended 31 March 1999 are given opposite.

	Rag plc £000	Tag Ltd £000	Bobtail Ltd £000
Turnover (*note 1*)	65 000	50 000	100 000
Cost of sales	(35 000)	(28 000)	(82 000)
Gross profit	30 000	22 000	18 000
Other operating expenses	(15 000)	(11 000)	(9 000)
Operating profit	15 000	11 000	9 000
Investment income (*note 2*)	3 000	1 200	–
Interest payable	(3 200)	(1 800)	(1 200)
Profit before taxation	14 800	10 400	7 800
Taxation	(3 600)	(2 800)	(2 400)
Profit after taxation	11 200	7 600	5 400
Proposed dividends	(6 000)	(4 000)	(3 000)
Retained profit	5 200	3 600	2 400
Retained profit – 1 April 1998	20 000	15 000	12 000
Retained profit – 31 March 1999	25 200	18 600	14 400

Notes to the profit and loss accounts
Note 1
Rag plc supplies a component which is used by both Tag Ltd and Bobtail Ltd. Because of the close relationships between the three companies, the component is supplied at a mark-up of only 10% on cost. Details of inter-company sales of the product for the year to 31 March 1999 were as follows:

- Rag plc to Tag Ltd   £8 million
- Rag plc to Bobtail Ltd   £4 million

Details of the stocks of the component supplied by Rag plc which were included in the books of Tag Ltd and Bobtail Ltd at the beginning and end of the year were:

Stocks of the component in the books at 31 March	1999 £000	1998 £000
Tag Ltd	2 200	1 980
Bobtail Ltd	1 100	990

Note 2
Details of inter-company shareholdings are as follows:

- On 15 July 1992 Rag plc purchased 4.5 million of the issued £1 equity shares of Tag Ltd for £14 million. The balance sheet of Tag Ltd at 15 July 1992 showed the following:

	£000
Share capital	6 000
Share premium	3 000
Profit and loss account	7 000
	16 000

- On 8 October 1993, Tag Ltd purchased 2 million of the issued £1 equity shares of Bobtail Ltd for £7.4 million. The balance sheet of Bobtail Ltd at 8 October 1993 showed the following:

	£000
Share capital	5 000
Share premium	3 000
Profit and loss account	8 000
	16 000

The policy of Rag plc is to amortise goodwill over 20 years with a full year's write-off in the year of acquisition. At the dates they joined the Rag group, the fair values of the net assets of Tag Ltd and Bobtail Ltd were the same as their book values.

Note 3
Both Rag plc and Tag Ltd recognise investment income on an accruals basis. The profit and loss accounts of Rag plc and Tag Ltd show dividend income as being the **cash** dividend receivable.

Your assistant is responsible for preparing the draft consolidated financial statements for your review. She is aware that Tag Ltd will be dealt with as a 75% subsidiary but is unsure of the way of dealing with Bobtail Ltd.

Requirements
(a) Write a memorandum to your assistant which
  • explains how Bobtail Ltd will be incorporated into the consolidated financial statements of Rag plc;
  • describes and justifies any disclosures which are required in the notes to the consolidated financial statements regarding the investment in Bobtail Ltd.
  Your memorandum should refer to relevant provisions of company law and Financial Reporting Standards to support your explanations. (10 marks)
(b) Prepare a working schedule for the consolidated profit and loss account of Rag plc for the year ended 31 March 1999. You should start with the turnover and end with the retained profit at the end of the year.
  Do not prepare notes to the consolidated profit and loss account. (30 marks)

CIMA, Financial Reporting, May 1999 **(Total Marks = 40)**

9.12 Wiltshire plc's draft accounts for the year ended 30 June 1993 disclosed profit before tax of £20 million, on turnover of £310 million, and net assets of £140 million. Wiltshire plc had made the following acquisitions during the year ended 30 June 1993, none of which has been accounted for in preparing the draft accounts referred to above:

(1) The shares in Nightingale Ltd not already owned by Wiltshire plc were acquired by Wiltshire plc on 1 January 1993 for £10 million – satisfied by the issue of 4 million ordinary £1 shares in Wiltshire plc with a market value on 1 January 1993 of £2.50 per share. 25% of Nightingale Ltd had been acquired by Wiltshire plc in 1979 for £3 million (in cash) when Nightingale Ltd's net assets were £8 million. Draft accounts for Nightingale Ltd, which has been treated as an associated undertaking by Wiltshire plc since 1979, for the year ended 30 June 1993 are:

Balance sheet	*£m*
Net assets	12
Share capital	1
Retained profits	11
	12
Profit and loss account	
Profit before tax	3
Taxation	(1)
Retained for the year	2

(2) The Adam partnership's trade, assets, liabilities and undertaking were acquired on 30 June 1993 for £1.4 million (in cash). The value of the net tangible assets acquired was £0.5 million. In arriving at the purchase consideration Wiltshire plc took into

account the Adam partnership's budget for the six month period to 31 December 1993 which envisages losses of some £75 000.

(3) On 1 April 1993 shares to the value of £28.6 million (11 million ordinary £1 shares, market value £2.60) were issued in respect of the acquisition of the entire issued share capital of Massen Ltd, a company with net assets of £12.5 million (comprising share capital of £8 million and accumulated reserves of £4.5 million) at 1 April 1993. The shares in Wiltshire plc were initially issued to the shareholders in Massen Ltd. They were then immediately offered by Wiltshire plc's merchant bankers to the existing shareholders in Wiltshire plc by way of a rights offer (in proportion to their existing shareholdings) which was fully taken up. The shareholders in Massen Ltd thereby received a cash consideration (of £28.6 million) for their shares from Wiltshire plc's merchant bankers.

Requirement
Write a report to the directors of Wiltshire plc detailing and discussing their accounting and reporting considerations and requirements in respect of the three acquisitions and in each case describe and explain the impact that accounting for the acquisition will have on Wiltshire plc's consolidated accounts.

ICAEW Financial Accounting 2, July 1993   (20 marks)

10 Overseas involvement

10.1 Groups of companies with overseas branches and subsidiaries have problems in determining the manner in which their results are included in the consolidated and parent company accounts.

Required
(a) Explain the two alternative methods of foreign currency translation now in general use, and distinguish the circumstances in which each is appropriately used. (19 marks)
(b) Give your views on the appropriateness of the two alternative methods of translating the 'foreign currency' annual accounts of an overseas branch or subsidiary. (6 marks)

ACCA Level 3 Advanced Financial Accounting, December 1987   (25 marks)

10.2 You are the Chief Accountant of JKL plc, a UK company that has three wholly-owned overseas subsidiaries.

● Company A is located in Spain. The company assembles computer terminals from materials provided by JKL plc. Once assembled, the computer terminals are shipped to the UK where JKL plc sells them.

● Company B is located in Singapore and produces computers using materials supplied by local companies. Company B sells the computers to customers throughout southeast Asia.

● Company C, operated on the same basis as Company A, is located in a country where recent legislation forbids the ownership of companies by foreign nationals and where strict currency and import/export controls have been introduced. These currency controls mean that JKL plc is unable to sell its interest in Company C.

You are required to explain how *each* of the three subsidiaries would be dealt with in the consolidated financial statements of JKL plc.

CIMA Advanced Financial Accounting, May 1994   (15 marks)

10.3 The balance sheets of UK plc and its subsidiary undertaking Germany GmbH at 31 March 1996 and their profit and loss accounts for the twelve months then ended are given overleaf:

Balance sheets at 31 March 1996

| | UK plc | | Germany GmbH | |
	£000	£000	DM000	DM000
Fixed assets				
Tangible assets	20 000		30 000	
Investments (*notes 1 and 2*)	5 500		–	
		25 500		30 000
Current assets				
Stocks	10 000		18 000	
Trade debtors	8 500		15 000	
Other debtors (*note 3*)	1 500		–	
	20 000		33 000	
Current liabilities				
Trade creditors	4 000		6 000	
Proposed dividends	3 900		4 400	
Bank overdraft	6 100		7 600	
	14 000		18 000	
Net current assets		6 000		15 000
Total assets less current liabilities		31 500		45 000
Creditors failing due after more				
than one year (*note 4*)		(10 000)		(20 000)
		21 500		25 000
Capital and reserves				
Called-up share capital				
(£1/1 DM shares)		9 000		15 000
Profit and loss account		12 500		10 000
		21 500		25 000

Profit and loss accounts – year ended 31 March 1996

| | UK plc | Germany GmbH |
	£000	DM000
Turnover	50 000	60 000
Cost of sales (*notes 2 and 5*)	(25 000)	(30 000)
Gross profit	25 000	30 000
Other operating expenses	(15 000)	(16 000)
Operating profit	10 000	14 000
Investment income (*note 3*)	1 500	–
Interest payable	(1 000)	(2 000)
Profit before taxation	10 500	12 000
Taxation	(3 600)	(4 200)
Profit after taxation	6 900	7 800
Proposed dividends	(3 900)	(4 400)
Retained profit for the year	3 000	3 400
Retained profit – 1 April 1995	9 500	6 600
Retained profit – 31 March 1996	12 500	10 000

Notes to the financial statements

(1) On 31 March 1992, UK plc purchased 11.25 million shares in Germany GmbH. The retained profits of Germany GmbH on this date stood at DM 5 million. Any premium or discount on acquisition was dealt with in the manner preferred by SSAP 22.

Germany GmbH operates as a fairly autonomous entity on a day-to-day basis although UK plc does control the long-term strategy of Germany GmbH.

(2) Since the date of the investment by UK plc, the £ sterling has depreciated against the DM. Exchange rates at relevant dates have been as follows:

Date	DM to the £
31 March 1992	3.0
Date on which Germany GmbH acquired its	
– fixed assets	2.8
– opening stock	2.5
– closing stock	2.25
31 March 1995	2.4
31 March 1996	2.2

(3) UK plc deals with investment income on an accruals basis.

(4) The creditors falling due after more than one year represent long-term borrowings. The long-term borrowings of Germany GmbH were raised in Germany and are repayable in DM.

(5) The profit and loss account of Germany GmbH includes depreciation as follows:
- DM 5 million included in cost of sales;
- DM 1 million included in other operating expenses.

Requirements

(a) Write a short memorandum which explains (with reasons) how Germany GmbH should be dealt with in the consolidated financial statements of UK plc, assuming the provisions of relevant UK accounting standards are followed.

Your memorandum should not contain a detailed exposition of the mechanics of the consolidation, but should concentrate on the implications of Germany GmbH being an overseas entity. (11 marks)

(b) Translate the balance sheet of Germany GmbH into £ sterling and then prepare the consolidated balance sheet of the UK plc group at 31 March 1996. (13 marks)

(c) Translate the profit and loss account of Germany GmbH into £ sterling and then prepare the consolidated profit and loss account of the UK plc group for the year ended 31 March 1996, starting with turnover and ending with retained profit for the year.

(6 marks)

(d) Prepare a statement reconciling the opening and closing balances on consolidated reserves. All figures in the statement should be supported by relevant workings.

(10 marks)

CIMA, Financial Reporting, May 1996 (Total Marks = 40)

10.4 Howard plc acquired 2 100 000 ordinary shares of Kroner 1 in Pau Ltd on 1 January 1985 when the reserves of Pau Ltd were Kr 1 500 000 and the exchange rate was Kr 10 to £1. Goodwill was eliminated against the consolidated reserves on 31 December 1985.

The profit and loss accounts of Howard plc and Pau Ltd for the year ended 31 December 1992 were as follows:

	Howard £000	Pau Kr 000
Turnover	9 225	94 500
Cost of sales	6 027	63 000
Gross profit	3 198	31 500
Distribution cost	1 290	7 550
Administrative expenses	1 469	2 520
Depreciation	191	2 100
	248	19 330
Dividends from subsidiary	315	
	563	19 330
Tax	195	7 570
Profit on ordinary activities after tax	368	11 760
Dividends paid 30.6.92	183	4 200
Retained profit for the year	185	7 560

The balance sheets of Howard plc and Pau Ltd as at 31 December 1992 were as follows:

	Howard £000	Pau Kr 000
Fixed assets		
Tangible assets	1 765	38 500
Investment in Pau Ltd	305	
Current assets		
Stock	2 245	3 675
Debtors	615	1 750
Cash	156	9 450
	3 016	14 875
Current liabilities		
Trade creditors	(2 245)	(4 375)
Creditors falling due after more than 1 year		
Loan	(1 230)	(8 680)
	1 611	40 320
Capital and reserves		
Share capital in £1 ordinary shares	600	
Share capital in Kr 1 ordinary shares		3 500
Profit and loss account	1 011	36 820
	1 611	40 320

The tangible assets of Pau Ltd were acquired 1 January 1985 and are stated at cost less depreciation.

Stocks represent six months purchases and at 31 December 1991 the stock held by Pau Ltd amounted to Kr 4 760 000.

Exchange rates have been as follows:

	Kroner to £1
1 January 1985	10
30 June 1991	10.5
30 September 1991	10
31 December 1991	9.5
Average for 1992	8

	Kroner to £1
30 June 1992	8
30 September 1992	7.5
31 December 1992	7

In determining the appropriate method of currency translation, it is established that the trade of Pau Ltd is more dependent on the economic environment of the investing company's currency than that of its own reporting currency.

Required

(a) Explain briefly how it would be established that the trade of Pau Ltd is more dependent on the economic environment of the investing company's currency than that of its own reporting currency. (4 marks)

(b) Prepare the consolidated profit and loss account for the year ended 31 December 1992 and a balance sheet as at that date, using the temporal method of translation. (22 marks)

(c) Calculate the amount to be included in the consolidated balance sheet of the Howard Group as at 31 December 1992 if Howard plc had sold goods to Pau Ltd on 30 September 1992 for £14 000 which had cost £10 000 and which remained unsold at 31 December 1992 using
   (i) the closing rate method;
   (ii) the temporal method. (4 marks)

ACCA Advanced Financial Accounting, June 1993 (30 marks)

10.5 The balance sheets of UK plc and its subsidiaries France SA and US Inc at 30 September 1998 (the accounting date for all three companies) are given below:

	UK plc		France SA		US Inc	
	£000	£000	Fr000	Fr000	$000	$000
Fixed assets						
Tangible assets	26 000		95 000		56 000	
Investments (*Notes 1 & 2*)	25 500		–		–	
		51 500		95 000		56 000
Current assets						
Stocks (*Note 3*)	15 000		44 000		25 000	
Debtors (*Note 4*)	10 000		30 000		16 000	
Cash in hand	2 000		6 000		3 000	
	27 000		80 000		44 000	
Current liabilities						
Trade creditors (*Note 4*)	6 000		12 000		8 000	
Taxation	3 000		6 000		4 000	
Proposed dividend	2 000		8 000		3 000	
Bank overdraft	8 000		10 000		9 000	
	19 000		36 000		24 000	
Net current assets		8 000		44 000		20 000
Long-term loans		(20 000)		–		(25 000)
		39 500		139 000		51 000
Capital and reserves						
Share capital (*Note 5*)		20 000		80 000		32 000
Profit and loss account		19 500		59 000		19 000
		39 500		139 000		51 000

Notes to the financial statements

Note 1

UK plc has owned 100% of the ordinary share capital of France SA since incorporation, subscribing for it at par. The date of incorporation of France SA was 25 May 1990. France SA acts as a selling agent for products manufactured in the UK by UK plc and has no manufacturing capacity of its own. UK plc has negotiated an overdraft facility for France SA and has guaranteed the overdraft. Apart from this overdraft, France SA receives all its funding from UK plc.

Note 2

On 30 September 1992, when the reserves of US Inc stood at $8 million, UK plc purchased 24 million shares in US Inc for $35 million. US Inc has a product range which is similar to that of UK plc and France SA, but is targeted more specifically towards the needs of the US market. The stock is manufactured in the USA, and US Inc negotiates its own day-to-day financing needs with US financial institutions. The $25 million loan which was outstanding at 30 September 1998 was originally taken out on 30 June 1976 for a 30-year period. The accounting policy of UK plc is to amortise premiums on acquisition over a 20-year period. In the case of US Inc, the first write-off took place in the year ended 30 September 1993.

Note 3

The stocks of France SA were acquired from UK plc on 31 August 1998. They represent a consignment which cost UK plc £3.6 million to manufacture but were invoiced to France SA at a price of 44 million Francs. This price represented the sterling transfer price of £4 million translated at the spot rate of exchange in force at 31 August 1998. The stocks of US Inc were all manufactured locally. The stock in hand of US Inc at 30 September 1998 represents 6 months' production.

Note 4

- The debtors of UK plc include dividends receivable from France SA and US Inc. These debtors have been translated into sterling using the rate of exchange in force at 30 September 1998.
- The trade creditors of France SA comprise 12 million Francs payable to UK plc.
  UK plc's debtors include the equivalent asset translated into sterling using the rate of exchange in force at 30 September 1998.
- There was no other inter-company trading.

Note 5

- The shares of UK plc are £1 shares.
- The shares of France SA are 1 Franc shares.
- The shares of US Inc are $1 shares.

Note 6

The dates of acquisition of the tangible fixed assets of France SA and US Inc were as follows:

30 September 1998 – Net Book Value of Fixed Assets

Date	France SA Fr million	US Inc $ million
25 May 1990	10 000	2 000
30 September 1993	45 000	20 000
30 September 1997	40 000	34 000
	95 000	56 000

Note 7
Exchange rates at relevant dates were as follows:

Date	£/Fr rate	£/$ rate
25 May 1990	10	2.4
30 September 1992	9.5	2.0
30 September 1993	9	1.7
30 September 1997	10	1.6
31 March 1998	10.5	1.7
31 August 1998	11	1.8
30 September 1998	12	1.8

Requirements
(a) **Explain how the financial statements [profit and loss account and balance sheet] of France SA and US Inc will be translated into sterling for the purposes of the consolidated financial statements of UK plc. Your answer should refer to relevant Accounting Standards and should explain the treatment of the exchange difference on translation in each case.** (10 marks)
(b) **Prepare the working schedule for the consolidated balance sheet of the UK plc group at 30 September 1998. Your schedule needs to show only one figure for consolidated reserves, so a separate analysis of the exchange differences is not required.** (30 marks)

CIMA, Financial Reporting, November 1998 (Total Marks = 40)

10.6 One of the frequent criticisms of SSAP 20, Foreign currency translation, is that exchange differences on net investments in foreign enterprises, and on borrowings which are a hedge, never pass through the profit and loss account.

Discuss the validity of this criticism and suggest a possible solution to the perceived problem.

ICAEW Financial Accounting 2, July 1993 (13 marks)

10.7 (a) Newton plc, to whom you are financial adviser, is preparing its financial statements for the year ended 31 March 1992. It has two wholly owned subsidiaries:
- An Italian company, Darwin SpA, which it acquired a number of years ago at a cost of 500m Lira. Newton plc incorporates the financial statements of Darwin SpA in its consolidated financial statements using the closing rate method. During 1989, Newton plc borrowed 1000 million Lira (repayable in 1999) to provide a hedge against the investment, which was then considered to be worth in excess of 1500 million Lira. The net assets of Darwin SpA at 31 March 1991 were 1200 million Lira.
- A German company, Hoyle GmbH, which it set up on 1 June 1991 at a cost of Dm 25 million. Newton plc is to incorporate Hoyle GmbH in its consolidated financial statements using the temporal method. The exchange loss for the period is £52 000. Newton plc partially financed the acquisition of the shares by borrowing Dm 20m repayable in 1997.

In addition, Newton plc has a 15% investment in a Japanese company, Gamow Inc, which it acquired in 1980 at a cost of Yen 220 million, financed by means of a Yen loan of the same amount. At 31 March 1992 none of the loan had been repaid.

The relevant exchange rates were:

	£1 = Lira	£1 = DM	£1 = Yen
31 March 1991	1000	–	230
1 June 1991	–	3.7	–
31 March 1992	950	4.0	290
Average – period to 31 March 1992	960	3.8	260

(b) The directors of Newton plc have asked your advice in respect of the following.

For sound commercial reasons Darwin SpA is to change its year end to 31 January with effect from 31 January 1993. The consolidated financial statements will hence forward include results for Darwin SpA drawn up for the period to 31 January. The directors wonder which 'closing exchange rate' to use for the purposes of the 31 March 1993 financial statements for the Newton plc group – that at 31 January 1993 or that at 31 March 1993.

Required

(a) **For the year ended 31 March 1992 calculate, in accordance with standard accounting practice, the exchange differences in respect of the investments/borrowings in (a) above and explain the treatment thereof in both the company and the consolidated financial statements for Newton plc.** (11 marks)

(b) **Prepare a paper advising the directors of Newton plc as to the accounting considerations to be taken into account in connection with Darwin SpA's change of year end; advise the directors of any appropriate accounting treatments for the purposes of the consolidated financial statements.** (10 marks)

Note: Ignore taxation

ICAEW Financial Accounting 2, July 1992 (**21 marks**)

11 Expansion of the annual report

11.1 In November 1996 the Accounting Standards Board issued FRS 1 (Revised) – *Cash Flow Statements*. The appendix to FRS 1 contains a number of examples of cash flow statements drawn up in accordance with the new Standard. The examples given present the cash flows under a number of standard headings, as shown below.

		£000
(i)	Cash flow from operating activities	X
(ii)	Returns on investments and servicing of finance	X
(iii)	Taxation	X
(iv)	Capital expenditure and financial investment	X
(v)	Acquisitions and disposals	X
(vi)	Equity dividends paid	X
		X
(vii)	Management of liquid resources	X
(viii)	Financing	X
	Decrease in cash in the period	X

Requirements

(a) **Describe the cash flows which are reported under each of the headings (i) to (viii), given above.** (10 Marks)

(b) **Summarise the changes which FRS 1 (Revised) made to the old FRS 1, and explain why each change was considered necessary by the Accounting Standards Board.**

(10 marks)

CIMA, Financial Reporting, November 1997   (Total Marks = 20)

11.2 Inverness plc has prepared the following draft financial statements for the year ended 31 October 1997:

Balance sheet as on 31 October 1997

	1997 £'000	1997 £'000	1996 £'000	1996 £'000
Fixed assets				
Freehold property – at cost/valuation	31 000		28 000	
– accumulated depreciation	–		(7 200)	
		31 000		20 800
Plant and machinery – at cost	20 000		16 400	
– accumulated depreciation	(8 600)		(5 400)	
		11 400		11 000
		42 400		31 800
Current assets				
Stock	7 200		5 600	
Trade debtors	4 800		5 200	
ACT recoverable	475		550	
Investments	2 000		1 600	
Cash at bank and in hand	3 000		1 400	
	17 475		14 350	
Creditors: amounts falling due within one year				
Trade creditors	(5 200)		(3 700)	
Corporation tax	(2 000)		(3 700)	
ACT payable	(475)		(550)	
Proposed dividends	(1 900)		(2 200)	
	(9 575)		(10 150)	
Net current assets		7 900		4 200
		50 300		36 000
Creditors: amounts falling due after more than one year				
Debentures		(7 000)		(2 000)
		43 300		34 000
Share capital		25 000		24 000
Share premium		4 600		3 900
Revalution reserve		9 000		–
Profit and loss account		4 700		6 100
		43 300		34 000

Profit and loss account for the year ended 31 October 1997

	£'000	£'000
Turnover		34 200
Change in stocks of finished goods and work in progress		(6 600)
Own work capitalised		500
Raw materials and consumables		(14 000)
Staff costs		(5 200)
Depreciation – freehold property	(800)	
– plant and machinery	(4 000)	
		(4 800)
Loss on sale of fixed assets		(600)
Interest receivable		500
Interest payable		(1 000)
Profit on ordinary activities before taxation		3 000
Taxation		(2 500)
Profit on ordinary activities after taxation		500
Dividends proposed		(1 900)
		(1 400)

Additional information

(1) During the year an item of plant and machinery with a cost of £1.9 million was sold.
(2) The freehold property was revalued on 31 October 1997.
(3) Interest of £400 000 was capitalised during the year as part of additions to freehold property.

Requirements

(a) **Prepare a cash flow statement and related notes for Inverness plc for the year ended 31 October 1997 in accordance with FRS 1 (Revised), Cash flow statements.**

(13 marks)

(b) **Briefly explain the main reasons for the recent changes to FRS 1.** (4 marks)

ICAEW Financial Reporting, November 1997 (17 marks)

11.3 You are the management accountant of Holmes plc and you are in the process of preparing the consolidated cash flow statement. Your Managing Director is aware that the statement is required by FRS 1 – *Cash flow statements*, and that a number of notes to the statement must also be included. She has a reasonable understanding of the rationale behind the cash flow statement but is not clear as to why so many notes to the statement are required.

Requirements

(a) **Prepare the consolidated cash flow statement of the Holmes group for the year ended 30 September 1999 in the form required by FRS 1 – *Cash flow statements*.**
Show your workings clearly.
Do not prepare notes to the cash flow statement. (30 marks)

(b) **Write a memorandum to your Managing Director which explains the need for the following notes to the cash flow statement:**
   • **reconciliation of operating profit to operating cash flows;**
   • **reconciliation of net cash flow to movement in net debt;**
   • **summary of the effect of the acquisition of Watson plc.**
Do not prepare any of these three notes for Holmes plc. (8 marks)

(Total Marks = 38)

Extracts from the consolidated financial statements of Holmes plc are given below:

Consolidated profit and loss accounts for the year ended	30 September 1999 £ million	£ million	30 September 1998 £ million	£ million
Turnover		600		500
Cost of sales		(300)		(240)
Gross profit		300		260
Other operating expenses (Note 1)		(150)		(130)
Group operating profit		150		130
Share of operating profit of associates		40		35
Interest payable:				
– group	50		45	
– associates	15		10	
		(65)		(55)
Profit before exceptional item		125		110
Exceptional item (Note 2)		10		–
Profit before taxation		135		110
Taxation:				
– group	35		25	
– associates	8		8	
		(43)		(33)
Profit after taxation		92		77
Minority interests		(10)		(6)
Group profit		82		71
Equity dividends		(25)		(25)
Retained profit for year		57		46

Consolidated balance sheets at	30 September 1999 £ million	£ million	30 September 1998 £ million	£ million
Fixed assets				
Intangible assets (Note 3)	25		19	
Tangible assets (Note 4)	240		280	
Investments in associates	80		70	
		345		369
Current assets				
Stocks	105		90	
Debtors	120		100	
Investments	20		70	
Cash in hand	10		5	
	255		265	
Creditors falling due within one year				
Trade creditors (Note 5)	40		30	
Taxation	10		8	
Proposed dividends	25		25	
Obligations under finance leases	25		20	
Other creditors (Note 6)	6		5	
Bank overdraft	20		80	
	126		168	
Net current assets		129		97
Carried forward		474		466

	30 September 1999 £ million	30 September 1998 £ million
Brought forward	474	466
Creditors falling due after more than one year		
Obligations under finance leases	(80)	(70)
12% loan stock	–	(90)
Provisions for liabilities and charges		
Deferred taxation	(30)	(24)
Minority interests	(65)	(40)
	299	242
Capital and reserves		
Called-up share capital	100	100
Revaluation reserve	–	20
Profit and loss account	199	122
	299	242

Notes to the financial statements:

Note 1 – other operating expenses

	1999 £ million	1998 £ million
Distribution costs	81	75
Administrative expenses	75	70
Investment income	(6)	(15)
	150	130

From time to time, the group invests cash surpluses in listed securities which are shown as current asset investments in the consolidated balance sheet.

Note 2 – exceptional item

This represents the gain on sale of a large freehold property sold by Holmes plc on 1 October 1998 and leased back on an operating lease in line with the practice adopted by the rest of the group. The property was not depreciated in the current year. The property had been revalued in 1990 and the revaluation surplus credited to a revaluation reserve. No other entries had been made in the revaluation reserve prior to the sale of the property.

Note 3 – intangible fixed assets

This comprises the unamortised balance of goodwill on consolidation which is written off over its useful economic life. During the year ended 30 September 1999, Holmes plc purchased 80% of the issued equity share capital of Watson plc for £100 million payable in cash. The net assets of Watson plc at the date of acquisition were assessed as having fair values as follows:

	£ million
Plant and machinery – owned	50
Fixture and fittings – owned	10
Stocks	30
Debtors	25
Cash at bank and in hand	10
Trade creditors	(15)
Taxation	(5)
	105

The goodwill arising was assessed as having a useful economic life of 16 years and a full year's write-off was made in the year ended 30 September 1999. Apart from the acquisition of Watson plc, there were no other changes to the group structure in the year.

Note 4 – tangible fixed assets

	30 September 1999	30 September 1998
	£ million	£ million
Freehold land and buildings	–	90
Plant and machinery – owned	130	100
Plant and machinery – leased	90	70
Fixtures and fittings – owned	20	20
	240	280

During the year the group entered into new finance lease agreements in respect of some items of plant and machinery. The amounts debited to fixed assets in respect of such agreements during the year totalled £40 million. No disposals of plant and machinery (owned or leased) or fixtures and fittings took place during the year. Depreciation of tangible fixed assets for the year totalled £58 million.

Note 5 – trade creditors
Trade creditors at 30 September 1999 and 30 September 1998 do not include any accrued interest.

Note 6 – other creditors
These comprise dividends payable to minority shareholders. ·

CIMA, *Financial Reporting, November 1999*

11.4 The following draft financial statements relate to the Baron Group plc.

Draft group profit and loss account for the year ended 30 November 1997

	£m	£m
Turnover		
Continuing operations	4458	
Discontinued operations	1263	
		5721
Cost of sales		(4560)
Gross profit		1161
Distribution costs	309	
Administration expenses	285	
		(594)
		567
Income from interests in joint venture		75
Defence costs of take-over bid		(20)
Operating profit		
Continuing operations	438	
Discontinued operations	184	
		622
Loss on disposal of tangible fixed assets	(7)	
Loss on disposal of discontinued operations (note a)	(25)	(32)
Interest receivable	27	
Interest payable	(19)	8
Profit on ordinary activities before taxation		598
Tax on profit on ordinary activities (note c)		(191)
Profit on ordinary activities after taxation		407
Minority interests – equity		(75)
Profit attributable to members of the parent company		332
Dividends – ordinary dividend		(130)
Retained profit for the year		202

Group statement of total recognised gains and losses for the year ended 30 November 1997

	£m
Profit attributable to members of the parent company	332
Deficit on revaluation of land and buildings	(30)
Deficit on revaluation of land and buildings in joint venture	(15)
Gain on revaluation of loan	28
Total recognised gains and losses relating to the year	315

Draft group balance sheet as at 30 November 1997

	£m 1997	£m 1996
Fixed assets		
Intangible assets	60	144
Tangible fixed assets (note d)	1 415	1 800
Investments (notes b and e)	600	–
	2 075	1 944
Current assets		
Stocks	720	680
Short term investments (note e)	152	44
Debtors (note f)	680	540
Cash at bank and in hand	24	133
	1 576	1 397
Creditors		
Amounts falling due within one year (note g)	(1 601)	(1 223)
Net current assets	(25)	174
Total assets less current liabilities	2 050	2 118
Creditors: amounts failing due after more than one year	(186)	(214)
Provision for liabilities and charges – bid defence costs	(30)	(15)
Minority interests – equity	(330)	(570)
	1 504	1 319
Capital and reserves		
Called up share capital	440	440
Share premium account	101	101
Revaluation reserve	33	50
Profit and loss account	930	728
Total shareholders' funds – equity	1 504	1 319

The following information is relevant to the Baron Group plc.

(a) The group disposed of a major subsidiary, Piece plc, on 1 September 1997. Baron held an 80% interest in the subsidiary at the date of disposal. Piece plc's results are classified as discontinued in the profit and loss account.

   The group required the subsidiary Piece plc to prepare an interim balance sheet at the date of the disposal and this is as follows:

	£m	£m
Tangible fixed assets (depreciation 30)		310
Current assets		
Stocks	60	
Debtors	50	
Cash at bank and in hand	130	
	240	
Creditors: amounts falling due within one year		
(including corporation tax – £25 million)	(130)	
		110
		420
Called up share capital		100
Profit and loss account		320
		420

The consolidated carrying values of all the assets and liabilities at that date are as above. The depreciation charge in the profit and loss account for the period was £9 million. The carrying amount relating to goodwill in the group accounts arising on the acquisition of Piece plc was £64 million at 1 December 1996. The loss on sale of discontinued operations in the group accounts comprises:

	£m
Sale proceeds	375
Net assets sold (80% × £420 million)	(336)
Goodwill	(64)
	(25)

The consideration for the sale of Piece plc was 200 million ordinary shares of £1 in Meal plc, the acquiring company, at a value of £300 million and £75 million in cash. The group's policy is to amortise goodwill arising on acquisition but not in the year of sale of a subsidiary. The amortisation for the year was £20 million on other intangible assets.

(b) During the year, Baron plc had transferred several of its tangible assets to a newly created company, Kevla Ltd which is owned jointly by three parties. The total investment at the date of transfer in the joint venture by Baron plc was £225 million at carrying value comprising £200 million in tangible fixed assets and £25 million in cash. The group has used equity accounting for the joint venture in Kevla Ltd. No dividends have been received from Kevla Ltd but the land and buildings transferred have been revalued at the year end.

(c) The taxation charge in the profit and loss account is made up of the following items:

	£m
Corporation tax	171
Tax attributable to joint venture	20
	191

(d) The movement on tangible fixed assets of the Baron Group plc during the year was as follows:

	£m
Cost or valuation 1 December 1996	2 100
Additions	380
Revaluation	(30)
Disposals and transfers	(680)
At 30 November 1997	1 770

Depreciation	
1 December 1996	300
Provided during year	150
Disposals and transfers	(95)
At 30 November 1997	355
Carrying value at 30 November 1997	1 415
Carrying value at 1 December 1996	1 800

(e) The investments included under fixed assets comprised the joint venture in Kevla Ltd (£265 million), the shares in Meal plc (£300 million), and investments in corporate bonds (£35 million). The bonds had been purchased in November 1997 and were deemed to be highly liquid, although Baron plc intended to hold them for the longer term as their maturity date is 1 January 1999.

The short term investments comprised the following items:

	1997 £m	1996 £m
Government securities (Repayable 1 April 1998)	51	23
Cash on seven day deposit	101	21
	152	44

(f) A prepayment of £20 million has been included in debtors against an exceptional pension liability which will fall due in the following financial year. Interest receivable included in debtors was £5 million at 30 November 1997 (£4 million at 30 November 1996).

(g) Creditors: amounts falling due within one year comprise the following items:

	1997 £m	1996 £m
Trade creditors	1 300	973
Corporation tax (including ACT)	181	150
Dividends	80	70
Accrued interest	40	30
	1 601	1 223

Required

(a) Prepare a group cash flow statement using the 'indirect method' for the Baron Group plc for the year ended 30 November 1997 in accordance with the requirements of FRS 1 (Revised 1996) 'Cash Flow Statements'. Your answer should include the following:

(i) Reconciliation of operating profit to operating cash flows.

(ii) An analysis of cash flows for any headings netted in the cash flow statement.
(Candidates should distinguish net cash flows from continuing and discontinued operations.) (26 marks)

The notes regarding the sale of the subsidiary and a reconciliation of net cash flow to movement in net debt are not required.

(b) Explain why the Accounting Standards Board feel that cash flow statements should focus on cash rather than a broader measure such as 'net debt'. (4 marks)

ACCA Financial Reporting Environment, December 1997 (30 marks)

11.5 Fogel Limited commenced trading as a carpet manufacturer on 1 November 1986. The accountant decided to produce a value added statement with the financial accounts for the year ended 31 October 1988.

The draft manufacturing and trading account for the year ended 31 October 1988 showed:

	£000	£000
Material in stock at 1 November 1987	47.00	
Purchases	470.00	
	517.00	
Material in stock at 31 October 1988	47.00	470.0
Direct labour		470.0
Overheads		
Material	117.50	
Labour	352.50	
Depreciation	235.00	705.0
		1 645.0
Add: Work in progress at 1 November 1987		
Material	117.50	
Labour	117.50	
Overheads	23.50	258.5
		1 903.5
Less: Work in progress at 31 October 1988		
Material	152.75	
Labour	152.75	
Overheads	47.00	352.5
		1 551.0
Sales		1 645.0
Finished goods in stock at 1 November 1987		
Material	235.00	
Labour	235.00	
Overheads	235.00	
	705.00	
Cost of production	1 551.00	
	2 256.00	

Less: Finished goods in stock at 31 October 1988			
Material	305.5		
Labour	305.5		
Overheads	235.0		
Cost of sales		846.0	
			1 410.0
Profit			235.0

The trainee accountant submitted an initial draft of a value added statement to the accountant as follows:

	£000
Sales	1 645.00
Materials consumed	481.75
	1 163.25
Cost of sales	928.25
Profit	235.00
	1 163.25

The accountant returned the draft with the following comments:

'Thank you

Please note that the statement has no heading and you have not submitted your workings to support the materials consumed and cost of sales figures.

Please redraft the value added statement to show:

Sales
Materials
Value added
Labour
Depreciation
Retained profit.'

Required

(a) Explain how the materials consumed of £481 750, and cost of sales of £928 250, were calculated in the initial draft. (5 marks)
(b) Prepare a statement of added value in the format suggested by the accountant. Explain clearly how each figure is arrived at. (5 marks)
(c) Calculate the ratio of employee rewards to value added and discuss how the ratio can be used in financial incentive schemes and wage negotiations. (7 marks)
(d) Comment on the usefulness of value added statements to users of financial reports with particular reference to differences between industries. (8 marks)

ACCA Level 3 Advanced Financial Accounting, December 1988 **(25 marks)**

11.6 Pitted Prunes plc merged with Rosy Plums plc and changed its name to Pitted Rosy Plums plc in June 1987. The figures included in the accounts for the year ended 31 December 1987 included the results of both companies from 1 January 1987.

The financial highlights printed in the annual report showed:

	1987 £000	1986 £000
Turnover		
Pitted Prunes plc	46434	43354
Rosy Plums plc	110420	78050
	156854	121404
Profit before taxation		
Pitted Prunes plc	4336	4171
Rosy Plums plc	2019	1144
	6355	5315
Shareholders' funds	38061	35772

	Pence per share	
Earnings per ordinary share	19.6	16.80
Dividends per ordinary share (net)	5.9	5.12

The five-year review showed:

	Pitted Rosy Plums		Pitted Prunes			
Year ended 31 December	1987 £000	1986 £000 restated	1986 £000	1985 £000	1984 £000	1983 £000
Turnover	156854	121404	43354	40959	34832	25209
Percentage exported	52%	49%	44%	45%	44%	38%
Operating profit	8437	6476	4174	3137	2607	1569
Profit on ordinary activities before taxation	6355	5315	4171	2667	2208	1205
Profit on ordinary activities after taxation	4538	3940	3040	2072	1836	952
Dividends:						
Preference	287	289	285	124	77	77
Ordinary	1288	1601	625	454	403	330
Shareholders' funds	38061	35772	15470	13529	10066	8590
Earnings per ordinary share	19.6p	16.8p	22.6p	16.0p	14.4p	7.1p
Dividends per ordinary share	8.1p	7.2p	7.2p	5.3p	4.7p	3.8p

Required
(a) Explain the current requirements for a company to produce a five year summary with its annual report and the circumstances in which it may be necessary to restate the actual figures. (5 marks)
(b) Discuss how historical summaries may be of interest and use to an investor or potential investor. (5 marks)
(c) Discuss the adequacy of the five year historical summary produced for Pitted Rosy Plums plc and the minimum content that you consider desirable. (10 marks)

ACCA Level 3 Advanced Financial Accounting, December 1989 (20 marks)

12 Capital reorganisation, reduction and reconstruction

12.1 In recent years several large listed companies have purchased their own ordinary shares.

You are required to summarise

(a) the accounting requirements for a public listed company when it purchases its own shares; (9 marks)

(b) six advantages of a company purchasing its own shares. (6 marks)

CIMA *Advanced Financial Accounting, November 1991* (15 marks)

12.2 Capital plc carried on business in four product segments, namely aircraft design, hairdressing salons, import agencies and beauty products.

The directors are now considering the dividend policy and the future capital structure of the company.

The draft accounts of Capital plc as at 30 November 1995 showed the following share capital and reserves:

Share capital		*£m*
Ordinary shares of £1 each	Note 1	500
8% Redeemable preference shares of £1 each	Note 2	50
Reserves – all credit balances		
Share premium		63
Capital redemption reserve		10
Fixed asset revaluation reserve	Note 3	43
Profit and loss account	Note 4	775

Note 1
The market value of ordinary shares as at 30 November 1995 was £1.60.

Note 2
The redeemable preference shares were issued in 1985. They are redeemable at par.

Note 3
A revaluation reserve of £45 million was created on 1 December 1994 on the revaluation of some of the buildings. A debit of £2 million was made to the reserve in 1995 arising from a permanent fall in value on the revaluation of certain computer equipment.

Note 4
The profit and loss account of Capital plc for the year ended 30 November 1995 contained the following items:

(i) Exchange gain on a long-term German mark loan
taken out on 1 December 1994 £6m
(ii) Depreciation based on historic cost of fixed assets £68m
Additional depreciation based on revalued amount of fixed assets £13m
(iii) Development costs for the year written off £22m
(iv) Profit attributed to long-term contracts in beauty products £9m

At their next meeting the directors will be considering proposals for:

(a) the purchase 'off market' at £1.50 per share of 30% of the issued ordinary shares of Capital plc which are currently held by Venture plc, a venture capital company. The directors consider that the shares are substantially undervalued and that the company should purchase the shares and hold them as an investment classified under 'own shares' in the balance sheet;

(b) the redemption of the preference shares;

(c) the distribution to the shareholders of Capital plc of shares in Kind plc, which have been held as an investment. The investment appears at cost, £15 million, in the balance sheet and the directors estimate that it has a market value of £24 million at 30 November 1995;

(d) a bonus issue of one ordinary share for every 20 ordinary shares held; and

(e) the amount of the final dividend to recommend for 1995.

The finance director has been requested to present a report in relation to these proposals.

Required

(a) (i) Advise the board on its proposed procedure for purchasing the issued shares in Capital plc held by Venture plc and on its intention to hold these as an investment.

(ii) Draft the journal entries to record the purchase transaction assuming that the board acts in accordance with the requirements of the Companies Act 1985.

(4 marks)

(b) (i) Explain the definition of distributable profits in a public company (ignore the rules relating to investment companies).

(ii) Identify which of the proposals (a) to (e) above would be classified as a distribution.

(iii) Describe the accounting treatment of proposal (c), distribution of shares held as an investment in Kind plc. (5 marks)

(c) Calculate the distributable profits as at 30 November 1995 on the assumption that the company had redeemed the preference shares and made the bonus issue but delayed action on the purchase of own shares and the distribution of the shares in Kind plc until 1996. Explain clearly your treatment of each item mentioned in the reserves. (11 marks)

ACCA, Financial Reporting Environment, December 1995   (20 marks)

12.3 Renewal plc was incorporated in 1985 to carry on business as manufacturers of designer jewellery. The company has incurred recent trading losses but has now returned to modest profitability. The directors estimate that raising new capital for additional investment in plant would produce an increase in profit from £1 000 000 to £1 750 000 per year but in order to be able to pay dividends it it necessary to eliminate the debit balance on the profit and loss account.

The balance sheet of Renewal plc as at 31 May 1996 showed:

	£000	£000	£000
Capital and reserves			
Ordinary shares of £1 each – 80p paid up			4 080
8% cumulative preference			
shares of £1 each			5 440
Profit and loss account balance			(5 046)
Profit attributable to arrears of preference			
dividends			1 306
			5 780
Fixed assets			
Freehold premises			2 890
Plant and machinery			2 040
Patents			578
Development expenditure			408
Current assets			
Stock	2 108		
Debtors	2 720		
		4 828	
Carried forward		4 828	5 916

	£000	£000	£000
Brought forward		4 828	5 916
Current liabilities; amounts due in less than one year			
Trade creditors	2 176		
Overdraft	1 768		
Loans from directors	1 020		
		4 964	
Net current liabilities			(136)
			5 780

The directors have formulated the following scheme:

(a) The unpaid capital on the £1 ordinary shares to be called up.
(b) The ordinary shareholders to agree to a reduction of 70p on each share held with new shares having a nominal value of 50p and treated as 30p paid up.
(c) The preference shareholders to agree to the cancellation of their three years' arrears of dividend.
(d) The preference shareholders to agree to a reduction of 20p on each share held with the new shares having a nominal value of 80p and treated as fully paid up.
(e) The dividend rate on preference shares to be increased from 8% to 11%.
(f) The debit balance on the profit and loss account to be eliminated.
(g) Freehold premises have been professionally valued at £3 800 000.
(h) Plant is to be written down by £850 000; patents are to be written down to £340 000; development expenditure is to be written off; stock is to be written down by £406 000; a provision for doubtful debts of 10% is to be created.
(i) New capital to be raised by a rights issue with existing ordinary shareholders subscribing for two shares for every one share held, 30p payable on application, and preference shareholders subscribing for one new 80p preference share for every four preference shares held.
(j) The directors to agree to £420 000 of their loans to be written off and to accept ordinary shares of 50p each, at a value of 30p (paid up), in settlement of the balance of their loans. These shares are not affected by the rights issue in (i) above.

Required
(a) (i) Explain the procedure that a company needs to follow to readjust the rights of members under ss. 425 and 426 of the Companies Act 1985.
    (ii) Advise the directors on an alternative course of action if the ordinary shareholders are not prepared to accept new obligations arising from the proposal to issue partly paid shares. (5 marks)
(b) Prepare the balance sheet for Renewal plc on the assumption that the directors' scheme has been put into effect. (7 marks)
(c) Advise the preference shareholders whether they should participate in the scheme. (8 marks)

ACCA Financial Reporting Environment, June 1996 (20 marks)

12.4 High plc acquired 60% of the issued ordinary shares of Low plc on 1 December 1989 at which date Low plc had a debit balance on reserves of £2 230 000. The directors of High plc expected to turn the company into profit by 1991. However, the losses continued and the debit balance on reserves in Low plc increased to £2 787 500 on 30 November 1990 and £3 791 000 on 30 November 1991. It was resolved to seek court approval to write off the accumulated losses of Low plc and to write down the plant and machinery in Low plc by £1 784 000 against paid up capital on 30 November 1991.

The balance sheets of High plc and Low plc as at 30 November 1991 immediately before the reduction are set out below:

Balance sheets as at 30 November 1991

	High plc £	Low plc £
Freehold property	14 495 000	–
Leasehold property	–	1 226 500
Plant and machinery	7 805 000	5 463 500
Investment in Low plc	5 575 000	–
Current assets	8 920 000	6 467 000
Current liabilities	(4 237 000)	(5 798 000)
Net current asset	4 683 000	669 000
Capital employed	32 558 000	7 359 000
Share capital		
Ordinary shares of £1 each	27 875 000	11 150 000
Reserves	4 683 000	(3 791 000)
	32 558 000	7 359 000

Required

(a) **Prepare the balance sheets for High plc, Low plc and the consolidated balance sheet as at 1 December 1991 immediately after the capital reduction. Show workings.**

(7 marks)

(b) **Prepare an analysis of the losses of Low plc for consolidation purposes at 30 November 1990 and 30 November 1991.** (3 marks)

(c) **Explain how the consolidated reserves would be calculated as at 30 November 1992 if, although when the reconstruction took place, the subsidiary was expected to be profitable, in the event it incurred losses but High plc continued its support.**

Illustrate your answer on the assumption that High plc increased its reserves by £1 600 000 and Low plc decreased its reserves by £6 000 000. (4 marks)

(d) **Discuss the legal and commercial obligations of a holding company to support an insolvent subsidiary.** (6 marks)

ACCA Advanced Financial Accounting, December 1992 **(20 marks)**

12.5 The Collapsible Chair Company Limited was incorporated in 1972 and traded profitably until the 1990s. During the early 1990s the entry of new competitors into the market led to a fall in demand for its product. Consequently, the company started making losses and no dividend has been paid to its equity shareholders since 1992.

A significant failure to co-ordinate production and sales, and a breakdown in credit control following staff illness, has led to an increase in stock and debtors. This, in turn, has led to an increase in the bank overdraft beyond the current limit of £1.3 million. Discussions with the bank have revealed a reluctance to increase the overdraft limit beyond the current level. The debentures, all of which are held by the bank, are due for repayment on 31 December 1997. Both the debentures and the overdraft are secured by a fixed charge over the premises. The bank has threatened to put the company into receivership so as to recover the amounts owed to it. The costs of a receivership and likely subsequent liquidation are estimated at £150 000.

The directors of the company approached a venture capitalist with the idea of using a new design to produce an alternative type of chair. With an investment of £1.2 million, production could begin to yield an annual operating profit before debenture interest and taxation of £600 000 which would result in a cash inflow of a roughly equal amount. However, the venture capitalist was reluctant to invest in the company unless a scheme of capital reorganisation was agreed, and did not wish to gain a controlling interest in the company.

The balance sheet of the company at 31 March 1997, before the implementation of the capital reorganisation scheme, was as follows:

	£000	£000
Fixed assets:		
Premises	3 000	
Plant	2 000	
		5 000
Current assets:		
Stocks	2 000	
Debtors	1 500	
	3 500	
Current liabilities:		
Trade creditors	1 800	
Bank overdraft	1 500	
8% debentures	2 500	
	5 800	
Net current liabilities		(2 300)
		2 700
Capital and reserves:		
Equity share capital (£1 each)		6 000
Profit and loss account		(3 300)
		2 700

The directors have obtained the following estimates for the value of the assets of the company as a going concern, and in a liquidation, at 31 March 1997.

Asset	Going concern value	Liquidation value
	£000	£000
Premises	3 500	3 500
Plant	1 600	400
Stock	1 500	500
Debtors	1 300	900

A scheme of capital reorganisation has been agreed with all interested parties and implemented by the directors. Details of the scheme are as follows:

(1) The equity shares of £1 were redesignated as 30p shares.
(2) The assets of the company were stated at their going concern values.
(3) The repayment date for the debentures was deferred to 31 December 2007 with the interest rate increased to 10% per annum.
(4) The bank was issued with 1 million 30p equity shares in return for its willingness to accept a deferred repayment of the debentures.
(5) The venture capitalist subscribed for 4 million new 30p equity shares at par.
(6) The accumulated losses were written off.

Requirements
(a) **Prepare the balance sheet of the company at 31 March 1997 which incorporates the scheme which has been implemented.** (13 marks)
(b) **Assess the effect of the scheme from the point of view of EACH of**
  ● **the equity shareholders;**
  ● **the bank;**
  ● **the venture capitalist.** (12 marks)

CIMA, Financial Reporting, May 1997 (**Total Marks = 25**)

12.6 Medical Equipment plc was incorporated in 1970 to assemble medical equipment used in hospitals. The directors of the company had a major shareholding and were all engaged full time in the operational management of the company. The company had experienced operating losses and the directors believed that profit improvement depended on reducing labour costs. They accordingly decided to automate the assembly process by investing in the development of an automatic machine known as 'Auto-Assembler'.

The 'Auto-Assembler' was tested and developed in 1990 and by 31 December 1990 development expenditure of £157 300 incurred in the development of the 'Auto-Assembler' has been capitalised. It was estimated that its operational use would result in cost savings of £130 000 per annum before tax and that it could be made operational in 1991 for a capital outlay of £75 000. The directors had been building up a short-term investment during 1989–1990 to cover this capital outlay.

The production engineer estimated that as a result of automation an additional £40 000 investment would be required for working capital to meet the additional cost of higher specification materials.

In December 1990 the manager of the bank informed the directors that he wanted the overdraft reduced to around £75 000 from its present level of £270 480.

The directors immediately approached Mr Jeremiah, a partner in the accounting firm of Hard Reality & Co. who were the company's auditors. They believed in the potential profitability of the new automated assembly process and advised Mr Jeremiah that they believed that they would be able to negotiate long-term loan finance to clear the overdraft. At the request of the accountants the company produced the following:

(i) draft accounts as at 31 December 1990
(ii) additional information on assets and liabilities.

Draft profit and loss account for the year ended 31 December 1990

	£	£
Sales		2 008 000
Cost of sales		
Materials	1 398 800	
Labour	300 000	
		1 698 800
Gross profit		309 200
Distribution costs		(213 200)
Administration expenses		(129 000)
Profit before interest and tax		(33 000)
Interest		(51 600)
Profit before tax		(84 600)

Draft balance sheet as at 31 December 1990

	£
Fixed assets	
Freehold land and buildings	312 000
Plant and machinery	197 600
Development cost of 'Auto-Assembler'	157 300
	666 900
Current assets	
Stock	302 400
Investments	52 000
Debtors	169 000
Cash	2 600
	526 000
Carried forward	1 192 900

631

	£
Brought forward	1 192 900
Current liabilities	
Creditors	(303 240)
Overdraft	(270 480)
	(573 720)
Non-current liabilities	
10% debentures	(208 000)
Capital employed	411 180
Capital and reserves	
Ordinary shares of £1 each	425 000
Share premium account	42 500
7% non-cumulative preference shares of £1 each	260 000
Profit and loss account	(316 320)
	411 180

Additional information on individual assets and liabilities as at 31 December 1990:

	Going concern values assuming 'Auto-Assembler' does NOT become operational £	Going concern values assuming 'Auto-Assembler' DOES become operational £	Values realisable on liquidation £
Freehold land and buildings	385 000	385 000	385 000
Plant and machinery	123 500	88 400	44 200
Stock	292 400	254 800	200 100
Debtors	149 000	149 000	119 840
Investments	52 000	52 000	81 000
Development costs	–	157 300	–

The creditors comprised:	£
Preferential creditors	34 700
Loan interest accrued on debentures	10 400
Trade creditors	258 140
	303 240

Trade creditors allow 60 days' credit.

The debentures were secured on the freehold land and buildings and were redeemable at par in 1997.

Mr Jeremiah was not convinced that the directors would be able to arrange long-term loan finance to replace the overdraft and was of the opinion that a scheme of internal reconstruction would become necessary. He requested one of his staff to draft a brief report to explain to the directors feasible ways forward.

Required

(a) Prepare a balance sheet as at 31 December 1990 on the basis that the company ceased trading on that date and explain its significance for the relevant parties. (5 marks)

(b) (i) Explain briefly the purposes of a scheme for reconstruction as it would apply to equity and loan stockholders. (4 marks)

   (ii) Propose a scheme for the capital reconstruction of Medical Equipment plc. Show your calculation of the loss involved in the scheme; state what you would do with this loss; calculate the working capital requirements of the company; calculate the possible additional equity capital that might be required.

Note: **The revised balance sheet after the implementation of the scheme is not required.** (16 marks)

(iii) **Explain briefly to the directors how the scheme will be fair to all relevant parties.**

(5 marks)

ACCA Advanced Financial Accounting, June 1992 (**30 marks**)

12.7 Aztec plc was incorporated in 1968 as an importer of silver artefacts from South America which it customised for the UK market. The company had sold its products in the luxury market and traded profitably until 1989. Since that date it has suffered continuous losses which have resulted in a negative balance on the profit and loss account. The balance sheet as at 31 December 1993 showed the following:

Share capital and reserves	£
Ordinary shares of 1 each	675 000
7% Preference shares of 1 each	135 000
Profit and loss account	(573 000)
Net capital employed	237 000
Fixed assets	
Leasehold premises	397 000
Vehicles and equipment	105 000
Machinery	250 000
Current assets	
Stock	295 000
Debtor	120 000
Current liabilities	
Suppliers	(288 000)
Wages VAT and PAYE	(80 000)
Hire-purchase liability on vehicles/equipment	(20 000)
Bank overdraft (secured by a fixed charge over the machinery)	(112 000)
Non-current liabilities	
Hire-purchase liability on vehicles and equipment	(25 000)
11% Debentures (secured by a floating charge)	(405 000)
Net assets	237 000

Since 1989 the company has been developing an export market for its products in Europe and the directors forecast that the company will return to profit in 1994. They expect profits before tax and debenture interest to be in the range of £70 000 to £140 000 per annum over the next three years. As a result of developing the export market, they expect that the company will require warehouse premises on the continent in 1996 at a forecast cost of £250 000.

However, the directors are concerned that even if the company achieves a profit of £70 000 per year it will be a number of years before a dividend could be distributed to the ordinary shareholders and it would be difficult to raise fresh funds from the shareholders in 1996 if there were to be little prospect of a dividend until the year 2000.

The directors have been considering various possible courses of action available under the Companies Act 1985 and the Insolvency Act 1986 and have had initial discussions with their auditors.

As a result of these discussions it was agreed that the finance director would produce a draft proposal for reorganisation; the auditors would let the finance director have their comments on the draft proposal: and the finance director would then submit a proposal to the board of directors for their consideration.

The following additional information was obtained by the finance director concerning the assets and liabilities at 31 December 1993 and estimated costs of liquidating or reorganising:

(a) Fair values and liquidation values of assets were:

	Fair values on a going concern basis £	Liquidation values on a forced sale basis £
Leasehold premises	360 000	100 000
Vehicles and equipment	85 000	35 000
Machinery	225 000	122 000
Current assets		
Stock	285 000	150 000
Debtors	110 000	100 000

(b) Preference dividends are four years in arrears.
(c) Wages, VAT and PAYE would be preferential creditors in a liquidation.
(d) The costs of liquidating Aztec plc were estimated at £55 000.
(e) The costs of reorganisation were estimated at £40 000; these would be paid by Aztec (Europe) plc and treated as part of the purchase consideration.

The finance director prepared the following draft proposal:

(i) A new company was to be formed Aztec (Europe) plc with a share capital of £270 000 in 10p shares to acquire the assets and liabilities of Aztec plc as at 31 December 1993.
(ii) The ordinary shareholders were to receive less than 25% of the ordinary shares in Aztec (Europe) plc so that the existing preference shareholders and debenture holders each had a significant interest and acting together had control of the new company.
(iii) The arrears of preference dividends were to be cancelled.
(iv) The new company was to issue:
  − 900 000 ordinary shares and £70 000 of 13% debentures to the existing preference shareholders
  − 1 200 000 ordinary shares and £200 000 of 13% debentures to the existing 11% debenture holders
  − 600 000 ordinary shares to the existing ordinary shareholders.
(v) The variation of the rights of the shareholders and creditors was to be effected under s.425 of the Companies Act 1985 which requires that the scheme should be approved by a majority in number and 75% in value of each class of shareholders, by a majority in number and 75% in value of each class of creditor affected and by the court.
(vi) The transfer of the assets to Aztec (Europe) plc was to be effected under s.427 of the Companies Act 1985 which would ensure that the court dealt with the transfer of the assets and liabilities and the dissolution of Aztec plc to avoid the costs of winding up that company.

Assume a corporation tax rate of 35% and an income tax rate of 25%. Ignore ACT.

Required

(a) Assuming that the necessary approvals have been obtained for assets and liabilities to be transferred on the proposed terms on 31 December 1993:
  (i) Prepare journal entries to close the books of Aztec plc: and
  (ii) Prepare the balance sheet of Aztec (Europe) plc after the transfer of assets and liabilities. (10 marks)
(b) Draft a memo to the finance director commenting on his draft proposals for a scheme of capital reduction and reorganisation. (16 marks)
(c) Advise the directors as to the course of action they should take in order to be able to proceed with their plans for reorganisation if they learn that a creditor has obtained a

judgment against the company and is considering seeking a compulsory winding-up order.   (4 marks)

ACCA Financial Reporting Environment, June 1994   (30 marks)

13 Interpretation of financial statements

13.1 The interpretation of financial statements is assisted by the use of ratio analysis. However, this process can be said to have inherent limitations and some ratios may not be appropriate in all circumstances.

Explain how users of published financial statements might best approach the interpretation of those statements, considering any inherent limitations of ratio analysis and to what extent these might be overcome.

ICAEW, Financial Reporting, November 1997   (10 marks)

13.2 The following companies carry on distribution businesses for the supermarket industry. Their draft accounts for the year ended 31 December 1997 were as follows:

Profit and loss accounts	*Truckers Ltd* £'000	*Distributors Ltd* £'000
Turnover	1 200	1 100
Cost of sales	(1 000)	(945)
Gross profit	200	155
Administrative and other expenses	(60)	(30)
Profit before taxation	140	125

Balance sheets	*Truckers Ltd* £'000	*Distributors Ltd* £'000
Fixed assets		
Freehold property	300	100
Fixtures and fittings	210	100
Commercial vehicles	400	200
Motor vehicles	30	40
	940	440
Current assets		
Stock	20	10
Debtors	150	90
Cash at bank and in hand	40	85
	210	185
Current liabilities		
Creditors	(20)	(10)
Net current assets	190	175
Total assets less current liabilities	1 130	615
Long term liabilities		
Loan stock 2001	(200)	–
	930	615
Shareholders' funds	930	615

Requirements

(a) Calculate suitable ratios on the profitability and financial position of the companies.

(6 marks)

(b) Comment on the results of your calculations, taking into account the nature of the companies' activities. State what further information would be useful in assisting your interpretation of the ratios calculated in (a).

(9 marks)

ICAEW, Financial Reporting, May 1998

(15 marks)

13.3 Arizona plc has carried on business for a number of years as a retailer of a wide variety of 'do it yourself' goods. The company operates from a number of stores around the United Kingdom.

In recent years, the company has found it necessary to provide credit facilities to its customers in order to achieve growth in turnover. As a result of this decision, the liability to the company's bankers has increased substantially.

The statutory accounts of the company for the year ended 31 March 1998 have recently been published, and extracts are provided below, together with comparative figures for the previous two years.

Profit and loss accounts for the years ended 31 March	1996 £ million	1997 £ million	1998 £ million
Turnover	1 850	2 200	2 500
Cost of sales	(1 250)	(1 500)	(1 750)
Gross profit	600	700	750
Other operating costs	(550)	(640)	(700)
Operating profit	50	60	50
Interest from credit sales	45	60	90
Interest payable	(25)	(60)	(110)
Profit before taxation	70	60	30
Taxation	(23)	(20)	(10)
Profit after taxation	47	40	20
Dividends	(30)	(30)	(20)
Retained profit	17	10	–

Balance sheets at 31 March	1996 £ million	1997 £ million	1998 £ million
Tangible fixed assets	278	290	322
Stocks	400	540	620
Debtors	492	550	633
Cash	12	12	15
Trade creditors	(270)	(270)	(280)
Taxation	(20)	(20)	(8)
Proposed dividends	(30)	(30)	(20)
Bank overdraft	(320)	(520)	(610)
Debentures	(200)	(200)	(320)
	342	352	352
Share capital	90	90	90
Reserves	252	262	262
	342	352	352

Other information

- Depreciation charged for the three years was as follows:

Year ended 31 March	1996 £ million	1997 £ million	1998 £ million
	55	60	70

- The debentures are secured by a floating charge over the assets of Arizona plc. Their repayment is due on 31 March 2008.
- The bank overdraft is unsecured. The bank has set a limit of £630 million on the overdraft.
- Over the past three years, the level of credit sales has been:

Year ended 31 March	1996 £ million	1997 £ million	1998 £ million
	213	263	375

Given the steady increase in the bank overdraft which has taken place in recent years, the company has recently written to its bankers to request an increase in the limit. The request was received by the bank on 15 May 1998, two weeks after the 1998 statutory accounts were published.

You are an accountant employed by the bankers of Arizona plc. The bank is concerned at the steep escalation in the level of the company's overdraft and your regional manager has asked for a report on the financial performance of Arizona plc for the last three years.

Requirement

Write a report to your regional manager which analyses the financial performance of Arizona plc for the period covered by the financial statements.

Your report may take any form you wish, but should specifically address the particular concern of the bank regarding the rapidly increasing overdraft. Therefore, your report should identify aspects of poor performance which could have contributed to the increase in the overdraft.

CIMA, Financial Reporting, May 1998 (20 marks)

13.4 The following information is available for a group classified within the 'Engineering, Vehicles' sector in the *Financial Times*.

	Years ended 31 March	
	1999	1998
Gross profit/sales	12.8%	13.6%
Operating profit/sales – total	4.5%	4.9%
– on continuing operations	8.4%	12.0%
– on discontinued operations	2.1%	2.1%
Current ratio	2.1:1	1.2:1
Quick (or acid test) ratio	1.2:1	0.3:1
Gearing ratio (debt:equity)	11.9%	14.9%
Return on capital employed	18.9%	36.4%
Stock turnover period	44 days	78 days
Debtors collection period	6 days	9 days
Creditors payment period	21 days	26 days
Sales/fixed assets	12 times	8 times
Earnings per share – basic	21.3p	42.3p
Earnings per share – adjusted for exceptional item	39.6p	42.3p
Turnover from continuing operations	£158.2m	£148.1m
Turnover from discontinued operations	£265.5m	£374.6m
Turnover – total	£423.7m	£522.7m

By the year end, the group's principal activities comprised public service vehicle manufacture and distribution. It is group policy to prepare its financial statements using the historical cost convention except for the revaluation of land and buildings which were last revalued in the year ended 31 March 1998.

Requirement

Comment on the performance of the group as far as you are able using the information above. You are not required to calculate any further ratios.

ICAEW, Financial Reporting, June 1999 (13 marks)

13.5 You are the chief financial accountant of Soda plc, a manufacturer and wholesaler of soft drinks. Soda plc is in direct competition with Fizz plc and Pop Ltd.

The finance director has informed you that the board of directors is considering purchasing an interest in one of their two competitors in order to increase market share. This decision will be based on forward-looking market and management information. However, the directors seek to use data from recent corporate reports to provide a firm audited foundation on which to construct the necessary estimates and forecasts leading to their decision.

The finance director has provided you with the following table of statistics calculated from the most recent financial statements of both competitors:

	Fizz plc	*Pop Ltd*
Gross profit margin	40%	40%
Net profit margin	15%	10%
Debt: Equity	15%	25%
Stock turnover	8 times	4 times
Debtor days	63 days	40 days
Creditor days	65 days	65 days
Dividend cover	3	2
Interest cover	7	5
Current ratio	1.25:1	1.75:1
Liquid ratio	0.9:1	1:1
Asset turnover	1.5 times	2 times

You are required, using the above information, to prepare a report for the board of directors,

(a) **comparing the results and the financial situation of the two competitors;** (20 marks)
(b) **suggesting, with reference to your comparison in (a) above, other items in the companies' corporate report which bear on this decision and which might merit further investigation.** (10 marks)

CIMA Advanced Financial Accounting, November 1994 (30 marks)

13.6 Recycle plc is a listed company which recycles toxic chemical waste products. The waste products are sent to Recycle plc from all around the world. You are an accountant (not employed by Recycle plc) who is accustomed to providing advice concerning the performance of companies, based on the data which is available from their published financial statements. Extracts from the financial statements of Recycle plc for the two years ended 30 September 1997 are given below:

Profit and loss accounts – year ended 30 September

	1997	1996
	£ m	£ m
Turnover	3 000	2 800
Cost of sales	(1 600)	(1 300)
Gross profit	1 400	1 500
Other operating expenses	(800)	(600)
Operating profit	600	900
Interest payable	(200)	(100)
Profit before taxation	400	800
Taxation	(150)	(250)
Profit after taxation	250	550
Proposed dividend	(200)	(200)
Retained profit	50	350
Retained profit b/fwd	900	550
Retained profit c/fwd	950	900

Balance sheets at 30 September

	1997		1996	
	£ m	£ m	£ m	£ m
Tangible fixed assets		4 100		3 800
Current assets				
Stocks	500		350	
Debtors	1 000		800	
Cash in hand	50		50	
	1 550		1 200	
Current liabilities				
Trade creditors	600		600	
Taxation payable	150		250	
Proposed dividend	200		200	
Bank overdraft	750		50	
	1 700		1 100	
Net current (liabilities)/assets		(150)		100
Long-term loans (repayable 1999)		(1 000)		(1 000)
		2 950		2 900
Capital and reserves				
Called-up share capital (£1 shares)		2 000		2 000
Profit and loss account		950		900
		2 950		2 900

You ascertain that depreciation of tangible fixed assets for the year ended 30 September 1997 was £1200 million. Disposals of fixed assets during the year ended 30 September 1997 were negligible.

You are approached by two individuals.

A is a private investor who is considering purchasing shares in Recycle plc. A considers that Recycle plc has performed well in 1997 compared with 1996 because turnover has risen and the dividend to shareholders has been maintained.

B is resident in the area immediately surrounding the premises of Recycle plc and is interested in the contribution, made by Recycle plc to the general well-being of the community. B is also concerned about the potential environmental effect of the recycling of chemical waste. B is uncertain how the published financial statements of Recycle plc might be of assistance in addressing social and environmental matters.

Requirements
(a) Write a report to A which analyses the financial performance of Recycle plc over the two years ended 30 September 1997.

Assume inflation is negligible.

Your report should specifically refer to the observations made by A concerning the performance of Recycle plc. (25 marks)
(b) Briefly discuss whether published financial statements satisfy the information needs of B.

You should consider published financial statements in general, not just the extracts which are provided in this question. (5 marks)

CIMA, *Financial Reporting, November 1997*   **Total Marks = 30**

13.7 Required
(a) Describe the current requirements for the disclosure of segmental information in the annual report. (7 marks)
(b) Discuss the advantages and disadvantages to the users and preparers of annual reports of disclosing segmental data classified by:
(i) Industry groupings;
(ii) Legal entities within the group structure. (9 marks)
(c) Discuss the importance of the disclosure of extraordinary items to the users of the annual report in addition to the operating profit. (9 marks)

ACCA *Level 3 Advanced Financial Accounting, June 1988*   **(25 marks)**

13.8 Travis plc is a large grocery retailing and wholesaling organisation. It is presently drawing up its financial statements for the year ended 31 October 1993 and, mindful of the requirements of SSAP 25, has drafted the following segmental report:

Segment information

	Turnover		Profit before tax		Operating net assets	
	31.10.93	31.10.92	31.10.93	31.10.92	31.10.93	31.10.92
	£m	£m	£m	£m	£m	£m
By category						
Retailing						
Food	5 650	6 126	300	295	2 925	2 964
Drinks	1 951	2 047	219	136	987	917
Consurnables	115	106	8	5	86	82
Wholesaling						
Warehousing	3 843	3 651	391	382	1 560	1 490
	11 559	11 930	918	818	5 558	5 453
By activity						
Retailing						
Hypermarkets	6 235	6 608	465	314	3 120	3 040
Large shops	545	534	43	40	560	538
Small shops	936	1 137	19	82	318	385
Wholesaling						
Warehousing	3 843	3 651	391	382	1 560	1 490
	11 559	11 930	918	818	5 558	5 453

Notes

Head office and service costs of £53 million (1992: £51 million) have been allocated according to the relative contribution of each segment to the total of continuing operations.

The group's borrowing requirements are centrally managed and so interest expense of £475 million (1992: £415 million) has been apportioned on the basis of average net assets for each segment.

Operating net assets represent the group's net assets adjusted to exclude interest bearing operating assets and liabilities.

Businesses discontinued during the year contributed £450 million (1992: £850 million) to turnover and £38 million (1992: £68 million) to profit before tax.

Requirements

(a) Discuss the objectives of segmental reporting in the context of each of the following user groups of financial statements:
   (i)   the shareholder group
   (ii) the investment analyst group
   (iii) the lender/creditor group
   (iv) Government.   (10 marks)
(b) Critically assess the presentation of Travis plc's draft 'Segment information' report, considering in particular its helpfulness to users of financial statements and its compliance with the requirements of SSAP 25. Outline any ways in which the information might be presented more effectively or in which the treatment of items might be improved.   (11 marks)

ICAEW Financial Accounting 2, December 1993   **(21 marks)**

13.9 Spreader plc is a UK parent company with a number of wholly-owned subsidiaries in the US and Europe. Extracts from the consolidated financial statements of the group for the year ended 30 April 1997 are given below.

Profit and loss account – year ended 30 April		1997	1996
		£000	£000
Turnover	(Note 1)	50 000	48 000
Cost of sales		(25 000)	(22 000)
Gross profit		25 000	26 000
Other operating expenditure		(15 000)	(14 200)
Operating profit		10 000	11 800
Interest payable		(1 000)	(900)
Profit before taxation	(Note 2)	9 000	10 900
Taxation		(2 800)	(3 600)
Profit after taxation		6 200	7 300
Dividend		(3 000)	(3 200)
Retained profit		3 200	4 100

Note 1 Analysis of turnover for the year by geographical segment

	UK		US		Rest of Europe		Total	
	1997	1996	1997	1996	1997	1996	1997	1996
	£000	£000	£000	£000	£000	£000	£000	£000
Total sales	15 000	20 000	10 000	8 000	30 000	25 000	55 000	53 000
Inter-segment sales	(2 000)	(2 500)	(1 000)	(500)	(2 000)	(2 000)	(5 000)	(5 000)
Sales to third parties	13 000	17 500	9 000	7 500	28 000	23 000	50 000	48 000

Note 2 Analysis of profit before tax for the year by geographical segment

	UK		US		Rest of Europe		Total	
	1997	*1996*	*1997*	*1996*	*1997*	*1996*	*1997*	*1996*
	£000	*£000*	*£000*	*£000*	*£000*	*£000*	*£000*	*£000*
Segment profit	3 000	6 000	1 500	1 200	6 000	5 000	10 500	12 200
Common costs							(500)	(400)
Operating profit							10 000	11 800
Interest payable							(1 000)	(900)
Profit before taxation							9 000	10 900

Note 3 Analysis of net assets at end of year by geographical segment

	UK		US		Rest of Europe		Total	
	1997	*1996*	*1997*	*1996*	*1997*	*1996*	*1997*	*1996*
	£000	*£000*	*£000*	*£000*	*£000*	*£000*	*£000*	*£000*
Segment net assets	15 000	13 500	6 000	5 000	20 000	20 000	41 000	38 500
Unallocated assets							2 000	1 800
Total net assets							43 000	40 300

Requirements
In your capacity as chief accountant of Spreader plc,

(a) prepare a report for the board of directors of the company which analyses the results of the group for the year ended 30 April 1997; (21 marks)
(b) explain why the segmental data which has been included in the extracts may need to be interpreted with caution. (4 marks)

CIMA, Financial Reporting, May 1997 **(Total Marks = 25)**

13.10 You are a management accountant who provides financial planning advice to a range of individual and corporate clients. One of your clients, Mr Green, owns 1000 shares in Prospect plc, a mining company with a listing on the London Stock Exchange. Prospect plc has interests all over the world through a number of wholly-owned subsidiaries. Extracts from the consolidated financial statements of Prospect plc for the year ended 30 June 1999 are given below. Mr Green has read these extracts and is dissatisfied with the performance of Prospect plc because profits and dividends have fallen even though turnover has increased. He is wondering whether he should sell his shares in the company.

Extracts from the consolidated financial statements of Prospect plc
Profit and loss accounts for the year ended

	30 June 1999	30 June 1998
	£ million	*£ million*
Turnover (*Note 1*)	1 300	7 000
Cost of sales	(700)	(450)
Gross profit	600	550
Distribution costs	(100)	(90)
Administrative expenses	(250)	(180)
Operating profit	250	280
Interest payable	(90)	(75)
Profit before taxation (*Note 2*)	160	205
Taxation	(50)	(60)
Profit after taxation c/fwd	110	145

	30 June 1999 £ million	30 June 1998 £ million
b/fwd	110	145
Equity dividends	(70)	(80)
Retained profit for the year	40	65
Retained profit brought forward	470	315
Foreign currency translation differences	140	90
Retained profit carried forward	650	470

Balance sheets at	30 June 1999 £ million	£ million	30 June 1998 £ million	£ million
Fixed assets				
Intangible assets (Note 4)	200		100	
Tangible assets	1 100		950	
		1 300		1 050
Current assets				
Stocks	380		300	
Debtors	460		400	
Cash at bank and in hand	35		35	
	875		735	
Creditors falling due within one year				
Trade creditors	115		95	
Taxation	50		60	
Proposed dividend	70		80	
Bank overdraft	90		80	
	325		315	
		550		420
Net current assets				
Creditors falling due after more than one year				
Loan stock		(1 000)		(800)
		850		670
Capital and reserves				
Called-up share capital (£1 shares)		100		100
Share premium account		100		100
Profit and loss account		650		470
		850		670

Selected notes to the financial statements

Note 1 – geographical analysis of turnover

	Europe		Africa		Far East		Total	
	1999 £ million	1998 £ million	1999 £ million	1998 £ million	1999 £ million	1998 £ million	1999 £ million	1998 £ million
Total sales	520	500	390	200	460	360	1 370	1 060
Inter-segment sales	(40)	(35)	(10)	(10)	(20)	(15)	(70)	(60)
Sales to third parties	480	465	380	190	440	345	1 300	1 000

Note 2 – geographical analysis of profit before tax

	Europe		Africa		Far East		Total	
	1999	1998	1999	1998	1999	1998	1999	1998
	£ million	£ million	£ million	£ million	£ million	£ million	£ million	£ million
Segment operating profit	70	145	100	55	100	100	270	300
Common costs							(20)	(20)
Group operating profit							250	280
Interest payable							(90)	(75)
Group profit before tax							160	205

Note 3 – geographical analysis of net assets

	Europe		Africa		Far East		Total	
	1999	1998	1999	1998	1999	1998	1999	1998
	£ million	£ million	£ million	£ million	£ million	£ million	£ million	£ million
Segment net assets	675	620	540	300	585	500	1 800	1 420
Unallocated assets							50	50
							1 850	1 470

Note 4 – intangible fixed assets

It is group policy to capitalise some direct costs of locating new mineral sources. These costs are amortised over the expected period during which the source will provide economic benefits for the group.

Requirement

Write a report to Mr Green which

- **highlights the major reasons for the decline in profits and dividends despite the increase in turnover;**
- **indicates the other factors which Mr Green may wish to take into account in making a hold or sell decision.**

While your report should include some analysis of the segmental data which has been provided in *Notes 1* to *3*, it is not necessary to compute any financial ratios based on that data.

CIMA, Financial Reporting, November 1999　　　　　　　　　　　　　　　　　**(24 marks)**

13.11　FRS 8 – *Related Party Disclosures* – was issued in October 1995. Prior to its existence, there were specific requirements for related-party disclosures contained in the 1985 Companies Act and the Listing Rules of the London Stock Exchange.

On 1 April 1997, Ace plc owned 75% of the equity share capital of Deuce Ltd and 80% of the equity share capital of Trey Ltd. On 1 April 1998, Ace plc purchased the remaining 25% of the equity shares of Deuce Ltd. In the two years ended 31 March 1999, the following transactions occurred between the three companies:

(i)　On 30 June 1997 Ace plc manufactured a machine for use by Deuce Ltd. The cost of manufacture was £20 000 The machine was delivered to Deuce Ltd for an invoiced price of £25 000. Deuce Ltd paid the invoice on 31 August 1997. Deuce Ltd depreciated the machine over its anticipated useful economic life of five years, charging a full year's depreciation in the year of purchase.

(ii)　On 30 September 1998, Deuce Ltd sold some goods to Trey Ltd at an invoiced price of £15 000. Trey Ltd paid the invoice on 30 November 1998. The goods had cost Deuce Ltd £12 000 to manufacture. By 31 March 1999, Trey Ltd had sold all the goods outside the group.

(iii) For each of the two years ended 31 March 1999, Ace plc provided management services to Deuce Ltd and Trey Ltd. Ace plc did not charge for these services in the year ended 31 March 1998 but in the year ended 31 March 1999 decided to impose a charge of £10 000 per annum to each company. The amounts of £10 000 are due to be paid by each company on 31 May 1999.

Requirements
(a) Explain why related-party disclosures are needed and why FRS 8 was considered necessary given the existing requirements of the 1985 Companies Act and the Listing Rules of the London Stock Exchange. (6 marks)
(b) Summarise the related-party disclosures which will be required in respect of transactions (i) to (iii) above for both of the years ended 31 March 1998 and 31 March 1999 in the financial statements of Ace plc, Deuce Ltd and Trey Ltd. (14 marks)
    You may assume that Ace plc presents consolidated financial statements for both of the years dealt with in the question.

CIMA, *Financial Reporting, May 1999* (Total Marks = 20)

14 The valuation of securities and businesses

14.1 The valuation of unlisted shares is highly subjective, especially when the object is to fix a fair price for acquisition by the company or by the owner's fellow-shareholders.

You are required
(a) to set out the principal bases commonly used for valuing unlisted shares, distinguishing the situations in which such bases are most appropriate; and (9 marks)
(b) to evaluate critically the theoretical soundness of the said bases of valuation, and the extent to which they achieve approximate justice as between buyer and seller.
(7 marks)

ACCA *Advanced Financial Accounting, Second paper, December 1983* (16 marks)

14.2 Charles Moon, the managing director of your client Neptune plc, is negotiating with a view to Neptune plc acquiring the entire share capital of Sirius Group Ltd ('Sirius').
    He has informed you that Sirius is the parent company of a diversified manufacturing group with overseas interests, and that he is considering making an offer at a price equivalent to the consolidated net assets disclosed by the most recent statutory accounts of Sirius as at 30 June 1987. He is also contemplating offering additional but deferred consideration based upon profits for the year ending 30 June 1988 as disclosed by the statutory accounts for that year.

Requirement
Prepare a report for Charles Moon to brief him on:

(a) four principal areas of accounting policy that could have a significant impact on the accounts of Sirius and thus on the total consideration to be paid; (8 marks)
(b) the usefulness and limitations of using statutory accounts as the basis for determining the amounts of both the initial and the deferred consideration for Sirius. (10 marks)

ICAEW *Financial Accounting II, December 1987* (18 marks)

14.3 Prentice Foods Ltd prepares ready-to-cook foods which are mainly sold as 'own label' products by one of the leading UK supermarket chains. Most of the company's shares are, owned by ten members of the Prentice family, but there are six senior managers who have very small holdings.

The company's 1996 annual report contained financial statements which can be outlined as follows:

Profit and loss account for the year ended 31 August 1996

	£'000
Turnover	82 360
Operating profit	11 242
Interest payable	(1 000)
	10 242
Tax	(3 286)
	6 956
Dividends	(2 600)
Retained profit for the year	4 356

Balance sheet as at 31 August 1996

	£'000	£'000
Fixed assets		44 890
Current assets	28 647	
Creditors: amounts falling due within one year	(26 319)	
		2 328
Total assets less current liabilities		47 218
Creditors: amounts falling due after more than one year		
(10% loan repayable in full in 2005)		(10 000)
		37 218
Share capital and reserves		
Ordinary shares of £1 each		10 000
Reserves		27 218
		37 218

Cash flow statement for the year ended 31 August 1996

	£'000	£'000
Net cash inflow from operating activities		13 472
Interest paid	(1 000)	
Dividends paid	(2 550)	
		(3 550)
Tax paid		(3 125)
New fixed assets, net of proceeds of disposals		(4 292)
Net cash inflow before financing		2 505
Financing		0
Increase in cash		2 505

The 1996 results are regarded as fairly typical of those over recent years and they are in line with expectations for the foreseeable future. Prentice Foods Ltd is a mature business. The company has a well-established policy of replacing its fixed assets on a rolling programme, so the amount spent on fixed assets each year is fairly constant.

Average figures for Stock Exchange listed companies in the food producing sector are:

Gross dividend yield	4.05%
Dividend cover	1.92
Cost of equity	11.52%

Requirements
(a) **Estimate the value of an ordinary share in Prentice Foods Ltd in three ways. Clearly explain the basis of your estimations and justify any assumptions which you have made.** (9 marks)
(b) **Suggest a suitable price per share for each of the following possible transactions:**
  (i) **The purchase of 500 shares by one manager from another manager. The shares represent each manager's only holding of the company's shares.**
  (ii) **The purchase of the entire share capital by a conglomerate.**
  Your suggested prices should be explained and justified.
  You should also outline any additional information which you feel would enable you to make a more informed valuation. (6 marks)

ICAEW, Business Planning and Finance, November 1996 (15 marks)

14.4 Look Ahead & Co were instructed to value as at 31 December 1992 a minority holding of 10 000 25p shares in Arbor Ltd held by D. Dodd who is considering disposing of his shareholding.

Arbor Ltd is a private company with an issued share capital of £125 000. The shareholdings are as follows:

Shareholder	Shareholding
A. Arny	61 250
B. Brady	30 000
D. Brady	20 000
E. Brady	11 250
D. Dodd	2 500

The following are extracts from the profit and loss accounts of Arbor Ltd for the four years ended 31 December 1992:

	1989 £000	1990 £000	1991 £000	1992 £000
Sales	4 200	5 600	8 470	11 700
Cost of sales	1 825	2 920	5 205	7 810
Gross profit	2 375	2 680	3 265	3 890
Administration expenses	900	1 000	1 200	1 400
Distribution costs	1 345	1 500	1 800	2 100
Profit before tax	130	180	265	390
Taxation	40	60	90	136
Profit after tax	90	120	175	254
Ordinary dividend	21.6	22.7	23.8	25.0

The following additional information is available:

The gross dividend yields on quoted companies operating in the same sector were 12% and the firm estimated that this yield should be increased to 18% to allow for lack of marketability.

Assume an income tax rate of 25%.

Required
(a) **Discuss the relevance of dividends in the valuation of D. Dodd's shareholding on the assumption that it is sold to his son W. Dodd. Illustrate your answer from the data given in the question.** (4 marks)

(b) Explain briefly the factors that the firm would take into account when:
   (i) estimating the future net dividends;
   (ii) estimating the investor's required gross yield. (8 marks)

(c) Explain how the approach adopted by the firm when valuing a minority interest might be influenced by the size of the shareholding or its relative importance to the other shareholdings. (8 marks)

ACCA Advanced Financial Accounting, June 1993 **(20 marks)**

14.5 You act in the capacity of financial adviser to a number of companies. One of them, Fig plc, whose managing director is not familiar with finance, has asked you to explain some financial terms which he does not understand and has also asked you to assist him in obtaining certain information. An extract of the letter received from the managing director of Fig plc is as follows:

'I should be grateful if you would briefly explain the following matters:

(1) For ordinary shares quoted in the *Financial Times*, the following particulars:

Company	Price	+ or –	Dividend Net	Cover	Yield Gross	P/E
x	x	x	x	x	x	x

(2) This extract from the quotations page of the *Financial Times*:

   "Price/earnings ratios are calculated on 'net' distribution basis . . .; bracketed figures indicate 10 per cent or more difference if calculated on 'nil' distribution. Covers are based on 'maximum' distribution."

In addition could you please inform me where I might obtain the following information:

(a) daily share prices for any share quoted on The Stock Exchange, London;
(b) recent dividends and rights issues of UK listed companies;
(c) copies of the financial statements of my competitors, which include both public and private companies in the UK.'

Requirement
Draft a letter in reply.

ICAEW Financial Accounting II, December 1985 **(17 marks)**

14.6 FRS 3, Reporting Financial Performance, requires that earnings per share should be calculated on the profit after tax, minority interest and extraordinary items. FRS 3 permits an additional measure of earnings per share to be disclosed provided it is presented on a consistent basis over time and reconciled to the amount required by the standard. There should also be an explanation of the reasons for calculating the additional version.

As a result, there is no longer a unique measure of performance. Is this a good thing and what problems might this give preparers and users of financial statements?

ICAEW Financial Accounting 2, July 1994 **(12 marks)**

14.7 A plc is a company which is listed on the UK Stock Exchange. Your client, Mr B, currently owns 300 shares in A plc. Mr B has recently received the published financial statements of A plc for the year ended 30 September 1998. Extracts from these published financial statements, and other relevant information, are given overleaf. Mr B is confused by the statements. He is unsure how the performance of the company during the year will affect the market value of his shares, but is aware that the published earnings per share (EPS) is a statistic which is often used by analysts in assessing the performance of listed companies.

Profit and loss accounts – year ended 30 September

	1998	1997
	£ million	£ million
Turnover	10 000	8 500
Cost of sales	(6 300)	(5 100)
Gross profit	3 700	3 400
Other operating expenses	(1 900)	(1 800)
Operating profit	1 800	1 600
Interest payable	(300)	(320)
Profit before taxation	1 500	1 280
Taxation	(470)	(400)
Profit after taxation	1 030	880
Equity dividend	(800)	(500)
Retained profit	230	380

Balance sheets at 30 September

	1998		1997	
	£ million	£ million	£ million	£ million
Fixed assets				
Intangible assets	3 000		–	
Tangible assets	4 000		3 700	
		7 000		3 700
Current assets				
Stocks	1 300		1 000	
Debtors	1 500		1 200	
Cash in hand and at bank	100		90	
	2 900		2 290	
Current liabilities				
Trade creditors	900		700	
Taxation	500		420	
Proposed dividend	800		500	
Bank overdraft	600		700	
	2 800		2 320	
Net current asssets		100		(30)
Total assets less current liabilities		7 100		3 670
Creditors: amounts failing due after more than one year:				
Loan stock		(2 000)		(2 000)
		5 100		1 670
Capital and reserves				
Called-up share capital		1 500		500
Share premium account		2 700		500
Profit and loss account		900		670
		5 100		1 670

Information regarding share capital
The called-up share capital of the company comprises £1 equity shares only. On 1 April 1998, the company made a rights issue to existing shareholders of two new shares for every one share held, at a price of £3.30 per share, paying issue costs of £100 000. The

market price of the shares immediately before the rights issue was £3.50 per share. No changes took place in the equity capital of A plc in the year ended 30 September 1997.

Requirements

(a) Compute the EPS figures (current year plus comparative) that will be included in the published financial statements of A plc for the year ended 30 September 1998.

(5 marks)

(b) Using the extracts with which you have been provided, write a short report to Mr B which identifies the key factors which have led to the change in the EPS of A plc since the year ended. 30 September 1997. (10 marks)

(c) Comment on the relevance of the EPS statistic to a shareholder like Mr B who is concerned about the market value of his shares. (5 marks)

CIMA, Financial Reporting, November 1998 (Total Marks = 20)

15–18 Accounting and price changes

18.1

(a) What do you consider to be the main weaknesses of historical cost accounting when prices are rising? (10 marks)

(b) State two ways in which firms have adopted different accounting policies for specific items in historical cost accounts so that they partly reflect rising price levels. (4 marks)

(c) The stewardship approach of traditional accounting has been said to have been replaced by a user-orientated approach. Briefly discuss this assertion in relation to historical cost accounts. (6 marks)

ACCA Level 2 The Regulatory Framework of Accounting, June 1988 (20 marks)

18.2 In the ASC's handbook, Accounting for the Effect of Changing Prices, accountants are faced with a choice of systems of accounting when dealing with the effects of inflation.

Requirements

(a) Briefly describe the three factors which combine to make up these systems of accounting. (3 marks)

(b) Explain the main advantages and disadvantages of two such systems. (6 marks)

ICAEW Financial Reporting II, May 1993 (9 marks)

18.3

(a) Explain the primary objective of current purchasing power accounting and outline the basic technique. (8 marks)

(b) What do you consider are the advantages and disadvantages of current purchasing power accounting as a method of adjusting financial statements for price level changes? (12 marks)

ACCA Level 2 The Regulatory Framework of Accounting, December 1988 (20 marks)

18.4

(a) Provide a definition of the deprival value of an asset. (2 marks)

(b) For a particular asset, suppose the three bases of valuation relevant to the calculation of its deprival value are (in thousands of pounds): £12, £10 and £8.

Construct a matrix of columns and rows showing all the possible alternative situations and, in each case, indicate the appropriate deprival value. (6 marks)

(c) **Justify the use of deprival value as a method of asset valuation, using the matrix in (b) above to illustrate your answer.** (12 marks)

ACCA Level 2 The Regulatory Framework of Accounting, December 1988 **(20 marks)**

18.5 An assistant accountant of Changeling plc has been requested to prepare a profit and loss account using the CPP model for the year ended 31 March 1991. He has calculated the net operating profit for the year and the remaining entries are yet to be completed.

The profit and loss accounts for the year ended 31 March 1991 are set out below, comprising the historic cost profit and loss account and partially completed CPP profit and loss account.

	Historic cost £000	Index factor	CPP units as at 31.3.91 000
Sales	6 500	2 000 / 1 875	6 933
Opening stock	700	2 000 / 1 700	824
Purchases	4 250	2 000 / 1 875	4 533
	4 950		5 357
Closing stock	(900)	2 000 / 1 937	(929)
	4 050		4 428
Gross profit	2 450		2 505
Expenses	1 150	2 000 / 1 875	1 227
Depreciation:			
Original equipment	500	2 000 / 1 025	976
New equipment	50	2 000 / 1 813	55
Net operating profit	750		247
Tax	338		
Profit (loss) after tax	412		
Gain (loss) on net monetary assets	–		
Gain (loss) on long-term loans	–		
Net profit (loss) for year	412		
Dividends	187		
Retained profit (loss) for year	225		
Retained profit brought forward	750		
Retained profit carried forward	975		

Balance sheet as at 31 March 1990

	Historic cost £000	Index factor	CPP units as at 31.3.90 000	Index factor	CPP units as at 31.3.91 000
Capital	2 500	1 750	4 605	2 000	5 263
Retained profit	750	950	1 142	1 750	1 305
	3 250		5 747		6 568
Fixed assets					
Equipment	5 000	1 750 / 1 025	8 537	2 000 / 1 750	9 757
Depreciation	(1 500)	1 750 / 1 025	(2 561)	2 000 / 1 750	(2 927)
Current assets					
Stock	700	1 750 / 1 700	721	2 000 / 1 750	824
Debtors	1 050	–	1 050	2 000 / 1 750	1 200
Current liabilities					
Trade creditors	(875)	–	(875)	2 000 / 1 750	(1 000)
Non-current liabilities					
Loan	(1 125)	–	(1 125)	2 000 / 1 750	(1 286)
	3 250		5 747	1 750	6 568

Balance sheet as at 31 March 1991

	Historic cost £000	Index factor	CPP units as at 31.3.91 000
Capital	2 500	2 000 / 950	5 263
Retained profit	975	–	1 142
	3 475		6 405
Fixed assets			
Equipment	5 000	2 000 / 1 025	9 757
Depreciation	(2 000)	2 000 / 1 025	(3 903)
New equipment	500	2 000 / 1 813	552
Depreciation	(50)	2 000 / 1 813	(55)
Current assets			
Stock	900	2 000 / 1 938	929
Debtors	1 150	–	1 150
Carried forward	5 500		8 430

	Historic cost £000	Index factor	CPP units as at 31.3.91 000
Brought forward	5 500		8 430
Current liabilities			
Trade creditors	(400)	–	(400)
Non-current liabilities			
Loan	(1 625)	–	(1 625)
	3 475		6 405

Assume that inflation index increased evenly throughout the year ended 31 March 1991.

Required
(a) Calculate the retained profit (loss) for the year using the CPP Model for the year ended 31 March 1991. (5 marks)
(b) Explain what the method of indexing is attempting to deal with and discuss the process from the viewpoint of both the entity and the proprietors. (5 marks)
(c) Write a brief report to the principal shareholder of Changeling Ltd who holds 20% of the issued share capital on the management of the company commenting on profitability, liquidity and financial structure. (10 marks)

ACCA Advanced Financial Accounting, December 1991 (20 marks)

18.6 'The recognition and correct treatment of holding gains in company financial statements are vital for a proper understanding of the position and performance of the business entity.'

You are required
(a) to explain briefly the significance of the treatment of holding gains for the measurement of business profit; (5 marks)
(b) to set out the arguments for and against the recognition or holding gains. (10 marks)

CIMA Advanced Financial Accounting, November 1994 (15 marks)

18.7 The accountant of Newsprint plc has produced three sets of accounts for the year ended 31 December 1988 using the historic cost, replacement cost with specific index adjustments and current purchasing power with general price index adjustments.

The historic and replacement cost accounts are set out below:

Profit and loss accounts for the year ended 31 December 1988

	Historic cost £	£	Specific index	Replacement cost £	£
Sales		357 500	–		357 500
Opening stock	41 250		240/200	49 500	
Purchases	178 750		–	178 750	
	220 000			228 250	
Closing stock	71 500			71 500	
Cost of sales		148 500			156 750
Gross profit		209 000			200 750
Wages	17 875			17 875	
Establishment and other charges	71 500			71 500	
Depreciation					
Fixtures	5 500		160/140	6 286	
Lease	5 500		220/160	7 563	
		100 375			103 224
Net profit	108 625		*Operating profit*	97 526	

653

Balance sheets as at 31 December 1988

	Historic cost £	£	Specific index	Replacement cost £	£
Fixed assets					
Leasehold					
Premises	55 000		220/160	75 625	
Amortisation	5 500	49 500		7 563	68 062
Fixtures	55 000		160/140	62 857	
Depreciation	5 500	49 500		6 286	56 571
Current assets					
Stock		71 500	280/240		83 416
Cash		55 825	–		55 825
		226 325			263 874
Share capital					
Ordinary shares		90 200			90 200
Profit and loss account		108 625			97 526
					11 099[1]
					37 549[2]
Loan		27 500			27 500
		226 325			263 874

Note 1	£
Stock	8 250
Fixtures	786
Lease	2 063
	11 099

Note 2
Closing Stock
$(71\,500 \times \frac{280}{240} - 71\,500)$ 11 916
Fixtures
$(49\,500 \times \frac{160}{140} - 49\,500)$ 7 071
Lease
$(49\,500 \times \frac{220}{160} - 49\,500)$ 18 562
   37 549

The historic and current purchasing power accounts are set out below.

Profit and loss accounts for the year ended 31 December 1988

	Historic cost £	£	General index	£CPP	£CPP
Sales		357 500	160/130		440 000
Opening stock	41 250		160/100	66 000	
Purchases	178 750		160/130	220 000	
	220 000			286 000	
Closing stock	71 500		160/130	88 000	
Cost of sales		148 500			198 000
Gross profit		209 000			242 000
Wages	17 875		160/130	22 000	
Establishment and					
other charges	71 500		160/130	88 000	
Carried forward	89 375	209 000		110 000	242 000

	Historic cost		General		
	£	£	index	£CPP	£CPP
Brought forward	89 375	209 000		110 000	242 000
Depreciation					
Fixtures	5 500		160/100	8 800	
Lease	5 500		160/100	8 800	
		100 375			127 600
	Net profit	108 625		Operating profit	114 400

Balance sheets as at 31 December 1988

	Historic cost		General		
Fixed assets	£	£	index	£CPP	£CPP
Leasehold premises	55 000		160/100	88 000	
Amortisation	5 500	49 500	160/100	8 800	79 200
Fixtures	55 000		160/100	88 000	
Depreciation	5 500	49 500	160/100	8 800	79 200
Current assets					
Stock		71 500	160/130		88 000
Cash		55 825	–		55 825
		226 325			302 225
Share capital					
Ordinary shares		90 200	160/100		144 320
Profit and loss account		108 625			114 400
					16 005[3]
Loan		27 500			27 500
		226 325			302 225

Note 3

Loan $(27\,500 \times \frac{160}{100} - 27\,500)$	16 500
Purchases $(178\,750 \times \frac{160}{130} - 178\,750)$	41 250
Fixtures $(55\,000 \times \frac{160}{100} - 55\,000)$	33 000
Lease $(55\,000 \times \frac{160}{100} - 55\,000)$	33 000
Expenses $(89\,375 \times \frac{160}{130} - 89\,375)$	20 625
Cash $(76\,450 \times \frac{160}{100} - 76\,450)$	(45 870)
Sales $(357\,500 \times \frac{160}{130} - 357\,500)$	(82 500)

Required

(a) Explain briefly what the following amounts relate to and why they are in the balance sheets:

   (i) in the replacement cost model
      £11 099
      £37 549;

   (ii) in the current purchasing power model
      £16 005.   (6 marks)

(b) Explain the case for and against the replacement cost model.   (8 marks)

(c) Consider the implication of the replacement cost model figures for 1988 to the management of Newsprint plc. (8 marks)

(d) Explain to a shareholder why the historic cost net profit is different from the CPP operating profit using the data in the question to illustrate your answer and explain which figure is to be regarded as the base for calculating earnings per share under each model. (8 marks)

ACCA Level 3 Advanced Financial Accounting, June 1989 (30 marks)

18.8 The Paraffin Supply Company Limited acquired freehold land as a depot for its delivery vans and started business on 1 January 1986. It collected sufficient paraffin from a wholesaler each day to satisfy known orders. The wholesaler was paid in cash and the customers paid cash on delivery. The opening balance sheet at 1 January 1986 showed the following:

Balance sheet of Paraffin Supply Company Limited as at 1 January 1986

	£
Freehold land for use as garage premises	100 000
Delivery vehicles	96 000
	196 000
Financed by: Share capital	150 000
Long-term loan	46 000
	196 000

The company traded for 2 years until 31 December 1987. All profits had been retained in the business. There were no creditors, debtors or stocks. At 31 December 1987 the directors were considering whether to cease trading at 31 December 1988.

The accountant produced the following estimated accounts for the year ended 31 December 1988 with the 1986 and 1987 actual comparative figures:

Profit and loss accounts for the years ended 31 December

	1986 £	1987 £	1988 £
Sales	140 000	184 000	248 000
Less: Purchases	70 000	90 000	124 000
Administration expenses	21 400	22 000	27 500
Selling expenses	21 000	30 000	42 500
Depreciation	24 000	24 000	24 000
	3 600	18 000	30 000

	1986	1987	1988
Return on equity	$\frac{3\,600}{150\,000} \times 100$	$\frac{18\,000}{153\,600} \times 100$	$\frac{30\,000}{171\,600} \times 100$
	= 2.4%	= 11.7%	= 17.5%

In preparing the accounts the following conventions and policies had been followed:

(a) The capital maintenance concept is that capital will be maintained if the cost of assets representing the initial monetary investment is recovered against operations.

(b) The concept of profit is that profit for the year is regarded as any gains arising during the year which may be distributed while maintaining the amount of the shareholders' interest in the company at the beginning of the year.

(c) The measurement unit used is the medium of exchange.

(d) Depreciation of delivery vans is over 4 years using the straight-line method.

The directors had recently attended a seminar on the treatment of inflation in financial reports and they required the profits to be calculated using the general purchasing power income model and the replacement cost model.

The accountant obtained the following information to allow him to redraft the profit and loss account using these two models:

(a) The retail price index was as follows:

1 January 1986	100
31 December 1986	110
31 December 1987	120
31 December 1988 (Estimated)	130

(b) The replacement cost of the assets was:

	Garage premises £	Delivery vehicles £
31 December 1986	120 000	102 000
31 December 1987	130 000	115 000
31 December 1988 (Estimated)	141 000	128 000

Required

(a) (i) Prepare the profit and loss account for the year ended 31 December 1988 using the general purchasing power income model and explain the following:
The concept of capital maintenance used.
The concept of profit used.
The measurement unit used. (8 marks)

  (ii) Mention four criteria for selecting an appropriate unit of measurement for financial reporting and briefly discuss whether the general purchasing power income model satisfies these criteria. (8 marks)

(b) (i) Prepare the profit and loss account for the year ended 31 December 1988 using the replacement cost model to show reported income on the assumption that backlog depreciation is not deducted in arriving at this reported income and explain the following:
The concept of capital maintenance used.
The concept of profit used.
The measurement unit used. (5 marks)

  (ii) Discuss the arguments for and against excluding backlog depreciation when calculating the reported income. (4 marks)

ACCA Level 3 Advanced Financial Accounting, December 1988 (**25 marks**)

18.9 Air Fare plc is the subsidiary of an American parent company. It had been incorporated in the United Kingdom in 1985 to provide in flight packed meals for American airlines on return flights from the United Kingdom.

The fixed assets in the annual accounts have been carried at cost less depreciation but the directors have been considering the production of supplementary statements that are based on current values and show a profit after maintaining the operating capital and also a profit that encompassed gains on holding assets to the extent that these were real gains after allowing for general/average inflation.

The following information (i) to (vi) was available when preparing the supplementary statements for the year ended 31 December 1993.

(i) Draft profit and loss account for the year ended 31 December 1993 prepared under the historic cost convention.

	£000
Sales	11 441
Cost of sales	10 292
	1 149
Loan interest	625
	524
Tax	124
	400
Less: Proposed dividend	100
	300

(ii) The current cost values of the net assets representing shareholders' funds was £25 million at 1 January 1993.

(iii) Freehold premises had cost £8 million in 1985 and were being depreciated over 40 years which was the group policy specified by the American parent. The current gross replacement cost was £14 million at 31 December 1993 and £13.8 million at 1 January 1993.

Equipment had cost £12 million in 1991 and was being depreciated over 15 years. The gross replacement cost was £12.6 million at 31 December 1993 and £12.5 million at 1 January 1993.

(iv) The cost of sales had increased by £412 000 during the year due to price increases. The costs and price increases occurred evenly during the year.

(v) The retail price index had risen by 3% during the year.

(vi) Stock at the beginning of the year was £660 000 at cost and £670 000 at current replacement cost and stock at the end of the year was £750 000 at cost and £795 000 at current replacement cost.

The following information relates to a consideration not to provide for depreciation on the freehold property.

The freehold property consisted of the premises where the meals were prepared and packed. When the directors were reviewing the information prepared for the current value supplementary statements they noted that the current value of the freehold property exceeded the book value and decided that it was appropriate not to provide for depreciation.

The chief accountant advised them that it was probable that the auditor would qualify the accounts if depreciation were not provided in accordance with the provisions of SSAP 12 Accounting for Depreciation.

The directors had been discussing the problem over lunch at the local hotel and were surprised when the owner of the hotel informed them that the auditor of the company that owned the hotel had not required depreciation to be provided on the hotel premises. Further enquiry by the directors established that there were a number of companies that were not providing depreciation on freehold properties from a range of industries that included hotels, retail shops and banks. They even discovered that the Financial Reporting Review Panel had accepted one company's policy on non-depreciation of freehold buildings in respect of the accounts of Forte plc. They had therefore formed the view that non-depreciation was acceptable provided the auditors were offered and accepted the company's reasons.

They accordingly requested the chief accountant to prepare a brief report for the board of reasons to support a decision by the company to adopt an accounting policy of non-depreciation which they could subsequently discuss with the auditors.

Required

(a) (i) Prepare a profit and loss account that shows a result after maintaining the operating capital and also a result that encompasses the gains for the year on holding assets to the extent that these are real gains after allowing for inflation.

(ii) Write a brief memo to the directors explaining the results disclosed in the profit and loss account prepared in (i) (10 marks)

(b) As chief accountant, prepare a brief report for the board giving reasons to support a decision by the company to adopt an accounting policy of non-depreciation of the freehold property. (10 marks)

ACCA Financial Reporting Enviornment, June 1994 (20 marks)

18.10 (A) The Bureau Limited is a company that is being incorporated to organise and manage a computer bureau operation. The directors are considering whether to finance the company by equity or equity and loan.

They estimate that the company will require £5 000 000 and that the rate of return on capital employed, calculated on the basis of profit before interest and tax to capital employed, could range from 10% to 20% as follows:

A return on capital employed of 20% if the company is able to obtain a contract with the government for processing monthly statistics, or

A return on capital employed of 15% if it is able to obtain a contract with a major commercial organisation for routine processing of the weekly payroll, or

A return on capital employed of 10% if it is only able to obtain a series of small contracts.

Required

(a) Calculate the earnings per share on the basis of the three possible rates of return on capital employed assuming that:

(i) The company is financed wholly by equity of £1 ordinary shares. Assume corporation tax at 30%.

(ii) The company is financed half by ordinary shares of £1 each issued at par and half by 10% loan stock. Assume corporation tax at 30%. (5 marks)

(b) Explain how the shareholders of Bureau Limited would be advantaged or disadvantaged by introducing a 50% gearing. (5 marks)

(B) Three proposals have been suggested to record the effect of gearing when accounts are prepared on an inflation accounting basis. These are:

(i) If current cost adjustments have been made to calculate a current operating profit, a gearing adjustment is allowed to abate the operating adjustments in the gearing proportion to derive a current cost operating profit.*

(ii) In addition to the abatement of the operating adjustments, required in part (i) above, an additional entry is to be made to recognise the proportion of the unrealised revaluation surpluses arising in the year that may be regarded as being financed by borrowing.

(iii) A gearing adjustment may be made to reflect the effect of general price changes on the net borrowings and net monetary assets other than those included in monetary working capital.

---

*There appears to be an error in the official version of this question. In the opinion of the authors, it should read:

'If current cost adjustments have been made to calculate a current cost operating profit, a gearing adjustment is allowed to abate the operating adjustments in the gearing proportion to derive a current cost profit attributable to the shareholders.'

Required
Discuss whether each of the above three proposals has a logical reason to support it and why there is difficulty in agreeing on a standard treatment to record the effect of gearing.

(15 marks)

ACCA Level 3 Advanced Financial Accounting, June 1988   **(25 marks)**

18.11 It has been stated that: 'Current cost accounts allow for the impact of specific price changes on the net operating assets and thus the operating capability of the business. The same tools of analysis as those applied to historical cost accounts are generally appropriate. The ratios derived from current cost accounts... will often differ substantially from those revealed in historical cost accounts but should be more realistic indicators when assessing an entity or making comparisons between entities'.

Required
(a) Explain, with reasons, whether the value of the following ratios might differ if calculated using current cost accounts rather than the historical cost accounts.
   (i)   Return on capital employed (ROCE)
   (ii) Stock turnover ratio (utilising the year end stock value)
   (iii) Debtors turnover ratio
   (iv) Gearing ratio (in the balance sheet)   (8 marks)
(b) Explain the principal limitations of the specific historical cost ratios set out in part (a) when utilising them for the purpose of inter-firm comparison.   (11 marks)
(c) Briefly discuss whether you feel that current cost based ratios are more realistic indicators of a company's performance than those ratios based upon historical cost accounts.   (6 marks)

ACCA, Accounting and Audit Practice, June 1995   **(25 marks)**

18.12 You are a financial analyst specialising in the analysis of the profitability of organisations in the engineering sector. One such company is D Ltd. The directors of D Ltd have always been interested in the impact of price changes on the performance of their business and have adopted the practice of including current cost accounts (using the 'Real Terms' system) alongside the historical cost accounts in the published financial statements. Extracts from the published financial statements for the year ended 31 March 1996 are given below:

Profit and loss accounts – year ended 31 March 1996

	Historical cost		Current cost
	£000	£000	£000
Sales	30 000		30 000
Operating costs (*Note 1*)	(16 000)		(19 000)
Operating profit	14 000		11 000
Interest payable	(2 000)		(2 000)
Profit before taxation	12 000		9 000
Taxation	(3 500)		(3 500)
Profit after taxation	8 500		5 500
Holding gains arising during the year	–	3 500	
Inflation adjustment to shareholders' funds	–	(2 000)	
Real gains	–		1 500
Profit for the year	8 500		7 000
Dividends	(7 000)		(7 000)
Retained profit	1 500		–

Balance sheet at 31 March 1996	*Historical cost*	*Current cost*
	£000	£000
Tangible fixed assets	20 000	24 000
Current assets (*Note 2*)	16 000	19 000
Current liabilities	(10 000)	(10 000)
Loans	(15 000)	(15 000)
	11 000	18 000
Shareholders' funds	11 000	18 000

Note 1		
Operating costs are as follows:	£000	£000
Cost of sales (excluding depreciation)	8 000	10 000
Depreciation	5 000	6 000
Other operating costs	3 000	3 000
	16 000	19 000

Note 2		
Current assets comprise:	£000	£000
Stocks	6 000	9 000
Debtors	9 000	9 000
Cash	1 000	1 000
	16 000	19 000

Requirements

(a) Compute (under both conventions) three accounting ratios for D Ltd which differ under the two conventions. (6 marks)

(b) Explain, for each ratio you have computed, the reason why the current cost elements included in the ratio differ from the historical cost elements. (9 marks)

(c) Explain the adjustments 'Holding gains arising during the year' and 'Inflation adjustment to shareholders' funds'. (5 marks)

CIMA, Financial Reporting, May 1996 (Total Marks = 20)

Index

AAA (American Accounting Association), 3, 4
abnormal items/transactions, 167, 170, 412, 414
   see also exceptional items *and* extraordinary items
accounting
   alternative rules, 254, 396
   choice in, 27–8, 39, 113, 397–8
   complexity, 131–2
   definitions of, 3–5
   limitations of, xii
   possibilities for development of, 66, 69,
     541–50, 552
Accounting Standards Board (ASB), ix, 30–3, 34, 298,
     320, 530, 550–2
   and capitalisation of finance costs, 80
   discussion papers, 146–7, 214, 217, 236, 242–3
   discussion paper 'Reporting Financial Performance:
     Proposals for Change', 18, 19, 32, 153, 154,
     167–70, 396
   discussion paper 'The Role of Valuation in Financial
     Reporting', 550
   drafts of Statement of Principles, ix, 4, 7, 9, 11–20,
     25, 27, 32, 164, 167, 192, 193, 217, 499, 551
     and assets, 74, 75, 76, 77
     and investments, 252–3
     and liabilities, 116, 117
     and prudence, 105
     and realisation, 68, 69
     standards and, 69
   Statement 'Interim Reports', 364–5
   Statement 'Operating and Financial Review',
     358, 359
   Statement 'Preliminary Announcements', 364,
     365, 366
   and valuation, 485
   views on historical cost accounting and alternatives,
     ix, 17–18, 499
Accounting Standards Committee (ASC), 10, 29–31,
     242, 254
Accounting for the Effects of Changing Prices: A
   Handbook, 452, 455–6, 496, 499–511,
     514–15, 517, 524, 525, 531, 534
accounting for inflation, 361, 455, 483, 533

Accounting Standards Steering Committee, 6, 28, 29,
     334–5
The Corporate Report, 6, 57, 335
   and employment report, 361
   and value added statements, 353, 354, 355
accounting theory/frameworks/principles, 5–11, 20,
     21, 24–7, 66
   see also under Accounting Standards Board
accounts
   objectives of, 55–60
   responsibility for, 29
   revision of, 31, 33
accruals concept, 26, 27
   and currency-related gains/losses, 300–1
   and deferred taxation, 206, 207
   and goodwill, 237–8
   and government grants, 112
acquisition accounting, 226–36, 262, 292
acquisitions, 161
   defining date of, 259
   motives for, 432
   in stages, 262–3
   treatment in cash flow statement, 339, 348–9
   treatment in consolidated accounts, 258–66
   valuation and, 432, 433
ACT (Advance Corporation Tax), 199–201, 202,
     203, 427
actuarial method, 119, 121, 147, 176, 180, 184–7
additivity, 542, 543
adjusted historical cost, 46
adjusting events, 150
adjustments, 157, 166, 170
   current cost, 489–90, 511–17
   historical summary and, 360–1
   necessity for comparability, 397–8
Advance Corporation Tax (ACT), 199–201, 202, 203,
     427
AEI, 28
Altman, E.I., 406
amalgamation, *see* business combinations
American Accounting Association, 3, 4
American Institute of Certifed Public Accountants, 312

amortisation of goodwill, 238, 239, 241–2, 243–4, 250
analysed reporting, *see* segmental reporting
annuity method, 176
Argenti, John, 405
ASB, *see* Accounting Standards Board
ASC, *see* Accounting Standards Committee
ASC Handbook, *see Accounting for the Effects of Changing Prices: A Handbook*
asset ratio test, 63
asset stripping, 220
assets, 73–113, 170–1
  businesses as, 431
  CCA and, 502–10
  combinations and inter-relationships of, 78, 81, 87, 89, 100, 245
  contingent, 132, 135–6
  control of, 94
  current, 488
  definitions of, 17, 74, 190, 192–6
  disposals of, taxation and, 215
  effects of inflation on, 461–2
  historical cost, 45–6
  identifiability, 94, 260
  intangible, 93–6, 236
  leased, *see* leases
  matching, 148
  monetary, 461, 462
  net operating, 489, 511
  and protection of creditors, 68
  as proxy, 47, 489, 511
  recognition and measurement of, 73–105, 190, 192–6
    following acquisitions, 260–3
    and tangible/intangible distinction, 74
  and segmental reporting, 408–9
  specific, 532–3, 543
  tangible/intangible distinction, 74
  tangible fixed, *see* tangible fixed assets
  valuation of, 44–8, 482, 483–8, 541, 542–3, 551, 552
    as approach to valuation of businesses, 435, 436–7
    CCA and, 500
    CPP accounting and, 474–5
    and measurement of wealth, 44–55
  values to different parties, 220
  whether likely to be replaced, 75–6, 483, 486, 510
  see also investments
assets and liabilities statement, proposed, 543–4, 547–8, 549–50

associates and joint ventures, 276, 277–92, 293
  treatment in cash flow statement, 350
  treatment in value added statement, 357
  see also JANE
Association of Chartered Certified Accountants, 29
Australia, 453
average net borrowing, 514–15
averaging method, 508–10, 512

backlog depreciation, CCA and, 503–5
balance sheet, 170–1, 550
  current cost, 488–9
  formats, 39
  intangible assets and, 171
  leases and, 190
  treatment of capital instruments, 117–18
  treatment of long-term contracts in, 109–10
bank balances, monetary working capital and, 512, 513
Baxter, W.T., 34, 56, 485, 534
Bell, P.W., 44, 55, 454, 477–84
beta values, 424
bias, 34
Blue Arrow, 240
Bonbright, J.C., 454, 484–5
bonus issues (scrip issues), 367, 443, 444–5
Bradfield, Robert, 161, 163
brands, 240
buildings
  CCA and, 505–7
  specialised/non-specialised, 83, 84, 505–6
  valuation of, 84–5
  see also investment properties
business combinations, 219–36, 439–41
  accounting for, 226–36
  methods of combining, 223–6
  see also groups
business contacts, information needs, 541
business units, 100, 543, 550
businesses
  different interests in, 501–2, 532
  valuation of, 43–4, 219–20, 250, 417, 431–42, 532–3, 543
  see also companies

Cadbury Report, 25
Canada, 234, 307, 313
capital, 50, 116
  cost of, 424–5
  government grants and, 112
  monetary/non-monetary, 461
  operating, 489

capital (*continued*)
  net operating assets as proxy for, 489, 511
  reduction/reorganisation of, 61, 367–91, 405
  working, 336
capital allowances, 208
Capital Asset Pricing Model, 423–4
capital expenditure, treatment in cash flow statement, 339
capital gains tax, 431, 432
capital instruments, 117–28
capital maintenance, 49–55, 474, 500–2, 536, 551
  dividends and, 58, 531–2
  inflation and, 452
capital reduction/reorganisation, 61, 367–91, 405
capital transfer tax, 441
capitalisation
  of development expenditure, 98
  of finance costs, 79–81
  of finance leases, 173
  of goodwill, 238, 239, 241–2, 243–4, 250
  of intangible assets, 94–5
  of leases, 190
  of subsequent expenditure on assets, 81
capitalisation, market, 542
CAPM (Capital Asset Pricing Model), 423–4
Carsberg, B.V., 65, 67–8, 69
cash
  definitions, 336, 337, 340
  and determination of dividends, 68–9
  and monetary working capital, 511–12, 513
  and realisation, 67, 68
cash equivalents, 340
cash flow
  forecast, 100–1, 102
  and ratio analysis, 403–4
cash flow statements, 333, 334, 335–53
  MCRV and, 545–6, 550
CCA, *see* current cost accounting
CCAB (Consultative Committee of Accountancy Bodies), 29
Centre for Interfirm Comparison, 397
Chambers, R.J., 484, 541
Chartered Institute of Management Accountants (CIMA), 29
Chartered Institute of Public Finance and Accountancy (CIPFA), 29
closing rate method of currency translation, 298, 303–4, 305, 306
closing rate/net investment method of currency translation, 306–12, 318–30, 331, 352
Cohen Committee, 25

Collins, Bill, 358
combinations, business, *see* business combinations
Combined Code on Corporate Governance (London Stock Exchange), 25–6
companies
  comparing, 425
  value-based, 501, 510
  see also businesses
Companies Acts, 22–5, 26, 31, 38, 39, 155
  and acquisitions, 161, 237
  and associated undertakings and joint ventures, 277, 281–2
  and business combinations, 226, 230–3, 234
  and capital reduction/reorganisation, 368–9, 375, 379, 382–3, 384
  and comparison, 359
  and distribution of profits, 43, 61–3
  and equity share capital, 124
  and goodwill, 239, 240, 241
  and government grants, 112, 113
  and group accounts, 253, 255–7, 261–2
  and post balance sheet events, 151
  and previous figures in accounts, 517
  and quasi-subsidiaries, 197
  and realisation, 65, 66, 300
  and research and development expenditure, 98–9
  and revaluation, 74, 82
  and segmental reporting, 408
  and share premium accounts, 120, 123
  and summary financial statements, 362
  and treatment of taxation, 202
  and valuation on acquisition, 237
comparisons and comparability, 58, 397–8, 425, 427, 436
  government grants and, 112
  see also interpretation
competition, 221–2
complexity, 532, 552
compound yield method, 121
consistency, 26–7, 157
  and treatment of goodwill, 239, 241
  and treatment of taxation, 205
consolidation/consolidated financial statements, 253, 256–7, 258–77, 407
  and currency translation, 294–5, 303–32
  EU and, 39–40
  liabilities in, 127
  and related party transactions, 413–14
  and timing differences, 206
  see also business combinations *and* proportional consolidation

constant purchasing power unit, 500
construction costs, 78–9, 80
constructive obligations, 117
Consultative Committee of Accountancy Bodies, 29
consumption, 59, 531–2
   see also dividends
contextual information, 541–2, 550
contingently issuable shares, 447
Continuously Contemporary Accounting (CoCoA), 484
contracts, long-term, *see* long-term contracts
control, 14, 19, 40, 57–8, 192, 253
   CCA and, 530–1
   through custody, 94
   and defining date of acquisitions/disposals, 259
   and definitions of subsidiary undertakings, 255–6
   in groups, 255–6, 267
   quasi-subsidiaries, 196–7
   value of, 441–2
convertible debt, 125–6
convertible preference shares, 446
COP, *see* current operating profit
Corporate Report, The, see under Accounting
   Standards Steering Committee
corporation tax, 200–1, 202, 203, 204, 205
correction of errors, 157, 170
COSA (cost of sales adjustment), 489, 491, 507–10,
   511–14
cost(s), 78–81, 103–4
   adjusted historical, 46
   of capital, 424–5
   of information, 533, 552
   see also finance costs, opportunity cost *and*
      replacement cost
costing systems, 507
courts
   and capital reduction/reorganisation, 378–80, 382–3
   and statutory valuation, 431
covenants, 123
CPP accounting, *see* current purchasing power
   accounting
creditors, 395
   and capital reduction/reorganisation, 378–80, 382–4
   effects of inflation on, 460–1, 462–5, 472–4
   information needs, 541
   protection of, 59, 61, 68
   treatment in CCA, 512
critical events, 164
cross-sectional analysis, 397
currencies, 295, 321–2
   functional, 306
   see also exchange rates, foreign currency financial
      statements *and* foreign currency transactions

currency options, 297–8
currency swaps, 297–8
currency translation methods, 304, 305, 306–30, 331
   and cash flow statement, 352
current cost accounting, 25, 451, 453, 454, 455,
   476–98, 502–29, 530–3, 541
   combining with CPP, 530, 534–40, 551, 552
   costs of, 533, 552
   real terms, 530, 534–40, 551, 552
current cost adjustments, 489–90, 511–17
current cost reserve account, 494, 495
current/non-current method of currency translation,
   304, 305, 306
current operating profit, 477–8, 480, 482–3
current purchasing power accounting, 46, 451, 453,
   454, 455, 456–75, 476, 500–1
   combining with CCA (real terms current cost
      accounting), 530, 534–40, 551, 552
current ratio, 402–3
current replacement cost, *see* replacement cost
current values of investments, 254
custody, *see under* control

dangling debits, 238
Davies, Mike, 13
Dearing Committee/Report, 30, 31
debentures, 119–22, 417–18
debt(s), 116, 118
   convertible, 125–6
   disclosure relating to, 127–8
   factoring of, 195
   liquidation and, 383–4
   maturity, 126
debtors
   effects of inflation on, 460–1, 462–5, 472–4
   treatment in CCA, 512
decision making, 5, 55–6, 58, 59, 353, 395
deferred taxation, 199, 200, 206–18
   partial/full provision methods of accounting for,
      200, 212–14, 217–18
depreciated replacement cost, 77
depreciation, 81, 85–93
   CCA and, 489, 491, 503–5, 506–7, 511
   CPP accounting and, 460
   disclosure, 90
   of intangible assets, 95–6
   of leased assets, 180
   and methods of currency translation, 304
   net realisable value and, 543
   and realised profit, 65–6
   and taxation, 208–9

depreciation adjustment, 489, 491, 511
deprival value, *see* value to the business
derivatives, 115, 128–32, 194, 446
development costs, 29, 97–9
dilution, 446
directors, 57, 358
   discretion, 408, 411, 482
   personal interests, 411, 502, 532
disaggregated reporting, *see* segmental reporting
disclosure, 196
   contingent assets, 136
   contingent liabilities, 136
   currency-related gains/losses, 301, 332
   debt, 127–8
   depreciation, 90
   financial instruments, 128–32
   goodwill, 241, 249
   government grants, 113
   impairment, 102
   intangible assets, 96
   investments, 290
   leases, 180–1, 188
   minority interests, 127, 163
   pension schemes and costs, 146, 148–9
   prior period adjustments, 157
   provisions, 135
   related parties, 411–15
   revaluation, 86
   shares, 127
   subsidiaries, 272–3
   taxation, 162–3, 201–4, 218
discontinued operations, 157–60, 161–2
   tests for, 160
discounted earnings approaches to valuation of
   businesses, 435–7
discounting and discount rates, 101, 135, 145, 148,
   218, 416, 418
discrete method in interim reports, 364–5
disposals
   costs of, 48
   deemed, 267
   defining date of, 259
   normal, 47–8
   partial, 273–7
   treatment in cash flow statement, 350
   treatment in consolidated accounts, 258, 267–77
distribution on liquidation, 383–4
distribution statement, proposed, 543, 545, 549
dividend cover, 427
dividend yield, 425, 426

dividends
   allowable, 59, 61–5
   treatment in cash flow statement, 338, 339–40
   CCA and, 531–2
   CPP accounting and, 473
   determining, 59, 61–5, 68–9
   from investments, 254
   from overseas companies, 204
   reporting of, 170
   and taxation, 205
      see also franked investment income
   tests for, 63
Dopuch, N., 483, 510
double taxation, 204
Drake, D.F., 483, 510

earnings per share, 427, 442–7
earnings yield, 428
economies of scale, 221
EDs (Exposure Drafts), *see following entries;*
   see also ASB, drafts of Statement of Principles
ED 3: Accounting for acquisitions and mergers, 226,
   230–1
ED 8: Accounting for changes in the purchasing power
   of money, 453, 454, 455
ED 11: Accounting for deferred taxation, 211
ED 14: Accounting for research and development, 98
ED 16: Supplement to extraordinary items and prior
   year adjustments, 295
ED 18: Current cost accounting, 454, 455
   guidance manual to, 506
ED 19: Accounting for deferred taxation, 211–12
ED 21: Accounting for foreign currency transactions,
   305–6
ED 24: Current cost accounting, 454, 455
ED 27: Accounting for foreign currency translations,
   302, 306, 307
ED 33: Accounting for deferred tax, 212
ED 35: Accounting for the effects of changing prices,
   454, 455
ED 42: Accounting for special purpose
   transactions, 171
ED 46: Disclosure of related party transactions, 412
ED 47: Accounting for goodwill, 241–2
ED 48: Accounting for acquisitions and mergers,
   226, 234
ED 49: Reflecting the substance of transactions in
   assets and liabilities, 171
ED 55: Accounting for investments, 254–5
ED (1997): Amendment to SSAP 8, 203
ED (1999): Amendment to SSAP 20, 298, 320

Edwards, E.O., 44, 55, 454, 477–84
Edwards, Ronald, 451
effective rate method, 121
efficient market hypothesis, 334
Egginton, D.A., 68
employee reports, 361–2
employees, 354, 502, 532
  information needs, 541
  as main asset of entity, 93
  and related party transactions, 414
  see also pensions and pension costs
employment reports, 334, 361, 362
enhancement of assets, 81
entities
  and currency translation, 331
  definitions of, 282
  and reporting, 14, 19
  as teams, 353–4
entity measure of profit, 51–2
equity, 116, 117, 118
  government grants and, 112
  inflation and, 461
equity accounting, 277–81, 283–7, 290, 291
  and methods of currency translation, 321
  where appropriate, 19, 258, 262–3, 276, 290,
    291, 293
Ernst & Young, 13
errors, correction of, see correction
Erskine House Group, 240
estimates, 46, 246–8, 249, 250–1, 550
European Commission, 41
European Union (and EEC/EC), 21, 22, 37–8, 40–1
  Second Directive, 61
  Fourth Directive, 22, 38–9, 40–1, 61
  Seventh Directive, 22, 39–41, 234, 255, 256
  Eighth Directive, 22
  Economic and Monetary Union, 295
  and 'true and fair view', 105
EUV (existing use value), 84–5
exceptional items, 156–7, 170
  see also abnormal items and extraordinary items
exchange rates, 294–332
  average rates, 305, 307
  examples, 318
expectation gap, 543
expected values, 134
Exposure Drafts, see EDs
extended statements, 334, 361
extraordinary items, 156, 157, 161, 170, 263
  taxation, 163
  see also abnormal items and exceptional items

factoring, 195
failure
  predicting, 405–7
  see also liquidation
fair values, 76–7, 95, 179, 260–3, 292
  and foreign currency translation, 331, 332
Fantl, Irving L., 36
FASB ([US] Financial Accounting Standards Board), 4
  and conceptual frameworks/principles, 6–10, 12, 14
  see also USA
FIFO, 507, 508, 509
Finance Act 1975, 431
Finance Act 1984, 173
finance costs, 79–81, 117, 118–23
finance leases, 172–8, 179–87, 188
  and sale and leaseback transactions, 189
financial accounting, definitions of, 3–5
financial capital maintenance, 50–2, 474, 496–8,
    500–2, 536, 551
financial instruments, 115, 117–32, 446, 552
  definitions, 129
Financial Reporting Council, 30
Financial Reporting Exposure Drafts, see FREDs
Financial Reporting Review Panel, 31, 33
Financial Reporting Standard for Smaller Entities
    (FRSSE), 23
Financial Reporting Standards, see FRSs
financial statements, 333–5
  fully stabilised, 534
  interpretation of, 395–411
  non-financial information in, 359, 541–2
  objectives, 14
  proposals for changes to, 168–9, 543–50, 552
  segmentation, 407–11
  summary/simplified, 334, 361–3
  users of, see users
  and valuation, 250
  see also specific statements
financing
  treatment in cash flow statement, 340–1
  see also finance costs
flexibility, 27–8, 39, 113
Flint, David, 25
foreign currency financial statements
  and historical cost accounting, 321–2
  translation of, 294–5, 303–32
  treatment in cash flow statement, 351–2
foreign currency transactions, 294–303, 331
  treatment in cash flow statement, 351–2
form and substance, 190–8
formats, 39, 400

forward exchange contracts, 297–8
franked investment income, 200, 201, 202–3, 204
FREDs (Financial Reporting Exposure Drafts):
FRED 4: Reporting the substance of transactions, 171
FRED 6: Acquisitions and mergers, 226, 234
FRED 8: Related party disclosures, 412
FRED 11: Associates and joint ventures, 282
FRED 12: Goodwill and intangible assets, 243
FRED 14: Provisions and contingencies, 132
FRED 17: Measurement of tangible fixed assets, 86
FRED 18: Current taxation, 200, 203, 204–5, 214
FRED 19: Deferred taxation, 200, 205, 214, 217–18
FRED 20: Retirement benefits, 146, 147, 148, 149, 168–9
FRSs (Financial Reporting Standards), 11–12, 32–3
FRS 1: Cash flow statements, 335, 336–41, 352, 353
FRS 2: Accounting for subsidiary undertakings, 197, 253, 257–8, 259, 262–3, 267, 292, 407
FRS 3: Reporting financial performance, 32, 86, 141, 153, 154, 155–70, 255, 259, 263, 265, 273, 398
FRS 4: Capital instruments, 33, 117–28, 131, 180
FRS 5: Reporting the substance of transactions, ix, 33, 131, 153, 171, 172, 190–8, 256
FRS 6: Acquisitions and mergers, 226, 227, 234–6, 262
FRS 7: Fair values in acquisition accounting, 76–7, 96, 227, 237, 241, 260–2
FRS 8: Related party disclosures, 412–15, 441
FRS 9: Accounting for associates and joint ventures, 237, 252–3, 277, 282–91, 293, 336, 338, 350, 357
FRS 10: Goodwill and intangible assets, ix, 34, 74, 93–7, 237, 238, 242, 243–4, 249, 250–1
FRS 11: Impairment of fixed assets and goodwill, ix, 74, 76, 81, 99–103, 244, 245–8, 249
FRS 12: Provisions, contingent liabilities and contingent assets, ix, 33, 113, 132–7, 162, 241, 260
FRS 13: Derivatives and other financial instruments: disclosures, 126, 128–32
FRS 14: Earnings per share, 443, 445, 446, 447
FRS 15: Tangible fixed assets, ix, 65, 74, 77–91, 92, 93, 95, 96, 208, 396, 482, 552
FRSSE, 23
functional currency, 306
funds, definitions of, 335–6
Future of Company Reports, The, 455
Future Shape of Financial Reports, The, 7

G4+1 group, 35, 167–70, 236
'GAAP, Big', 23
GAAP, US, 37, 293
gains
    on exchange, 298–303
    not in profit and loss account, 164
    revaluation, 85
game theory, 461
gearing, 171, 404, 515
gearing adjustment, 490, 493–4, 495, 511, 514–17, 532, 536
    and taxation, 531
gearing gain, 52
GEC, 28
geographical segmentation, 409
Germany, 453
gifts, 116
going concern concept, 26
goodwill, 44, 45, 74, 93, 236–51
    amortisation of, 238, 239, 241–2, 243–4, 250
    related to buildings, 505
    calculating following acquisitions in stages, 262
    CCA and, 532
    and currency translation, 331, 332
    immediate write-off of, 238, 239, 240, 250
    internal, 236, 237, 239
    negative, 95, 237, 241, 248–9
        eliminating, 248
    reviews of, 241, 245–8, 250
    suggestions for treatment of, 250–1
government, 21, 31
government grants, 111–13, 116, 189
government securities, 461
Grand Metropolitan, 240
grants, 111–13, 116, 189
Greenbury Report, 25
gross current replacement cost, 502
gross equity accounting, 283, 287–8, 290, 291
groups, 253, 255–77
    cash flow statements, 348–50
    changes in, 258–77
    definitions concerning, 255–8
    EU and, 39–40
    and related parties, 413–14
    structures, 223–4
    and summary financial statements, 362–3
    value added statements, 356–7
    see also business combinations
Guidance Manual on Current Cost Accounting (Inflation Accounting Steering Group), 506

Guidelines for Financial Reporting Standards (Solomons), 7

Heath, Loyd C., 336
hedging and hedge accounting, 129, 302, 320, 331
Hendriksen, E.S., 6
hire purchase, 171, 179, 180, 187, 188
historical cost, 45–6
historical cost accounting, ix, 10, 17–18, 451–6, 552
  ASB and, 550
  comparability, 58
  dangers of, 532, 541
  legislation and, 24–5
  and methods of currency translation, 321–2
  modified, 73–4, 82, 83
  and negative goodwill, 248
  profit measurement, 56–60
  recognition of UHGs in, 482
  valuation and, 60
historical cost profits and losses, note of, 166–7
historical rate of exchange, 303–4, 305
historical summary, 333–4, 359–61, 517
holding gains, 477, 480, 482–3, 510
holding intervals, 477
Hyde guidelines, 454, 455
hyper-inflation, 321

IASs (International Accounting Standards):
IAS 1: Presentation of financial statements, 172
IAS 7: Cash flow statements, 337, 353
IAS 12: Income taxes, 216–17
IAS 14: Reporting financial information by segments, 36, 408, 409
IAS 16: Property, plant and equipment, 77, 90–1
IAS 18: Revenue recognition, 36
IAS 19: Employee benefits, 147, 148, 149
IAS 20: Accounting for government grants and disclosure of government assistance, 112
IAS 21: The effects of changes in foreign exchange rates, 331–2
IAS 22: Business combinations, 236, 249, 250, 292–3
IAS 23: Borrowing costs, 80, 90
IAS 24: Related party disclosures, 412
IAS 25: Accounting for investments, 292
IAS 27: Consolidated financial statements and accounting for investments in subsidiaries, 292
IAS 28: Accounting for investments in associates, 292, 293
IAS 29: Financial reporting in hyper-inflationary economies, 321
IAS 31: Financial reporting of interests in joint ventures, 292, 293

IAS 32: Financial instruments: disclosure and presentation, 125, 131
IAS 33: Earnings per share, 447
IAS 36: Impairment of assets, 102–3, 249
IAS 38: Intangible assets, 96, 99, 249
IAS 39: Financial instruments: recognition and measurement, 37, 131, 331
IASC (International Accounting Standards Committee), ix, 35–7
  European Commission and, 41
  Framework for the Preparation and Presentation of Financial Statements, 7, 10–11, 12, 190
  and G4+1 group, 167
  USA and, 37, 41
ICAEW (Institute of Chartered Accountants in England and Wales), 7, 28, 29, 295, 454, 455
  Accounting for Stewardship in a Period of Inflation, 453
  research paper *The Reporting of Profits and the Concept of Realization*, 65, 67–8, 69
  'Statement of intent on accounting standards in the 1970s', 28–9
ICAS (Institute of Chartered Accountants of Scotland), 7, 29
  see also Making Corporate Reports Valuable
impairment, disclosure relating to, 102
impairment reviews, 87, 88, 91, 95, 96, 99–103, 245–8, 250, 543
income-generating units, 100, 543, 550
index-linked agreements, 460
index-linked securities, 461
indices, *see* price indices
inflation, 60, 74, 321, 451–2, 500, 501, 534
  adjusting for, 360–1
  and discount rates, 101
  effects of, 58, 460–1, 462–5, 472–4, 500
  financial capital maintenance bases and, 496
  historical summary and, 360–1
  taxation and, 60
  see also current cost accounting *and* current purchasing power accounting
Inflation Accounting Committee, *see* Sandilands Committee/Report
Inflation Accounting Steering Group, *Guidance Manual on Current Cost Accounting*, 506
information
  comparability, 14–16
  contextual, 541–2, 550
  costs of, 533, 552
  needs for, 541
  relevance, 14–16

information (*continued*)
reliability, 14–16
and share prices, 334
structure and balance of, 163
timeliness, 16, 150, 363–4
understandability, 14–16, 334, 357–8, 361–2, 543, 550, 552
information set, 161, 165, 250–1, 552
infrastructure systems, 89–90
inheritance tax, 431, 432
Insolvency Act 1986, 383–4
Institute of Chartered Accountants in England and Wales, *see* ICAEW
Institute of Chartered Accountants in Ireland, 29
Institute of Chartered Accountants of Scotland, *see* ICAS
Institute of Cost and Management Accountants, 29
insurance, 432
intangible assets, 93–6
capitalisation of, 94–5
depreciation of, 95–6
importance of, xii
integral method in interim reports, 364, 365
interest method, 121
interest rates, real, 461, 472–4
interests/interested parties, 396, 411–15
controlling/minority, 441–2
differing, 501–2, 532
interim reports, 334, 363–5, 366
International Accounting Standards Committee, *see* IASC
International Accounting Standards, *see* IASs
International Association of Financial Executives Institutes, 36
International Confederation of Free Trade Unions, 36
International Organisation of Securities Commissions, 37
internationalisation, 37, 167, 217
interpretation of financial statements, 395–411
inter-segmental trading, 408, 411
intra-group sales, 267
investment companies, 62–3
investment income, franked, 200, 201, 202–3, 204
investment period method, 187
investment properties, 87, 91–3
investments, 19, 252–6, 293
in associates and joint ventures, 276, 277–92, 293
categories of, 252–5, 277
CCA and, 507
effects of inflation on, 462
fixed asset, 253–4, 277, 291

intention and treatment of, 253–4
treatment in cash flow statement, 338, 339–40
valuation of, 254
see also net investment *and* subsidiaries
IOSCO (International Organisation of Securities Commissions), 37
issue costs, 122–3

JANE (Joint Arrangement that is Not an Entity), 253, 282–3, 291
Jenkins Committee, 120
joint ventures
definitions of, 281–2, 293
see also associates and joint ventures *and* JANE

Kearton, Frank, 28

land, 87
CCA and, 505, 506–7
see also investment properties
Leach, Ronald, 28
Leasco, 28
leases, 153, 171–90
earnings on, 182, 183, 187
see also sale and leaseback transactions
Lee, G.A., 25
Lee, T.A., 44
legislation, 21–5, 31, 173, 383–4, 431
Lennard, A.C., 360
lessors, accounting by, 181–8
liabilities, 115, 116–32
contingent, 132, 135, 136
convertible debt and, 125–6
definitions, 17, 116–17, 190, 192–6
monetary/non-monetary, 461
pension funds and, 147
provisions and, 133–4, 136, 137
recognition of, 190, 192–6, 260–3
and shareholders' funds, 123–4
valuation of, 49, 260–3, 542–3, 551
linked presentation, 195–6
liquid resources, 340, 353
liquidation, 383–4
capital reconstruction schemes to avoid, 367, 383–91
liquidators, 383–4
liquidity, 340, 398, 402–5
London Business School, 424
London Stock Exchange, *see* Stock Exchange
long-term contracts, 105–11
long-term loans, 119–22

long-term/short-term monetary items, and currency-related gains/losses, 300
Lorensen, Leonard, 312
losses
    on exchange, 298–303
    not in profit and loss account, 164
    revaluation, 85–6

McGregor, Warren, 189–90
McKinnon Report, 29–30
McMonnies, Peter N., 7
    see also Making Corporate Reports Valuable
Macve, Richard, 10, 254
maintainable profit, 436
maintenance, capital, see capital maintenance
Making of Accounting Standards, The (Dearing Report), 30, 31
Making Corporate Reports Valuable, 7, 250, 484, 530, 541–50
    proposals for financial statements, 543–50, 552
management accounting, 3–4
manipulation, 159–60, 162
    see also off balance sheet financing
market approach to measuring pension fund assets, 147
market capitalisation, 542
market comparisons, 47, 48
market values, 77, 419
materiality, 180
    of related party transactions, 412, 414–15
    of segments, 408, 410
Maxwell, Robert, 411
MCRV, see Making Corporate Reports Valuable
measurement, bases of, 9–10, 17–18
merger accounting, 226–36
minority interests, 127
    and acquisition accounting, 236
    disclosure concerning, 163
Mirror Group, 411
monetary items
    and currency-related gains/losses, 300
    definitions, 461, 462
monetary working capital, 511
monetary/non-monetary method of currency translation, 304, 305, 306
money financial capital maintenance, 50–2, 59, 452
monopolies, 221–2
Morley, M.F., 357
multi-columnar accounts, 32, 483, 552
multinational companies, 322
multivariate analysis, 396, 405–7

Mumford, Michael, 452
MWCA (monetary working capital adjustment), 489–90, 491, 511–14, 536

net current replacement cost, 502, 503, 506
net investment
    lessors', 181–2, 183–4
    see also closing rate/net investment method of currency translation
net operating assets, 489, 511
net realisable value, 47–8, 105, 483, 484, 486, 487–8, 508, 541, 542–3, 550
    and methods of currency translation, 304
Noke, C.W., 65, 67–8, 69
nominal money, capital maintenance, 50
non-adjusting events, 150
non-specialised buildings, 506
normal course of business, 47–8
notes to the accounts, 165–7
NRV, see net realisable value

obligations, 116, 117, 123
OECD, 35, 97
off balance sheet finance, 171, 256
Office for National Statistics, 502
offsets, 196, 203, 302, 320
OMV (open market value), 84–5
operating and financial review, 334, 357–9
    in interim reports, 364
operating capital, net operating assets as proxy for, 489, 511
operating capital maintenance, 50, 51–2, 501–2, 511
    and current cost profit and loss account, 489–96
operating gains, revaluation surpluses and, 510
operating leases, 171, 172, 178, 180, 181
    and sale and leaseback transactions, 189
operations statement, proposed, 543, 544, 548, 550
opportunity cost, 425, 473–4
options, 115, 128–32, 194, 446
ordinary activities, 156
Organisation for Economic Co-operation and Development (OECD), 35, 97
overdrafts, monetary working capital and, 512, 513
overseas taxation, 204, 205
ownership, non-financial aspects, 441–2
ownership interest, 117

parent companies, 255–8
partnerships, 432–3
Paterson, Ron, 13
payment ratio, 427

pensions and pension costs, 137–50
  disclosure concerning, 146, 148–9
  and related party transactions, 414
  and taxation, 206, 214
Pensions Research Accountants Group, 149
Pergamon, 28, 411
physical capital, 50
pooling of interests, *see* merger accounting
post balance sheet events, 150–1
Prakash, P., 483, 510
prediction, 154
  of failure, 405–7
  segmental reporting and, 407–8
  see also decision making
preference shares, 50, 417, 446, 461
preliminary announcements, 334, 364, 365–6
present value, 48, 102, 416, 433, 486, 487, 488
price changes, 451, 452
  see also inflation *and* price indices
Price Index Numbers for Current Cost Accounting,
  502
price indices, 456, 500, 502–3
  averaging, 508–10
  and buildings, 506
  see also Retail Price Index
price/earnings ratio, 222–3, 427–8, 436
prior period adjustments, 157, 170
private companies
  and capital, 367, 369
  distribution of profit, 61–2
  and segmental reporting, 409
profit, 42–62, 68–9
  accounting and taxable, 206
    see also deferred taxation
  currency translation and, 300–1, 319–20
  current operating, 477–8, 480
  distributable, and distribution policies, 43, 61–5,
    68–9, 452
  long-term contracts and, 105–8
  maintainable, 436
  measurement of, 42–62, 68–9, 483–4
  realisation of, 35–6, 61–2, 65–9, 105–8, 164
  reporting on more than one basis, 483–4
  super-profit, 437–9
profit and loss account, 550
  current cost, 489–98
  discontinued operations and, 159–60
  formats, 39, 400
  and pension funds, 148, 149
  reserve accounting and, 154–5
  revaluations and, 85, 86

STRGL and, 153
  treatment of taxation in, 162–3
profit maximising principle, 441–2
profitability, 398–402
property
  overseas, 302
  see also buildings, investment properties *and* land
proportional consolidation, 277–81, 283, 293
proprietary capital maintenance, 51–2
Provisional Statement of Standard Accounting Practice
  (PSSAP) 7: Accounting for changes in the
    purchasing power of money, 453, 454, 456, 461
provisions, 65, 132–5, 136, 137, 162, 260
  disclosure concerning, 135
  for reorganisation costs, 241
prudence concept, 27, 105
  and CCA, 493
  and currency-related gains/losses, 300–1
  and determination of profit, 66, 67
  and goodwill, 238
  and government grants, 112
  and provisions, 134
  and research and development, 97–8
PSSAP 7, *see* Provisional Statement of Standard
  Accounting Practice 7: Accounting for changes in
    the purchasing power of money
  see also disclosure
purchase method, *see* acquisition accounting
purchasing power, 50, 456
  see also current purchasing power accounting
PV, *see* present value

quasi-subsidiaries, 196–7, 256

Rank Hovis McDougall, 240
ratios and ratio analysis, 398–407, 426–30
RC, *see* replacement cost
real financial capital maintenance, 50–1, 474,
  536, 551
real terms current cost accounting, 530, 534–40,
  551, 552
realisable cost saving, *see* holding gains
realisation, 65–9, 164, 254
  concerning foreign currency transactions, 300
  recognition and, 69
  see also realised holding gains *and* unrealised
    holding gains
realised holding gains/losses, 480, 482, 508, 551
reality
  as basis for valuation, 542, 543
  perceptions of, 552

rearranged and simplified statements, 334, 361–3

recognition, 9–10, 17, 94–5, 164

reconciliation of movements in shareholders' funds, 165–6

record-keeping, and currency translation, 319, 331

recoverable amount, 76, 77, 79, 81, 99, 100, 102, 245, 261

reduction of capital, 61, 367–91, 405

related parties, 396, 411–15, 441

renewals accounting, 89–90

rentals, 179–80, 181
    see also leases

reorganisation of capital, 61, 367–91, 405

reorganisation costs, 241, 260

replacement cost, 46–7, 48, 77, 105, 483–8, 542–3
    depreciated, 77
    net current, 502, 503, 506

research and development costs, 29, 97–9

reserve accounting, 154–5

reserves, 154–5
    bonus issues and, 367
    currency translation and, 307
    government grants and, 112
    revaluation, 240, 254
    and write-off of goodwill, 240–1

Retail Price Index, 360, 451, 456, 500, 501

return on capital employed, 398–9
    segmented, 409–10

revaluation, 65, 73, 82–6, 96, 164, 167, 254, 396, 552
    ASB and, 550
    CPP accounting and, 474–5
    currency translation and, 304
    disclosure, 86
    frequency of, 83
    taxation and, 215

revaluation reserves, 240, 254

revaluation surpluses, see holding gains

Review of the Standard Setting Process (McKinnon Report), 29–30

reviews, impairment, see impairment reviews

revision of accounts, 31, 33

RHGs, see realised holding gains

RICS (Royal Institute of Chartered Surveyors), 83, 84

rights issues, 367, 444

risk, 101, 115, 129–32, 135, 192, 423, 425
    business combinations and, 222

risk premium, 423–4

Royal Institute of Chartered Surveyors, 83, 84

RPI, see Retail Price Index

'Rule of 78', 176, 179–80, 187

Saatchi and Saatchi, 239–40

sale and leaseback transactions, 188–9

sales of discontinued operations, 160, 161

sales moments, 477

sales with options to repurchase, 190, 194

Sandilands Committee/Report, 6, 454, 455, 476, 485, 500

scale, economies of, 221

scrip issues (bonus issues), 367, 443, 444–5

SEC (Securities and Exchange Commission, USA), 37, 453

securities
    valuation of, 259, 416–31
    see also shares

Securities and Exchange Commission (USA), 37, 453

segmental reporting, 407–11, 546

sensitivity analysis, 132

set-offs, 196, 203, 302, 320

Setting Accounting Standards: A Consultative Document (Watts Report), 29, 31

share premium accounts, 120–2, 123, 240

shareholders, 57, 58, 123–5, 541–2

shares
    companies' purchase/redemption of own, 367, 368–79
    disclosure relating to, 127
    equity/non-equity, 122–3, 124–5
    prices, 334, 542
    valuation of, 259, 416–31
    'warehousing', 233
    see also earnings per share

short-term/long-term monetary items, and currency-related gains/losses, 300

simplified statements, 334, 361–3

small and medium-sized companies, 22–3, 39, 414, 532

small and medium-sized groups, 256

SOIs (Statements of Intent), 30

Solomons, David, 7, 10

SORPs (Statements of Recommended Accounting Practice), 30, 149

specialised buildings, see under buildings

SSAPs (Statements of Standard Accounting Practice), see following entries ; see also PSSAP

SSAP 1: Accounting for the results of associated companies, 277, 281

SSAP 2: Disclosure of accounting policies, 26–7, 67, 97, 98, 105, 113, 206, 300

SSAP 3: Earnings per share, 442–3

SSAP 4: Accounting for government grants, 111–13, 116

SSAP 5: Accounting for value added tax, 199
SSAP 6: Extraordinary items and prior year adjustments, 91, 141, 154–5, 156, 161
SSAP 8: The treatment of taxation under the imputation system in the accounts of companies, 199–200, 201–4
SSAP 9: Stocks and long-term contracts, 74, 103–9, 487
SSAP 10: Statements of source and application of funds, 335–6
SSAP 11: Deferred tax, 211
SSAP 12: Accounting for depreciation, 86, 87, 91, 92
SSAP 13: Accounting for research and development, 74, 97–9
SSAP 15: Accounting for deferred taxation, 199, 200, 212–15, 217–18
  amendment to, 214
SSAP 16: Current cost accounting, 30, 454, 455, 476, 511–12, 533
SSAP 17: Accounting for post balance sheet events, 150–1
SSAP 18: Accounting for contingencies, 113, 136
SSAP 19: Accounting for investment properties, 74, 87, 91–3
SSAP 20: Foreign currency translation, 67, 294, 295–303, 306–7, 312, 313, 315, 319–21, 331–2
SSAP 21: Accounting for leases and hire purchase contracts, 121, 171, 172, 178–89, 190
SSAP 22: Accounting for goodwill, 34, 238–42, 250
SSAP 23: Accounting for acquisitions and mergers, 226, 232–4
SSAP 24: Accounting for pension costs, 137–8, 139–41, 145–9, 206, 214
SSAP 25: Segmental reporting, 36, 408, 409–10
stakeholders, 4, 57–8
Stamp, Edward, 28
standard costing systems, 507
standardisation, advantages and disadvantages of, 33–4, 36
standards, ix-x, 6–7, 34, 69, 302
  effects on economic behaviour, 29
  financing for, 30
  international, 34–41
  legislation and, 25
  sources of, 21–41, 533
  see also individual standards and standard-setting bodies
statement of changes in financial wealth, proposed, 543, 544–5, 548–9
statement of source and application of funds, 353

statement of total recognised gains and losses, 12, 19, 86, 153, 155, 164–5, 168, 255, 358, 396, 551
  and pension funds, 148, 149
  revaluations and, 85, 86
  users and, 168
statements, financial, see financial statements
Statements of Intent, 30
Statements of Recommended Accounting Practice (SORPs), 30, 149
Statements of Standard Accounting Practice, see SSAPs
statutory valuation, 431
Sterling, R.J., 541
stewardship, 4, 57–8
stock, 103–5, 483, 488, 507–10, 513
Stock Exchange, 21, 25–6, 334, 359
  and financing for standard setting, 30
  and interim reports/preliminary announcements, 364, 365–6
  and segmental reporting, 408
  and valuation of shares, 418–19
STRGL, see statement of total recognised gains and losses
subsidiaries, 253, 255–92, 293
  foreign, 303–33
  and related party transactions, 414
  treatment in cash flow statement, 348–50
  see also quasi-subsidiaries
substance of transactions, reflecting, 190–8
sum of year's digits method ('Rule of 78'), 176, 179–80, 187
summary financial statements, 334, 361–3
Sunder, S., 483, 510
super-profit, 437–9
Sweeney, F.N., 453, 454
synergy, 431–2, 439

Taffler, R.J., 407
tangible fixed assets, 77–93
  acquired/constructed, 79
  initial costs, 78–81
  subsequent expenditure on, 81
taxation, 199–218
  and calculation of dividend cover, 427
  treatment in cash flow statement, 339
  CCA and, 531
  and discontinued operations, 161, 162–3
  disposals and, 267, 271–2
  treatment in interim reports, 365
  and off balance sheet financing, 171
  overseas/double, 204, 205
  treatment in profit and loss account, 162–3

taxation (*continued*)
  profit measurement and, 56, 59–60
  proposals for treatment of, in financial statements,
    169–70
  and valuation of businesses, 432, 441
  and valuation of securities, 417, 431
  treatment in value added statement, 355–6
temporal method of currency translation, 304, 305,
    306, 312–22, 331
  and cash flow statement, 352
Thorn EMI, 239–40
TI Group, 240
time series analysis, 397
timeliness, 16, 150, 363–4
Tisshaw, H., 407
transactions
  involving related parties, 411–15
  normal/abnormal, 412, 414
  substance of, 190–8
translation of foreign currency financial statements,
    294–5, 303–32
  and historical cost accounting, 321–2
  treatment in cash flow statement, 351–2
trend analysis, 397
'true and fair view', 25, 27, 34, 105, 113
  and definition of realisation, 66
  EU and, 38–9
Tweedie, David P., 66

UHGs, *see* unrealised holding gains
UITF (Urgent Issues Task Force), 31, 33
UITF Abstract 9: Accounting for operations in hyper-
    inflationary economies, 321
understandability, 14–16, 334, 357–8, 361–2, 543,
    550, 552
United Nations, 35
United States of America, *see* USA
uniting of interests, *see* merger accounting
univariate analysis, 395–405
unrealised holding gains/losses, 480, 482, 551
unusual items, *see* abnormal items
Urgent Issues Task Force, *see* UITF
US GAAP, 37, 293
USA
  and cash flow statements, 336, 337
  and companies' purchase/redemption of own
    shares, 368
  and CPP accounting, 453
  and currency translation, 297, 306, 307, 312, 319,
    320, 331

FASB (Financial Accounting Standards Board), 4
  and conceptual frameworks/principles, 6–10,
    12, 14
  and treatment of goodwill, 248
gross domestic product implicit price deflator, 456
  and IASC, 37, 41
  and treatment of inflation, 453
  and leases, 189–90
  and LIFO, 104
  and treatment of long-term loans, 121
  reporting periods for interim reports, 364
  and revaluation, 82
  Securities and Exchange Commission, 37, 453
  and segmental reporting, 408
users of financial statements, 4, 8–9, 167, 168, 360,
    362, 395
  and cash flow statement, 353
  and CCA, 533
  differing interests, 501–2, 532
  information needs, 541
  understanding, 360, 543, 550, 552

valuation, 60, 416, 542–3
  acquisitions and, 237, 259–63
  of businesses, *see under* businesses
  CCA and, 532–3
  and comparison, 397
  of control, 441–2
  EU and, 38, 39
  financial statements and, 250
  of intangible assets, 95
  of investment properties, 92
  of investments, 254
  of liabilities, 49, 551
  and methods of currency translation, 304
  present value model, 44, 77
  of securities, 259, 416–31
  statutory, 431
  see also fair values, historical cost accounting,
    recoverable amount, value to the business *and*
    under assets
value
  expected, 134
  material change in, 83
  true and market, 77, 419
value added, 354
value added statements, 333, 334, 353–7
value added tax, 199
value in use, *see* present value
value to the business, 12, 75–7, 261, 484–8, 534,
    551, 552

value-based companies, 501, 510
VAT, 199
vendor placing schemes, 233–4
vendor rights schemes, 233–4
Virgin Music Group, 239–40

Walker, D.P., 320
'warehousing' shares, 233
warrants, 123–4, 446

Watts, Tom, 29
Watts Report, 29, 31
wealth/well-offness, measuring, 43–55
Weetman, Pauline, 358
Wilkins, R.M., 360
Wilson, Allister, 13
work-in-progress, 486–7, 507
working capital, 336
World Bank, 36